T0184047

Lecture Notes in Computer Science 11147

Commenced Publication in 1973
Founding and Former Series Editors:
Gerhard Goos, Juris Hartmanis, and Jan van Leeuwen

More information about this series at http://www.springer.com/series/7407

Travis Gagie · Alistair Moffat
Gonzalo Navarro · Ernesto Cuadros-Vargas (Eds.)

String Processing
and Information Retrieval

25th International Symposium, SPIRE 2018
Lima, Peru, October 9–11, 2018
Proceedings

 Springer

Editors
Travis Gagie 🄳
Diego Portales University
Santiago
Chile

Gonzalo Navarro 🄳
University of Chile
Santiago
Chile

Alistair Moffat 🄳
The University of Melbourne
Melbourne, VIC
Australia

Ernesto Cuadros-Vargas
Universidad de Ingeniería y Tecnología
Lima
Peru

ISSN 0302-9743   ISSN 1611-3349   (electronic)
Lecture Notes in Computer Science
ISBN 978-3-030-00478-1   ISBN 978-3-030-00479-8   (eBook)
https://doi.org/10.1007/978-3-030-00479-8

Library of Congress Control Number: 2018954071

LNCS Sublibrary: SL1 – Theoretical Computer Science and General Issues

This Springer imprint is published by the registered company Springer Nature Switzerland AG
The registered company address is: Gewerbestrasse 11, 6330 Cham, Switzerland

Preface

This volume contains the papers presented at the 25th International Symposium on String Processing and Information Retrieval (SPIRE), held in Lima, Peru, October 9–11, 2018. The annual SPIRE symposium provides an opportunity for researchers to present original contributions in the three complementary areas of string processing, information retrieval, and computational biology. SPIRE has its origins in the South American Workshop on String Processing, which was first held in 1993. Starting in 1998, the focus of the symposium was broadened to include the area of information retrieval due to the growing emphasis on information processing. The first 24 meetings were held in Belo Horizonte (Brazil, 1993), Valparaiso (Chile, 1995), Recife (Brazil, 1996), Valparaiso (Chile, 1997), Santa Cruz (Bolivia, 1998), Cancun (Mexico, 1999), A Coruña (Spain, 2000), Laguna San Rafael (Chile, 2001), Lisbon (Portugal, 2002), Manaus (Brazil, 2003), Padua (Italy, 2004), Buenos Aires (Argentina, 2005), Glasgow (UK, 2006), Santiago (Chile, 2007), Melbourne (Australia, 2008), Saariselkä (Finland, 2009), Los Cabos (Mexico, 2010), Pisa (Italy, 2011), Cartagena de Indias (Colombia, 2012), Jerusalem (Israel, 2013), Ouro Preto (Brazil, 2014), London (UK, 2015), Beppu (Japan, 2016), and Palermo (Italy, 2017).

The 28 papers accepted for presentation at SPIRE 2018 were selected from 51 submissions received in response to the call for papers. Each submission was reviewed by at least three referees. After discussion, 22 full papers were accepted, as well as a further 6 short papers. The program also included three talks by invited speakers: Philip Bille, from the Technical University of Denmark; Nataša Pržulj, from University College London; and Rossano Venturini, from the Università di Pisa.

While many people helped make this conference possible, we particularly thank the members of the Program Committee and the additional reviewers who worked diligently to ensure the timely review of all submitted manuscripts. We are also grateful to the conference sponsors: Google and eBay, who each donated 5000 USD, which recompensed two of the invited speakers and sponsored ten 500 USD student travel grants; the Chilean Centro de Biotecnología y Bioingeniería (CeBiB), who contributed 2500 USD for the third invited speaker; Springer, who sponsored the 1000-euro best-paper award; and the Bioinformatics and Information Retrieval Data Structures Analysis and Design (BIRDS) project, who sponsored the colocated 13th Workshop on Compression, Text and Algorithms (WCTA) with funding from the European Union's Horizon 2020 research and innovation programme under the Marie Skłodowska-Curie grant agreement No. 690941. Submissions were managed and the proceedings produced using the EasyChair conference system.

August 2018

Travis Gagie
Alistair Moffat
Gonzalo Navarro
Ernesto Cuadros-Vargas

Organization

Program Committee

Diego Arroyuelo	Universidad Técnica Federico Santa María, Chile
Ricardo Baeza-Yates	NTENT, USA; Northeastern University, USA
Hideo Bannai	Kyushu University, Japan
Ilaria Bordino	UniCredit R&D, Italy
Christina Boucher	University of Florida, USA
Broňa Brejová	Comenius University in Bratislava, Slovakia
Nieves R. Brisaboa	Universidade da Coruña, Spain
Ruey-Cheng Chen	SEEK, Australia
Shane Culpepper	RMIT University, Australia
Fabio Cunial	MPI Molecular Cell Biology and Genetics, Germany
Antonio Fariña	Universidade da Coruña, Spain
David Fernández-Baca	Iowa State University, USA
Allyx Fontaine	Université de Guyane, France
Travis Gagie (Chair)	Universidad Diego Portales, Chile
Simon Gog	eBay, USA; KIT, Germany
Roberto Grossi	Università di Pisa, Italy
Inge Li Gørtz	Technical University of Denmark, Denmark
Cecilia Hernandez	Universidad de Concepción, Chile
Wing-Kai Hon	National Tsing Hua University, Taiwan
Tomohiro I	Kyushu Institute of Technology, Japan
Katharina Jahn	ETH Zürich, Switzerland
Dominik Kempa	University of Helsinki, Finland
Roberto Konow	eBay, USA
Gregory Kucherov	Université Paris-Est Marne-la-Vallée, France
Susana Ladra	Universidade da Coruña, Spain
Gad M. Landau	University of Haifa, Israel; NYU, USA
Yiqun Liu	Tsinghua University, China
Veli Mäkinen	University of Helsinki, Finland
Alistair Moffat (Chair)	The University of Melbourne, Australia
Gonzalo Navarro (Chair)	Universidad de Chile, Chile
Matthias Petri	The University of Melbourne, Australia
Cinzia Pizzi	Università di Padova, Italy
Giovanna Rosone	Università di Pisa, Italy
Leena Salmela	University of Helsinki, Finland
Diego Seco	Universidad de Concepción, Chile
Julian Shun	Massachusetts Institute of Technology, USA
Jouni Sirén	University of California, Santa Cruz, USA
Wing-Kin Sung	National University of Singapore, Singapore

Sharma Thankachan   University of Central Florida, USA
Andrew Trotman   University of Otago, New Zealand
Przemysław Uznański   ETH Zürich, Switzerland
Michal Ziv-Ukelson   Ben Gurion University of the Negev, Israel
Guido Zuccon   Queensland University of Technology, Australia

Steering Committee

Ricardo Baeza-Yates   NTENT, USA; Northeastern University, USA
Gabriele Fici   Università di Palermo, Italy
Costas Iliopoulos   King's College London, UK
Shunsuke Inenaga   Kyushu University, Japan
Simon J. Puglisi   University of Helsinki, Finland
Berthier Ribeiro-Neto   Google Inc., Brazil; Universidade Federal Minas
                                  Gerais, Brazil
Kunihiko Sadakane   University of Tokyo, Japan
Tetsuya Sakai   Waseda University, Japan
Marinella Sciortino   Università di Palermo, Italy
Rossano Venturini   Università di Pisa, Italy
Emine Yilmaz   University College London, UK
Nivio Ziviani   Universidade Federal Minas Gerais, Brazil

Additional Reviewers

Paniz Abedin   Avivit Levy
Jarno Alanko   Noa Lewenstein
Amir Carmel   Felipe A. Louza
Bastien Cazaux   Shima Moghtasedi
Panagiotis Charalampopoulos   Yuto Nakashima
Sriram Chockalingam   Takaaki Nishimoto
Francisco Claude   Alberto Ordóñez Pereira
Laxman Dhulipala   José Ramón Paramá
Gabriele Fici   Solon P. Pissis
Samah Ghazawi   Utkarsh Porwal
Adrián Gómez-Brandón   Nicola Prezza
Sahar Hooshmand   Dina Sokol
Shunsuke Inenaga   Dina Svetlitsky
Dmitry Kosolobov   Balaji Venkatachalam
Alan Kuhnle   Tomáš Vinař

Abstracts of Invited Talks

Techniques for Grammar-Based Compression

Philip Bille

Technical University of Denmark

Abstract. Grammar-based compression, where one replaces a long string by a small context-free grammar that generates the string, is a classic, simple, and powerful paradigm that captures many popular compression schemes with little or no reduction in compression rate. One of the most basic problems for grammar-based compression is to compactly represent the grammar while supporting efficient access to any character or substring without decompressing the string. The access problem naturally appears as a computational primitive in wide range of other problems for grammar-based compression such as indexing and pattern matching. Despite several recent breakthroughs and significant interest in the area many important open questions remain. In this talk we give an overview of the main techniques and results for the access problem and its variants. The talk is targeted to an audience with a general algorithmic background and we highlight the main general techniques, connections to other areas (e.g. graph decompositions and data structures), and a selection of open problems.

Mining the Integrated Connectedness
of Biomedical Systems

Nataša Pržulj

University College London

Abstract. We are faced with a flood of molecular and clinical data. Various bio-molecules interact in a cell to perform biological function, forming large, complex systems. Large-scale patient-specific omics datasets are increasingly becoming available, providing heterogeneous, but complementary information about cells, tissues and diseases. The challenge is how to mine these interacting, complex, complementary data systems to answer fundamental biological and medical questions. Dealing with them is nontrivial, because many questions we ask to answer from them fall into the category of computationally intractable problems, necessitating the development of heuristic methods for finding approximate solutions.

We develop methods for extracting new biomedical knowledge from the wiring patterns of systems-level, heterogeneous, networked biomedical data. Our methods link the patterns in molecular networks and the multi-scale network organization with biological function. In this way, we translate the information hidden in the wiring patterns into domain-specific knowledge. In addition, we introduce a versatile data fusion (integration) framework that can effectively integrate the information obtained from mining molecular networks with patient-specific somatic mutation data and drug chemical data to address key challenges in precision medicine: stratification of patients, prediction of driver genes in cancer, and re-purposing of approved drugs to particular patients and patient groups. Our new methods stem from novel network science approaches coupled with graph-regularized non-negative matrix tri-factorization, a machine learning technique for dimensionality reduction and co-clustering of heterogeneous datasets. We utilize our new framework to develop methodologies for performing other related tasks, including disease re-classification from modern, heterogeneous molecular level data, inferring new Gene Ontology relationships, and aligning multiple molecular networks.

Data Compression: The Whole is Larger than the Sum of Its Parts

Rossano Venturini

Department of Computer Science, University of Pisa

Abstract. More than 70 years of research in data compression led to the design of several effective classes of compressors to deal with sequences of different types and with different characteristics. Their use in practice is widespread as encoding data to save space is of utmost importance to enable the effective exploitation of the very large datasets managed by today's systems.

Only recently, however, it has been investigated the possibility of boosting the performance of a given compressor by partitioning its input sequence. Indeed, as data compressors are very sensitive to changes of characteristics in the underlying sequence, we can achieve better results by partitioning the input sequence into homogeneous parts and compressing them separately rather than compressing the entire sequence at once.

Consider the following toy example to appreciate the benefits of this approach. We are given a sequence of n zeros followed by n ones to be compressed with arithmetic coding, the most effective entropy encoder. Encoding the whole sequence gives no compression at all as the output has size $2n$ bits. Instead, partitioning it in two halves and compressing them independently gives a compressed size of $\Theta(\log n)$ bits. An exponential improvement!

Among all the possible partitions, we are looking for an optimal one, i.e., a partition that minimizes the compressed size. Several optimization algorithms have been introduced in order to compute an optimal partition for the most important classes of compressors, e.g., zero-th and k-th order encoders [4], Burrows-Wheeler Transform-based compressors [3, 6], Lempel-Ziv '77 and '78 [1, 2, 5, 7], Elias-Fano representation [8], and so on. In this talk we will present those solutions and we will introduce the most important open problems.

References

1. Buchsbaum, A.L., Caldwell, D.F., Church, K.W., Fowler, G.S., Muthukrishnan, S.: Engineering the compression of massive tables: an experimental approach. In: Proceedings of the 11th ACM-SIAM Symposium on Discrete Algorithms, SODA 2000, pp. 175–184 (2000)
2. Buchsbaum, A., Fowler, G., Giancarlo, R.: Improving table compression with combinatorial optimization. J. ACM **50**(6), 825–851 (2003)
3. Ferragina, P., Giancarlo, R., Manzini, G., Sciortino, M.: Boosting textual compression in optimal linear time. J. ACM **52**, 688–713 (2005)

4. Ferragina, P., Nitto, I., Venturini, R.: On optimally partitioning a text to improve its compression. Algorithmica **61**(1), 51–74 (2011)
5. Ferragina, P., Nitto, I., Venturini, R.: On the bit-complexity of Lempel-Ziv compression. SIAM J.Comput. (SICOMP) **42**, 1521–1541 (2013)
6. Kärkkäinen, J., Puglisi, S.J.: Fixed block compression boosting in FM-indexes. In: Proceedings of the 18th International Symposium on String Processing and Information Retrieval, SPIRE 2011, pp. 174–184 (2011)
7. Matias, Y., Sahinalp, S.C.: On the optimality of parsing in dynamic dictionary based data compression. In: Proceedings of the Tenth Annual ACM-SIAM Symposium on Discrete Algorithms, SODA 1999, pp. 943–944 (1999)
8. Ottaviano, G., Venturini, R.: Partitioned Elias-Fano indexes. In: Proceedings of the 37th Annual International ACM SIGIR Conference on Research and Development in Information Retrieval, SIGIR 2014, pp. 273–282 (2014), (Best Paper Award)

Contents

Recoloring the Colored de Bruijn Graph

Bahar Alipanahi$^{(\boxtimes)}$, Alan Kuhnle, and Christina Boucher

Department of Computer and Information Science and Engineering,
University of Florida, Gainesville, FL 32611, USA
{baharpan,kuhnle,christinaboucher}@ufl.edu

Abstract. The colored de Bruijn graph, an extension of the de Bruijn graph, is routinely applied for variant calling, genotyping, genome assembly, and various other applications [11]. In this data structure, the edges are labeled with one or more colors from a set $\{c_1, \ldots, c_\alpha\}$, and are stored as a $m \times \alpha$ matrix, where m is the number of edges. Recently, there has been a significant amount of work in developing compacted representations of this color matrix but all existing methods have focused on compressing the color matrix [3,10,12,14]. In this paper, we explore the problem of recoloring the graph in order to reduce the number of colors, and thus, decrease the size of the color matrix. We show that finding the minimum number of colors needed for recoloring is not only NP-hard but also, difficult to approximate within a reasonable factor. These hardness results motivate the need for a recoloring heuristic that we present in this paper. Our results show that this heuristic is able to reduce the number of colors between one and two orders of magnitude. More specifically, when the number of colors is large (>5,000,000) the number of colors is reduced by a factor of 136 by our heuristic. An implementation of this heuristic is publicly available at https://github.com/baharpan/cosmo/tree/Recoloring.

1 Introduction

The colored de Bruijn graph was introduced by Iqbal et al. [11] for detecting genetic variation in one or more individual(s) of a population and then used to disambuigate the traversal of the de Bruijn graph [2]. It extends the traditional de Bruijn graph in that each edge in the graph has a set of one or more color(s), each of which corresponds to an individual of the population.

We first give a constructive definition of the traditional de Bruijn graph and show it can be extended to include color information. Given a set of DNA sequences R of length ℓ, a de Bruijn graph is constructed on R as follows: first, a directed edge $e = (u, v)$ is constructed for each unique k-length subsequence (k-mer) in R, where u and v (the nodes or $(k-1)$-mers) are labeled with the prefix and suffix of that k-mer, and next, after all possible edges have been constructed, nodes with the same label are glued together to a single node. Hence, in this paper we restrict interest to the DNA alphabet consisting of the symbols A, C, G, and T. The set of DNA sequences in R are referred to as *sequence reads*. An

© Springer Nature Switzerland AG 2018
T. Gagie et al. (Eds.): SPIRE 2018, LNCS 11147, pp. 1–11, 2018.
https://doi.org/10.1007/978-3-030-00479-8_1

example of gluing is as follows: if for $k = 4$, node u_1 with label ATG has outgoing edge A and node u_2 with the same label ATG, has outgoing edge G, since the labels are the same, to make sure that all of the labels in de Bruijn graph are distinctive, we glue them. This means that the outgoing edge of u_2 will be added to u_1, so u_1 has two outgoing edges with labels A and G, and u_2 will be deleted. In order to construct the colored de Bruijn graph, we assign a set of colors to each edge (k-mer) in the de Bruijn graph. More specifically, we view the colored de Bruijn graph as a de Bruijn graph $G = (V, E)$ with a $m \times \alpha$ binary matrix C (m is the number of distinct k-mers, and α is the number of colors), where there exists a row for each edge (k-mer), and a column for each color such that $C[j, a] = 1$ if edge $e_j \in E$ contains color c_a and $C[j, a] = 0$ otherwise. We refer to C as the *color matrix*. Figure 2 (left) illustrates an example of colored de Bruijn graph with four colors.

In this paper, we consider the case in which the colored de Bruijn graph is used to disambiguate the traversal of the graph by assigning each sequence read in R a unique color. We note that the necessity of colors arises from the fact that constructing the de Bruijn graph requires that reads are split to k-mers—making them indistinguishable from each other. Thus, the information that ties a particular k-mer to the originating sequence(s) is lost. This problem is circumvented in the colored de Bruijn graph by storing this information in the color matrix. Due to the number of reads—or individuals in the original use case of the colored de Bruijn graph—the size of the color matrix can be immense. Typically, the number of distinct k-mers is in the order of several millions and the number of reads or number of individuals is at least 100,000—as in the case of the 100,000 Genome Project [1].

Given the typical size of current datasets, a significant amount of attention has been spent on constructing and storing the colored de Bruijn graph efficiently with respect to both memory and time. Vari [14] was the first succinct representation of the colored de Bruijn graph. It views the colored de Bruijn graph as the union graph of several de Bruijn graphs $G_{c_1}, G_{c_2}, \dots, G_{c_\alpha}$, each of which corresponds to the de Bruijn graph of a single color in color set $\{c_1, \dots, c_\alpha\}$. It uses FM-index [17] and Burrows-Wheeler Transform (BWT) [6], to efficiently construct and store the de Bruijn graph, and stores the color matrix as a one-dimensional row-based bit vector (the rows of C, are concatenated), which is compressed using Elias-Fano [7,13,15] encoding. In this construction, the color matrix is compressed during the construction to decrease the peak memory usage. Rainbowfish [3] is another method to construct the colored de Bruijn graph in a memory-efficient manner which is an extension of Vari. After storing the distinct sets of colors in a table, this method is able to index the color sets for each edge in the de Bruijn graph using variable length bit patterns similar to Huffman coding. Bloom filter tries [10] is another tool to encode the sets of colors along with the de Bruijn graph. This method assigns a reference to the color set, and if the reference takes fewer bits than the set itself, the reference will be stored. All of these methods, with some penalty to runtime, can reduce the memory required for storage of colors without reducing the number of them.

In this paper, we investigate a different approach for decreasing the size of colored de Bruijn graph, namely recoloring the graph with a smaller number of colors; to differentiate the new colors from the original, the former are called labels. First, we prove that finding the minimum number of labels needed to recolor a colored de Bruijn graph is not only NP-hard but also difficult to approximate within a factor of $|R|^{1-\epsilon}$, where R is the set of reads and $\epsilon > 0$; since a trivial approximation ratio is at most $|R|$ by coloring each read with a unique color, this is a strong inapproximability result. Given the computational hardness of this problem, we present a polynomial-time heuristic that recolors the graph by greedily giving the same label to *compatible* colors (defined in Sect. 2), but still allows for the reads to be efficiently distinguished. We implement the heuristic and demonstrate that it reduces the number of colors by up to two orders of magnitude. In particular, when the number of colors was 5,000,000 and 10,000,000 the number of labels needed to recolor the graph was 36,686 and 75,281, respectively—which reduces the size of the color matrix by more than half. Lastly, the recoloring algorithm uses less than 7 GB of memory and 4 hours of CPU time, even when the number of colors is large. In Sect. 2, we give an overview of the definitions and terminology that will be used in our paper. Next, in Sect. 3 we show that not only is determining the minimum number of colors needed *exactly* is NP-complete, it is also computationally hard to determine the number within a reasonable factor. In Sect. 4 we describe a polynomial heuristic for recoloring a colored de Bruijn graph, and show it reduces the number of original colors by up to 136 times. Lastly, we conclude in Sect. 5 and discuss directions for future work.

2   Preliminaries

In this section we formally define the main concepts used in this paper.

Strings. Throughout we consider a string $s = s[1 \ldots x] = s[1]s[2] \ldots s[x]$ of $|s| = x$ symbols drawn from the alphabet $[0 \ldots \sigma-1]$. For $i = 1, \ldots, n$ we write $s[i \ldots x]$ to denote the *suffix* of s of length $x - i + 1$, that is $s[i \ldots x] = s[i]s[i+1] \ldots s[x]$. Similarly, we write $s[1 \ldots i]$ to denote the *prefix* of s of length i, that starts at the first position and ends at i.

Given a string $s[i \ldots x]$ we denote the set of all unique k-mers of s as s_k, the set of all unique prefixes of length $k - 1$ of s_k as $\mathsf{prefix}(s_k)$ and the set of all unique suffixes of length $k - 1$ of s_k as $\mathsf{suffix}(s_k)$.

Binary Strings. We let x and y be two binary characters, we denote $x \oplus y$ as the XOR of these characters. Next, we let $s_1[1 \ldots a]$ and $s_2[1 \ldots a]$ be two binary vectors (bit-vectors) of length a, we denote $s_1 \oplus s_2$ be equal to $[s_1[1] \oplus s_2[1], s_1[2] \oplus s_2[2], \ldots, s_1[a] \oplus s_2[a]]$.

Color Compatibility. As previously mentioned, in this paper we focus on colored de Bruijn graphs in which each read is assigned a unique color and the k-mers corresponding to that read contain the associated color. Hence, given a colored de Bruijn graph G constructed for read set R, we let $\{c_1, \ldots, c_x\}$ be such that a k-mer (edge) contains color c_i if it occurs in read r_i.

Therefore, given two reads r_i and r_j with colors c_i and c_j, we call the colors *compatible* if for any pair of k-mers in r_i and r_j, say $s_i^k \in r_i$ and $s_j^k \in r_j$, it follows that $\text{prefix}(s_i^k) \cap \text{suffix}(s_j^k) = \emptyset$—meaning there does not exist a k-mer in r_i whose prefix is equal to the suffix of a k-mer in r_j. Given any two reads r_i and r_j with colors c_i and c_j, we call the colors *incompatible* if they are not compatible.

Recoloring and Labels. Given a colored de Bruijn graph G with colors $\{c_1, \ldots, c_\alpha\}$, we refer to a *recoloring* of G as a function $F : \{c_1, \ldots, c_\alpha\} \to \{\ell_1, \ldots, \ell_y\}$ that maps each color to one element in $\{\ell_1, \ldots, \ell_y\}$. In order to distinguish between the original set of colors, and the (smaller) set of colors obtained by recoloring, we use the term *label* to refer to the latter. We denote $\{\ell_1, \ldots, \ell_y\}$ as the set of labels and the correspond $m \times y$ label matrix as L.

Valid Recoloring. Given a colored de Bruijn graph G with colors $\{c_i, \ldots, c_\alpha\}$ and recoloring F with label set $\{\ell_1, \ldots, \ell_y\}$, we refer to F as a *valid recoloring* if there exists a label ℓ_j for each c_i such that $\ell_j = F(c_i)$, and $F(c_i) = F(c_j)$ if and only if c_i and c_j are compatible. An example of a valid recoloring is in Fig. 2; here, by recoloring with a set of compatible colors the number of colors—or labels—is reduced from 4 to 2.

3 Recoloring a Colored de Bruijn Graph with the Minimum Number of Colors

We begin by formally defining the problem of recoloring a colored de Bruijn graph with a minimum number of labels.

CDBG-Recoloring

 Input: A read-colored de Bruijn graph (CDBG) $G = (V, E)$ constructed from a set of sequence reads R with the set of colors $\{c_1, \ldots, c_\alpha\}$.

Question: What is the minimum α', such that there exist a valid recoloring of G that uses α' labels?

Notice that the original number of colors α is irrelevant to the minimum number of colors α'. As we show in the following theorem, any approximation algorithm for *CDBG-Recoloring* problem may be used to approximate the classical *Graph-Coloring* problem for arbitrary graphs. A t-coloring of a graph $G' = (V', E')$ is a mapping $H : V' \to \{1, 2, \ldots, t\}$ such that $H(u) \neq H(v)$ for all edges $(u, v) \in E'$. We say G' is t-colorable if G' has a t-coloring. Figure 1 illustrates an instance of graph coloring.

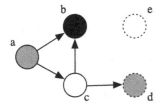
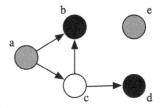

Fig. 1. In this figure, we illustrate the coloring of an arbitrary graph. (Left): Each node has a unique color, thus five colors are used for coloring five nodes (solid Black, solid Grey, solid White, dashed Grey, dashed White). (Right): This graph can be colored using only 3 colors—is 3-colorable (solid Black, solid Grey, solid White).

Graph-Coloring
   Input: A graph $G' = (V', E')$.
   Question: What is the minimum t such that G' is t-colorable?

For a given graph G', the solution of *Graph-Coloring* is termed the *chromatic index* of G'. For the decision version of this problem, we write t-*Graph-Coloring*, which is known to be NP-complete for any value of t greater than 2 [16]. For *Graph-Coloring*, it is known that there is no approximation within $|V'|^{1-\epsilon}$ unless NP=ZPP[1] [8], for any $\epsilon > 0$.

Theorem 1. *Any γ-approximation algorithm for* CDBG-Recoloring *yields a γ-approximation for* Graph-Coloring; *the decision version of* CDBG-Recoloring *is NP-complete.*

Proof. First, we give a reduction from *Graph-Coloring* to *CDBG-Recoloring*. In particular, we show how, given an instance of *Graph-Coloring* $G' = (V', E')$, in polynomial time we can find a set S of $|V'|$ ternary strings such that the following statements are equivalent:

- each node in G' can be assigned one of t colors such that if two vertices are neighbours then those vertices are different colors;
- each string in S can be assigned one of t labels such that if one string contains a k-mer s_{k_1} and another contains a k-mer s_{k_2} with the last $k-1$ characters of s_{k_1} equal to the first $k-1$ characters of s_{k_2}, then those strings are different colors.

Let m be the number of edges in G' and assume $m \geq 1$ without loss of generality. We number the edges from 0 to $m - 1$ and label each edge with the concatenation of two copies of the $(\lfloor \lg m \rfloor + 1)$-bit binary representation of its number, separated by \$. For each node $v \in V'$ we build a string s_v by concatenating its incident edges' labels, separated by copies of \$. Finally, we make S the set of these strings and set $k = 2(\lfloor \lg m \rfloor + 1) + 2$.

---

[1] ZPP is the complexity class of problems solvable by a randomized algorithm in expected polynomial time.

If u and v share an edge e in G, then s_u contains $\$\gamma\$\gamma$ and s_v contains $\gamma\$\gamma\$$, where γ is the $(\lfloor \lg m \rfloor + 1)$-bit binary representation of e's number. Now suppose s_u and s_v contain k-mers s_{uk} and s_{vk}, respectively, with the $k-1$-length suffix of s_{uk} is equal to the $k-1$-length prefix of s_{vk}. Since any substring of length $k - 1 = 2(\lfloor \lg m \rfloor + 1) + 1$ of any string consisting of $(\lfloor \lg m \rfloor + 1)$-bit binary numbers separated by copies of $\$$ contains at least one complete number, s_u and s_v must contain the same number, so u and v must share an edge. That is, u and v share an edge if and only if s_u and s_v contain k-mers s_{uk} and s_{vk}, respectively, with the last $k-1$ characters of α equal to the first $k-1$ characters of β. It follows that we can obtain a valid coloring of G from any valid coloring of S, or vice versa, by making each node the same color as the corresponding string. By this one-to-one correspondence between colorings, the minimum number of colors for both problems is the same, and the solution of any γ-approximation for *CDBG-Recoloring* can be transformed in polynomial time into a solution for *Graph-Coloring* with the same number of colors, yielding an approximation algorithm with the same ratio γ for *Graph-Coloring*.

Given an instance of and a certificate in the form of an assignment of colors to the strings, it is easy to check the certificate in polynomial time, so α'-*CDBG-Recoloring* is also in NP and thus NP-complete.   □

Corollary 1. *For any $\epsilon > 0$, there is no $|R|^{1-\epsilon}$-approximation for* CDBG-Recoloring *unless NP=ZPP.*

Corollary 1 follows from Feige and Kilian [8] and Theorem 1; since the number of reads $|R|$ is usually large (in our experimental evaluation, up to 10^7), this is a strong inapproximability result. At first, it may appear surprising since the a classical de Bruijn graph on an alphabet of four symbols has chromatic index 8 [5]. However, in the *CDBG-Recoloring* problem, the coloring does not correspond to edges of the de Bruijn graph; instead, it corresponds to coloring the reads, which form paths in the graph; as shown in the proof of Theorem 1, these paths can encode an arbitrary graph structure.

4   Recoloring the Colored de Bruijn Graph

Given the computational hardness of finding the minimum number of colors, we present a heuristic for recoloring a colored de Bruijn graph. Our algorithm constructs a label matrix by greedily giving the same label to the colors that are deemed to be compatible, and thus, avoids constructing the original (significantly larger) color matrix. Each column of the label matrix is constructed one column (per label) at a time and compressed using Elias-Fano vector encoding [7,13,15]. Thus, the algorithm avoids constructing the color matrix or the uncompressed color matrix at any point.

4.1   A Practical Algorithm

We recall that the color matrix C is defined such that $C[j, a] = 1$, if k-mer k_j (jth k-mer in lexicographical order) is present in r_a. Hence, colors c_a and c_b

corresponding to r_a and r_b are compatible if there does exist any pair of k-mers $s_a^k \in r_a$ and $s_b^k \in r_b$ such that $\mathsf{prefix}(s_a^k) \cap \mathsf{suffix}(s_b^k) = \emptyset$. It follows that colors c_a and c_b are guaranteed to be compatible if $\mathsf{C}[j,a] \oplus \mathsf{C}[j,b] = \emptyset$ for all $j = 1, \ldots, m$. This condition is stronger than color compatibility condition.

Our algorithm works as follows. We first initialize L to be equal to the empty set. Then, we extract all unique k-mers from $r_1 \in R$, add a new label ℓ_1 to L, and set $F(c_1) = \ell_1$. Next, for each subsequent $r_i \in R$, we extract the k-mers of r_i and assign a temporary color t to the corresponding k-mers. We check whether t is compatible with any label in L by determining whether $\mathsf{L}[j,a] \oplus t[j] = \emptyset$, $j = 1, \ldots, m$. If there exists a $\ell' \in \mathsf{L}$ compatible with t then we label r_i with ℓ'. We note that in this case the number of labels in L remains unchanged. Otherwise, it follows that t is incompatible with all labels in L, necessitating the creation of a new label ℓ_t that will be added to L. We continue on this process until all reads in R have been considered.

Figure 2 illustrates the original colored de Bruijn graph (left) with 4 colors, which using the recoloring algorithm is colored (labeled) by only 2 colors (right). Similarly, on Fig. 3, the original color matrix (left) and the recolored matrix (right) are shown.

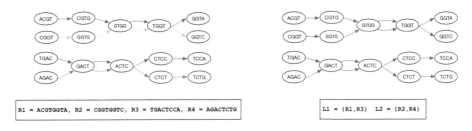

Fig. 2. (Left): This graph is an illustration of colored de Bruijn graph with $k = 5$, in which the colors are sequence reads. Note that there is actually only one edge GTGGT from GTGG to TGGT in the real de Bruijn graph, while in this figure we drew 2 individual edges each with different color (solid Black and dashed Black) due to better showing the concept of the color. The same is true for the edge GACTC. (Right): Since read R1 (solid Black) and R3 (dashed Grey) in left graph does not share any edges (k-mers), they are compatible and can be labeled same L1 (solid Grey). The same is correct for R2 and R4 which are labeled by L2 (solid Black).

4.2   Implementation and Datasets

We demonstrate the ability of the recoloring algorithm to reduce the number colors using real shotgun metagenomic data. We implemented the algorithm in C++ and tested it on a machine with two Xeon E5-2640 v4 chips, each having 10 2.4 GHz cores. The system contains 755 GB of RAM and two ZFS RAID pools of 9 disk each for storage. We report CPU time and maximum resident set size from Linux. We use the SDSL-Lite library [9] to store all succinct vectors.

	R1	R2	R3	R4
ACG	1	0	1	0
AGT	0	1	0	0
ATT	0	0	0	1
CGT	1	0	1	0
GAC	0	0	1	0
GTC	1	0	0	0
GTG	0	1	0	0
TAG	0	1	0	0
TAT	0	0	0	1
TTG	0	0	0	1

	L1	L2
ACG	1	1
AGT	1	0
ATT	1	
CGT	1	1
GAC	0	1
GTC	1	0
GTG	1	0
TAG	1	0
TAT	1	0
TTG	1	0

R1 = ACGTC, R2 = TAGTG, R3 = GACGT, R4 = TATTG

L1 = {R1, R2, R4}, L2 = {R3}

Fig. 3. (Left) The color matrix constructed on four colors (reads), with $k = 4$. (Right) The recoloring matrix. The compatible colors R1, R2 and R4 have same label L1, while the color R3 has the label L2. In this example, the number of colors drops from 4 (Left) to 2 (right).

Our test dataset consists of 87 metagenomic datasets that were obtained from sequencing on an Illumina HiSeq 2500 system. The biological samples were selected across a beef production system, which contain various interventions aimed at decreasing pathogenic and antibiotic-resistant bacteria in consumable beef. Standardized filtering and data cleaning was first done by removing contaminant DNA (e.g., human and bovine DNA), and filtering for k-mers ($k = 32$) that have low multiplicity (< 12).

We expect the reduction in the size of the color matrix will become more significant as the number of colors increases. In order to test this hypothesis, we assigned a unique color to each sequence read—which, as previously mentioned, is the use case of LueVari [2]—and varied the number of sequence reads from 25,000 to 10,000,000. The number of colors is shown in the leftmost column of Table 1. We emphasize that our method does not need to construct the color matrix first, and is able to directly build the recolored matrix from the beginning.

4.3 Experiments

We demonstrate the performance of the recoloring algorithm in Table 1. As shown in the table, the recoloring heuristic produces a number of labels that is between one and two orders of magnitude smaller than the number of colors. The reduction witnessed from recoloring steadily increased as the number of original colors increased. To illustrate this point, we see the number of labels produced by recoloring was 414 when there was 25,000 colors (a 60 times reduction), whereas, the number of labels produced by recoloring was 26,239 when there was 2,000,000 colors (a 80 times reduction). The largest reduction was witnessed with > 5,000,000 colors. For instance, in experiment with 5,000,000 and 10,000,000 reads the number of labels is 36,686, and 75,281, respectively—a reduction by 136 and 133 times.

We show both the CPU time and peak memory usage of the recoloring algorithm in Table 1. Our method required between 0.26 CPU seconds and 1.24 MB of memory, and 3.5 CPU hours and 6.2 GB of memory. Finally, in last two columns of this table we see that with recoloring, the resulting matrix is almost half in all experiments. Both the color matrix and the label matrix were compressed using Elias-Fano encoding [7, 13, 15].

Table 1. Results of the recoloring algorithm. In this table, we report the number of colors before running the recoloring heuristic (Colors), the number of labels needed to recolor (Labels), the CPU time needed to recolor (Time), peak memory usage of constructing and recoloring the colored de Bruijn graph (Memory), the size of the original color matrix in MB (Color Matrix) and the size of the label matrix produced after recoloring in MB (Label Matrix). In all experiments, the k-mer size is 32 and reads are 60 bp and 150 bp in length.

Colors	Labels	Time (hh.mm.ss)	Memory	Color matrix (MB)	Label matrix (MB)
25,000	414	0.26 s	1.24 MB	0.0071	0.0033
100,000	1,315	00:00:02	1.24 MB	0.0288	0.0147
250,000	3,029	00:00:07	1.24 MB	0.0901	0.0488
500,000	6,126	00:00:26	1.24 MB	0.1989	0.1204
1,000,000	12,875	00:02:22	379.68 MB	0.5408	0.2978
2,000,000	26,239	00:10:27	783.42 MB	1.5263	0.8470
5,000,000	36,686	00:37:52	2.54 GB	20.3215	7.82015
10,000,000	75,281	03:48:15	6.21 GB	69.8746	27.5117

5   Conclusion

The colored de Bruijn graph has become an increasingly important data structure in bioinformatics in the past several years [11]. Due to this, there have been several independent efforts to represent the colored de Bruijn graph in a compressed manner. In this paper, we present a different approach to reducing the size of structure—which we show is complementary to existing compression techniques.

We first demonstrate that determining the minimum number of colors needed to unambiguously color the graph in NP-complete, and unlikely to be approximated within a reasonable factor in polynomial time. In light of these results, we give a polynomial-time heuristic to recolor the colored de Bruijn graph in a manner that compatible colors have same labels. By applying this approach, we show the number of colors is greatly reduced—between 60 and 136 times. By applying Elias-Fano encoding [7, 13, 15], we are able to represent the color matrix in less than 1 GB for even very large datasets (e.g., >5,000,000 reads). We implemented our recoloring approach in the column-based manner. The respective row-based recoloring algorithm would require an auxiliary data structure that checks the color compatibility—thus, increasing the space usage to store the recolored de Bruijn graph.

We emphasize that recoloring the de Bruijn graph—which is effective in reducing the number of colors—is complementary to compression and succinct representations of the color matrix. Lastly, due to the recent interest in dynamic de Bruijn graphs [4], studying how to represent the color matrix in a compressed—yet, mutable—manner is worthy of future study.

References

1. The 100,000 Genomes Project Protocol v3 (2017). https://doi.org/10.6084/m9. figshare.4530893.v2
2. Alipanahi, B., et al.: Resistome SNP calling via read colored de Bruijn graphs. In: RECOMB-Seq (2018)
3. Almodaresi, F., Pandey, P., Patro, R.: Rainbowfish: a succinct colored de Bruijn graph representation. In: WABI, pp. 251–256 (2017)
4. Belazzougui, D., Gagie, T., Mäkinen, V., Previtali, M.: Fully dynamic de Bruijn graphs. In: Inenaga, S., Sadakane, K., Sakai, T. (eds.) SPIRE 2016. LNCS, vol. 9954, pp. 145–152. Springer, Cham (2016). https://doi.org/10.1007/978-3-319-46049-9_14
5. Bermond, J.C., Hell, P.: On even factorizations and the chromatic index of the Kautz and de Bruijn digraphs. J. Graph Theory **17**(5), 647–655 (1993)
6. Burrows, M., Wheeler, D.J.: A block sorting lossless data compression algorithm. Technical report 124, Digital Equipment Corporation (1994)
7. Elias, P.: Efficient storage and retrieval by content and address of static files. J. ACM (JACM) **21**(2), 246–260 (1974)
8. Feige, U., Kilian, J.: Zero knowledge and the chromatic number. In: Conference on Computational Complexity, pp. 278–287 (1996)
9. Gog, S., Beller, T., Moffat, A., Petri, M.: From theory to practice: plug and play with succinct data structures. In: Gudmundsson, J., Katajainen, J. (eds.) SEA 2014. LNCS, vol. 8504, pp. 326–337. Springer, Cham (2014). https://doi.org/10.1007/978-3-319-07959-2_28
10. Holley, G.: Bloom filter Trie: an alignment-free and reference-free data structure for pan-genome storage. Algorithms Mol. Biol. **11**, 3 (2016)
11. Iqbal, Z.: De novo assembly and genotyping of variants using colored de Bruijn graphs. Nat. Genet. **44**(2), 226–232 (2012)
12. Marcus, S.: Splitmem: a graphical algorithm for pan-genome analysis with suffix skips. Bioinformatics **30**, 3476–3483 (2014)

13. Mario, F.R.: On the number of bits required to implement an associative memory. Massachusetts Institute of Technology, Project MAC (1971)
14. Muggli, M.D., et al.: Succinct colored de Bruijn graphs. Bioinformatics **33**, 3181–3187 (2017)
15. Okanohara, D., Sadakane, K.: Practical entropy-compressed rank/select dictionary. In: Proceedings of the Meeting on Algorithm Engineering & Expermiments, pp. 60–70 (2007)
16. Sánchez-Arroyo, A.: Determining the total colouring number is NP-hard. Discret. Math. **78**, 315–319 (1989)
17. Simpson, J.T., Durbin, R.: Efficient construction of an assembly string graph using the FM-index. Bioinformatics **26**(12), i367–i373 (2010)

Efficient Computation of Sequence Mappability

Mai Alzamel[1,2] , Panagiotis Charalampopoulos[1] , Costas S. Iliopoulos[1] ,
Tomasz Kociumaka[3] , Solon P. Pissis[1] , Jakub Radoszewski[3] ,
and Juliusz Straszyński[3(✉)]

[1] Department of Informatics, King's College London, London, UK
{mai.alzamel,panagiotis.charalampopoulos,
c.iliopoulos,solon.pissis}@kcl.ac.uk
[2] Computer Science Department, King Saud University, Riyadh, Saudi Arabia
[3] Institute of Informatics, University of Warsaw, Warsaw, Poland
{kociumaka,jrad,jks}@mimuw.edu.pl

Abstract. Sequence mappability is an important task in genome re-sequencing. In the (k, m)-mappability problem, for a given sequence T of length n, our goal is to compute a table whose ith entry is the number of indices $j \neq i$ such that length-m substrings of T starting at positions i and j have at most k mismatches. Previous works on this problem focused on heuristic approaches to compute a rough approximation of the result or on the case of $k = 1$. We present several efficient algorithms for the general case of the problem. Our main result is an algorithm that works in $\mathcal{O}(n \min\{m^k, \log^{k+1} n\})$ time and $\mathcal{O}(n)$ space for $k = \mathcal{O}(1)$. It requires a careful adaptation of the technique of Cole et al. [STOC 2004] to avoid multiple counting of pairs of substrings. We also show $\mathcal{O}(n^2)$-time algorithms to compute *all* results for a fixed m and all $k = 0, \ldots, m$ or a fixed k and all $m = k, \ldots, n - 1$. Finally we show that the (k, m)-mappability problem cannot be solved in strongly subquadratic time for $k, m = \Theta(\log n)$ unless the Strong Exponential Time Hypothesis fails.

Keywords: Sequence mappability · Hamming distance
Genome sequencing · Longest common substring with k mismatches
Suffix tree

1 Introduction

Analyzing data derived from massively parallel sequencing experiments often depends on the process of genome assembly via re-sequencing; namely, assembly with the help of a reference sequence. In this process, a large number of reads (or

---

J. Radoszewski and J. Straszyński—Supported by the "Algorithms for text processing with errors and uncertainties" project carried out within the HOMING programme of the Foundation for Polish Science co-financed by the European Union under the European Regional Development Fund.

© Springer Nature Switzerland AG 2018
T. Gagie et al. (Eds.): SPIRE 2018, LNCS 11147, pp. 12–26, 2018.
https://doi.org/10.1007/978-3-030-00479-8_2

short sequences) derived from a DNA donor during these experiments must be mapped back to a reference sequence, comprising a few gigabases, to establish the section of the genome from which each read has been derived. An extensive number of short-read alignment techniques and tools have been introduced to address this challenge emphasizing on different aspects of the process [10].

In turn, the process of re-sequencing depends heavily on how mappable a genome is given a set of reads of some fixed length m. Thus, given a reference sequence, for every substring of length m in the sequence, we want to count how many additional times this substring appears in the sequence when allowing for a small number k of errors. This computational problem and a heuristic approach to approximate the solution were first proposed in [7] (see also [3]). A great variance in genome mappability between species and gene classes was revealed in [7].

More formally, let T_i^m denote the length-m substring of T that starts at position i. In the (k, m)-mappability problem, for a given string T of length n, we are asked to compute a table $A_{\leq k}^m$ whose ith entry $A_{\leq k}^m[i]$ is the number of indices $j \neq i$ such that the substrings T_i^m and T_j^m are at Hamming distance at most k. In the previous study [7] the assumed values of parameters were $k \leq 4$, $m \leq 100$, and the alphabet of T was $\{\mathtt{A}, \mathtt{C}, \mathtt{G}, \mathtt{T}\}$.

Example 1. Consider the string $T = \mathtt{aababba}$ and $m = 3$. The following table shows the (k, m)-mappability counts for $k = 1$ and $k = 2$.

Position	i	1	2	3	4	5
Substring	T_i^3	aab	aba	bab	abb	bba
$(1, 3)$-mappability	$A_{\leq 1}^3[i]$	2	2	1	2	1
$(2, 3)$-mappability	$A_{\leq 2}^3[i]$	3	3	3	4	3
Difference	$A_{=2}^3[i]$	1	1	2	2	2

For instance, consider the position 1. The $(1, 3)$-mappability is 2 due to the occurrence of bab at position 3 and occurrence of abb at position 4. The $(2, 3)$-mappability is 3 since only the substring bba, occurring at position 5, has three mismatches with aab.

For convenience, in our algorithms we compute an array $A_{=k}^m$ whose ith entry $A_{=k}^m[i]$ is the number of positions $j \neq i$ such that substrings T_i^m and T_j^m are at Hamming distance *exactly* k. Note that $A_{\leq k}^m[i] = \sum_{k'=0}^{k} A_{=k'}^m[i]$; see the "difference" row in the example above. Henceforth we refer to this modified problem as to the (k, m)-mappability problem.

Using the well-known LCP table [14,15,17], the $(0, m)$-mappability problem can be solved in $\mathcal{O}(n)$ time and space. Manzini [18] proposed an algorithm working in $\mathcal{O}(mn \log n / \log \log n)$ time and $\mathcal{O}(n)$ space for strings over a constant-sized alphabet for the case of $k = 1$. This was later improved in [2] with two algorithms that require worst-case time $\mathcal{O}(mn)$ and $\mathcal{O}(n \log n \log \log n)$, respectively, and space $\mathcal{O}(n)$ for the case of $k = 1$. Moreover, the authors presented another algorithm requiring average-case time and space $\mathcal{O}(n)$ for uniformly random strings over a linearly-sortable integer alphabet of size σ if $k = 1$ and $m = \Omega(\log_\sigma n)$. In addition, they showed that their algorithm is generalizable for arbitrary k, requiring average-case time $\mathcal{O}(kn)$ and space $\mathcal{O}(n)$ if $m = \Omega(k \log_\sigma n)$. In [1] the authors introduced an efficient construction of a *genome mappability array* B_k in which $B_k[\mu]$ is the smallest length m such that at least μ of the length-m substrings of T do not occur elsewhere in T with at most k mismatches.

Our Contributions. We present several algorithms for the general case of the (k, m)-mappability problem. More specifically, our contributions are as follows:

1. In Sect. 3 we present an algorithm for the (k, m)-mappability problem that works in $\mathcal{O}(n\binom{\log n + k + 1}{k+1} 4^k k)$ time and $\mathcal{O}(n 2^k k)$ space for a string over an ordered alphabet. It requires a careful adaptation of the technique of recursive heavy-path decompositions in a tree [6].
2. In Sect. 4 we show an algorithm for the same problem that works in $\mathcal{O}(n\binom{m}{k} \sigma^k)$ time and $\mathcal{O}(n)$ space for a string over an integer alphabet. Together with the previous one, this yields an $\mathcal{O}(n \min\{m^k, \log^{k+1} n\})$-time and $\mathcal{O}(n)$-space algorithm for $\sigma, k = \mathcal{O}(1)$.
3. In Sect. 5 we describe $\mathcal{O}(n^2)$-time algorithms to compute *all* (k, m)-mappability results: for a fixed m and all $k = 0, \ldots, m$; or for a fixed k and all $m = k, \ldots, n - 1$.
4. Finally, in Sect. 6 we show that the (k, m)-mappability problem cannot be solved in strongly subquadratic time for $k, m = \Theta(\log n)$ unless the Strong Exponential Time Hypothesis [12,13] fails.

In contributions 1 and 4 we apply very recent advances in the Longest Common Substring with k Mismatches problem that were presented in [5,16], respectively (see also [21]). In particular, in addition to [5], our contribution 1 requires careful counting of substring pairs to avoid multiple counting and a thorough analysis of the space usage. Technically this is the most involved contribution.

2   Preliminaries

Let $T = T[1]T[2] \cdots T[n]$ be a *string* of length $|T| = n$ over a finite ordered alphabet Σ of size $|\Sigma| = \sigma$. For two positions i and j on T, $T[i] \cdots T[j]$ is the *substring* (sometimes called *factor*) of T that starts at position i and ends at position j (it is of length 0 if $j < i$). A *prefix* of T is a substring that starts at position 1 and a *suffix* of T is a substring that ends at position n. We denote the suffix that starts at position i by T_i and its prefix of length m by T_i^m.

The *Hamming distance* between two strings T and S, $|T| = |S|$, is defined as $d_H(T, S) = |\{i : T[i] \neq S[i], \ i = 1, 2, \ldots, |T|\}|$. If $|T| \neq |S|$, we set $d_H(T, S) = \infty$.

By $\mathsf{lcp}(S, T)$ we denote the length of the longest common prefix of S and T and by $\mathsf{lcp}(r, s)$ we denote $\mathsf{lcp}(T_r, T_s)$ for a fixed string T. By $k\text{-}\mathsf{lcp}(r, s)$ we denote the length of the longest common prefix of T_r and T_s when k mismatches are allowed, that is, the maximum ℓ such that $d_H(T_r^\ell, T_s^\ell) \leq k$.

Compact Trie. A compact trie $\mathcal{T}$ of a collection of strings C is obtained from the trie of C by removing all non-branching nodes, excluding the root and the leaves. The nodes of the trie which become nodes of $\mathcal{T}$ are called *explicit* nodes, while the other nodes are called *implicit*. Each edge of $\mathcal{T}$ can be viewed as an upward maximal path of implicit nodes starting with an explicit node. The string label of an edge is a substring of one of the strings in C; the label of an edge is its first letter. Each node of the trie can be represented in $\mathcal{T}$ by the edge it belongs to and an index within the corresponding path. We let $\mathcal{L}(v)$ denote the *path-label* of a node v, i.e., the concatenation of the edge labels along the path from the root to v. Additionally, $\mathcal{D}(v) = |\mathcal{L}(v)|$ is the *string-depth* of node v.

Suffix Tree. The suffix tree $\mathcal{T}(T)$ of a string T is a compact trie representing all suffixes of T. A node v is a *terminal* node if its path-label is a suffix of T, that is, $\mathcal{L}(v) = T_i$ for some $1 \leq i \leq n$; here v is also labeled with index i. Each substring of T is uniquely represented by either an explicit or an implicit node of $\mathcal{T}(T)$. The *suffix link* of a node v with path-label $\mathcal{L}(v) = \alpha Y$ is a pointer to the node with path-label Y, where $\alpha \in \Sigma$ is a single letter and Y is a string. The suffix link of v exists if v is a non-root explicit node of $\mathcal{T}(T)$.

The suffix tree of a string of length n over an integer alphabet (together with the suffix links) can be computed in time and space $\mathcal{O}(n)$ [9]. In standard suffix tree implementations, we assume that each node of the suffix tree is able to access its parent. For non-constant alphabets, in order to access the children of an explicit node by the first letter of their edge label, perfect hashing [11] can be used. Once $\mathcal{T}(T)$ is constructed, it can be traversed in a depth-first manner to compute $\mathcal{D}(v)$ for each node v.

3 $\mathcal{O}(n \log^{k+1} n)$-Time and $\mathcal{O}(n)$-Space Algorithm

Our algorithm operates on so-called modified strings. A *modified string* α is a string U with a set of modifications M. Each element of the set M is a pair of the form (i, c) which denotes a substitution "$U[i] := c$". We assume that the first components of the pairs in M are pairwise distinct. By $val(\alpha)$ we denote the string U after all the substitutions and by $M(\alpha)$ we denote the set M.

The algorithm processes *modified substrings* of T that are modified strings originating from the substrings T_i^m. The index of origin of a modified substring α is denoted by $idx(\alpha)$ (that is, α is a modification of T_i^m for $i = idx(\alpha)$).

Overview of the Algorithm. Intuitively, the algorithm performs the task by efficiently simulating transformations of a compact trie initially containing all substrings T_i^m. The operation we would like to perform efficiently is copying one subtree unto its sibling, changing the first letter on the appropriate label. This process effectively results in registering one mismatch for a large batch of substrings at once. Combining it together with the *smaller-to-larger* principle, this yields a foundation to solve the main problem in the aforementioned time.

More precisely, the algorithm navigates a compact trie of modified substrings.[1] The trie is constructed top-down recursively, and the final set of modified substrings that are present in the trie is known only when all the leaves of the trie have been reached.

In a recursive step, a node v of the trie stores a set of modified substrings $MS(v)$. Initially, the root r stores all substrings T_i^m in its set $MS(r)$. The path-label $\mathcal{L}(v)$ is the longest common prefix of all the modified substrings in $MS(v)$ and the string-depth $\mathcal{D}(v)$ is the length of this prefix. None of the strings in $MS(v)$ contains a modification at a position greater than $\mathcal{D}(v)$. The children of v are determined by subsets of $MS(v)$ that correspond to different letters at position $\mathcal{D}(v) + 1$. Furthermore, additional modified substrings with modifications at position $\mathcal{D}(v) + 1$ are created and inserted into the children's MS-sets. This corresponds to the intuition of copying subtrees unto their siblings.

The goal is to put multiple appropriate modified substrings in a single leaf, where they will be processed in such way that every pair of substrings (T_i^m, T_j^m) differing on exactly k positions will be registered exactly once.

Now, we will describe the recursive routine for visiting a node.

Processing an Internal Node. Assume that our node v has children $u_1, \ldots, u_a$. First, we distinguish a child of v with maximum-size set MS; let it be u_1. We will refer to this child as *heavy* and to every other as *light*. We will recursively branch into each child to take care of all pairs of modified strings contained in any single subtree. We need to make sure that all relevant pairs satisfy this condition.

For this, we create an extra child u_{a+1} that contains all modified substrings from $MS(u_2) \cup \cdots \cup MS(u_a)$ with the letters at position $\mathcal{D}(v) + 1$ replaced by a common wildcard character \$. Note that each modified substring in u_{a+1} contains one more substitution compared to its source in one of the light subtrees. Hence, we refrain from copying any modified substring which already has k substitutions. This way, we will consider pairs of modified substrings that originate from different light children.

Additionally, we insert all modified substrings from $MS(u_2) \cup \cdots \cup MS(u_a)$ into $MS(u_1)$, substituting the letter at position $\mathcal{D}(v) + 1$ with the common letter at this position of modified substrings in $MS(u_1)$. This transformation will take care of pairs between the heavy child and the light ones.

Finally, the algorithm branches into the subtrees of $u_1, \ldots, u_{a+1}$. A pseudocode of this process is presented as Algorithm 1. Note that in the special case of a binary alphabet the child u_{a+1} need not be created.

Processing a Leaf. Each modified substring α stores its index of origin $idx(\alpha)$ and information about modified positions. As we have seen, the substitutions

---

[1] The true course of the algorithm will not actually perform much of its operations on a compact trie, but the intuition is best conveyed by visualizing them this way.

Algorithm 1. A recursive procedure of processing a trie node

Procedure `processNode(v)`

  `lcp(v)`: computes the longest common prefix of all the strings in $MS(v)$
  `insert(v, α)`: inserts α into $MS(v)$
  `splitByLetter(v, index)`: splits $MS(v)$ into groups having the same
                            index-th letter, returning a list of groups

  depth ← `lcp(v)`
  if depth = m **then**
  │   `processLeaf(v)`
  └   **return**
  children ← `splitByLetter(v, depth + 1)`
  heavyChild ← `findHeaviest(children)`
  heavyLetter ← `least(heavyChild)[depth+1]`
  wildcardTree ← ∅
  foreach lightChild ∈ children \ {heavyChild} **do**
  │   **foreach** α ∈ MS(lightChild) **do**
  │   │   **if** $|M(\alpha)| < k$ **then**
  │   │   │ $\alpha' \leftarrow \alpha$
  │   │   │ α'[depth+1] ← \$
  │   │   │   `insert(wildcardTree, α')`
  │   │   │ $\alpha'' \leftarrow \alpha$
  │   │   │ α''[depth+1] ← heavyLetter
  │   │   └   `insert(heavyChild, α'')`
  foreach child ∈ children ∪ {wildcardTree} **do**
  └   `processNode(child)`

---

introduced in the recursion are of two types: of wildcard origin and heavy origin. For a modified substring α, we introduce a partition $M(\alpha) = W(\alpha) \cup H(\alpha)$ into modifications of these kinds. For all modified strings α in the same leaf, $val(\alpha)$ is the same and, hence, $W(\alpha)$ is the same. Finally, by $W^{-1}(\alpha)$ we denote the set $\{(j, T^m_{idx(\alpha)}[j]) : (j, \$) \in W(\alpha)\}$. In the end, we count the pairs of modified substrings (α, β) that satisfy the following conditions:

$$H(\alpha) \cap H(\beta) = \emptyset, \quad W^{-1}(\alpha) \cap W^{-1}(\beta) = \emptyset, \quad |H(\alpha)| + |H(\beta)| + |W(\alpha)| = k. \tag{1}$$

Modified substrings α and β that satisfy (1) are called *compatible*. For a given modified substring α, the number of compatible pairs (α, β) obtained in the same leaf is counted using the inclusion-exclusion principle as follows.

For convenience, let $R(\alpha)$ denote the disjoint union of $H(\alpha)$ and $W^{-1}(\alpha)$. Let $Count(s, B)$ denote the number of modified substrings $\beta \in MS(v)$ such that $|H(\beta)| = s$ and $B \subseteq R(\beta)$. All the non-zero values are stored in a hashmap. They can be generated by iterating through all the subsets of $R(\beta)$ for all modified substrings $\beta \in MS(v)$, with a multiplicative $\mathcal{O}(2^k k)$ overhead in time and space.

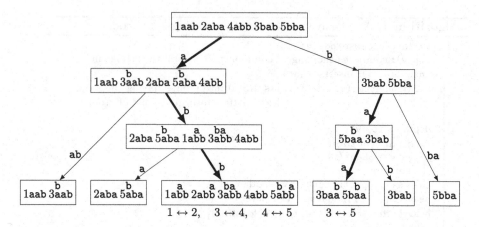

Fig. 1. Computation of $(2,3)$-mappability for the string $T = $ aababba from Example 1. Note that in this case the alphabet is binary, so wildcard subtrees do not need to be introduced. Edges leading to heavy children are drawn in bold. The only substitutions are from a light child to a heavy child. The letters shown above are the original letters before the substitutions. The pairs of modified substrings are counted as shown; in the end, $A^3_{=2}[1] = A^3_{=2}[2] = 1$ and $A^3_{=2}[3] = A^3_{=2}[4] = A^3_{=2}[5] = 2$ as expected.

Finally, the result for a modified substring α—by which $A[idx(\alpha)]$ is increased—can be computed using the formula:

$$\sum_{B \subseteq R(\alpha)} (-1)^{|B|} \, Count(k - |M(\alpha)|, B).$$

Examples. Examples of the execution of the algorithm for a binary and a ternary string can be found in Figs. 1 and 2, respectively.

Correctness. Let us start with an observation that lists some basic properties of our algorithm. Both parts can be shown by straightforward induction.

Observation 2. *(a) If a node v stores modified substrings $\alpha, \beta \in MS(v)$, then it has a descendant v' with $\mathcal{D}(v') = lcp(val(\alpha), val(\beta))$ and $\alpha, \beta \in MS(v')$.*
(b) Every node stores at most one modified substring with the same idx value.

The following lemma shows that the above approach correctly computes the (k, m)-mappability array $A^m_{\leq k}$.

Lemma 3. *If $d_H(T_i^m, T_j^m) = k$, then there is exactly one leaf v and exactly one pair of compatible modified strings $\alpha, \beta \in MS(v)$ with $i = idx(\alpha)$ and $j = idx(\beta)$. Otherwise, there is no such leaf v and pair α, β.*

Proof. Suppose that $\alpha, \beta \in MS(v)$ are compatible, $i = idx(\alpha)$, and $j = idx(\beta)$. Since $W^{-1}(\alpha) \cap W^{-1}(\beta) = \emptyset$, we conclude that T_i^m and T_j^m differ at positions in $W(\alpha) = W(\beta)$. They differ at positions in $H(\beta)$ since at the nodes corresponding to these positions, an ancestor of α (that is, the

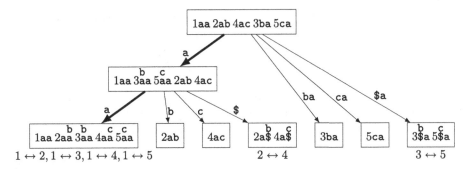

Fig. 2. Computation of $(1, 2)$-mappability for the string $T = \text{aabaca}$. This example shows how wildcard symbols are used in the algorithm. We have $A^2_{=1}[1] = 4$ and $A^2_{=1}[2] = A^2_{=1}[3] = A^2_{=1}[4] = A^2_{=1}[5] = 2$.

modified substring from which α originates) was in the heavy child (because $H(\alpha) \cap H(\beta) = \emptyset$ due to (1)) and an ancestor of β originated from a light child. Symmetrically, T^m_i and T^m_j differ at positions in $H(\alpha)$. In conclusion, they differ at positions in $H(\alpha) \cup H(\beta) \cup W(\alpha)$. The three sets are disjoint, so $|H(\alpha) \cup H(\beta) \cup W(\alpha)| = |H(\alpha)| + |H(\beta)| + |W(\alpha)| = k$ by (1). This shows that $d_H(T^m_i, T^m_j) \geq k$. With $val(\alpha) = val(\beta)$, we conclude that $d_H(T^m_i, T^m_j) = k$.

For a proof in the other direction, assume that $d_H(T^m_i, T^m_j) = k$ and let $1 \leq x_1 < x_2 < \cdots < x_k \leq m$ be the indices where the two substrings differ. Further let $x_{k+1} = m + 1$.

First of all, let us show that there is at least one leaf that contains compatible modified substrings α and β with $idx(\alpha) = i$ and $idx(\beta) = j$.

Claim. For every $p = 1, \ldots, k+1$, there exists a node v_p and modified substrings $\alpha_p, \beta_p \in MS(v_p)$ such that:

- $idx(\alpha_p) = i$ and $idx(\beta_p) = j$;
- $\mathsf{lcp}(val(\alpha_p), val(\beta_p)) = x_p - 1 = \mathcal{D}(v_p)$;
- for each position $x_1, \ldots, x_{p-1}$, both $M(\alpha_p)$ and $M(\beta_p)$ contain modifications of wildcard origin, or exactly one of these sets contains a modification of heavy origin;
- there are no other modifications in $M(\alpha_p)$ or $M(\beta_p)$.

Proof (of Claim). The proof goes by induction on p. As α_1 and β_1 we take modified substrings such that $idx(\alpha_1) = i$, $idx(\beta_1) = j$, and $M(\alpha_1) = M(\beta_1) = \emptyset$. They are stored in the set $MS(r)$ for the root r, so Observation 2(a) guarantees existence of a node v_1 with $\mathcal{D}(v_1) = \mathsf{lcp}(\alpha_1, \beta_1)$ and $\alpha_1, \beta_1 \in MS(v_1)$.

Let $p > 1$. By the inductive hypothesis, the set $MS(v_{p-1})$ contains modified substrings α_{p-1} and β_{p-1}. The node v_{p-1} has children w_1, w_2 corresponding to letters $T^m_i[x_{p-1}]$ and $T^m_j[x_{p-1}]$, respectively. If w_1 is the heavy child, then w_2 is a light child and a modified string β' such that $idx(\beta') = j$ and $M(\beta') = M(\beta_{p-1}) \cup \{(x_{p-1}, T^m_i[x_{p-1}])\}$ is created for the recursive call in w_1.

Then, we take $\alpha' = \alpha_{p-1}$. The case that w_2 is the heavy child is symmetric. Finally, if both w_1 and w_2 are light children, a child u of v_{p-1} is created along the wildcard symbol \$. There exist modified substrings $\alpha', \beta' \in MS(u)$ such that: $idx(\alpha') = i$, $idx(\beta') = j$, $M(\alpha') = M(\alpha_{p-1}) \cup \{(x_{p-1}, \$)\}$, and $M(\beta') = M(\beta_{p-1}) \cup \{(x_{p-1}, \$)\}$.

In either case, we have $\mathsf{lcp}(val(\alpha'), val(\beta')) = x_p - 1$. The set $(M(\alpha') \cup M(\beta')) \setminus (M(\alpha_{p-1}) \cup M(\beta_{p-1}))$ contains either a modification of heavy origin in one of the modified substrings or modifications of wildcard origin in both. Hence, by the inductive hypothesis we can set $\alpha_p = \alpha'$, $\beta_p = \beta'$. The node v_p with $\mathcal{D}(v_p) = \mathsf{lcp}(val(\alpha_p), val(\beta_p))$ and $\alpha_p, \beta_p \in MS(v_p)$ must exist due to Observation 2(a).   □

It suffices to apply the claim for $k = p + 1$. The node v_{k+1} is a leaf that contains compatible modified substrings $\alpha = \alpha_{k+1}$ and $\beta = \beta_{k+1}$.

Now, let us check that there is no other pair of compatible modified substrings $(\alpha', \beta') \neq (\alpha, \beta)$ that would be present in some leaf u and satisfy $idx(\alpha') = i$ and $idx(\beta') = j$. Let us first note that $M(\alpha') \cup M(\beta')$ must contain the positions $x_1, \ldots, x_k$ (since $val(\alpha') = val(\beta')$) and no other positions (otherwise, $|H(\alpha')| + |H(\beta')| + |W(\alpha')|$ would exceed k). Let p be the greatest index in $\{1, \ldots, k+1\}$ such that $x_p \le \mathsf{lcp}(val(\alpha), val(\alpha'))$. By Observation 2(b), $u \neq v_{k+1}$, so $p < k$.

Thus the node v_p is an ancestor of the leaf u, but the node v_{p+1} is not. Let us consider the children w_1, w_2 of v_p corresponding to letters $T_i^m[x_{p-1}]$ and $T_j^m[x_{p-1}]$, respectively. If w_1 is the heavy child, β' must contain a modification of heavy origin at position x_{p+1}, so v_{p+1} is an ancestor of u; a contradiction. The same contradiction is obtained in the symmetric case that w_2 is the heavy child. Finally, if both w_1 and w_2 are light, then either both α' and β' contain a modification of wildcard origin at position x_{p+1}, which again gives a contradiction, or they both contain a modification of heavy origin, which contradicts the first part of condition (1).   □

Remark 4. The authors also attempted to adapt the approach of [21] but failed due to multiple counting of substring pairs, e.g., for $T = \mathsf{aabbab}$, $k = 2$, $m = 3$.

Implementation and Complexity. Our Algorithm 1, excluding the counting phase in the leaves, has exactly the same structure as Algorithm 1 in [5]. Proposition 13 from [5] provides a bound on the total size of the generated compact trie and an efficient implementation based on finger-search trees. We apply that proposition for a family $\mathcal{F}$ of size $\mathcal{O}(n)$ composed of substrings T_i^m to obtain the following bounds.

Fact 5 ([5]). *Algorithm 1 applied up to the leaves takes $\mathcal{O}(n\binom{\log n + k + 1}{k + 1} 2^k)$ time.*

Let us further analyze the space complexity of the algorithm.

Lemma 6. *Algorithm 1 applied up to the leaves uses $\mathcal{O}(nk)$ working space.*

Proof. We inductively bound the working space of any recursive call. For a node v, let us define the potential

$$\Phi(v) = C \sum_{\alpha \in MS(v)} (k + 1 - |M(\alpha)|),$$

where C is a constant which depends on the implementation details.

We shall prove that the space consumption of a recursive call to v is bounded by $\Phi(v)$. We ignore the working space for the procedure processing leaves, so this is trivially true if v is a leaf. Next, let us analyze an internal node with children $u_1, \ldots, u_a, u_{a+1}$, where u_1 is the heavy child, $u_2, \ldots, u_a$ are the light children, and u_{a+1} corresponds to the wildcard character. Moreover, let $LS(v) = MS(u_2) \cup \cdots \cup MS(u_a)$.

Outside the recursive calls, the working space is $\mathcal{O}(|MS(v)|)$, which is below $\Phi(v)$ provided that C is large enough. Thus, let us analyze the space consumption during a recursive call to u_i. By the inductive hypothesis, the call uses $\Phi(u_i)$ working space. On top of that, we need to store the input for the remaining branches, which takes $\mathcal{O}(\sum_{i' \neq i} |MS(u_{i'})|)$ space.

If u_i is light, we observe that $\Phi(v) - \Phi(u_i) \geq C(|MS(v)| - |MS(u_i)|) \geq \frac{1}{2}C|MS(v)|$, which is sufficient to cover the total size $\mathcal{O}(|MS(v)|)$ of the input for the remaining branches. Similarly, if $i = a + 1$, then $\Phi(v) - \Phi(u_i) \geq C|MS(v)|$, because each modified string in $MS(u_i)$ has more changes than its original in $MS(v)$. Finally, to analyze the case $i = 1$ when u_i is heavy, we observe that $\sum_{i' > 1} |MS(u_{i'})| \leq 2|LS(v)|$. However, $\Phi(v) - \Phi(u_1) \geq C|LS(v)|$, because each modified substring from $LS(v)$ inserted to $MS(u_1)$ has an additional substitution. In the root call, we have $\Phi(r) = C \cdot (k + 1) \cdot |MS(r)| = \mathcal{O}(nk)$, as claimed. □

Fact 5 and Lemma 6 yield the complexity of Algorithm 1. Note that, due to the application of the inclusion-exclusion principle in the leaves, we need to multiply the time complexity of the algorithm by $2^k k$ and increase the space complexity by $\mathcal{O}(n2^k k)$.

Theorem 7. *Given a string of length n, the (k, m)-mappability problem can be solved in $\mathcal{O}(n\binom{\log n + k + 1}{k+1} 4^k k)$ time and $\mathcal{O}(n2^k k)$ space. For $k = \mathcal{O}(1)$, the time becomes $\mathcal{O}(n \log^{k+1} n)$ and the space is $\mathcal{O}(n)$.*

4 $\mathcal{O}(nm^k)$-Time and $\mathcal{O}(n)$-Space Algorithm

In this section we generalize the $\mathcal{O}(nm)$-time algorithm for $k = 1$ and integer alphabets from [2]. We start off with a simple $\mathcal{O}(nm\binom{m}{k}(\sigma - 1)^k)$-time and $\mathcal{O}(n)$-space algorithm. We first construct the suffix tree $\mathcal{T}(T)$ in $\mathcal{O}(n)$ time. Within the same time complexity, we use a post-order traversal of $\mathcal{T}(T)$, to compute, for each explicit node v, a value $C(v)$ denoting the number of terminal nodes in the subtree rooted at v. For each T_i^m, we generate all possible $\binom{m}{k}$ combinations of substitution positions, create all $(\sigma - 1)^k$ distinct strings per combination, and then spell each created string from the root of $\mathcal{T}(T)$. Generating all combinations can be done in $\mathcal{O}(\binom{m}{k})$ time [8] and creating and querying the strings can be done in $\mathcal{O}(m)$ time per string. If we successfully spell the whole string arriving at an explicit node v or an implicit node along an edge (u, v), we increment $A[i]$ by $C(v)$. The whole process takes $\mathcal{O}(nm\binom{m}{k}(\sigma - 1)^k)$ time and $\mathcal{O}(n)$ space. For $k, \sigma = \mathcal{O}(1)$, the time becomes $\mathcal{O}(nm^{k+1})$. The counting of this algorithm is correct as we do the above for all $\binom{m}{k}(\sigma - 1)^k$ pairwise distinct strings.

We next show how to shave a factor m from the time complexity. The main idea comes from observing that in the algorithm described above, after spelling from the root of $\mathcal{T}(T)$ a string of length m created by a combination of substitution positions, we start again from the root to spell a (potentially) completely different string. We can instead make use of the maximal match achieved in each spelling to query efficiently for another string. Intuitively, we construct $\sigma^k\binom{m}{k}$ strings of length n and spell them utilizing suffix links. When we reach string-depth m, we increment the respective counter if needed. Then the algorithm presented below correctly counts the number of times each length-m substring occurs in T with exactly k mismatches.

Consider a specific combination of k substitution positions with a sequence of k letters assigned to these k positions. We apply this "mask" to all non-overlapping length-m substrings of T (including, possibly, a suffix of length smaller than m) thus creating a new string S of length n. We start by spelling S from the root of $\mathcal{T}(T)$ until either we have a mismatch or we are at string-depth m. Let us denote the current depth by $d \leq m$. If $d < m$, we follow the suffix link of the last visited explicit node and traverse the edges down until we reach depth $\max\{d - 1, 0\}$. If $d = m$, we have successfully spelled S_1^m arriving at an explicit node v or an implicit node along an edge (u, v). In this case, we increment $A[1]$ by $C(v)$ if and only if $d_H(S_1^m, T_1^m) = k$. If $\mathcal{D}(v) = m$, we follow its suffix link arriving by construction to a node of depth $m-1$; if not, we follow the suffix link of its parent u and traverse the edges down until we reach depth $m-1$. (Note that we know which edges we need to traverse by looking at S.) From this point onward, we process substring S_i^m, for all $2 \leq i \leq n - m + 1$, analogously. Processing S takes time $\mathcal{O}(n)$ using an amortization argument analogous to the suffix tree construction of McCreight [19]. The working space is clearly $\mathcal{O}(n)$.

It remains to argue that for each length-m substring all different combinations with their different substitutions of k letters are induced by our construction of S. This is easy to see by considering a sliding window of length m running through S: it always contains k altered positions and these are uniquely determined by the combination used for the length-m substrings starting at positions equal to 1 *modulo* m. The final array A becomes $A_{=k}^m$. We arrive at the following result.

Theorem 8. *Given a string of length n over an integer alphabet, the (k, m)-mappability problem can be solved in $\mathcal{O}(n\binom{m}{k}\sigma^k)$ time and $\mathcal{O}(n)$ space. For $k, \sigma = \mathcal{O}(1)$, the time becomes $\mathcal{O}(nm^k)$.*

Combining Theorems 7 and 8 gives the following result for $\sigma, k = \mathcal{O}(1)$.

Corollary 9. *Given a string of length n over a constant-sized alphabet, the (k, m)-mappability problem can be solved in $\mathcal{O}(n \min\{m^k, \log^{k+1} n\})$ time and $\mathcal{O}(n)$ space for $k = \mathcal{O}(1)$.*

5 Computing (k, m)-Mappability for All k or for All m

Theorem 10. *The (k, m)-mappability for a given m and all $k = 0, \ldots, m$ can be computed in $\mathcal{O}(n^2)$ time using $\mathcal{O}(n)$ space.*

Proof. We first present an algorithm which solves the problem in $\mathcal{O}(n^2)$ time using $\mathcal{O}(n^2)$ space and then show how to reduce the space usage to $\mathcal{O}(n)$.

We initialize an $n \times n$ matrix M in which $M[i, j]$ will store the Hamming distance between substrings T_i^m and T_j^m. Let us consider two letters $T[i] \neq T[j]$ of the input string, where $i < j$. Such a pair contributes to a mismatch between the following pairs of strings: $(T_{i-m+1}^m, T_{j-m+1}^m), (T_{i-m+2}^m, T_{j-m+2}^m), \ldots, (T_i^m, T_j^m)$. This list of strings is represented by a diagonal interval in M, the entries of which we need to increment by 1. We process all $\mathcal{O}(n^2)$ pairs of letters and update the information on the respective intervals. Then $A_{=k}^m[i] = |\{j : M[i, j] = k\}|$.

To achieve $\mathcal{O}(1)$ time of a single addition on a diagonal interval, we use a well-known trick from an analogous problem in one dimension. Suppose that we would like to add 1 on the diagonal interval from $M[x_1, y_1]$ to $M[x_2, y_2]$. Instead, we can simply add 1 to $M[x_1, y_1]$ and -1 to $M[x_2 + 1, y_2 + 1]$. Every cell will then represent the difference of its actual value to the actual value of its predecessor on the diagonal. After all such operations are performed, we can retrieve the actual values by computing prefix sums on each diagonal in a top-down manner.

To reduce space usage to $\mathcal{O}(n)$, it suffices to observe that the value of $M[i, j]$ depends only on the value of $M[i - 1, j - 1]$ and at most two letter comparisons which can add $+1$ and/or -1 to the cell. Recall that $M[i, j] = d_H(T_i^m, T_j^m)$. We need to subtract 1 from the previous result if the first characters of the previous substrings were equal and add 1 if the last characters of the new substrings were different. Therefore, we can process the matrix row by row, from top to bottom, and compute the values $A_{=0}^m[i], \ldots, A_{=m}^m[i]$ while processing the ith row.   □

Theorem 11. *The (k, m)-mappability for a given k and all $m = k, \ldots, n - 1$ can be computed in $\mathcal{O}(n^2)$ time and space.*

Proof. We first prove the following claim.

Claim. The longest common prefixes with k mismatches for all pairs of suffixes of T can be computed in $\mathcal{O}(n^2)$ time.

Proof (of Claim). We process the pairs in batches B_δ for $\delta = 1, 2, \ldots, n - 1$ so that the pair (T_i, T_j), which we denote by (i, j), is in $B_{|j-i|}$. It now suffices to show how to process a single batch B_δ in $\mathcal{O}(n)$ time. We will do so by comparing pairs of letters of T at distance δ from left to right. We first compute $k\text{-lcp}(1, 1 + \delta)$ naively. Then, given that $k\text{-lcp}(i, j) = \ell$, where $j - i = \delta$, we will retrieve $k\text{-lcp}(i + 1, j + 1)$ using the following simple observation: either $j + \ell - 1 = n$, or T_i^ℓ and T_j^ℓ have exactly k mismatches and $T[i + \ell] \neq T[j + \ell]$. In the former case, we trivially have that $k\text{-lcp}(i + 1, j + 1) = \ell - 1$. In the latter case, we first check whether $T[i] = T[j]$, in which case $d_H(T_{i+1}^{\ell-1}, T_{j+1}^{\ell-1}) = k$ and hence $k\text{-lcp}(i + 1, j + 1) = \ell - 1$. If $T[i] \neq T[j]$, then $d_H(T_{i+1}^{\ell-1}, T_{j+1}^{\ell-1}) = k - 1$ and we perform letter comparisons to extend the match. The pairs of letters compared in this step have not been compared before; the complexity follows.   □

We store the information on $k\text{-lcp}$'s as follows. We initialize an $n \times n$ matrix Q. Then, for a pair (i, j) such that $k\text{-lcp}(i, j) = \ell$, we increment by 1 the entries $Q[\ell, i]$ and $Q[\ell, j]$. Note that if $k\text{-lcp}(i, j) = \ell$, then i (resp. j) will contribute 1 to the (k, m)-mappability values $A_{\leq k}^m[j]$ (resp. $A_{\leq k}^m[i]$) for all $1 \leq m \leq \ell$. Thus, starting from the last row of Q, we iteratively add row ℓ to row $\ell - 1$. In the end, by the above observation, row m stores the (k, m)-mappability array $A_{\leq k}^m$.   □

6   Conditional Hardness for $k, m = \Theta(\log n)$

We will show that (k, m)-mappability cannot be computed in strongly subquadratic time in case that the parameters are $\Theta(\log n)$, unless the Strong Exponential Time Hypothesis (SETH) of Impagliazzo, Paturi and Zane [12,13] fails. Our proof is based on the conditional hardness of the following decision version of the Longest Common Substring with k Mismatches problem.

Common Substring of Length d with k Mismatches
Input: Strings T_1, T_2 of length n over binary alphabet and integers k, d
Output: Is there a factor of T_1 of length d that occurs in T_2 with k mismatches?

Lemma 12 ([16]). *Suppose there is $\varepsilon > 0$ such that Common Substring of Length d with k Mismatches can be solved in $\mathcal{O}(n^{2-\varepsilon})$ time on strings over binary alphabet for $k = \Theta(\log n)$ and $d = 21k$. Then SETH is false.*

Theorem 13. *If the (k, m)-mappability can be computed in $\mathcal{O}(n^{2-\varepsilon})$ time for binary strings, $k, m = \Theta(\log n)$, and some $\varepsilon > 0$, then SETH is false.*

Proof. We make a Turing reduction from Common Substring of Length d with k Mismatches. Let T_1 and T_2 be the input to the problem. We compute the (k, d)-mappabilities of strings $T_1 \cdot T_2$ and $T_1 \cdot T_2[1..d - 1]$ and store them in arrays A and B, respectively. For each $i = 1, \ldots, n - d + 1$, we subtract $B[i]$ by $A[i]$. Then, $A[i]$ holds the number of factors of T_2 of length d that are at Hamming distance k from $T_1[i..i + d - 1]$. Hence, Common Substring of Length d with k Mismatches has a positive answer if and only if $A[i] > 0$ for any $i = 1, \ldots, n - d + 1$.

By Lemma 12, an $\mathcal{O}(n^{2-\varepsilon})$-time algorithm for Common Substring of Length d with k Mismatches with $k = \Theta(\log n)$ and $d = 21k$ would refute SETH. By the shown reduction, an $\mathcal{O}(n^{2-\varepsilon})$-time algorithm for (k, m)-mappability with $k, m = \Theta(\log n)$ would also refute SETH.   □

7   Final Remarks

Our main contribution is an $\mathcal{O}(n \min\{m^k, \log^{k+1} n\})$-time and $\mathcal{O}(n)$-space algorithm for solving the (k, m)-mappability problem. Let us recall that genome mappability, as introduced in [7], counts the number of substrings that are at Hamming distance at most k from every length-m substring of the text. One may also be interested to consider mappability under the edit distance model. This question relates also to very recent contributions on approximate matching under edit distance [4,20]. In the case of the edit distance, in particular, a decision needs to be made whether sufficiently similar substrings only of length exactly m or of all lengths between $m - k$ and $m + k$ should be counted. We leave the mappability problem under edit distance for future investigation.

References

1. Alamro, H., Ayad, L.A.K., Charalampopoulos, P., Iliopoulos, C.S., Pissis, S.P.: Longest common prefixes with k-mismatches and applications. In: Tjoa, A.M., Bellatreche, L., Biffl, S., van Leeuwen, J., Wiedermann, J. (eds.) SOFSEM 2018. LNCS, vol. 10706, pp. 636–649. Springer, Cham (2018). https://doi.org/10.1007/978-3-319-73117-9_45

2. Alzamel, M., Charalampopoulos, P., Iliopoulos, C.S., Pissis, S.P., Radoszewski, J., Sung, W.-K.: Faster algorithms for 1-mappability of a sequence. In: Gao, X., Du, H., Han, M. (eds.) COCOA 2017. LNCS, vol. 10628, pp. 109–121. Springer, Cham (2017). https://doi.org/10.1007/978-3-319-71147-8_8

3. Antoniou, P., Daykin, J.W., Iliopoulos, C.S., Kourie, D., Mouchard, L., Pissis, S.P.: Mapping uniquely occurring short sequences derived from high throughput technologies to a reference genome. In: Information Technology and Applications in Biomedicine, ITAB 2009. IEEE (2009). https://doi.org/10.1109/itab.2009.5394394

4. Ayad, L.A.K., Barton, C., Charalampopoulos, P., Iliopoulos, C.S., Pissis, S.P.: Longest common prefixes with k-errors and applications. In: Gagie, T., et al. (eds.) SPIRE 2018. LNCS, vol. 11147, pp. 27–41. Springer, Cham (2018). https://doi.org/10.1007/978-3-030-00479-8_3

5. Charalampopoulos, P., et al.: Linear-time algorithm for long LCF with k mismatches. In: Navarro, G., Sankoff, D., Zhu, B. (eds.) Combinatorial Pattern Matching, CPM 2018. LIPIcs, vol. 105, pp. 23:1–23:16. Schloss Dagstuhl-Leibniz-Zentrum für Informatik (2018). https://doi.org/10.4230/LIPIcs.CPM.2018.23

6. Cole, R., Gottlieb, L., Lewenstein, M.: Dictionary matching and indexing with errors and don't cares. In: Babai, L. (ed.) 36th Annual ACM Symposium on Theory of Computing, STOC 2004, pp. 91–100. ACM (2004). https://doi.org/10.1145/1007352.1007374

7. Derrien, T.: Fast computation and applications of genome mappability. PLoS ONE **7**(1), e30377 (2012). https://doi.org/10.1371/journal.pone.0030377

8. Eades, P., McKay, B.D.: An algorithm for generating subsets of fixed size with a strong minimal change property. Inf. Process. Lett. **19**(3), 131–133 (1984). https://doi.org/10.1016/0020-0190(84)90091-7

9. Farach, M.: Optimal suffix tree construction with large alphabets. In: 38th IEEE Annual Symposium on Foundations of Computer Science, FOCS 1997, pp. 137–143. IEEE Computer Society (1997). https://doi.org/10.1109/SFCS.1997.646102

10. Fonseca, N.A., Rung, J., Brazma, A., Marioni, J.C.: Tools for mapping high-throughput sequencing data. Bioinformatics **28**(24), 3169–3177 (2012). https://doi.org/10.1093/bioinformatics/bts605

11. Fredman, M.L., Komlós, J., Szemerédi, E.: Storing a sparse table with $O(1)$ worst case access time. J. ACM **31**(3), 538–544 (1984). https://doi.org/10.1145/828.1884

12. Impagliazzo, R., Paturi, R.: On the complexity of k-SAT. J. Comput. Syst. Sci. **62**(2), 367–375 (2001). https://doi.org/10.1006/jcss.2000.1727

13. Impagliazzo, R., Paturi, R., Zane, F.: Which problems have strongly exponential complexity? J. Comput. Syst. Sci. **63**(4), 512–530 (2001). https://doi.org/10.1006/jcss.2001.1774

14. Kärkkäinen, J., Sanders, P., Burkhardt, S.: Linear work suffix array construction. J. ACM **53**(6), 918–936 (2006). https://doi.org/10.1145/1217856.1217858

15. Kasai, T., Lee, G., Arimura, H., Arikawa, S., Park, K.: Linear-time longest-common-prefix computation in suffix arrays and its applications. In: Amir, A., Landau, G.M. (eds.) CPM 2001. LNCS, vol. 2089, pp. 181–192. Springer, Heidelberg (2001). https://doi.org/10.1007/3-540-48194-X_17

16. Kociumaka, T., Radoszewski, J., Starikovskaya, T.A.: Longest common substring with approximately k mismatches (2017). arxiv.1712.08573

17. Manber, U., Myers, E.W.: Suffix arrays: a new method for on-line string searches. SIAM J. Comput. **22**(5), 935–948 (1993). https://doi.org/10.1137/0222058

18. Manzini, G.: Longest common prefix with mismatches. In: Iliopoulos, C., Puglisi, S., Yilmaz, E. (eds.) SPIRE 2015. LNCS, vol. 9309, pp. 299–310. Springer, Cham (2015). https://doi.org/10.1007/978-3-319-23826-5_29

19. McCreight, E.M.: A space-economical suffix tree construction algorithm. J. ACM **23**(2), 262–272 (1976). https://doi.org/10.1145/321941.321946

20. Thankachan, S.V., Aluru, C., Chockalingam, S.P., Aluru, S.: Algorithmic framework for approximate matching under bounded edits with applications to sequence analysis. In: Raphael, B.J. (ed.) RECOMB 2018. LNCS, vol. 10812, pp. 211–224. Springer, Cham (2018). https://doi.org/10.1007/978-3-319-89929-9_14

21. Thankachan, S.V., Apostolico, A., Aluru, S.: A provably efficient algorithm for the k-mismatch average common substring problem. J. Comput. Biol. **23**(6), 472–482 (2016). https://doi.org/10.1089/cmb.2015.0235

Longest Common Prefixes with k-Errors and Applications

Lorraine A. K. Ayad[1], Carl Barton[2], Panagiotis Charalampopoulos[1(✉)], Costas S. Iliopoulos[1], and Solon P. Pissis[1]

[1] Department of Informatics, King's College London, London, UK
{lorraine.ayad,panagiotis.charalampopoulos,c.iliopoulos, solon.pissis}@kcl.ac.uk
[2] European Molecular Biology Laboratory, European Bioinformatics Institute (EMBL-EBI), Wellcome Genome Campus, Hinxton, Cambridge, UK
carl@ebi.ac.uk

Abstract. Although real-world text datasets, such as DNA sequences, are far from being uniformly random, string searching average-case algorithms perform significantly better than worst-case ones in most applications of interest. In this paper, we study the problem of computing the longest prefix of each suffix of a given string of length n that occurs elsewhere in the string with k-errors. This problem has already been studied under the Hamming distance model. Our first result is an improvement upon the state-of-the-art average-case time complexity for *non-constant* k and using only *linear space* under the Hamming distance model. Notably, we show that our technique can be extended to the edit distance model with the same time and space complexities. Specifically, our algorithms run in $\mathcal{O}(n\frac{(c\log n)^k}{k!})$ time on average, where $c > 1$ is a constant, using $\mathcal{O}(n)$ space. Finally, we show that our technique is applicable to several algorithmic problems found in computational biology and elsewhere. The importance of our technique lies on the fact that it is the first one achieving this bound for non-constant k and using $\mathcal{O}(n)$ space.

Keywords: Longest common prefix · Longest common substring
Longest common factor · k-mismatches · k-errors

1 Introduction

The longest common prefix (LCP) array is a commonly used data structure alongside the suffix array (SA). The LCP array stores the length of the longest common prefix between two adjacent suffixes of a given string as they are stored (in lexicographic order) in the SA [27]. A typical use combining the SA and the LCP array is to simulate the suffix tree functionality using less space [2].

However, there are many practical scenarios where the LCP array may be applied without making use of the SA. The LCP array provides us with essential

© Springer Nature Switzerland AG 2018
T. Gagie et al. (Eds.): SPIRE 2018, LNCS 11147, pp. 27–41, 2018.
https://doi.org/10.1007/978-3-030-00479-8_3

information regarding *repetitiveness* in a given string and is therefore a useful data structure for analysing textual data in areas such as molecular biology, musicology, or natural language processing (see [28] for some applications).

It is also quite common to account for potential alterations within textual data (sequences). For example, alterations can be the result of DNA replication or sequencing errors in DNA sequences. In this context, it is natural to define the longest common prefix with k-errors. Given a string $x[0 .. n - 1]$, the longest common prefix with k-errors for every suffix $x[i .. n - 1]$ is the length of the longest common prefix of $x[i .. n - 1]$ and any $x[j .. n - 1]$, $j \neq i$, allowing for up to k substitution operations [28]. Some applications are given below.

Interspersed Repeats. Repeated sequences are a common feature of genomes. One type in particular, interspersed repeats, are known to occur in all eukaryotic genomes. These repeats have no repetitive pattern and appear irregularly within DNA sequences [23]. Single nucleotide polymorphisms result in the existence of interspersed repeats that are not identical [26]. Identifying these repeats has been linked to genome folding locations and phylogenetic analysis [33].

Genome Mappability Data Structure. In [3] the authors showed that using the longest common prefixes with k-errors they can construct, in $\mathcal{O}(n)$ worst-case time, an $\mathcal{O}(n)$-sized data structure answering the following type of queries in $\mathcal{O}(1)$ time per query: find the smallest m such that at least μ of the substrings of x of length m do not occur more than once in x with at most k errors. This is a data structure version of the genome mappability problem [4,5,13,28].

Longest Common Substring with k-Errors. The longest common substring with k-errors problem has received much attention recently, in particular due to its applications in bioinformatics [25,36,37]. We are asked to find the longest substrings of two strings that are at distance at most k. The notion of longest common prefix with k-errors is thus *closely related* to the one of longest common substring with k-errors. For the latter see [1,10,18,19,22,34,35].

All-Pairs Suffix/Prefix Overlaps with k-Errors. Finding approximate overlaps is the first stage of most genome assembly methods. Given a set of strings and an error-rate ϵ, the goal is to find, for all pairs of strings, their suffix/prefix matches (overlaps) that are within distance $k = \lceil \epsilon \ell \rceil$, where ℓ is the length of the overlap [24,32,38]. By concatenating the strings to form one single string x and then computing longest common prefixes with k-errors for x only against the prefixes of the strings we have all the information we need to solve this problem.

1.1   Our Model

We assume the standard word-RAM model with word size $w = \Omega(\log n)$. Although real-world text datasets are far from being uniformly random, string searching average-case algorithms perform significantly better than worst-case ones in most applications of interest [16]. When we state time complexities for our algorithms, we assume that the input is a string x of length n over an alphabet Σ of size $\sigma > 1$ with the letters of x being independent random variables, uniformly distributed over Σ. In molecular biology we typically have that $\Sigma = \{\texttt{A},\texttt{C},\texttt{G},\texttt{T}\}$ and so we assume that $\sigma = \mathcal{O}(1)$ throughout unless stated otherwise.

1.2 Related Work

The problem of computing longest common prefixes with k-errors was first studied by Manzini for the restricted case of $k = 1$ [28]. We distinguish the following techniques that can be applied to solve this and other related problems for $k > 1$.

Non-constant k and $\omega(n)$ space: We can make use of the well-known k-errata data structure by Cole et al. [11]. The size of the data structure is $\mathcal{O}(n\frac{(c \log n)^k}{k!})$, where $c > 1$ is a constant.

Constant k and $\mathcal{O}(n)$ space: We can make use of the techniques in [10,34,35] which build heavily on the k-errata data structure [11]. The working space is *exponential in k* but $\mathcal{O}(n)$ for $k = \mathcal{O}(1)$.

Non-constant k and $\mathcal{O}(n)$ space: In this case, only a simple $\mathcal{O}(n^2 k)$-time worst-case algorithm exists to solve the problem. The fastest known average-case algorithm was presented in [3]. It requires $\mathcal{O}(n(\sigma R)^k \log\log n(\log k + \log\log n))$ time on average, where $R = \lceil (k+2)(\log_\sigma n + 1) \rceil$.

Other related work: In [22] it was shown that a strongly sub-quadratic-time algorithm for the longest common substring with k-errors problem, for $k = \Omega(\log n)$ and binary strings, would refute the Strong Exponential Time Hypothesis. Thus sub-quadratic-time solutions for approximate variants of the problem have been developed [22]. A non-deterministic algorithm based on the polynomial method is also known for the same problem [1].

1.3 Our Results

We continue the line of research for non-constant k and $\mathcal{O}(n)$ space, in particular in the absence of any worst-case strongly sub-quadratic-time approach with these parameters. In all algorithmic results we assume that $k = o(\log n)$, since these are the values for which we can obtain *strongly sub-quadratic-time* algorithms:

1. We first show a non-trivial upper bound of independent interest: the maximal length of the longest common prefix with k-errors between all pairs of suffixes of x is $\mathcal{O}(k + \log_\sigma n)$ with high probability (w.h.p.).
2. By applying this result, we significantly improve upon the state-of-the-art algorithm for non-constant k and using $\mathcal{O}(n)$ space [3]. Specifically, our algorithm runs in $\mathcal{O}(n\frac{(c \log n)^k}{k!})$ time on average, where $c > 1$ is a constant, using $\mathcal{O}(n)$ space.
3. Notably, we extend our results to the *edit distance* model with no extra cost.
4. As a bonus we give an algorithm for Hamming distance and general ordered alphabets working in $\mathcal{O}(n\frac{(c \log_\sigma n)^k}{k!})$ time on average using $\mathcal{O}(n)$ space.

The importance of our technique lies on the fact that it is the first one achieving the $\mathcal{O}(n\frac{(c\log n)^k}{k!})$-time bound for $k = o(\log n)$ using $\mathcal{O}(n)$ space; thus solving the genome mappability data structure problem, the longest common substring with k-errors problem, and the all-pairs suffix/prefix overlaps with k-errors problem.

Moreover, since our technique avoids the classic recursive heavy-path tree decompositions [11], it is efficiently implementable. A C++ implementation of contribution 4 is made available at https://github.com/lorrainea/PLCP.

2   Preliminaries

We begin with some basic definitions and notation. Let $x = x[0]x[1] \ldots x[n-1]$ be a *string* of length $|x| = n$ over a finite ordered alphabet Σ of size $|\Sigma| = \sigma$. For two positions i and j on x, we denote by $x[i \mathinner{.\,.} j] = x[i] \ldots x[j]$ the *substring* (sometimes called *factor*) of x that starts at position i and ends at position j. We recall that a *prefix* of x is a substring that starts at position 0 ($x[0 \mathinner{.\,.} j]$) and a *suffix* of x is a substring that ends at position $n-1$ ($x[i \mathinner{.\,.} n-1]$). Let y be a string of length m with $0 < m \leq n$. We say that there exists an *occurrence* of y in x, or, more simply, that y *occurs in* x, when y is a substring of x. Every occurrence of y can be characterised by a starting position in x. We thus say that y occurs at the *starting position* i in x when $y = x[i \mathinner{.\,.} i + m - 1]$.

The *Hamming distance* between two strings x and y, $|x| = |y|$, is defined as $d_H(x, y) = |\{i : x[i] \neq y[i],\ i = 0, 1, \ldots, |x|-1\}|$. If $|x| \neq |y|$, we set $d_H(x, y) = \infty$. The *edit distance* between x and y is the minimum total cost of a sequence of edit operations (insertions, deletions, substitutions) required to transform x into y. It is known as *Levenshtein distance* for unit cost operations. We consider this special case here. If two strings x and y are at (Hamming or edit) distance at most k we say that x and y match with *k-errors* or match with *at most $k$errors*.

We denote by SA the *suffix array* of x. SA is an integer array of size n storing the starting positions of all (lexicographically) sorted non-empty suffixes of x, i.e. for all $1 \leq r < n$ we have $x[\mathsf{SA}[r-1] \mathinner{.\,.} n-1] < x[\mathsf{SA}[r] \mathinner{.\,.} n-1]$ [27]. Let $\mathsf{lcp}(r, s)$ denote the length of the longest common prefix between $x[\mathsf{SA}[r] \mathinner{.\,.} n-1]$ and $x[\mathsf{SA}[s] \mathinner{.\,.} n-1]$ for positions r, s on x. We denote by LCP the *longest common prefix* array of x defined by $\mathsf{LCP}[r] = \mathsf{lcp}(r-1, r)$ for all $1 \leq r < n$, and $\mathsf{LCP}[0] = 0$. The inverse iSA of the array SA is defined by $\mathsf{iSA}[\mathsf{SA}[r]] = r$, for all $0 \leq r < n$. It is known that SA, iSA, and LCP of a string of length n can be computed in time and space $\mathcal{O}(n)$ [17,30]. A range minimum query (RMQ) data structure over the LCP array, that can be constructed in $\mathcal{O}(n)$ time and $\mathcal{O}(n)$ space [8], can answer lcp-queries in $\mathcal{O}(1)$ time per query [27]. The lcp queries are also known as *longest common extension* (LCE) queries.

The *permuted* LCP *array*, denoted by PLCP, has the same contents as the LCP array but in different order. Let i^- denote the starting position of the lexicographic predecessor of $x[i \mathinner{.\,.} n-1]$. For $i = 0, \ldots, n-1$, we define $\mathsf{PLCP}[i] = \mathsf{LCP}[\mathsf{iSA}[i]] = \mathsf{lcp}(\mathsf{iSA}[i^-], \mathsf{iSA}[i])$, that is, $\mathsf{PLCP}[i]$ is the length of the longest common prefix between $x[i \mathinner{.\,.} n-1]$ and its lexicographic predecessor. For the starting position j of the lexicographically smallest suffix we set $\mathsf{PLCP}[j] = 0$.

For any $k \geq 0$, we define $\mathsf{lcp}_k(y, z)$ as the largest $\ell \geq 0$ such that $y[0 .. \ell - 1]$ and $z[0 .. \ell - 1]$ exist and are at *Hamming distance* at most k; note that this is defined for a pair of strings. We analogously define the *permuted LCP array with k-errors*, denoted by PLCP_k. For $i = 0, \ldots, n - 1$, we have that

$$\mathsf{PLCP}_k[i] = \max_{j=0,\ldots,n-1, \; j \neq i} \mathsf{lcp}_k(x[i .. n - 1], x[j .. n - 1]).$$

The main computational problem in scope can be formally stated as follows.

PLCP WITH k-ERRORS
Input: A string x of length n and a positive integer $k = o(\log n)$
Output: PLCP_k and P_k; $\mathsf{P}_k[i] \neq i$, for $i = 0, \ldots, n - 1$, is such that $x[i .. i + \ell - 1] \approx_k x[\mathsf{P}_k[i] .. \mathsf{P}_k[i] + \ell - 1]$, where $\ell = \mathsf{PLCP}_k[i]$

---

3 Computing PLCP_k

In this section we propose a new algorithm for the PLCP WITH k-ERRORS problem under both the Hamming and the edit distance (Levenshtein distance) models. Our algorithms are based on a deeper look into the behaviour of the longest common prefixes with k-errors. These turn out to be usually short, a fact that allows us to make use of the connection between longest common prefix values and predecessor/successor queries. We already know the following result for errors under the Hamming distance model.

Theorem 1 ([3]). *The PLCP WITH k-ERRORS problem can be solved in time $\mathcal{O}(n(\sigma R)^k \log^2 \log n)$ on average, where $R = \lceil (k + 2)(\log_\sigma n + 1) \rceil$, using $\mathcal{O}(n)$ extra space.*

In the rest of this section, we show the following result for errors under both the Hamming and edit distance models.

Theorem 2. *The PLCP WITH k-ERRORS problem can be solved in $\mathcal{O}(n \frac{(c \log n)^k}{k!})$ time on average, where $c > 1$ is a constant, using $\mathcal{O}(n)$ extra space.*

For clarity of presentation, we first do the analysis and present the algorithm under the Hamming distance model in Sects. 3.1 and 3.2. We then show how to extend our technique to work under the edit distance model in Sect. 3.3.

3.1 Bounding the PLCP_k Values

The expected maximal value in the LCP array is $2 \log_\sigma n + \mathcal{O}(1)$ [21]. We can thus obtain a trivial $\mathcal{O}(k \log_\sigma n)$ bound on the maximal expected length of the longest common prefix with k-errors for arbitrary k and σ. A related result was recently presented in [9]; the authors show that the maximal value in the LCP array is $2 \log_\sigma n + \mathcal{O}(\log_\sigma \log_\sigma n)$ w.h.p. In this section, by looking deeper into the behaviour of the longest common prefixes with k-errors, we show the following non-trivial result of independent interest.

Theorem 3. *Let x be a string of length n over an alphabet of size $\sigma > 1$ and $1 \leq k \leq n$ be an integer.*

(a) *The maximal expected length of the longest common prefix with k-errors between all pairs of suffixes of x is $\mathcal{O}(k + \log_\sigma n)$.*

(b) *The maximal length of the longest common prefix with k-errors between all pairs of suffixes of x is $\mathcal{O}(k + \log_\sigma n)$ w.h.p.*

Proof (of (a)). Let us denote the ith suffix of x by $x_i = x[i \mathinner{.\,.} n - 1]$. Further let us define the following random variables:

$$X_{i,j} = \mathsf{lcp}_k(x_i, x_j) \text{ and } Y = \max_{0 \leq i < j \leq n-1} X_{i,j}.$$

Claim. $\Pr(X_{i,j} \geq m) \leq \binom{m}{k} \frac{1}{\sigma^{m-k}}$.

Proof (of Claim). Each possible set of positions where a substitution is allowed is a subset of one of the $\binom{m}{k}$ subsets of m of size k. For each of these subsets, we can disregard what happens in the k chosen positions; in order to yield a match with k-errors, the remaining $m - k$ positions must match and each of them matches with probability $\frac{1}{\sigma}$. The claim follows by applying the Union-Bound (Boole's inequality). □

By applying the Union-Bound again we have that

$$\Pr(Y \geq m) = \Pr\left(\bigcup_{i<j}\{X_{i,j} \geq m\}\right) \leq \sum_{i<j} \Pr\left(X_{i,j} \geq m\right) \leq n^2 \binom{m}{k} \frac{1}{\sigma^{m-k}},$$

for $m \geq k$ and $\Pr(Y \geq m) = 1$ for $m \leq k$.

The expected value of Y is given by:

$$E[Y] = \sum_{m=1}^{\infty} \Pr(Y \geq m) = \underbrace{\sum_{m=1}^{\alpha(\log_\sigma n + k)} \Pr(Y \geq m)}_{\leq \alpha(\log_\sigma n + k)} + \sum_{m=\alpha(\log_\sigma n + k)+1}^{\infty} \Pr(Y \geq m).$$

(Note that we bound the first summand using that $\Pr(Y \geq m) \leq 1$ for all m.)

Claim. Let $r_{m,k} = \binom{m}{k}$. We have that $\frac{r_{m,k}}{r_{m-1,k}} \leq \frac{3}{2}$ for $m \geq 3k$.

Proof (of Claim).

$$\frac{r_{m,k}}{r_{m-1,k}} = \frac{m}{(m-k)} \leq \frac{3k}{(3k-k)} = \frac{3}{2}.$$

□

Let $\beta = \alpha(\log_\sigma n + k) + 1 \geq 4k$, for some $\alpha > 4$. We apply the above claim to bound the second summand[1].

$$\sum_{m=\beta}^{\infty} \Pr(Y \geq m) \leq \sum_{m=\beta}^{\infty} n^2 \binom{m}{k} \frac{1}{\sigma^{m-k}} \leq \sum_{m=\beta}^{\infty} n^2 \binom{4k}{k} \left(\frac{3}{2}\right)^{m-4k} \frac{1}{\sigma^{m-k}}$$

$$= \sum_{m=\beta}^{\infty} n^2 \binom{4k}{k} \left(\frac{2}{3}\right)^{3k} \left(\frac{3}{2\sigma}\right)^{m-k} \leq n^2 \binom{4k}{k} \left(\frac{2}{3}\right)^{3k} \left(\frac{3}{2\sigma}\right)^{\beta-k} \sum_{m=0}^{\infty} \left(\frac{3}{2\sigma}\right)^m$$

$$\leq An^2 \binom{4k}{k} \left(\frac{3}{2\sigma}\right)^{\beta-k} \leq An^2 2^{4k} \left(\frac{3}{2\sigma}\right)^{\alpha \log_\sigma n + (\alpha-1)k}$$

$$= \frac{An^2}{n^{\alpha(1-1/\log_{3/2}\sigma)}} \cdot \left(16 \left(\frac{3}{2\sigma}\right)^{\alpha-1}\right)^k$$

for some constant A since $\sigma \geq 2$. Then $1 - 1/\log_{3/2}\sigma > 0$ and $\frac{3}{2\sigma} < 1$ and thus, for any $\epsilon > 0$, we can pick an α large enough such that this sum is $\mathcal{O}(n^{-\epsilon})$. □

Proof (of (b)). It suffices to note that

$$\sum_{m=\beta}^{\infty} \Pr(Y = m) \leq \sum_{m=\beta}^{\infty} \Pr(Y \geq m),$$

which we can bound as above. □

Remark 4. The above result can be also derived by adapting the analysis presented in the Appendix of [29].

3.2 Improved Algorithm for Hamming Distance

Main Idea. In light of Theorem 3 it suffices on average to only consider the multiset X_λ of all substrings of x of length $\lambda = \alpha \log_\sigma n$, $\alpha > 0$ (recall that $k = o(\log n)$). By our assumptions each of these λ-digit numbers fits in a computer word; note that we can simulate a word-RAM machine with word size $\mathcal{O}(\beta)$ using a word-RAM machine with word size β with only a constant factor slowdown.

The main idea is to exploit the connection between longest common prefix values and predecessor/successor queries: the maximal length of the longest common prefix between a queried string of length λ that is not in X_λ and any of the strings in X_λ can be found in the time required to answer a single predecessor/successor query assuming X_λ has been sorted. We can thus query for each string that is within distance k from each of the elements of X_λ. If the length of the longest prefix value returned is λ, we switch to any polynomial-time algorithm. By Theorem 3 this will happen for $\mathcal{O}(n^{-\epsilon})$ inputs for some $\epsilon > 0$ based on our choice of α. Thus in what follows we assume that this does not happen.

---

[1] The reason for imposing "$\alpha > 4$" instead of "$\alpha > 3$" becomes clear in Sect. 3.3.

y-Fast Trie Implementation. First let us note that we can compute the length of the longest common prefixes with k-errors for the last $\lambda - 1$ positions of x using LCE queries. We thus update PLCP_k and P_k for each i accordingly. The whole process takes time $\mathcal{O}(nk\lambda) = \mathcal{O}(nk\log n)$.

The y-fast trie supports insert, delete and search (exact, predecessor and successor) operations in time $\mathcal{O}(\log\log U)$ w.h.p., using $\mathcal{O}(n)$ space, where n is the number of stored values and U is size of the universe [39]. We have that $U = \sigma^\lambda$, $\lambda = \alpha \log_\sigma n$, and hence $\log\log U = \mathcal{O}(\log\log n + \log\alpha) = \mathcal{O}(\log\log n)$.

We initialise the y-fast trie by inserting all elements of X_λ to it. This procedure takes time $\mathcal{O}(n\log\log n)$ in total. We further construct the SA and LCP array of x in time $\mathcal{O}(n)$. We then want to find a longest prefix of the $\sigma^k\binom{\lambda}{k}$ strings of length at most λ that are at Hamming distance at most k from $x[i\mathinner{.\,.}i+\lambda-1]$ that occurs elsewhere in x as well as an occurrence of it. If this prefix is of length λ, we find all positions $t \neq i$ in x for which $d_H(x[i\mathinner{.\,.}i+\lambda-1], x[t\mathinner{.\,.}t+\lambda-1]) \leq k$ and treat each of them individually.

We query for all $\sigma^k\binom{\lambda}{k}$ possible strings; including $x[i\mathinner{.\,.}i+\lambda-1]$ itself. We view each string z created after at most k substitution operations as a number; the aim is to find its longest prefix that occurs elsewhere in x. To this end we perform at most three queries over the y-fast trie: an exact; a predecessor; and a successor query. One of these three queries will return an element z' of X_λ that attains the longest common prefix that any element of X_λ has with z of maximal length. If it is the case that z' only occurs at position i, we retrieve the predecessor and successor of $x[i\mathinner{.\,.}i+\lambda-1]$ from the SA and use these instead.

Having found z', we can then compute the length of the longest common prefix between z and z' in constant time using standard bit-level operations. An XOR operation between z and z' provides us with an integer d specifying the positions of errors (bits set on when d is viewed as binary). If $d \neq 0$, we take $\delta = \lfloor \log d \rfloor$, which provides us with the index of the leftmost bit set on which in turn specifies the length of the longest common prefix between z and z'; specifically $\mathsf{lcp}_0(z, z') = \lfloor \frac{\lambda\lceil\log\sigma\rceil - \delta - 1}{\lceil\log\sigma\rceil} \rfloor$.

The combinations can be generated in $\mathcal{O}(\binom{\lambda}{k})$ time [14]; creating and querying the $\sigma^k\binom{\lambda}{k}$ strings can be done in $\mathcal{O}(1)$ time using standard bit-level operations and $\mathcal{O}(\log\log n)$ time using the y-fast trie per string, respectively. We have $\lambda = \alpha\log_\sigma n$ positions where we need to consider the k errors, yielding an overall time of $\mathcal{O}(n\sigma^k\binom{\alpha\log n}{k}\log\log n) = \mathcal{O}(n\frac{(\alpha\sigma)^k}{k!}\log^k n\log\log n)$.

Remark 5. The procedure for all $x[i\mathinner{.\,.}i+\lambda-1]$ is parallelisable in the CREW PRAM model; each of the p processors is assigned $\lceil n/p \rceil$ or $\lfloor n/p \rfloor$ such positions.

Off-Line Implementation. We next show how to shave the $\log\log n$ factor by answering the exact, predecessor and successor queries in an off-line manner. We know the lexicographic order of the elements of X_λ by the SA of x. We then process a set B, consisting of at most one generated string per position of x, as a batch. We allow the substitutions for each position in the same order so that we can store them globally.

Given a set B of at most n λ-digit numbers we can find the exact, predecessor and successor elements of each of them in a sorted list of n integers in $\mathcal{O}(n)$ time as follows. We first sort the numbers in B using radix sort in time $\mathcal{O}(n\frac{\lambda}{\log n}) = \mathcal{O}(n)$ [12]. We then apply a single step of mergesort to merge the two sorted lists, corresponding to B and X_λ, and finally we scan the merged list once and answer the queries. If for position i the query returns an element of the batch occurring at position i, we retrieve the predecessor and successor of $x[i..i+\lambda-1]$ from the SA similarly to the description in Sect. 3.2. By using this to process the generated strings as batches, we answer each query in $\mathcal{O}(1)$ time after $\mathcal{O}(n)$-time pre-processing per $\mathcal{O}(n)$-sized batch, thus arriving at the following result.

Theorem 2. *The* PLCP WITH k-ERRORS *problem can be solved in* $\mathcal{O}(n\frac{(c\log n)^k}{k!})$ *time on average, where $c > 1$ is a constant, using $\mathcal{O}(n)$ extra space.*

Remark 6. The obtained time complexity is upper bounded by $n^{1+\epsilon}$ for any $\epsilon > 0$ when $k = o(\log n)$. Let $m = ce\log n/k$. Using Stirling's approximation we get

$$\frac{c^k}{k!}\log^k n \leq \frac{1}{\sqrt{2\pi k}}m^{ce\log n/m} \leq n^{ce\log m/m},$$

which is upper bounded by n^ϵ, for any $\epsilon > 0$, if $\log m/m \leq \frac{\epsilon}{ce}$, which is true for sufficiently large n if $k = o(\log n)$.

Remark 7. We have that $\frac{c^k}{k!} \leq c^c = \mathcal{O}(1)$ and hence the required time is $\mathcal{O}(n\log^k n)$. Notably, this complexity is $o(n\log^k n)$ for super-constant k.

Large Alphabets Implementation. In this section, we assume a general ordered alphabet. The SA of a string of length n, over a general ordered alphabet, can be computed in $\mathcal{O}(n\log n)$ time and $\mathcal{O}(n)$ space [15]. We consider in total $\binom{\lambda}{k}$ position sets of size k each denoting where the k errors may occur. For each set $\{\ell_0, \ldots, \ell_{k-1}\}$ of error positions we want to find the longest prefix of *maximum* length λ that occurs elsewhere in the string with k-errors. Let us show the process of finding this for a single set. Considering the suffixes of x, all letters that occur at the $\ell_0, \ldots, \ell_{k-1}$th positions of every suffix are disregarded to intuitively obtain n suffixes split into $k + 1$ substrings each. Recall that the first error occurs at the ℓ_0th position of every suffix. Using the SA and starting with the first n substrings of length ℓ_0, a new rank is assigned to each of them according to the lexicographical ordering of these substrings; this can be easily derived from the SA. Clearly, two suffixes y and z are given the same rank if $\mathsf{lcp}_0(y, z) \geq \ell_0$. Again considering that the first error occurs at the ℓ_0th position of every suffix, the new rank for the first n substrings will be identical to the original SA if each substring has a unique rank i.e. no two substrings are the same. We proceed to the next position ℓ_i of our set analogously to consider n substrings of length $\ell_i - \ell_{i-1} - 1$. To maintain $\mathcal{O}(n)$ space, for every consecutively considered pair of error positions, a bucket sort is applied to the n pairs of ranks corresponding to the n suffixes to obtain a new ranking, and the process continues. In the end, we have a new lexicographical ordering of the suffixes of x that disregards the letters at the $\ell_0, \ldots, \ell_{k-1}$th positions of every suffix. LCE queries are applied between successive suffixes in the new ordering to obtain the longest prefixes with k-mismatches for this set of positions. The process takes $\mathcal{O}(kn)$ time.

We next describe how to shave a factor of k from the time complexity. We show in Appendix A how to generate all distinct subsets of $\{0, \ldots, \lambda - 1\}$ of size at most k in a structured manner in time $\mathcal{O}(\binom{\lambda}{k})$ such that consecutively generated subsets only differ on whether they contain the largest element of their union.

Let us denote by SA_P an integer array storing the starting positions of all lexicographically sorted suffixes of x when the ith letter of every suffix, for all $i \in P$, is disregarded. We similarly denote by $\mathsf{LCP}_P[r]$ the longest common prefix of the suffixes with starting positions $\mathsf{SA}_P[r-1]$ and $\mathsf{SA}_P[r]$ when the ith letter of both suffixes, for all $i \in P$, is disregarded. The only thing we need to show is that from SA_{L_i} and LCP_{L_i}, where $L_i = \{\ell_0, \ldots, \ell_i : \ell_0 < \ldots < \ell_i\}$, $L_{i+1} = L_i \cup \{\ell_{i+1}\}$ and $\ell_{i+1} > \ell_i$, we can compute $\mathsf{SA}_{L_{i+1}}$ and $\mathsf{LCP}_{L_{i+1}}$ in $\mathcal{O}(n)$ time and the opposite. We get the ranks for the substrings of length $\ell_{i+1} - 1$ from SA_{L_i} and LCP_{L_i} and the ranks after position ℓ_{i+1} from SA and LCP, and so we can compute $\mathsf{SA}_{L_{i+1}}$. By preprocessing LCP_{L_i} for RMQs it easy to see how we can obtain $\mathsf{LCP}_{L_{i+1}}$ with $\mathcal{O}(n)$ LCE queries over LCP_{L_i} and $\mathcal{O}(n)$ LCE queries over LCP. The opposite direction is similar; we can get the ranks for SA_{L_i} by getting ranks for substrings of length $\ell_{i+1} - 1$ from $\mathsf{SA}_{L_{i+1}}$, and the rest from the original SA. LCP_{L_i} can also be computed similarly. Throughout the computation we need to maintain only $\mathsf{SA}_{L_i}, \mathsf{LCP}_{L_i}, \mathsf{SA}_{L_{i+1}}$ and $\mathsf{LCP}_{L_{i+1}}$.

Theorem 8. *The* PLCP *with* k-ERRORS *problem, under the Hamming distance model and for an alphabet of size* $\sigma > 1$, *can be solved in time* $\mathcal{O}(n\frac{(c\log_\sigma n)^k}{k!})$ *on average, where* $c > 1$ *is a constant, using* $\mathcal{O}(n)$ *extra space.*

3.3   Extension to Edit Distance

We next consider computing PLCP_k under the edit distance model; however in this case we observe that $x[i..n-1]$ and $x[i+d..n-1]$ are at edit distance $|d|$ for $-k \leq d \leq k$. We hence slightly amend the definition so that $\mathsf{PLCP}_k[i]$ refers to the length of the longest common prefix of $x[i..n-1]$ with k-errors occurring at some position $j \notin S_{i,k} = \{i-k, \ldots, i+k\}$.

The proof of Theorem 3 can be extended to allow for k-errors under the edit distance model. In this case we have that $\Pr(X_{i,j} \geq m) \leq \binom{m}{k}\frac{3^k}{\sigma^{m-k}}$; this can be seen by following the same reasoning as in the first claim of the proof with two extra considerations: (a) each deletion/insertion operation conceptually shifts the letters to be matched (giving the 3^k factor); (b) the letters to be matched are m minus the number of deletions and substitutions and hence at least $m - k$. The extra 3^k factor gets consumed by $(2/3)^{3k}$ later in the proof since $2\sqrt[3]{3}/3 < 1$.

On the algorithmic side, to obtain Theorem 2 for edit distance, we modify the algorithm of Sect. 3.2 for Hamming distance and constant-sized alphabets:

1. At each considered position, except for $\sigma - 1$ substitutions, we also consider σ insertions and 1 deletion. This yields an extra multiplicative 2^k factor in the time complexity. We keep counters ins for insertions and del for deletions; for each obtained length, we add del and subtract ins.
2. When querying for a string z, while processing position i, we now have to check that we do not return a position $j \in S_{i,k}$.

y-Fast Trie Implementation. When we start processing position i, we create an array of size $\mathcal{O}(k)$ storing, for each position $j \in S_{i,k}$, a position $f_j \notin S_{i,k}$ that has a longest common prefix with $x[j .. n - 1]$ of maximal length using the SA and the LCP array. When a query returns a position $j \in S_{i,k}$, we instead consider f_j. This takes $\mathcal{O}(k)$ time per position i.

Off-Line Implementation. Recall that we process a batch consisting of at most one generated string per position of x. For a fixed position i in X_λ, we essentially even query for $x[j .. j + \lambda - 1]$, $j \in S_{i,k}$. However we show that with one more predecessor query in X_λ we usually obtain a position $r \notin S_{i,k}$. For the rare cases that we do not, we can afford to precompute the answer by performing $\mathcal{O}(k^3)$ predecessor queries in total. The probability that the predecessor of j in X_λ is in $S_{j,2k}$ (which is a superset of $S_{i,k}$ for $j - k < i < j + k$) is no more than $\frac{4k}{n-\lambda-1}$. We do precomputations for all such pairs (i, j) in $\mathcal{O}(n + k^2 \cdot \frac{4k}{n-\lambda-1} n) = \mathcal{O}(n + k^3)$. The successor queries are handled analogously. We arrive at Theorem 2.

Remark 9. The technique leading to Theorem 8 that works for general ordered alphabets is generalisable to edit distance with an overhead factor only dependent on k (exponentially); we leave the details for the full version of the paper.

4   Applications

In what follows we demonstrate some algorithmic implications of our results.

4.1   Genome Mappability Data Structure

The *genome mappability* problem has already been studied under the Hamming distance model [4,5,13,28]. We can also define the problem under the edit distance model as follows. Given a string x of length n and integers $m < n$ and $k < m$, we are asked to count, for each length-m substring $x[i .. i + m - 1]$ of x, the number occ of other substrings of x occurring at a position $j \notin S_{i,k} = \{i - k, \ldots, i + k\}$ that are at edit distance at most k from $x[i .. i + m - 1]$. We then say that this substring has k-mappability equal to occ. Specifically, we consider a data structure version of this problem [3]. Given x and k, construct a data structure, which, for a query value μ given on-line, returns the minimal value of m that forces at least μ length-m substrings of x to have k-mappability equal to 0.

Theorem 10 ([3]). *An $\mathcal{O}(n)$-sized data structure answering genome mappability queries in $\mathcal{O}(1)$ time per query can be constructed from PLCP_k in time $\mathcal{O}(n)$.*

By combining Theorems 2 with 10 we obtain the first efficient algorithm for the genome mappability data structure under the edit distance model.

4.2 Longest Common Substring with k-Errors

In the *longest common substring with k-errors* problem we are asked to find the longest substrings of two strings that are at distance at most k. The Hamming distance version has received much attention due to its applications in computational biology [6,7,25,36,37]. Under edit distance, the problem is less explored [34]. The *average k-error common substring* is an alignment-free method based on this notion for measuring string dissimilarity under Hamming distance; we denote the induced distance by $\text{Dist}_k(x, y)$ for two strings x and y (see [37] for the definition). $\text{Dist}_k(x, y)$ can be computed in time $\mathcal{O}(|x| + |y|)$ from arrays $\Lambda_{x,y}$ and $\Lambda_{y,x}$, defined as $\Lambda_{x,y}[i] = \max_{0 \le j \le |y|-1}(\text{lcp}_k(x[i \mathbin{..} |x| - 1], y[j \mathbin{..} |y| - 1]))$.

A worst-case and more practical average-case algorithms for the computation of $\Lambda_{x,y}$ have been presented in [31,35,36]. This measure was extended to allow for *wildcards* (don't care letters) in the strings in [20]. Here we consider a natural generalisation of this measure: the average k-error common substring under the edit distance model. The sole change is in the definition of $\Lambda_{x,y}[i]$: except for substitution, we also allow for insertion and deletion operations.

The algorithm of Sect. 3.3 can be applied to compute $\Lambda_{x,y}$ under the edit distance model within the same complexities. We start by constructing X_λ, using $\lambda = \alpha \log_\sigma(|x| + |y|)$ as above for x and then do the queries for the suffixes of y. We obtain the following result.

Theorem 11. *Given two strings x and y of length at most n and a distance threshold k, arrays $\Lambda_{x,y}$ and $\Lambda_{y,x}$ and $\text{Dist}_k(x, y)$ can be computed in time $\mathcal{O}(n\frac{(c \log n)^k}{k!})$ on average, where $c > 1$ is a constant, using $\mathcal{O}(n)$ extra space.*

Remark 12. By applying Theorem 11 we essentially solve the longest common substring with k-errors for x and y within the same complexities. A similar *worst-case* time bound for *constant k* was recently shown in [34].

4.3 All-Pairs Suffix/Prefix Overlaps with k-Errors

Given a set of strings and an error-rate ϵ, the goal is to find, for all pairs of strings, their suffix/prefix matches (overlaps) that are within distance $k = \lceil \epsilon \ell \rceil$, where ℓ is the length of the overlap [24,32,34,38].

Using our technique but setting X_λ to be the set of *prefixes* of length λ of the strings and querying for all starting positions (*suffixes*) in a similar manner as in Sect. 3.1, we obtain the following result (see also [34] for constant k).

Theorem 13. *Given a set of strings of total length n and a distance threshold k, the maximal length of the longest suffix/prefix overlaps of every string against all other strings within distance k can be computed in time $\mathcal{O}(n\frac{(c \log n)^k}{k!})$ on average, where $c > 1$ is a constant, using $\mathcal{O}(n)$ extra space.*

Acknowledgements. We warmly thank Cyril Nicaud (Université Paris-Est) for useful discussions.

A K-Combinations Generation Process

We generate all combinations of size K of the set $[N]$ using the following folklore algorithm. We build a tree in a recursive way. Each node v has a label $\ell(v) \in [N]$, apart from the root which is labeled with 0. We say that a node v represents the set $r(v) = \{\ell(v)\} \cup \{\ell(u)|u \text{ is an ancestor of } v\} \setminus \{0\}$. By construction, no two nodes will represent the same set. At the end of the process each of the $\mathcal{O}(\binom{N}{K})$ leaves will represent a distinct K-combination. The procedure works as follows:

1. It takes as input a node v with satellite data $\ell(v)$ and $|r(v)|$.
2. It creates $N - \ell(v) - K + |r(v)|$ child nodes of v, labeled $\ell(v) + 1$ to $N - K + |r(v)| + 1$.
3. For each newly created node u, if $|r(u)| = |r(v)| + 1 < K$, the procedure recursively calls itself.

Initiating this procedure with an input node u, with $\ell(u) = 0$ and $|r(u)| = 0$, all K-combinations are generated in time $\mathcal{O}(\binom{N}{K})$ if $K \leq N/2$ as shown below. Note that each node of the tree is associated with a unique subset of $[N]$ and neighbouring nodes only differ on whether they contain the largest element of their union.

To upper bound the time complexity, it suffices to bound the number of nodes in the tree with a single child, since the rest internal nodes are trivially upper bounded by the number of leaves. A node with label $N - i$ will have a single child only if it is the $(K - i)$th element added in a combination. This can happen $\mathcal{O}(\binom{N-i-1}{K-i-1})$ times. Given our assumption that $K \leq N/2$ and using Pascal's identity $\binom{m}{j} = \binom{m-1}{j-1} + \binom{m-1}{j}$, we bound the number of nodes with a single child as follows:

$$\sum_{i=1}^{K-1} \binom{N-i-1}{K-i-1} = 1 + \sum_{i=1}^{K-2} \binom{N-i}{K-i-1} - \sum_{i=1}^{K-2} \binom{N-i-1}{K-i-2}$$

$$= 1 + \sum_{i=1}^{K-2} \binom{N-i}{K-i-1} - \sum_{i=2}^{K-1} \binom{N-i}{K-i-1} = 1 + \binom{N-1}{K-2} - 1 = \frac{K(K-1)}{N(N-K+1)} \binom{N}{K} \leq \binom{N}{K}.$$

References

1. Abboud, A., Williams, R., Yu, H.: More applications of the polynomial method to algorithm design. In: SODA, SODA 2015, pp. 218–230. Society for Industrial and Applied Mathematics (2015)
2. Abouelhoda, M.I., Kurtz, S., Ohlebusch, E.: Replacing suffix trees with enhanced suffix arrays. J. Discret. Algorithms **2**(1), 53–86 (2004)

3. Alamro, H., Ayad, L.A.K., Charalampopoulos, P., Iliopoulos, C.S., Pissis, S.P.: Longest common prefixes with k-mismatches and applications. In: Tjoa, A.M., Bellatreche, L., Biffl, S., van Leeuwen, J., Wiedermann, J. (eds.) SOFSEM 2018. LNCS, vol. 10706, pp. 636–649. Springer, Cham (2018). https://doi.org/10.1007/978-3-319-73117-9_45

4. Alzamel, M., et al.: Efficient computation of sequence mappability. In: Gagie, T., et al. (eds.) SPIRE 2018. LNCS, vol. 11147, pp. 12–26. Springer, Cham (2018)

5. Alzamel, M., Charalampopoulos, P., Iliopoulos, C.S., Pissis, S.P., Radoszewski, J., Sung, W.-K.: Faster algorithms for 1-mappability of a sequence. In: Gao, X., Du, H., Han, M. (eds.) COCOA 2017. LNCS, vol. 10628, pp. 109–121. Springer, Cham (2017). https://doi.org/10.1007/978-3-319-71147-8_8

6. Apostolico, A., Guerra, C., Landau, G.M., Pizzi, C.: Sequence similarity measures based on bounded hamming distance. Theor. Comput. Sci. **638**, 76–90 (2016). Pattern Matching, Text Data Structures and Compression

7. Apostolico, A., Guerra, C., Pizzi, C.: Alignment free sequence similarity with bounded hamming distance. In: DCC, pp. 183–192. IEEE (2014)

8. Bender, M.A., Farach-Colton, M.: The LCA problem revisited. In: Gonnet, G.H., Viola, A. (eds.) LATIN 2000. LNCS, vol. 1776, pp. 88–94. Springer, Heidelberg (2000). https://doi.org/10.1007/10719839_9

9. Bollobás, B., Letzter, S.: Longest common extension. Eur. J. Comb. **68**, 242–248 (2018)

10. Charalampopoulos, P., et al.: Linear-time algorithm for long LCF with k mismatches. In: CPM. LIPIcs, vol. 105, pp. 23:1–23:16. Schloss Dagstuhl-Leibniz-Zentrum fuer Informatik (2018)

11. Cole, R., Gottlieb, L.-A., Lewenstein, M.: Dictionary matching and indexing with errors and don't cares. In: STOC, STOC 2004, pp. 91–100. ACM (2004)

12. Cormen, T.H., Leiserson, C.E., Rivest, R.L., Stein, C.: Introduction to Algorithms, 3rd edn. MIT Press, Cambridge (2009)

13. Derrien, T., et al.: Fast computation and applications of genome mappability. PLoS ONE **7**(1), e30377 (2012)

14. Eades, P., McKay, B.D.: An algorithm for generating subsets of fixed size with a strong minimal change property. Inf. Process. Lett. **19**(3), 131–133 (1984)

15. Farach, M.: Optimal suffix tree construction with large alphabets. In: FOCS, pp. 137–143. IEEE Computer Society (1997)

16. Faro, S., Lecroq, T.: The exact online string matching problem: a review of the most recent results. ACM Comput. Surv **45**(2), 13:1–13:42 (2013)

17. Fischer, J.: Inducing the LCP-array. In: Dehne, F., Iacono, J., Sack, J.-R. (eds.) WADS 2011. LNCS, vol. 6844, pp. 374–385. Springer, Heidelberg (2011). https://doi.org/10.1007/978-3-642-22300-6_32

18. Flouri, T., Giaquinta, E., Kobert, K., Ukkonen, E.: Longest common substrings with k mismatches. Inf. Process. Lett. **115**(6–8), 643–647 (2015)

19. Grabowski, S.: A note on the longest common substring with k-mismatches problem. Inf. Process. Lett. **115**(6–8), 640–642 (2015)

20. Horwege, S., et al.: Spaced words and kmacs: fast alignment-free sequence comparison based on inexact word matches. Nucleic Acids Res. **42**(Webserver-Issue), 7–11 (2014)

21. Karlin, S., Ghandour, G., Ost, F., T, S., Korn, L.J.: New approaches for computer analysis of nucleic acid sequences. Proc. Natl. Acad. Sci. USA **80**, 5660–5664 (1983)

22. Kociumaka, T., Radoszewski, J., Starikovskaya, T.A.: Longest common substring with approximately k mismatches. CoRR, abs/1712.08573 (2017)

23. Kolpakov, R., Bana, G., Kucherov, G.: MREPS: efficient and flexible detection of tandem repeats in DNA. Nucleic Acids Res. **31**(13), 3672–3678 (2003)
24. Kucherov, G., Tsur, D.: Improved filters for the approximate suffix-prefix overlap problem. In: Moura, E., Crochemore, M. (eds.) SPIRE 2014. LNCS, vol. 8799, pp. 139–148. Springer, Cham (2014). https://doi.org/10.1007/978-3-319-11918-2_14
25. Leimeister, C., Morgenstern, B.: Kmacs: the k-mismatch average common substring approach to alignment-free sequence comparison. Bioinformatics **30**(14), 2000–2008 (2014)
26. Liang, K.-H.: Bioinformatics for Biomedical Science and Clinical Applications. Woodhead Publishing Series in Biomedicine. Woodhead Publishing (2013)
27. Manber, U., Myers, E.W.: Suffix arrays: a new method for on-line string searches. SIAM J. Comput. **22**(5), 935–948 (1993)
28. Manzini, G.: Longest common prefix with mismatches. In: Iliopoulos, C., Puglisi, S., Yilmaz, E. (eds.) SPIRE 2015. LNCS, vol. 9309, pp. 299–310. Springer, Cham (2015). https://doi.org/10.1007/978-3-319-23826-5_29
29. Navarro, G., Baeza-Yates, R.A.: A hybrid indexing method for approximate string matching. J. Discret. Algorithms **1**(1), 21–49 (2000)
30. Nong, G., Zhang, S., Chan, W.H.: Linear suffix array construction by almost pure induced-sorting. In: DCC, pp. 193–202. IEEE (2009)
31. Pizzi, C.: Missmax: alignment-free sequence comparison with mismatches through filtering and heuristics. Algorithms Mol. Biol. **11**(1), 6 (2016)
32. Rasmussen, K.R., Stoye, J., Myers, E.W.: Efficient q-gram filters for finding all epsilon-matches over a given length. J. Comput. Biol. **13**(2), 296–308 (2006)
33. Smit, A.F.: Interspersed repeats and other mementos of transposable elements in mammalian genomes. Curr. Opin. Genet. Dev. **9**(6), 657–663 (1999)
34. Thankachan, S.V., Aluru, C., Chockalingam, S.P., Aluru, S.: Algorithmic framework for approximate matching under bounded edits with applications to sequence analysis. In: Raphael, B.J. (ed.) RECOMB 2018. LNCS, vol. 10812, pp. 211–224. Springer, Cham (2018). https://doi.org/10.1007/978-3-319-89929-9_14
35. Thankachan, S.V., Apostolico, A., Aluru, S.: A provably efficient algorithm for the k-mismatch average common substring problem. J. Comput. Biol. **23**(6), 472–482 (2016)
36. Thankachan, S.V., Chockalingam, S.P., Liu, Y., Apostolico, A., Aluru, S.: ALFRED: a practical method for alignment-free distance computation. J. Comput. Biol., **23**(6), 452–460 (2016)
37. Ulitsky, I., Burstein, D., Tuller, T., Chor, B.: The average common substring approach to phylogenomic reconstruction. J. Comput. Biol. **13**(2), 336–350 (2006)
38. Välimäki, N., Ladra, S., Mäkinen, V.: Approximate all-pairs suffix/prefix overlaps. Inf. Comput. **213**, 49–58 (2012)
39. Willard, D.E.: Log-logarithmic worst-case range queries are possible in space theta(n). Inf. Process. Lett. **17**(2), 81–84 (1983)

Longest Property-Preserved Common Factor

Lorraine A. K. Ayad[1], Giulia Bernardini[2], Roberto Grossi[3],
Costas S. Iliopoulos[1], Nadia Pisanti[3,4(✉)], Solon P. Pissis[1],
and Giovanna Rosone[3]

[1] Department of Informatics, King's College London, London, UK
{lorraine.ayad,c.iliopoulos,solon.pissis}@kcl.ac.uk
[2] Department of Informatics, Systems and Communication, University of
Milan-Bicocca, Milan, Italy
giulia.bernardini@unimib.it
[3] Department of Computer Science, University of Pisa, Pisa, Italy
{grossi,pisanti}@di.unipi.it, giovanna.rosone@unipi.it
[4] ERABLE Team, INRIA, Lyon, France

Abstract. In this paper we introduce a new family of string processing
problems. We are given two or more strings and we are asked to compute
a factor common to all strings that preserves a specific property and has
maximal length. Here we consider two fundamental string properties:
square-free factors and periodic factors under two different settings, one
per property. In the first setting, we are given a string x and we are asked
to construct a data structure over x answering the following type of on-
line queries: given string y, find a longest square-free factor common to
x and y. In the second setting, we are given k strings and an integer
$1 < k' \leq k$ and we are asked to find a longest periodic factor common to
at least k' strings. We present linear-time solutions for both settings. We
anticipate that our paradigm can be extended to other string properties.

Keywords: Longest common factor · Periodicity · Squares
Algorithms

1 Introduction

In the longest common factor problem, also known as longest common factor
problem, we are given two strings x and y, each of length at most n, and we are
asked to find a maximal-length string occurring in both x and y. This is a classical
and well-studied problem in computer science arising out of different practical
scenarios. It can be solved in $\mathcal{O}(n)$ time and space [8,15] (see also [18,23]).
Recently, the same problem has been extensively studied under distance metrics;
that is, the sought factors (one from x and one from y) must be at distance at
most k and have maximal length [1,7,21,22,24,25] (and references therein).

In this paper we initiate a new related line of research. We are given two or
more strings and our goal is to compute a *factor* common to all strings that preserves a specific *property* and has maximal length. An analogous line of research

© Springer Nature Switzerland AG 2018
T. Gagie et al. (Eds.): SPIRE 2018, LNCS 11147, pp. 42–49, 2018.
https://doi.org/10.1007/978-3-030-00479-8_4

was introduced in [9]. It focuses on computing a *subsequence* (rather than a factor) common to all strings that preserves a specific property and has maximal length. Specifically, in [2,9,16], the authors considered computing a longest common palindromic subsequence and in [17] computing a longest common square subsequence.

We consider two fundamental string properties: *square-free* factors and *periodic* factors [20] under two different settings, one per property. In the first setting, we are given a string x and we are asked to construct a data structure over x answering the following type of on-line queries: given string y, find a longest square-free factor common to x and y. In the second setting, we are given k strings and an integer $1 < k' \leq k$ and we are asked to find a longest periodic factor common to at least k' strings. We present linear-time solutions for both settings. We anticipate that our paradigm can be extended to other string properties.

1.1 Definitions and Notation

An *alphabet* Σ is a non-empty finite ordered set of letters of size $\sigma = |\Sigma|$. In this work we consider that $\sigma = \mathcal{O}(1)$ or that Σ is a linearly-sortable integer alphabet. A *string* x on an alphabet Σ is a sequence of elements of Σ. The set of all strings on an alphabet Σ, including the *empty string* ε of length 0, is denoted by Σ^*. For any string x, we denote by $x[i..j]$ the *substring* (sometimes called *factor*) of x that starts at position i and ends at position j. In particular, $x[0..j]$ is the *prefix* of x that ends at position j, and $x[i..|x|-1]$ is the *suffix* of x that starts at position i, where $|x|$ denotes the *length* of x. A string uu, $u \in \Sigma^*$, is called a *square*. A *square-free* string is a string that does not contain a square as a factor.

A *period* of $x[0..|x|-1]$ is a positive integer p such that $x[i] = x[i+p]$ holds for all $0 \leq i < |x| - p$. The smallest period of x is denoted by $\mathsf{per}(x)$. String u is called *periodic* if and only if $\mathsf{per}(u) \leq |u|/2$. A *run* of string x is an interval $[i,j]$ such that for the smallest period $p = \mathsf{per}(x[i..j])$ it holds that $2p \leq j - i + 1$ and the periodicity cannot be extended to the left or right, *i.e.*, $i = 0$ or $x[i-1] \neq x[i+p-1]$, and, $j = |x| - 1$ or $x[j-p+1] \neq x[j+1]$.

1.2 Algorithmic Toolbox

The maximum number of runs in a string of length n is less than n [3], and, moreover, all runs can be computed in $\mathcal{O}(n)$ time [3,19].

The *suffix tree* $\mathsf{ST}(x)$ of a non-empty string x of length n is a compact trie representing all suffixes of x. $\mathsf{ST}(x)$ can be constructed in $\mathcal{O}(n)$ time [12]. We can analogously define and construct the *generalised suffix tree* $\mathsf{GST}(x_0, x_1, \ldots, x_{k-1})$ for a set of k strings. We assume the reader is familiar with these data structures.

The matching statistics capture all matches between two strings x and y [6]. More formally, the *matching statistics* of a string $y[0..|y|-1]$ with respect to a string x is an array $\mathsf{MS}_y[0..|y|-1]$, where $\mathsf{MS}_y[i]$ is a pair (ℓ_i, p_i) such that (i) $y[i..i+\ell_i-1]$ is the longest prefix of $y[i..|y|-1]$ that is a factor of x; and (ii)

$x[p_i..p_i + \ell_i - 1] = y[i..i + \ell_i - 1]$. Matching statistics can be computed in $\mathcal{O}(|y|)$ time for $\sigma = \mathcal{O}(1)$ by using $\mathsf{ST}(x)$ [5,14,15].

Given a rooted tree T with n leaves coloured from 0 to $k - 1$, $1 < k \leq n$, the *colour set size* problem is finding, for each internal node u of T, the number of different leaf colours in the subtree rooted at u. In [8], the authors present an $\mathcal{O}(n)$-time solution to this problem.

In the *weighted ancestor* problem, introduced in [13], we consider a rooted tree T with an integer weight function μ defined on the nodes. We require that the weight of the root is zero and the weight of any other node is strictly larger than the weight of its parent. A weighted ancestor query, given a node v and an integer value $\ell \leq \mu(v)$, asks for the highest ancestor u of v such that $\mu(u) \geq \ell$, i.e., such an ancestor u that $\mu(u) \geq \ell$ and $\mu(u)$ is the smallest possible. When T is the suffix tree of a string x of length n, we can locate the locus of any factor of $x[i..j]$ using a weighted ancestor query. We define the weight of a node of the suffix tree as the length of the string it represents. Thus a weighted ancestor query can be used for the terminal node corresponding to $x[i..n - 1]$ to create (if necessary) and mark the node that corresponds to $x[i..j]$. Given a collection Q of weighted ancestor queries on a weighted tree T on n nodes with integer weights up to $n^{\mathcal{O}(1)}$, all the queries in Q can be answered *off-line* in $\mathcal{O}(n + |Q|)$ time [4].

2   Square-Free-Preserved Matching Statistics

In this section, we introduce the square-free-preserved matching statistics problem and provide a linear-time solution. In the *square-free-preserved matching statistics* problem we are given a string x of length n and we are asked to construct a data structure over x answering the following type of on-line queries: given string y, find the longest square-free prefix of $y[i..|y| - 1]$ that is a factor of x, for all $0 \leq i < |y| - 1$. (For related work see [10].) We represent the answer using an integer array $\mathsf{SQMS}_y[0..|y| - 1]$ of lengths, but we can trivially modify our algorithm to report the actual factors. It should be clear that a maximum element in SQMS gives the length of some longest square-free factor common to x and y.

Construction. Our data structure over string x consists of the following:

- An integer array $L_x[0..n - 1]$, where $L_x[i]$ stores the length of the longest square-free factor starting at position i of string x.
- The suffix tree $\mathsf{ST}(x)$ of string x.

The idea for constructing array L_x efficiently is based on the following crucial observation.

Observation 1. *If $x[i..n-1]$ contains a square then $L_x[i]+1$, for all $0 \leq i < n$, is the length of the shortest prefix of $x[i..n - 1]$ (factor f) containing a square. In fact, the square is a suffix of f, otherwise f would not have been the shortest. If $x[i..n - 1]$ does not contain a square then $L_x[i] = n - i$.*

We thus shift our focus to computing the shortest such prefixes. We start by considering the runs of x. Specifically, we consider squares in x observing that a run $[\ell, r]$ with period p contains $r - \ell - 2p + 2$ squares of length $2p$ with the leftmost one starting at position ℓ. Let $r' = \ell + 2p - 1$ denote the ending position of the leftmost such square of the run. In order to find, for all i's, the shortest prefix of $x[i..n-1]$ containing a square s, and thus compute $L_x[i]$, we have two cases:

1. s is part of a run $[\ell, r]$ in x that starts *after* i. In particular, $s = x[\ell..r']$ such that $r' \leq r$, $\ell > i$, and r' is minimal. In this case the shortest factor has length $\ell + 2p - i$; we store this value in an integer array $C[0..n-1]$. If no run starts after position i we set $C[i] = \infty$. To compute C, after computing in $\mathcal{O}(n)$ time all the runs of x with their p and r' [3,19], we sort them by r'. A right-to-left scan after this sorting associates to i the closest r' with $\ell > i$.
2. s is part of a run $[\ell, r]$ in x and $i \in [\ell, r]$. This implies that if $i \leq r - 2p + 1$ then a square *starts at* i and we store the length of the shortest such square in an integer array $S[0..n-1]$. If no square starts at position i we set $S[i] = \infty$. Array S can be constructed in $\mathcal{O}(n)$ time by applying the algorithm of [11].

Since we do not know which of the two cases holds, we compute both C and S. By Observation 1, if $C[i] = S[i] = \infty$ ($x[i..n-1]$ does not contain a square) we set $L_x[i] = n - i$; otherwise ($x[i..n-1]$ contains a square) we set $L_x[i] = \min\{C[i], S[i]\} - 1$.

Finally, we build the suffix tree $\mathsf{ST}(x)$ of string x in $\mathcal{O}(n)$ time [12]. This completes our construction.

Querying. We rely on the following fact for answering the queries efficiently.

Fact 2. *Every factor of a square-free string is square-free.*

Let string y be an on-line query. Using $\mathsf{ST}(x)$, we compute the matching statistics MS_y of y with respect to x. For each $j \in [0, |y| - 1]$, $\mathsf{MS}_y[j] = (\ell_i, i)$ indicates that $x[i..i + \ell_i - 1] = y[j..j + \ell_i - 1]$. This computation can be done in $\mathcal{O}(|y|)$ time [5,15]. By applying Fact 2, we can answer any query y in $\mathcal{O}(|y|)$ time for $\sigma = \mathcal{O}(1)$ by setting $\mathsf{SQMS}_y[j] = \min\{\ell_i, L_x[i]\}$, for all $0 \leq j \leq |y| - 1$.

We arrive at the following result.

Theorem 3. *Given a string x of length n over an alphabet of size $\sigma = \mathcal{O}(1)$, we can construct a data structure of size $\mathcal{O}(n)$ in time $\mathcal{O}(n)$, answering SQMS_y on-line queries in $\mathcal{O}(|y|)$ time.*

Proof. The time complexity of our algorithm follows from the above discussion. We next show the correctness of our algorithm. Let us first show the correctness of computing array L_x. The square contained in the shortest prefix of $x[i..n-1]$ (containing a square) starts by definition either at i or after i. If it starts at i this is correctly computed by the algorithm of [11] which assigns the length of the shortest such square in $S[i]$. If it starts after i it must be the leftmost square of another run by the runs definition. $C[i]$ stores the length of the shortest prefix containing such a square. Then by Observation 1, $L_x[i]$ is computed correctly.

It suffices to show that, if w is the longest square-free substring common to x and y occurring at position i_x in x and at position i_y in y, then (i) $\mathsf{MS}_y[i_y] = (\ell, i_x)$ with $\ell \geq |w|$ and $x[i_x..i_x + \ell - 1] = y[i_y..i_y + \ell - 1]$; (ii) w is a prefix of $x[i_x..i_x + L_x[i_x] - 1]$; and (iii) $\mathsf{SQMS}_y[i_y] = |w|$. Case (i) directly follows from the correctness of the matching statistics algorithm. For Case (ii), since w occurs at i_x and w is square-free, $L_x[i_x] \geq |w|$. For Case (iii), since w is square-free we have to show that $|w| = \min\{\ell_i, L_x[i]\}$. We know from (i) that $\ell \geq |w|$ and from (ii) that $L_x[i_x] \geq |w|$. If $\min\{\ell_i, L_x[i]\} = \ell$, then w cannot be extended because the possibly longer than $|w|$ square-free string occurring at i_x does not occur in y, and in this case $|w| = \ell$. Otherwise, if $\min\{\ell_i, L_x[i]\} = L_x[i_x]$ then w cannot be extended because it is no longer square-free, and in this case $|w| = L_x[i_x]$. Hence we conclude that $\mathsf{SQMS}_y[i_y] = |w|$. The statement follows. □

The following example provides a complete overview of the workings of our algorithm.

Example 4. Let $x = $ **aababaababb** and $y = $ **babababbaaab**. The length of a longest common square-free factor is 3, and the factors are **bab** and **aba**.

i	0	1	2	3	4	5	6	7	8	9	10	
$x[i]$	a	a	b	a	b	a	a	b	a	b	b	
$C[i]$	5	6	5	4	3	5	5	4	3	∞	∞	
$S[i]$	2	4	4	6	∞	2	4	∞	∞	2	∞	
$L_x[i]$	1	3	3	3	2	1	3	3	2	1	1	
j	0	1	2	3	4	5	6	7	8	9	10	11
$y[j]$	b	a	b	a	b	a	b	b	a	a	a	b
$\mathsf{MS}_y[j]$	(4,2)	(5,1)	(4,2)	(5,6)	(4,7)	(3,8)	(2,9)	(3,4)	(2,0)	(3,0)	(2,1)	(1,2)
$\mathsf{SQMS}_y[j]$	3	3	3	3	3	2	1	2	1	1	2	1

3   Longest Periodic-Preserved Common Factor

In this section, we introduce the longest periodic-preserved common factor problem and provide a linear-time solution. In the *longest periodic-preserved common factor* problem, we are given $k \geq 2$ strings $x_0, x_1, \ldots, x_{k-1}$ of total length N and an integer $1 < k' \leq k$, and we are asked to find a longest periodic factor common to at least k' strings. We represent the answer $\mathsf{LPCF}_{k'}$ by the length of a longest factor, but we can trivially modify our algorithm to report an actual factor. Our algorithm, denoted by LPCF, works as follows.

1. Compute the runs of string x_j, for all $0 \leq j < k$.
2. Construct the generalised suffix tree $\mathsf{GST}(x_0, x_1, \ldots, x_{k-1})$ of $x_0, x_1, \ldots, x_{k-1}$.

3. For each string x_j and for each run $[\ell, r]$ with period p_ℓ of x_j, augment GST with the explicit node spelling $x[\ell..r]$, decorate it with p_ℓ, and mark it as a *candidate* node. This can be done as follows: for each run $[\ell, r]$ of x_j, for all $0 \leq j < k$, find the leaf corresponding to $x_j[\ell..|x_j|-1]$ and answer the weighted ancestor query in GST with weight $r - \ell + 1$. Let aGST be this tree.
4. Mark as *good* the nodes of aGST having at least k' different colours on the leaves of the subtree rooted there.
5. Return as LPCF$_{k'}$ the string depth of a candidate node in aGST which is also a good node, and that has maximal string depth (if any, otherwise return 0).

Theorem 5. *Given k strings of total length N on alphabet $\Sigma = \{1, \ldots, N^{\mathcal{O}(1)}\}$, and an integer $1 < k' \leq k$, algorithm LPCF returns LPCF$_{k'}$ in time $\mathcal{O}(N)$.*

Proof. Let us assume wlog that $k' = k$, and let w with period p be the longest periodic factor common to all strings. By the construction of aGST (Steps 1-4 of LPCF), the path spelling w leads to a good node n_w as w occurs in all the strings. We make the following observation.

Observation 6. *Each periodic factor with period p of string x is a factor of $x[i..j]$, where $[i, j]$ is a run with period p.*

By Observation 6, in all strings, w is included in a run having the same period. Observe that for at least one of the strings, there is a run ending with w, otherwise we could extend w obtaining a longer periodic common factor. Therefore n_w is *both* a good and a candidate node. By definition, n_w is at string depth at least $2p$ and, by construction, LPCF$_{k'}$ is the string depth of a deepest such node; thus $|w|$ will be returned by Step 5.

As for the time complexity, Step 1 [3,19] and Step 2 [12] can be done in $\mathcal{O}(N)$ time. Since the total number of runs is less than N [3], Step 3 can be done in $\mathcal{O}(N)$ time using off-line weighted ancestor queries [4], and the size of the aGST is still in $\mathcal{O}(N)$. Step 4 can be done in $\mathcal{O}(N)$ time [8]. Step 5 can be done in $\mathcal{O}(N)$ by a post-order traversal of aGST. $\qquad\qquad\square$

The following example provides a complete overview of the workings of our algorithm.

Example 7. Consider $x = \text{ababbabba}$, $y = \text{ababaab}$, and $k = k' = 2$. The runs of x are: $r_0 = [0, 3]$, per(abab) $= 2$, $r_1 = [1, 8]$, per(babbabba) $= 3$, $r_2 = [3, 4]$, per(bb) $= 1$, and $r_3 = [6, 7]$, per(bb) $= 1$; those of y are $r_4 = [0, 4]$, per(ababa) $= 2$ and $r_5 = [4, 5]$, per(aa) $= 1$. Figure 1 shows aGST for x, y, and $k = k' = 2$. Algorithm LPCF outputs $4 = |\text{abab}|$, with per(abab) $= 2$, as the node spelling abab is the deepest good one that is also a candidate.

4   Final Remarks

We introduced a new family of string processing problems. The goal is to compute factors common to a set of strings preserving a specific property and having

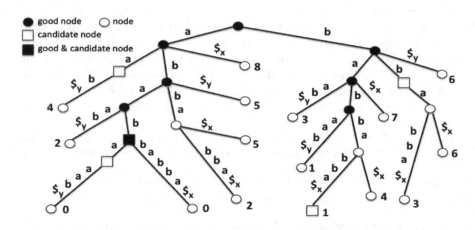

Fig. 1. aGST for $x = \texttt{ababbabba}$, $y = \texttt{ababaab}$, and $k = k' = 2$.

maximal length. We showed linear-time algorithms for square-free and periodic factors. We anticipate that our paradigm can be extended to other string properties.

Acknowledgements. Solon P. Pissis and Giovanna Rosone are partially supported by the Royal Society project IE 161274 "Processing uncertain sequences: combinatorics and applications". Giovanna Rosone and Nadia Pisanti are partially supported by the project Italian MIUR-SIR CMACBioSeq ("Combinatorial methods for analysis and compression of biological sequences") grant n. RBSI146R5L.

References

1. Ayad, L.A.K., Barton, C., Charalampopoulos, P., Iliopoulos, C.S., Pissis, S.P.: Longest common prefixes with k-errors and applications. In: Gagie, T., et al. (eds.) SPIRE 2018. LNCS, vol. 11147, pp. 27–41. Springer, Heidelberg (2018)
2. Bae, S.W., Lee, I.: On finding a longest common palindromic subsequence. Theor Comput Sci **710**, 29–34 (2018). Advances in Algorithms and Combinatorics on Strings (Honoring 60th birthday for Prof. Costas S, Iliopoulos)
3. Bannai, H., I, T., Inenaga, S., Nakashima, Y., Takeda, M., Tsuruta, K.: The "runs" theorem. SIAM J. Comput. **46**(5), 1501–1514 (2017)
4. Barton, C., Kociumaka, T., Liu, C., Pissis, S.P., Radoszewski, J.: Indexing weighted sequences: neat and efficient. CoRR, arXiv:abs/1704.07625 (2017)
5. Belazzougui, D., Cunial, F.: Indexed matching statistics and shortest unique substrings. In: Moura, E., Crochemore, M. (eds.) SPIRE 2014. LNCS, vol. 8799, pp. 179–190. Springer, Cham (2014). https://doi.org/10.1007/978-3-319-11918-2_18
6. Chang, W.I., Lawler, E.L.: Sublinear approximate string matching and biological applications. Algorithmica **12**(4), 327–344 (1994)
7. Charalampopoulos, P., et al.: Linear-time algorithm for long LCF with K mismatches. In: CPM. LIPIcs, vol. 105, pp. 23:1–23:16. Schloss Dagstuhl - Leibniz-Zentrum fuer Informatik (2018)

8. Chi, L., Hui, K.: Color set size problem with applications to string matching. In: Apostolico, A., Crochemore, M., Galil, Z., Manber, U. (eds.) CPM 1992. LNCS, vol. 644, pp. 230–243. Springer, Heidelberg (1992). https://doi.org/10.1007/3-540-56024-6_19

9. Chowdhury, S.R., Hasan, M.M., Iqbal, S., Rahman, M.S.: Computing a longest common palindromic subsequence. Fundam. Inf. **129**(4), 329–340 (2014)

10. Dumitran, M., Manea, F., Nowotka, D.: On prefix/suffix-square free words. In: Iliopoulos, C., Puglisi, S., Yilmaz, E. (eds.) SPIRE 2015. LNCS, vol. 9309, pp. 54–66. Springer, Cham (2015). https://doi.org/10.1007/978-3-319-23826-5_6

11. Duval, J.-P., Kolpakov, R., Kucherov, G., Lecroq, T., Lefebvre, A.: Linear-time computation of local periods. Theor. Comput. Sci. **326**(1), 229–240 (2004)

12. Farach, M.: Optimal suffix tree construction with large alphabets. In: 38th Annual Symposium on Foundations of Computer Science (FOCS), pp. 137–143 (1997)

13. Farach, M., Muthukrishnan, S.: Perfect hashing for strings: formalization and algorithms. In: Hirschberg, D., Myers, G. (eds.) CPM 1996. LNCS, vol. 1075, pp. 130–140. Springer, Heidelberg (1996). https://doi.org/10.1007/3-540-61258-0_11

14. Federico, M., Pisanti, N.: Suffix tree characterization of maximal motifs in biological sequences. Theor. Comput. Sci. **410**(43), 4391–4401 (2009)

15. Gusfield, D.: Algorithms on Strings, Trees, and Sequences - Computer Science and Computational Biology. Cambridge University Press, Cambridge (1997)

16. Inenaga, S., Hyyrö, H.: A hardness result and new algorithm for the longest common palindromic subsequence problem. Inf. Process. Lett. **129**, 11–15 (2018)

17. Inoue, T., Inenaga, S., Hyyrö, H., Bannai, H., Takeda, M.: Computing longest common square subsequences. In: 29th Symposium on Combinatorial Pattern Matching (CPM), LIPIcs, vol. 105, pp. 15:1–15:13 (2018)

18. Kociumaka, T., Starikovskaya, T., Vildhøj, H.W.: Sublinear space algorithms for the longest common substring problem. In: Schulz, A.S., Wagner, D. (eds.) ESA 2014. LNCS, vol. 8737, pp. 605–617. Springer, Heidelberg (2014). https://doi.org/10.1007/978-3-662-44777-2_50

19. Kolpakov, R., Kucherov, G.: Finding maximal repetitions in a word in linear time. In: 40th Symposium on Foundations of Comp Science, pp. 596–604 (1999)

20. Lothaire, M.: Applied Combinatorics on Words. Encyclopedia of Mathematics and its Applications. Cambridge University Press, Cambridge (2005)

21. Peterlongo, P., Pisanti, N., Boyer, F., do Lago, A.P., Sagot, M.: Lossless filter for multiple repetitions with hamming distance. J. Discr. Alg. **6**(3), 497–509 (2008)

22. Peterlongo, P., Pisanti, N., Boyer, F., Sagot, M.-F.: Lossless filter for finding long multiple approximate repetitions using a new data structure, the Bi-factor array. In: Consens, M., Navarro, G. (eds.) SPIRE 2005. LNCS, vol. 3772, pp. 179–190. Springer, Heidelberg (2005). https://doi.org/10.1007/11575832_20

23. Starikovskaya, T., Vildhøj, H.W.: Time-space trade-offs for the longest common substring problem. In: Fischer, J., Sanders, P. (eds.) CPM 2013. LNCS, vol. 7922, pp. 223–234. Springer, Heidelberg (2013). https://doi.org/10.1007/978-3-642-38905-4_22

24. Thankachan, S.V., Aluru, C., Chockalingam, S.P., Aluru, S.: Algorithmic framework for approximate matching under bounded edits with applications to sequence analysis. In: Raphael, B.J. (ed.) RECOMB 2018. LNCS, vol. 10812, pp. 211–224. Springer, Cham (2018). https://doi.org/10.1007/978-3-319-89929-9_14

25. Thankachan, S.V., Apostolico, A., Aluru, S.: A provably efficient algorithm for the k-mismatch average common substring problem. J. Comput. Biol. **23**(6), 472–482 (2016)

Adaptive Computation of the Discrete Fréchet Distance

Jérémy Barbay$^{(\boxtimes)}$ (iD)

Departamento de Ciencias de la Computación, University of Chile, Santiago, Chile
jeremy@barbay.cl

Abstract. The discrete Fréchet distance is a measure of similarity between point sequences which permits to abstract differences of resolution between the two curves, approximating the original Fréchet distance between curves. Such distance between sequences of respective length n and m can be computed in time within $O(nm)$ and space within $O(n + m)$ using classical dynamic programming techniques, a complexity likely to be optimal in the worst case over sequences of similar length unless the Strong Exponential Time Hypothesis is proved incorrect. We propose a parameterized analysis of the computational complexity of the discrete Fréchet distance in function of the area of the dynamic program matrix relevant to the computation, measured by its *certificate width* ω. We prove that the discrete Fréchet distance can be computed in time within $O((n + m)\omega)$ and space within $O(n + m)$.

Keywords: Adaptive algorithm · Dynamic programming
Fréchet distance

1 Introduction

Measuring the similarity between two curves has applications in areas such as handwriting recognition [14], protein structure alignment [10], quantifying macro-molecular pathways [13], morphing [3], movement analysis [7], and many others [15]. One of the most popular solutions, the FRÉCHET DISTANCE is a measure of similarity between two curves $\mathcal{P}$ and $\mathcal{Q}$, that takes into account the location and ordering of the points along the curves. It permits, among other features, to abstract the difference of resolution between $\mathcal{P}$ and $\mathcal{Q}$, with application to morphing, handwriting recognition and protein structure alignment, among others [15]. In 1995, Art and Godau [9] described an algorithm computing the FRÉCHET DISTANCE between two polygonal curves composed of n and m segments respectively in time within $O(mn \log(mn))$.

One year before (1994), Eiter and Mannila [4] had extended the notion of the FRÉCHET DISTANCE between curves to the DISCRETE FRÉCHET DISTANCE

See a longer version at the url http://arxiv.org/abs/1806.01226 (pdf) and https://gitlab.com/FineGrainedAnalysis/Frechet (sources).

J. Barbay—Supported by project Fondecyt Regular no. 1170366 from Conicyt.

T. Gagie et al. (Eds.): SPIRE 2018, LNCS 11147, pp. 50–60, 2018.
https://doi.org/10.1007/978-3-030-00479-8_5

between sequences of points of respective sizes n and m, demonstrating that the latter can be used to approximate the former in time within $O(nm)$ and space within $O(n + m)$ using classical dynamic programming techniques. Two decades later (2014), Bringmann [2] showed that this worst case complexity is likely to be optimal, unless a bunch of other problems (among which CNF SAT) can be computed faster than usually expected. Hence, the bounds about the computational complexity of the DISCRETE FRÉCHET DISTANCE in the worst case over instances of input sizes n and m are reasonably tight.

Yet, for various restricted classes of curves (e.g. κ-bounded, backbone, c-packed and long-edged [8] curves), both the FRÉCHET DISTANCE and the DISCRETE FRÉCHET DISTANCE are known to be easier to compute. Among other examples, we consider the FRÉCHET DISTANCE DECISION problem, which consists in deciding whether the FRÉCHET DISTANCE between two curves is equal to a given value f. In 2018, Gudmundsson et al. [8] described an algorithm deciding if the FRÉCHET DISTANCE is equal to a given value f in time linear in the size of the input curves when each edge is longer than the FRÉCHET DISTANCE between those two curves. Those results easily project to the DISCRETE FRÉCHET DISTANCE.

Those results for the mere computation of the DISCRETE FRÉCHET DISTANCE suggest that one does not always need to compute the $n \times m$ values of the dynamic program. **Can such approaches be applied to more general instances**, such that the **area of the dynamic program which *needs* to be computed** measures the *difficulty* of the instance?

In this work we perform a parameterized analysis of the computational complexity of the DISCRETE FRÉCHET DISTANCE, in function of the area of the dynamic program matrix relevant to the computation, measured by its *certificate width* ω. After describing summarily the traditional way to compute the DISCRETE FRÉCHET DISTANCE and the particular case of long edged curves (Sect. 2), we describe an optimization of the classical dynamic program based on two simple techniques, banded dynamic programming and thresholding (Sect. 3), and we prove that this program runs in time within $O((n + m)\omega)$ and space within $O(n + m)$ (Sect. 4). We conclude with a discussion in Sect. 5 of how our results generalize those of Gudmundsson et al. [8], and the potential applications and generalizations of our techniques to other problems where dynamic programs have given good results.

2 Preliminaries

Before describing our results, we describe some classical results upon which we build: the classical dynamic program computing the DISCRETE FRÉCHET DISTANCE, and the "easy" case of long-edged curves described by Gudmundsson et al. [8].

Classical Dynamic Program: Let $P[1..n]$ and $Q[1..m]$ be sequences of n and m points with $n \geq m$. The DISCRETE FRÉCHET DISTANCE between P and Q is the minimal width of a traversal of P and Q, where the width of a traversal is the maximal distance separating two points $u \in P$ and $v \in Q$, where u and v progress independently, but always forward.

Such a distance is easily computed using classical techniques from dynamic programming. Algorithm 1 (page 4) describes a simple implementation in Python, executing in time within $O(nm)$.

Algorithm 1 Classical algorithm to compute the DISCRETE FRÉCHET DISTANCE between two sequences of points P and Q. The implementation is decomposed in two parts: the computation function initializes the array of values, which is filled recursively by the recursive function. For the sake of space, the documentation strings and unit tests were not included, but the source file including those is available at https://gitlab.com/FineGrainedAnalysis/Frechet.

```python
def recursive(dpA,i,j,P,Q):
    if dpA[i,j] > -1:
        return dpA[i,j]
    elif i == 0 and j == 0:
        dpA[i,j] = distance(P[0],Q[0])
    elif i > 0 and j == 0:
        dpA[i,j] = max(
            recursive(dpA,i-1,0,P,Q),
            distance(P[i],Q[0]))
    elif i == 0 and j > 0:
        dpA[i,j] = max(
            recursive(dpA,0,j-1,P,Q),
            distance(P[0],Q[j]))
    elif i > 0 and j > 0:
        dpA[i,j] = max(
            min(
                recursive(dpA,i-1,j,P,Q),
                recursive(dpA,i-1,j-1,P,Q),
                recursive(dpA,i,j-1,P,Q)),
            distance(P[i],Q[j]))
    else:
        dpA[i,j] = float("inf")
    return dpA[i,j]

def computation(P,Q):
    dpA = numpy.ones((len(P),len(Q)))
    dpA = numpy.multiply(dpA,-1)
    d = recursive(dpA,len(P)-1,len(Q)-1,P,Q)
    return d
```

While such a simple algorithm also requires space within $O(nm)$, a simple optimization yields a space within $O(n+m)$, by computing the DISCRETE FRÉCHET DISTANCE between $P[1..i]$ and $Q[1..j]$ for increasing values of i and j, one column and row at the time, keeping in memory only the previous column and row. We describe in Sect. 3 a more sophisticated algorithm which avoids computing some of the $n \times m$ values computed by Algorithm 1.

Easy Instances of the Fréchet Distance: For various restricted classes of curves, such as long-edged [8] curves, both the FRÉCHET DISTANCE and the DISCRETE FRÉCHET DISTANCE are known to be easier to compute (or approximate). In 2018, Gudmundsson et al. [8] showed that in the special case where all the edges of the polygonal curve are longer than the FRÉCHET DISTANCE, the latter can be decided (i.e., checking a value of the FRÉCHET DISTANCE) in linear time in the size of the input, computed in time within $O((n + m) \lg(n + m))$.

In the next section, we describe a quite simple algorithm which not only takes advantage of long edged curves, but of any pair of curves for which a consequent part of the array of the dynamic program can be ignored.

3   An Opportunistic Dynamic Program

We describe an algorithm based on two complementary techniques: first, a *banded dynamic program*, which *approximates* the value computed by a classical dynamic program by considering only the values of the dynamic program within a range of width w (for some parameter w) around the diagonal (a technique previously introduced for the computation of the EDIT DISTANCE between two strings); and second, a *thresholding* process, which *accelerates* the computation by cutting the recurrence any time the distance computed becomes larger or equal to a threshold t (for some parameter t corresponding to a distance already achieved by some traversal of the two curves). The combination of those two techniques, combined with a parametrization of the problem, yields the parameterized upper bound on the computational complexity of the DISCRETE FRÉCHET DISTANCE.

Banded Dynamic Program: When computing the EDIT DISTANCE (e.g., the DELETE INSERT EDIT DISTANCE, or the LEVENSHTEIN EDIT DISTANCE [1]) between similar strings $S \in [1..\sigma]^n$ and $T \in [1..\sigma]^m$ (i.e., their EDIT DISTANCE d is small), it is possible to compute less than $n \times m$ cells of the dynamic program array, and hence compute the EDIT DISTANCE in time within $O(d(n + m)) \subseteq O(nm)$. The "trick" is based on the following observation: when the distance between the two strings is d, the "paths" corresponding to d operations transforming S into T in the matrix of the dynamic program errs at most at distance d from the diagonal between the cell $(1, 1)$ and the cell (n, m). Based on this observation, it is sufficient to compute the number of operations corresponding to paths inside a "band" of width d around such a diagonal [1]. This technique needs some adaptation to be applied to the computation of the DISCRETE FRÉCHET DISTANCE f between two curves, for two reasons: first, f is a real number (it corresponds to the Euclidean distance between two points) and not an integer as the number of edition operations, and this number is independent of the number of cells of the dynamic program being computed; and second, the definition of the DISCRETE FRÉCHET DISTANCE is based on a maximum rather than a sum, which actually makes another optimization possible, described in the next paragraph.

Thresholding: Given two sequences of points $P[1..n]$ and $Q[1..m]$, consider the *Euclidean matrix* $E(P, Q)$ of all $n \times m$ distances between a point $u \in P$ and a point $v \in Q$. Any parallel traversal of P and Q corresponds to a path in $E(P, Q)$ from the top left cell $(1, 1)$ to the bottom right cell (n, m); the width of such a traversal is the maximum value in $E(P, Q)$ on this path; and the DISCRETE FRÉCHET DISTANCE is the minimum width achieved over all such traversals.

Now suppose that, as for the EDIT DISTANCE between two similar strings, the traversal of the Euclidean matrix $E(P, Q)$ corresponding to the DISCRETE FRÉCHET DISTANCE f between P and Q is close to the diagonal from $(1, 1)$ to (n, m), and that any traversal diverging from such a path "encounters" a pair of points (u, v) at euclidean distance larger than f (in particular, this happens when the two curves are "long edged" compared to f). Then, some of the values of the cells of the dynamic program matrix outside of this diagonal can be ignored for the computation of the DISCRETE FRÉCHET DISTANCE between P and Q.

In the following paragraph we describe how to combine those two techniques into an adaptive algorithm taking advantage of "easy" instances where a large quantity of cells of the dynamic program can be ignored.

Combining the Two Techniques: The solution described consists of two algorithms: an approximation Algorithm 2 which computes a parameterized upper bound on the DISCRETE FRÉCHET DISTANCE, and a computation Algorithm 3 which calls the previous one iteratively with various parameter values, in order to compute the real DISCRETE FRÉCHET DISTANCE of the instance.

Algorithm 2 lists an implementation in `Python` of an algorithm which, given as parameters two arrays of points P and Q, an `integer` *width* w, and a `float` *threshold* t; computes an upper bound of the DISCRETE FRÉCHET DISTANCE between P and Q, obtained by computing only the cells within a band of width $2w$ around the diagonal from the top left cell $(1, 1)$ to the bottom right cell (n, m), and cutting all sequences of recursive calls when reaching a distance of value t or above. This algorithm uses space within $(n + m)$ as it computes the values from $(1, 1)$ to (n, m) by updating and switching alternatively two arrays of size n and two arrays of size m (respectively corresponding to rows and columns of the dynamic program matrix). Its running time is within $O(w(n + m))$, as it computes at most $w(n + m)$ cells of the dynamic program array. Furthermore, it not only returns the value of the upper bound computed, but also a Boolean `breached` indicating if the border of the banded diagonal has been reached during this computation. When such a border has *not* been reached (and the threshold value t is smaller than or equal to the DISCRETE FRÉCHET DISTANCE between P and Q), the value returned is equal to the DISCRETE FRÉCHET DISTANCE between P and Q.

Algorithm 2 Parameterized Algorithm to approximate the DISCRETE FRÉCHET DISTANCE between two sequences of points by computing only values of the dynamic program within a band of width w around the diagonal, and limiting the recursion to distances smaller than a threshold t.

```python
def approximation(P,Q,w,t):
    bReached = False
    n = len(P)
    m = len(Q)
    assert( m <= n )
    assert( m > 0 )
    def e(i,j):
        d = utils.distance(P[i],Q[j])
        if d < t:
            if (i-j) >= w or (j-i) >= w:
                bReached = True
            return d
        else:
            return float("inf")
    oldRow = np.ones(n)
    oldColumn = np.ones(m)
    oldRow[0] = oldColumn[0] = e(0,0)
    for s in range(1,m):
        newRow = np.ones(n)
        for i in range(max(1,s-w+1),s):
            newRow[i]  = max(e(i,s),min(
                oldRow[i],
                oldRow[i-1],
                newRow[i-1]))
        newColumn = np.ones(m)
        for j in range(max(1,s-w+1),s):
            newColumn[j]  = max(e(s,j),min(
                newColumn[j-1],
                oldColumn[j-1],
                oldColumn[j]))
        newColumn[s] = newRow[s] = max(e(s,s),min(
            newRow[s-1],
            newColumn[s-1],
            oldRow[s-1]))
        oldRow = newRow
        oldColumn = newColumn
    for s in range(m,n):
        newColumn = np.ones(m)
        for j in range(max(1,s-w+1),m):
            newColumn[j]  = max(e(s,j),min(
                oldColumn[j],
                oldColumn[j-1],
                newColumn[j-1]))
        oldColumn = newColumn
    return bReached,newRow[n-1]
```

Algorithm 3 lists an implementation in Python of an algorithm which, given as parameters two sequences of points P and Q, calls the approximation Algorithm 2 on P and Q for widths of exponentially increasing value (by a factor of two). The first call is performed with an infinite threshold (no information is available on the similarity of the curve at this point), but each successive call uses the best upper bound on the DISCRETE FRÉCHET DISTANCE between P and Q previously computed as a threshold.

Algorithm 3 Adaptive algorithm to compute the DISCRETE FRÉCHET DISTANCE between two sequences of points, by iteratively approximating it with increasing width, using the value of the previous approximation to potentially reduce the number of distances being computed.

```python
def computation(P,Q):
    if len(P)<len(Q):
        P,Q = Q,P
    if len(Q) == 0:
        return float("inf")
    w = 1
    bReached,t=approximation(P,Q,w,float("inf"))
    while bReached and w < len(Q):
        w = 2*x
        bReached,t=approximation(P,Q,w,t)
    return t
```

In the next section, we analyze the running time of Algorithm 3, and describe a parameterized upper bound on it.

4 Parameterized Upper Bound

The running time of the approximation Algorithm 2 when given parameter w is clearly within $O(w(n + m))$: it computes within $O(w)$ cells in at most $n + m$ rounds, each in constant time. A finer upper bound taking into account the value of the parameter t requires more hypothesis on the relation between P and Q, for which we need to consider the running time of the computation Algorithm 3. We model such hypothesis on the instance in the form of a *certificate*, and more specifically in the form of a *certificate area* of the Euclidean matrix corresponding to a set of values which suffice to *certify* the value of the DISCRETE FRÉCHET DISTANCE.

Definition 1. *Given two sequences of points $P[1..n]$ and $Q[1..m]$ of respective lengths n and m and of DISCRETE FRÉCHET DISTANCE f, a Certificate Area of the instance formed by P and Q is an area of the Euclidean matrix of P and Q containing both $(1,1)$ and (n,m), and delimited by two paths (one above and one below), both such that the minimum value on this path is larger than or equal to f. The width of such a certificate area is the minimal width of a banded diagonal containing both paths.*

The surface of such an area is a good measure of the difficulty to certify the DISCRETE FRÉCHET DISTANCE, but the minimal width of such an area lends itself better to an analysis of the running time of the computation Algorithm 3:

Definition 2. *Given two sequences of points $P[1..n]$ and $Q[1..m]$, the* Certificate Width ω *of* (P, Q) *is the minimum width of a certificate area, taken over all possible certificate areas of* (P, Q).

Such a width can be as large as $n + m$ in the worst case over instances formed by sequences of points of respective lengths n and m, but the smaller this *certificate width* is, the faster Algorithm 3 runs:

Theorem 1. *Given two sequences of points $P[1..n]$ and $Q[1..m]$ forming an instance of certificate width ω, Algorithm 3 computes the* DISCRETE FRÉCHET DISTANCE *between P and Q in time within $O((n + m)\omega)$ and space within $O(n + m)$.*

Beyond the necessity to measure experimentally the certificate width of practical instances of the DISCRETE FRÉCHET DISTANCE, and the exact running time of Algorithm 3 on such instances, we discuss some more subtle options for future work in the next section.

5   Discussion

The results described in this work are by far only preliminary. Among the various questions that those preliminary results raise, we discuss here the relation to the long edged sequences recently described by Gudmundsson et al. [8]; a potential parameterized conditional lower bound matching our parameterized upper bound on the computational complexity of the DISCRETE FRÉCHET DISTANCE; (the not so) similar results on the ORTHOGONAL VECTOR decision problem; and the possibility of a theory of reductions between parameterized versions of polynomial problems without clear (parameterized or not) computational complexity lower bounds.

Relation to Long Edged Sequences: In 2018, Gudmundsson et al. [8] described an algorithm deciding if the Fréchet distance is equal to a given value f in time linear in the size of the input curves when each edge is longer than the FRÉCHET DISTANCE between those two curves. Algorithm 3 is more general than Gudmundsson et al.'s algorithm [8], but it also performs in linear time on long-edged instances: the traversal corresponding to the FRÉCHET DISTANCE of such an instance is along the diagonal, implying a *certificate width* of 1. See Figs. 1, 2 and 3 for the Euclidean matrix, Fréchet Matrix and Dynamic Program Matrix of a random instance formed of 5 points, each edge of length 100 with a FRÉCHET DISTANCE of 13.45.

The ratio between the FRÉCHET DISTANCE and the minimal edge length of the curves might prove to be a more "natural" parameter than the *certificate width* to measure the "difficulty" of computing the FRÉCHET DISTANCE of a pair of curves: we focused on the *certificate width* in the hope that such a technique can find applications in the analysis of other problems on which dynamic programming has yield good solutions (Fig. 4).

1.41	101.43	193.97	294.66	199.17	227.36
100.14	**13.45**	94.67	195.37	99.5	142.89
199.48	97.99	**5.39**	105.43	6.13	113.25
290.44	192.56	104.04	**6.0**	97.26	109.6
193.23	93.14	13.17	104.98	**10.44**	99.05
232.69	156.27	112.89	104.58	107.64	**6.4**

Fig. 1. Euclidean matrix for a long edged instance: the 6 points from the first curve were randomly generated at distance 100 of each other, while the points from the second curve were generated by perturbing within a distance of 10 from the points of the first curve.

1.41	101.43	193.97	294.66	294.66	294.66
100.14	**13.45**	94.67	195.37	195.37	195.37
199.48	97.99	**13.45**	105.43	105.43	113.25
290.44	192.56	104.04	**13.45**	97.26	109.6
290.44	192.56	104.04	104.98	**13.45**	99.05
290.44	192.56	112.89	104.58	107.64	**13.45**

Fig. 2. Fréchet matrix for the same long edged instance as Fig. 1: the traversal corresponding to the FRÉCHET DISTANCE of the instance is along the diagonal (highlighted in bold here), resulting in a FRÉCHET DISTANCE of 13.45.

1.41	*inf*	*inf*	−1.0	−1.0	−1.0
inf	**13.45**	*inf*	*inf*	−1.0	−1.0
inf	*inf*	**13.45**	*inf*	6.13	−1.0
−1.0	*inf*	*inf*	**13.45**	*inf*	*inf*
−1.0	−1.0	13.17	*inf*	**13.45**	*inf*
−1.0	−1.0	−1.0	*inf*	*inf*	**13.45**

Fig. 3. Dynamic program matrix for the same long edged instance as Fig. 1, with width 3 and threshold 20: "inf" denotes interrupted recurrences because the distance found is already larger than the threshold, meanwhile values outside of the band of width 3 are marked with "−1".

9.43	19.48	19.48	−1.0	−1.0	−1.0
18.81	**11.31**	11.31	16.86	−1.0	−1.0
18.81	14.26	**11.31**	11.31	*inf*	−1.0
−1.0	*inf*	16.07	**11.31**	16.5	13.77
−1.0	−1.0	*inf*	11.31	**11.31**	11.31
−1.0	−1.0	−1.0	3.17	14.06	**11.31**

Fig. 4. Dynamic program matrix for a general instance. The 6 points from the first curve were randomly generated at distance 10 of each other, the points from the second curve by perturbing within a distance of 10 the points of the first curve. The computation of the matrix is performed with width 3 and threshold 20 as before.

Parameterized Conditional Lower Bound: The original motivation for this work was to prove a parameterized conditional lower bound on the computational complexity of the DISCRETE FRÉCHET DISTANCE as a step-stone for doing the same for the computation of various EDIT DISTANCES. The first step in this direction was the identification of a parameter for this problem: the *certificate width*, that seems to be a good candidate. The next step is to refine the reduction from

CNF SAT to the DISCRETE FRÉCHET DISTANCE described by Bringmann [2], in order to define a reduction from (a potential parameterized version of) CNF SAT to a parameterized version of the DISCRETE FRÉCHET DISTANCE.

Parameterized Upper and Lower Bound for the Computation of Orthogonal Vectors: Bringmann [2] mentions that the reduction from SAT CNF to the computation of the DISCRETE FRÉCHET DISTANCE is similar to Williams' reduction from SAT CNF to the (polynomial) problem of deciding if two sets of vectors contain an ORTHOGONAL VECTOR pair, and that there might be a reduction from the ORTHOGONAL VECTOR decision problem to the computation of the DISCRETE FRÉCHET DISTANCE. This mention called the ORTHOGONAL VECTOR decision problem to our attention, and in particular (1) the possibility of a parametrization of the analysis of this problem, and (2) a potential linear (or parameterized) reduction from such a parameterized ORTHOGONAL VECTOR decision problem to the parameterized computation of the DISCRETE FRÉCHET DISTANCE described in this work. It turns out that there exists an algorithm solving the ORTHOGONAL VECTOR decision problem in time within $O((n + m)(\delta + \log(n) + \log(m)))$, where n and m are the respective sizes of the sets of vectors forming the instance, and δ is the *certificate density* measuring the proportion of cells from the dynamic program which are sufficient to compute in order to certify the answer to the program. The reduction of this to the DISCRETE FRÉCHET DISTANCE will be more problematic: the two measures of difficulty seem completely unrelated.

A Theory of Reduction Between Polynomial Parameterized Problems: The study of the *parameterized complexity* of NP-hard problems [6,11] yields a theory of reduction between pairs formed by a decision problem P and a parameter k. The study of *adaptive sorting* algorithms [5,12] yields a theory of reductions between parameters measuring the existing disorder in an array to be sorted (which can also be seen as a theory of reductions between pairs of problems and parameters, but where all the problems are equal). Considering the theory of reductions between polynomial problems such as the DISCRETE FRÉCHET DISTANCE, the various EDIT DISTANCES between strings, the ORTHOGONAL VECTOR decision problem, and many others, one can imagine that it would be possible to define a theory of reductions between parameterized versions of these problems.

Acknowledgements. The author would like to thank Travis Gagie for interesting discussions and for pointing out Gudmundsson et al.'s work [8].

Funding. Jérémy Barbay is partially funded by the project Fondecyt Regular no. 1170366 from Conicyt.

Data and Material Availability. The sources of this article, along with the unabridged code, will be made publicly available upon publication at the url https://gitlab.com/FineGrainedAnalysis/Frechet.

References

1. Bergroth, L., Hakonen, H., Raita, T.: A survey of longest common subsequence algorithms. In: Proceedings of the 11th Symposium on String Processing and Information Retrieval (SPIRE), pp. 39–48 (2000)
2. Bringmann, K.: Why walking the dog takes time: Fréchet distance has no strongly subquadratic algorithms unless SETH fails. In: Proceedings of the 2014 IEEE 55th Annual Symposium on Foundations of Computer Science, FOCS 2014, pp. 661–670. IEEE Computer Society, Washington, DC (2014)
3. Efrat, A., Guibas, L., Har-Peled, S., Mitchell, J., Murali, T.: New similarity measures between polylines with applications to morphing and polygon sweeping. Discret. Comput. Geom. **28**(4), 535–569 (2002)
4. Eiter, T., Mannila, H.: Computing discrete Fréchet distance. Technical report, Christian Doppler Labor für Expertensyteme, Technische Universität Wien (1994)
5. Estivill-Castro, V., Wood, D.: A survey of adaptive sorting algorithms. ACM Comput. Surv. (ACMCS) **24**(4), 441–476 (1992)
6. Flum, J., Grohe, M.: Parameterized Complexity Theory. Texts in Theoretical Computer Science. An EATCS Series. Springer-Verlag New York Inc., Secaucus (2006). https://doi.org/10.1007/3-540-29953-X
7. Gudmundsson, J., Laube, P., Wolle, T.: Movement patterns in spatio-temporal data. In: Shekhar, S., Xiong, H. (eds.) Encyclopedia of GIS, pp. 1362–1370. Springer, Cham (2017). https://doi.org/10.1007/978-0-387-35973-1_823
8. Gudmundsson, J., Mirzanezhad, M., Mohades, A., Wenk, C.: Fast Fréchet distance between curves with long edges. In: Proceedings of the International Workshop on Interactive and Spatial Computing (WISC), IWISC 2018, pp. 52–58. ACM, New York (2018). Best Paper Award IWISC'18
9. Alt, H., Godau, M.: Computing the Fréchet distance between two polygonal curves. Int. J. Comput. Geom. Appl. (IJCGA) **5**(1–2), 75–91 (1995)
10. Jiang, M., Xu, Y., Zhu, B.: Protein structure-structure alignment with discrete Fréchet distance. J. Bioinform. Comput. Biol. **6**(1), 51–64 (2008)
11. Marx, D.: Parameterized complexity of constraint satisfaction problems. In: Proceedings of 19th Annual IEEE Conference on Computational Complexity (CCC), pp. 139–149 (2004)
12. Moffat, A., Petersson, O.: An overview of adaptive sorting. Aust. Comput. J. (ACJ) **24**(2), 70–77 (1992)
13. Seyler, S.L., Kumar, A., Thorpe, M.F., Beckstein, O.: Path similarity analysis: a method for quantifying macromolecular pathways. PLoS Comput. Biol. **11**, e1004568 (2015)
14. Sriraghavendra, E., Karthik, K., Bhattacharyya, C.: Fréchet distance based approach for searching online handwritten documents. In: Proceedings of the Ninth International Conference on Document Analysis and Recognition, ICDAR 2007, vol. 01, pp. 461–465. IEEE Computer Society, Washington, DC (2007). http://dl.acm.org/citation.cfm?id=1304595.1304769
15. Wikipedia: Frechet_distance. https://en.wikipedia.org/wiki/Fr'echet_distance

Indexed Dynamic Programming to Boost Edit Distance and LCSS Computation

Jérémy Barbay$^{(\boxtimes)}$ ⓘ and Andrés Olivares

Departamento de Ciencias de la Computación, University of Chile, Santiago, Chile
jeremy@barbay.cl, aolivare@dcc.uchile.cl

Abstract. There are efficient dynamic programming solutions to the computation of the Edit Distance from $S \in [1..\sigma]^n$ to $T \in [1..\sigma]^m$, for many natural subsets of edit operations, typically in time within $O(nm)$ in the worst-case over strings of respective lengths n and m (which is likely to be optimal), and in time within $O(n + m)$ in some special cases (e.g., disjoint alphabets). We describe how indexing the strings (in linear time), and using such an index to refine the recurrence formulas underlying the dynamic programs, yield faster algorithms in a variety of models, on a continuum of classes of instances of intermediate difficulty between the worst and the best case, thus refining the analysis beyond the worst case analysis. As a side result, we describe similar properties for the computation of the Longest Common Sub Sequence $\mathtt{LCSS}(S, T)$ between S and T, since it is a particular case of Edit Distance, and we discuss the application of similar algorithmic and analysis techniques for other dynamic programming solutions. More formally, we propose a parameterized analysis of the computational complexity of the Edit Distance for various sets of operators and of the Longest Common Sub Sequence in function of the area of the dynamic program matrix relevant to the computation.

Keywords: Adaptive algorithm · Dynamic programming
Edit distance · Longest Common Sub-Sequence

1 Introduction

Given a set of edition operators on strings, a source string $S \in [1..\sigma]^n$ and a target string $T \in [1..\sigma]^m$ of respective lengths n and m on the alphabet $[1..\sigma]$, the EDIT DISTANCE is the minimum number of such operations required to transform the string S into the string T. Introduced in 1974 by Wagner and Fischer [14], such computation is a fundamental problem in Computer Science, with a wide range of applications, from text processing and information retrieval to computational biology. The typical edit distance between two strings is defined by the minimum

---

A longer version is available at the urls https://arxiv.org/abs/1806.04277 (pdf) and https://gitlab.com/FineGrainedAnalysis/EditDistances (pdf and sources).

J. Barbay—Supported by project Fondecyt Regular no. 1170366 from Conicyt.

T. Gagie et al. (Eds.): SPIRE 2018, LNCS 11147, pp. 61–73, 2018.
https://doi.org/10.1007/978-3-030-00479-8_6

number of `insertions`, `deletions` (in both cases, of a character at an arbitrary position of S) and `replacement` (of one character of S by some other) needed to transform the string S into T. Many generalizations have been defined in the literature, including weighted costs for the edit operations, and different sets of edit operations – the standard set is {`insertion`, `deletion`, `replacement`}.

Operators	(n, m)-Worst Case Complexity	Finer Results	
		Distance	Parikh vectors
Swap	$O(n^2)$ [14]	$O(n(1 + \lg d/n) \lg n)$	DNA
Delete, Insert	$O(nm)$ [6]	$O(d^2)$	$O(\sum n_\alpha m_\alpha \lg nm)$
Delete, Replace	$O(nm)$ [17]	$O(d^2)$	$O(\sum n_\alpha m_\alpha \lg nm)$
Delete, Swap	NP-complete [15]	$O(1.6181^d m)$ [1]	$O(\sigma^2 nm\gamma^{\sigma-1})$ [3]
Replace, Swap	$O(nm)$ [17]	$O(d^2)$	$O(\sum n_\alpha m_\alpha \lg nm)$
Delete, Insert, Replace	$O(nm)$ [6]	$O(d^2)$	$O(\sum n_\alpha m_\alpha \lg nm)$
Delete, Insert, Swap	$O(nm)$ [15]	$O(d^2)$	
Delete, Replace, Swap	$O(nm)$ [15]	$O(d^2)$	
Insert, Replace, Swap	$O(nm)$ [15]	$O(d^2)$	
Delete, Insert, Replace, Swap	$O(nm)$ [6]	$O(d^2)$	

Fig. 1. Summary of results for various combinations of operators from the basic set {`Insert`, `Delete`, `Replace`, `Swap`}. The column labeled "(n, m)-Worst Case Complexity" presents results in the worst case over instances of fixed sizes n and m, while the columns labeled "Finer Results" present results where the analysis was refined by various parameters: the distance d, the size σ of the alphabet, and some form of imbalance $\gamma = \max_{\alpha \in [1..\sigma]} \min\{n_\alpha, m_\alpha - n_\alpha\}$ between the Parikh vectors of S and T. For brevity, the only distance based on a single operator presented is the SWAP EDIT DISTANCE, as the computation of the others is always linear in the size of the input.

Each distinct set of correction operators yields a distinct correction distance on strings (see Fig. 1 for a summary). For instance, Wagner and Fischer [14] showed that for the three following operations, the `insertion` of a symbol at some arbitrary position, the `deletion` of a symbol at some arbitrary position, and the `replacement` of a symbol at some arbitrary position, the EDIT DISTANCE can be computed in time within $O(nm)$ and space within $O(n + m)$ using traditional dynamic programming techniques. As another variant of interest, Wagner and Lowrance [15] introduced the `Swap` operator (`S`), which exchanges the positions of two contiguous symbols. For two of the newly defined distances, the INSERT SWAP EDIT DISTANCE and the DELETE SWAP EDIT DISTANCE (equivalent by symmetry), the best known algorithms take time exponential in the input size [3,4], which is likely to be optimal [14]. The EDIT DISTANCE itself is linked to many other problems: for instance, given the two same strings $S \in [1..\sigma]^n$ and $T \in [1..\sigma]^m$, the computation of the LONGEST COMMON SUB-SEQUENCE (LCSS) L between S and T is equivalent to the computation of the DELETE INSERT EDIT DISTANCE d, as the symbols deleted from S and inserted from T in order to "edit" S into T are exactly the same as the symbols deleted from S and

T in order to produce L. Hence, the LCSS between S and T can be computed in time within $O(nm)$ and space within $O(n + m)$ using traditional dynamic programming techniques.

Most of these computational complexities are likely to be optimal in the worst case over instances of size (n, m): the algorithms computing the three basic distances in linear time are optimal as any algorithm must read the whole strings; the INSERT SWAP EDIT DISTANCE and its symmetric the DELETE SWAP EDIT DISTANCE are NP-hard to compute [16]; and in 2015 Backurs and Indyk [2] showed that the $O(n^2)$ upper bound for the computation of the DELETE INSERT REPLACE EDIT DISTANCE is optimal up to a sub-polynomial factor unless the *Strong Exponential Time Hypothesis* (SETH) is false.

More recently, Barbay and Pérez-Lantero [3,4], complementing Meister's previous results [12] by the use of an index supporting the operators rank and select on strings, described an algorithm computing this distance in time within $O(\sigma^2 nm\gamma^{\sigma-1})$ in the worst case over instances where σ, n, m and γ are fixed, where $\gamma = \max_{\alpha \in [1..\sigma]} \min\{n_\alpha, m_\alpha - n_\alpha\}$ measures a form of imbalance between the frequency distributions of each string.

Hypothesis: Given this situation, is it possible to **take advantage of** indexing techniques supporting **rank and select** in order **to speed up the computation of** other **edit distances**? Can a similar analysis to that of Barbay and Pérez-Lantero [3,4] be applied to other edit distances? **Are there instances for which the edit distance is easier to compute**, and **do such instances occur in real applications** of the computation of the edit distance?

Our Results: We answer all those questions positively, and describe general techniques to refine the analysis of dynamic programs beyond the traditional analysis in the worst case over inputs of fixed size. More specifically, we analyze the computational cost of four EDIT DISTANCES using various rank and select text indices, as a function of the Parikh vector [13] of the source S and target T strings. As a side result, this yields similar properties for the computation of the LONGEST COMMON SUB SEQUENCE LCSS(S, T) between S and T, and definitions and techniques which can be applied to other dynamic programs. After defining formally the notion of Parikh's vector and various index data structures supporting rank and select on strings in Sect. 2, we describe the algorithms taking advantage of such techniques in Sect. 3: for the LONGEST COMMON SUB SEQUENCE and DELETE-INSERT EDIT DISTANCE (Sect. 3.1), the DELETE INSERT REPLACE EDIT DISTANCE (Sect. 3.2), and finally for the DELETE-REPLACE EDIT DISTANCE and its dual, the INSERT-REPLACE EDIT DISTANCE (Sect. 3.3). We describe some preliminary experiments and their results, which seem to indicate that those instances are not totally artificial and occur naturally in practical applications in Sect. 4. We conclude in Sect. 5 with a discussion of other potential refinement of the analysis, and the extension of our results to other EDIT DISTANCES.

2   Preliminaries

Before describing our proposed algorithms to compute various EDIT DISTANCES, we describe formally in Sect. 2.1 the notion of `Parikh vector` which is essential to our analysis technique; and in Sect. 2.2 two key implementations of indices supporting the `rank` and `select` operators on strings.

2.1   Parikh Vector

Given positive integers σ and n, a string $S \in [1..\sigma]^n$, and the integers $n_1, \ldots, n_\sigma$ such that n_α denotes the number of occurrences of the letter $\alpha \in [1..\sigma]$ in the string S, the `Parikh vector` of S is defined [13] as $p(S) = (n_1, \ldots, n_\sigma)$.

Barbay and Pérez-Lantero [3] refined the analysis of the INSERT SWAP EDIT DISTANCE from a string $S \in [1..\sigma]^n$ to a string $T \in [1..\sigma]^m$ via a function of the `Parikh vectors` $(n_1, \ldots, n_\sigma)$ of S and $(m_1, \ldots, m_\sigma)$ of T, the local imbalance $\gamma_\alpha = \min\{n_\alpha, m_\alpha - n_\alpha\}$ for each symbol $\alpha \in [1..\sigma]$, projected to a global measure of imbalance, $\gamma = \max_{\alpha \in [1..\sigma]} \gamma_\alpha$. In the worst case among instances of fixed `Parikh vector`, they describe an algorithm to compute the INSERT SWAP EDIT DISTANCE in time within $O(\sigma^2 nm\gamma^{\sigma-1})$ in the worst case over instances where σ, n, m and γ are fixed.

Such a vector is essential to the fine analysis of dynamic programs for computing EDIT DISTANCES when using operators whose running time depends on the number of occurrence of each symbol, such as for the `rank` and `select` operators described in the next section.

2.2   Rank and Select in Strings

Given a symbol $\alpha \in [1..\sigma]$, an integer $i \in [1..|X|]$ and an integer $k > 0$, the operation $rank(X, i, \alpha)$ denotes the number of occurrences of the symbol α in the substring $X[1..i]$, and the operation $select(X, k, \alpha)$ denotes the value $j \in [1..|X|]$ such that the k-th occurrence of α in X is precisely at position j, if j exists. If j does not exist, then $select(X, k, \alpha)$ is *null*.

A simple way to support the `rank` and `select` operators in reasonably good time consists in, for each symbol $\alpha \in [1..\sigma]$, listing all the occurrences of α in a sorted array (called a "Posting List" [17]): supporting the `select` operator reduces to a simple access to the sorted array corresponding to the symbol α; while supporting the `rank` operator reduces to a SORTED SEARCH in the same array, which can be simply implemented by a `Binary Search`, or more efficiently in practice by a `Doubling Search` [5] in time within $O(q_\alpha \lg(n_\alpha/q_\alpha))$ when supporting q_α monotone queries in a posting list of size n_α (for a given symbol $\alpha \in [1..\sigma]$).

Golynski *et al.* [9] described a more sophisticated (but asymptotically more efficient) way to support the `rank` and `select` operators in the RAM model, via a clever reduction to Y-Fast Trees on permutations supporting the operators in time within $O(\lg \lg \sigma)$. We describe how to use those techniques to speed up the computation of various EDIT DISTANCES in the following sections.

3   Adaptive Dynamic Programs

For each of the problems considered, we describe how to compute a subset of the values computed by classical dynamic programs. We start with the computation of the LONGEST COMMON SUB SEQUENCE (LCSS) and the DELETE INSERT (DI) EDIT DISTANCE (Sect. 3.1) because it is the simplest; extend its results to the computation of the LEVENSHTEIN EDIT DISTANCE (Sect. 3.2); and project those to the computation of the DELETE REPLACE (DR) EDIT DISTANCE and its symmetric INSERT REPLACE (IR) EDIT DISTANCE (Sect. 3.3).

3.1   LCSS and DI-Edit Distance

The DELETE INSERT EDIT DISTANCE is a classical problem in Stringology [6], if only as a variant of the LONGEST COMMON SUB SEQUENCE problem. It is classically computed using dynamic programming: we describe the classical solution first, which we then refine.

Classical Solution: Given two strings $S \in [1..\sigma]^n$ and $T \in [1..\sigma]^m$, we note $d_{DI}(n, m)$ the DELETE INSERT EDIT DISTANCE from S to T. If the last symbols of S and T match, the edit distance is the same as the edit distance between the prefixes of respective lengths $n - 1$ and $m - 1$ of S and T. Otherwise, the edit distance is the minimum between the edit distance when inserting a copy of the last symbol of T in S (i.e. deleting this symbol in T) and the edit distance when deleting the mismatching symbol in T. More formally:

$$d_{DI}(S[1..n], T[1..m]) = \begin{cases} n \text{ if } m == 0; \\ m \text{ if } n == 0; \\ d_{DI}(S[1..n-1], T[1..m-1]) \text{ if } S[n] == T[m]; \text{ and} \\ 1 + \min \left\{ \begin{matrix} d_{DI}(S[1..n-1], T[1..m]), \\ d_{DI}(S[1..n], T[1..m-1]) \end{matrix} \right\} \text{ otherwise.} \end{cases}$$

This recursive definition directly yields an algorithm to compute the DELETE INSERT EDIT DISTANCE from S to T in time within $O(nm)$ and space within $O(n + m)$. We describe in the next section a technique taking advantage of the discrepancies between the `Parikh vectors` of S and T.

Refined Analysis: It is natural to wonder if techniques described in the previous section can be used in to take advantage of cases where a symbol occurs many times in one string, but occurs only once in the other: at some point, the dynamic program will reduce to the case described in the previous section. To be able to notice when this happens, one would need to maintain dynamically the counters of occurrences of each symbol during the execution of the dynamic program, or more simply pre-compute an index on S and T supporting the operators `rank` and `select` on it.

Given the support for the `rank` and `select` operators on both S and T, we can refine the dynamic program to compute the distance $d_{DI}(n, m)$ as follows:

$$
\begin{cases}
n \text{ if } m == 0; \\
m \text{ if } n == 0; \\
d_{DI}(n-1, m-1) \text{ if } S[n] == T[m]; \\
1 + d_{DI}(n-1, m) \text{ if } \mathtt{rank}(S, T[m]) == 0; \\
1 + d_{DI}(n, m-1) \text{ if } \mathtt{rank}(T, S[n]) == 0; \\
\min
\begin{cases}
1 + d_{DI}(n-1, m-1), \\
n - \mathtt{select}(S, T[m]) \\
\quad + d_{DI}(\mathtt{select}(S, T[m], \mathtt{rank}(S, T[m]) - 1) - 1, m - 1), \\
m - \mathtt{select}(T, S[n]) \\
\quad + d_{DI}(n - 1, \mathtt{select}(T, S[n], \mathtt{rank}(T, S[n]) - 1)) - 1)
\end{cases}
\text{ otherwise.}
\end{cases}
$$

The running time of the algorithm can then be expressed as a function of the number of recursive calls, the number of `rank` and `select` operations performed on the strings, in order to yield various running times depending upon the solution used to support the `rank` and `select` operators.

Theorem 1. *Given two strings $S \in [1..\sigma]^n$ and $T \in [1..\sigma]^m$ of respective **Parikh** vectors $(n_a)_{a \in [1..\sigma]}$ and $(m_a)_{a \in [1..\sigma]}$, the dynamic program above computes the* DELETE INSERT EDIT DISTANCE *from S to T and the* LONGEST COMMON SUB SEQUENCE *between S and T*

1. *through at most $4 \sum_{a \in [1..\sigma]} n_a m_a$ recursive calls;*
2. *within $O(\sum_{a \in [1..\sigma]} n_a m_a)$ operations `rank` or `select`;*
3. *in time within $O(\sum_{a \in [1..\sigma]} n_a m_a \times \lg(\max_a\{n_a, m_a\}) \times \lg(nm))$ in the comparison model; and*
4. *in time within $O(\sum_{a \in [1..\sigma]} n_a m_a \times \lg \lg \sigma \times \lg(nm))$ in the RAM memory model.*

Proof. We prove point (1) by an amortization argument. Point (2) is a direct consequence of point (1), given that each recursive call performs a finite number of calls to the `rank` and `select` operators. Point (3) is a simple combination of Point (2) with the classical *inverted posting list* implementation [17] of an index supporting the `select` operator in constant time and the `rank` operator via *doubling search* [5]; while point (4) is a simple combination of Point (2) with the index described by Golynski *et al.* [9] to support the `rank` and `select` operators.

Albeit quite simple, this results corresponds to real improvement in practice: see in Fig. 2 how the number of recursive calls is reduced by using such indexes. Moreover, such a refinement of the analysis and optimization of the computation can be applied to more than the DELETE INSERT EDIT DISTANCE: in the next sections, we describe a similar one for computing the LEVENSHTEIN DISTANCE (Sect. 3.2) and the DELETE REPLACE and INSERT REPLACE EDIT DISTANCE (Sect. 3.3).

3.2   Levenshtein Distance, or DIR-Edit Distance

In information theory, linguistics and computer science, the LEVENSHTEIN DISTANCE is a string metric for measuring the difference between two sequences [6]. It generalizes the DELETE INSERT EDIT DISTANCE explored in the previous section by adding the `Replace` operator to the operators `Delete` and `Insert` (so that it can be also called the DELETE INSERT REPLACE EDIT DISTANCE, or DIR for short). The recursion traditionally used is a mere extension from the one described in the previous section, and the adaptive version only a technical extension of the one for the DELETE INSERT EDIT DISTANCE: we will compute the distance $d_{DIR}(n, m)$ as

$$
\begin{cases}
n \text{ if } m == 0; \\
m \text{ if } n == 0; \\
d_{DIR}(n-1, m-1) \text{ if } S[n] == T[m]; \\
1 + d_{DIR}(n-1, m-1) \quad \begin{array}{l} \text{if } \mathbf{rank}(S, T[m]) == 0 \\ \text{and } \mathbf{rank}(T, S[n]) == 0; \end{array} \\
1 + d_{DIR}(n-1, m) \quad \begin{array}{l} \text{if } \mathbf{rank}(S, T[m]) == 0 \\ \text{but } \mathbf{rank}(T, S[n]) > 0; \end{array} \\
1 + d_{DIR}(n, m-1) \quad \begin{array}{l} \text{if } \mathbf{rank}(T, S[n]) == 0 \\ \text{but } \mathbf{rank}(S, T[m]) > 0; \end{array} \\
\min \left\{ \begin{array}{l} n - \mathbf{select}(S, T[m]) \\ \quad + d_{DIR}(\mathbf{select}(S, T[m], \mathbf{rank}(S, T[m]) - 1) - 1, m - 1), \\ m - \mathbf{select}(T, S[n]) \\ \quad + d_{DIR}(n - 1, \mathbf{select}(T, S[n], \mathbf{rank}(T, S[n]) - 1)) - 1), \\ 1 + d_{DIR}(n - 1, m - 1) \end{array} \right\} \text{otherwise.}
\end{cases}
$$

The refined analysis yields similar results (we omit the proof for lack of space):

Theorem 2. *Given two strings $S \in [1..\sigma]^n$ and $T \in [1..\sigma]^m$ of respective Parikh vectors $(n_a)_{a \in [1..\sigma]}$ and $(m_a)_{a \in [1..\sigma]}$, the dynamic program above computes the* LEVENSHTEIN EDIT DISTANCE *from S to T*

1. *through at most $4 \sum_{a \in [1..\sigma]} n_a m_a$ recursive calls;*
2. *within $O(\sum_{a \in [1..\sigma]} n_a m_a)$ operations $\mathbf{rank}$ or $\mathbf{select}$;*
3. *in time within $O(\sum_{a \in [1..\sigma]} n_a m_a \times \lg(\max_a\{n_a, m_a\}) \times \lg(nm))$ in the comparison model; and*
4. *in time within $O(\sum_{a \in [1..\sigma]} n_a m_a \times \lg \lg \sigma \times \lg(nm))$ in the RAM memory model.*

It is important to note that for two strings S and T, the computation of the LEVENSHTEIN EDIT DISTANCE from S to T actually generates more recursive calls than the computation of the DELETE INSERT EDIT DISTANCE from S to T, but that the analysis above does not capture this difference. In the following section, we project this result to two equivalent edit distances, the DELETE REPLACE and INSERT REPLACE EDIT DISTANCES, for which the dynamic program explores only half of the position in the dynamic program matrix compared to the LEVENSHTEIN EDIT DISTANCE or DELETE INSERT EDIT DISTANCE.

3.3 DR-Edit Distance and IR-Edit Distance

Given a source string $S \in [1..\sigma]^n$ and a target string $T \in [1..\sigma]^m$, the DELETE REPLACE EDIT DISTANCE from S to T and the INSERT-REPLACE EDIT DISTANCE from T to S are the same, as the sequence of `Insert` or `Replace` operations transforming S into T is the symmetric to the sequence of `Delete` or `Replace` operations transforming T back into S.

As before, if the last symbols of S and T match, the edit distance is the same as the edit distance between the prefixes of respective lengths $n-1$ and $m-1$ of S and T. Otherwise, the edit distance is the minimum between the edit distance when inserting a copy of the last symbol of T in S (i.e. deleting this symbol in T) and the edit distance when replacing the mismatching symbol in S by the corresponding one in T.

As in the two previous sections, given the support for the `rank` and `select` operators on both S and T, we can refine the dynamic program to compute the DELETE REPLACE EDIT DISTANCE $d_{DR}(n, m)$ as follows:

$$
\begin{cases}
n \text{ if } m == 0; \\
\infty \text{ if } n < m; \\
d_{DR}(n-1, m-1) \text{ if } S[n] == T[m]; \\
1 + d_{DR}(n-1, m) \text{ if } \texttt{rank}(T, S[n]) == 0; \\
1 + d_{DR}(n-1, m-1) \text{ if } \texttt{rank}(S, T[n]) == 0; \\
\min \left\{ \begin{array}{l} n - \texttt{select}(S, T[m]) \\ \quad + d_{DR}(\texttt{select}(S, T[m], \texttt{rank}(S, T[m]) - 1) - 1, m - 1), \\ 1 + d_{DR}(n-1, m-1) \end{array} \right\} \text{ otherwise.}
\end{cases}
$$

The analysis from the two previous sections projects to a similar result.

Theorem 3. *Given two strings $S \in [1..\sigma]^n$ and $T \in [1..\sigma]^m$ of respective* **Parikh** *vectors $(n_a)_{a \in [1..\sigma]}$ and $(m_a)_{a \in [1..\sigma]}$, the dynamic program above computes the* DELETE REPLACE EDIT DISTANCE *from S to T*

1. *through at most $4 \sum_{a \in [1..\sigma]} n_a m_a$ recursive calls;*
2. *within $O(\sum_{a \in [1..\sigma]} n_a m_a)$ operations* **rank** *or* **select;**
3. *in time within $O(\sum_{a \in [1..\sigma]} n_a m_a \times \lg(\max_a\{n_a, m_a\}) \times \lg(nm))$ in the comparison model; and*
4. *in time within $O(\sum_{a \in [1..\sigma]} n_a m_a \times \lg \lg \sigma \times \lg(nm))$ in the RAM memory model.*

Parameterizing the analysis of the computation of the LONGEST COMMON SUB SEQUENCE, of the LEVENSHTEIN EDIT DISTANCE and of the DELETE REPLACE or INSERT REPLACE EDIT DISTANCE would be only of moderate theoretical interest, if it did not correspond to some correspondingly "easy" instances in practice. In the next section we describe some preliminary experimental results which seem to indicate the existence of such "easy" instances in information retrieval.

4   Experiments

In order to test the practicality of the parameterization and algorithms described in the previous section, we performed some preliminary experiments on some public data sets from the GUTENBERG project [11]. We considered each text as a sequence of words (hence considering as equivalent all the word separations, from blank spaces to punctuations and line jumps), which results in large alphabets. Due to some problems with the implementation, we could not run the algorithms for texts larger than 32 kB (a memory issue with a library in Python), so we extracted the first 32 kB of the texts "Romeo & Juliet" (English), "Romeo & Julia" (German), "Hamlet" (German), and "The hound of the Baskervilles" (English), "The war of the worolds" (English); the last two texts being randomly picked non Shakespeare texts.

Figures 2, 3 and 4 show the runtime for five pairs of texts for each algorithm described in Sect. 3, the main difference is the use of constant time rank and select: "Hamlet" (English) vs "Hamlet" (German), "The hound of the Baskervilles" (English) vs "The war of the worlds" (English), "The hound of the Baskervilles" (English) vs "Romeo and Juliet" (English), "Romeo & Juliet" (English) vs "Romeo & Julia" (German), and "Romeo & Juliet" (English) vs "Hamlet" (German).

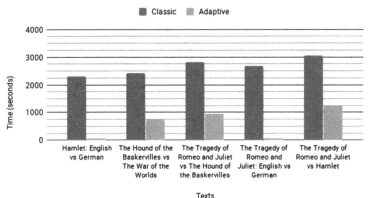

Fig. 2. Experimental results for the DELETE INSERT EDIT DISTANCE with constant rank and select.

For the two types of EDIT DISTANCES and the five pairs of texts, the adaptive variant is faster. In the case of the DELETE REPLACE EDIT DISTANCE, since the rank and select structures take from 15 to 18 s of preprocessing time, the adaptive variant is slower in 3 cases. For the three types of EDIT DISTANCES, the speedup of the adaptive variant is less between two texts from the same author (i.e. "Romeo & Juliet" (English) vs "Hamlet" (English)), because the vocabulary

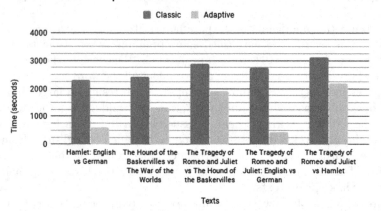

Fig. 3. Experimental results for the LEVENSHTEIN EDIT DISTANCE with constant `rank` and `select`.

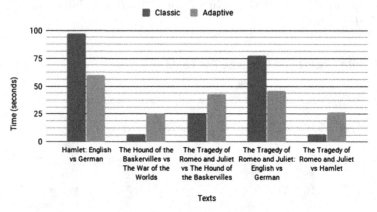

Fig. 4. Experimental results for the DELETE REPLACE EDIT DISTANCE with constant `rank` and `select`.

is the same, and is the most between texts of distinct languages (i.e. "Romeo & Juliet" (English) vs "Romeo & Julia" (German) and "Hamlet" (English) vs "Hamlet" (German)), because the vocabulary (i.e. the alphabet) is mostly distinct, there seems to be a correlation between alphabet intersection and speedup. Still, for two texts in the same language, but from distinct authors (i.e. "The hound of the Baskervilles" (English) vs "The war of the worlds" (English)), the difference is quite sensible for DELETE INSERT and DELETE INSERT REPLACE edit distances. Obviously, those experimental results are only preliminary, and a more thorough study is needed (and underway), both with a larger data set and with a larger range of measures, from the *running time* with various indexing data structures supporting the operators `rank` and `select`, to the number of entries of the dynamic program matrix being effectively computed. We discuss additional perspectives for future work in the next section.

5   Discussion

We have shown how the computation of other EDIT DISTANCES than the INSERT SWAP and DELETE SWAP EDIT DISTANCE is also sensitive to the `Parikh vectors` of the input. We discuss here various directions in which these results can be extended, from the possibility of proving conditional lower bounds in the refined analysis model, to further refinements of the analysis for these same EDIT DISTANCES, and to the analysis of other dynamic programs.

Adaptive Conditional Lower Bounds: Backurs and Indyk [2] showed that the $O(n^2)$ upper bound for the computation of the DELETE INSERT REPLACE EDIT DISTANCE is optimal unless the *Strong Exponential Time Hypothesis* (SETH) is false, and since then the technique has been applied to various other related problems. Should the reduction from the SETH to the EDIT DISTANCE computation be refined as shown here for the upper bound, it would speak in favor of the optimality of the analysis.

Other Measures of Difficulty: Abu-Khzam et al. [1] described an algorithm computing the INSERT SWAP EDIT DISTANCE d from S to T in time within $O(1.6181^d m)$, which is polynomial in the size of the input and exponential in the output size d. The output distance d itself can be as large as n, but such instances are not necessarily difficult: Barbay and Pérez-Lantero [3] showed that the gap vector between the `Parikh vectors` separate the hard instances from the easy ones, and we showed that the same can be applied to other EDIT DISTANCES.

But still, among instances of fixed input size, output distance, and imbalance between the `Parikh vectors`, there are instances easier than others (e.g. the computation of the INSERT SWAP EDIT DISTANCE on an instance where all the `insertions` are in the left part of S while all the `swaps` are in the right part of S). A measure which to refine the analysis would be the cost of encoding a *certificate* of the EDIT DISTANCE, one which is easier to check than recomputing the distance itself.

Indexed Dynamic Programming: Our results are close in spirit to those in fixed-parameter complexity, but with an important difference, namely, trying to spot one or more parameters that explain what makes an instance hard or easy. For the computation of the INSERT SWAP and DELETE SWAP EDIT DISTANCES, the size of the alphabet d makes the difference between polynomial time and NP-hardness. However, Barbay and Pérez-Lantero [3] showed that different instances of the same size can exhibit radically different costs-for a given fixed algorithm. The parameterized analysis captures in parameters the cause for such cost differences. We described how the same logic applies to other types of EDIT DISTANCES, and it is likely that similar situations happen with many other algorithms based on dynamic programming, such as the computation of the FRÉCHET DISTANCE [10], the DISCRETE FRÉCHET DISTANCE [8] and the decision problem ORTHOGONAL VECTOR [7].

Acknowledgement. The author would like to thank Pablo Pérez-Lantero for introducing the problem of computing the EDIT DISTANCE between strings; Felipe Lizama for a semester of very interesting discussions about this approach; and an anonymous referee from the journal Transaction on Algorithms for his positive feedback and encouragement.

Funding. Jérémy Barbay is partially funded by the project Fondecyt Regular no. 1170366 from Conicyt.

Data and Material Availability. The source of this article, along with the code and data used for the experiments described within, will be made publicly available upon publication at the url https://gitlab.com/FineGrainedAnalysis/EditDistances.

References

1. Abu-Khzam, F.N., Fernau, H., Langston, M.A., Lee-Cultura, S., Stege, U.: Charge and reduce: a fixed-parameter algorithm for string-to-string correction. Discret. Optim. (DO) **8**(1), 41–49 (2011)
2. Backurs, A., Indyk, P.: Edit distance cannot be computed in strongly subquadratic time (unless SETH is false). In: Proceedings of the Annual ACM Symposium on Theory of Computing (STOC) (2015)
3. Barbay, J., Pérez-Lantero, P.: Adaptive computation of the swap-insert correction distance. In: Proceedings of the Annual Symposium on String Processing and Information Retrieval (SPIRE), pp. 21–32 (2015)
4. Barbay, J., Pérez-Lantero, P.: Adaptive computation of the swap-insert correction distance. ACM Trans. Algorithms (TALG) (2018, to appear). Accepted 25 May 2018
5. Bentley, J.L., Yao, A.C.C.: An almost optimal algorithm for unbounded searching. Inf. Process. Lett. (IPL) **5**(3), 82–87 (1976)
6. Bergroth, L., Hakonen, H., Raita, T.: A survey of longest common subsequence algorithms. In: Proceedings of the 11th Symposium on String Processing and Information Retrieval (SPIRE), pp. 39–48 (2000)
7. Bringmann, K.: Why walking the dog takes time: Fréchet distance has no strongly subquadratic algorithms unless SETH fails. In: Proceedings of the 2014 IEEE 55th Annual Symposium on Foundations of Computer Science, FOCS 2014, pp. 661–670. IEEE Computer Society, Washington, DC (2014)
8. Eiter, T., Mannila, H.: Computing discrete Fréchet distance. Technical report, Christian Doppler Labor für Expertensyteme, Technische Universität Wien (1994)
9. Golynski, A., Munro, J.I., Rao, S.S.: Rank/select operations on large alphabets: a tool for text indexing. In: Proceedings of the Seventeenth Annual ACM-SIAM Symposium on Discrete Algorithm, SODA 2006, pp. 368–373. Society for Industrial and Applied Mathematics, Philadelphia (2006)

10. Alt, H., Godau, M.: Computing the Fréchet distance between two polygonal curves. Int. J. Comput. Geom. Appl. (IJCGA) **5**(1–2), 75–91 (1995)
11. Hart, M.: Gutenberg project. https://www.gutenberg.org/. Accessed 27 May 2018
12. Meister, D.: Using swaps and deletes to make strings match. Theor. Comput. Sci. (TCS) **562**, 606–620 (2015)
13. Parikh, R.J.: On context-free languages. J. ACM (JACM) **13**(4), 570–581 (1966). https://doi.org/10.1145/321356.321364
14. Wagner, R.A., Fischer, M.J.: The string-to-string correction problem. J. ACM (JACM) **21**(1), 168–173 (1974)
15. Wagner, R.A., Lowrance, R.: An extension of the string-to-string correction problem. J. ACM (JACM) **22**(2), 177–183 (1975)
16. Wagner, R.A.: On the complexity of the extended string-to-string correction problem. In: Proceedings of the Annual ACM Symposium on Theory of Computing, STOC 1975, pp. 218–223. ACM (1975)
17. Witten, I.H., Moffat, A., Bell, T.C.: Managing Gigabytes: Compressing and Indexing Documents and Images. The Morgan Kaufmann Series in Multimedia Information. Morgan Kaufmann Publishers, San Francisco (1999)

Compressed Communication Complexity
of Longest Common Prefixes

Philip Bille[1], Mikko Berggreen Ettienne[1], Roberto Grossi[2]([⊠]),
Inge Li Gørtz[1], and Eva Rotenberg[1] [iD]

[1] DTU Compute, AlgoLoG, Technical University of Denmark,
2800 Kongens Lyngby, Denmark
[2] Dipartimento di Informatica, Università di Pisa, Pisa, Italy
grossi@di.unipi.it

Abstract. We consider the communication complexity of fundamental longest common prefix (LCP) problems. In the simplest version, two parties, Alice and Bob, each hold a string, A and B, and we want to determine the length of their longest common prefix $\ell = \mathrm{LCP}(A, B)$ using as few rounds and bits of communication as possible. We show that if the longest common prefix of A and B is compressible, then we can significantly reduce the number of rounds compared to the optimal uncompressed protocol, while achieving the same (or fewer) bits of communication. Namely, if the longest common prefix has an LZ77 parse of z phrases, only $O(\lg z)$ rounds and $O(\lg \ell)$ total communication is necessary. We extend the result to the natural case when Bob holds a set of strings $B_1, \ldots, B_k$, and the goal is to find the length of the maximal longest prefix shared by A and any of $B_1, \ldots, B_k$. Here, we give a protocol with $O(\log z)$ rounds and $O(\lg z \lg k + \lg \ell)$ total communication. We present our result in the public-coin model of computation but by a standard technique our results generalize to the private-coin model. Furthermore, if we view the input strings as integers the problems are the greater-than problem and the predecessor problem.

Keywords: Communication complexity · LZ77 · Compression
Upper bound · Output sensitive · Longest common prefix · Predecessor

1 Introduction

Communication complexity is a basic, useful model, introduced by Yao [14], which quantifies the total number of bits of communication and rounds of communication required between two or more players to compute a function, where each player holds only part of the function's input. A detailed description of the model can be found, for example, in the book by Kushilevitz and Nisam [5].

Communication complexity is widely studied and has found application in many areas, including problems such as equality, membership, greater-than, and predecessor (see the recent book by Rao and Yehudayoff [9]). For the approximate string matching problem, the paper by Starikovskaya [12] studies its

© Springer Nature Switzerland AG 2018
T. Gagie et al. (Eds.): SPIRE 2018, LNCS 11147, pp. 74–87, 2018.
https://doi.org/10.1007/978-3-030-00479-8_7

deterministic one-way communication complexity, with application to streaming algorithms, and provides the first sublinear-space algorithm. Apart from these results, little work seems to have been done in general for the communication complexity of string problems [13].

In this paper, we study the fundamental *longest common prefix problem*, denoted LCP, where Alice and Bob each hold a string, A and B, and want to determine the length of the longest common prefix of A and B, that is, the maximum $\ell \geq 0$, such that $A[1..\ell] = B[1..\ell]$ (where $\ell = 0$ indicates the empty prefix). This problem is also called the *greater than problem*, since if we view both A and B as integers, the position immediately after their longest common prefix determines which is larger and smaller. The complexity is measured using the number of rounds required and the total amount of bits exchanged in the communication. An optimal randomized protocol for this problem uses $O(\lg n)$ communication and $O(\lg n)$ rounds [8,11] where n is the length of the strings. Other trade-offs between communication and rounds are also possible [10]. Buhrman et al. [2] describe how to compute LCP in $O(1)$ rounds and $O(n^\epsilon)$ communication.

We show that if A and B are compressible we can significantly reduce the number of needed rounds while simultaneously matching the $O(\lg n)$ bound on the number of bits of communication. With the classic and widely used Lempel-Ziv 77 (LZ77) compression scheme [15] we obtain the following bound.

Theorem 1. *The* LCP *problem has a randomized public-coin $O(\lg z)$-round protocol with $O(\lg \ell)$ communication complexity, where $\ell \leq n$ is the length of the longest common prefix of A and B and $z \leq \ell$ is the number of phrases in the LZ77 parse of this prefix.*

Compared to the optimal uncompressed bound we reduce the number of rounds from $O(\lg n)$ to $O(\lg z)$ (where typically z is much smaller than ℓ). At the same time we achieve $O(\lg \ell) = O(\lg n)$ communication complexity and thus match or improve the $O(\lg n)$ uncompressed bound. Note that the number of rounds is both compressed and output sensitive and the communication is output sensitive.

As far as we know, this is the first result studying the communication complexity problems in LZ77 compressed strings. A previous result by Bar-Yossef et al. [1] gives some impossibility results on compressing the text for (approximate) string matching in the sketching model, where a sketching algorithm can be seen as a public-coin one-way communication complexity protocol. Here we exploit the fact that the common prefixes have the same parsing into phrases up to a certain point, and that the "mismatching" phrase has a back pointer to the portion of the text represented by the previous phrases: Alice and Bob can thus identify the mismatching symbol inside that phrase without further communication (see the "techniques" paragraph).

We extend the result stated in Theorem 1 so as to compute longest common prefixes when Bob holds a set of k strings $B_1, \ldots, B_k$, and the goal is to compute the maximal longest common prefix between A and any of the strings

$B_1, \ldots, B_k$. This problem, denoted LCP^k, naturally captures the distributed scenario, where clients need to search for query strings in a text database stored at a server. To efficiently handle many queries we want to reduce both communication and rounds for each search. If we again view the strings as integers this is the *predecessor problem*. We generalize Theorem 1 to this scenario.

Theorem 2. *The* LCP^k *problem has a randomized public-coin* $O(\lg z)$ *round communication protocol with* $O(\lg z \lg k + \lg \ell)$ *communication complexity, where* ℓ *is the maximal common prefix between* A *and any one of* $B_1, \ldots, B_k$, *and* z *is the number of phrases in the LZ77 parse of this prefix.*

Compared to Theorem 1 we obtain the same number of rounds and only increase the total communication by an additive $O(\lg z \lg k)$ term. As $z \le \ell$ the total communication increases by at most a factor $\lg k$.

The mentioned results hold only for LZ77 parses without self-references (see Sect. 2). We also show how to handle self-referential LZ77 parses and obtain the following bounds, where we add either extra $O(\lg \lg \ell)$ rounds or extra $O(\lg \lg \lg |A|)$ communication.

Theorem 3. *The* LCP *problem has a randomized public-coin protocol with*

1. $O(\lg z + \lg \lg \ell)$ *rounds and* $O(\lg \ell)$ *communication complexity,*
2. $O(\lg z)$ *rounds and* $O(\lg \ell + \lg \lg \lg |A|)$ *communication complexity*

where ℓ *is the length of the longest common prefix of* A *and* B, *and* z *is the number of phrases in the* self-referential *LZ77 parse of this prefix.*

Theorem 4. *The* LCP^k *problem has a randomized public-coin protocol with*

1. $O(\lg z + \lg \lg \ell)$ *rounds and* $O(\lg z \lg k + \lg \ell)$ *communication complexity,*
2. $O(\lg z)$ *rounds and* $O(\lg z \lg k + \lg \ell + \lg \lg \lg |A|)$ *communication complexity*

where ℓ *is the length of the maximal common prefix between* A *and any one of* $B_1, \ldots, B_k$, *and* z *is the number of phrases in the* self-referential *LZ77 parse of this prefix.*

Turning again to LZ77 parses without self-references we also show the following trade-offs between rounds and communication.

Theorem 5. *For any constant* $\epsilon > 0$ *the* LCP *problem has a randomized public-coin protocol with*

1. $O(1)$ *rounds and* $O(z_A^\epsilon)$ *total communication where* z_A *is the number of phrases in the LZ77 parse of* A,
2. $O(\lg \lg \ell)$ *rounds and* $O(z^\epsilon)$ *total communication where* z *is the number of phrases in the LZ77 parse of the longest common prefix between* A *and* B.

We note that all the given bounds are in expectation. Using the standard transformation technique by Newman [7] all of the above results can be converted into private-coin results for bounded length strings: If the sum of the lengths of the strings is $\leq n$, then, Newman's construction adds an $O(\lg n)$ term in communication complexity, and only gives rise to 1 additional round.

Techniques. Our results rely on the following key idea. First, we want to perform a binary search over the LZ77-parses of the strings, to find the first phrase where Alice and Bob disagree. Then, the longest common prefix must end somewhere in the next phrase (see Fig. 1). So Alice needs only to send the offset and length of her next phrase, and Bob can determine the longest common prefix with his string or strings (as proven in Lemma 6).

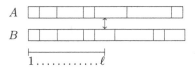

Fig. 1. If the longest common prefix L of A and B has z phrases, then the first $z - 1$ phrases of A, B, and L are identical.

To implement the idea efficiently, we use standard techniques that allow Alice and Bob to check if a specific prefix of their strings match using $O(1)$ communication, with only constant probability of error (we call this the EQUALITY problem). Similarly, if Bob holds k strings, they can check whether any of the k strings matches Alice's string with only $O(\log k)$ communication, with constant error probability (we call this the MEMBERSHIP problem). This leads to the following $O(\log z)$ round communication protocol.

1. Alice and Bob do an exponential search, comparing the first, two first, four first, etc., phrases of their strings using EQUALITY or MEMBERSHIP, until they find a mismatch.
2. Alice and Bob do a binary search on the last interval of phrases from Step 1, again, using EQUALITY or MEMBERSHIP, until they find their longest common prefix up to a phrase border.
3. Alice sends the offset and length of her next phrase, and Bob uses this to determine the longest common prefix.

To efficiently cope with errors in each step (which can potentially accumulate), we show how to extend techniques for *noisy binary search* [4] to an exponential search. Our new *noisy exponential search* only increases the number of rounds by a constant factor.

Paper Outline. In Sect. 2, we review protocols for EQUALITY and MEMBERSHIP. Section 2 also contains a formal definition of the LZ77-parse of a string. In Sect. 3, we recall efficient techniques to handle errors using noisy binary search, and extend them to exponential search. In Sect. 4 we go on to prove Theorems 1 and 2. In Sect. 5, we show how to extend our results to self-referencing LZ77 (Theorems 3 and 4). Finally, in Sect. 6, we give the constant-round and near-constant round protocols promised in Theorem 5.

2   Definition and Preliminaries

A string S of length $n = |S|$ is a sequence of n symbols $S[1] \cdots S[n]$ drawn from an alphabet Σ. The sequence $S[i, j]$ is the *substring* of S given by $S[i] \cdots S[j]$ and, if $i = 1$, this substring is a *prefix* of S. Strings can be concatenated, i.e. $S = S[1, k]S[k+1, n]$. Let $\text{LCP}(A, B)$ denote the length of the longest common prefix between strings A and B. Also, denote by $[u]$ the set of integers $\{1, 2, \ldots, u\}$.

Communication Complexity Primitives. We consider the public-coin and private-coin randomized communication complexity models. In the public-coin model the parties share an infinite string of independent unbiased coin tosses and the parties are otherwise deterministic. The requirement is that for every pair of inputs the output is correct with probability at least $1 - \epsilon$ for some specified $1/2 > \epsilon > 0$, where the probability is on the shared random string. We note that any constant probability of success can be amplified to an arbitrarily small constant at the cost of a constant factor overhead in communication. In the private-coin model, the parties do not share a random string, but are instead allowed to be randomized using private randomness. Newman [7] showed that any result in the public-coin model can be transformed into private-coin model result at the cost of an additive $O(\log \log T)$ bits of communication, where T is the number of different inputs to the players. In our results this leads to an $O(\log n)$ additive overhead, if we restrict our input to bounded length strings where the sum of the lengths of the strings is $\leq n$.

In the MEMBERSHIP problem, Alice holds a string A of length $|A| \leq n$, and Bob holds a set $\mathcal{B}$ of k strings. The goal is to determine whether $A \in \mathcal{B}$ (we assume that n and k are known to both parties) [9].

Lemma 1. *The* MEMBERSHIP *problem has a public-coin randomized 1-round communication protocol with* m *communication complexity and error probability* $k2^{-m}$, *for any integer* $m > 0$.

Proof Sketch. Let $F : \{0, 1\}^n \to \{0, 1\}^m$ be a random linear function over $GF(2)$ where the coefficients of F are read from the shared random source (public coin). Alice applies F to A and sends the resulting m bits to Bob, i.e., she computes the product between a random $m \times n$ matrix and her string as a vector. Bob applies the same function to each of his strings, i.e., he computes the product between the same random matrix and each of his strings. If one of these products is the same as the one he received from Alice he sends a "1" to Alice indicating a match. This protocol has no false-negatives and by union bound the probability of a false-positive is at most $k2^{-m}$. For further details see e.g. [2, 6].   □

In the EQUALITY problem, Alice holds a string A of size $|A| \leq n$, and Bob holds a string B. The goal is to determine whether $A = B$ (we assume that n is known to both parties). Lemma 1 implies the following corollary.

Corollary 1. *The* EQUALITY *problem has a public-coin randomized 1-round communication protocol with m communication complexity and error probability 2^{-m}.*

Lempel-Ziv Compression. The *LZ77 parse* [15] of a string S of length n divides S into z substrings $f_1 f_2 \ldots f_z$, called *phrases*, in a greedy left-to-right order. The ith phrase f_i starting at position u_i is the longest substring having at least one occurrence starting to the left of u_i plus the following symbol. To compress S, we represent each phrase as a tuple $(s_i, l_i, \alpha_i) \in ([n] \times [n] \times \Sigma)$, such that s_i is the position of the previous occurrence, l_i is the length of the previous occurrence, and α_i is the symbol at position $u_i + l_i$. It follows that $s_1 = l_1 = 0, u_1 = 1, \alpha_1 = S[1]$ and we define $e_i = u_i + l_i$ for $i \in z$. That is, the ith phrase of S ends at position e_i. We call the positions $e_1, \ldots, e_z$ the *borders* of S and the substring $S[s_i, s_i + l_i - 1]$ is the *source* of the ith phrase $f_i = S[u_i, u_i + l_i]$.

When a phrase is allowed to overlap with its source, the parse is *self-referential*. A more restricted version does not allow self-references and thus requires that $s_i + l_i \leq u_i$ for $i \in [z]$. We consider LZ77 parse without self-references unless explicitly stated. An LZ77 parse of S can be found greedily in $O(n \log |\Sigma|)$ time from the suffix tree of S. It is easy to see that $z = \Omega(\lg n)$ if self-references are not allowed, while $z = \Omega(1)$ for self-referential parses.

3   Noisy Search

The *noisy binary search* problem is to find an element x_t among a sequence of elements $x_1, \ldots, x_n$ where $x_i \leq x_{i+1}$ using only comparisons in a binary search. Each comparison may fail with a constant probability less than $1/2$ and faults are independent.

Lemma 2 (Feige et al. [4, Theorem 3.2]). *For every constant $Q < 1/2$, we can solve the noisy binary search problem on n elements with probability at least $1 - Q$ in $O(\lg(n/Q))$ steps.*

We now show how to generalize the algorithm by Feige et al. to solve the *noisy exponential search* problem. That is, given a sequence $x_1, x_2, \ldots$ where $x_i \leq x_{i+1}$ and an element x_ℓ find an element x_r such that $\ell \leq r \leq 2\ell$ using exponential search.

Lemma 3. *For every constant $Q < 1/2$, we can solve the noisy exponential search problem searching for x_ℓ with probability at least $1 - Q$ in $O(\lg(\ell/Q))$ steps.*

Proof. In case of no errors we can find x_r on $O(\lg \ell)$ steps comparing x_ℓ and x_i for $i = 1, 2, 4, 8 \ldots$ until $x_i \geq x_\ell$. At this point we have $\ell \leq i \leq 2\ell$.

Consider the decision tree given by this algorithm. (See Fig. 2). This tree is simply a path $v_0, v_1, v_2, \ldots$ and when reaching vertex v_i the algorithm compares elements x_ℓ and x_{2^i}. In order to handle failing comparisons we transform this tree by adding a path with length l_i (to be specified later) as a child of vertex v_i. Denote such a path with p_i. The search now performs a walk in this tree starting in the root and progresses as follows: Reaching vertex v_i we first check if $x_\ell \geq x_{2^{i-1}}$. If not, this reveals an earlier faulty comparison and we backtrack by moving to the parent. Otherwise, we check if $x_\ell \geq x_{2^i}$. If so we move to vertex v_{i+1}. Otherwise, we move to the first vertex on the path p_i. Reaching a vertex u on a path p_i we test if $x_\ell \geq x_{2^{i-1}}$ and if $x_\ell < x_{2^i}$. If both tests are positive, we move to the only child of u. Otherwise, this reveals an earlier faulty comparison and we backtrack by moving to the parent of u. When reaching a leaf on path p_i we terminate and report the element corresponding to v_i.

The search can be modeled as a Markov process. Assume that $\lceil \lg \ell \rceil = j$ and thus $j = O(\lg \ell)$ and direct all edges towards the leaf u on the path p_j. For every vertex $v \neq u$, exactly one adjacent edge is directed away from v and the remaining edges are directed towards v. Without loss of generality we can assume that the transition probability along an outgoing edge of a vertex is greater than $1/2$ and the transition probability along the remaining edges is less than $1/2$ (this probability can be achieved by taking the majority of $O(1)$ comparisons).

Let b be the number of backward transitions and f the number of forward transitions. We need to show that $f - b \geq j + l_j$ with probability at least $1 - Q$ for $Q < 1/2$ implying that the search terminates in the leaf u. Setting $l_i = i c_1$ this follows after $c_2(\lg(2^j/Q)) = O(\lg(\ell/Q))$ rounds from Chernoff's bound [3] with suitable chosen constants c_1 and c_2.   □

Fig. 2. In the proof of Lemma 3, the decision tree for exponential search (left) is transformed to a fault-tolerant decision tree (right).

4   Communication Protocol for LCP

We now present our protocol for the LCP problem without self-references. We consider the case with self-references in the next section. First, we give an efficient uncompressed output sensitive protocol that works for an arbitrary alphabet (Lemma 4). Secondly, we show how to encode LZ77 strings as strings from a small alphabet (Lemma 5) which allows us to efficiently determine the first phrase where Alice and Bob disagree. Thirdly, we show that given this phrase Alice and Bob can directly solve LCP (Lemma 6). Combining these results leads to Theorem 1. Finally, we generalize the results to the LCP^k case.

First we show how to solve the LCP problem with output-sensitive complexity for both the number of rounds and the amount of bits of communication.

Lemma 4. *Let A and B be strings over an alphabet Σ known to the parties. The LCP problem has a public-coin randomized $O(\lg \ell)$-round communication protocol with $O(\lg \ell)$ communication complexity, where ℓ is the length of the longest common prefix between A and B.*

Proof. Alice and Bob compare prefixes of exponentially increasing length using equality, and stop after the first mismatch. Let t be the length of the prefixes that do not match and observe that $t \leq 2\ell$. They now do a binary search on the interval $[0, t]$, using equality to decide if the left or right end of the interval should be updated to the midpoint in each iteration. The parties use Corollary 1 with $m = 2$, and new random bits from the shared random source for every equality check. Thus, the probability of a false-positive is at most $1/4$, and the faults are independent. Using Lemmas 3 and 2 we get that we can solve the problem in $O(\lg(\ell/Q))$ rounds of communication with probability at least $1 - Q$ for any constant $Q < 1/2$. □

Note that the size of the alphabet Σ does not affect the complexity of this protocol. Alice and Bob do however need to agree on how many bits to use per symbol in order to use the same number of random bits for the equality checks. Because Σ is known to the parties, they sort the alphabet and use $\lg |\Sigma|$ bits per symbol.

We move on to consider how to handle LZ77 compressed strings. Recall that the ith phrase in the LZ77 parse of a string S is represented as a tuple (s_i, l_i, α_i) consisting of the source s_i, the length l_i of the source, and a symbol $\alpha_i \in \Sigma$. Observe that the LZ77 parse can be seen as a string where each tuple describing a phrase corresponds to a symbol in this string. Because we consider LZ77 without self-references a phrase is never longer than sum of the lengths of the previous phrases and we can thus bound the number of bits required to write a phrase.

Lemma 5. *Let $Z_i = (s_1, l_1, \alpha_1), \ldots, (s_i, l_i, \alpha_i)$ be the first i elements in the LZ77 parse of a string S. Then, s_i and l_i can be written in binary with i bits.*

Proof. Recall that e_j is the position in S of the last symbol in the jth phrase. Since we have no self-references s_i and l_i are both no larger than e_{i-1} they can be written with $\lg e_{i-1}$ bits. By definition $u_j = e_{j-1}+1$. Therefore, $e_j = u_j + l_j = e_{j-1} + 1 + l_j \leq 2e_{j-1} + 1$, and it follows that $e_{i-1} \leq 2e_{i-2} + 1 \leq \cdots \leq 2^i - 1$ since $e_1 = 1$. □

We show that $\ell = \text{LCP}(A, B)$ can be determined from $\text{LCP}(Z_A, Z_B)$ with only one round and $O(\lg \ell)$ communication, where Z_A and Z_B are the respective LZ77 parses of A and B.

While a LZ77 parse of a string is not necessarily unique, in this case, we can assume that the parties as part of the protocol agree deterministically upon their same decisions on LZ77-compression algorithm (e.g. taking always the leftmost source when there are multiple possibilities). This ensures that we obtain the same parsing for equal strings, independently and without any communication.

Lemma 6. *Let A and B be strings and let Z_A and Z_B be their respective LZ77 parses. If Alice knows A and Bob knows B and the length of the longest common prefix $\text{LCP}(Z_A, Z_B)$, then they can determine the length $\ell = \text{LCP}(A, B)$ of the longest common prefix of A and B in $O(1)$ rounds and $O(\lg \ell)$ communication.*

Proof. First, Z_A and Z_B themselves can be seen as strings over the special alphabet $\Sigma' \equiv ([n] \times [n] \times \Sigma)$ of tuples. Letting $z = \text{LCP}(Z_A, Z_B)$, these LZ77 parses of A and B are identical up until but no longer than their z^{th} tuple. Now, let $\ell = \text{LCP}(A, B)$. Let a_i and b_i denote the ith phrase border in the LZ77 parse of A and B respectively.

Observe that $A[1, a_z] = B[1, b_z]$ but $A[1, a_{z+1}] \neq B[1, b_{z+1}]$ because of how we choose z and, thus, $a_z = b_z \leq \ell < a_{z+1}, b_{z+1}$. Let s_{z+1}, l_{z+1} be the source and length of the $(z+1)^{th}$ phrase in Z_A. Alice sends s_{z+1}, l_{z+1} to Bob in one round with $O(\lg a_z) = O(\lg \ell)$ bits of communication since $s_{z+1}, l_{z+1} \leq a_z$. At this point, it is crucial to observe that Bob can recover $A[1, a_{z+1}]$ by definition of LZ77 parsing: he deduces that $A[1, a_{z+1}] = B[1, b_z]B[s_{z+1}, s_{z+1} + l_{z+1}]$, from which he can compute $\text{LCP}(A[1, a_{z+1}], B[1, b_{z+1}]) = \text{LCP}(A, B)$. $\qquad\square$

We can now combine Lemmas 4, 5, and 6 to prove Theorem 1. Alice and Bob construct the LZ77 parse of their respective strings and interpret the parse as a string. Denote these strings by Z_A and Z_B. They first use Lemma 4 to determine $\text{LCP}(Z_A, Z_B)$, where the parties decide to use $2i + \lg |\Sigma|$ random bits for the equality check of the ith symbols (from Σ'), which suffices by Lemma 5. Then they apply Lemma 6 to determine $\text{LCP}(A, B)$. In conclusion this proves Theorem 1.

4.1 The LCP^k Case

In this section we generalize the result on LCP to the case where Bob holds multiple strings. Here, Alice knows a string A and Bob knows strings $B_1, \ldots, B_k$, where all strings are drawn from an alphabet Σ known to the parties.

The main idea is to substitute the equality-tests by membership queries. We first generalize Lemma 4 to the LCP^k-case.

Lemma 7. *The LCP^k-problem has a randomized public-coin $O(\lg \ell)$-round communication protocol with $O(\lg \ell \lg k)$ communication complexity, where ℓ is the length of the maximal longest common prefix between A and any B_i.*

Proof. Along the same lines as the proof of Lemma,4, Alice and Bob perform membership-queries on exponentially increasing prefixes, and then, perform membership-queries to guide a binary search. They use Lemma 1 with $m = 2 \lg k$, and exploit shared randomness as in the previous case. Again, the probability of a false positive is $\leq 1/4$, and the faults are independent. Thus Lemmas 3 and 2 gives us an $O(\lg \ell/Q)$ round communication protocol with total error probability $1 - Q$ for any constant choice of $Q < 1/2$.

Since there are $O(\lg \ell)$ rounds in which we spend $O(\lg k)$ communication, the total communication becomes $O(\lg \ell \lg k)$. $\qquad\qquad\square$

We go on to show that the maximal $\text{LCP}(A, B_i)$ can be determined from solving LCP^k on Z_A and $\{Z_{B_1}, \ldots, Z_{B_k}\}$ with only one additional round and $O(\lg n)$ communication.

Lemma 8. *Let $Z_A, Z_{B_1}, \ldots, Z_{B_k}$ be the LZ77 parses of the strings $A, B_1, \ldots,$ B_k. If Alice knows A, and Bob knows $B_1, \ldots, B_k$ and the length of the maximal longest common prefix between Z_A and any Z_{B_i}, they can find $\max_i \text{LCP}(A, B_i)$ in $O(1)$ rounds and $O(\lg n)$ communication.*

Proof. In this case, Bob holds a set, $\mathcal{B}'$, of at least one string that matches Alice's first z phrases, and no strings that match Alice's first $z+1$ phrases. Thus, if Alice sends the offset and length of her next phrase, he may determine $\text{LCP}(A, B_i)$ for all strings $B_i \in \mathcal{B}'$. Since the maximal LCP among $B_i \in \mathcal{B}'$ is indeed the maximal over all $B_i \in \mathcal{B}$, we are done. $\qquad\qquad\square$

Combining Lemmas 7 and 8 we get Theorem 2.

5   Self-referencing LZ77

We now consider how to handle LZ77 parses with self-references. The main hurdle is that Lemma 5 does not apply in this case as there is no bound on the phrase length except the length of the string. This becomes a problem when the parties need to agree on the number of bits to use per symbol when computing LCP of Z_A and Z_B, but also when Alice needs to send Bob the source and length of a phrase in order for him to decide $\text{LCP}(A, B)$.

First we show how Alice and Bob can find a bound on the number of random bits to use per symbol when computing $\text{LCP}(Z_A, Z_B)$.

Lemma 9. *Bob and Alice can find an upper bound ℓ' on the length of the longest common prefix between A and B where*

1. *$\ell' \leq \ell^2$ using $O(\lg \lg \ell)$ rounds and $O(\lg \lg \ell)$ total communication,*
2. *$\ell' \leq |A|^2$ using $O(1)$ rounds and $O(\lg \lg \lg |A|)$ total communication.*

Proof. Part (1): Alice and Bob do a double exponential search for ℓ and find a number $\ell \leq \ell' \leq \ell^2$ using equality checks on prefixes of their uncompressed strings in $O(\lg \lg \ell)$ rounds. Again, at the cost of only a constant factor, we apply Lemma 3 to deal with the probability of false positives.

Part (2): Alice sends the minimal i such that $|A| \leq 2^{2^i}$ thus $i = \lceil \lg \lg |A| \rceil$ can be written in $O(\lg \lg \lg |A|)$ bits. Alice and Bob can now use $n = 2^{2^i}$ as an upper bound for ℓ, since $\ell \leq |A| \leq 2^{2^i} < |A|^2$. □

Assume that Alice and Bob find a bound ℓ' using one of those techniques, then they can safely truncate their strings to length ℓ'. Now they know that every symbol in Z_A and Z_B can be written with $O(\lg \ell' + \lg |\Sigma|)$ bits, and thus, they agree on the number of random bits to use per symbol when doing equality (membership) tests. Using Lemma 4 they can now find the length of the longest common prefix between Z_A and Z_B in $O(\lg \ell)$ rounds with $O(\lg \ell)$ communication.

We now show how to generalize Lemma 6 to the case of self-referential parses.

Lemma 10. *Let A and B be strings and let Z_A and Z_B be their respective self-referential LZ77 parses. If Alice knows A and Bob knows B and the length of the longest common prefix between Z_A and Z_B, then they can determine the length ℓ of the longest common prefix of A and B in*

1. *$O(1 + \lg \lg \ell)$ rounds and $O(\lg \ell)$ communication,*
2. *$O(1)$ rounds and $O(\lg \ell + \lg \lg \lg |A|)$ communication.*

Proof. Let s_i, e_i and l_i be the respective source, border and length of the ith phrase in Z_A. The proof is the same as in Lemma 6 except that the length l_{z+1} of the $(z+1)^{th}$ phrase in Z_A that Alice sends to Bob is no longer bounded by ℓ.

There are two cases. If $l_{z+1} \leq 2e_z$, then $l_{z+1} \leq 2\ell$, and Alice can send l_{z+1} to Bob in one round and $O(\lg \ell)$ bits and we are done.

If $l_{z+1} > 2e_z$ then the source of the $(z+1)^{th}$ phrase must overlap with the phrase itself and thus the phrase is periodic with period length at most e_z and has at least 2 full repetitions of its period. Alice sends the starting position of the source of the phrase s_{i+1} along with a message indicating that we are in this case to Bob in $O(\lg \ell)$ bits. Now Bob can check if they agree on next $2e_z$ symbols. If this is not the case, he has also determined $\text{LCP}(A, B)$ and we are done. Otherwise, they agree on the next $2e_z$ symbols and therefore $(z+1)^{th}$ phrases of both A and B are periodic with the same period. What remains is to determine which phrase that is shorter. Let l_a and l_b denote the lengths of respectively Alice's and Bob's next phrase. Then (1) follows from Alice and Bob first computing a number $\ell' \leq \ell^2$ using a double exponential search and equality checks in $O(\lg \lg \ell)$ rounds and total communication. Clearly either l_a or l_b must be shorter than ℓ' and the party with the shortest phrase sends its length to the other party in $O(\lg \ell)$ bits and both can then determine $\text{LCP}(A, B)$. To get the result in (2) Alice sends the smallest integer i such that $l_a \leq 2^{2^i}$ in a single round and $O(\lg \lg \lg |A|)$ bits of communication. Bob then observes that if $l_b \leq 2^{2^{i-1}}$, then $l_b = \ell$ and he sends ℓ to Alice using $O(\lg \ell)$ bits. If $l_b > 2^{2^i}$ then $l_a = \ell$ and he informs Alice to send him l_a in $O(\lg \ell)$ bits. Finally, if $2^{2^{i-1}} < l_b$ and $l_a \leq 2^{2^i} \leq \ell^2$ he sends l_b to Alice using $O(\lg \ell)$ bits. □

Theorem 3 now follows from Lemmas 4, 9, and 10.

5.1 LCP^k in the Self-referential Case

Finally, we may generalize Theorem 2 to the self-referential case. Substituting equality with membership, we may directly translate Lemma 9:

Lemma 11. *Bob and Alice can find an upper bound on the length ℓ' of the maximal longest common prefix between A and $B_1, \ldots, B_k$ where*

1. *$\ell' \leq \ell^2$ using $O(\lg \lg \ell)$ rounds and $O(\lg \lg \ell \log k)$ total communication,*
2. *$\ell' \leq |A|^2$ using $O(1)$ round and $O(\lg \lg \lg |A|)$ total communication.*

Using the lemma above, we can generalize Corollary 10 to the LCP^k-case.

Lemma 12. *Let A and $B_1, \ldots, B_k$ be strings, and let Z_A and Z_{B_i} be their respective self-referential LZ77 parses. If Alice knows A and Bob knows $B_1, \ldots, B_k$ and Bob knows the length of the maximal longest common prefix between Z_A and any Z_{B_i}, then they can determine ℓ in*

1. *$O(1 + \lg \lg \ell)$ rounds and $O(\lg \ell \lg k)$ communication,*
2. *$O(1)$ rounds and $O(\lg \ell \lg k + \lg \lg \lg |A|)$ communication.*

Proof tweak.. Alice and Bob have already found a common prefix of size e_z – question is whether a longer common prefix exists. As before, if Alice's next phrase is shorter than $2e_z$, she may send it. Otherwise, she sends the offset, and indicates we are in this case. Now, Bob can check if *any* of his strings agree with Alice's on the next $2e_z$ symbols. If none do, we are done. If several do, he forgets all but the one with the longest $(z + 1)^{st}$ phrase, and continue as in the proof of Corollary 10. □

Theorem 4 now follows from the combination of Lemmas 11 and 12.

6 Obtaining a Trade-Off via D-ary Search

We show that the technique of Buhrman et al. [2], to compute LCP of two strings of length n in $O(1)$ rounds and $O(n^\epsilon)$ communication, can be used to obtain a compressed communication complexity. Note that we again consider LZ77 compression without self-references. We first show the following generalization of Lemma 4.

Lemma 13. *Let A and B be strings over an alphabet Σ known to the parties. The LCP problem has a public-coin randomized communication protocol with*

1. *$O(1)$ rounds and $O(|A|^\epsilon)$ communication*
2. *$O(\lg \lg \ell)$ rounds and $O(\ell^\epsilon)$ communication*

where ℓ is the length of the longest common prefix between A and B, and $\epsilon > 0$ is any arbitrarily small constant.

Proof. Assume the parties agree on some parameter C and have previous knowledge of some constant ϵ' with $0 < \epsilon' < \epsilon$ (i.e. ϵ' and ϵ are plugged into their protocol). They perform a D-ary search in the interval $[-1, C]$ with $D = C^{\epsilon'}$. In each round, they split the feasible interval into D chunks, and perform equality tests from Corollary 1 with $m = 2\lg(D/\epsilon')$ on the corresponding prefixes. The feasible interval is updated to be the leftmost chunk where the test fails. There are $\lg_D C = 1/\epsilon' = O(1)$ rounds. The communication per round is $2D\lg(D/\epsilon')$ and the total communication is $1/\epsilon' \cdot 2D\lg(D/\epsilon') = O(C^{\epsilon'}\lg C)$. The probability of a false positive for the equality test is 2^{-m}, and thus, by a union bound over D comparisons in each round and $1/\epsilon'$ rounds, the combined probability of failure becomes $1/4$.

1. Alice sends $|A|$ to Bob in $\lg|A| = O(|A|^\epsilon)$ bits and they use $C = |A|$. The total communication is then $O(C^{\epsilon'}\lg C) = O(|A|^\epsilon)$ with $O(1)$ rounds.
2. Alice and Bob use Lemma 9 to find an ℓ' such that $\ell \le \ell' \le \ell^2$ in $O(\lg\lg\ell)$ rounds and communication. They run the D-ary search protocol where $\epsilon' < \epsilon/4$, setting $C = \ell'$. The extra communication is $O(C^{\epsilon'}\lg C) = O(\ell^\epsilon)$.

$\square$

We can now combine Lemmas 13, 5, and 6 to prove Theorem 5. Alice and Bob construct the LZ77 parse of their respective strings and interpret the parses as strings, denoted by Z_A and Z_B. They first use Lemma 13 to determine $\mathrm{LCP}(Z_A, Z_B)$, and then Lemma 6 to determine $\mathrm{LCP}(A, B)$. The parties use $2i+\lg|\Sigma|$ random bits for the ith symbol, which suffices by Lemma 5. This enables them to apply Lemma 13 to Z_A and Z_B. In conclusion this proves Theorem 5.

We note without proof that this trade-off also generalizes to self-referential parses by paying an additive extra $O(\lg\lg\lg|A|)$ in communication for Theorem 5 (1) and an additive $O(\lg\ell)$ communication cost for Theorem 5 (2). The same goes for LCP^k where the communication increases by a factor $O(\lg k)$ simply by increasing m by a factor $\lg k$ and using the techniques already described.

References

1. Bar-Yossef, Z., Jayram, T.S., Krauthgamer, R., Kumar, R.: The sketching complexity of pattern matching. In: Jansen, K., Khanna, S., Rolim, J.D.P., Ron, D. (eds.) APPROX/RANDOM -2004. LNCS, vol. 3122, pp. 261–272. Springer, Heidelberg (2004). https://doi.org/10.1007/978-3-540-27821-4_24
2. Buhrman, H., Koucký, M., Vereshchagin, N.: Randomised individual communication complexity. In: Proceedings of the 23rd CCC, pp. 321–331 (2008)
3. Chernoff, H.: A measure of asymptotic efficiency for tests of a hypothesis based on the sum of observations. Ann. Math. Stat. **23**, 493–507 (1952)
4. Feige, U., Raghavan, P., Peleg, D., Upfal, E.: Computing with noisy information. SIAM J. Comput. **23**(5), 1001–1018 (1994)
5. Kushilevitz, E., Nisan, N.: Communication Complexity. Cambridge University Press, Cambridge (1997)
6. Miltersen, P.B., Nisan, N., Safra, S., Wigderson, A.: On data structures and asymmetric communication complexity. J. Comp Syst. Sci. **57**(1), 37–49 (1998)

7. Newman, I.: Private vs. common random bits in communication complexity. Inf. Proc. Lett. **39**(2), 67–71 (1991)
8. Nisan, N.: The communication complexity of threshold gates. Comb. Paul Erdos Eighty **1**, 301–315 (1993)
9. Rao, A., Yehudayoff, A.: Communication Complexity (Early Draft) (2018). https://homes.cs.washington.edu/~anuprao/pubs/book.pdf
10. Sena, P., Venkatesh, S.: Lower bounds for predecessor searching in the cell probe model. J. Comput. Syst. Sci. **74**, 364–385 (2008)
11. Smirnov, D.V.: Shannon's information methods for lower bounds for probabilistic communication complexity. Master's thesis, Moscow University (1988)
12. Starikovskaya, T.A.: Communication and streaming complexity of approximate pattern matching. In: Proceedings of the 28th CPM, pp. 13:1–13:11 (2017)
13. Starikovskaya, T.A.: Streaming and property testing algorithms for string processing. In: 26th London Stringology Days (2018)
14. Yao, A.C.-C.: Some complexity questions related to distributive computing (preliminary report). In: Proceedings of the 11th STOC, pp. 209–213 (1979)
15. Ziv, J., Lempel, A.: A universal algorithm for sequential data compression. IEEE Trans. Inf. Theory **23**(3), 337–343 (1977)

New Structures to Solve Aggregated Queries for Trips over Public Transportation Networks

Nieves R. Brisaboa[1], Antonio Fariña[1(✉)], Daniil Galaktionov[1,2],
Tirso V. Rodeiro[1], and M. Andrea Rodríguez[3,4]

[1] Fac. Informática, CITIC, Universidade da Coruña, A Coruña, Spain
antonio.farina@udc.es
[2] Enxenio S.L., A Coruña, Spain
[3] Computer Science Department, Universidad de Concepcion, Concepción, Chile
[4] Millennium Institute for Foundational Research on Data, Santiago, Chile

Abstract. Representing the trajectories of mobile objects is a hot topic from the widespread use of smartphones and other GPS devices. However, few works have focused on representing trips over public transportation networks (buses, subway, and trains) where user's trips can be seen as a sequence of stages performed within a vehicle shared with many other users. In this context, representing vehicle journeys reduces the redundancy because all the passengers inside a vehicle share the same arrival time for each stop. In addition, each vehicle journey follows exactly the sequence of stops corresponding to its line, which makes it unnecessary to represent that sequence for each journey.

To solve data management for transportation systems, we designed a conceptual model that gave us a better insight into this data domain and allowed us the definition of relevant terms and the detection of redundancy sources among those data. Then, we designed two compact representations focused on users' trips (**TTCTR**) and on vehicle trips (**AcumM**), respectively. Each approach owns some strengths and is able to answer some queries efficiently.

We include experimental results over synthetic trips generated from accurate schedules obtained from a real network description (from the bus transportation system of Madrid) to show the space/time trade-off of both approaches. We considered a wide range of different queries about the use of the transportation network such as counting-based/aggregate queries regarding the load of any line of the network at different times.

Funded in part by European Union's Horizon 2020 research and innovation programme under the Marie Sklodowska-Curie grant agreement No 690941 (project BIRDS). The Spanish group is also partially funded by Xunta de Galicia/FEDER-UE [CSI: ED431G/01 and GRC: ED431C 2017/58]; by MINECO-AEI/FEDER-UE [Datos 4.0: TIN2016-78011-C4-1-R; Velocity: TIN2016-77158-C4-3-R; and ETOME-RDFD3: TIN2015-69951-R]; by MINECO-CDTI/FEDER-UE [INNTERCONECTA: uForest ITC-20161074]; and by FPI Program [BES-C-2017-0085]. M. A. Rodríguez is partially funded by Fondecyt-Conicyt grant number 1170497 and by the Millennium Institute for Foundational Research on Data.

© Springer Nature Switzerland AG 2018
T. Gagie et al. (Eds.): SPIRE 2018, LNCS 11147, pp. 88–101, 2018.
https://doi.org/10.1007/978-3-030-00479-8_8

1   Introduction

The management of public transportation systems is a complex problem that has been typically faced from the point of view of the **offer** (lines, stops, schedules of journeys for each line, ...). In the last decade, the widespread use of new technologies allowing somehow the tracking of users' movements along a network transportation system (mobile phones with GPS, use of RFID technologies, smart cards used to pay and enter buses/trains, ...) brings new opportunities to gather the actual usage of the transportation systems allowing to study the problem from the point of view of **users' demand**. In consequence, it is now possible to develop new applications to exploit those data in order to effectively handle the resources of the transportation system and to give a better service to the users.

The management of the transportation system has become a Big Data problem in many important cities around the world, where millions of passengers use the public transportation network every day. Therefore, even though we can assume the gathered data is reliable (even in the case of depending on the smart cards provided to users that typically gather only the entry point to the network, the end point can commonly be derived using historical data from user trips and transportation models [9]), the problem lies now on how to represent user trips in such a way that not only we provide a compact representation but also we enable performing queries in an efficient way.

While there exist many works that tackle the problem of representing trajectories of mobile objects constrained to networks [5,6,12], they typically aim at locating the position of those objects from the underlying trajectories. Others [7,8] focus on solving *strict and approximate path queries* that permit to find the trajectories that follow a given line pattern within a given time interval. The latter work [7] is, to the best of our knowledge, the first work using a compact data structure to represent the spatial data (a FM-index [4]). Yet, none of them have been designed to tackle the analysis of the usage of the transportation network and would hardly support queries such as *count the number of user trips that went from stop X to stop Y*, or *show the load of the lines at a given hour*.

In [1], a representation for user trips along a transportation network referred to as CTR was presented. The different stops from bus lines were given a *node-ID*. Then, each user trip was associated a string composed of the sequence of *node-IDs* traversed. Finally, a CSA-based representation [13] was used to represent the collection with all users' trips, and a Wavelet Matrix (WM) [2] aligned with the CSA represented, for each trip, the time instant when every node from that trip was reached. CTR enabled answering counting-based aggregated queries (number of users that started/ended a trip at a given node within a given time interval, number of users that used a node, top-k most used nodes, etc.). In addition, since it represented the actual trips in a compact self-indexed way, CTR still possessed enough flexibility to support more complex queries. CTR succeeded at providing a compact representation for general trips. Yet, it still represented trips in a redundant way when considering public transportation by bus, train, and subway. This happens because it does not exploit the fact that all the passengers in the same bus/train traverse each stop at the same time, nor the topology of the network (for all the users' trips from a stop X to a stop Y along a given line, all the intermediate stops are always the same).

In this work, we have analyzed the problem of representing both *offer* (stops, lines, schedule for each line) and *users' demand* (user trips, and stages that include stops where users get on/off or switch lines) within a public transportation network. We present a conceptual model that provides valuable insights into this domain and shows both the data needed and the relationships among them.

Then, we present two complementary structures to represent those data and show how they handle some useful queries in this context. The first solution is named Topology&Trip − aware CTR (TTCTR) and is based on a modification of CTR that also represents all the user trips but exploits both the network topology and the fact that all the passengers of the same vehicle journey reach the same stops at the same time, hence temporal information can be related to the vehicle journey rather than to each user trip. Therefore, it still makes up a general representation focused on users' trips. The second solution, named Accumulated − Matrix (AcumM), does not actually represents user's trips. It focuses on the journeys of each line, and accumulates the number of passengers that get on/off in each stop of each journey. Therefore, AcumM is a summarization of the load each line had considering each of its journeys, in the same way a data warehouse is a summarization of the operational data in a database.

The structure of the paper is as follows. In Sect. 2 we discuss the conceptual model associated to the network transportation problem and provide some definitions. In Sect. 3, we present our representation of the *offer* (lines, stops and journeys) which is then used in our two solutions. The next sections describe both TTCTR and AcumM and discuss the types of queries they are designed for. Section 7 includes experimental results to show the space/time trade-offs of our proposals. And finally, conclusions and future work are discussed in Sect. 8.

2   A Model to Describe a Public Transportation Network

The E-R conceptual model at Fig. 1 represents the relevant data of any public transportation system including data related with both the *offer* and the *demand*. We did not include entities such as vehicles or drivers, as they are out of the scope of this work. To create that model we have defined the following concepts:

- **Stop (or Stop-place).** Places were passengers can get on/off from a vehicle.
- **Lines.** A line (or route) is a sequence of stops that starts at a given stop X and ends in another stop Y. We consider a line and its *return* line as different lines because they include different sequences of stops.
- **Journeys.** We define a journey (or vehicle journey, or line trip) as a trip that a vehicle performs. It departs at a given day and time from the first stop of a specific line and follows the complete sequence of stops of that line until the ending stop, allowing passengers to get on and to get off in each stop. For instance, a *journey* is the trip that a bus performed along line $L1$ departing at 9:00 am on 2017/05/05, and stopping at each stop of the line. In addition to the day and time each journey starts, it could be interesting to have the

time at which each stop was reached by each specific journey of the line. Yet, if such an accurate time is not needed, we can save a large amount of space by only storing, for each stop of a line, the average accumulated time needed to reach that stop from the initial stop (as in the examples shown along this paper). Some other solutions, with different trade-off between accuracy of the temporal data and storage space, are possible. For example, we could store the average time to get to each stop of a line in peak and non-peak hours. In any case, all those strategies enable us to associate temporal data to the user-trips done within a given vehicle journey.

- **Stages.** A stage represents the pair of stops where a given user respectively gets on/off to/from a vehicle doing a given journey of a given line.
- **User_trip.** We define a user trip as a sequence of stages. That is, a user trip can begin at stop A from line 3 and continue up to stop B (first stage), then change to line 2 up to stop C (second stage), and so on. This enables tracking user trips from an origin to a destination. Note that, since stages refer to a given journey, and we can know the time when a journey traverses a stop X, we can also know when a given user trip reached such stop X.

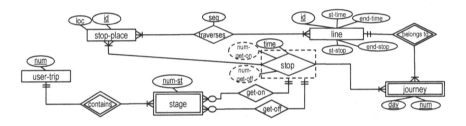

Fig. 1. E-R model for a public transportation network.

3   Towards a Practical Representation: Common Structures to Represent the *Offer*

In Sects. 4 and 5, we present two representations. The first one is focused on the representation of user trips, whereas the second one is focused on the journeys of each line and basically stores the number of users that get on/off at any given stop for each journey of a any line. Both techniques require some common structures that handle the data that represents the *offer* of public transportation the network provides. Such *offer* refers to the structure of the network and includes the representation of the lines, and, for each line, the schedule of its journeys; that is, their departure time from the starting stop. In addition, we use two aligned arrays for each line, one with the sequence of stops, and another with the average accumulated time to reach each stop from the first stop of the line. Note that instead of assigning a unique sequence of estimated times to reach any stop from the line, we could have dealt with several, probably more accurate, estimations for peak/low periods, or even we could have stored the actual time each journey reached each stop. In any case, we can estimate the time when each journey reaches each stop.

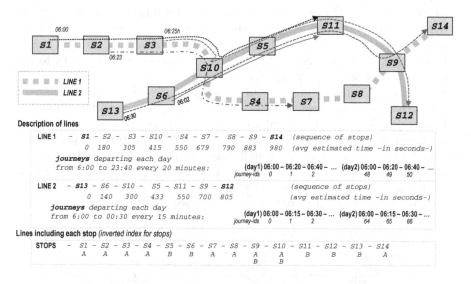

Fig. 2. Example of (bus) public transportation network.

Figure 2 includes an example of a bus network with two lines (1 and 2). For each line we show the stops that compose it (e.g. Line 2 contains the sequence of stops $\langle S13, S6, S10, S5, S11, S9, S14 \rangle$) and the accumulated times from the initial stop (e.g. the average time to reach the fourth stop $S5$ from the starting stop of the line is 433 s). We also include the starting times for each journey of each line. In this case, Line 1 has 48 journeys per day, the first one starts at 6:00 am, the second one at 6:20 am, etc.

Note that given a line X we have direct access to the information related to the i-th stop. Yet, given a stop, we do not know the line/s it belongs to. To overcome this issue, we include, for each stop Y, the list of lines that include such stop Y. It is referred to as *inverted index for stops* in the bottom of Fig. 2.

To sum up, we saw that to represent the network offer we need: *(i)* a sequence of stops for each line[1]; *(ii)* a schedule with the starting times of the journeys of each line; and *(iii)*, an inverted index to mark the lines each stop belongs to.

Apart from the network offer, in Fig. 2 we also include (arrows) five user trips done along the network. For example, there is a user trip (dashed arrow from $S3$) that starts at stop $S3$ at 06:25 am on *day-1* (6:20 am + 305 sec.), and follows the journey of line 1 until $S10$, where the user switches to line 2 at time 6:35 am (6:30 am + 300 sec.) and continues the corresponding journey of line 2 (the one started as 06:30 h in $S13$) up to stop $S12$. That is, it includes two stages.

---

[1] We also store average estimated times to reach each stop from first stop of the line.

4   Topology&Trip − Aware CTR (TTCTR): A Representation Focused on User's Trips

A previous representation for user trips along a transportation network, named CTR [1], basically associates an integer s_i to each stop in the network, and represents a user trip t_i as the sequence of the stops traversed plus a terminator $ (t_i = s_1, s_2, \ldots, s_k$)$. Finally, a CSA-based representation is used to represent the collection with all users' trips, and a Wavelet Matrix (WM) aligned with the CSA keeps, for each trip, the (discretized) time instant in which every stop from that trip was reached. For example, the trip from Fig. 2 that started at $S3$ would be represented as $\langle S3, S10, S5, S11, S9, S12, $\rangle$ and the times associated to those stops would be discretized into 5-min time periods. CTR exploited the indexing capabilities of the underlying CSA and WM to solve counting-based spatial, temporal, and spatio-temporal queries.

Our TTCTR is an adaptation of CTR that represents a user trip as a sequence of stages rather than as a sequence of stops (hence exploiting the topology of the network). Furthermore, instead of having to represent the time each user trip reaches a stop, we will only store a reference/id of the journey (within a vehicle of a line) that the user used. The building process of TTCTR is presented below.

Let us assume a network with n_s stops (S) numbered $s \in [1, n_s]$; n_l lines (L) numbered $[1, n_l]$, and that there are n_j^l journeys (J^l) for each line $l \in L$ numbered $[0, n_j^l - 1]$. Additionally, we have the starting times for each journey and the accumulated average times for the stops of each line as discussed in the previous section. We can define that a user gets on/off from a vehicle following the journey j of line l at a given stop s, as a triple (s, l, j) where $l \in L, s \in S, j \in J^l$.

Let us define $\mathcal{T} = \{t_1, t_2, \ldots, t_z\}$ as a set of z user trips. Since we want to represent a user trip t_x as a sequence of k stages, but it holds that the final stop of a stage and the starting stop of the next stage are the same (or close in walking distance), it is not necessary to explicitly represent the final stop of each stage, except for the final stop. We define $t_x = \langle (s_1, l_1, j_1), (s_2, l_2, j_2), \ldots, (s_{k+1}, l_{k+1}, j_{k+1}) \rangle$, $k \geq 1$. That is, we have a sequence of k triples that indicate that the user got on a vehicle corresponding to the j_i-th journey of line l_i at stop s_i. The last triple indicates where the user finally got off. Note that, for the last two triples, $l_k = l_{k+1}$, and $j_k = j_{k+1}$ since the beginning of the last stage is represented by the k-th triple, and its end by the $(k+1)$-th triple.

Example 1. Assuming that all the user trips depicted in Fig. 2 belong to our 1st-day, those user trips can be represented as: $t_1 = \langle (1, 1, \mathbf{0}), (10, 2, 1), (11, 2, 1) \rangle$, $t_2 = \langle (2, 1, \mathbf{1}), (7, 1, 1) \rangle$, $t_3 = \langle (3, 1, \mathbf{1}), (10, 2, 2), (12, 2, 2) \rangle$, $t_4 = \langle (6, 2, \mathbf{0}), (11, 2, \mathbf{0}) \rangle$, and $t_5 = \langle (13, 2, \mathbf{2}), (9, 1, \mathbf{2}), (14, 1, \mathbf{2}) \rangle$. Note that, for example, $(13, 2, \mathbf{2})$ from t_5 indicates that, at stop 13, the user got on a vehicle from line 2, that corresponds to the **2**-nd journey. We know it is the **2**-nd journey because t_5 started at 06:30 h, which is the departure time of journey **2**. Note also that the line and journey ids of the last triple of each trip are identical to the ones in the previous triple.   □

In TTCTR, we represent both the spatial (lines and stops) and the temporal component (journeys) of the user trips of our collection of trips $\mathcal{T}$ using respectively a CSA and a WM aligned with the CSA. In the following sections we show how we handle such components, and how we solve some queries of interest.

4.1   Representing the Spatial Component of TTCTR with a CSA

We use a variant of the CSA [3] for integer alphabets to represent the spatial component, i.e. the sequence of pairs (s_i, l_i) that compose each user trip in $\mathcal{T}$. However, in order to create a CSA we need to assign each pair $(stop, line)$ a unique integer id. This will allow us to create an integer sequence $S[1, n]$ (ended by a $ terminator) over which our CSA will be built. For this purpose we create a vocabulary V (with $1 + n_s(1 + n_l)$ entries) as follows:

- Entry $V[0]$ is reserved for the terminator symbol $.
- Entries $\langle V[1], V[2], \ldots V[n_s] \rangle$ are associated to stops $\langle 1, 2, \ldots, n_s \rangle$ and are used to represent the final stops of the trips. That is, when a given stop x ends a user trip, it is given $id \leftarrow x$.
- The last $n_l \times n_s$ entries are associated to the sequence composed of the pairs $(s, l) \in S \times L$ considering that those pairs are sorted by s and l respectively. That is, entry $V[n_s+1]$ is given to $(s, l) = (1, 1)$; $V[n_s+2]$ to $(1, 2)$; $V[n_s+3]$ to $(1, 3)$; $\ldots$; $V[n_s+n_l]$ to $(1, n_l)$; $V[n_s+n_l+1]$ to $(s, l) = (2, 1)$, $V[n_s+n_l+2]$ to $(2, 2)$, and so on. In practice, in this case, the $id/pos\text{-}in\text{-}V$ for a pair (s, l) is obtained as $id \leftarrow n_s + n_l(s - 1) + l$.

Note that there will be a large number of unused entries (holes) in V. Yet, this can be efficiently handled by a bitvector B with rank/select capabilities that marks the used entries from V. Therefore, once we gather the position (id) corresponding to a pair (s, l) in V, we obtain its final position (id') in a *vocabulary without holes* (V') as $id' \leftarrow rank_1(B, id)$. Our id' assignment ensures that the used pairs (s_i, l), corresponding to a given stop s_i, receive contiguous id's. This will be interesting at query time.

The next step processes each user trip $t_i \in \mathcal{T}$, $i \in [1, z]$ replacing all the pairs $(stop, line)$ in t_i (except in the last one where the line is already known and we only need s) by their corresponding id'. After each trip, a 0 (id' for terminator $) is added. That is, a trip t_i with k stages is regarded as a string $s_1 s_2 \ldots s_k s_{last}$, where $1 \leq s_{last} \leq rank_1(B, n_s)$ is the id' of ending stop given to stop s.

Once this process has completed, a sequence $S[1, n]$ that contains only values from V' is obtained, and a CSA can be built on S.

In parallel with the construction of S, we create a sequence $Jcodes[1, n]$ aligned to S where we set, for each trip t_i, the *journey-id* corresponding to each stage in t_i. Recall the *journey-id* is the third term from the triples (s_i, l_i, j_i), $i \in [1, k]$ from t_i. In addition, assuming that $S[p]$ contains the 0 corresponding to the terminator $ for the trip, we set $Jcodes[p] \leftarrow j_1$ (i.e. the same journey-id as the starting stop of the trip). According to the discussion above, Fig. 3 shows, for the user trips in Example 1: *(step-1)* the sequence of pairs $(stop, line)$ for each

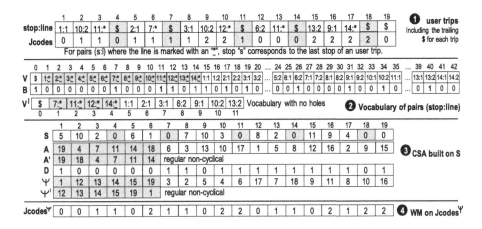

Fig. 3. Structures involved in the creation of a TTCTR.

trip, and the corresponding *Jcodes*; *(step-2)* the vocabularies, including V, B, and V' (ending stops s of trips do not need the line, therefore we use "s:*".);[2] and *(step-3)* the structures involved in the creation of CSA from which TTCTR uses Ψ, D, (and V', B).

As in CTR [1], we sort the terminators considering that each trip is a cyclical string. For instance in Fig. 3, $S[18] = 0$ would traditionally be followed by $S[19] = 0$, but for sorting purposes we consider it is instead followed by $S[15] = 11$. After that, we make Ψ cyclical in the terms of each user trip. That is, let us assume that a user trip lays on $S[i] \dots S[i + k + 1]$, i.e. the terminator of the trip is at position $e = i + k + 1$ in S. Therefore, being $A[j] = e$, we modify $\Psi[j]$ in such a way that $A[\Psi[j]]$ points not to the initial position $e + 1$ of the next user trip, but it cyclically points to the beginning of the same trip; that is, we set $\Psi[j] \leftarrow \Psi[A^{-1}[i]]$.[3] Using a cyclical Ψ will enable searching efficiently for user trips that started at a stop X and ended at a stop Y, as we will see below.

4.2 Representing the Temporal Component of TTCTR with a WM

The temporal component of TTCTR includes the sequence *Jcodes* described above. Recall *Jcodes* contains *journey-ids* aligned to the values in S, and that, for every line l there are n_j^l journeys sorted by their starting time and numbered as $0 \dots n_j^l - 1$, and also we have average accumulated times to reach each stop in the line. Therefore, this representation allows us to describe exact times for each stop. In practice, we use *Jcodes*$^\Psi$, which is aligned to Ψ rather than to S. See *step-4* in Fig. 3. Note that *Jcodes*$[8] = 1$ corresponds to *Jcodes*$^\Psi[14] = 1$, since $A[14] = 8$; *Jcodes*$[9] = 2$ corresponds to *Jcodes*$^\Psi[18] = 2$, since $A[18] = 9$;

---

[2] In this example, with only 5 trips, we have only 11 *used pairs* in V, but in a real scenario for each stop of each line (*existing pair* (s, l)) there will be a 1 in B.

[3] Note that A^{-1} is the inverse of the suffix array A; i.e. $A^{-1}[i] = j$ iff $A[j] = i$.

and so on. We represent the sequence $Jcodes^\Psi$ with a WM. This saves space, and provides indexing capabilities to the temporal component.

5   Dealing with Aggregated Data: **Accumulated** − **Matrix**

We propose AcumM as an intuitive solution for the representation of two-dimensional matrices of integers with support to aggregated queries by row, column, or window/range. In the context of a public transportation network we found queries referred to a given line where data must be aggregated either by *stop* (e.g. number of users that got on a vehicle at stop X); by *time-interval*, hence referred to a sequence of consecutive journeys within that time-interval (e.g. number of users got on at any stop of the line on 2017/03/24); or by *stop and time-interval*.

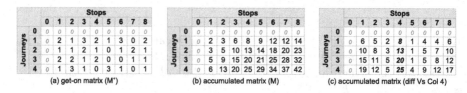

Fig. 4. Example, **for a given line**, of get-on matrix (a), accumulated matrix (b), and compact representation with gaps (c). Stop and column **0** are virtual. The values in column/row **0** are set to *zero* to simplify operations.

Let us assume that, for a given line, we have a matrix M^+ that stores the number of users that got-on at each stop (column) from each journey (row). Figure 4(a) includes an example. To efficiently support aggregated queries, we create, for each line, the accumulated get-on matrix M for M^+. We compute the value of a cell $M(r,c) \leftarrow \sum_{i=1}^{r}\sum_{j=1}^{c} M^+(i,j)$. That is, each cell contains the sum of all the values from position $(1,1)$ to position (r,c). M is depicted in Fig. 4(b). The accumulated matrix M allows us to solve a range count query over M^+ in $O(1)$ time by computing: $\mathsf{countRange}((x_1,y_1),(x_2,y_2)) \leftarrow M(x_2,y_2) - M(x_2,y_1-1) - M(x_1-1,y_2) + M(x_1-1,y_1-1)$. In AcumM, we actually represent, for each line, two accumulated matrices that count, respectively, the passengers that get on and get off to/from a journey in each stop.

$\mathsf{countRange}$ allows us to add: *(i)* consecutive values of a column (e.g. users that got on in a stop X in consecutive journeys, such as those in one day); *(ii)* consecutive values in a row (e.g. users that, for a given journey, got on along a consecutive sequence of stops, such as those in a neighborhood); and *(iii)* values in a window (e.g. users that got on in a consecutive sequence of stops in consecutive journeys).

Being C the capacity of a vehicle, a simple way to decrease space usage on M (it has $n_s \times n_j^l$ integers) consists in keeping the middle column $m \leftarrow (n_s + 1)/2$ explicitly, and representing the values in the other columns $m \pm k$

as the difference with respect to column m. This is depicted in Fig. 4(c). The differences in columns $m \pm k$ require at most $\lceil \log_2 kC \rceil$ bits, while retaining direct access.

6 Performing Queries on **TTCTR** and **AcumM**

AcumM and TTCTR are designed for different purposes and therefore each highlight in different types of queries.

Queries for Accumulated – Matrix: This data structure resembles a data-warehouse, i.e. it stores aggregated values (rather than individual trips) to efficiently answer aggregated queries about the number of users (load of the network) in a given stop or group of stops over one or more journeys. Recall countRange efficiently sums the values of any submatrix. Yet, some useful queries could need more than one countRange operation, and then to either aggregate or compute the average of those results. For example, if we want to know the *average number of users that got on in line L in stops of a neighborhood (consecutive stops) between 8:00 and 9:00 along the last month*, we will need a countRange operation for each window including the consecutive stops and the consecutive journeys inside that period for each day. Finally, we add the results of those countRange operations (one per day) and divide the result by the number of days in the month.

Since we have both the accumulated matrix for users getting on and getting off, we can easily compute queries about the load of the journeys. For example, to know *how many users were inside the vehicle of journey j from line L, between the stops X and X + 1*, we compute: $tot\_up \leftarrow$ *how many users got on in such journey j between stops 1 and X* (inclusive), using the accumulated get-on matrix for line L (countRange of a row); in the same way, using the accumulated get-off matrix, we compute $tot\_down \leftarrow$ *how many users got off in the same journey and range of stops*; and finally, we return the value $total \leftarrow tot\_up - tot\_down$.

Queries for TTCTR: Recall that TTCTR actually stores all the individual trips. This allows it to answer queries about the patterns users follow when using the transportation network. For example, queries about *how many users start their trips in stop X*, or *end their trips in stop Y*, or even *started their trips in stop X and ended in stop Y*, can be efficiently answered because CSA easily locates the subsection devoted to each stop, and the cyclic encoding of the trips allows to ask for patters such as $\$X$ or $Y\$$ or even $Y\$X$. Note also that our way to encode the pairs *stop:line* guaranties that the occurrences of a stop for different lines are consecutive in the CSA, therefore, we can ask both *how many users start their trips in stop X* or *how many users start their trips in stop X of line L*. Finally, using the WM we can filter out those queries by time using the journeys.

Note that none of those queries can be answered by AcumM, which stores the number of passengers getting on to (off from) a journey in each stop but cannot track individual trips. On the other hand, in TTCTR, queries about the load of the transportation network, such as *number of passengers into the vehicle in journey j between stops X and X + 1*, would become very time consuming.

7   Experimental Evaluation

We created a synthetic collection of user trips generated from a GTFS[4] description of urban and medium-distance buses[5] from Madrid, with 1049 different lines and 10913 stop locations. We used real stop times from the journeys provided by the GTFS to generate ten million user trips over the span of a month. Each user trip created had one or more stages, defined as pairs *(stop_in, stop_out)*, being *stop_in* and *stop_out* respectively triples *(stop, line, journey)* that determine the stop, line, and the journey where the user got on and got off.

The created user trips started from a random stop on a random journey, and followed the stops on that journey. After at least two traversed stops, we used a probability table to determine if the stage ends and user switch lines. In such case, we simulate the user getting off from that journey and either waiting on the same stop (at most 30 min) or walking to a nearby (100 m) stop to get on to a new journey. We ensured there were no inconsistencies in our generated trips (i.e. users getting on the same line from which they just got off). Trip lengths were limited to 100 stops. Yet, after each traversed stop, the probability for ending the trip was 0.01λ, where λ is the number of previously traversed stops.

Finally, we represented all those trips using TTCTR and AcumM.

Implementation Details: Due to the relatively small size of the network, the common structures were built using plain arrays of fixed size integers. Table 1 shows the space occupied by these structures.

For TTCTR, we used the CSA from [3] tuned the sampling rate for Ψ (t_Ψ) to the values $t_\Psi = \{32, 128, 512\}$. To represent bitvector D we used a *SDArray* [10]. In Table 2 (left) we show the space required by Ψ, D, B, and V' for an input of 35,702,981 entries in S and $Jcodes$, when compared to a baseline that uses fixed width integers to represent the pairs *(line, stop)* in the trips (that is, of $\lceil \log_2 |V| \rceil$ bits/entry, where V is the vocabulary defined in Sect. 4.1). In the WM of the TTCTR we used a *RRR* bitvector to compress the bitmaps [11]. We set sampling parameter $s \in \{32, 64, 128\}$, as shown in the Table 2 (right), where we compare the space of WM with a plain representation of the *journey-ids* that uses the number of bits needed to represent the maximum number of journeys on any line, $\arg\max_{l \in L} \lceil \log_2 J^l \rceil$:

For AcumM, we consider both the simple *accumulated-matrix* and the version using differential encoding. In the former case we have a simple matrix of integers. In the latter one, the middle column is kept apart as an integer array. For the rest of columns in the *differential matrix* values in each cell are encoded with $\lceil \log_2 N \rceil$ bits, being N the maximum difference (i.e. value on those columns). The space requirements of those structures are shown in Table 3.

---

[4] https://developers.google.com/transit/gtfs/reference.
[5] Provided by CRTM (http://www.crtm.es).

Table 1. Size of common structures (in KiB).

	(i) Lines	(ii) Schedules	(iii) Inverted index of stops	Overall size
Size (KiB)	176.54	7299.66	139.96	7616.17

Table 2. Compression of the CSA (left) and WM (right) components from TTCTR. Percentages refer to the sizes with respect to the size of the uncompressed baseline

	t_Ψ		
	32	128	512
iCSA	27.13 MB	21.91 MB	20.58 MB
	(39.84)%	(32.17)%	(30.22)%

	RRR sampling		
	32	64	128
WM	42.35 MB	39.43 MB	37.98 MB
	(71.07)%	(66.18)%	(63.73)%

Table 3. Sizes of the different AcumM variants.

	Accumulated matrix	Differential matrix
Get-on matrix	11189 KB (100%)	5596 KB (50.01%)
Get-off matrix	11189 KB (100%)	5596 KB (50.01%)

Query Execution Times: We run experiments to show the query execution times of our proposals. An Intel Xeon E5-2620v4@2.1 GHz machine was used.

On TTCTR, we tested several configurations for the query *number of user trips from stop X to stop Y*, labeled as xy$_*$ in Table 4. The entry for xy with no subindices applies no line nor time restriction. xy$_S$ and xy$_E$ restrict, respectively, the Starting and Ending stop to a specific line. xy$_T$ denotes a Temporal restriction (at one random day). Therefore, combinations of these subindices stand for combinations of these three restrictions. We randomly generated a set of 10, 000 query patterns by choosing trips from all the available user trips. In the densest setup ($t_\Psi = 32$, RRR $= 32$) all the queries are answered in around 6–30 μs.

The last row also includes the times to solve the query: *How many users got on in a stop X on a given line during a given day?* (J^kS^1). We also implemented this query in AcumM to compare the efficiency for these type of queries.

Table 4. Performance at query time shown in μsecs/query for TTCTR.

	RRR = 32			RRR = 64			RRR = 128		
	$t_\Psi = 32$	$t_\Psi = 128$	$t_\Psi = 512$	$t_\Psi = 32$	$t_\Psi = 128$	$t_\Psi = 512$	$t_\Psi = 32$	$t_\Psi = 128$	$t_\Psi = 512$
xy	6.94	10.28	22.89	6.90	10.23	22.80	6.87	10.21	22.82
xy$_S$	6.89	10.23	22.95	6.86	10.22	22.82	6.90	10.21	22.74
xy$_E$	29.37	62.63	192.86	29.13	62.60	192.01	29.14	62.38	192.28
xy$_{SE}$	29.21	61.84	192.11	28.88	61.83	190.46	28.92	62.05	190.47
xy$_T$	31.85	64.66	195.62	31.63	65.52	195.06	31.95	65.47	195.31
xy$_{ST}$	31.61	63.83	193.41	31.12	65.05	193.14	31.54	64.78	194.23
xy$_{ET}$	31.73	65.04	195.53	31.66	65.73	195.15	32.01	65.09	195.45
xy$_{SET}$	31.36	63.96	194.12	31.17	64.99	193.11	31.42	64.42	193.40
J^kS^1	5.05	5.85	9.14	5.20	6.01	9.30	5.41	6.31	9.63

Table 5. Performance at query time for the variants of AcumM (in ns per query).

	Accumulated matrix	Differential matrix
$J^k S^1$(column)	131	211
$J^1 S^*$ (rows)	107	221
$J^k S^k$ (window)	76	182

To test AcumM we considered three types of queries: The query $J^k S^1$ discussed above; *total number of passengers that got on in all the stops of a given journey (1-row)*, labeled $J^1 S^*$; and *total passengers that got on along a range of consecutive stops from several consecutive journeys (window)*, labeled $J^k S^k$. We generated 20,000 query patterns based on the real data (line number, stop number, and journeys), and then run the tests obtaining query times around $0.1\,\mu s$ when using the accumulated matrix. As expected, the differential accumulated matrix performs around twice slower. Yet, AcumM performs more than one order of magnitude faster than TTCTR on query $J^k S^1$. Table 5 shows the results.

8 Conclusions and Future Work

We have analyzed the problem of representing trips over a public transportation network and presented two data structures designed to efficiently answer two subsets of useful queries. Both approaches use some common data structures defined to represent the transportation network, that is the *offer* (lines, schedule of their journeys and stops) it provides.

The first proposal, TTCTR, represents the whole set of user trips during a period of time. Each user trip is composed of stages performed over specific journeys of different lines. This data structure is useful to analyze user trip patterns, that represent the real *demand* over the transportation network. Yet, TTCTR enables not only counting-based queries for the number of passengers related to any stop of the network, but also queries for stops or stops-lines were users start/end trips or switch lines. It also allows to retrieve individual trips.

The second structure (AcumM) focuses on the usage of lines. For each line, it keeps in an accumulated fashion, the number of passengers that, at each stop, get on/off from the vehicle performing a specific journey of the line. This simplifies solving queries regarding the load of the different journeys and therefore to analyze when specific lines must be reinforced with a more frequent schedule.

We understand more research is needed in this topic. Even we can see AcumM as a data warehouse were we store basically the same information but in an aggregated way, we consider that avoiding the redundancy between both structures would be desirable. As future work, we are interested in developing a unique self-indexed structure providing the functionality included in both TTCTR and *acumM*.

References

1. Brisaboa, N.R., Fariña, A., Galaktionov, D., Rodriguez, M.A.: A compact representation for trips over networks built on self-indexes. Inf. Syst. **78**, 1–22 (2018). https://doi.org/10.1016/j.is.2018.06.010
2. Claude, F., Navarro, G., Ordóñez, A.: The wavelet matrix: an efficient wavelet tree for large alphabets. Inf. Syst. **47**, 15–32 (2015)
3. Fariña, A., Brisaboa, N.R., Navarro, G., Claude, F., Places, Á.S., Rodríguez, E.: Word-based self-indexes for natural language text. ACM Trans. Inf. Syst. **30**(1) (2012). Article no. 1. https://doi.org/10.1145/2094072.2094073
4. Ferragina, P., Manzini, G.: Opportunistic data structures with applications. In: Proceedings of the 41st IEEE Symposium on Foundations of Computer Science (FOCS), pp. 390–398 (2000)
5. Funke, S., Schirrmeister, R., Skilevic, S., Storandt, S.: Compass-based navigation in street networks. In: Gensel, J., Tomko, M. (eds.) W2GIS 2015. LNCS, vol. 9080, pp. 71–88. Springer, Cham (2015). https://doi.org/10.1007/978-3-319-18251-3_5
6. Kellaris, G., Pelekis, N., Theodoridis, Y.: Map-matched trajectory compression. J. Syst. Softw. **86**(6), 1566–1579 (2013). https://doi.org/10.1016/j.jss.2013.01.071
7. Koide, S., Tadokoro, Y., Yoshimura, T.: SNT-index: spatio-temporal index for vehicular trajectories on a road network based on substring matching. In: Proceedings of the 1st International ACM SIGSPATIAL Workshop on Smart Cities and Urban Analytics (UrbanGIS@SIGSPATIAL), pp. 1–8 (2015). https://doi.org/10.1145/2835022.2835023
8. Krogh, B., Pelekis, N., Theodoridis, Y., Torp, K.: Path-based queries on trajectory data. In: Proceedings of the 22nd ACM SIGSPATIAL International Conference on Advances in Geographic Information Systems (SIGSPATIAL), pp. 341–350 (2014)
9. Munizaga, M.A., Palma, C.: Estimation of a disaggregate multimodal public transport origin-destination matrix from passive smartcard data from Santiago, Chile. Transp. Res. Part C: Emerg. Technol. **24**, 9–18 (2012). https://doi.org/10.1016/j.trc.2012.01.007
10. Okanohara, D., Sadakane, K.: Practical entropy-compressed rank/select dictionary. In: Proceedings of the 9th Workshop on Algorithm Engineering and Experiments (ALENEX), pp. 60–70 (2007). https://doi.org/10.1137/1.9781611972870.6
11. Raman, R., Raman, V., Rao, S.S.: Succinct indexable dictionaries with applications to encoding k-ary trees and multisets. In: Proceedings of the 13th Annual ACM-SIAM Symposium on Discrete Algorithms (SODA), pp. 233–242 (2002)
12. Richter, K.F., Schmid, F., Laube, P.: Semantic trajectory compression: representing urban movement in a nutshell. J. Spat. Inf. Sci. **4**(1), 3–30 (2012). https://doi.org/10.5311/JOSIS.2012.4.62
13. Sadakane, K.: New text indexing functionalities of the compressed suffix arrays. J. Algorithms **48**(2), 294–313 (2003)

3DGraCT: A Grammar-Based Compressed Representation of 3D Trajectories

Nieves R. Brisaboa[1], Adrián Gómez-Brandón[1(✉)], Miguel A. Martínez-Prieto[2], and José Ramón Paramá[1]

[1] CITIC, Universidade da Coruña, A Coruña, Spain
{brisaboa,adrian.gbrandon,jose.parama}@udc.es
[2] Universidad de Valladolid, Valladolid, Spain
migumar2@infor.uva.es

Abstract. Much research has been published about trajectory management on the ground or at the sea, but compression or indexing of flight trajectories have usually been less explored. However, air traffic management is a challenge because airspace is becoming more and more congested, and large flight data collections must be preserved and exploited for varied purposes. This paper proposes 3DGraCT, a new method for representing these flight trajectories. It extends the GraCT compact data structure to cope with a third dimension (altitude), while retaining its space/time complexities. 3DGraCT improves space requirements of traditional spatio-temporal data structures by two orders of magnitude, being competitive for the considered types of queries, even leading the comparison for a particular one.

1 Introduction

Geopositioned data is ubiquitously and continuously generated to describe different types of trajectories; e.g. routes of professional transportation vehicles or our daily running paths. Obviously, large and varied trajectory datasets are being consolidated, and they are exploited for different and innovative purposes. Disregarding their final application, managing trajectory datasets poses many challenges that have attracted much research efforts.

A prominent domain that demands efficient trajectory management is Air Traffic Management (ATM). ATM systems analyze very large flight-related datasets to make decisions to improve air traffic performance, reducing costs, or making safer and environmentally friendly airspaces. Currently, ATM services are

This work was funded in part by EU H2020 MSCA RISE BIRDS: 690941; MINECO-AEI/FEDER-UE: TIN2016-78011-C4-1-R; MINECO-CDTI/FEDER-UE CIEN IDI-20141259; MINECO-CDTI/FEDER-UE CIEN IDI-20150616; MINECO-CDTI/FEDER-UE INNTERCONECTA ITC-20161074; Xunta de Galicia/FEDER-UE ED431C 2017/58 and ED431G/01.

T. Gagie et al. (Eds.): SPIRE 2018, LNCS 11147, pp. 102–116, 2018.
https://doi.org/10.1007/978-3-030-00479-8_9

evolving to support and leverage "next generation" technologies like *Automatic Dependent Surveillance-Broadcast (ADS-B)*. ADS-B is a surveillance technology in which aircrafts determine flight parameters (latitude, longitude, altitude, etc.) via navigation systems, and broadcast them to ground stations, that then deliver this data to ADS-B providers; e.g. the OpenSky Network [16], that is the provider of the ADS-B datasets used in our experiments.

ADS-B has been progressively adopted by many aircraft manufacturers, and more ground stations have been deployed around the world. It has increased ADS-B coverage, and also the size of ADS-B datasets, whose storage and querying has become more difficult. Storage issues were first addressed using columnar compression [20,22]. Although their numbers are moderately successful, the resulting representations can not be efficiently queried. More recently, a compressed index for ADS-B (called ADS-BI) has been proposed [21]. It performs block partitioning and stores descriptive metadata about the block to enable some types of queries. Block contents are then encoded by columns using universal compression (e.g. gzip or p7zip), reporting competitive numbers. Although ADS-BI resolves some type of queries by time or 2D-position, it does not support altitude-based searches, which is highly desirable for ATM systems; for instance, when a controller looks for aircrafts flying at certain flight level in a given region.

Therefore, our main objective is to propose a data structure that allows 3D trajectories to be effectively compressed, and searches to be performed by time and/or any of the three positional dimensions. It is not a new problem [7], and some researches have been previously published about 2D *(latitude, longitude)*, and 3D (including *altitude*) trajectory management. Data structures like 3DR-tree [19], HR-tree [13], the MVR-tree [17], or PIST [2] have been successfully used for many years, but currently show scalability issues when they are used to manage larger trajectory datasets. The Douglas-Peucker algorithm [8] has been used to make trajectories more compact; other examples are dead reckoning [18], TrajStore [6] and Trajic [15].

Our approach, called 3DGraCT, proposes a new compact data structure that stores and indexes 3D trajectories in compressed space. 3DGraCT enhances GraCT [14] to manage altitude information, and also to enable query resolution by this dimension. Our experiments, using different-size ADS-B datasets, show that 3DGraCT improves space requirements of traditional spatiotemporal data structures by two orders of magnitude, and competes with them in query performance, leading the comparison for queries asking for large time intervals.

2   Background

k^2-**tree.** The k^2-tree [5] is conceptually an unbalanced k^2-ary tree constructed from a binary matrix by recursively subdividing the matrix into k^2 submatrices of the same size, if $k = 2$, it is a space/time efficient version of a region quadtree. First, the original matrix is divided into k^2 submatrices of size n^2/k^2, being $n \times n$ the size of the matrix. Each of these submatrices generates a child of the root node whose value is 1, if there is at least one 1 in the cells of that submatrix, and 0 otherwise. The subdivision continues recursively for each child with value 1 until a submatrix full of 0s is found or the cells of the original matrix (i.e., submatrices of size 1×1) ar reached. Figure 1 shows an example of this subdivision (left) and the resulting conceptual k^2-ary tree (right up) for $k = 2$.

The k^2-tree is stored using two bitmaps T and L (see Fig. 1). T stores all the bits of the k^2-tree, except those in the last level, following a level-wise traversal: first the k^2 binary values of the children of the root node, then the values of the second level, and so on. L stores the last level of the tree.

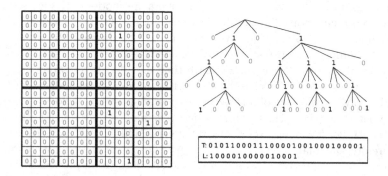

Fig. 1. Example of a binary matrix (left), the k^2-tree conceptual representation (top right), and the compact representation (bottom right), where $k = 2$.

k^3-**tree.** The k^2-tree can be generalized to deal with a three-dimensional binary cube, instead of a two-dimensional binary matrix. It can be trivially done by extending the space partitioning, while maintaining the representation techniques used for k^2-trees. Thus, each 1 in the binary cube of the k^3-tree [1] represents a tuple $\langle x, y, z \rangle$, where (x, y) are the coordinates in the 2D space, and z is the altitude. It is possible to obtain efficiently the value of a cell, a cube, or slices of the cube, by just performing *rank* and *select* operations [10] over T and L.

Re-Pair. Re-Pair [12] compresses a sequence by recursively substituting pairs of symbols by a new one. Given a sequence of integers I (called *terminals*) the compression process is as follows: (1) it obtains the most frequent pair of integers ab in I; (2) it adds rule $W \rightarrow ab$ to dictionary R, where W is a new symbol not present in I (called a *non-terminal*); (3) every occurrence of ab in I is replaced by W, and (4) it repeats steps 1–3 until all pairs in I appear only once (see Fig. 2). The resulting sequence after compressing I is called C.

GraCT. GraCT [4] is a compact data structure to represent and query trajectories of moving objects in a free space of two dimensions. It requires that all objects declare their positions at regular time instants (e.g. each minute), but interpolation is used when an object does not inform its position in a given

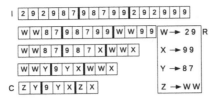

Fig. 2. Example of Re-Pair compression.

instant. GraCT uses a raster model to represent the space; i.e. it is divided into cells (squares) of a fixed size, and it is assumed that objects fit in one of these cells. The size of the cells and the time elapsed between consecutive instants are parameters that can be adapted to particular cases.

To store absolute positions of all objects, every d time instants, GraCT uses a data structure based on the k^2-tree, which is called *snapshot*. The distance, d, between snapshots is another parameter of GraCT. Between two consecutive snapshots, the trajectory of each moving object is represented as a *log*, which is an array of relative movements with respect to the previous time instant.

3   3DGraCT

3DGraCT proposes an extension of GraCT to three dimensions, so the space is divided into cells (small cubes) of fixed length, that form a bigger cube.

Snapshots. Each d time instants, there is a snapshot $\mathcal{S}_k$, where k is the time instant represented by the snapshot. These snapshots are organized as k^3-trees. A leaf of the k^3-tree set to 1 (i.e., a 1 in the bitmap L) means that one or more aircrafts[1] are placed in the corresponding cell, but the snapshot needs to determine which objects are located in that cell. Following the order of 1s in L, an array of object identifiers (aircrafts) holds that information. This array is denoted as *perm*, since it is a permutation [11]. An additional bitmap, called Q, is aligned with *perm*. It marks with 0 that the aligned object identifier in *perm* is the last object in the corresponding cell, and 1 means that more objects are located in that cell.

Figure 3 shows an example of snapshot.[2] The two matrices models the first two slices of an $8 \times 8 \times 8$ cube representing the 3D space. Each slice contains the horizontal positions of all aircrafts flying at a given altitude. Each matrix shows object identifiers at certain positions, and the corresponding k^3-tree encodes this information by assuming that no objects are contained in the remaining slices. Each non-empty position in matrix corresponds to a bit set to 1 in L. The object identifiers corresponding to the first 1 in L (which is at position 3 of L) are stored starting at position 1 of *perm*. Q is then accessed to count the number of objects

---

[1] From now on, we will refer to them simply as objects or moving objects.

[2] Note that only shaded structures are used to encode the snapshot, the other ones are used for illustration purposes.

that are located in this cell: a sequential search is performed from $Q[1]$ until the first 0 (located at $Q[2]$). Thus, there are two objects in the inspected cell. The corresponding object identifiers are retrieved from *perm[1] = 3* and *perm[2] = 6*. Now, in position 3 of *perm* starts the object identifiers corresponding to the second 1 in L, and so on.

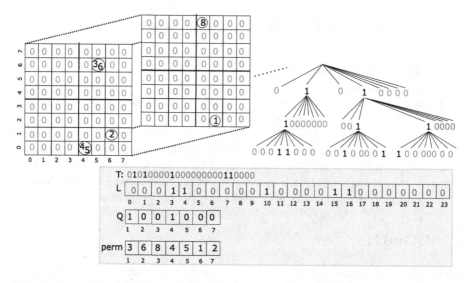

Fig. 3. The position of objects in the 3D space (top left), the conceptual k^3-tree (top right), and the snapshot (bottom).

These structures allow 3DGraCT to address two types of queries:

– *Find the objects in a box of the 3D space.* The k^3-tree is traversed from the root to the leaves to obtain positions $n_1, n_2, \ldots n_m$, in L, that corresponds to positions marked with 1 in the queried box. For each n_i, we count the number of 1s in the array of leaves L until the position n_i; it obtains the number of non-empty leaves up to the n_i^{th} leaf, $x = rank_1(L, n_i)$. Then, the position of the $(x - 1)$th 0 in Q is obtained, which indicates the last bit of the previous leaf (with objects), and by adding 1, we get the first position in *perm* with the objects of the leaf corresponding to n_i, $p = select_0(Q, x - 1) + 1$. From p, object identifiers aligned with 1s in Q are retrieved, until a 0 is reached (it marks the last object identifier located in a leaf).

– *Find the position in the 3D space of a given object.* The desired object identifier is first searched in *perm*. Our permutation is enhanced with *shortcuts* to avoid sequential searches. Assuming the object identifier is located at position k, the following step looks for its corresponding position in L. We calculate the number of leaves before the object at *perm[k]*: $y = rank_0(Q, k - 1)$. Then we find in L the position of the $(y+1)^{th}$ 1, that is, $select_1(L, y+1)$. This value is used to traverse the k^3-tree upwards in order to obtain the cell position in the 3D space, and thus the horizontal position and altitude of the object.

Log of Relative Movements. The use of a snapshot for encoding each time instant would consume too much space, instead, between snapshots, 3DGraCT stores for each aircraft the relative movements with respect to the last known position. A relative movement consists of 3 values, $\langle x, y, z \rangle$, which are the number of cells of difference between the new position and the last known position, in each dimension. Probably, $\langle x, y, z \rangle$ will be numbers with a small magnitude, as the differences between consecutive time instants cannot be very big. Instead of using 32 bits for each value, we fit the three values into a 32-bit integer using 12 bits for the x and y values and 8 bits for the z component. In Fig. 4(a), we can see a relative movement of 1 cell up on the y-coordinate, 3 cells to the right on the x-coordinate and 2 cells down on the z-coordinate. Below, observe that those values are encoding using Zig-Zag encoding ($-1 \rightarrow 1, 1 \rightarrow 2, -2 \rightarrow 3, \dots$), and then they are packed in a 32-bit integer.

Obviously, this works well as long as the assumption that there are small differences between two consecutive positions is maintained. However, there may be periods of time without information about the positions of the aircraft (for example, the aircraft is in an area without reception stations). In those cases, the 32-bit integer comprising $\langle x, y, z \rangle$ would not be enough. Observe that, to save space, our method does not explicitly store the time instant of a recorded position, it can be derived from its position inside the log. Therefore, 3DGraCT requires a method to manage that disappearances/appearances.

Between two consecutive snapshots $\mathcal{S}_k$ and $\mathcal{S}_{k+d}$, each object is represented by a log, $\mathcal{L}_{k,k+d}(id_j)$, where id_j is the identifier of the object. It is a sequence of codewords of the following types: (1) an integer encoding a relative movement; (2) *Disappearance* (D) codeword, which means that we have no information about the position object id_j from one time instant of $\mathcal{L}_{k,k+d}(id_j)$ until its end; (3) *Absolute appearance* (AA), which means that we have no information about the position of id_j from the beginning of $\mathcal{L}_{k,k+d}(id_j)$ until a time instant covered by $\mathcal{L}_{k,k+d}(id_j)$, where that information appears; (4) *Relative disappearance*, which means that the information about the position of id_j disappears in a time instant of $\mathcal{L}_{k,k+d}(id_j)$, but reappears in a time instant of the same portion of the log.

In order to maintain the synchronization of the sequences of values in $\mathcal{L}_{k,k+d}(id_j)$, the appearances and disappearances require the storage of their corresponding time instant. In addition, they also require the storage of the absolute position of the appearance/disappearance. The relative disappearances imply the storage of the number of time instants they lasted and the relative movement with respect to the last known position.

In Fig. 4(b), it is shown an example. The relative movements are depicted with the three relative displacements $\langle z, x, y \rangle^3$. The array $\mathcal{D}$ stores the duration of a relative disappearance and the exact time instant of absolute appearances and disappearances. For example, in $\mathcal{L}_{0,4}(1)$, there is a relative disappearance that lasts two instants, and in $\mathcal{L}_{0,4}(7)$, the object appears at time instant 3. In addition, array $\mathcal{P}$ stores the relative movements of relative disappearances

---

^{3} $\langle z, x, y \rangle$ notation indicated that these three values are packed in a 32-bit integer.

and the absolute position of absolute appearances or disappearances. For example, in $\mathcal{L}_{0,4}(1)$, the $\langle 1,4,1 \rangle$ tuple in $\mathcal{P}_{0,4}(1)$ means that the object reappeared 1 cell upwards in the z-coordinate, 4 cells to the right in the x-coordinate, and 1 cell upwards in the y-coordinate. In $\mathcal{L}_{0,4}(7)$, the object appears in the absolute position $(0,5,2)$ (see $\mathcal{P}_{0,4}(7)$). In the figure, the values are aligned to their corresponding time instants, but this is only for illustration purposes, thanks to the array $\mathcal{D}$, for one object, all the logs are stored as a sequence. $\mathcal{D}$ and $\mathcal{P}$ are compressed with DACs [3], a compressor for sequences of integers that provides direct access to any position without the need of decompressing the previous numbers.

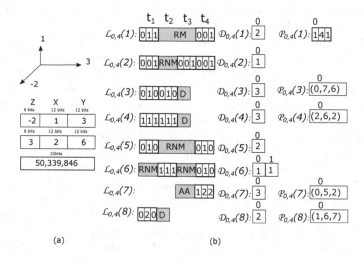

Fig. 4. The encoding of relative movements (left) and logs of objects (right).

Compressing the Log. Logs represent an important saving in space with respect to snapshots, but it is possible to obtain additional compression taking advantage the following fact: aircrafts spend most of the time following the same course at a constant speed. This situation will be represented in the logs as sequences of repetitive numbers, that is, the same relative displacements with respect to the previous time instant. These series of similar numbers are compressed very efficiently using a grammar compressor, such as Re-Pair.

To improve the query processing, the Re-Pair rules in 3DGraCT are enriched with additional information. Each rule in R has the following information: $s \to a, b, \#t, x, y, z, MBB$, where: (1) s, a and b are the components of a normal rule of Re-Pair, (2) $\#t$ is the number of instants covered by the rule, (3) $\langle z, x, y \rangle$ are the relative coordinates of the final position of the object after the application of the rule (that is, the displacement considering $(0, 0, 0)$ the initial position before the application of the rule) and, (4) MBB is the Minimum Bounding

Box enclosing the movements of the rule. MBB is represented by six coordinates $(z1, x1, y1, z2, x2, y2)$, which are the points at the ends of a diagonal of the box.

For example, in Fig. 4, in $\mathcal{L}_{0,4}(4)$, the two $\langle 1, 1, 1 \rangle$ consecutive relative movements produce a rule, $W \rightarrow \langle 1,1,1 \rangle, \langle 1,1,1 \rangle, 2, \langle 2,2,2 \rangle, (0,0,0,2,2,2)$, and then $\mathcal{L}_{0,4}(4) = W, D$. Thanks to the additional information, the non-terminal symbols of the logs do not need to be decompressed in many cases. For example, if we wish to know the position of object 4 at t_2, we obtain its absolute position in the snapshot $\mathcal{S}_0$ (Fig. 3), which is (0,4,0), and then the first symbol of $\mathcal{L}_{0,4}(4)$ (W) is applied. Since W covers 2 time instants, its application to the position at t_0 produces the position of the object at the queried time instant. For this, the relative displacement $(2, 2, 2)$ is added to the original position, obtaining the position $(2, 6, 2)$.

4   Querying

Obtain the Position of an Object. To obtain the position of an object at a given time instant t_q, first, the algorithm retrieves the position of the object in the closest snapshot to t_q. If the snapshot does not represent t_q, then the algorithm follows the movements through the log until it reaches t_q, as it was explained in the previous section, using the relative coordinates included in the rules when possible. When the nearest snapshot is located before t_q, the process follows a forward traversal of the log, otherwise, the process performs a backward traversal.

Obtain the Trajectory of an Object. Given an interval of time $[t_s, t_e]$ and an object, this query obtains all the positions of the object between t_s and t_e. First, the query obtains the position of the object at t_s using the algorithm explained for the previous query, and then it applies the movements of the log until it reaches the position at t_e. Since the additional information of the rules does not contain the detailed positions of the trajectory, the algorithm has to decompress every non-terminal value of the log containing a $t_i \in [t_s, t_e]$.

Time Slice Query. Let $r = [x_1, y_1, z_1] \times [x_2, y_2, z_2]$ be a rectangular cuboid (or box) and t_q a time instant, this query returns all objects within r at t_q. Let (s_x, s_y, s_z) be the maximum speed vector of any object in our dataset, that is, the maximum speed in each of the three axes of the space achieved by any object in the dataset. We denote $E_r(t_k, t_q)$, the *expanded region* of r from t_k to t_q, as the area that contains any object active at t_k capable of being located within r at t_q. Hence, $E_r(t_k, t_q)$ is r extended in the three dimensions; in the x-axis to the coordinates $[x_1 - s_x \cdot (t_q - t_k), x_2 + s_x \cdot (t_q - t_k)]$, and repeat the same for the y-axis and z-axis. Assuming that the closest snapshot is $\mathcal{S}_k$ and that $t_k \leq t_q$, the algorithm obtains the candidate objects $\mathcal{C}$ inside $E_r(t_k, t_q)$ at t_k. If $t_k = t_q$, the algorithm returns $\mathcal{C}$. Otherwise, it tracks the movements in $\mathcal{L}_{k,k+d}$ for each object in $\mathcal{C}$ until it reaches t_q. During this process, after obtaining the position of an object c_j at t_i, we can discard c_j if it is outside $E_r(t_i, t_q)$. The position at t_q can be given by a terminal or a non-terminal value. In the first case, we apply the movement and check if the object is within r. In the second case, the object is part of the solution when the MBB of the additional information of the rule defining the non-terminal value is completely contained in r, and the object can be pruned if its MBB does not intersect r. However, when the MBB intersects r (but it is not completely contained), the algorithm has to decompress the non-terminal symbol using the Re-Pair rule to obtain the exact position of the object at t_q. If the closest snapshot to t_q is after it, then the algorithm performs the same process backwards.

Time Interval Query. Given a box r and an interval of time $[t_s, t_e]$, this query obtains all objects within r at any $t_i \in [t_s, t_e]$. This query could be solved in a similar way to the previous one. However, to avoid large expanded regions, that lead to track too many candidate objects, the query interval $[t_s, t_e]$ is divided into as many queries as portions of log overlaps. Then, each one of these portions $[t'_s, t'_e]$ can be solved in a similar way to time-slice. First, the algorithm obtains the candidates from the closest snapshot, using the expanded region with respect to t'_e; then it applies the movements of the log. During the processing of the log of a candidate object c_j, the algorithm has to take into account that when the traversal reaches a symbol s_m that after its application obtains the position (x_i, y_i, z_i) at a time instant $t_i \in [t_s, t_e]$: (1) c_j is part of the solution if (x_i, y_i, z_i) is within r; (2) if (x_i, y_i, z_i) is not within $E_r(t_i, t'_e)$, then c_j can be discarded of the processing of the current portion; (3) if (x_i, y_i, z_i) is outside r but within $E_r(t_i, t'_e)$, then c_j continues as a candidate that needs to be tracked. If s_m is a non-terminal symbol that produces a position at $t_i > t'_e$ and covers the time interval $[t_u, t_i]$, where $t_u \le t'_e$: (1) if the MBB of s_m is fully within r, then c_j is part of the solution (2) if the MBB of s_m does not intersect r, then c_j is discarded in the processing of the current portion. (3) if the MBB of s_m intersects r, the algorithm has to decompress s_m to check if s_m involves any $t_l \in [t_u, t'_e]$ whose position is within r.

5   Experimental Evaluation

Our experiments analyze space/time tradeoffs of 3DGraCT using real-world ADS-B data. We also evaluate the use of interpolation to fill in large periods of missing data during the trajectory. For comparison purposes, we propose a baseline including the MVR-tree [17], but we do not include ADS-BI [21] because it does not provide altitude-based queries, and its inner index stores some string dimensions which are not covered by 3DGraCT.

Both 3DGraCT and the MVR-tree are coded in C++. 3DGraCT uses some structures from SDSL [9] and MVR-tree is obtained from the spatialindex library (libspatialindex.github.io). All experiments were run on an Intel® Core™ i7-3820 CPU@3.60 GHz (4 cores), 10 MB of cache and 64 GB of RAM, over Ubuntu 12.04.5 LTS (kernel 3.2.0-115, 64 bits), using gcc 4.6.4 with -O9 flag.

Dataset Details. We use four real ADS-B datasets including descriptive data of flights between different airports of Europe (see details in Appendix A). Each dataset covers a different period of time, namely *one day, one week, two weeks,* and *one month.* Positions are discretized into a cube where the cell size is 5 km in x-axis, 5 km in y-axis, and 100 m in z-axis. Since aircraft positions can contain incorrect information and they can be emitted at different time rates, we discard incorrect positions and normalize timestamps to obtain regular instants every 15 s.

Gate-to-gate trajectories are difficult to reconstruct from ADS-B data because some broadcasted positions are lost, mainly due to lack of coverage. Although we use disappearance and reappearance codewords to represent these situations, we consider relevant to understand how they affect to 3DGraCT tradeoffs. We use the original datasets to generate a new ones, where aircraft positions are interpolated when no information is available during, at least, 15 minutes. As consequence, we have eight datasets: four real-world datasets (*1D, 1W, 2W, 1M*) and four interpolated datasets (*1D-I, 1W-I, 2W-I, 1M-I*). Table 1 shows the details of each dataset. Note that the fourth and fifth rows give, respectively, dataset sizes of binary and p7zip-compressed representations.

Table 1. Dataset details.

Dataset	1D	1D-I	1W	1W-I	2W	2W-I	1M	1M-I
Time	1 day	1 day	1 week	1 week	2 weeks	2 weeks	1 month	1 month
Objects	1082	1082	1764	1764	2003	2003	2263	2263
Interpolated	No	Yes	No	Yes	No	Yes	No	Yes
Binary	7.31M	7.68M	55.32M	58.27M	115.57M	122.03M	261.01M	275.35M
p7zip	1.71M	1.86M	12.58M	13.09M	26.03M	27.18M	57.45M	60.14M
(ratio)	23.41%	24.19%	22.73%	22.47%	22.53%	22.27%	22.01%	21.84%

Compression Ratio. We define compression ratio as the ratio between the binary size and the compressed size. The last row of Table 1 gives compression ratios reported by p7zip for all datasets, while Fig. 5(a) illustrates 3DGraCT numbers for *one day* and *one month* datasets, using different periods of snapshot (120, 240, 360 and 720 time instants). p7zip report stable ratios around 22–24%, but 3DGraCT effectiveness is clearly influenced by the distance between snapshots, because snapshot encoding requires more space than log compression. Thus, the more-distanced the snapshots are, the better the results are. In our experiments, 3DGraCT reports its best ratios using a separation of 720 time instants between snapshots, outperforming p7zip in all datasets. For instance, 3DGraCT reports 22.29% for *1D* and p7zip 23.41%. This gap increases for larger datasets: 3DGraCT only needs 14.73% of the original *1M* size, while p7zip demands 22.01%. Thus, 3DGraCT is more effective than a powerful compressor like p7zip, while retaining search capabilities.

This comparison also applies for interpolated datasets. Note that, in this case, 3DGraCT reports slightly better results, meaning that missing information adds an small overhead ($\approx 2\%$) to our structure.

Query Times. Query times are averaged over the following settings: (1) *Object t: 20,000 queries* that obtain the position of an object at a given time instant, (2)

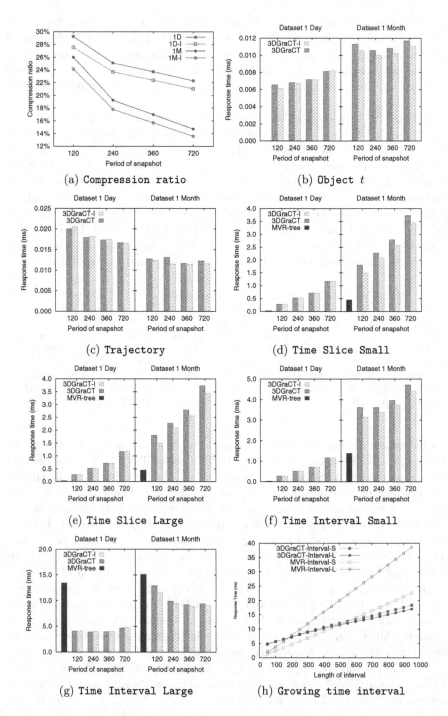

Fig. 5. Compression ratio and query times (ms).

Trajectory: *10,000 queries* obtaining trajectories that cover 2,000 time instants, (3) *Time Slice S*: *1,000 time slice queries* involving a small region ($20 \times 20 \times 20$), (4) *Time Slice L*: *1,000 time slice queries* specifying large regions ($160 \times 160 \times 160$), (5) *Time Interval S*: *1,000 time interval queries* involving small regions and intervals of 50 time instants, (6) *Time Interval L*: *1,000 time interval queries* specifying large regions and intervals of 400 time instants. Query times for 3D-GraCT over real-world (3D-GraCT) and interpolated (3D-GraCT-I) datasets are distinguished in the following figures.

Figure 5(b) shows that query times of *Object t* increase with distance between snapshots because larger log portions must be processed. On the contrary, Fig. 5(c) shows that *Trajectory* queries are slowler for less distanced snapshots because more snapshots must be checked.

In region queries, Time Slice and Time Interval, the number of candidates depends on the period between snapshots. *Time Slice* is slower as the distance between snapshot gets larger (see Figs. 5(d) and (e)), because the extended region grows and the number of candidates that are tracked is also larger. Figures 5(f) and (g) show that *Time Interval* queries behave similar to Time Slice ones, except in the right part of Fig. 5(g). In this case, the expanded region covers the whole space for each period of snapshot, so the number of candidates between different settings remains constant. Thus, traversing the log demands the same computation, but less snapshots are checked for larger periods.

Finally, it is worth noting that the effect of interpolation is not very relevant to 3DGraCT performance. It is only a slight improvement for region queries and large datasets. Thus, we conclude that the interpolation of missing positions avoids the cost of managing appearances and reappearances, improves Re-Pair effectiveness, and allows logs to be processed faster. For this reason, querying real-world datasets are 3%–10% slower.

Comparison with MVR-Tree. 3DGraCT and MVR-tree are compared over the real-world datasets of our setup: *1D*, *1W*, *2W* and *1M*. It is worth noting that MVR-Tree space requirements are 250–300 times larger than 3DGraCT one, but we tune MVR-Tree to run on main-memory.

Our analysis show that MVR-tree is only efficient for Time Slice, Time Interval, and knn queries. Although MVR-tree can obtain the position of an object at a given time instant, or can follow the trajectory of the object in a given interval, these are expensive queries.

MVR-tree can be enhanced with an auxiliary 3DR-tree [17], but the resulting structure would consume even more space. Thus, we only analyze queries where MVR-tree is efficient.

Figures 5(d) and (e) show that MVR-tree outperforms 3DGraCT in Time Slice queries. However, our structure is better in Time Interval queries for large intervals (Fig. 5(g)). We study the turning point where the 3DGraCT starts to improve the MVR-tree, by increasing the time interval length. Figure 5(h) shows this comparison for the *1M* dataset, and a period of snapshot of 720. 3DGraCT outperforms MVR-tree for time intervals over 550 and 200 time instants in small and large regions, respectively.

6   Conclusions

This paper introduces 3DGraCT, a new data structure capable of compressing and querying 3D trajectories with no prior decompression. 3DGraCT extends an existing 2D compact data structure (GraCT) to support a third dimension, enabling object positions to be enhanced with descriptive altitude data. Our improvements to GraCT are more than just improving object descriptions because 3DGraCT also enables for resolving altitude-based queries.

3DGraCT has been evaluated using real-world trajectories reconstructed from ADS-B descriptions. 3DGraCT reports better compression ratios than universal compressors like p7zip (3DGraCT uses up to 50% less space), while retaining search capabilities. Compared to traditional spatio-temporal solutions, 3DGraCT needs 2 orders of magnitude less space than MVR-tree, being competitive in query performance. Finally, we also study the effect of missing subtrajectories, concluding that interpolation is effective in different cases.

A   Appendix

The datasets used in our experimentaion have been obtained from the OpenSky Network[4]. We have chosen ADS-B messages broadcasted by aircrafts of 30 different airlines and describe flights between 30 European airports:

- Airlines (ICAO code): AEA, AEE, AFR, AUA, AZA, BAW, BEE, BEL, BER, DLH, EIN, EWG, EZS, EZY, FDX, FIN, GWI, IBE, IBK, IBS, KLM, LOT, NAX, NLY, RYR, SAS, SHT, SWR, TAP, and VLG.
- Airports (ICAO code): EBBR, EDDF, EDDK, EDDL, EDDM, EDDT, EFHK, EGCC, EGKK, EGLL, EGPH, EGSS, EHAM, EIDW, EKCH, ENGM, EPWA, ESSA, LEBL, LEMD, LEPA, LFPG, LFPO, LGAV, LIMC, LIRF, LOWW, LPPT, LSGG, and LSZH.

ADS-B messages were captured from 2017-01-02 to 2017-01-31, and sampled as follows:

- 1day : 2017-01-02.
- 1week: 2017-01-02 -- 2017-01-08.
- 2weeks: 2017-01-02 -- 2017-01-15.
- 1month: 2017-01-02 -- 2017-01-31.

References

1. de Bernardo, G., Álvarez-García, S., Brisaboa, N.R., Navarro, G., Pedreira, O.: Compact querieable representations of raster data. In: Kurland, O., Lewenstein, M., Porat, E. (eds.) SPIRE 2013. LNCS, vol. 8214, pp. 96–108. Springer, Cham (2013). https://doi.org/10.1007/978-3-319-02432-5_14

---

[4] https://opensky-network.org/.

2. Botea, V., Mallett, D., Nascimento, M.A., Sander, J.: PIST: an efficient and practical indexing technique for historical spatio-temporal point data. GeoInformatica **12**(2), 143–168 (2008)
3. Brisaboa, N., Ladra, S., Navarro, G.: DACs: bringing direct access to variable-length codes. Inf. Process. Manag. **49**(1), 392–404 (2013)
4. Brisaboa, N.R., Gómez-Brandón, A., Navarro, G., Paramá, J.R.: GraCT: a grammar based compressed representation of trajectories. In: Inenaga, S., Sadakane, K., Sakai, T. (eds.) SPIRE 2016. LNCS, vol. 9954, pp. 218–230. Springer, Cham (2016). https://doi.org/10.1007/978-3-319-46049-9_21
5. Brisaboa, N.R., Ladra, S., Navarro, G.: Compact representation of web graphs with extended functionality. Inf. Syst. **39**(1), 152–174 (2014)
6. Cudre-Mauroux, P., Wu, E., Madden, S.: Trajstore: an adaptive storage system for very large trajectory data sets. In: Proceedings of the IEEE 26th International Conference on Data Engineering (ICDE 2010), pp. 109–120 (2010)
7. Deng, K., Xie, K., Zheng, K., Zhou, X.: Trajectory indexing and retrieval. In: Zheng, Y., Zhou, X. (eds.) Computing with Spatial Trajectories, pp. 35–60. Springer, New York (2011). https://doi.org/10.1007/978-1-4614-1629-6_2
8. Douglas, D.H., Peuker, T.K.: Algorithms for the reduction of the number of points required to represent a line or its caricature. Can. Cartogr. **10**(2), 112–122 (1973)
9. Gog, S., Beller, T., Moffat, A., Petri, M.: From theory to practice: plug and play with succinct data structures. In: Gudmundsson, J., Katajainen, J. (eds.) SEA 2014. LNCS, vol. 8504, pp. 326–337. Springer, Cham (2014). https://doi.org/10.1007/978-3-319-07959-2_28
10. Jacobson, G.: Space-efficient static trees and graphs. In: IEEE Symposium on Foundations of Computer Science (FOCS), pp. 549–554 (1989)
11. Knuth, D.E.: Efficient representation of perm groups. Combinatorica **11**, 33–43 (1991)
12. Larsson, N.J., Moffat, A.: Off-line dictionary-based compression. Proc. IEEE **88**(11), 1722–1732 (2000)
13. Nascimento, M.A., Silva, J.R.O.: Towards historical R-trees. In: Proceedings of the 1998 ACM Symposium on Applied Computing. SAC 1998, pp. 235–240. ACM (1998)
14. Navarro, G.: Compact Data Structures - A Practical Approach. Cambridge University Press, Cambridge (2016)
15. Nibali, A., He, Z.: Trajic: an effective compression system for trajectory data. IEEE Trans. Knowl. Data Eng. **27**(11), 3138–3151 (2015)
16. Schäfer, M., Strohmeier, M., Lenders, V., Martinovic, I., Wilhelm, M.: Bringing up OpenSky: a large-scale ADS-B sensor network for research. In: Proceedings of the 13th International Symposium on Information Processing in Sensor Networks. IPSN 2014, pp. 83–94. IEEE Press, Piscataway (2014). http://dl.acm.org/citation.cfm?id=2602339.2602350
17. Tao, Y., Papadias, D.: MV3R-tree: a spatio-temporal access method for timestamp and interval queries. In: 2001 Proceedings of the 27th International Conference on Very Large Data Bases, VLDB, pp. 431–440 (2001)
18. Trajcevski, G., Cao, H., Scheuermann, P., Wolfson, O., Vaccaro, D.: On-line data reduction and the quality of history in moving objects databases. In: Proceedings of the Fifth ACM International Workshop on Data Engineering for Wireless and Mobile Access, pp. 19–26 (2006)
19. Vazirgiannis, M., Theodoridis, Y., Sellis, T.K.: Spatio-temporal composition and indexing for large multimedia applications. ACM Multimed. Syst. J. **6**(4), 284–298 (1998)

20. Wandelt, S., Sun, X.: Efficient compression of 4D-trajectory data in air traffic management. IEEE Trans. Intell. Transp. Syst. **16**(2), 844–853 (2015)
21. Wandelt, S., Sun, X., Fricke, H.: ADS-BI: compressed indexing of ADS-B data. IEEE Trans. Intell. Transp. Syst. **99**, 1–12 (2018)
22. Wandelt, S., Sun, X., Gollnick, V.: SO6C: compressed trajectories in air traffic management. Air Traffic Control Q. **22**(2), 157–178 (2014)

Towards a Compact Representation of Temporal Rasters

Ana Cerdeira-Pena[1], Guillermo de Bernardo[1,2], Antonio Fariña[1],
José Ramón Paramá[1(✉)], and Fernando Silva-Coira[1]

[1] Fac. Informática, CITIC, Universidade da Coruña, A Coruña, Spain
jose.parama@udc.es
[2] Enxenio S.L., A Coruña, Spain

Abstract. Big research efforts have been devoted to efficiently manage spatio-temporal data. However, most works focused on vectorial data, and much less, on raster data. This work presents a new representation for raster data that evolve along time named Temporal k^2raster. It faces the two main issues that arise when dealing with spatio-temporal data: the space consumption and the query response times. It extends a compact data structure for raster data in order to manage time and thus, it is possible to query it directly in compressed form, instead of the classical approach that requires a complete decompression before any manipulation. In addition, in the same compressed space, the new data structure includes two indexes: a spatial index and an index on the values of the cells, thus becoming a self-index for raster data.

1 Introduction

Spatial data can be represented using either a raster or a vector data model [6]. Basically, vector models represent the space using points and lines connecting those points. They are used mainly to represent man-made features. Raster models represent the space as a tessellation of disjoint fixed size tiles (usually squares), each one storing a value. They are traditionally used in engineering, modeling, and representations of real-word elements that were not made by men, such as pollution levels, atmospheric and vapor pressure, temperature, precipitations, wind speed, land elevation, satellite imagery, etc.

Temporal evolution of vectorial data has been extensively studied, with a large number of data structures to index and/or store spatio-temporal data. Examples are the 3DR-tree [14], HR-tree [10], the MVR-tree [13], or PIST [3].

Funded in part by European Union's Horizon 2020 research and innovation programme under the Marie Sklodowska-Curie grant agreement No 690941 (project BIRDS); by Xunta de Galicia/FEDER-UE [CSI: ED431G/01 and GRC: ED431C 2017/58]; by MINECO-AEI/FEDER-UE [Datos 4.0: TIN2016-78011-C4-1-R; Velocity: TIN2016-77158-C4-3-R; and ETOME-RDFD3: TIN2015-69951-R]; and by MINECO-CDTI/FEDER-UE [INNTERCONECTA: uForest ITC-20161074].

T. Gagie et al. (Eds.): SPIRE 2018, LNCS 11147, pp. 117–130, 2018.
https://doi.org/10.1007/978-3-030-00479-8_10

In [9] the classical Map Algebra of Tomlin for managing raster data is extended to manage raster data with a temporal evolution. The conceptual solution is simple, instead of considering a matrix, it considers a cube, where each slice of the temporal dimension is the raster corresponding to one time instant.

Most real systems capable of managing raster data, like Rasdaman, Grass, or even R are also capable of managing time-series of raster data. These systems, as well as raster representation formats such as NetCDF (standard format of the OGC[1]) and GeoTiff, rely on classic compression methods such as run length encoding, LZW, or Deflate to reduce the size of the data. The use of these compression methods poses an important drawback to access a given datum or portion of the data, since the dataset must be decompressed from the beginning.

Compact data structures [7,11] are capable of storing data in compressed form and enable us to access a given datum without the need for decompressing from the beginning. In most cases, compact data structures are equipped with an index that provides fast access to data. There are several compact data structures designed to store raster data [2,8]. In this work, we extend one of those compact data structures, the k^2raster [8], to support representing time-series of rasters.

2   Related Work

In this section, we first revise the k^2tree, a compact data structure that can be used to represent binary matrices. Then, we also present several compact data structures for representing raster data containing integers in the cells. We pay special attention to discuss one of them, the k^2raster, which is the base of our proposal Temporal k^2raster ($T-k^2$raster).

k^2tree: The k^2tree [5] was initially designed to represent web graphs, but it also allows to represent binary matrices, that is, rasters where the cells contain only a bit value. It is conceptually a non-balanced k^2-ary tree built from the binary matrix by recursively dividing it into k^2 submatrices of the same size. First, the original matrix is divided into k^2 submatrices of size n^2/k^2, being $n \times n$ the size of the matrix. Each submatrix generates a child of the root whose value is 1 if it contains at least one 1, and 0 otherwise. The subdivision continues recursively for each node representing a submatrix that has at least one 1, until the submatrix is full of 0s, or until the process reaches the cells of the original matrix (i.e., submatrices of size 1×1).

The k^2tree is compactly stored using just two bitmaps T and L. T stores all the bits of the conceptual k^2tree, except the last level, following a level-wise traversal: first the bit values of the children of the root, then those in the second level, and so on. L stores the last level of the tree.

It is possible to obtain any cell, row, column, or window of the matrix very efficiently, by running *rank* and *select* operations [7] over the bitmaps T and L.

k^3tree: The k^3tree [2] is obtained by simply adding a third dimension to the k^2tree, and thus, it conceptually represents a binary cube. This can be trivially

---

[1] http://www.opengeospatial.org/standards/netcdf.

done by using the same space partitioning and representation techniques from the k^2tree, yet applied to cubes rather than to matrices.

Thus, each 1 in the binary cube represents a tuple $\langle x, y, z \rangle$, where (x, y) are the coordinates of the cell of the raster and z is the value stored in that cell.

k^2acc: The k^2acc [2] representation for a raster dataset is composed by as many k^2trees as different values can be found in the raster. Given t different values in the raster: $v_1 < v_2 < \cdots < v_t$, k^2acc contains $K_1, K_2, \ldots, K_t$ k^2trees, where each K_i has a value 1 in those cells whose value is $v \leq v_i$.

2D-1D Mapping: In [12], it is presented a method that uses a space-filling curve to reduce the raster matrix to an array, and the use of one dimensional index (for example a B-tree) over that array to access the data.

k^2raster: k^2raster has proven to be superior in both space and query time [8, 12] to all the other compact data structures for storing rasters. In [8], it was also compared with NetCDF. It drew slightly worse space needs than the compressed version (that uses Deflate) of NetCDF, but queries performed noticeably faster.

k^2raster is based in the same partitioning method of the k^2tree, that is, it recursively subdivides the matrix into k^2 submatrices and builds a conceptual tree representing these subdivisions. Now, in each node, instead of having a single bit, it contains the minimum and maximum values of the corresponding submatrix. The subdivision stops when the minimum and maximum values of the submatrix are equal, or when the process reaches submatrices of size 1×1. Again the conceptual tree is compactly represented using, in addition to binary bitmaps, efficient encoding schemes for integer sequences.

More in detail, let $n \times n$ be the size of the input matrix. The process begins by obtaining the minimum and maximum values of the matrix. If these values are different, they are stored in the root of the tree, and the matrix is divided into k^2 submatrices of size n^2/k^2. Each submatrix produces a child node of the root storing its minimum and maximum values. If these values are the same, that node becomes a leaf, and the corresponding submatrix is not subdivided anymore. Otherwise, this procedure continues recursively until the maximum and minimum values are the same, or the process reaches a 1×1 submatrix.

Figure 1 shows an example of the recursive subdivision (top) and how the conceptual tree is built (centre-top), where the minimum and maximum values of each submatrix are stored at each node. The root node corresponds to the original raster matrix, nodes at level 1 correspond to submatrices of size 4×4, and so on. The last level of the tree corresponds to cells of the original matrix. Note, for instance, that all the values of the bottom-right 4×4 submatrix are equal; thus, its minimum and maximum values are equal, and it is not further subdivided. This is the reason why the last child of the root node has no children.

The compact representation includes two main parts. The first one represents the topology of the tree (T) and the second one stores the maximum/minimum values at the nodes $(Lmin/Lmax)$. The topology is represented as in the k^2tree, except that the last level (L) is not needed. The maximum/minimum values are differentially encoded with respect to the values stored at the parent node.

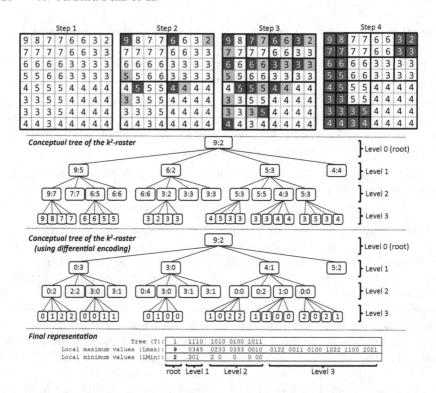

Fig. 1. Example (using $k = 2$) of integer raster matrix (top), conceptual tree of the k^2 raster, conceptual tree with differential encoding, and final representation of the raster matrix. *Lmax* and *Lmin* contain the maximum and minimum values of each node following a level-wise order and using differential encoding.

Again, these values are stored as arrays following the same method of the k^2tree, that is, following the same level-wise order of the conceptual tree. By using differential encoding, the numbers become smaller. *Directly Addressable Codes* (DACs) [4] take advantage of this, and at the same time, provide direct access. The last two steps to create the final representation of the example matrix are also illustrated in Fig. 1. In the center-bottom and bottom parts, we respectively show the tree with the differences for both the maximum and minimum values, and the data structures that compose the final representation of the k^2raster. Therefore, the original raster matrix is compactly stored using just a bitmap T, which represents the tree topology, and a pair of integer arrays (*Lmax* and *Lmin*), which contain the minimum and maximum values stored at the tree. Note that when the raster matrix contains uniform areas, with large areas of equal or similar values, this information can be stored very compactly using differential encoding and DACs.

The maximum/minimum values provide indexation of the stored values, this technique is usually known as lightweight indexation. It is possible to query the structure only decompressing the affected areas. Queries can be efficiently computed navigating the conceptual tree by running $rank$ and $select$ operations on T and, in parallel, accessing the arrays $Lmax$ and $Lmin$.

3   T$-$k^{2}raster: A Temporal Representation for Raster Data

Let $\mathcal{M}$ be a raster matrix of size $n \times n$ that evolves along time with a timeline of size τ time instants. We can define $\mathcal{M} = \langle \mathcal{M}_\infty, \mathcal{M}_\in, \ldots, \mathcal{M}_\tau \rangle$ as the sequence of raster matrices M_i of size $n \times n$ for each time instant $i \in [1, \tau]$.

A rather straightforward baseline representation for the temporal raster matrix $\mathcal{M}$ can be obtained by simply representing each raster matrix M_i in a compact way with a k^{2}raster. In this section we use a different approach. The idea is to use sampling at regular intervals of size t_δ. That is, we represent with a k^{2}raster all the raster matrices $M_s, s = 1 + i\ t_\delta$, $i \in [0, (\tau - 1)/t_\delta]$. We will refer to those M_i rasters as *snapshots of* $\mathcal{M}$ *at time* i. The $t_\delta - 1$ raster matrices $M_t, t \in [s + 1, s + t_\delta - 1]$ that follow a snapshot M_s are encoded using M_s as a reference. The idea is to create a modified k^{2}raster$'$ to represent M_t where, at each step of the construction process, the values in the submatrices are encoded as differences with respect to the corresponding submatrices in M_s rather than as differences with respect to the parent node as usual in a regular k^{2}raster.

With this modification, we still expect to encode small gaps for the maximum and minimum values in each node of the conceptual tree of M_t. Yet, in addition, when a submatrix in M_t is identical to the same submatrix in M_s, or when all the values in both submatrices differ only in a unique gap value α, we can stop the recursive splitting process and simply have to keep a reference to the corresponding submatrix of M_s and the gap α (when they are identical, we simply set $\alpha = 0$). In practice, keeping that reference is rather cheap as we only have to mark, in the conceptual tree of M_t, that the subtree rooted at a given node p has the same structure of the one from the conceptual tree of M_s. For such purpose, in the final representation of k^{2}raster$'$, we include a new bitmap eqB, aligned to the zeroes in T. That is, if we have $T[i] = 0$ (node with no children), we set $eqB[rank_0(T, i)] \leftarrow 1,$[2] and set $Lmax[i] \leftarrow \alpha$. Also, if we have $T[i] = 0$, we also can set $eqB[rank_0(T, i)] \leftarrow 0$ and $Lmax[i] \leftarrow \beta$ (where β is the gap between the maximum values of both submatrices) to handle the case in which the maximum and minimum values in the corresponding submatrix are identical (as in a regular k^{2}raster).

The overall construction process of the k^{2}raster$'$ for the matrix M_t related to the snapshot M_s can be summarized as follows. At each step of the recursive process, we consider a submatrix of M_t and the related submatrix in M_s. Let the corresponding maximum and minimum values of the submatrix of M_t be max_t and min_t, and those of M_s be max_s and min_s respectively. Therefore:

---

[2] From now on, assume $rank_b(B, i)$ returns the number of bits set to b in $B[0, i - 1]$, and $rank_b(B, 0) = 0$. Note that the first index of T, eqB, $Lmax$, and $Lmin$ is 0.

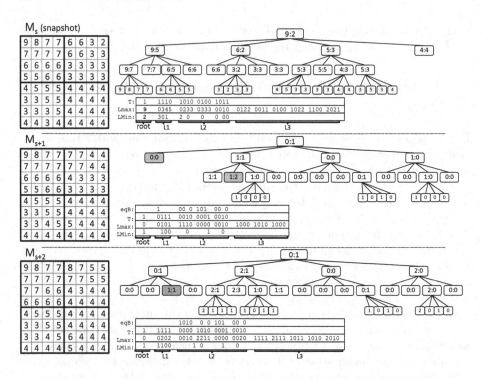

Fig. 2. Structures involved in the creation of a $T-k^2$raster considering $\tau = 3$.

- If max_t and min_t are identical (or if we reach a 1×1 submatrix), the recursive process stops. Being z_t the position in the final bitmap T, we set $T[z_t] \leftarrow 0$, $eqB[rank_0[T, z_t]] \leftarrow 0$, and $Lmax[z_t] \leftarrow (max_t - max_s)$.[3]
- If all the values in M_s and M_t differ only in a unique value α (or if they are identical, hence $\alpha = 0$), we set $T[z_t] \leftarrow 0$, $eqB[rank_0[T, z_t]] \leftarrow 1$, and $Lmax[z_t] \leftarrow (max_t - max_s)$.
- Otherwise, we split the submatrix M_t into k^2 parts and continue recursively. We set $T[z_t] \leftarrow 1$, and, as in the regular k^2raster, $Lmax[z_t] \leftarrow (max_t - max_s)$, and $Lmin[rank_1(z_t)] \leftarrow (min_t - min_s)$.

Figure 2 includes an example of the structures involved in the construction of a $T-k^2$raster over a temporal raster of size 8×8, with $\tau = 3$. The raster matrix corresponding to the first time instant becomes a *snapshot* that is represented exactly as the k^2raster in Fig. 1. The remaining raster matrices M_{s+1} and M_{s+2} are represented with two k^2raster' that are built taking M_s as a reference. We have highlighted some particular nodes in the differential conceptual trees corresponding to M_{s+1} and M_{s+2}. *(i)* the shaded node labeled $\langle 0 : 0 \rangle$ in M_{s+1} indicates that the first 4×4 submatrix of both M_s and M_{s+1} are identical.

---

[3] Since in k^2raster' we have to deal both with positive and negative values, we actually apply a *zig-zag* encoding for the gaps ($max_t - max_s$).

Therefore, node $\langle 0: 0 \rangle$ has no children, and we set: $T[2] \leftarrow 0$, $eqB[1] \leftarrow 1$, and $Lmax[2] \leftarrow 0$. *(ii)* the shaded node labeled $\langle 1: 1 \rangle$ in M_{s+2} illustrates the case in which all the values of a given submatrix are increased by $\alpha \leftarrow 1$. In this case values $\langle 6, 6, 5, 5 \rangle$ in M_s become $\langle 7, 7, 6, 6 \rangle$ in M_{s+2}. Again, the recursive traversal stops at that node, and we set: $T[8] \leftarrow 0$, $eqB[3] \leftarrow 1$, and $Lmax[8] \leftarrow 1$ (values are increased by 1). *(iii)* the shaded node labeled $\langle 1: 2 \rangle$ in M_{s+1} corresponds to the node labeled $\langle 3: 2 \rangle$ in M_s. In this case, when we sum the maximum and minimum values of both nodes we obtain that node in M_{s+1} has the same maximum and minimum values (set to 4). Consequently the recursive process stops again. In this case, we set $T[7] \leftarrow 0$, $eqB[3] \leftarrow 0$, and $Lmax[7] \leftarrow 1$.

4   Querying Temporal Raster Data

In this section, we show two basic queries over $\mathsf{T}-\mathsf{k}^2$raster.

Obtaining a Cell Value in a Time Instant: This query retrieves the value of a cell (r, c) of the raster at time instant t: $v \leftarrow getCellValue(r, c, t)$. For solving this query, there are two cases: if t is represented by a snapshot, then the algorithm to obtain a cell in the regular k^2raster is used, otherwise, a synchronized top-down traversal of the trees representing that time instant (M_t) and the closest previous snapshot (M_s) is required.

Focusing on the second case, the synchronized traversal inspects the two nodes at each level corresponding to the submatrix that contains the queried cell. The problem is that due to parts of M_t or M_s having the same value, the shape of the trees representing them can be different. Therefore, it is possible that one of the two traversals reaches a leaf, whereas the other does not. In such a case, the traversal that did not reach a leaf, continues, but the process must remember the value in the reached leaf, since that is the value that will be added or subtracted to the value found when the continued traversal reaches a leaf.

Indeed, we have three cases: (a) the processed submatrix of M_t is uniform, (b) the original submatrix of M_s is uniform and, (c) the processed submatrix after applying the differences with the snapshot has the same value in all cells.

Algorithm 1 shows the pseudocode of this case. To obtain the value stored at cell (r, c) of the raster matrix M_t, it is invoked as **getCell**$(n, r, c, 1, 1, Lmax_s[0], Lmax_t[0])$, assuming that the cell at position $(0, 0)$ of the raster is that in the upper-left corner.

z_s is used to store the current position in the bitmap T of M_s (T_s) during the downward traversal at any given step of the algorithm, similarly, z_t is the position in T of M_t (T_t). When z_s (z_t) has a -1 value, it means that the traversal reached a leaf and, in $maxval_s$ $(maxval_t)$ the algorithm keeps the maximum value stored at that leaf node. Note that, T_s, T_t, $Lmax_s$, $Lmax_t$, and k are global variables.

In lines 1–11, the algorithm obtains the child of the processed node that contains the queried cell, provided that in a previous step, the algorithm did not reach a leaf node (signaled with z_s/z_t set to -1). In $maxval_s$ $(maxval_t)$, the algorithm stores the maximum value stored in that node.

Algorithm 1. getCell($n, r, c, z_s, z_t, maxval_s, maxval_t$) returns the value at cell (r, c)

```
 1  if z_s ≠ -1 then
 2      z_s ← (rank_1(T_s, z_s) - 1) · k² + 1
 3      z_s ← z_s + ⌊r/(n/k)⌋ · k + ⌊c/(n/k)⌋ + 1
 4      val_s ← Lmax_s[z_s - 1]
 5      maxval_s ← maxval_s - val_s
 6  end
 7  if z_t ≠ -1 then
 8      z_t ← (rank_1(T_t, z_t) - 1) · k² + 1
 9      z_t ← z_t + ⌊r/(n/k)⌋ · k + ⌊c/(n/k)⌋ + 1
10      maxval_t ← Lmax_t[z_t - 1])
11  end
12  if (z_s > |T_s| or z_s = -1 or T_s[z_s] = 0) and (z_t > |T_t| or z_t = -1 or T_t[z_t] = 0) then
    /* Both leafs */
13      return maxval_s + ZigZag_Decoded(maxval_t)
14  end
15  else if z_s > |T_s| or z_s = -1 or T_s[z_s] = 0 then   /* Leaf in Snapshot */
16      z_s ← -1
17      return getCell(n/k, r mod (n/k), c mod (n/k), z_s, z_t, maxval_s, maxval_t)
18  end
19  else if z_t > |T_t| or z_t = -1 or T_t[z_t] = 0 then   /* Leaf in time instant */
20      if z_t ≠ -1 and T_t[z_t] = 0 then
21          eq ← eqB[rank_0(T_t, z_t)]
22          if eq = 1 then z_t ← -1 ;
23          else return maxval_s + ZigZag_Decoded(maxval_t) ;
24      end
25      return getCell(n/k, r mod (n/k), c mod (n/k), z_s, z_t, maxval_s, maxval_t)
26  end
27  else  /* Both internal nodes */
28      return getCell(n/k, r mod (n/k), c mod (n/k), z_s, z_t, maxval_s, maxval_t)
29  end
```

If the condition in line 12 is true, the algorithm has reached a leaf in both trees, and thus the values stored in $maxval_s$ and $maxval_t$ are added/subtracted to obtain the final result. If the condition of line 15 is true, the algorithm reaches a leaf in the snapshot. This is signaled by setting z_s to -1 and then a recursive call continues the process.

The *If* in line 19 treats the case of reaching a leaf in M_t. If the condition of line 20 is true, the algorithm uses bitmap eqB to check if the uniformity is in the original M_t submatrix or if it is in the submatrix resulting from applying the differences between the corresponding submatrix in M_s and M_t. A 1 in eqB implies the latter case, and this is solved by setting z_t to -1 and performing a recursive call. A 0 means that the treated original submatrix of M_t has the same value in all cells, and that value can be obtained adding/subtracting the values stored in $maxval_s$ and $maxval_t$, since the unique value in the submatrix of M_t is encoded as a difference with respect to the maximum value of the same submatrix of M_s, and thus the traversal ends.

The last case is that the treated nodes are not leaves, that simply requires a recursive call.

Retrieving Cells with Range of Values in a Time Instant: $\langle[r_i, c_i]\rangle \leftarrow$ $getCells(v_b, v_e, r_1, r_2, c_1, c_2, t)$ obtains from the raster of the time instant t, the positions of all cells within a region $[r_1, r_2] \times [c_1, c_2]$ containing values in the range $[v_b, v_e]$.

Again, if t is represented with a snapshot, the query is solved with the normal algorithm of the k^2raster. Otherwise, as in the previous query, the search involves a synchronized top-down traversal of both trees. This time requires two main changes: (i) the traversal probably requires following several branches of both trees, since the queried region can overlap the submatrices corresponding to several nodes of the tree, (ii) at each level, the algorithm has to check whether the maximum and minimum values in those submatrices are compatible with the queried range, discarding those that fall outside the range of values sought.

5 Experimental Evaluation

In this section we provide experimental results to show how $T-k^2$raster handles a dataset of raster data that evolve along time. We discuss both the space requirements of our representation and its performance at query time.

We used several synthetic and real datasets to test our representation, in order to show its capabilities. All the datasets are obtained from the TerraClimate collection [1], that contains high-resolution time series for different variables, including temperature, precipitations, wind speed, vapor pressure, etc. All the variables in this collection are taken in monthly snapshots, from 1958 to 2017. Each snapshot is a 4320×8640 grid storing values with $1/24°$ spatial resolution. From this collection we use data from two variables: TMAX (maximum temperature) is used to build two synthetic datasets, and VAP (vapor pressure) is compressed directly using our representation. Variable TMAX is a bad scenario for our approach, since most of the cells change their value between two snapshots. In this kind of dataset, our $T-k^2$raster would not be able to obtain good compression. Hence, we use TMAX to generate two synthetic datasets that simulate a slow, and approximately constant, change rate, between two real snapshots. We took the snapshots for January and February 2017 and built two synthetic datasets called T_100 and T_1000, simulating 100 and 1000 intermediate steps between both snapshots; however, note that to make comparisons easier we only take the first 100 time steps in both datasets. We also use a real dataset, VAP, that contains all the monthly snapshots of the variable VAP from 1998 to 2017. Note that, although we choose a rather small number of time instants in our experiments, the performance of our proposal is not affected by this value: it scales linearly in space with the number of time instants, and query times should be unaffected as long as the change rate is similar.

We compared our representation with two baseline implementations. The first, called k^2raster[4] is a representation that stores just a full snapshot for each time instant, without trying to take advantage of similarities between close time instants. The second baseline implementation, NetCDF, stores the different raster datasets in NetCDF format, using straightforward algorithms on

---

[4] https://gitlab.lbd.org.es/fsilva/k2-raster.

top of the NetCDF library[5] (v.4.6.1) to implement the query operations. Note that NetCDF is a classical representation designed mainly to provide compression, through the use of Deflate compression over the data. Therefore, it is not designed to efficiently answer indexed queries.

We tested cell value queries (*getCellValue*) and range queries (*getCells*). We generated sets of 1000 random queries for each query type and configuration: 1000 random cell value queries per dataset, and sets of 1000 random range queries for different spatial window sizes (ranging from 4×4 windows to the whole matrix), and different ranges of values (considering cells with 1 to 4 possible values). To achieve accurate results, when the total query time for a query set was too small, we repeated the full query set a suitable number of times (in practice, 100 or 1000 times) and measured the average time per query.

All tests were run on an Intel (R) Core TM i7-3820 CPU @ 3.60 GHz (4 cores) with 10 MB of cache and 64 GB of RAM, over Ubuntu 12.04.5 LTS with kernel 3.2.0-126 (64 bits). The code is compiled using gcc 4.7 with -O9 optimizations.

Table 1. Space requirements (in MB) of $T-k^2raster$, $k^2raster$ and NetCDF over synthetic datasets.

	$T-k^2raster$ (varying t_δ)						$k^2raster$	NetCDF (varying deflate level)			
	4	6	8	10	20	50		0	2	5	9
T_100	398.2	407.0	429.6	456.7	584.4	820.8	769.3	14241.3	615.3	539.5	528.0
T_1000	170.4	152.5	151.2	154.6	196.2	304.6	496.6	14241.3	435.0	344.7	323.6

Table 1 displays the space requirements for the datasets T_100 and T_1000 in all the representations. We tested our $T-k^2raster$ with several sampling intervals t_δ, and also show the results for NetCDF using several deflate levels, from level 0 (no compression) to level 9. Our representation achieves the best compression results in both datasets, especially in T_1000, as expected, due to the slower change rate. In T_100, our approach achieves the best results for $t_\delta = 4$, since as the number of changes increases our differential approach becomes much less efficient. In T_1000, the best results are also obtained for a relatively small t_δ (6–8), but our proposal is still smaller than $k^2raster$ for larger t_δ. NetCDF is only competitive when compression is applied, otherwise it requires roughly 20 times the space of our representations. In both datasets, NetCDF with compression enabled becomes smaller than the $k^2raster$ representation, but $T-k^2raster$ is able to obtain even smaller sizes.

Figure 3 shows the space/time trade-off for the datasets T_100 and T_1000 in cell value queries. We show the results only for NetCDF with compression enabled (deflate level 2 and 5), and for $T-k^2raster$ with a sampling interval of 6 and 50. The $T-k^2raster$ is slower than the baseline $k^2raster$, but is much smaller if a good t_δ is selected. Note that we use two extreme sampling intervals to show the consistency of query times, since in practice only the best approach in space

---

[5] https://www.unidata.ucar.edu/software/netcdf/.

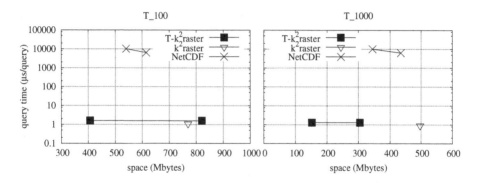

Fig. 3. Space/time trade-off on T_100 and T_1000 datasets for cell value queries.

would be used for a given dataset. In our experiments we work with a fixed t_δ, but straightforward heuristics could be used to obtain an space-efficient $T-k^2$raster without probing for different periods: for instance, the number of nodes in the tree of differences and in the snapshot is known during construction, so a new snapshot can be built whenever the size of the tree of differences increases above a given threshold.

Table 2. Range query times over T_100 and T_1000 datasets. Times shown in μs/query for different spatial windows (wnd) and range of values (rng).

		T_100					T_1000				
		$T-k^2$raster		k^2raster	NetCDF		$T-k^2$raster		k^2raster	NetCDF	
wnd	rng	6	50		2	5	6	50		2	5
16	1	3.6	3.8	2.8	6130	10070	3.3	3.4	2.5	6160	10020
	4	5.1	5.5	3.6	6240	10100	3.5	3.5	2.6	6160	10100
256	1	222.9	248.1	163.9	9610	15330	207.1	228.9	167.6	9370	15110
	4	429.3	489.4	301.7	9340	14790	213.4	234.3	172.7	9510	15240
All	1	111450	126220	78250	443830	580660	79650	89380	63350	436400	568730

Table 2 shows an extract of the range query times for all the representations in datasets T_100 and T_1000. We only include here the results for $T-k^2$raster with a t_δ of 6 and 50, and for NetCDF with deflate level 2 and 5, since query times with the other parameters report similar conclusions. We also show the results for some relevant spatial window sizes and ranges of values. In all the cases, $T-k^2$raster is around 50% slower than k^2raster, due to the need of querying two trees to obtain the results. However, the much smaller space requirements of our representation compensate for this query time overhead, especially in T_1000. NetCDF, that is not designed for this kind of queries, cannot take advantage of spatial windows or ranges of values, so it is several orders of magnitude slower than the other approaches. The last query set (ALL) involves retrieving all the cells in the raster that have a given value (i.e. the spatial window covers the complete raster). In this context, NetCDF must traverse and decompress the whole raster, but our representation cannot take advantage of its spatial indexing capabilities, so this provides a fairer comparison. Nevertheless, both $T-k^2$raster and k^2raster are still several times faster than NetCDF in this case, and our proposal remains very close in query times to the k^2raster baseline.

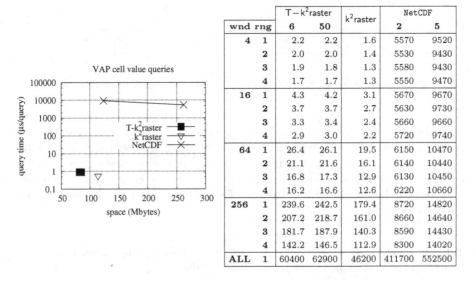

		$T-k^2$raster		k^2raster	NetCDF	
wnd	rng	6	50		2	5
4	1	2.2	2.2	1.6	5570	9520
	2	2.0	2.0	1.4	5530	9430
	3	1.9	1.8	1.3	5580	9430
	4	1.7	1.7	1.3	5550	9470
16	1	4.3	4.2	3.1	5670	9670
	2	3.7	3.7	2.7	5630	9730
	3	3.3	3.4	2.4	5660	9660
	4	2.9	3.0	2.2	5720	9740
64	1	26.4	26.1	19.5	6150	10470
	2	21.1	21.6	16.1	6140	10440
	3	16.8	17.3	12.9	6130	10450
	4	16.2	16.6	12.6	6220	10660
256	1	239.6	242.5	179.4	8720	14820
	2	207.2	218.7	161.0	8660	14640
	3	181.7	187.9	140.3	8590	14430
	4	142.2	146.5	112.9	8300	14020
ALL	1	60400	62900	46200	411700	552500

Fig. 4. Results for VAP dataset. Left plot shows space/time tradeoff for cell value queries. Right table shows query times for range queries. Times in μs/query.

Figure 4 (left) shows the space/time trade-off for the real dataset VAP. Results are similar to those obtained for the previous datasets: our representation, $T-k^2$raster, is a bit slower in cell value queries than k^2raster, but also requires significantly less space. The NetCDF baseline is much slower, even if it becomes competitive in space when deflate compression is applied.

Finally, Fig. 4 (right) displays the query times for all the alternatives in range queries over the VAP dataset. The k^2raster is again a bit faster than the $T-k^2$raster, as expected, but the time overhead is within 50%. NetCDF is much slower, especially in queries involving small windows, as it has to traverse and decompress a large part of the dataset just to retrieve the values in the window. Note that even if the window covers the complete raster, $T-k^2$raster and k^2raster achieve significantly better query times.

6 Conclusions and Future Work

In this work we introduce a new representation for time-evolving raster data. Our representation, called $T-k^2$raster, is based on a compact data structure for raster data, the k^2raster, that we extend to efficiently manage time series. Our proposal takes advantage of similarities between consecutive snapshots in the series, so it is especially efficient in datasets where few changes occur between consecutive time instants. The $T-k^2$raster provides spatial and temporal indexing capabilities, and is also able to efficiently filter cells by value. Results show that, in datasets where the number of changes is relatively small, our representation can compress the raster and answer queries very efficiently. Even if its space efficiency depends on the dataset change rate, the $T-k^2$raster is a good alternative to compress raster data with high temporal resolution, or slowly-changing datasets, in small space.

As future work, we plan to apply to our representation some improvements that have already been proposed for the k^2raster, such as the use of specific compression techniques in the last level of the tree. We also plan to develop an adaptive construction algorithm, that selects an optimal, or near-optimal, distribution of snapshots to maximize compression.

References

1. Abatzoglou, J.T., Dobrowski, S.Z., Parks, S.A., Hegewisch, K.C.: TerraClimate, a high-resolution global dataset of monthly climate and climatic water balance from 1958–2015. Sci. Data **5**, 170191 (2017)
2. de Bernardo, G., Álvarez-García, S., Brisaboa, N.R., Navarro, G., Pedreira, O.: Compact querieable representations of raster data. In: Kurland, O., Lewenstein, M., Porat, E. (eds.) SPIRE 2013. LNCS, vol. 8214, pp. 96–108. Springer, Cham (2013). https://doi.org/10.1007/978-3-319-02432-5_14
3. Botea, V., Mallett, D., Nascimento, M.A., Sander, J.: PIST: an efficient and practical indexing technique for historical spatio-temporal point data. GeoInformatica **12**(2), 143–168 (2008)
4. Brisaboa, N.R., Ladra, S., Navarro, G.: DACs: bringing direct access to variable-length codes. Inf. Process. Manag. **49**(1), 392–404 (2013)
5. Brisaboa, N.R., Ladra, S., Navarro, G.: Compact representation of web graphs with extended functionality. Inf. Syst. **39**(1), 152–174 (2014)
6. Couclelis, H.: People manipulate objects (but cultivate fields): beyond the raster-vector debate in GIS. In: Frank, A.U., Campari, I., Formentini, U. (eds.) GIS 1992. LNCS, vol. 639, pp. 65–77. Springer, Heidelberg (1992). https://doi.org/10.1007/3-540-55966-3_3
7. Jacobson, G.: Succinct static data structures. Ph.D. thesis, Carnegie-Mellon (1988)
8. Ladra, S., Paramá, J.R., Silva-Coira, F.: Scalable and queryable compressed storage structure for raster data. Inf. Syst. **72**, 179–204 (2017)
9. Mennis, J., Viger, R., Tomlin, C.D.: Cubic map algebra functions for spatio-temporal analysis. Cartogr. Geogr. Inf. Sci. **32**(1), 17–32 (2005)
10. Nascimento, M.A., Silva, J.R.O.: Towards historical R-trees. In: Proceedings of the 1998 ACM Symposium on Applied Computing. SAC 1998, pp. 235–240. ACM, New York (1998)
11. Navarro, G.: Compact Data Structures - A Practical Approach. Cambridge University Press, Cambridge (2016)
12. Pinto, A., Seco, D., Gutiérrez, G.: Improved queryable representations of rasters. In: Proceedings of the 2017 Data Compression Conference (DCC), pp. 320–329 (2017)

13. Tao, Y., Papadias, D.: MV3R-tree: a spatio-temporal access method for timestamp and interval queries. In: Proceedings of the 27th International Conference on Very Large Data Bases (VLDB), pp. 431–440 (2001)
14. Vazirgiannis, M., Theodoridis, Y., Sellis, T.K.: Spatio-temporal composition and indexing for large multimedia applications. ACM Multimed. Syst. J. **6**(4), 284–298 (1998)

On Extended Special Factors of a Word

Panagiotis Charalampopoulos[1], Maxime Crochemore[1,2], and Solon P. Pissis[1(✉)]

[1] Department of Informatics, King's College London, London, UK
{panagiotis.charalampopoulos,maxime.crochemore,solon.pissis}@kcl.ac.uk
[2] Université Paris-Est, Marne-la-Vallée, France

Abstract. An *extended special* factor of a word x is a factor of x whose longest infix can be extended by at least two distinct letters to the left or to the right and still occur in x. It is called *extended bispecial* if it can be extended in *both* directions and still occur in x. Let $\rho(n)$ be the maximum number of extended bispecial factors over all words of length n. Almirantis et al. have shown that $2n - 6 \leq \rho(n) \leq 3n - 4$ [WABI 2017]. In this article, we show that there is no constant $c < 3$ such that $\rho(n) \leq cn$. We then exploit the connection between extended special factors and minimal absent words to construct a data structure for computing minimal absent words of a specific length in optimal time for integer alphabets generalising a result by Fujishige et al. [MFCS 2016]. As an application of our data structure, we show how to compare two words over an integer alphabet in optimal time improving on another result by Charalampopoulos et al. [Inf. Comput. 2018].

Keywords: Special factors · Minimal absent words · String algorithms

1 Introduction

We begin with basic definitions and notation, generally following [14]. Let $x = x[0]x[1] \ldots x[n-1]$ be a *word* of *length* $n = |x|$ over a finite ordered *alphabet* Σ of size σ, i.e. $\sigma = |\Sigma|$. In particular, we consider the case of an *integer alphabet*; in this case each letter is replaced by its rank such that the resulting word consists of integers in the range $\{1, \ldots, n\}$. In what follows we assume without loss of generality that $\Sigma = \{0, 1, \ldots, \sigma - 1\}$. We also define Σ_x to be the alphabet of word x and $\sigma_x = |\Sigma_x|$. For two positions i and j on x, we denote by $x[i \mathrel{..} j] = x[i] \ldots x[j]$ the *factor* (sometimes called *subword*) of x that starts at position i and ends at position j (it is empty if $j < i$), and by ε the *empty word*, word of length 0. We recall that a *prefix* of x is a factor that starts at position 0 ($x[0 \mathrel{..} j]$) and a *suffix* is a factor that ends at position $n - 1$ ($x[i \mathrel{..} n - 1]$). A factor of x is called *proper* if it is not x itself. If a word y is both a proper prefix and a proper

---

P. Charalampopoulos—Partially supported by a Studentship from the Faculty of Natural and Mathematical Sciences at King's College London and an A. G. Leventis Foundation Educational Grant.

T. Gagie et al. (Eds.): SPIRE 2018, LNCS 11147, pp. 131–138, 2018.
https://doi.org/10.1007/978-3-030-00479-8_11

suffix of a non-empty word x, then y is called a *border* of x. A factor $x[i..j]$ of x that is neither a prefix nor a suffix of x is called an *infix* of x.

Let $w = w[0..m-1]$ be a word, $0 < m \le n$. We say that there exists an *occurrence* of w in x, or, more simply, that w *occurs in* x, if w is a factor of x. Every occurrence of w can be characterised by a starting position in x. Thus we say that w occurs at (starting) position i in x when $w = x[i..i+m-1]$.

A factor $u \ne \varepsilon$ of a word x is called *bispecial* if there exist $a, b, c, d \in \Sigma$ with $a \ne b$ and $c \ne d$ such that au, bu, uc and ud occur in x. The notion of special factors has been extensively studied in literature, mainly in the case of infinite words or infinite languages [4,8–10,18–20]. We extend this definition here as follows. We call *extended left-special* the factors ayb, where $a, b \in \Sigma$, $y \ne \varepsilon$ is a factor of x and cy occurs in x for some $c \in \Sigma \setminus \{a\}$. Similarly, we call *extended right-special* the factors ayb, where $a, b \in \Sigma$, $y \ne \varepsilon$ is a factor and yd occurs in x for some $d \in \Sigma \setminus \{b\}$. Factors that are both extended left-special and extended right-special are called *extended bispecial*. The following result is known.

Lemma 1. ([2]). *For any word x of length n the number of extended right-special factors is no more than $3n - 2 - 2\sigma_x$.*

By symmetry the same bound holds for extended left-special factors. It also holds for extended bispecial factors, since these are a subset of extended right-special factors. In [2], the authors provide a word with a linear number of extended bispecial factors: $\mathrm{ba}^{n-2}\mathrm{b}$ which has $2n - 6$ of them. Let $\rho(n)$ be the maximum number of extended bispecial factors over all words of length n.

Theorem 2. ([2]). $2n - 6 \le \rho(n) \le 3n - 4$.

The main algorithm presented in [2] computes statistically overabundant words of a word over an integer alphabet in linear time, by first computing all extended right-special factors of the word and then filtering out some of them based on a simple computation. We can easily adapt the algorithm to compute the extended left-special factors; the extended bispecial factors can be then retrieved easily within the same complexity. We thus know the following.

Theorem 3. ([2]). *Given a word of length n over an integer alphabet all extended left-, right-special and bispecial factors can be computed in $\mathcal{O}(n)$ time.*

2   A Lower Bound on Extended Bispecial Factors

In this section, we improve the lower bound of Theorem 2.

Definition 4. *A word x over an alphabet Σ of size σ is a de Bruijn sequence of order k if and only if all words of length k over Σ occur exactly once in x.*

By definition, a de Bruijn sequence of order k has length $\sigma^k + k - 1$.

Theorem 5. *There is no constant $c < 3$ such that $\rho(n) \le cn$.*

Proof. In a de Bruijn sequence of order k all words over Σ of lengths 3 to k (inclusive) are extended bispecial factors. In addition, by the definition of de Bruijn sequences, the $\sigma^k - 1$ subwords of x of length $k + 1$ are all distinct and each of them is an extended bispecial factor as its longest infix is of length $k - 1$ and hence it can be extended by all letters in Σ in any direction and still occur in x. We thus have at least

$$\sigma^3 + \ldots + \sigma^k + \sigma^k - 1 = \sigma^k - 1 + \sigma^3 \cdot \sum_{i=0}^{k-3} \sigma^i = \sigma^k - 1 + \sigma^3 \cdot \frac{\sigma^{k-2} - 1}{\sigma - 1}$$

extended bispecial factors. By letting $\sigma = 2$, the above formula becomes $2^k - 1 + 2(2^k - 4) = 3 \cdot 2^k - 9$. We now look at the ratio of the number of bispecial factors over the length of the sequence as k increases and have that

$$\lim_{k \to \infty} \frac{3 \cdot 2^k - 9}{2^k + k - 1} = 3$$

by L'Hôpital's rule.   □

3 Minimal Absent Words via Extended Special Factors

The word y is an *absent word* of x if it does not occur in x. The absent word y of x is *minimal* if and only if all its proper factors occur in x. The set of all minimal absent words for a word x is denoted by $\mathcal{M}_x$. The set of all minimal absent words of length ℓ for a word x is denoted by $\mathcal{M}_x^\ell$. For example, if $x = \mathsf{abaab}$, then $\mathcal{M}_x = \{\mathsf{aaa}, \mathsf{aaba}, \mathsf{bab}, \mathsf{bb}\}$ and $\mathcal{M}_x^3 = \{\mathsf{aaa}, \mathsf{bab}\}$. If we suppose that all the letters of Σ appear in x and $|x| = n$, the length of a minimal absent word of x lies between 2 and $n + 1$. It can be equal to $n + 1$ if and only if x is of the form a^n, $a \in \Sigma$. So, if x contains occurrences of at least two different letters, the length of any minimal absent word of x is upper bounded by n. In what follows, we perform the computations considering all minimal absent words of length at least 3; the ones of length 2 can be handled separately in the same manner.

The upper bound on the number of minimal absent words is $\mathcal{O}(\sigma n)$ and it is tight for integer alphabets [12]; in fact, for large alphabets, such as when $\sigma \geq \sqrt{n}$, this bound is also tight even for minimal absent words of the same length [1].

In many real-world applications of minimal absent words, such as in sequence comparison [12], data compression [17], on-line pattern matching [15], and identifying pathogen-specific signatures [24], only a subset of minimal absent words may be considered, and, in particular, the minimal absent words of length (at most) ℓ. State-of-the-art algorithms compute all minimal absent words of x in $\mathcal{O}(\sigma n)$ time [3,16] or in $\mathcal{O}(n + |\mathcal{M}_x|)$ time [23]. There also exist space-efficient data structures based on the Burrows-Wheeler transform of the input that can be applied for this computation [5,6]. In the worst case, the number of minimal absent words of x is $\Theta(\sigma n)$ and we would thus need $\Omega(\sigma n)$ space to represent them explicitly.

3.1   The Data Structure

We next present an alphabet-independent data structure that stores information related to extended special factors. It allows for *counting* and *reporting* minimal absent word queries in optimal time. Specifically, we show the following result.

Theorem 6. *Given a word x of length n over an integer alphabet, we can construct in $\mathcal{O}(n)$ time an $\mathcal{O}(n)$-sized data structure that outputs, for a given on-line query ℓ, $\mathcal{M}_x^\ell$ in $\mathcal{O}(1 + |\mathcal{M}_x^\ell|)$ time or $|\mathcal{M}_x^\ell|$ in $\mathcal{O}(1)$ time.*

Let us start with a simple but crucial lemma. It unveils the connection between extended special factors and minimal absent words (see also [4], Sect. 2).

Lemma 7. *Given a minimal absent word awb of x, where $a, b \in \Sigma$ and $w \in \Sigma^*$, either (i) w occurs as an infix of x and any word cwd, $c, d \in \Sigma$, that occurs in x is an extended left- or right-special factor of x; or (ii) wb is a prefix of x, aw is a suffix of x and w occurs only twice in x.*

Proof. If w occurs as infix of x at position i, then $x[i - 1 .. i + |w|] \neq awb$ and since aw and wb occur in x, $x[i - 1 .. i + |w|]$ is an extended left- or right-special factor; this is case (i). If w does not occur as infix in x, we are at case (ii).   □

Proposition 8. [22]. *In a word x of length n there is at most one minimal absent word awb of type (ii) (Lemma 7) and we can compute it in $\mathcal{O}(n)$ time.*

Proof. The word w must be a border of x that does not occur elsewhere in x[1]; this can only be the longest border u of x: any other border of x is also a border of u [22]. We locate u and check if it has another occurrence in x in $\mathcal{O}(n)$ time [14], thus retrieving this minimal absent word of type (ii), if there is one.   □

Main Idea. For each word w that is the longest infix of a minimal absent word, we compute the letters that precede it in x, the ones that succeed it and the pairs of letters (a, b) such that awb occurs in x. The total size of these sets is $\mathcal{O}(n)$ by Lemmas 1 and 7. If the minimal absent words with longest infix w are no more than twice the number of factors of the form awb of x we pre-compute them in $\mathcal{O}(n)$ time in total; otherwise we off-load the computation to the query.

Construction. Since word x is stored in internal memory, in what follows, we assume a constant-sized representation of arbitrary-length factors and minimal absent words of x. We first compute all extended left- and right-special factors in $\mathcal{O}(n)$ time using Theorem 3. We form their union U, assign their longest infix w as their representative, group the elements of U based on their representatives' length, and sort them lexicographically based on the representatives in each group. The sorting can be done in $\mathcal{O}(n)$ time, for all groups together, using standard tools that exploit longest common prefix information [14] and radix

---

[1] In this case, x is called *closed*. Such words are an object of combinatorial interest [21].

sort. We then identify in $\mathcal{O}(n)$ time the prefixes P_x (resp. suffixes S_x) of x of the form wb (resp. aw), where $cwd \in U$, $a, b, c, d \in \Sigma$ and $w \in \Sigma^*$, that do not occur elsewhere in x. This can also be implemented using longest common prefix information [14]. We assign the longest proper prefix (resp. suffix) of each element of P_x (resp. S_x) as its representative.

We then group the elements of $V = U \cup S_x \cup P_x$ based on their representatives' length and store them in each such group based on the representatives. We do this by inferring the representatives' lexicographical order in $\mathcal{O}(n)$ time by using the same tools. The size of V is $\mathcal{O}(n)$ by Lemma 1.

For each such representative w, we construct the following sets:

- $B(w) = \{(\alpha, \beta) | \alpha, \beta \in \Sigma \cup \{\varepsilon\}$ and $\alpha w \beta \in V$ with representative $w\}$;
- $B'(w) = \{(\alpha, \beta) | (\alpha, \beta) \in B(w), \alpha \neq \varepsilon, \beta \neq \varepsilon\}$;
- $L(w) = \{\alpha | \alpha \in \Sigma, (\alpha, \beta) \in B(w)\}$ and $R(w) = \{\beta | \beta \in \Sigma, (\alpha, \beta) \in B(w)\}$.

We also construct these sets for the single minimal absent word of type (ii) if there is one. By definition, the minimal absent words whose longest infix is w are the ones of the form $\alpha w \beta$, where $\alpha \in L(w), \beta \in R(w)$, and $(\alpha, \beta) \notin B'(w)$. We lexicographically sort the elements in $L(w)$, $R(w)$ and $B'(w)$, for all w together, in $\mathcal{O}(n)$ time using radix sort. Then if

$$|B'(w)| \geq |L(w)| \cdot |R(w)| - |B'(w)| \iff |L(w)| \cdot |R(w)| \leq 2|B'(w)|,$$

we pre-compute all minimal absent words with longest infix w in $\mathcal{O}(|B'(w)|)$ time by generating all possible awb, $a \in L(w), b \in R(w)$ in lexicographical order, filtering out awb such that $(a, b) \in B'(w)$ by scanning $B'(w)$ at the same time. We store these words in the linked list $\Lambda_1(|w|)$.

Otherwise, if $|L(w)| \cdot |R(w)| > 2|B'(w)|$, we store $L(w)$, $R(w)$ and $B'(w)$ as an element in the linked list $\Lambda_2(|w|)$. This requires $\mathcal{O}(n)$ time in total by Lemma 1; and the total size of Λ_1 and Λ_2 is $\mathcal{O}(n)$.

By definition, the number of minimal absent words whose longest infix is w is $|L(w)| \cdot |R(w)| - |B'(w)|$. We can thus maintain this information per length in an integer array C initialised to zeros, by adding this number to $C[|w|]$, for all representatives w. This requires $\mathcal{O}(n)$ time in total and the array is of size $\mathcal{O}(n)$.

Querying. For a *reporting* on-line query ℓ, we can output $\mathcal{M}_x^\ell$ in $\mathcal{O}(1 + |\mathcal{M}_x^\ell|)$ time as follows. We locate the elements in V with representatives of length $\ell - 2$. For the representatives for which we have already pre-computed the minimal absent words we output them from $\Lambda_1(\ell - 2)$; for the rest, we perform the computation described above for each w based on the sets $L(w), R(w)$ and $B'(w)$, which are stored in $\Lambda_2(\ell - 2)$. For a *counting* on-line query ℓ, we output $|\mathcal{M}_x^\ell| = C[\ell - 2]$.

Lemma 7 guarantees the correctness of the algorithm and we thus arrive at Theorem 6. If we apply Theorem 6 for pre-processing and then query for $\ell = 2, \ldots, n + 1$, we obtain the respective result of [23], which is based on constructing the directed acyclic word graph for x [7,13] and on refining the algorithm of [16].

Corollary 9. ([23]). *Given a word x of length n over an integer alphabet, $\mathcal{M}_x$ can be computed in the optimal $\mathcal{O}(n + |\mathcal{M}_x|)$ time.*

3.2 Sequence Comparison

In [11], the authors introduced a measure of similarity between two words x and y based on the notion of minimal absent words. Let $\mathcal{M}_x^\ell$ (resp. $\mathcal{M}_y^\ell$) denote the set of minimal absent words of length at most ℓ of x (resp. y). The authors made use of a length-weighted index to provide a measure of similarity between x and y, using their sample sets $\mathcal{M}_x^\ell$ and $\mathcal{M}_y^\ell$, by considering the length of each member in the symmetric difference $\mathcal{M}_x^\ell \triangle \mathcal{M}_y^\ell$ of the sample sets. In [12] the authors considered a more general measure of similarity for two words x and y. It is based on the set $\mathcal{M}_x \triangle \mathcal{M}_y$, and is defined by

$$\mathsf{LW}(x,y) = \sum_{w \in \mathcal{M}_x \triangle \mathcal{M}_y} \frac{1}{|w|^2},$$

so without any restriction on the lengths of minimal absent words. The smaller the value of $\mathsf{LW}(x,y)$, the more similar we assume x and y to be; in fact, $\mathsf{LW}(x,y)$ is a metric on Σ^* [12]. Note that $\mathsf{LW}(x,y)$ is affected by both the cardinality of $\mathcal{M}_x \triangle \mathcal{M}_y$ and the lengths of its elements; longer words in $\mathcal{M}_x \triangle \mathcal{M}_y$ contribute less in the value of $\mathsf{LW}(x,y)$ than shorter ones. Hence, intuitively, the shorter the words in $\mathcal{M}_x \triangle \mathcal{M}_y$, the more dissimilar x and y are.

One of the main results of [12] is that $\mathsf{LW}(x,y)$ can be computed in $\mathcal{O}(\sigma(|x|+|y|))$ time. In what follows, we improve this result for integer alphabets by avoiding to compute the minimal absent words explicitly. We rather exploit the connection between minimal absent words and extended special factors, and thus remove the dependency on the alphabet size—a somewhat surprising result.

Theorem 10. *Given two words x and y over an integer alphabet, $\mathsf{LW}(x,y)$ can be computed in the optimal $\mathcal{O}(|x| + |y|)$ time.*

Proof. It suffices to compute the size of the set $\mathcal{M}_x^\ell \triangle \mathcal{M}_y^\ell$, for all $2 \leq \ell \leq n+1$. We will do that by computing the number of words $awb \in \mathcal{M}_x^\ell \triangle \mathcal{M}_y^\ell$, $a, b \in \Sigma$ for each w that is the longest infix of some minimal absent word of x or of y.

Let us denote by $\mathcal{M}_{z,w}$ the minimal absent words of z whose longest infix is w. By definition we have that

$$\mathcal{M}_{x,w} \triangle \mathcal{M}_{y,w} = (\mathcal{M}_{x,w} \cup \mathcal{M}_{y,w}) \setminus (\mathcal{M}_{x,w} \cap \mathcal{M}_{y,w}).$$

This implies

$$|\mathcal{M}_{x,w} \triangle \mathcal{M}_{y,w}| = |\mathcal{M}_{x,w} \cup \mathcal{M}_{y,w}| - |\mathcal{M}_{x,w} \cap \mathcal{M}_{y,w}| =$$
$$|\mathcal{M}_{x,w}| + |\mathcal{M}_{y,w}| - 2|\mathcal{M}_{x,w} \cap \mathcal{M}_{y,w}|.$$

We further denote the sets $L(w)$, $R(w)$, $B'(w)$ for word z by $L_z(w)$, $R_z(w)$, $B'_z(w)$. By the definition of minimal absent words, we have that

$$|\mathcal{M}_{x,w}| = |L_x(w)| \cdot |R_x(w)| - |B'_x(w)|.$$

This can be computed, for all w, in $\mathcal{O}(|x|)$ time by applying the data structure of Theorem 6. We obtain $|\mathcal{M}_{y,w}|$ analogously. We thus only need to compute:

$$|\mathcal{M}_{x,w} \cap \mathcal{M}_{y,w}| =$$
$$|\{(a,b)|(a,b) \in (L_x(w) \times R_x(w)) \cap (L_y(w) \times R_y(w)), (a,b) \notin B'_x(w) \cup B'_y(w)\}| =$$
$$|\{(a,b)|(a,b) \in (L_x(w) \cap L_y(w)) \times (R_x(w) \cap R_y(w)), (a,b) \notin B'_x(w) \cup B'_y(w)\}|.$$

The quantities $|(L_x(w) \cap L_y(w)) \times (R_x(w) \cap R_y(w))|$ can be computed in $\mathcal{O}(|x| + |y|)$ time, for all w, since we store the elements of the sets sorted. We can then check for each $(\alpha, \beta) \in B'_x(w) \cup B'_y(w)$ whether it occurs in $(L_x(w) \cap L_y(w)) \times (R_x(w) \cap R_y(w))$, for all w, within the same complexity as follows. Since all our sets are sorted, we can check whether $\alpha \in L_x(w) \cap L_y(w)$ in time linear in the total size of $B'_x(w)$, $B'_y(w)$, $L_x(w)$ and $L_y(w)$, for all pairs (α, β); if so, we keep (α, β). After we do this for all w, we (globally) sort the surviving pairs based on their second element—using integer identifiers for representatives w so that we can regroup them—and conclude in an analogous manner as before by employing $R_x(w) \cap R_y(w)$. The result then follows from Theorem 3.   □

Acknowledgements. The authors would like to acknowledge the financial support towards travel and subsistence from the Laboratoire d'Informatique Gaspard-Monge at the Université Paris-Est, where part of this work has been conducted.

References

1. Almirantis, Y., et al.: On avoided words, absent words, and their application to biological sequence analysis. Algorithms Mol. Biol. **12**(1), 5:1–5:12 (2017)
2. Almirantis, Y., et al.: Optimal computation of overabundant words. In: Schwartz, R., Reinert, K. (eds.) 17th International Workshop on Algorithms in Bioinformatics (WABI 2017), Leibniz International Proceedings in Informatics (LIPIcs), Dagstuhl, Germany, vol. 88, pp. 4:1–4:14. Schloss Dagstuhl-Leibniz-Zentrum fuer Informatik (2017)
3. Barton, C., Héliou, A., Mouchard, L., Pissis, S.P.: Linear-time computation of minimal absent words using suffix array. BMC Bioinform. **15**, 388 (2014)
4. Béal, M.-P., Mignosi, F., Restivo, A.: Minimal forbidden words and symbolic dynamics. In: Puech, C., Reischuk, R. (eds.) STACS 1996. LNCS, vol. 1046, pp. 555–566. Springer, Heidelberg (1996). https://doi.org/10.1007/3-540-60922-9_45
5. Belazzougui, D., Cunial, F.: A framework for space-efficient string kernels. Algorithmica **79**(3), 857–883 (2017)
6. Belazzougui, D., Cunial, F., Kärkkäinen, J., Mäkinen, V.: Versatile succinct representations of the bidirectional burrows-wheeler transform. In: Bodlaender, H.L., Italiano, G.F. (eds.) ESA 2013. LNCS, vol. 8125, pp. 133–144. Springer, Heidelberg (2013). https://doi.org/10.1007/978-3-642-40450-4_12
7. Blumer, A., Blumer, J., Haussler, D., Ehrenfeucht, A., Chen, M.T., Seiferas, J.I.: The smallest automaton recognizing the subwords of a text. Theor. Comput. Sci. **40**, 31–55 (1985)

8. Carpi, A., de Luca, A.: Special factors, periodicity, and an application to Sturmian words. Acta Inf. **36**(12), 983–1006 (2000)
9. Carpi, A., de Luca, A.: Words and special factors. Theor. Comput. Sci. **259**(1–2), 145–182 (2001)
10. Cassaigne, J., Fici, G., Sciortino, M., Zamboni, L.Q.: Cyclic complexity of words. J. Comb. Theory Ser. A **145**, 36–56 (2017)
11. Chairungsee, S., Crochemore, M.: Using minimal absent words to build phylogeny. Theor. Comput. Sci. **450**, 109–116 (2012)
12. Charalampopoulos, P., Crochemore, M., Fici, G., Mercaş, R., Pissis, S.P.: Alignment-free sequence comparison using absent words. Inf. Comput. (2018, in Press)
13. Crochemore, M.: Transducers and repetitions. Theor. Comput. Sci. **45**(1), 63–86 (1986)
14. Crochemore, M., Hancart, C., Lecroq, T.: Algorithms on Strings. Cambridge University Press, New York (2007)
15. Crochemore, M., Héliou, A., Kucherov, G., Mouchard, L., Pissis, S.P., Ramusat, Y.: Minimal absent words in a sliding window and applications to on-line pattern matching. In: Klasing, R., Zeitoun, M. (eds.) FCT 2017. LNCS, vol. 10472, pp. 164–176. Springer, Heidelberg (2017). https://doi.org/10.1007/978-3-662-55751-8_14
16. Crochemore, M., Mignosi, F., Restivo, A.: Automata and forbidden words. Inf. Process. Lett. **67**(3), 111–117 (1998)
17. Crochemore, M., Navarro, G.: Improved antidictionary based compression. In: 22nd International Conference of the Chilean Computer Science Society (SCCC 2002), 6–8 November 2002, Copiapo, Chile, pp. 7–13. IEEE Computer Society (2002)
18. de Luca, A., Mione, L.: On bispecial factors of the Thue-Morse word. Inf. Process. Lett. **49**(4), 179–183 (1994)
19. de Luca, A., Varricchio, S.: On the factors of the Thue-Morse word on three symbols. Inf. Process. Lett. **27**(6), 281–285 (1988)
20. de Luca, A., Varricchio, S.: Some combinatorial properties of the Thue-Morse sequence and a problem in semigroups. Theor. Comput. Sci. **63**(3), 333–348 (1989)
21. Fici, G.: Open and closed words. Bull. EATCS **123** (2017). http://eatcs.org/beatcs/index.php/beatcs/article/view/508
22. Fici, G., Mignosi, F., Restivo, A., Sciortino, M.: Word assembly through minimal forbidden words. Theor. Comput. Sci. **359**(1–3), 214–230 (2006)
23. Fujishige, Y., Tsujimaru, Y., Inenaga, S., Bannai, H., Takeda, M.: Computing DAWGs and minimal absent words in linear time for integer alphabets. In: Faliszewski, P., Muscholl, A., Niedermeier, R. (eds.) 41st International Symposium on Mathematical Foundations of Computer Science. MFCS 2016, LIPIcs, 22–26 August 2016, Kraków, Poland, vol. 58, pp. 38:1–38:14. Schloss Dagstuhl - Leibniz-Zentrum fuer Informatik (2016)
24. Silva, R.M., Pratas, D., Castro, L., Pinho, A.J., Ferreira, P.J.S.G.: Three minimal sequences found in ebola virus genomes and absent from human DNA. Bioinformatics **31**(15), 2421–2425 (2015)

Truncated DAWGs and Their Application to Minimal Absent Word Problem

Yuta Fujishige[1]([✉]), Takuya Takagi[2], and Diptarama Hendrian[3]

[1] Department of Informatics, Kyushu University, Fukuoka, Japan
`yuta.fujishige@inf.kyushu-u.ac.jp`
[2] Graduate School of Information Science and Technology, Hokkaido University, Sapporo, Japan
[3] Graduate School of Information Sciences, Tohoku University, Sendai, Japan
`diptarama@tohoku.ac.jp`

Abstract. The *directed acyclic word graph* (*DAWG*) of a string y is the smallest (partial) DFA which recognizes all suffixes of y and has $O(n)$ nodes and edges. Na et al. [11] proposed k-truncated suffix tree which is a compressed trie that represents substrings of a string whose length up to k. In this paper, we present a new data structure called k-*truncated DAWGs*, which can be obtained by pruning the DAWGs. We show that the size complexity of the k-truncated DAWG of a string y of length n is $O(\min\{n, kz\})$ which is equal to the truncated suffix tree's one, where z is the size of LZ77 factorization of y. We also present an $O(n \log \sigma)$ time and $O(\min\{n, kz\})$ space algorithm for constructing the k-truncated DAWG of y, where σ is the alphabet size. As an application of the truncated DAWGs, we show that the set $MAW_k(y)$ of all minimal absent words of y whose length is smaller than or equal to k can be computed by using k-truncated DAWG of y in $O(\min\{n, kz\} + |MAW_k(y)|)$ time and $O(\min\{n, kz\})$ working space.

1 Introduction

Text indexes are fundamental data structures for string processing that allow for efficient processing of string data. Several data structures have been developed for string processing such as suffix trees [13], suffix arrays [9] and directed acyclic word graphs (DAWGs) [1,4]. Na et al. [11] proposed k-*truncated suffix trees* which are the truncated version of suffix trees that require less space than the suffix trees. The k-truncated suffix tree of y is a compressed trie that represents substrings of y whose length is less than or equal to k. They also show an application of truncated suffix trees for LZ77 [14] that compresses using a sliding window of a fixed size [11]. Later, Tanimura et al. [12] showed that the k-truncated suffix tree of a string y of length n can be represented in $O(\min\{n, kz\})$ space, where z is the size of LZ77 factorization of y.

In this paper, we focus on *directed acyclic word graphs* (*DAWGs*) [1]. The DAWG of a string y, denoted by $DAWG(y)$, is an edge-labeled directed acyclic graph obtained by merging isomorphic subtrees of the suffix trie of y. It is known

© Springer Nature Switzerland AG 2018
T. Gagie et al. (Eds.): SPIRE 2018, LNCS 11147, pp. 139–152, 2018.
https://doi.org/10.1007/978-3-030-00479-8_12

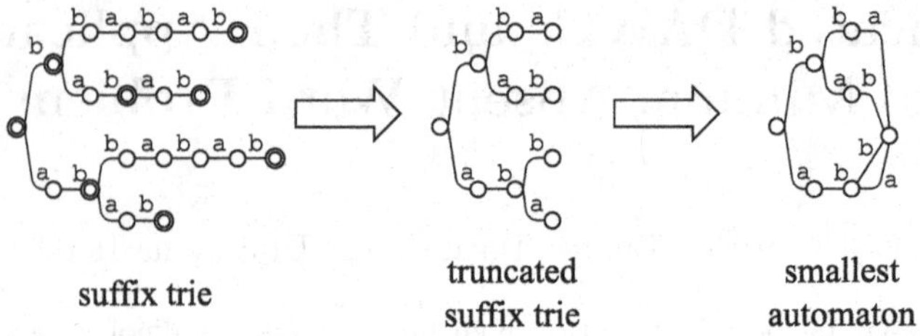

suffix trie

truncated
suffix trie

smallest
automaton

Fig. 1. The smallest automaton which represents all substrings of $y = $ `abbabab` of length 3 or less.

that each node in $DAWG(y)$ represents strings that have the same set of ending positions in the string y. $DAWG(y)$ also can be seen as the smallest automaton recognizing all suffixes of y. We can make the smallest automaton recognizing all substrings of length k or less, by minimizing the trie representing substrings of y whose length less than or equal to k (see Fig. 1). However, it is difficult to construct the smallest automaton in an online manner and sometimes it does not become small e.g. when all characters in y are different from another (see Fig. 2). This problem can be solved by representing some substrings whose length is more than k.

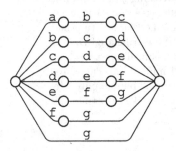

Fig. 2. The smallest automaton which represents all substrings of $y = $ `abcdefg` of length 3 or less.

In this paper, we propose a new data structure called k-*truncated DAWG*, which is the DAWG with some of its nodes and edges omitted. The k-truncated DAWG of y, denoted by k-$TDAWG(y)$, is a subgraph of $DAWG(y)$ where a node in $DAWG(y)$ is also a node in k-$TDAWG(y)$ if and only if the length of the shortest string represented by the node in $DAWG(y)$ is k or less. We show that k-$TDAWG(y)$ can be stored in $O(\min\{n, kz\})$ space, where n is the length of y and z is the size of the LZ77 factorization of y. We also present an $O(n \log \sigma)$ time and $O(\min\{n, kz\})$ space algorithm for constructing k-$TDAWG(y)$, where σ is the alphabet size. The proposed algorithm is based on the online DAWG construction algorithm by Blumer et al. [1]. We add node and edge deletion operations to the algorithm and show that these deletion operations can be performed safely while maintaining $O(\min\{n, kz\})$ working space.

For a string y, it is known that the suffix links of the $DAWG(y)$ coincide with the edges of the suffix tree of y^R [6], where y^R is the reverse string of y. We show that this property also holds between the truncated DAWG of y and the truncated suffix tree of y^R. Moreover, truncated DAWGs contain secondary edges, which do not present in truncated suffix trees. Therefore, truncated DAWGs contain more information than suffix trees for the same space complexity.

As an application of $k\text{-}TDAWG(y)$, we present an algorithm to compute the set $MAW_k(y)$ of all minimal absent words of y whose size is smaller than or equal to k by using $k\text{-}TDAWG(y)$. A string x is said to be a minimal absent word of another string y if x does *not* occur in y and all proper substrings of x occur in y. Minimal absent words have some applications such as to build phylogeny [3] and pattern matching [5]. Let $MAW(y)$ be the set of minimal absent words of y. Fujishige et al. [7] proposed an algorithm to compute $MAW(y)$ from $DAWG(y)$ in $O(n + |MAW(y)|)$ time. Their algorithm uses $DAWG(y)$ and its suffix links. This problem cannot be solved with the suffix tree of y and its suffix links in the same time and space complexity. We show that $MAW_k(y)$ can be computed from k-truncated DAWG in $O(\min\{n, kz\} + |MAW_k(y)|)$ time. Similar to $MAW(y)$, $MAW_k(y)$ cannot be computed with the truncated suffix tree of y with its suffix links in the same time and space complexity.

2   Preliminaries

2.1   Strings

Let Σ denotes the alphabet. An element of Σ^* is called a *string*. Let ε denotes the empty string and $\Sigma^+ = \Sigma^* \setminus \{\varepsilon\}$. For any string y, we denote its length by $|y|$. For any $1 \le i \le |y|$, we use $y[i]$ to denote the i-th character of y. For any string y, we denote the reverse string of y by $y^R = y[|y|] \ldots y[1]$. For any $u, v, w \in \Sigma^*$ such that $y = uvw$, then u, v, and w are a *prefix*, *substring*, and *suffix* of y, respectively. For any $1 \le i \le j \le |y|$, $y[i..j]$ denotes the substring of y which begins at position i and ends at position j. For convenience, let $y[i..j] = \varepsilon$ if $i > j$. Let $Prefix(y)$, $Substr(y)$ and $Suffix(y)$ denote the set of all prefixes, all substrings, and all suffixes of y, respectively. Moreover, let $Substr_k(y)$ denotes the set of substrings of y of length k and suffixes of y whose length is less than or equal to k, namely $Substr_k(y) = \{y[i.. \min\{i + k - 1, |y|\}] \mid 1 \le i \le |y|\}$. Throughout this paper, we will use y to denote the input string.

For any string $x \in \Sigma^*$, we define $BegPos(x) = \{i \mid i \in [1, |y| - |x| + 1], y[i..i + |x| - 1] = x\}$ and $EndPos(x) = \{i \mid i \in [|x|, |y|], y[i - |x| + 1..i] = x\}$, i.e., the set of beginning and end positions of occurrences of x in y, respectively. For any strings s, t, we write $s \equiv_L t$ (resp. $s \equiv_R t$) iff $BegPos(s) = BegPos(t)$ (resp. $EndPos(s) = EndPos(t)$). For any string $x \in \Sigma^*$, the equivalence classes with respect to $\equiv_L$ and $\equiv_R$ that x belongs to, are respectively denoted by $[x]_L$ and $[x]_R$. Also, $\overrightarrow{x}$ and $\overleftarrow{x}$ respectively denote the longest elements of $[x]_L$ and $[x]_R$.

For any set S of strings where no two strings are of the same length, let $\mathsf{long}(S) = \arg\max\{|x| \mid x \in S\}$ and $\mathsf{short}(S) = \arg\min\{|x| \mid x \in S\}$.

In this paper, we assume that the input string y of length n is over the ordered alphabet Σ of size σ. We use the standard word RAM model, thus the space complexities will be evaluated by the number of words (not bits).

2.2   LZ77 Factorization

The *Lempel-Ziv 77 factorization* (*LZ77 factorization*) with self-references [14] of a string y is a sequence $f_1 f_2 \cdots f_z = y$ that satisfies the following conditions:

- $f_1 = y[1]$,
- $f_i = y[|f_1 \cdots f_{i-1}| + 1]$ if $y[|f_1 \cdots f_{i-1}| + 1]$ does not occur in $f_1 \cdots f_{i-1}$,
- otherwise, f_i is the longest prefix of $y[|f_1 \cdots f_{i-1}| + 1..|y|]$ such that f_i begins at a position inside $y[1..|f_1 \cdots f_{i-1}|]$.

In this paper, z denotes the size of LZ77 factorization of y. For example, for string $y = $ ababbbabbba, LZ77 factorization of y is $f_1 = $ a, $f_2 = $ b, $f_3 = $ ab, $f_4 = $ bb, $f_5 = $ abbba and this factorization size is 5.

2.3   Suffix Trees and DAWGs

Suffix trees [13] and directed acyclic word graphs (*DAWGs*) [1] are fundamental text data structures. Both of these data structures are based on suffix tries. The *suffix trie* for string y, denoted by $STrie(y)$, is a trie representing $Substr(y)$, formally defined as follows.

Definition 1. *$STrie(y)$ for a string y is an edge-labeled rooted tree (V_T, E_T) s.t.*

$$V_T = \{x \mid x \in Substr(y)\}$$
$$E_T = \{(x, b, xb) \mid x, xb \in V_T, b \in \Sigma\}.$$

The second element b of each edge (x, b, xb) is the label of the edge. We also define the set L_T of labeled "reversed" edges called the suffix links *of $STrie(y)$ by*

$$L_T = \{(ax, a, x) \mid x, ax \in Substr(y), a \in \Sigma\}.$$

As can be seen in the above definition, each node v of $STrie(y)$ can be identified with the substring of y that is represented by v. Assuming that string y terminates with a unique character that appears nowhere else in y, for each suffix $y[i..|y|] \in Suffix(y)$ there is a unique leaf ℓ_i in $STrie(y)$ such that the suffix $y[i..|y|]$ is spelled out by the path from the root to ℓ_i.

It is well known that $STrie(y)$ requires $O(n^2)$ space and this bound is tight. One idea to reduce its space to $O(n)$ is to compress each path consisting only of non-branching edges into a single edge labeled with a non-empty string. This leads to the suffix tree $STree(y)$ of string y. Following [2,8], $STree(y)$ is defined as follows.

Definition 2. *$STree(y)$ for string y is an edge-labeled rooted tree (V_S, E_S) s.t.*

$$V_S = \{[x]_L \mid x \in Substr(y)\}$$
$$E_S = \{([x]_L, \beta, [x\beta]_L) \mid [x]_L, [x\beta]_L \in V_S, x \not\equiv_L x\beta, \beta \in \Sigma^+, b = \beta[1], \overrightarrow{xb} = x\beta\}.$$

The second element β of each edge $([x]_L, \beta, [x\beta]_L)$ is the label of the edge. We also define the set L_S of labeled "reversed" edges called the suffix links *of $STree(y)$ by*

$$L_S = \{([ax]_L, a, [x]_L) \mid [x]_L, [ax]_L \in V_S, a \in \Sigma\},$$

and denote the tree (V_S, L_S) of the suffix links by $SLT(y)$.

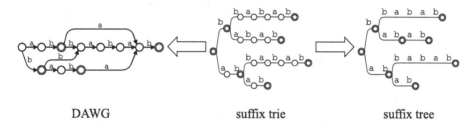

Fig. 3. $STrie(y)$, $STree(y)$, and $DAWG(y)$ for $y = $ abbabab.

Observe that each internal node of $STree(y)$ is a branching internal node in $STrie(y)$. Assuming that y terminates with a unique character, the leaves in the subtree rooted at $[x]_L$ correspond to $BegPos(x)$ for any $x \in Substr(y)$. By representing each edge label β with a pair of integers (i, j) such that $y[i..j] = \beta$, $STree(y)$ can be represented with $O(n)$ space.

An alternative way to reduce the size of $STrie(y)$ to $O(n)$ is by regarding $STrie(y)$ as a partial DFA which recognizes $Suffix(y)$ and minimizing it. This leads to the directed acyclic word graph $DAWG(y)$ of string y. Following conventions from [2,8], $DAWG(y)$ is defined as follows.

Definition 3. $DAWG(y)$ *of string* y *is an edge-labeled DAG* (V_D, E_D) *s.t.*

$$V_D = \{[x]_R \mid x \in Substr(y)\}$$
$$E_D = \{([x]_R, b, [xb]_R) \mid x, xb \in Substr(y), b \in \Sigma\}.$$

We define the set L_D *of labeled "reversed" edges called the* suffix links *of* $DAWG(y)$ *by*

$$L_D = \{([ax]_R, a, [x]_R) \mid x, ax \in Substr(y), a \in \Sigma, [ax]_R \neq [x]_R\}.$$

For any node $v \in V_D$ of $DAWG(y)$ and character $b \in \Sigma$, we write $\delta_D(v, b) = u$ if $(v, b, u) \in E_D$ for some $u \in V_D$, and $\delta_D(v, b) = nil$ otherwise. For any suffix link $(u, a, v) \in L_D$ of $DAWG(y)$, we write $sl_D(u) = v$. Note that there is exactly one suffix link coming out from each node $u \in V_D \backslash \{[\epsilon]_R\}$ of $DAWG(y)$, so the character a is unique for each node u.

An edge $e = (u, a, v) \in E_D$ of $DAWG(y)$ is called *secondary* if $|\mathsf{long}(u)| + 1 < |\mathsf{long}(v)|$. See Fig. 3 for examples of $STrie(y)$, $STree(y)$, and $DAWG(y)$.

Minimization of $STrie(y)$ to $DAWG(y)$ can be done by merging isomorphic subtrees of $STrie(y)$ which are rooted at nodes connected by a chain of suffix links of $STrie(y)$. Since the substrings represented by these merged nodes end at the same positions in y, each node of $DAWG(y)$ forms an equivalence class $[x]_R$.

2.4 k-truncated Suffix Trees

Na et al. [11] proposed k-*truncated suffix trees* which are pruned suffix trees. The k-truncated suffix tree of y is a compressed trie that represents substrings of y whose length is less or equal to k. Formally, the k-truncated suffix tree k-$TSTree(y)$ for string y is defined as follows.

Definition 4. k-$TSTree(y)$ for string y is an edge-labeled rooted tree $(V_{k\text{-}TS}, E_{k\text{-}TS})$ such that

$$V_{k\text{-}TS} = \{[x]_L \mid x \in Substr(y), |x| \le k\}$$
$$E_{k\text{-}TS} = \{([x]_L, \beta, [x\beta]_L) \mid [x]_L, [x\beta]_L \in V_{k\text{-}TS}, x \not\equiv_L x\beta, b = \beta[1],$$
$$(\overrightarrow{xb} = x\beta \wedge |x\beta| \le k) \vee (|\overrightarrow{xb}| > k \wedge |x\beta| = k \wedge x\beta \in Prefix(\overrightarrow{xb}))\}.$$

Figure 4 shows an example of k-truncated suffix tree. The truncated suffix trees is useful for LZ77 that compresses using a sliding window of a fixed size [11]. Since basic operations of suffix tree can be simulated against strings of length k or less on truncated suffix tree, it can be used as suffix trees for some algorithms such as data compression [11] and pattern matching [12]. The k-truncated suffix tree can be computed in $O(n \log \sigma)$ time [11]. The following lemma holds for the size of k-$TSTree(y)$.

Lemma 1 ([12]). *The k-truncated suffix tree of y can be represented in $O(|Substr_k(y)|)$ space, where $|Substr_k(y)| = O(\min\{n, kz\})$.*

3 k-truncated DAWGs

In this chapter, we present a new data structure called *truncated DAWGs*, that is data structures that can be obtained by pruning the DAWGs, and also show the truncated DAWGs properties. First, we define k-truncated DAWG as follows.

Definition 5. k-$TDAWG(y)$ for string y is a DAG $(V_{k\text{-}TD}, E_{k\text{-}TD})$ such that

$$V_{k\text{-}TD} = \{[x]_R \mid x \in Substr(y), |x| \le k\}$$
$$E_{k\text{-}TD} = \{([x]_R, b, [xb]_R) \mid x, xb \in Substr(y), |xb| \le k, b \in \Sigma\}.$$

For any node $v \in V_{k\text{-}TD}$ of k-$TDAWG(y)$ and character $b \in \Sigma$, we write $\delta_{TD}(v, b) = u$ if $(v, b, u) \in E_{k\text{-}TD}$ for some $u \in V_{k\text{-}TD}$, and $\delta_{TD}(v, b) = nil$ otherwise.

We also define the set $L_{k\text{-}TD}$ of labeled "reversed" edges called the *suffix links* of k-$TDAWG(y)$ by

$$L_{k\text{-}TD} = \{([ax]_R, a, [x]_R) \mid x, ax \in Substr(y), [ax]_R \in V_{k\text{-}TD}, a \in \Sigma, [ax]_R \ne [x]_R\}.$$

For any suffix link $(u, a, v) \in L_{k\text{-}TD}$ of k-$TDAWG(y)$, we write $sl_{TD}(u) = v$. Note that there is exactly one suffix link coming out from each node $u \in V_{k\text{-}TD} \setminus \{[\epsilon]_R\}$ of k-$TDAWG(y)$, so the character a is unique for each node u.

By the definition, clearly $V_{k\text{-}TD} \subseteq V_D$, $E_{k\text{-}TD} \subseteq E_D$, and $L_{k\text{-}TD} \subseteq L_D$ hold. See Fig. 5 for examples of $DAWG(y)$ and 3-$TDAWG(y)$. Because it is a subgraph of DAWG, the size of k-$TDAWG(y)$ is smaller than or equal to the size of

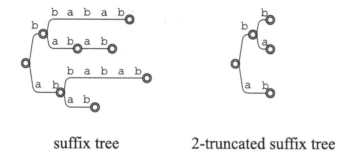

suffix tree   **2-truncated suffix tree**

Fig. 4. The suffix tree and 2-truncated suffix tree for $y =$ abbabab.

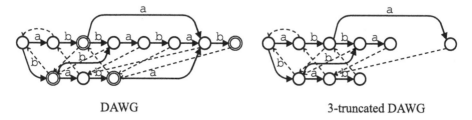

DAWG   3-truncated DAWG

Fig. 5. The DAWG and 3-truncated DAWG for $y =$ abbabab. The solid arcs represent edges and the broken arcs represent suffix links.

$DAWG(y)$. From the definition of k-truncated DAWG, k-$TDAWG(y)$ can simulate δ_D and sl_D on strings of length k or less similar to $DAWG(y)$.

For a string y, it is known that the number of nodes of $DAWG(y)$ coincides with the number of nodes of $STree(y^R)$ [6]. From the definition, this property also holds between k-$TDAWG(y)$ and k-$TSTree(y^R)$.

Lemma 2. *For any string y, the number of nodes of k-$TDAWG(y)$ coincides with the number of nodes of k-$TSTree(y^R)$.*

Proof. For convenience, let $BegPos^R(x)$ be the set of beginning positions of x in y^R, $s \equiv_L^R t$ iff $BegPos^R(s) = BegPos^R(t)$ and $[x]_L^R$ be equivalence classes with respect to $\equiv_L^R$. $BegPos^R(x^R)$ can be defined as $\{n-i+1 \mid i \in EndPos(x)\}$. Since $EndPos(s) = EndPos(t)$ iff $BegPos^R(s^R) = BegPos^R(t^R)$, $s \equiv_R t$ iff $s^R \equiv_L^R t^R$. Because $[x]_R$ to $[x^R]_L^R$ mapping is a one-to-one correspondence, the number of nodes of k-$TDAWG(y)$ is equal to the number of nodes of k-$TSTree(y^R)$.   □

By using the above property, we can show that the following theorem holds for the space complexity of k-truncated DAWGs.

Theorem 1. *Given a string y of length n and natural number k, k-$TDAWG(y)$ can be stored in $O(\min\{n, kz\})$ space, where z is the size of LZ77 factorization of y.*

Proof. First, we prove $|V_{k\text{-}TD}| \in O(\min\{n, kz\})$. From Lemma 2, the number of nodes of k-$TDAWG(y)$ is the same as the number of nodes of k-$TSTree(y^R)$.

Algorithm 1. $O(n \log \sigma)$-time construction algorithm of $TDAWG(y)$

Input: string y of length n.
Output: $k\text{-}TDAWG(y) = (V_{k\text{-}TD}, E_{k\text{-}TD})$ and $L_{k\text{-}TD}$
1 V, E and L are empty;
2 make new node v;
3 $V \leftarrow V \cup \{v\}$;
4 **for** $i = 1$ **to** n **do**
5       $u \leftarrow v$;
6   make a new node v;
7       $V \leftarrow V \cup \{v\}$;
8   **while** $\delta_{TD}(u, y[i]) = nil$ and $sl_{TD}(u) \neq nil$ and $|long(u)| < k$ **do**
9           $E \leftarrow E \cup \{(u, y[i], v)\}$;
10          $u \leftarrow sl_{TD}(u)$;
11   **if** $(u, y[i], \delta_{TD}(u, y[i]))$ is a secondary edge **then**
12   **if** $short(u) = k$ **then**
13              $E \leftarrow E \backslash \{(u, a, \delta_{TD}(u, a)) \mid \forall a \in \Sigma\}$;
14          $split(u, \delta_{TD}(u, y[i]))$;
15   **if** there is no in-degree edge of v **then**
16          $V \leftarrow V \backslash v$;
17          $v \leftarrow \delta_{TD}(u, y[i])$;
18      $L \leftarrow L \cup \{(v, \delta_{TD}(u, y[i]))\}$;
19 Output (V, E) and L;

Since $|Substr_k(y^R)| = |Substr_k(y)| = O(\min\{n, kz\})$ and the number of nodes of $k\text{-}TSTree(y^R)$ is $O(|Substr_k(y^R)|)$ by Lemma 1, thus $|V_{k\text{-}TD}| \in O(\min\{n, kz\})$. Next, we prove $|E_{k\text{-}TD}| \in O(\min\{n, kz\})$. Let $l(v)$ be $\arg\min_x\{|x| \mid x \in v\}$ for each node $v \in V_{k\text{-}TD}$. Consider a spanning tree T on the $k\text{-}TDAWG$ consisting of the shortest path from the root to each node, the number of edges in T is obviously $O(\min\{n, kz\})$. Let E be the set of edges of truncated DAWG of y not included in T. For $\lambda = ([x]_R, b, [xb]_R) \in E$, consider a function f, $f(\lambda) = short([x]_R) \cdot s$, where $|short([x]_R) \cdot s| = k$, $s[1] = b$ and $short([x]_R) \cdot s \in Substr(y)$. Since, f is injective function from E to k-mers of y, $|E| \in O(kz)$. Moreover, $E_{k\text{-}TD} \in O(n)$ because $E_{k\text{-}TD} \subset E_D$. Therefore, $|E_{k\text{-}TD}| \in O(\min\{n, kz\})$. □

4 Construction of Truncated DAWG

In this section, we present a construction algorithm of k-truncated DAWGs. As previously mentioned, $k\text{-}TDAWG(y)$ is a subgraph of $DAWG(y)$. Therefore, $k\text{-}TDAWG(y)$ can be constructed in $O(n \log \sigma)$ time and $O(n)$ working space by traversing all edges and vertices of $DAWG(y)$ and deleting unnecessary ones, but the working space is not optimal. Therefore, we propose an optimal working space algorithm that can construct $k\text{-}TDAWG(y)$ in $O(\min\{n, kz\})$ working

---

Algorithm 2. $O(n \log \sigma)$-time construction algorithm of $DAWG(y)$ [1]

Input: string y of length n.
Output: $DAWG(y) = (V_D, E_D)$ and L_D

1 V, E and L are empty;
2 make new node v;
3 $V \leftarrow V \cup \{v\}$;
4 **for** $i = 1$ **to** n **do**
5      $u \leftarrow v$;
6   make a new node v;
7      $V \leftarrow V \cup \{v\}$;
8   **while** $\delta_D(u, y[i]) = nil$ *and* $sl_D(u) \neq nil$ **do**
9         $E \leftarrow E \cup \{(u, y[i], v)\}$;
10        $u \leftarrow sl_D(u)$;
11   **if** $(u, y[i], \delta_D(u, y[i]))$ *is a secondary edge* **then**
12        $split(u, \delta_D(u, y[i]))$;
13     $L \leftarrow L \cup \{(v, \delta_D(u, y[i]))\}$;
14 Output (V, E) and L;

---

space Our algorithm is based on the online DAWG construction algorithm by Blumer et al. [1].

The main idea of our algorithm is that the algorithm deleting unnecessary nodes and edges while creating new nodes and edges similarly to $DAWG(y)$ construction algorithm. In order to construct $k\text{-}TDAWG(y)$ similarly to $DAWG(y)$, first we show the following lemma.

Lemma 3. *Let v be a node of both $DAWG(y[1..i])$ and $DAWG(y[1..i+1])$. If v does not exist in $k\text{-}TDAWG(y[1..i])$, v does not exist in $k\text{-}TDAWG(y[1..i+1])$.*

Proof. Let, $[x]_R^i$ be the equivalence class represented by v in $DAWG(y[1..i])$ and $[x]_R^{i+1}$ be the equivalence class represented by v in $DAWG(y[1..i+1])$. Assume that v does not exist in $k\text{-}TDAWG(y[1..i])$ and exists in $k\text{-}TDAWG(y[1..i+1])$. From the assumption, there is a string w such that $w \notin [x]_R^i$, $w \in [x]_R^{i+1}$, and $|w| \leq k$. However, $[x]_R^{i+1} \subseteq [x]_R^i$ holds from the definition, which is a contradiction. $\qquad\square$

By Lemma 3, we can safely delete nodes whose exist in $k\text{-}TDAWG(y[1..i-1])$ but not in $k\text{-}TDAWG(y[1..i])$ and do not need to consider the nodes that have been deleted when constructing $k\text{-}TDAWG(y)$ in an online manner. Thus, we can construct $k\text{-}TDAWG(y[1..i+1])$ from $k\text{-}TDAWG(y[1..i])$ online in a similar way to the DAWG construction algorithm in [1]. Algorithm 1 shows a pseudo-code of the proposed algorithm, provided that the function *split* is defined by Blumer et al. [1]. For strings s and t ($|s| < |t|$) which holds $[s]_R^{i-1} = [t]_R^{i-1}$ and $[s \cdot y[i]]_R^i \neq [t \cdot y[i]]_R^i$, the function *split* compute $[sy[i]]_R^i$ and $[ty[i]]_R^i$ by splitting the node $[s]_R^{i-1} = \delta_D(u, y[i])$. Figure 6 shows a snapshot during the construction of $3\text{-}TDAWG$ for $y = \text{abbabab}$.

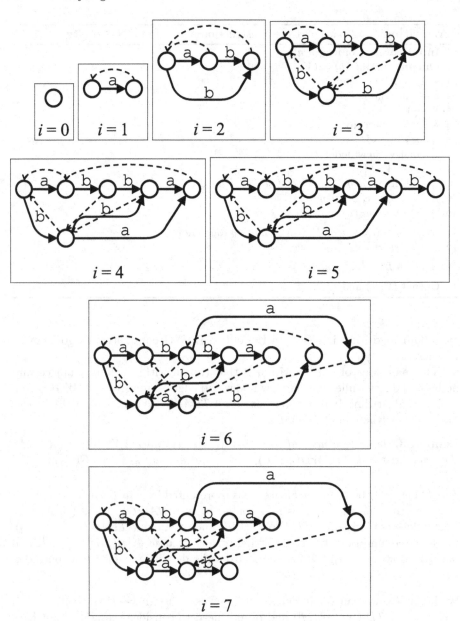

Fig. 6. Snapshots during the construction of 3-$TDAWG(y)$ for $y =$ **abbabab** on Algorithm 1.

Algorithm 1 satisfies the following theorem.

Theorem 2. *Given a string y of length n over an ordered alphabet and a natural number k, Algorithm 1 computes k-$TDAWG(y)$ in $O(n \log \sigma)$ time and*

Algorithm 3. An $O(\min\{n, kz\} + |MAW_k(y)|)$-time algorithm for computing $MAW_k(y)$

Input: k-truncated DAWG $k\text{-}TDAWG(y)$ of y.
Output: All minimal absent words of length up to k for y

1   $MAW_k \leftarrow \emptyset$;
2   **for each** *non-source node u of $k\text{-}TDAWG(y)$* **do**
3   **for each** *character b such that $\delta_{TD}(sl_{TD}(u), b) \neq nil$* **do**
4   **if** $\delta_{TD}(u, b) = nil \wedge |\mathsf{long}(sl_{TD}(u))| \leq k - 2$ **then**
5            $x \leftarrow \mathsf{long}(sl_{TD}(u))$;
6            $MAW_k \leftarrow MAW_k \cup \{axb\}$;   // $(u, a, sl_{TD}(u)) \in L_{k\text{-}TD}$

7   Output MAW_k;

$O(\min\{n, kz\})$ *working space in an online manner, where z is the size of LZ77 factorization of y.*

Proof. Algorithm 1 shows construction algorithm of $k\text{-}TDAWG(y)$ and Algorithm 2 shows construction algorithm of $DAWG(y)$. Basically, the differences between these algorithms are operations of deleting nodes and edges in line 12–13 and line 15–17 of Algorithm 1. First, we show the correctness of our algorithm. By the definition of truncated DAWGs, it is clear that truncated DAWGs moves in the same manner as DAWGs for $u \in V_{k\text{-}TD}$. For each step, because algorithm runs on the nodes u which corresponded to $y[i-k..i-1]$ and connected nodes by suffix links, any nodes v such that $|\mathsf{short}(v)| > k$ is never visited (see Lemma 3). Therefore the nodes and edges which corresponded only to strings whose length is greater than k can be deleted immediately. Thus we can construct truncated DAWGs in an online manner by adding delete operation of nodes and edges in each the step.

Next, we prove the working space in $O(\min\{n, kz\})$. The nodes and edges are deleted only in line 13 and 16. These deleted nodes and edges are made in line 6 or line 14, their size is obviously not over the size of k-truncated DAWG of $y[1..i-1]$. Thus working space complexity is $O(kz)$.   □

5   Applications of Truncated DAWGs for Minimal Absent Words

In this section, we show an algorithm to compute the set of all minimal absent words with length k or less of a given string as an application of k-truncated DAWG.

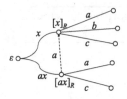

Fig. 7. Computing minimal absent words from a truncated DAWG.

For two strings x and y, x is said to be an *absent word* of y if $x \notin Substr(y)$. An absent word x of y is said to be a *minimal absent word* (*MAW*) of y if and only if $Substr(x) \setminus \{x\} \subset Substr(y)$. The set of all MAWs of y is denoted by $MAW(y)$. For example, given $\Sigma = \{a, b, c\}$ and $y = \mathtt{abaab}$, then $MAW(y) = \{\mathtt{aaa}, \mathtt{aaba}, \mathtt{bab}, \mathtt{bb}, \mathtt{c}\}$.

Given a string y, the following lemma holds for the number of MAWs of y.

Lemma 4 ([10]). *For any string $y \in \Sigma^*$, $\sigma \leq |MAW(y)| \leq (\sigma_y - 1)(|y| - 1) + \sigma$, where $\sigma = |\Sigma|$ and σ_y is the number of distinct characters occurring in y. This bound is tight.*

MAWs can be computed from DAWGs with suffix links in linear time.

Lemma 5 ([7]). *Given a DAWG of string y of length n, $MAW(y)$ can be computed in $O(n + |MAW(y)|)$ time with $O(n)$ working space.*

Let the MAWs of y which length k or less be $MAW_k(y)$. Now we show that $MAW_k(y)$ can be computed from k-$TDAWG(y)$ including the suffix links. Algorithm 3 shows an algorithm for computing $MAW_k(y)$.

Theorem 3. *Given a k-truncated DAWG of string y of length n, Algorithm 3 computes $MAW_k(y)$ in $O(\min\{n, kz\} + |MAW_k(y)|)$ time with $O(\min\{n, kz\})$ working space, where z is the size of LZ77 factorization of y.*

Proof. First, we show the correctness of our algorithm. For any node u of k-$TDAWG(y)$ where $\mathsf{short}(u)$ is less than k, $EndPos(sl_D(u)) \supset EndPos(u)$ holds since every string in $sl_D(u)$ is a suffix of the strings in u. Thus, if there is an out-edge of u labeled c, then there is an out-edge of $sl_D(u)$ labeled c. Hence, the task is to find every character b such that there is an out-edge of $sl_D(u)$ labeled b but there is no out-edge of u labeled b. The for loop of Line 3 of Algorithm 3 tests all such characters and only those. Hence, Algorithm 3 computes $MAW_k(y)$ correctly.

Let Fig. 7 shows k-$TDAWG(y)$. The string ax occurs in y, $ax \not\equiv_R x$ and $[x]_R$ has out-going edges labeled a, b, and c. So xa, xb, and xc occur in y. On the other hand, $[ax]_R$ has out-going edges labeled a and c, but not b, i.e. axa and axc occur in y and axb not. Because ax and xb occur in y and axb not, axb is a minimal absent word of y.

Second, we analyze the efficiency of our algorithm. As mentioned above, minimal absent words of length 1 for y can be found in $O(n + \sigma)$ time and $O(1)$ working space. By Lemma 4, $\sigma \leq |MAW_k(y)|$ and hence the σ-term is dominated by the output size $|MAW_k(y)|$. Now we consider the cost of finding minimal absent words of length at least 2 and k or less by Algorithm 3. Let b be any character such that there is an out-edge e of $sl_{TD}(u)$ labeled b.

There are two cases: (1) If there is no out-edge of u labeled b, then we output a MAW, so we can charge the cost to check e to an output. (2) If there is an out-edge e' of u labeled b, then the trick is that we can charge the cost to check e to e'. Since each node u has exactly one suffix link going out from it, each out-edge of u is charged only once in Case (2). Moreover, since the out-edges of every node u and those of $sl_{TD}(u)$ are both sorted, we can compute their difference for every node u in k-$TDAWG(y)$ in overall $O(\min\{n, kz\})$ time. Overall, Algorithm 3 runs in $O(\min\{n, kz\} + |MAW_k(y)|)$ time. The space requirement is clearly $O(\min\{n, kz\})$.   □

6   Conclusion

In this paper, we proposed a new data structure called truncated DAWGs. We show that the k-truncated DAWG of y, denoted by k-$TDAWG(y)$, is a subgraph of $DAWG(y)$, and can be stored in $O(\min\{n, kz\})$ space. We also present an $O(n \log \sigma)$ time and $O(\min\{n, kz\})$ space algorithm for constructing k-$TDAWG(y)$, where n is the length of y, σ is the alphabet size, and z is the size of LZ77 factorization of y. As an application of k-$TDAWG(y)$, we present an $O(\min\{n, kz\} + |MAW_k(y)|)$ time algorithm to compute the set $MAW_k(y)$ of all minimal absent words of y whose size is smaller than or equal to k by using k-$TDAWG(y)$.

Our future work is to find a way to construct truncated DAWGs in $O(\min\{n, kz\})$ time by using compressed strings such as LZ77 factorization.

Acknowledgements. We thank the organizers of StringMasters in Fukuoka, 2016, where we had fruitful discussions on this topic.

References

1. Blumer, A., Blumer, J., Haussler, D., Ehrenfeucht, A., Chen, M.T., Seiferas, J.I.: The smallest automaton recognizing the subwords of a text. Theor. Comput. Sci. **40**, 31–55 (1985)
2. Blumer, A., Blumer, J., Haussler, D., McConnell, R.M., Ehrenfeucht, A.: Complete inverted files for efficient text retrieval and analysis. J. ACM **34**(3), 578–595 (1987)
3. Chairungsee, S., Crochemore, M.: Using minimal absent words to build phylogeny. Theor. Comput. Sci. **450**, 109–116 (2012). https://doi.org/10.1016/j.tcs.2012.04.031
4. Crochemore, M.: Transducers and repetitions. Theor. Comput. Sci. **45**(1), 63–86 (1986)
5. Crochemore, M., Héliou, A., Kucherov, G., Mouchard, L., Pissis, S.P., Ramusat, Y.: Minimal absent words in a sliding window and applications to on-line pattern matching. In: Klasing, R., Zeitoun, M. (eds.) FCT 2017. LNCS, vol. 10472, pp. 164–176. Springer, Heidelberg (2017). https://doi.org/10.1007/978-3-662-55751-8_14
6. Crochemore, M., Rytter, W.: Jewels of Stringology. World Scientific Publishing Co., Pte. Ltd., Singapore (2002)

7. Fujishige, Y., Tsujimaru, Y., Inenaga, S., Bannai, H., Takeda, M.: Computing DAWGs and minimal absent words in linear time for integer alphabets. In: 41st International Symposium on Mathematical Foundations of Computer Science, MFCS 2016, 22–26 August 2016, Kraków, Poland, pp. 38:1–38:14 (2016). https://doi.org/10.4230/LIPIcs.MFCS.2016.38

8. Inenaga, S., et al.: On-line construction of compact directed acyclic word graphs. Discret. Appl. Math. **146**(2), 156–179 (2005)

9. Manber, U., Myers, E.W.: Suffix arrays: a new method for on-line string searches. SIAM J. Comput. **22**(5), 935–948 (1993)

10. Mignosi, F., Restivo, A., Sciortino, M.: Words and forbidden factors. Theor. Comput. Sci. **273**(1–2), 99–117 (2002)

11. Na, J.C., Apostolico, A., Iliopoulos, C.S., Park, K.: Truncated suffix trees and their application to data compression. Theor. Comput. Sci. **304**(1–3), 87–101 (2003). https://doi.org/10.1016/S0304-3975(03)00053-7

12. Tanimura, Y., Nishimoto, T., Bannai, H., Inenaga, S., Takeda, M.: Small-space LCE data structure with constant-time queries. In: 42nd International Symposium on Mathematical Foundations of Computer Science, MFCS 2017, 21–25 August 2017, Aalborg, Denmark, pp. 10:1–10:15 (2017). https://doi.org/10.4230/LIPIcs.MFCS.2017.10

13. Weiner, P.: Linear pattern matching algorithms. In: 14th Annual Symposium on Switching and Automata Theory, 15–17 October 1973, Iowa City, Iowa, USA, pp. 1–11 (1973)

14. Ziv, J., Lempel, A.: A universal algorithm for sequential data compression. IEEE Trans. Inf. Theory IT **23**(3), 337–343 (1977)

The Colored Longest Common Prefix Array Computed via Sequential Scans

Fabio Garofalo[1], Giovanna Rosone[2($\boxtimes$)], Marinella Sciortino[1], and Davide Verzotto[2]

[1] University of Palermo, Palermo, Italy
`garofalo_uni@yahoo.it, marinella.sciortino@unipa.it`
[2] University of Pisa, Pisa, Italy
`giovanna.rosone@unipi.it, davide.verzotto@di.unipi.it`

Abstract. Due to the increased availability of large datasets of biological sequences, tools for sequence comparison are now relying on efficient alignment-free approaches to a greater extent. Most alignment-free approaches require the computation of statistics when comparing sequences, even if such computations may not scale well in in internal memory when very large collections of long sequences are considered. In this paper, we present a new conceptual data structure, the *colored longest common prefix array* (cLCP), that allows to efficiently tackle several problems with an alignment-free approach. In fact, we show that such a data structure can be computed via sequential scans in semi-external memory. By using cLCP, we propose an efficient lightweight strategy to solve the *multi-string Average Common Substring (ACS) problem*, that consists in the pairwise comparison of a single string against a collection of m strings simultaneously, in order to obtain m ACS induced distances. Experimental results confirm the high practical efficiency of our approach.

Keywords: Longest common prefix · Average Common Substring
Matching statistics · Burrows-Wheeler transform
Alignment-free methods

1 Introduction

The rapid increase in the availability of large sets of biological sequences observed in the last two decades, particularly triggered by the human sequencing project, posed several challenges in the analysis of such data. So far, traditional methods based on sequence alignment worked well for small and closely related sequences, but scaling these approaches up to multiple divergent sequences, especially of large genomes and proteomes, is a difficult task. To keep pace with this, several

G.R. and M.S. are partially supported and D.V. is supported by the project Italian MIUR-SIR CMACBioSeq ("Combinatorial methods for analysis and compression of biological sequences") grant n. RBSI146R5L.

T. Gagie et al. (Eds.): SPIRE 2018, LNCS 11147, pp. 153–167, 2018.
https://doi.org/10.1007/978-3-030-00479-8_13

algorithms that go beyond the concept of sequence alignment have been developed, called alignment-free [37]. Alignment-free approaches have been explored in several large-scale biological applications ranging, for instance, from DNA sequence comparison [12,14,17,21,29,30] to whole-genome phylogeny construction [13,15,25,35,36] and the classification of protein sequences [14,18]. Most alignment-free approaches aforementioned require, each with its own specific approach and with the use of appropriate data structures, the computation of statistics of the sequences of the analyzed collections. However, it is interesting to note that the increasing number of completely sequenced genomes is causing the computation of many statistics that do not scale well in internal memory, determining the need for lightweight strategies for the comparative analysis of very large collections of long sequences.

In this paper, we propose a new conceptual data structure, the *colored longest common prefix array* (cLCP), that implicitly stores all the information necessary to compute statistics on distinguishing, repeating, or matching substrings within a collection or different collections of strings. Loosely speaking, given a collection S, in which each string (or subset of strings) is identified by a specific color, we can generally define cLCP as an integer array representing the longest common prefix between any specific suffix of a string $s_r \in S$ and the nearest suffixes of a specific string $s_t \in S$ in the sorted list of suffixes of S. Here, we assume that S is partitioned in two subsets and consider the comparison of suffixes of strings belonging to different subsets, but we remark that one can consider any situation and note also that the definition can be easily adapted to more than two sets. We also show that cLCP can be computed via sequential scans and therefore acquires the characteristics of an appropriate structure for analyzing large collections of strings stored in external memory.

cLCP can be used in several application contexts. In this paper we explore the multi-string Average Common Substring (ACS) [36] problem. More specifically, the ACS measure is a simple and effective alignment-free method for pairwise string comparison [13,35], based on the concept of *matching statistics* (MS) [12, 15,24,30]. Given two strings s and t, it can be defined by the arrays $MS(s,t)$ and $MS(t,s)$, which store, at each position i, the length of the longest substring that starts at position i of the string given as first parameter that is also a substring of the string given as second parameter.

ACS approach has been employed in several biological applications [15,16, 19,25,36]. Generalization of measures based on longest matches with mismatches have been proposed in [7], also with distributed approaches [23]. Similarly to [33], we define the *multi-string* ACS *problem* as the pairwise comparison of a single string, say $s_\chi \in S^0$ of length n_χ, against a set of m strings, say $s_r \in S^1$ with $1 \leq r \leq m$, by considering the strings in S^1 all together, in order to obtain m ACS induced distances at once. A major bottleneck in the computation (and application) of ACS and MS initially consisted in the construction of a suffix tree. More recent approaches use efficient indexing structures [9], CDAWG [10], backward search [30] or enhanced suffix arrays [25]. However, to the best of our knowledge, the above mentioned approaches would require a great effort, especially in terms of RAM space, when applied to compare very large collections of long strings.

In this paper we use cLCP to efficiently solve the above mentioned multi-string ACS problem. Preliminary experimental results show that our algorithm is a competitive tool for the lightweight simultaneous computation of pairwise distances between a single string and all strings in another collection, allowing us to suppose that this data structure and its computational strategy can be used for more general versions of the multi-string ACS problem.

2   Preliminaries

Let $\Sigma = \{c_1, c_2, \ldots, c_\sigma\}$ be a finite ordered alphabet with $c_1 < c_2 < \ldots < c_\sigma$, where $<$ denotes the standard lexicographic order. We consider finite strings such as $s \in \Sigma^*$, where $s[1], s[2], \ldots, s[n]$ denote its characters and $|s| = n$ its length. A *substring* of a string s is written as $s[i,j] = s[i] \cdots s[j]$, with a substring $s[1,j]$ being called a *prefix*, while a substring $s[i,n]$ is referred to as a *suffix*. A range is delimited by a square bracket if the correspondent endpoint is included, whereas a parenthesis means that the endpoint is excluded.

The BWT [11] is a well known reversible string transformation widely used in data compression. The BWT can be extended to a collection of strings $\mathcal{S} = \{s_1, s_2, \ldots, s_m\}$. Such an extension, known as EBWT or multi-string BWT, is a reversible transformation that produces a string (denoted by $\mathsf{ebwt}(\mathcal{S})$) that is a permutation of the characters of all strings in $\mathcal{S}$ [28]. Lightweight implementations of EBWT have been proposed [8,22,26]. We append to each string s_i of length n_i a distinct end-marker symbol $\$_i < c_1$ (for implementation purposes, we could simply use a unique end-marker $\$$ for all strings in $\mathcal{S}$). The output string $\mathsf{ebwt}(\mathcal{S})$ is the concatenation of the symbols (circularly) preceding each suffix of the strings in $\mathcal{S}$, sorted according to the lexicographic order. More in detail, the length of $\mathsf{ebwt}(\mathcal{S})$ is denoted by $N = \sum_{i=1}^m n_i + m$ and $\mathsf{ebwt}(\mathcal{S})[i] = x$, with $1 \leq i \leq N$, if x circularly precedes the i-th suffix $s_j[k, n_j + 1]$ (for some $1 \leq j \leq m$ and $1 \leq k \leq n_j + 1$), according to the lexicographic sorting of the suffixes of all strings in $\mathcal{S}$. In this case we say the suffix $s_j[k, n_j+1]$ is associated with the position i in $\mathsf{ebwt}(\mathcal{S})$. We can associate to each string $s_i \in \mathcal{S}$ a color i in $ID = \{1, 2, \ldots, m\}$. The output string $\mathsf{ebwt}(\mathcal{S})$, enhanced with the array $\mathsf{id}(\mathcal{S})$ of length N where $\mathsf{id}(\mathcal{S})[i] = r$, with $1 \leq r \leq m$ and $1 \leq i \leq N$, if $\mathsf{ebwt}(\mathcal{S})[i]$ is a symbol of the string $s_r \in \mathcal{S}$, is called *colored* EBWT.

The *longest common prefix* (LCP) array of the collection $\mathcal{S}$ [20,26,32] is the array $\mathsf{lcp}(\mathcal{S})$ of length $N + 1$, such that $\mathsf{lcp}(\mathcal{S})[i]$, with $2 \leq i \leq N$, is the length of the longest common prefix between the suffixes associated to the positions i and $i - 1$ in $\mathsf{ebwt}(\mathcal{S})$ and $\mathsf{lcp}(\mathcal{S})[1] = \mathsf{lcp}(\mathcal{S})[N + 1] = -1$ set by default. We denote by $\mathrm{LCP}(i,j)$ the length of the LCP between the suffixes associated with positions i and j in $\mathsf{ebwt}(\mathcal{S})$, i.e. $\min\{\mathsf{lcp}(\mathcal{S})[l] : i < l \leq j\}$. An interval $[i,j]$ with $1 \leq i < j \leq N$, is an k-*lcp interval* if $\mathsf{lcp}(\mathcal{S})[i] < k$, $\mathrm{LCP}(i,j) = k$, $\mathsf{lcp}(\mathcal{S})[j + 1] < k$. The set $\mathcal{S}$ will be later omitted if it is clear from the context.

3   Colored Longest Common Prefix Array

In this section we present a novel data structure, the *colored longest common prefix* array (cLCP). Loosely speaking, the cLCP array represents the longest common prefix between a suffix that belongs to a string of the collection $\mathcal{S}$ and the nearest suffixes belonging to another string of $\mathcal{S}$, in the list of sorted suffixes of $\mathcal{S}$. In this paper, for simplicity of description, we assume that $\mathcal{S}$ is partitioned into two subsets and consider the comparison of suffixes of strings belonging to different subsets, but we remark that one can consider any situation and note also that the definition can be easily adapted for more than two sets.

For $i = 1, \ldots, N$ and $t = 1, \ldots m$, let $prev(i, t) = \max\{x \,|\, 1 \leq x < i, \mathrm{id}(\mathcal{S})[x] = t\}$ and $next(i, t) = \min\{x \,|\, i < x \leq N, \mathrm{id}(\mathcal{S})[x] = t\}$ (if such an x exists, and null otherwise).

In order to give the notion of the cLCP array, we first define the *Upper colored LCP array* (UcLCP) and the *Lower colored LCP array* (LcLCP), as follows.

Definition 1. *The* upper *(resp.* lower*) colored longest common prefix array (UcLCP) (resp. LcLCP) is a $(N \times m)$-integer array where, for each $i_r \in \{1, 2, \ldots, N\}$ with $id[i_r] = r$ and $t \in ID$, $\mathsf{UcLCP}[i_r][t] = \mathrm{LCP}(prev(i_r, t), i_r)$ (resp. $\mathsf{LcLCP}[i_r][t] = \mathrm{LCP}(i_r, next(i_r, t)))$. Both $\mathrm{LCP}(\mathtt{null}, i_r)$ and $\mathrm{LCP}(i_r, \mathtt{null})$ are set equal to 0.*

Definition 2. *The* colored longest common prefix *array (cLCP) is a $(N \times m)$-integer array where, for each $i_r \in \{1, 2, \ldots, N\}$ with $id[i_r] = r$ and $t \in ID$, $\mathsf{cLCP}[i_r][t] = \max(\mathsf{UcLCP}[i_r][t], \mathsf{LcLCP}[i_r][t])$.*

For simplicity UcLCP, LcLCP, and cLCP are also defined when $r = t$. For all i_r such that $id[i_r] = r$, $\mathsf{UcLCP}[i_r][t]$ coincides with the corresponding value in the usual $\mathrm{lcp}(\{s_r\})$. As mentioned before, the notion of UcLCP, LcLCP, and cLCP can be also given for a pair of disjoint collections of strings $\mathcal{S}^0$ and $\mathcal{S}^1$ by obtaining an array defined for the pairs (i_r, t), where $id[i_r] = r$ and $t \in ID$ such that s_r and s_t belong to a different collection.

A given string $s_\chi \in \mathcal{S}^0$ with color χ implicitly induces a partition of $\mathrm{lcp}(\mathcal{S})$ into open intervals delimited by consecutive suffixes having color χ (or the positions 1 and $N+1$ of lcp), called χ-*intervals*. Let us consider a position i_r contained within a χ-interval such that $id[i_r] = r$ and $s_r \in \mathcal{S}^1$. Then, we can use a similar procedure as the one employed in [25], such that

$$\mathsf{UcLCP}[i_r][\chi] = \mathrm{LCP}(prev(i_r, \chi), i_r) = \min\{\mathrm{lcp}[x] : prev(i_r, \chi) < x \leq i_r\}, \quad (1)$$
$$\mathsf{LcLCP}[i_r][\chi] = \mathrm{LCP}(i_r, next(i_r, \chi)) = \min\{\mathrm{lcp}[x] : i_r < x \leq next(i_r, \chi)\}. \quad (2)$$

Additionally, we notice that there exists a relationship between the values of UcLCP related to the suffixes of s_r and the values of LcLCP related to the suffixes of s_χ. Indeed, if j_χ is a position where $id[j_\chi] = \chi$, then

$$\mathsf{LcLCP}[j_\chi][r] = \mathrm{LCP}(j_\chi, next(j_\chi, r)) = \mathsf{UcLCP}[next(j_\chi, r)][\chi]. \quad (3)$$

Table 1. Let $\Sigma = \{A, C, G, T\}$, $s_\chi = ACGCGCC\$_\chi \in \mathcal{S}^0$, $s_1 = ACGAGACGAT\$_1 \in \mathcal{S}^1$, and $s_2 = AACGCCGCCGGCA\$_2 \in \mathcal{S}^1$. Then, $\mathsf{Score}(s_\chi, s_1) = 11/7$, $\mathsf{Score}(s_\chi, s_2) = 19/7$, $\mathsf{Score}(s_1, s_\chi) = 15/10$, $\mathsf{Score}(s_2, s_\chi) = 30/13$, and thus $\mathrm{ACS}(s_\chi, s_1) = 0.67$ and $\mathrm{ACS}(s_\chi, s_2) = 0.34$. In bold are all positions associated with suffixes of s_χ (i.e. the limits of the χ-intervals)

#	id	S	ebwt	lcp	D	lcp$_\chi$	α	ζ	UcLCP χ	UcLCP 1	UcLCP 2	LcLCP χ	LcLCP 1	LcLCP 2	cLCP χ	cLCP 1	cLCP 2	Sorted suffixes of $\mathcal{S}$
1	**χ**	**1**	**C**	**-1**	**0**	**-1**	∞	0		0	0		0	0		0	0	$\$_\chi$
2	1	0	T	0	0		0	0				0			0			$\$_1$
3	2	0	A	0	0		0	0				0			0			$\$_2$
4	2	0	C	0	2		0	1				1			1			$A\ \$_2$
5	2	0	$\$_2$	1	0		0	1				1			1			$A\ A\ C\ G\ C\ C\ G\ C\ C\ G\ G\ C\ A\ \$_2$
6	1	0	$\$_1$	1	4		0	3				3			3			$A\ C\ G\ A\ G\ A\ C\ G\ A\ T\ \$_1$
7	1	0	G	4	0		0	3				3			3			$A\ C\ G\ A\ T\ \$_1$
8	2	0	A	3	5		0	4				4			4			$A\ C\ G\ C\ C\ G\ C\ C\ G\ G\ C\ A\ \$_2$
9	**χ**	**1**	**$\$_0$**	**4**	**0**	**0**	∞	0		3	4		1	0		3	4	$A\ C\ G\ C\ G\ C\ C\ \$_\chi$
10	1	0	G	1	0		1	0				0			1			$A\ G\ A\ C\ G\ A\ T\ \$_1$
11	1	0	G	1	0		1	0				0			1			$A\ T\ \$_1$
12	**χ**	**1**	**C**	**0**	**2**	**0**	∞	0		0	0		1	1		1	1	$C\ \$_\chi$
13	2	0	C	1	0		1	0							1			$C\ A\ \$_2$
14	**χ**	**1**	**G**	**1**	**3**	**1**	∞	0		0	1		1	2		1	2	$C\ C\ \$_\chi$
15	2	0	G	2	0		2	0				1			2			$C\ C\ G\ C\ C\ G\ G\ C\ A\ \$_2$
16	2	0	G	3	0		2	0				1			2			$C\ C\ G\ G\ C\ A\ \$_2$
17	1	0	A	1	3		1	2				2			2			$C\ G\ A\ G\ A\ C\ G\ A\ T\ \$_1$
18	1	0	A	3	0		1	2				2			2			$C\ G\ A\ T\ \$_1$
19	**χ**	**1**	**G**	**2**	**5**	**1**	∞	0		2	1		0	4		2	4	$C\ G\ C\ C\ \$_\chi$
20	2	0	A	4	0		4	0				3			4			$C\ G\ C\ C\ G\ C\ C\ G\ G\ C\ A\ \$_2$
21	2	0	C	5	0		4	0				3			4			$C\ G\ C\ C\ G\ G\ C\ A\ \$_2$
22	**χ**	**1**	**A**	**3**	**0**	**3**	∞	0		2	3		0	2		2	3	$C\ G\ C\ G\ C\ C\ \$_\chi$
23	2	0	C	2	0		2	0				0			2			$C\ G\ G\ C\ A\ \$_2$
24	1	0	A	0	2		0	1				1			1			$G\ A\ C\ G\ A\ T\ \$_1$
25	1	0	C	2	0		0	1				1			1			$G\ A\ G\ A\ C\ G\ A\ T\ \$_1$
26	1	0	C	2	0		0	1				1			1			$G\ A\ T\ \$_1$
27	2	0	G	1	3		0	2				2			2			$G\ C\ A\ \$_2$
28	**χ**	**1**	**C**	**2**	**4**	**0**	∞	0		1	2		0	3		1	3	$G\ C\ C\ \$_\chi$
29	2	0	C	3	0		3	2				2			3			$G\ C\ C\ G\ C\ C\ G\ G\ C\ A\ \$_2$
30	2	0	C	4	0		3	3				2			3			$G\ C\ C\ G\ G\ C\ A\ \$_2$
31	**χ**	**1**	**C**	**2**	**0**	**2**	∞	0		1	2		0	1		1	2	$G\ C\ G\ C\ C\ \$_\chi$
32	2	0	C	1	0		1	0							1			$G\ G\ C\ A\ \$_2$
33	1	0	A	0	0		0	0							0			$T\ \$_1$
				-1		-1												

Similarly, there exists a relationship between the values of UcLCP related to suffixes of s_χ and the values of LcLCP related to suffixes of s_r. In particular,

$$\mathsf{UcLCP}[j_\chi][r] = \mathrm{LCP}(prev(j_\chi, r), j_\chi) = \mathsf{LcLCP}[prev(j_\chi, r)][\chi]. \qquad (4)$$

Table 1 shows the values of UcLCP, LcLCP and cLCP of the running example, in which the collection $\mathcal{S}$ is partitioned into two subsets $\mathcal{S}^0 = \{ACGCGCC\$_\chi\}$ and $\mathcal{S}^1 = \{ACGAGACGAT\$_1, AACGCCGCCGGCA\$_2\}$.

4 Lightweight Computation of cLCP

In this section we describe a lightweight strategy to compute the colored longest common prefix array cLCP. For sake of simplicity we consider the case in which the collection $\mathcal{S}$ is partitioned into two subsets $\mathcal{S}^0$ and $\mathcal{S}^1$, and $\mathcal{S}^0$ consists of a single string s_χ of length n_χ. The general case can be treated analogously.

Definition 3. *A colored k-lcp interval is a k-lcp interval $[i, j]$ such that, among all the suffixes associated to the range $[i, j]$, at least one suffix belongs to S^0 and at least one suffix belongs to S^1.*

Definition 4. *Let $D[1, N + 1]$ denote an integer array such that $D[i] = k$ if a colored $(k-1)$-lcp interval starts at position i and for every colored h-lcp interval starting at position i then $h \leq k - 1$.*

Table 1 highlights the conceptual blocks of suffixes that are associated to the positions i of D such that $D[i] \neq 0$.

Note that the array D can be easily computed in $\Theta(N)$ time by linearly scanning the arrays $\mathsf{lcp}(S)$ and $\mathsf{id}(S)$, and using a stack that simulates the computation of the colored k-lcp intervals. During the sequential scan, each element can be inserted or deleted from the stack at most once. Furthermore, considering that each suffix could take part into no more than $\max \mathsf{lcp}(S)$ nested blocks, the stack requires $O(\max \mathsf{lcp}(S))$ space, at most. We note that this upper bound in space is unlikely to be reached in practice, especially since the stack is emptied when two consecutive values of id corresponding to strings of different subsets are found. It is important to specify that the above mentioned stack could be stored in external memory.

In the following we describe a sequential strategy to construct the cLCP array of the collection S from the arrays $\mathsf{id}(S)$, $\mathsf{lcp}(S)$, and $D(S)$.

Without loss of generality, let us consider a generic string $s_r \in S^1$ and $s_\chi \in S^0$. Assume that $\mathsf{ebwt}[i_r]$, with $1 \leq i_r \leq N$, is associated with a suffix of s_r, i.e. $\mathsf{id}[i_r] = r \neq \chi$, and let $\chi_1 = prev(i_r, \chi)$ and $\chi_2 = next(i_r, \chi)$. Moreover, for simplicity, let UcLCP_r (resp. LcLCP_r) denote UcLCP of s_r versus s_χ (resp. LcLCP of s_r versus s_χ), i.e. the values $\mathsf{UcLCP}[i_r][\chi]$ (resp. $\mathsf{LcLCP}[i_r][\chi]$) for all such i_r; and LcLCP_χ (resp. UcLCP_χ) denote LcLCP (resp. UcLCP) of s_χ versus s_r, i.e. the values $\mathsf{LcLCP}[j_\chi][r]$ (resp. $\mathsf{UcLCP}[j_\chi][r]$) for all $1 \leq j_\chi \leq N$ such that $\mathsf{id}[j_\chi] = \chi$.

UcLCP_r *computation* — This is the easiest case, since Eq. 1 allows us to directly compute UcLCP_r sequentially and linearly in the total size N of lcp. This enables us to scan lcp forward only once for all suffixes of all m strings in S^1, by keeping track of the minimum value found since the beginning of each conceptual χ-interval (see column α in Table 1). If we consider the χ-interval (χ_1, χ_2), by employing a variable α we can iteratively compute the minimum value among consecutive elements of lcp and determine, for every $i_r \in (\chi_1, \chi_2)$, the LCP between the suffix associated with position i_r and the suffix associated with position χ_1: $\mathsf{UcLCP}[i_r][\chi] = \mathsf{LCP}(\chi_1, i_r) = \min\{\mathsf{lcp}[x] : x \in (\chi_1, i_r]\} = \alpha$.

Example 1 (Running example). If the χ-interval is $(14, 19)$ and $i_r = 18$, then $\mathsf{UcLCP}[18][\chi] = \mathsf{LCP}(14, 18) = \min\{\mathsf{lcp}[x] : x \in (14, 18]\} = \alpha[18] = 1$.

LcLCP_χ *computation* — Since LcLCP_χ is strictly related to UcLCP_r by Eq. 3, we would like to compute it sequentially and linearly as well. Suppose that we have just computed $\mathsf{UcLCP}[i_r][\chi]$ and i_r represents the first suffix of s_r encountered since the beginning in (χ_1, χ_2). Then, by Eq. 3, $\mathsf{LcLCP}[\chi_1][r] = \mathsf{UcLCP}[i_r][\chi]$. To keep track of the first instance of every $s_r \in \mathcal{S}^1$ in the interval, we could resort to a bit-array of m elements for χ_1.

Nevertheless, this is not sufficient to complete the construction of LcLCP_χ, because there might be no suffixes of a particular string $s_r \in \mathcal{S}^1$ within (χ_1, χ_2), but other suffixes of s_r might exist at positions $> \chi_2$. To tackle this issue, once we have thoroughly read lcp and filled LcLCP_χ using the above procedure, we can propagate the computed values of LcLCP_χ backward from lower to higher lexicographically ranked suffixes of χ, in order to complete LcLCP_χ. For example, to propagate the information from χ_2 to χ_1, we must compute:

$$\mathsf{LcLCP}[\chi_1][r] = \min\{\mathrm{LCP}(\chi_1, \chi_2), \mathsf{LcLCP}[\chi_2][r]\}. \tag{5}$$

Thus, iteratively, we can propagate the information backward from the lowest ranked suffixes of χ to the top of LcLCP_χ.

Example 2 (Running example). After the first scan of lcp in the example of Table 1, $\mathsf{LcLCP}[12][1]$ (i.e. suffix of s_χ in row 12 versus string $s_1 \in \mathcal{S}^1$) would be 0, whereas by propagating the information back from the suffix of s_χ in row 14, we obtain: $\mathsf{LcLCP}[12][1] = \min\{\mathrm{LCP}(12, 14), \mathsf{LcLCP}[14][1]\} = \min\{1, 2\} = 1$.

LcLCP_r *computation* —The most interesting part is computing LcLCP_r in such a way as to avoid the backward scan of id and lcp suggested by Eq. 2 and, concomitantly, for particular applications such as the multi-string ACS problem discussed below, to reduce the memory footprint required to keep both UcLCP_r and LcLCP_r to a somehow negligible one. Thus, we show how to sequentially determine, for every $i_r \in (\chi_1, \chi_2)$, the LCP between the suffix associated with position i_r and the suffix associated with position χ_2.

Let us consider the array D introduced in Definition 4. Intuitively, D provides an interlacing forward information that could be exploited to compute $\mathsf{LcLCP}[i_r][\chi]$ sequentially, as soon as we reach position i_r. Firstly, observe that, for any $1 \le i_r \le N$ with $\mathsf{id}[i_r] = r$ and any $\chi_1 < x < \chi_2$, $prev(x, \chi) = prev(i_r, \chi) = \chi_1$ and $next(x, \chi) = next(i_r, \chi) = \chi_2$.

Remark 1. For any $x_1 < x_2$, with $\chi_1 \le x_1 < \chi_2$ and $\chi_1 < x_2 \le \chi_2$, $\mathrm{LCP}(x_1, x_2) \ge \mathrm{LCP}(\chi_1, \chi_2)$.

Lemma 1. *For any* $1 \le i_r \le N$, *if* $\mathrm{LCP}(i_r, \chi_2) = k - 1$ *then there exists an* x, *with* $\chi_1 < x \le i_r$, *such that* $\mathsf{D}[x] = k \ne 0$ *if and only if* $\mathrm{LCP}(\chi_1, \chi_2) < k - 1$.

Moreover, it follows that $\mathsf{D}[x]$ would be (the only) maximum in the range $(\chi_1, i_r]$ and its value is ≥ 2. Hence, we can determine $\mathsf{LcLCP}[i_r][\chi] = \mathrm{LCP}(i_r, \chi_2)$.

Theorem 1. *For any* $1 \le i_r \le N$ *such that* $\mathsf{id}[i_r] = r$, *if* $\mathrm{LCP}(\chi_1, i_r) > \mathrm{LCP}(\chi_1, \chi_2)$ *then* $\mathrm{LCP}(i_r, \chi_2) = \mathrm{LCP}(\chi_1, \chi_2)$, *otherwise* $\mathrm{LCP}(i_r, \chi_2) = \max\{\max\{\mathsf{D}[x] : \chi_1 < x \le i_r\} - 1, \mathrm{LCP}(\chi_1, \chi_2)\}$.

By using Theorem 1 we need to keep track of the maximum value (decreased by 1) among consecutive D values since the beginning of each conceptual χ-interval (see column ζ in Table 1). An immediate example of Theorem 1 is given in column $\mathsf{LcLCP}[\cdot][\chi]$ of Table 1, which provides the final values of LcLCP_r, where $\mathrm{LCP}(\chi_1, i_r)$ is computed using Eq. 1 and $\mathrm{LCP}(\chi_1, \chi_2)$ through $\mathsf{lcp}(\mathcal{S}^0)$ (or, shortly, lcp_χ).

Example 3 (Running example). Let $i_r = 16$ (with $prev(i_r, \chi) = 14$ and $next(i_r, \chi) = 19$) such that $\mathrm{LCP}(14, 16) = \mathsf{UcLCP}[16][\chi] = 2 > \mathrm{LCP}(14, 19) = \mathsf{lcp}_\chi[5] = 1$; then, $\mathsf{LcLCP}[17][\chi] = \mathrm{LCP}(16, 19) = \mathrm{LCP}(14, 19) = 1$. Conversely, by considering $i_r = 17$ (with $prev(i_r, \chi) = 14$ and $next(i_r, \chi) = 19$, as before), $\mathrm{LCP}(14, 17) = \mathsf{UcLCP}[17][\chi] = 1 = \mathrm{LCP}(14, 19) = \mathsf{lcp}_\chi[5] = 1$; therefore, $\mathsf{LcLCP}[17][\chi] = \mathrm{LCP}(17, 19) = \max\{\max\{D[x] : 14 < x \leq 17\} - 1, \mathrm{LCP}(14, 19)\} = \max\{2, 1\} = 2$. Furthermore, we consider the third case of Theorem 1 such that, for $i_r = 13$ (where $prev(i_r, \chi) = 12$ and $next(i_r, \chi) = 14$), $\mathrm{LCP}(12, 13) = \mathsf{UcLCP}[13][\chi] = 1 = \mathrm{LCP}(12, 14) = \mathsf{lcp}_\chi[4] = 1$ and thus $\mathsf{LcLCP}[13][\chi] = \mathrm{LCP}(13, 14) = \max\{\max\{D[x] : 12 < x \leq 13\} - 1, \mathrm{LCP}(12, 14)\} = \max\{-1, 1\} = 1$.

UcLCP_χ *computation* —Similarly to LcLCP_χ, we can compute UcLCP_χ by exploiting Eq. 4 and the previously computed LcLCP_r within each χ-interval (compare columns $\mathsf{UcLCP}[\cdot][1]$ and $\mathsf{UcLCP}[\cdot][2]$ against column $\mathsf{LcLCP}[\cdot][\chi]$ in Table 1). To complete the construction of UcLCP_χ, we need then to propagate forward the information from higher to lower lexicographically ranked suffixes of χ. For example, to propagate the information from χ_1 to χ_2, we must compute $\mathsf{UcLCP}[\chi_2][r] = \min\{\mathrm{LCP}(\chi_1, \chi_2), \mathsf{UcLCP}[\chi_1][r]\}$.

To reduce the memory footprint, for instance for applications such as multi-string ACS, we could use a single matrix $\mathsf{cLCP}_\chi[1, n_\chi][1, m]$ (initialized with all 0s) to keep track of the maximum values between the corresponding positions of UcLCP_χ and LcLCP_χ, which could be then refined at most twice by propagation. Observe that UcLCP_χ, alone, can be directly computed sequentially, eventually reducing the additional space to a negligible one of size $O(m)$, as seen before for UcLCP_r and LcLCP_r.

Example 4 (Running example). After the first scan of lcp, $\mathsf{UcLCP}[22][1]$ (i.e. suffix of s_χ in row 22 versus string $s_1 \in \mathcal{S}^1$) would be 0, whereas by propagating the information forward from the suffix of s_χ at row 19, we obtain: $\mathsf{UcLCP}[22][1] = \min\{\mathrm{LCP}(19, 22), \mathsf{UcLCP}[19][1]\} = \min\{3, 2\} = 2$.

Computational complexity — The first phase of the algorithm consists of the semi-external memory computation of the D array in $\Theta(N)$ time and $O(\max \mathsf{lcp}(\mathcal{S}))$. Notice that UcLCP_r and LcLCP_r can be determined sequentially (forward) requiring nothing but to update variables α and ζ, while keeping track, respectively, of the minimum among consecutive lcp values and of the maximum among consecutive D values since the last s_χ suffix encountered. Moreover one can observe that also in UcLCP_χ and LcLCP_χ computation both lcp_χ and cLCP_χ are actually accessed either sequentially forward or sequentially backward, up to one position before or after the currently processed one, allowing them to reside in external memory too. This means that we need $O(m)$ additional space in RAM. In order to optimally use the available size M of RAM, assuming $Q \geq 2$

is the number of m-elements rows of cLCP_χ that we could accommodate in RAM, at any moment we could just keep in memory and process only a single block of lcp_χ and cLCP_χ of size proportional to Q. Such a block, together with the bit-array of size m required in first part of LcLCP_χ computation, yield $O(mQ + \max \mathsf{lcp}(\mathcal{S}))$ overall required space (with Q a configurable parameter). Furthermore, since cLCP_χ values could be refined at most twice by propagation, a global cost of $O(N + mn_\chi)$ time is deduced. Note that, instead, a straightforward approach that just uses Eqs. 1 and 2 would have required to process in RAM at least three data structures, each of size $\sim N$, using $O(n_\chi N)$ time (without propagation). In order to evaluate the number of I/O operations, we denote by B the disk block size and we assume that both the RAM size and B are measured in units of $(\log N)$-bit words. The overall complexity of the algorithm, including the number of I/O operations need to process the arrays $\mathsf{id}(\mathcal{S})$, $\mathsf{lcp}(\mathcal{S})$, $\mathsf{D}(\mathcal{S})$, lcp_χ, and cLCP_χ, is summarized by the following theorem.

Theorem 2. *Let $\mathcal{S}$ a collection of m strings. Given $\mathsf{id}(\mathcal{S})[1, N]$, $\mathsf{lcp}(\mathcal{S})[1, N+1]$ and $\mathsf{lcp}(s_\chi)[1, n_\chi + 1]$, $\mathsf{cLCP}(\mathcal{S})$ can be computed by sequential scans in $\mathcal{O}(N + mn_\chi)$ time and $\mathcal{O}(m + L_1)$ additional space, where $L_1 = \max \mathsf{lcp}(\mathcal{S})$. The total number of I/O disk operations is $O\left(\frac{1}{B \log N}(N \log m + N \log L_1 + n_\chi \log L_2 + n_\chi m \log L_1) \right)$, where $L_2 = \max \mathsf{lcp}(s_\chi)$.*

5   Multi-string ACS Computation by cLCP

The cLCP is a data structure that implicitly stores information useful to compute distinguishing and repeating strings in different collections. Its lightweight computation described in previous section enables the use of cLCP in several contexts in which large collections of long strings are considered.

Here, we describe its use for computing the *matching statistics* (MS) [12,24] and therefore the *Average Common Substring* measure (ACS). Indeed, the ACS induced distance is typically computed from the matching statistics by proceeding in two steps. Let us first consider two strings s_r, of length n_r, and s_t, of length n_t, over the alphabet Σ of size σ. In the first step, ACS asymmetrically computes the longest match lengths of s_r versus s_t, $\mathsf{MS}(s_r, s_t)$, where s_r is the base string. $\mathsf{MS}(s_r, s_t)[1, n_r]$ is an integer array such that, for any position j_r of s_r, $\mathsf{MS}(s_r, s_t)[j_r]$ is the length of the longest prefix of the suffix of s_r starting at position j_r that is also a substring of s_t (see Table 2). In the second step, ACS takes the average of these scores $\mathsf{Score}(s_r, s_t) = \frac{\sum_{j_r=1}^{n_r} \mathsf{MS}(s_r,s_t)[j_r]}{n_r}$; normalizes it by the lengths of s_r, s_t, and σ $Norm(\mathsf{Score}(s_r, s_t)) = \frac{\log_\sigma n_t}{\mathsf{Score}(s_r,s_t)} - \frac{2 \log_\sigma n_r}{(n_r+1)}$; and finally makes the measure symmetrical by defining $\mathrm{ACS}(s_r, s_t) = \frac{Norm(\mathsf{Score}(s_r,s_t))+Norm(\mathsf{Score}(s_t,s_r))}{2}$, in order to achieve an induced distance. We observe that ACS is not a metric, because the triangular inequality might not hold in general. Nevertheless, if we assume s_r and s_t be generated by finite-state Markovian probability distributions, it follows that ACS is a natural distance measure between these distributions [36].

Table 2. Matching statistics $MS(s_0, s_1)$ and $MS(s_1, s_0)$ for $s_0 = ACGCGCC\$_0$ and $s_1 = ACGAGACGAT\$_1$ on $\Sigma = \{A, C, G, T\}$. It follows that $Score(s_0, s_1) = 11/7$, $Score(s_1, s_0) = 15/10$ and, thus, $ACS(s_0, s_1) = 0.67$.

$s_0[j_0]$	A	C	G	C	G	C	C			
$MS(s_0, s_1)[j_0]$	3	2	1	2	1	1	1			
$s_1[j_1]$	A	C	G	A	G	A	C	G	A	T
$MS(s_1, s_0)[j_1]$	3	2	1	1	1	3	2	1	1	0

For simplicity, we assume that we have a set consisting of only one string $S^0 = \{s_\chi\}$, of length n_χ, and a set of strings $S^1 = \{s_1, s_2, \ldots, s_m\}$, of length $N^1 = \sum_{1 \le r \le m} n_r$, and we want to compute the pairwise ACS induced distances between S^0 (or, more explicitly, s_χ) and every other string in S^1 simultaneously, as in the multi-string ACS problem. Our approach could be also applied to a more general case.

Firstly, we observe that there is a clear correspondence between the cLCP array previously described, computed for s_χ versus all strings in S^1, and MS. More precisely:

Proposition 1. *Given any two strings $s_r, s_\chi \in S$, $MS(s_r, s_\chi)$ is a permutation of all values in $cLCP(S)$ related to the suffixes of s_r (the base string) versus s_χ: $MS(s_r, s_\chi)[j_r] = cLCP[i_r][\chi]$, where $1 \le i_r \le N$ such that $id(S)[i_r] = r$, and j_r is the starting position in s_r of the suffix associated with $ebwt(S)[i_r]$.*

Indeed, for each suffix of every string $s_r \in S^1$, associated with $ebwt[i_r]$, $cLCP[i_r]$ would account for the longest prefix that is a substring of s_χ, and this must correspond to one of the nearest suffixes belonging to s_χ immediately above $(prev(i_r, \chi))$ or below $(next(i_r, \chi))$ row i_r in the sorted suffixes list, in particular to the closest prefix matching one.

We can thus exploit the above proposition to compute MS using cLCP, by using the strategy described in previous section. In fact, computing MS by straightly using the Eqs. 1 and 2 would require to explicitly keep track of cLCP for each χ-interval, which could have width $\Theta(N)$ in the worst case. In this section we show that this additional space can be controlled and reduced by using our lightweight computation of cLCP.

Using the construction described in Sect. 4 we can determine $UcLCP_r$ and $LcLCP_r$ sequentially (forward) and these values are definitive (they are not subject to refinement by propagation). We can thus reduce the multi-string ACS memory footprint by summing up all the maximum values between the respective positions in $UcLCP_r$ and $LcLCP_r$ for every specific string $s_r \in S^1$, and for every position i_r, and storing them into an array $Score_r$ of size m as they are computed during forward phase, without explicitly maintaining the $cLCP_r$ values in either internal or external memory. On the other hand, since $UcLCP_\chi$ and $LcLCP_\chi$ require propagation to be completed, we need to maintain (a Q-sized portion of) $cLCP_\chi$ matrix and similarly cumulate $cLCP_\chi$ values for every position

j_χ and for every string $s_r \in \mathcal{S}^1$ into an array Score_χ of size m, as these values became definitive during backward phase. Accordingly, multi-string ACS computation does not add to cLCP construction more than $\Theta(m)$ space and $O(mn_\chi)$ time. Note that in a typical application, m can be assumed $\ll N$ and negligible compared to the internal memory available. Here, we show a simplified version of our strategy described in Sect. 5. For simplicity, we index the files as arrays but the reader can note that we only access to them sequentially. We need to keep in memory the length of the strings for the m ACS scores.

6 Preliminary Experiments

As a proof-of-concept, we tested our new data structure (cLCP) using a prototype C++ tool, named CLCP-MACS [1], designed to specifically solve the multi-string ACS problem.

To assess the performance of our algorithm we consider the two collections of genomes listed in [1] and described in Table 3. All tests were done on a MacBook Pro (13-inch), Intel Core i7 at 3, 5 GHz, with 16 GB of RAM, HDD of type SSD and with O.S. macOS 10.13.5.

We show that our preliminary experiments confirm the effectiveness of our approach for the multi-string ACS problem, that consists in the pairwise comparison of a single string against a set of m strings simultaneously, in order to obtain m ACS induced distances. This is not a limitation, because the computation of pairwise distances between strings of a collection $\mathcal{S}$ can be treated analogously, in the sense that one could execute our tool more times, without computing the data structures of the preprocessing step.

We experimentally observed that the preprocessing step is more computationally expensive than the step for computing the m ACS distances via cLCP. The problem of computing the $\mathsf{ebwt}(\mathcal{S}), \mathsf{lcp}(\mathcal{S}), \mathsf{id}(\mathcal{S})$ has been extensively studied, and improving its efficiency is out of the aim of this paper. Therefore, we omit time/space requirements of the preprocessing step, since (i) these data structures can be reused and (ii) different programs [2–5] are used to construct them with different space-time trade-offs. So, we solely focus on the phase of computation of the matrix distances.

Notice that an entirely like-for-like comparison between our implementation and the below existing implementation is not possible, since, for the best of our knowledge, our tool is the first lightweight tool.

ACS has been implemented in the k-Mismatch Average Common Substring approach tool (KMACS) [6], which has been shown to be one of the most performing ones to compute the classic ACS problem (with $k = 0$) [25]. Other algorithms besides KMACS [31,35] have been designed to compute alignment-free distances based on longest matches with mismatches, but for the special case $k = 0$ KMACS is the software that has the better change to scale with the dataset size. We remark that the current implementation of KMACS works completely in internal memory (and not in sequential way), but can be easily adapted to solve the multi-string ACS problem (with $k = 0$), even though not

Table 3. The first collection contains 932 genomes, the second one contains 4,983 genomes. Note that $|s_\chi| = 5,650,368$ for the first collection and $|s_\chi| = 3,571,103$ for the second one. In both cases these values are greater than the average length of the strings in the respective collection. The amount of time elapsed from the start to the completion of the instance. The column memory is the peak Resident Set Size (RSS). Both values were taken with `/usr/bin/time` command.

|ebwt(S)| (Gbytes)	Min length	Max length	Max lcp	Program	Wall clock (mm:ss)	Memory (kbytes)
1	3.434	1,080,084	10,657,107	1,711,194	cLCP-mACS	13:37	10,716
					KMACS	23:30	4,213,364
2	9.258	744	14,782,125	5,714,157	cLCP-mACS	40:21	10,780
					KMACS	57:43	9,637,964

natively. Indeed, it shows a high intrinsic redundancy in the multiple creation of the same supporting data structures and thus when loading these structures into RAM. More in detail, it works in m steps, at each step it builds the suffix array [27] and the lcp array of two strings s_i and s_j (for $1 \le i < j \le m$) in order to compute the ACS distance between s_i and s_j. We modified the current implementation, which takes in input multiple sequences, by fixing $s_\chi = s_1$ to achieve a more fair assessment and thus compare only s_χ with s_j, for all $2 \le j \le m+1$. Note that the performance in terms of time of KMACS could be improved by separately considering the computation of the auxiliary data structures. However, the occupation of RAM as well as its redundancy would remain almost the same.

The experimental results shown in Table 3 indicate that our algorithm is a competitive tool for the lightweight simultaneous computation of the pairwise ACS distance of a string versus all strings in another collection. In cLCP-mACS, the auxiliary external disk space used was 34 GB for the first collection and 108 GB for the second one. Moreover, since D tends to be typically a sparse array, one could reduce its size in external memory by storing only non-zero values the number of consecutive empty slots, or using an alternative encoding such as Sadakane's encoding [34].

7   Conclusion and Future Work

We have first introduced the colored longest common prefix array (cLCP): given a collection of strings S, the cLCP array stores the length of the longest common prefix between the suffix of any string in S and the nearest suffixes of another string in S, by exploiting the lexicographically sorted list of suffixes in the lcp array and some other combinatorial properties of it. This notion has been then extended in a natural way to compute the longest common prefix between any pair of strings in two different collections of strings S^0 and S^1. We have further provided a versatile, lightweight method to compute cLCP via sequential scans when $\mathcal{S}^0$ consists of a single string, which could be further extended to cope with the more general case. This makes cLCP suitable for computing several kinds of statistics on large collections of long strings, while dramatically reducing the amount of computational resources used. In particular, we have proved that cLCP($\mathcal{S}$) produces a permutation of the matching statistics (MS) for the strings of the collection of $\mathcal{S}$ and exploited it to efficiently solve the multi-string ACS problem — i.e. computing pairwise MS between a string in $\mathcal{S}^0$ and all m strings in $\mathcal{S}^1$ simultaneously, — that is nowadays crucial in many practical applications, but demanding for large string comparisons. This is also supported by experimental results.

Moreover, it is interesting to note that cLCP and its sequential strategy of computation are intrinsically dynamic, i.e. cLCP can be efficiently updated when the collection is modified by inserting or removing a string. In particular, after the removal of a string, cLCP can be updated by exploiting the mathematical properties of the permutation associated with the EBWT. The insertion of a new string in the collection can be managed by using the merging strategy proposed in [22], which works in semi-external memory. In this case, the intermediate array D used to compute cLCP can be constructed directly during this merging phase. Finally, we plan to extend our framework to solve the many-to-many pairwise ACS problem on a collection $\mathcal{S}$ of m sequences or between all strings of a collection versus all strings of another collection simultaneously.

References

1. https://github.com/giovannarosone/cLCP-mACS
2. https://github.com/BEETL/BEETL
3. https://github.com/giovannarosone/BCR_LCP_GSA
4. https://github.com/felipelouza/egsa
5. https://github.com/felipelouza/egap
6. http://kmacs.gobics.de/
7. Apostolico, A., Guerra, C., Pizzi, C.: Alignment free sequence similarity with bounded hamming distance. In: Data Compression Conference, DCC 2014, pp. 183–192. IEEE (2014)
8. Bauer, M., Cox, A., Rosone, G.: Lightweight algorithms for constructing and inverting the BWT of string collections. Theor. Comput. Sci. **483**, 134–148 (2013)
9. Belazzougui, D., Cunial, F.: Indexed matching statistics and shortest unique substrings. In: Moura, E., Crochemore, M. (eds.) SPIRE 2014. LNCS, vol. 8799, pp. 179–190. Springer, Cham (2014). https://doi.org/10.1007/978-3-319-11918-2_18
10. Belazzougui, D., Cunial, F.: Fast label extraction in the CDAWG. In: Fici, G., Sciortino, M., Venturini, R. (eds.) SPIRE 2017. LNCS, vol. 10508, pp. 161–175. Springer, Cham (2017). https://doi.org/10.1007/978-3-319-67428-5_14
11. Burrows, M., Wheeler, D.: A block sorting data compression algorithm. Technical report, DEC Systems Research Center (1994)
12. Chang, W.I., Lawler, E.L.: Sublinear approximate string matching and biological applications. Algorithmica **12**(4), 327–344 (1994)
13. Cohen, E., Chor, B.: Detecting phylogenetic signals in eukaryotic whole genome sequences. J. Comput. Biol. **19**(8), 945–956 (2012)

14. Comin, M., Verzotto, D.: The irredundant class method for remote homology detection of protein sequences. J. Comput. Biol. **18**(12), 1819–1829 (2011)
15. Comin, M., Verzotto, D.: Alignment-free phylogeny of whole genomes using underlying subwords. Algorithms Mol. Biol. **7**(1), 34 (2012)
16. Comin, M., Verzotto, D.: Whole-genome phylogeny by virtue of unic subwords. In: DEXA, pp. 190–194. IEEE (2012)
17. Comin, M., Verzotto, D.: Comparing, ranking and filtering motifs with character classes: application to biological sequences analysis. In: Biological Knowledge Discovery Handbook: Preprocessing, Mining and Postprocessing of Biological Data, chap. 13. Wiley (2013)
18. Comin, M., Verzotto, D.: Filtering degenerate patterns with application to protein sequence analysis. Algorithms **6**(2), 352–370 (2013)
19. Comin, M., Verzotto, D.: Beyond fixed-resolution alignment-free measures for mammalian enhancers sequence comparison. IEEE/ACM Trans. Comput. Biol. Bioinform. **11**(4), 628–637 (2014)
20. Cox, A.J., Garofalo, F., Rosone, G., Sciortino, M.: Lightweight LCP construction for very large collections of strings. J. Discret. Algorithms **37**, 17–33 (2016)
21. Cox, A.J., Jakobi, T., Rosone, G., Schulz-Trieglaff, O.B.: Comparing DNA sequence collections by direct comparison of compressed text indexes. In: Raphael, B., Tang, J. (eds.) WABI 2012. LNCS, vol. 7534, pp. 214–224. Springer, Heidelberg (2012). https://doi.org/10.1007/978-3-642-33122-0_17
22. Egidi, L., Louza, F.A., Manzini, G., Telles, G.P.: External memory BWT and LCP computation for sequence collections with applications. ArXiv e-prints (2018)
23. Ferraro Petrillo, U., Guerra, C., Pizzi, C.: A new distributed alignment-free approach to compare whole proteomes. Theor. Comput. Sci. **698**, 100–112 (2017)
24. Gusfield, D.: Algorithms on Strings, Trees, and Sequences: Computer Science and Computational Biology. Cambridge University Press, Cambridge (1997)
25. Leimeister, C.A., Morgenstern, B.: Kmacs: the k-mismatch average common substring approach to alignment-free sequence comparison. Bioinformatics **30**(14), 2000–2008 (2014)
26. Louza, F., Telles, G., Hoffmann, S., Ciferri, C.: Generalized enhanced suffix array construction in external memory. Algorithms Mol. Biol. **12**(1), 26 (2017)
27. Manber, U., Myers, G.: Suffix arrays: a new method for on-line string searches. In: Proceedings of the First Annual ACM-SIAM Symposium on Discrete Algorithms, SODA 1990, pp. 319–327. Society for Industrial and Applied Mathematics (1990)
28. Mantaci, S., Restivo, A., Rosone, G., Sciortino, M.: An extension of the Burrows-Wheeler transform. Theor. Comput. Sci. **387**(3), 298–312 (2007)
29. Mantaci, S., Restivo, A., Rosone, G., Sciortino, M.: A new combinatorial approach to sequence comparison. Theory Comput. Syst. **42**(3), 411–429 (2008)
30. Ohlebusch, E., Gog, S., Kügel, A.: Computing matching statistics and maximal exact matches on compressed full-text indexes. In: Chavez, E., Lonardi, S. (eds.) SPIRE 2010. LNCS, vol. 6393, pp. 347–358. Springer, Heidelberg (2010). https://doi.org/10.1007/978-3-642-16321-0_36
31. Pizzi, C.: MissMax: alignment-free sequence comparison with mismatches through filtering and heuristics. Algorithms Mol. Biol. **11**, 6 (2016)
32. Puglisi, S.J., Turpin, A.: Space-time tradeoffs for longest-common-prefix array computation. In: Hong, S.-H., Nagamochi, H., Fukunaga, T. (eds.) ISAAC 2008. LNCS, vol. 5369, pp. 124–135. Springer, Heidelberg (2008). https://doi.org/10.1007/978-3-540-92182-0_14
33. Ren, J., Song, K., Sun, F., Deng, M., Reinert, G.: Multiple alignment-free sequence comparison. Bioinformatics **29**(21), 2690–2698 (2013)

34. Sadakane, K.: Compressed suffix trees with full functionality. Theory Comput. Syst. **41**(4), 589–607 (2007)
35. Thankachan, S., Chockalingam, S., Liu, Y., Apostolico, A., Aluru, S.: ALFRED: a practical method for alignment-free distance computation. J. Comput. Biol. **23**(6), 452–460 (2016)
36. Ulitsky, I., Burstein, D., Tuller, T., Chor, B.: The average common substring approach to phylogenomic reconstruction. J. Comput. Biol. **13**(2), 336–350 (2006)
37. Zielezinski, A., Vinga, S., Almeida, J., Karlowski, W.: Alignment-free sequence comparison: benefits, applications, and tools. Genome Biol. **18**(1), 186 (2017)

Early Commenting Features for Emotional Reactions Prediction

Anastasia Giachanou[1]([✉]), Paolo Rosso[2], Ida Mele[3], and Fabio Crestani[1]

[1] Faculty of Informatics, Università della Svizzera italiana, Lugano, Switzerland
{anastasia.giachanou,fabio.crestani}@usi.ch
[2] PRHLT Research Center, Universitat Politècnica de València, Valencia, Spain
prosso@dsic.upv.es
[3] ISTI-CNR, Pisa, Italy
ida.mele@isti.cnr.it

Abstract. Nowadays, one of the main sources for people to access and read news are social media platforms. Different types of news trigger different emotional reactions to users who may feel happy or sad after reading a news article. In this paper, we focus on the problem of predicting emotional reactions that are triggered on users after they read a news post. In particular, we try to predict the number of emotional reactions that users express regarding a news post that is published on social media. In this paper, we propose features extracted from users' comments published about a news post shortly after its publication to predict users' the triggered emotional reactions. We explore two different sets of features extracted from users' comments. The first group represents the activity of users in publishing comments whereas the second refers to the comments' content. In addition, we combine the features extracted from the comments with textual features extracted from the news post. Our results show that features extracted from users' comments are very important for the emotional reactions prediction of news posts and that combining textual and commenting features can effectively address the problem of emotional reactions prediction.

1 Introduction

In recent years, social media platforms have become an integral part of news industry. News agents post news articles on social media platforms such as Facebook[1] and Twitter[2]. These news articles are accessible to users who can comment or express their opinion about them. Some of the news articles posted on social networks trigger a large number of emotional reactions whereas others do not. Predicting the number of emotional reactions that will be triggered on users is very useful for information spreading and fake news detection. For example, fake news are written to attract users' attention and to trigger emotions to a large

---

[1] https://www.facebook.com/.
[2] https://twitter.com/.

© Springer Nature Switzerland AG 2018
T. Gagie et al. (Eds.): SPIRE 2018, LNCS 11147, pp. 168–182, 2018.
https://doi.org/10.1007/978-3-030-00479-8_14

number of people [24]. Therefore, the number of emotional reactions can be used as an additional information for fake news or clickbait detection.

Emotional reactions prediction is a challenging problem. The structure of the network or other external factors such as users' location are some of the factors that can affect the number of the triggered emotional reactions. Intuitively, the content of the news post is one of the most important factors that influences the emotional reactions that will be triggered [1]. However, content is not sufficient alone since there are other factors that may influence the triggered reactions. Information extracted from users' *early comments* (i.e., comments published within the first ten minutes after the publication of the news post) can be very useful for an effective emotional reaction prediction.

The problem of *emotional reactions prediction* is related to online content popularity prediction. Most prior work on news articles' popularity prediction is based on early-stage measurements, whereas little effort has been made on the pre-publication prediction scenario [4,5]. Although the problem of predicting the number of emotional reactions has apparent similarities with predicting the popularity of a piece of news, the two problems are not the same. A piece of news that triggers emotional reactions has certainly higher probabilities of receiving attention compared to news articles that do not trigger any emotional reaction. However, predicting the triggered emotional reactions depends on many factors such as, for example, the affective words that the news post contains, the structure of the network and the early commenting activity. Therefore, for an effective prediction it is very important to combine features extracted from the news post content and the comments that are posted after the news post is published.

In this paper, we focus on the problem of predicting the ordinal level in regards to the number of the emotional reactions triggered on users after reading a news post per emotion (e.g., low, medium, high number of anger reactions). We propose two different sets of features extracted from users' early comments to perform the prediction on five standard emotional reactions (*love, surprise, joy, sadness, anger*). The two proposed sets of features capture two different aspects of information: the commenting activity (e.g., when the first comment is published) and the content of the comments (e.g., relevance to the post). In addition, we combine the features extracted from *early comments* with the *terms* of the news post and we show that this combination can effectively address the problem of emotional reactions prediction.

2   Related Work

One aspect that is relevant to the emotional reaction prediction is popularity prediction. Prior work tried to predict the popularity of different web items such as images, videos or tweets prior and after their publication. A wide range of features have been explored and the most informative have shown to be those extracted from early activity [8]. To this end, a large number of researchers tackled the online content prediction after publication by modeling the early users' behavior [18] or by using temporal patterns of online content [29].

Tsagkias et al. [27] explored different features such as the length of the article and the number of authors to address the problem of news articles' popularity prediction. Tsagkias et al. addressed the problem as a binary classification where the news articles were classified as having low or high popularity. Bandari et al. [5] tackled the prediction task as both regression and classification, and used various features including category of the article and named entities. Bandari et al. reached the conclusion that predicting the popularity of web items is feasible without any early activity signals. However, recently Arapakis et al. [4] extended the study of Bandari et al. and they showed that predicting the popularity of news articles prior to their publication is not a viable task.

The problem of the emotional reactions prediction is also related to opinion and emotion analysis that have been applied on different social media platforms, including blogs [10], forums [28] and microblogs [12,14,17]. Prior work on emotion and sentiment analysis include classification and lexicon-based approaches [11]. The classification based approaches [3,17,22] leverage classifiers that are trained on several features such as n-grams, stylistic features (e.g., number of exclamation and question marks), negation, or part-of-speech tags. Lexicon-based approaches use list of words known as opinion or sentiment lexicons which convey a specific sentiment or emotion to label the text [26].

Regarding emotional reactions, Clos et al. [9] proposed a unigram mixture model to create an emotional lexicon that was used to predict the probabilities of five different emotional reactions. In addition, Alam et al. [1] focused on mood level prediction of readers on news articles (ranging from 0 to 1) using features such as character, words and affect scores. Alam et al. showed that n-grams and stylometric features are the most important. More recently, Goel et al. [15] focused on predicting the intensity of emotions in tweets using an ensemble of three neural-network approaches. However, our problem is not the same as emotional intensity, since an article may trigger an emotion that is intense to only a small number of people. Consider the case of a strike in the means of transportation in a small city. In such a case, some people may feel very angry (e.g., "I got stuck in traffic for an hour and a half! #busStrike") but such intense emotion might be triggered only in a small number of people.

The study that is the most similar to ours is the one presented by Giachanou et al. [13] who also focused on predicting the ordinal level regarding the number of emotional reactions triggered by news posts. However, in their study they only explored pre-publication features including similarities and entities extracted from the article's content. Different from Giachanou et al., we focus on features that are extracted from the users' comments to understand how effective they are in predicting the emotional reactions of the news post. We study the effectiveness of two groups of features extracted from users' comments regarding the post. In addition, we propose combining simple textual and early commenting features for effectively predicting the triggered emotional reactions.

3   Problem Definition

The problem of *emotional reactions prediction* of news posts published on a social network is defined as: *Given a news article post and data about users' early comments published regarding the post, the task consists in predicting the qualitative ordinal level of emotional reactions that the post will trigger.* Note that the main aim is to classify a news post with regards to the volume of the emotional reactions it will trigger per emotion. We focus on the following five different emotions: *love, surprise, joy, sadness, anger.* We address the problem as both 3-class and 5-class ordinal classification task to capture the different levels of the reactions. Hence, given a news post we assign to it one of these labels: *low, medium, high* for the 3-class task and one of these labels *very low, low, medium, high, very high* for the 5-class task. The labels refer to the number of reactions that the post will collect per emotion.

4   Features

Intuitively, content is very important for predicting if a news article will trigger a high number of a certain emotional reaction. To this end, in our study we start with *terms* extracted from the news post. Terms can be very important to understand why a specific article triggered massive emotions. Furthermore, we extract features from users' comments published shortly after the publication of the post to investigate if there is any pattern in commenting that can be useful for predicting the emotional reactions' popularity.

4.1   Term Frequencies

The first feature we use is the *terms* of the news post. Although *terms* is a simple feature, it is one of the most important features for news articles' popularity prediction [1, 27] as well as similar information retrieval tasks [2, 20]. For *terms* feature we use the bag-of-words representation of a news post. In particular, we use the classic term frequency-inverse document frequency (TF-IDF) approach [23] that considers how important is a term in a corpus to represent the content of the post. On the contrary to other studies [27] that used only a small percentage of the vocabulary to represent textual features, we are using all the terms that appear in the collection after stopwords removal. In the rest of the paper, we use *terms* to refer to the TF-IDF representation of the post's content.

4.2   Early Commenting Features

As already mentioned, once a news post is published on a social network, the users can publish their comments regarding the post. These comments usually appear below the post. We explore two groups of features extracted from users' comments. The first group represents the commenting activity and includes features such as how fast the users publish a comment. For the second group we extract features from the content of the comments such as their relevance to the news post.

Here we should note that activity of emotional reactions can also be very useful (e.g., number of sadness reactions in the first ten minutes). However, we do not have access to these data. Therefore, we use features from the early comments of users to capture early patterns in the users' comments. To extract the commenting features we use three different time range settings: 10, 20, and 30 min after the publication date of the news post to explore how useful the different time ranges are and if there is any improvement in performance when a wider time range is used. Finally, we do not differentiate between comments and replies to comments.

Early Commenting Activity. The early commenting activity features aim to capture the patterns in the activity of publishing comments below the news post. We explore the following features:

1. *First comment.* Time difference in seconds between publication date of the post and the first comment, if the first comment is published within the specified time range.
2. *Number of comments.* Number of comments published within the specified time range.
3. *Commenting ratio.* Mean time of commenting for those published within the specified time range.
4. *Unique authors.* Number of unique authors for the comments published within the specified time range. This feature can partially capture the discussion activity in the comments since a certain author will post more than one comments when there is a discussion.

Early Comments' Content Features. In this section we propose features that are extracted from the comments' content. These features can reveal if there is any pattern in the content of the comments that are posted about a news post and the emotional reactions it triggers. We propose three features: the length of the comments, the relevance to the post and the sentiment expressed in the comments.

1. *Length of comments.* This feature is calculated based on the average length of the comments published. The length of a comment is represented by the number of words it contains. This feature is useful because users might tend to post shorter or longer comments regarding the news posts that trigger specific emotional reactions. In addition, longer comments might express stronger emotional reactions that may relate to the reactions triggered regarding the news post.
2. *Relevance to the post.* This feature represents the average relevance of the comments published within the specified time range to the post. This feature is important since there may be comments not related to the post. To calculate the relevance, we use the word2vec model that is an embedding model

proposed by Mikolov et al. [19] and which learns word vectors via a neural network with a single hidden layer. First, we calculate the average vector for all words in the comment and the post and then we use cosine similarity between the vectors to calculate the similarity score. We use the pre-trained word embeddings that are publicly available and which are generated from news articles[3] to generate the word vectors.

3. *Sentiment in comments.* We also measure the sentiment expressed in the comments published within the specified time range. In particular, we calculate the positive, neutral and negative sentiment ratio of the comments. We use an opinion lexicon [16] to calculate the sentiment expressed in a comment. More formally, let $N_t(z, s)$ be the number of comments that express a sentiment s towards the news post z posted during a particular time period t and $N_t(z)$ the number of total comments posted regarding z at t. Then, we can define the ratio of comments that share a common sentiment s as:

$$r_t(z, s) = \frac{N_t(z, s)}{N_t(z)}$$

We calculate the ratio for all the three sentiment polarities: positive, neutral and negative.

5   Experimental Setup

In this section, we describe the experimental setup of the study. First, we describe the dataset and next we present the experimental settings we applied for our study.

5.1   Dataset

For this study, we collected news posts from *The New York Times* group[4] in Facebook together with the number of 5 different emotional reactions: *love, surprise, joy, sadness,* and *anger* for each post. We used Facebook API[5] to collect the posts, the reactions, and the comments[6]. The number of reactions are used to determine how many reactions each post has triggered. Other types of posts, such as tweets, do not contain information about the emotional reactions, and therefore, they need to be manually annotated, a process that is very costly in time and resources.

Our collection consists of 26,560 news posts that span from April 2016 to September 2017. We use a 10-fold cross validation to perform the experiments. We keep training and test sets always separate. As an example, Fig. 1 shows the distribution of the posts with regards to the emotional reaction *love.* More

---

[3] https://code.google.com/p/word2vec/.
[4] https://www.facebook.com/nytimes/.
[5] https://developers.facebook.com/.
[6] Facebook allows users to select an emotional reaction with regards to a post.

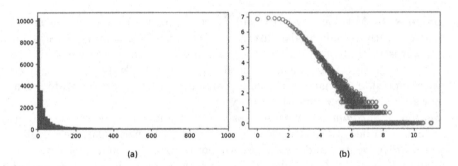

(a)   (b)

Fig. 1. (a). Frequency of posts versus number of the emotional reaction *love* (binned). (b). Number of *love* reactions per post versus number of posts with that number of *love* reactions (log-scale).

specifically, Fig. 1(a) shows the number of posts versus the number of the *love* reactions triggered. For clarity, we show only the first part of the distribution and cut the long tail after 1,000 *love* reactions. Figure 1(b) shows the number of *love* reactions per post versus the number of posts that triggered that number of *love* reactions. The other emotional reactions follow similar distributions. From the figures, we can observe that the number of reactions per post follows a long-tail distribution. In other words, few posts collect a high number of reactions, while the majority of posts get very few.

5.2   Experimental Settings

In this study, we performed two tasks: a 3-class and 5-class emotional reaction ordinal classification task. For those tasks, we divided the collection into 3 (and 5) balanced classes with regards to the number of each emotional reaction. A balanced classification formulation has also been chosen by several prior studies on popularity prediction [8,25]. For the 3-class task a news post can get one of the following labels: *low, medium, high*, while for the 5-class one of: *very low, low, medium, high, very high*. We predicted the number of the following five different emotional reactions: *love, surprise, joy, sadness,* and *anger*. The emotional reactions were addressed individually.

Table 1 shows the boundaries of the different classes. From the table, we observe that the range of the *high* and *very high* classes of the 3-class and 5-class task respectively is wide. For example, the class *very high* of the 5-class task contains posts that received from 122 to 67K *love* reactions. This is due to the long-tail distribution of the data and the balanced classes setting.

For the ordinal classification of the emotional reactions, we used Random Forest [7], a decision tree meta classifier[7]. For all the experiments, we used the

---

[7] We use Random Forest because it obtained the best results on the run trained on terms among the various classifiers that we tried including SVM and Logistic Regression.

Table 1. Boundaries of the different classes.

3-class					
	Love	Surprise	Joy	Sadness	Anger
Low	0–9	0–8	0–3	0–2	0–2
Medium	10–47	9–39	4–21	3–31	3–35
High	48–67K	40–23K	22–27K	32–50K	36–67K

5-class					
	Love	Surprise	Joy	Sadness	Anger
Very low	0–5	0–4	0–1	0–0	0–0
Low	6–13	5–11	2–4	1–4	1–3
Medium	14–33	12–28	5–13	5–18	4–17
High	34–121	29–89	15–63	19–110	18–134
Very high	122–67K	90–23K	64–27K	111–50K	135–67K

open source machine learning toolkit scikit-learn[8]. To generate the word vectors we used publicly available pre-trained word embeddings (see footnote 3). To calculate the sentiment expressed in a comment, we used the opinion lexicon described in [16]. Pre-processing of the posts involved stop-words removal and stemming with Porter stemmer [21].

Mean Absolute Error (MAE) is reported for both 3-class and 5-class tasks and for each emotional reaction. We used the runs trained on *terms* and *activity+content$_{t=10}$* as our baselines. Significance is measured with the non-parametric Wilcoxon signed-rank test that is appropriate for the ordinal classification.

6   'Results and Discussion

Tables 2 and 3 show the results using the early commenting features on predicting the number of emotional reactions triggered on users regarding a news post for the 3-class and 5-class ordinal classification respectively. The tables show the MAE scores (the lower the value, the better the approach performs) for three different groups of features: the commenting activity features (*activity*), the comments' content features (*content*) and their combination (*activity+content*). The approach based on post's terms is used as a baseline.

From the results we observe that post's *terms* are better predictors compared to using only the *early commenting activity* or the *comments' content* in the case of *love, sadness* and *anger*. However, in case of *surprise* and *joy* the *early commenting activity* runs perform better compared to *terms* and in fact in some cases the difference is statistically better (e.g., 5-class classification of *surprise* and *joy*). Also, we observe, that in general the runs that use the *comments'*

---

8 http://scikit-learn.org/.

Table 2. Performance results (MAE) for the 3-class ordinal classification using early commenting features. Scores with * indicate statistically significant improvements with respect to the *terms* approach.

Post's terms	Love	Surprise	Joy	Sadness	Anger
	0.629	0.649	0.542	0.565	0.503
activity$_{t=10}$	0.743	0.631	0.517*	0.730	0.596
activity$_{t=20}$	0.732	0.616	0.504*	0.699	0.560
activity$_{t=30}$	0.724	0.602	0.493*	0.690	0.544
content$_{t=10}$	0.697	0.655	0.556	0.633	0.507
content$_{t=20}$	0.686	0.660	0.583	0.618	0.507
content$_{t=30}$	0.683	0.664	0.590	0.609	0.505
activity+content$_{t=10}$	0.612*	0.568*	0.448*	0.586	0.442*
activity+content$_{t=20}$	0.581*	0.539*	0.426*	0.551*	0.408*
activity+content$_{t=30}$	0.555*	0.534*	0.413*	0.539*	0.388*

Table 3. Performance results (MAE) for the 5-class ordinal classification using early commenting features. Scores with * indicate statistically significant improvements with respect to the *terms* approach.

Post's terms	Love	Surprise	Joy	Sadness	Anger
	1.232	1.269	1.101	1.059	0.982
activity$_{t=10}$	1.396	1.195*	1.009*	1.334	1.122
activity$_{t=20}$	1.377	1.161*	0.989*	1.300	1.070
activity$_{t=30}$	1.362	1.142*	0.956*	1.275	1.044
content$_{t=10}$	1.334	1.249 *	1.078*	1.175	0.989
content$_{t=20}$	1.311	1.250*	1.114	1.151	0.972*
content$_{t=30}$	1.298	1.256*	1.125	1.124	0.960*
activity+content$_{t=10}$	1.177*	1.093*	0.895*	1.103	0.857*
activity+content$_{t=20}$	1.112*	1.039*	0.846*	1.042*	0.794*
activity+content$_{t=30}$	1.074*	1.021*	0.822*	1.014*	0.766*

content features obtain a lower performance compared to *terms*. One exception is the case of *surprise* and *joy* on the 5-class task where there are runs that perform statistically better to *terms* (e.g., *content$_{t=10}$* run).

Regarding the performance between the runs that are based only on the *activity* and those based only on the *comments' content*, we observe that the emotional reactions perform in a different way. More specifically, *activity* leads to a better performance compared to *comments' content* in case of *surprise* and *joy*, whereas regarding *love*, *sadness* and *anger*, the *comments' content* features are better predictors compared to *activity*. This result shows that users' follow different patterns in commenting regarding the different emotional reactions and they probably tend to write more useful comments regarding *love, sadness* and *anger.*

More importantly, the majority of runs that use all the early commenting features (i.e. *activity+content*) perform statistically better compared to the ones trained on the *terms* of the post. The only exception is the case of *sadness* in the $activity+content_{t=10}$ run. This suggests that in case of *sadness* the terms from the post are stronger predictors compared to commenting activity. However, the results also prove that for most of the reactions the features that are extracted from the users' commenting activity shortly after the post is published can effectively predict the number of emotional reactions.

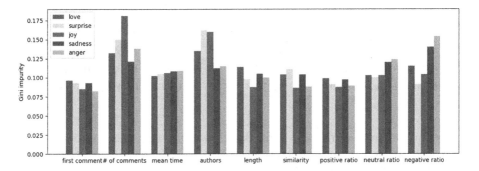

Fig. 2. Gini impurity score for the $activity+content_{t=10}$ run for the 3-class ordinal classification per each emotional reaction.

To understand the contribution of each feature on the prediction, we calculated the Gini impurity scores as described in [6]. Figure 2 shows the Gini impurity score for each feature in the $activity+content_{t=10}$ run for the 3-class classification per each emotional reaction. From the figure we observe that the *number of comments* that have been published in the first ten minutes are good predictors for all the five emotional reactions. Indeed for the reaction *joy*, the *number of comments* is the best predictor. Similarly, the *number of unique authors* feature is important for the reactions *joy* and *surprise.*

An interesting observation is that in case of *sadness* and *anger*, the *negative ratio* has the highest Gini impurity score. This result suggests that users tend to express their feelings in comments to the posts that trigger *sadness* or *anger.*

Tables 4 and 5 show the performance of runs trained on combining the *terms* extracted from the news post with the *early commenting* features (*activity+content*$_{t=10}$) for the 3-class and 5-class tasks respectively. We use features from the first ten minutes (i.e. $t = 10$) because we believe that they are very important for the prediction while keeping the advantage of quick access after the post is published.

From the results, we observe that the performance after combining the *terms* with the *early commenting* features leads to significant improvements over both

Table 4. Performance results (MAE) for the 3-class ordinal classification on combining terms with early commenting features. Scores with ∗ and † indicate statistically significant improvements with respect to *terms* and *activity+content*$_{t=10}$ respectively.

	Love	Surprise	Joy	Sadness	Anger
Post's terms	0.629	0.649	0.542	0.565	0.503
activity+content$_{t=10}$	0.612	0.568	0.448	0.586	0.442
terms+activity+content$_{t=10}$	0.540∗†	0.510∗†	0.405∗†	0.499∗†	0.403∗†

Table 5. Performance results (MAE) for the 5-class ordinal classification on combining terms with early commenting features. Scores with ∗ and † indicate statistically significant improvements with respect to *terms* and *activity+content*$_{t=10}$ respectively.

	Love	Surprise	Joy	Sadness	Anger
Post's terms	1.232	1.269	1.101	1.059	0.982
activity+content$_{t=10}$	1.177	1.093	0.895	1.103	0.857
terms+activity+content$_{t=10}$	1.078∗†	1.012∗†	0.830∗†	0.949∗†	0.789∗†

terms and *activity+content*$_{t=10}$ runs. Also, we notice that this improvement is not consistent across the emotional reactions. For example, the least improvements over *terms* are observed for the reaction *sadness* (e.g., regarding the 3-class classification, the improvement of *terms+activity+content*$_{t=10}$ over the *terms* is 12.41%) whereas the largest improvements are observed for *joy* (28.93%).

One possible explanation for this inconsistency could be that in case of news that trigger a large number of *anger* and *sadness*, the textual features are very important predictors regardless if they are extracted from the news post or the comments' content. To investigate if there are any different patterns in commenting across the different reactions, we display the boxplot of the number of comments published in the first ten minutes for each class and for each emotional reaction in Fig. 3. The figure suggests that there is a difference in the distributions of *sadness* compared to *joy* and *surprise*. Therefore, we also calculate the statistical differences in the number of comments published in the first ten minutes for the posts that triggered a high number of *sadness* compared to *surprise* and *joy*. The results showed that there is a statistical difference between *sadness* and *surprise* (2-sample t-test, p-value < 0.001) as well as *sadness* and *joy* (2-sample t-test, p-value < 0.001). This suggests that users may have different commenting patterns on news posts that trigger *sadness* compared to those that trigger *surprise* or *joy*.

Analysis on Terms. We also carried out further analysis to explore which terms were the most informative for the prediction. As an example, we present the top 20 terms that are the most informative for the 3-class classification of the emotional reactions *surprise* and *sadness*. Figure 4 shows the most informative terms sorted by their Gini impurity score [6] for the reactions of (a) *surprise*, and

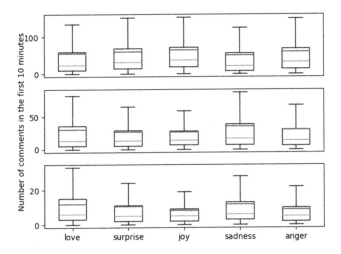

Fig. 3. Boxplot showing the number of comments published in the first ten minutes for the five emotional reactions and the classes *low, medium, high*. The yellow and black line refer to median and mean number of comments respectively. (Color figure online)

(b) *sadness*. We observe that in both cases the most informative terms are *donald, trump* and *president*. We believe that this happens because of the time range of our collection that contains a lot of articles referring to US Elections 2016. In addition, we observe that there are also some terms that convey sentiment, such as the terms *kill* and *attack* that are informative for the emotional reaction *sadness*.

What is important to mention is that there are some words that are informative for both emotions (e.g., breaking, Donald, Trump, president). This observation suggests that there are terms that in general trigger either a large or a small number of emotional reactions regardless of the emotion. In addition to

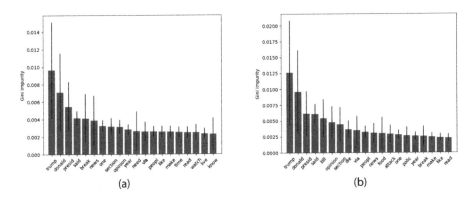

Fig. 4. Top 20 most important *terms* for the 3-class ordinal classification for (a) *surprise* and (b) sadness.

those terms, there are also terms (e.g., excited, attack, etc.) that are important only for a specific emotion (e.g. sadness).

7   Conclusions and Future Work

In this study, we presented a methodology for predicting the ordinal level regarding the number of emotional reactions triggered on users by news posts. For our study, we focused on the following five emotional reactions: *love, surprise, joy, sadness,* and *anger.* We studied the prediction task by using features extracted from the *comments* of users. In addition, we studied the effectiveness of combining *early commenting* features with news posts' *terms* on predicting the emotional reactions.

Our results suggested that features extracted from *comments* are very important for the emotional prediction task. More importantly, we showed that the *commenting* features contain more predictive power compared to *terms* for all the reactions except for *sadness.* In addition, we showed that the different features extracted from *comments* are not equally important for the different emotional reactions because there are different commenting patterns across reactions. For example, we found that the negative ratio is the most important feature for *sadness* and *anger.* Finally, our results suggested that the most effective prediction models are those trained on both *terms* and *comments.*

In the future, we plan to address the prediction task as a regression problem and we will try to predict the exact number of each emotional reaction. In addition, we would like to explore the effect of time on the prediction task since news articles are extremely sensitive to time and temporal information can be very useful.

Acknowledgments. This paper was partially funded by the Swiss National Science Foundation (SNSF) under the project OpiTrack.

The work of the second author was partially funded by the the Spanish MINECO under the research project SomEMBED (TIN2015-71147-C2-1-P).

This paper is partially supported by the BIGDATAGRAPES project (grant agreement N. 780751) that received funding from the European Union's Horizon 2020 research and innovation programme under the Information and Communication Technologies programme.

References

1. Alam, F., Celli, F., Stepanov, E.A., Ghosh, A., Riccardi, G.: The social mood of news: self-reported annotations to design automatic mood detection systems. In: PEOPLES 2016, pp. 143–152 (2016)
2. Aliannejadi, M., Crestani, F.: Venue suggestion using social-centric scores. CoRR abs/1803.08354 (2018)
3. Alm, C.O., Roth, D., Sproat, R.: Emotions from text: machine learning for text-based emotion prediction. In: HLT 2005, pp. 579–586 (2005)

4. Arapakis, I., Cambazoglu, B.B., Lalmas, M.: On the feasibility of predicting popular news at cold start. J. Assoc. Inf. Sci. Technol. **68**(5), 1149–1164 (2017)
5. Bandari, R., Asur, S., Huberman, B.A.: The pulse of news in social media: forecasting popularity. In: ICWSM 2012, pp. 26–33 (2012)
6. Breiman, L., Friedman, J., Stone, C., Olshen, R.: Classification and Regression Trees. The Wadsworth and Brooks-Cole Statistics-probability Series (1984)
7. Breiman, L.: Random forests. Mach. Learn. **45**(1), 5–32 (2001)
8. Cheng, J., Adamic, L., Dow, P.A., Kleinberg, J.M., Leskovec, J.: Can cascades be predicted? In: WWW 2014, pp. 925–936 (2014)
9. Clos, J., Bandhakavi, A., Wiratunga, N., Cabanac, G.: Predicting emotional reaction in social networks. In: Jose, J.M., et al. (eds.) ECIR 2017. LNCS, vol. 10193, pp. 527–533. Springer, Cham (2017). https://doi.org/10.1007/978-3-319-56608-5_44
10. Gerani, S., Carman, M., Crestani, F.: Aggregation methods for proximity-based opinion retrieval. ACM Trans. Inf. Syst. (TOIS) **30**(4), 1–36 (2012)
11. Giachanou, A., Crestani, F.: Like it or not: a survey of twitter sentiment analysis methods. ACM Comput. Surv. **49**(2), 28:1–28:41 (2016)
12. Giachanou, A., Harvey, M., Crestani, F.: Topic-specific stylistic variations for opinion retrieval on Twitter. In: Ferro, N., et al. (eds.) ECIR 2016. LNCS, vol. 9626, pp. 466–478. Springer, Cham (2016). https://doi.org/10.1007/978-3-319-30671-1_34
13. Giachanou, A., Rosso, P., Mele, I., Crestani, F.: Emotional influence prediction of news posts. In: ICWSM 2018 (2018)
14. Go, A., Bhayani, R., Huang, L.: Twitter sentiment classification using distant supervision. Technical report, Standford (2009)
15. Goel, P., Kulshreshtha, D., Jain, P., Shukla, K.K.: Prayas at EmoInt 2017: an ensemble of deep neural architectures for emotion intensity prediction in tweets. In: WASSA 2017, vol. 17, pp. 58–65 (2017)
16. Hu, M., Liu, B.: Mining and summarizing customer reviews. In: KDD 2004, pp. 168–177 (2004)
17. Kiritchenko, S., Zhu, X., Mohammad, S.M.: Sentiment analysis of short informal texts. J. Artif. Intell. Res. **50**(1), 723–762 (2014)
18. Lee, J.G., Moon, S., Salamatian, K.: Modeling and predicting the popularity of online contents with cox proportional hazard regression model. Neurocomputing **76**(1), 134–145 (2012)
19. Mikolov, T., Sutskever, I., Chen, K., Corrado, G., Dean, J.: Distributed representations of words and phrases and their compositionality. In: NIPS 2013, USA, pp. 3111–3119 (2013)
20. Paltoglou, G., Giachanou, A.: Opinion retrieval: searching for opinions in social media. In: Paltoglou, G., Loizides, F., Hansen, P. (eds.) Professional Search in the Modern World. LNCS, vol. 8830, pp. 193–214. Springer, Cham (2014). https://doi.org/10.1007/978-3-319-12511-4_10
21. Porter, M.F.: An algorithm for suffix stripping. Program **14**(3), 130–137 (1980)
22. Roberts, K., Roach, M.A., Johnson, J., Guthrie, J., Harabagiu, S.M.: EmpaTweet: annotating and detecting emotions on Twitter. In: LREC 2012, pp. 3806–3813 (2012)
23. Salton, G.: Automatic Text Processing: The Transformation, Analysis, and Retrieval of Information by Computer. Addison-Wesley Longman Publishing Co., Inc., Boston (1989)
24. Shu, K., Sliva, A., Wang, S., Tang, J., Liu, H.: Fake news detection on social media: a data mining perspective. SIGKDD Explor. Newsl. **19**(1), 22–36 (2017)

25. Shulman, B., Sharma, A., Cosley, D.: Predictability of popularity: gaps between prediction and understanding. In: ICWSM 2016, pp. 348–357 (2016)
26. Taboada, M., Brooke, J., Tofiloski, M., Voll, K., Stede, M.: Lexicon-based methods for sentiment analysis. Comput. Linguist. **37**(2), 267–307 (2011)
27. Tsagkias, M., Weerkamp, W., De Rijke, M.: Predicting the volume of comments on online news stories. In: CIKM 2009, pp. 1765–1768 (2009)
28. Wen, M., Yang, D., Rose, C.: Sentiment analysis in MOOC discussion forums: what does it tell us? In: EDM 2014 (2014)
29. Yang, J., Leskovec, J.: Patterns of temporal variation in online media. In: WSDM 2011, pp. 177–186 (2011)

Block Palindromes: A New
Generalization of Palindromes

Keisuke Goto[1]([✉]), I Tomohiro[2], Hideo Bannai[3], and Shunsuke Inenaga[3]

[1] Fujitsu Laboratories Ltd., Kawasaki, Japan
goto.keisuke@jp.fujitsu.com
[2] Kyushu Institute of Technology, Iizuka, Japan
tomohiro@ai.kyutech.ac.jp
[3] Kyushu University, Fukuoka, Japan
{bannai,inenaga}@inf.kyushu.ac.jp

Abstract. We study a new generalization of palindromes and gapped palindromes called *block palindromes*. A block palindrome is a string that becomes a palindrome when identical substrings are replaced with a distinct character. We investigate several properties of block palindromes and in particular, study substrings of a string which are block palindromes. In so doing, we introduce the notion of a *maximal block palindrome*, which leads to a compact representation of all block palindromes that occur in a string. We also propose an algorithm which enumerates all maximal block palindromes that appear in a given string T in $O(|T| + \|MBP(T)\|)$ time, where $\|MBP(T)\|$ is the output size, which is optimal unless all the maximal block palindromes can be represented in a more compact way.

Keywords: Palindrome · Enumeration algorithm
Factorization

1 Introduction

A palindrome is a string that is equal to its reverse, e.g., "Able_was_I_ere_ I_saw_Elba" (we treat upper and lower characters are the same for simple explanations). Palindromes have been studied in combinatorics on words and stringology.

Many research focused on finding palindromic structure of a string. Manacher [12] proposed a beautiful algorithm that enumerates all maximal palindromes of a string. Kosolobov et al. [11] proved that, a language P^k can be recognizable in $O(kN)$ time, where P is the language of all nonempty palindromes and N is the length of an input string. Alatabbi et al. [2] considered maximal palindromic factorization in which all factors are maximal palindromes. They also consider a problem of computing the fewest palindromic factorization, and proposed off-line linear-time algorithms. Later, I et al. [9] and Fici et al. [4] independently proposed on-line $O(N \log N)$-time algorithms, where N is the length

© Springer Nature Switzerland AG 2018
T. Gagie et al. (Eds.): SPIRE 2018, LNCS 11147, pp. 183–190, 2018.
https://doi.org/10.1007/978-3-030-00479-8_15

of an input string. Similar problems were also considered, such as, computing palindromic length [3], computing palindromic covers [9], computing palindromic pattern matching [8].

A gapped palindrome is a generalization of a palindrome that becomes a palindrome when a center substring is replaced by a character, where the center substring is a substring whose beginning and ending positions are equally far from the beginning and ending positions of the input string, respectively. For example, "Madam,_he_is_Adam" is a gapped palindrome, and it becomes a palindrome if the center substring "m,_he_is_" is replaced by a character. Gapped palindromes play an important role in molecular biology since they model a hairpin data structure of DNA and RNA sequences, see e.g. [14]. Several problems were considered such as, enumeration of exact gapped palindromes of a string [10] and also enumeration of approximate gapped palindromes [7,13], finding maximal length of long armed or and constrained length gapped palindrome [5].

In this paper, we consider the notion of block palindromes [1], which is a new generalization of palindromes and also gapped palindromes [1]. A block palindrome is a string that becomes a palindrome when identical substrings are replaced with a distinct character. More precisely, a block palindrome is a "symmetric" factorization $f = f_{-n} \cdots f_{-1} f_0 f_1 \cdots f_n$ of a string with the center factor f_0 is a string (which may be empty) and each of other factor $f_{-i} = f_i$ is a non-empty string for any $1 \leq i \leq n$. We also call a factor a block. For convenience, let $f = f_0$ when $n = 0$. For example, a factorization "To|kyo|_|and|_|Kyo|to" is a block palindrome, where "|" is a mark to distinguish adjacent blocks. Palindromes and gapped palindromes are special cases of block palindromes: For a palindrome, all blocks are characters, and for a gapped palindrome, the center block f_0 is a string and the other blocks are characters.

We investigate several properties of block palindromes. We introduce the notion of maximal block palindromes to concisely represent all block palindromes in a string, and propose an algorithm which enumerates all maximal block palindromes in a string T in $O(|T| + \|MBP(T)\|)$ time, where $\|MBP(T)\|$ is the output size. This is optimal unless all the maximal block palindromes can be represented in a more compact way.

2   Preliminaries

Let Σ be an integer alphabet. An element of Σ^* is called a *string*. The string of length 0 is called the *empty* string, and is denoted by ε. Although ε is not contained in Σ, we sometimes call ε the empty character for convenience. For a string $T = xyz$, x, y and z are called a *prefix*, *substring*, and *suffix* of T, respectively. In particular, a prefix (resp. suffix) x of T is called a *proper* prefix (resp. suffix) iff $x \neq T$. A non-empty string that is a proper prefix and also a proper suffix of T is called a *border* of T. Hence, a string of length N can have at most $N - 1$ borders of length ranging from 1 to $N - 1$. A string which does not

---

[1] Block palindromes were firstly introduced in a problem of 2015 British Informatics Olympiad [1], but we did not know the existence at the first version of this paper.

have any borders is called an *unbordered* string. For $1 \le i \le j \le |T|$, a substring of T which begins at position i and ends at position j is denoted by $T[i \ldots j]$. For convenience, let $T[i \ldots j] = \varepsilon$ if $j < i$.

In this paper, we also consider *half-positions* $k + 1/2$ for integers $0 \le k \le |T|$. For convenience, for a half-position i and an integer r such that $1/2 \le i - r \le i + r \le |T| + 1/2$, let $T[i - r \ldots i + r] = T[\lceil i - r \rceil \ldots \lfloor i + r \rfloor]$. Note that $T[i]$ for a half-position i is the empty character. The position $c = (|T| + 1)/2$ is called the *center position* of T, $T[c]$ is called the *center character* of T, and $T[c - d \ldots c + d]$ for an integer d is called a *center substring* of T.

For a string T and integers $1 \le i, j \le |T|$, a *longest common extension* (LCE) query $LCE_T(i, j)$ asks the length of the longest common prefix of the two suffixes $T[i \ldots |T|]$ and $T[j \ldots |T|]$ of T. When clear from the context, $LCE_T(i, j)$ is abbreviated as $LCE(i, j)$. It is well known that if T is drawn from an integer alphabet of size polynomially bounded in $|T|$, then LCE queries for T can be answered in constant time after an $O(|T|)$-time preprocessing, e.g., by constructing the suffix tree of T and a data structure for lowest common ancestor queries on the tree [6].

For a block palindrome $f = f_{-n} \cdots f_{-1} f_0 f_1 \cdots f_n$, the length of f denoted by $|f|$ is the total length of blocks, and the size of f denoted by $\|f\|$ is the number of non-empty blocks. A block palindrome is *even* if its size is even (that is, the center block f_0 is the empty string), and otherwise *odd* (that is, the center block f_0 is non-empty).

3   Properties of Block Palindromes

In this section, we investigate the properties of block palindromes. We assume that T is an input string of length N in the rest of the paper.

Since there are $O(2^N)$ factorization of T and block palindromes are symmetric, there are $O(2^{N/2})$ block palindromes of T. Moreover, there is a tight example that T consists of only the same characters.

Although there are a huge number of block palindromes of a string, they are very redundant. To look for more essential properties of block palindromes, we define the *largest block palindrome* which is a representative of other block palindromes. A block palindrome $f = f_{-n} \cdots f_n$ of T that has the largest number of blocks among all block palindromes of T is called the largest block palindrome. Note that each block f_i for $0 \le i \le n$ is an unbordered substring and f_i for $0 < i \le n$ is the shortest border of $T[k + 1 \ldots N - k]$, where $k = 0$ if $i = n$ and $k = |f_{i+1} \cdots f_n|$ otherwise. So, the largest block palindrome of T is unique. The largest block palindrome is a representative of all block palindromes in the sense that all block palindromes can be represented as block palindromes of f.

A natural and prompt question would be about how to efficiently compute the largest block palindrome of T. The following theorem answers this question.

Theorem 1. *The largest block palindrome* $f_{-n} \cdots f_n$ *of* T *can be computed in* $O(N)$ *time.*

Proof. We construct a data structure in $O(N)$ time that can answer any LCE query in constant time.

We greedily compute the blocks from outside f_n to inner f_1 by LCE queries. We assume that we compute the shortest border f_i of $T[b \ldots e]$. For $k = 1$ to $\lfloor (e - b + 1)/2 \rfloor$, we check whether $T[b \ldots b + k - 1]$ is the border of $T[b \ldots e]$ or not by checking whether $LCE(b, e - k + 1) \geq k$ or not. If $T[b \ldots e]$ does not have any border, we obtain $f_0 = T[b \ldots e]$. Otherwise, we obtain the shortest border $f_i = T[b \ldots b + k - 1]$ of $T[b \ldots e]$, and compute the more inner blocks for $T[b + k \ldots e - k]$. Since the number of LCE queries is $O(N)$ and each LCE query takes constant time, the largest block palindrome of T can be computed in $O(N)$ time. □

So far, we have considered only block palindromes that are equal to T itself. Next, we consider block palindromes that appear as substrings in T. We define a *maximal block palindrome* which is a representative of some block palindromes in T, and study how many maximal block palindromes can appear in T.

For a half-position $1 \leq c \leq N$ and an integer $1 \leq d \leq N/2$, let $F_T(c, d) = \{f \mid f = f_{-n} \cdots f_0 \cdots f_n$ is the largest block palindrome, $f_0 = T[c - d + 1 \ldots c + d - 1], f = T[c - d - k + 1 \ldots c + d + k - 1], k = |f_1 \cdots f_n|\}$ be the set of largest block palindromes whose center positions are the same and whose center blocks appear at $T[c - d + 1 \ldots c + d - 1]$. When context is clear, we denote F_T by F. For a string T, a largest block palindrome $f \in F(c, d)$ such that $|f|$ is the longest, namely the number of blocks are maximal among all largest block palindromes of $F(c, d)$, is called a *maximal block palindrome*.

We remark that the maximal block palindrome of $F(c, d)$ is a representative of all the largest block palindromes of $F(c, d)$.

Remark 1. *For a half-position $1 \leq c \leq N$ and an integer $1 \leq d \leq N/2$, any largest block palindrome $f = f_{-n} \cdots f_n \in F(c, d)$ is a sub-factorization of the maximal block palindrome $g = g_{-m} \cdots g_m \in F(c, d)$, that is, $n \leq m$ and $f_i = g_i$ for $0 \leq i \leq n$.*

Proof. We assume that the statement does not hold. Let f_j be a block that $f_j \neq g_j$, and $j = 0$ or $f_i = g_i$ for $0 \leq i < j \leq n$. If $|f_j| < |g_j|$, f_j is a border of g_j and it contradicts that g_j is the largest block palindrome. We can say the same things for the case $|f_j| > |g_j|$. Therefore, such f_j and g_j do not exist and this statement holds. □

We are interested in how many maximal block palindromes can appear in T. It is trivially upper bounded by $O(N^2)$ since there are $O(N^2)$ substrings which can be center substrings. If there is no limitation on the size of maximal block palindromes, we can easily see that it is tight. For a string T of length N in which the characters are all distinct, any substring w is unbordered, and there is at least one maximal block palindrome that contains w as a center block. Thus, T can contain $\Theta(N^2)$ maximal block palindromes. The following example says that the number of maximal block palindromes having three blocks has also the same tight upper bound.

Example 1. *The number of maximal block palindromes in $T = \mathtt{a}^n\mathtt{b}^n\mathtt{aba}^n\mathtt{b}^n$ that have at least three blocks is $\Theta(N^2)$, where c^n for a character c denotes run of c of length n, and $n = (N-2)/4$.*

For convenience, we denote T by $T = A_0 B_1 A_1 B_2 A_2 B_3$, where A_0, B_1, A_1, B_2, A_2, and B_3 are strings $\mathtt{a}^n$, $\mathtt{b}^n$, $\mathtt{a}$, $\mathtt{b}$, $\mathtt{a}^n$, and $\mathtt{b}^n$, respectively. There are maximal block palindromes of size three that, for $1 < i \leq n$, $1 < j \leq n$, $T[n-j+1 \ldots N - n+i-1] = (A_0[n-j+1 \ldots n]B_1[1..i-1])(B_1[i \ldots n]A_1 B_2 A_2[1 \ldots j])(A_2[n-j+1 \ldots n]B_3[1 \ldots i-1])$ and they are unbordered, where the parentheses indicate blocks.

Remark that the upper bound is reduced to $O(N)$ if we impose a limitation on the lengths of center blocks.

Remark 2. *For any constant $k \geq 0$, a string of length N can contain $\Theta(N)$ maximal block palindromes whose center blocks are of length $\leq k$ because there are $O(N)$ possible center blocks. In particular, a string contains at most $N-1$ maximal block palindromes of even size (i.e., the center blocks must be empty) because the number of occurrences of center blocks are at most $N-1$.*

The following lemma shows an interesting property of maximal block palindromes, and this property can be used for the proof of Lemma 2.

Lemma 1. *For a half-position $1 \leq c \leq N$ and two integers $1 \leq d < d' \leq N/2$, two largest block palindromes $f = f_{-n} \cdots f_n \in F(c, d)$ and $g = g_{-m} \cdots g_m \in F(c, d')$ do not share the block boundaries, namely, the ending positions of blocks k_i and k'_i such that $k_i = c+d-1+|f_1 \cdots f_i|$ and $k'_i = c+d'-1+|g_1 \cdots g_j|$ do not equal for any $1 \leq i \leq n$ and $1 \leq j \leq m$.*

Proof. Similar to Remark 1, if we assume that this lemma does not hold, a block of f or g must have a border and it contradicts that f and g are the largest block palindromes. □

Let $\|MBP(T)\|$ denote the sum of the sizes of all maximal block palindromes in T.

Lemma 2. *For any string T of length N, $\|MBP(T)\| \leq N(2N - 1)$.*

Proof. From Lemma 1, any two largest block palindromes, whose center positions are same but center blocks are different, do not share the block boundaries. This implies that, for a half-position c, the number of blocks of maximal block palindromes whose center position is c is up to N. Since there are $2N-1$ center positions, we have $\|MBP(T)\| \leq N(2N-1)$. □

4   Enumeration of Maximal Block Palindromes

In this section, we consider how to enumerate all the maximal block palindromes $MBP(T)$. A brute-force approach based on Theorem 1 would compute the largest block for every possible substring $T[b \ldots b + \ell - 1]$ (while suppressing output of non-maximal ones), which takes $\Theta(\sum_{\ell=1}^{N} \ell(N - \ell)) = \Theta(N^3)$ time.

We propose an optimal solution running in $o(N^3)$ time.

Theorem 2. *All maximal block palindromes that appear in T can be enumerated in $O(N + \|MBP(T)\|)$ time, where $\|MBP(T)\|$ is the output size.*

We actually consider a variant of the problem: We propose an algorithm to enumerate all the maximal block palindromes of size ≥ 2, whose total output size is denoted by $\|MBP_{\geq 2}(T)\|$, in optimal $O(N + \|MBP_{\geq 2}(T)\|)$ time. That is to say, we can completely ignore maximal block palindromes of size 1, which might not be interesting if we focus on palindromic structures in T. If we want to enumerate $MBP(T)$, we can do that by slightly modifying the algorithm.

Our algorithm proceeds in two steps: (i) enumerate all the pairing unbordered blocks for all center positions in a batch processing, and (ii) build maximal block palindromes from the enumerated blocks.

In Step (i), we firstly enumerate every pair of occurrences of an unbordered substring in T. Note that the pair will be a component of a maximal block palindrome, and the total number of enumerated pairs is $O(\|MBP_{\geq 2}(T)\|)$. We preprocess T in $O(N)$ time and space to support LCE queries in constant time. We also compute, for every character in T, the list storing all the occurrences of the character in increasing order, all of which can be obtained by sorting the positions i of T with the key $T[i]$ by radix sort in $O(N)$ time and space.

Now we focus on an occurrence b of $T[b]$, and identify every pair of occurrences of an unbordered substring such that the left one starts at b. Let $b < b_1 < b_2 < \cdots < b_k$ be the occurrences of $T[b]$ in $T[b \ldots N]$. We process $b_i \in \{b_1, \ldots, b_k\}$ in increasing order to identify common unbordered substrings starting at b and b_i using LCE queries. At the first round for b_1, we see that for any ℓ with $1 \leq \ell \leq \min(LCE(b, b_1), b_1 - b)$, the common substring of length ℓ starting at b and b_1 is unbordered, and thus, we report each pair of such unbordered substrings. While processing $b_i \in \{b_1, \ldots, b_k\}$ in increasing order, we maintain a set L of positive integers ℓ (by a sorted list of intervals) such that $T[b \ldots b + \ell - 1]$ has a border caused by the common substrings starting at b and b_i's processed so far. We use L to efficiently skip ℓ's such that $T[b \ldots b + \ell - 1]$ has a border in the later rounds. For example, in the first round, we add the interval $[b_1 - b + 1 \ldots b_1 - b + LCE(b, b_1)]$ to L (which is initially empty) as, for any $\ell \in [b_1 - b + 1 \ldots b_1 - b + LCE(b, b_1)]$, $T[b \ldots b + \ell - 1]$ has a border caused by the common substring starting at b and b_1. When processing b_i for $1 < i \leq k$, we see that for any $\ell \in [1 \ldots \min(LCE(b, b_i), b_i - b)] \setminus L$, the common substring of length ℓ starting at b and b_i is unbordered. Updating L can be easily done in $O(1)$ time by adding (merging if necessary) the interval $[b_i - b + 1 \ldots b_i - b + LCE(b, b_i)]$ to L (observe that the new interval is always pushed back to L or merged with the last interval of L as we process $\{b_1, \ldots, b_k\}$ in increasing order). Note that $[1 \ldots \min(LCE(b, b_i), b_i - b)] \setminus L$ always contains 1, and we can incrementally enumerate its element in constant time per element because L is maintained as a sorted list of intervals. Thus, the computation cost can be charged to the number of output, i.e., it runs in $O(N + \|MBP_{\geq 2}(T)\|)$ time in total.

When we find a pair of occurrences $b_l < b_r$ of an unbordered substring of length ℓ, we list it up as a triple $(c, b_r, b_r + \ell)$, where $c = (b_l + b_r + \ell - 1)/2$ is the center of the pairing blocks. After listing up all those triples, we sort them using the first and second elements as keys by radix sort, which can be done in $O(N + \|MBP_{\geq 2}(T)\|)$ time and space.

Now we are ready to proceed to Step (ii) in which we build the maximal block palindromes from the sorted list of triples computed in Step (i). For building the maximal block palindromes with center c, we scan the sublist of triples having center c and connect the pairing blocks whose beginning and ending positions are adjacent using the information of the second (the beginning position of the block) and third (the ending position of the block plus one) elements of the triples. We build all the c-centered maximal block palindromes by extending their blocks outwards simultaneously with a 0-initialized array A of length N. When we look at a triple $(c, b_r, b_r + \ell)$, we write b_r to $A[b_r + \ell]$, and connect the block with the block ending at $b_r - 1$ if such exists (which can be noticed by the information $A[b_r] \neq 0$). Since the block boundaries are not shared due to Lemma 1, the information written in A can be propagated correctly to extend the blocks. It runs in time linear to the size of the sublist. We can also clear A in the same time by scanning the sublist again while writing 0 to the entries we touched.

Since the initialization cost $O(N)$ of A is payed once in the very beginning of Step (ii) and the other computation cost can be charged to the output size, the total time complexity is $O(N + \|MBP_{\geq 2}(T)\|)$.

For enumerating $MBP(T)$, we modify Step (ii). While scanning the sublist for center c, we can identify all the positions $e \geq c$ such that e is not an ending position of some pairing block, for which the substring $T[2c - e \ldots e]$ is unbordered. If the unbordered substring cannot be extended outwards by blocks (which can also be checked while scanning the sublist), it is the maximal block palindrome of size 1 to output for $MBP(T)$. The algorithm runs in $O(N + \|MBP(T)\|)$ time in total as the additional cost can be charged to the output size.

5   Conclusions

In this paper, we investigated several properties of block palindromes which are the generalization of palindromes and gapped palindromes. We also proposed an optimal-algorithm to enumerate all maximal block palindromes appearing in a given string. As mentioned in Remark 2, if we impose a limitation on the lengths of center blocks, the upper bound of the number of maximal block palindromes is reduced to $O(N)$, where N is the length of an input string. In particular, for maximal block palindromes of even size, the center blocks are super restricted to be empty. The situation is similar to considering ordinal palindromes (in which the center blocks are strict) versus maximal gapped palindromes (in which the restriction on the center blocks are relaxed). It would be interesting to investigate the properties of maximal block palindromes whose center blocks have restricted lengths and develop efficient algorithms to enumerate only such a subset of maximal block palindromes.

References

1. The 2015 British Informatics Olympiad (2015). http://olympiad.org.uk/2015/index.html. Accessed 13 June 2018
2. Alatabbi, A., Iliopoulos, C.S., Rahman, M.S.: Maximal palindromic factorization. In: Holub, J., Žďárek, J. (eds.) Proceedings of the Prague Stringology Conference 2013, pp. 70–77. Czech Technical University in Prague, Czech Republic (2013)
3. Borozdin, K., Kosolobov, D., Rubinchik, M., Shur, A.M.: Palindromic length in linear time. In: CPM. LIPIcs, vol. 78, pp. 23:1–23:12. Schloss Dagstuhl - Leibniz-Zentrum fuer Informatik (2017)
4. Fici, G., Gagie, T., Kärkkäinen, J., Kempa, D.: A subquadratic algorithm for minimum palindromic factorization. J. Discret. Algorithms **28**, 41–48 (2014)
5. Gupta, S., Prasad, R.: Searching gapped palindromes in DNA sequences using Burrows Wheeler type transformation. J. Inf. Optim. Sci. **37**(1), 51–74 (2016). https://doi.org/10.1080/02522667.2015.1103044
6. Gusfield, D.: Algorithms on Strings, Trees, and Sequences - Computer Science and Computational Biology. Cambridge University Press, Cambridge (1997)
7. Hsu, P., Chen, K., Chao, K.: Finding all approximate gapped palindromes. Int. J. Found. Comput. Sci. **21**(6), 925–939 (2010)
8. I, T., Inenaga, S., Takeda, M.: Palindrome pattern matching. Theor. Comput. Sci. **483**, 162–170 (2013). https://doi.org/10.1016/J.TCS.2012.01.047
9. I, T., Sugimoto, S., Inenaga, S., Bannai, H., Takeda, M.: Computing palindromic factorizations and palindromic covers on-line. In: Kulikov, A.S., Kuznetsov, S.O., Pevzner, P. (eds.) CPM 2014. LNCS, vol. 8486, pp. 150–161. Springer, Cham (2014). https://doi.org/10.1007/978-3-319-07566-2_16
10. Kolpakov, R., Kucherov, G.: Searching for gapped palindromes. Theor. Comput. Sci. **410**(51), 5365–5373 (2009). https://doi.org/10.1016/j.tcs.2009.09.013
11. Kosolobov, D., Rubinchik, M., Shur, A.M.: Pa^k is linear recognizable online. In: Italiano, G.F., Margaria-Steffen, T., Pokorný, J., Quisquater, J.-J., Wattenhofer, R. (eds.) SOFSEM 2015. LNCS, vol. 8939, pp. 289–301. Springer, Heidelberg (2015). https://doi.org/10.1007/978-3-662-46078-8_24
12. Manacher, G.K.: A new linear-time "on-line" algorithm for finding the smallest initial palindrome of a string. J. ACM **22**(3), 346–351 (1975)
13. Narisada, S., Diptarama, Narisawa, K., Inenaga, S., Shinohara, A.: Computing longest single-arm-gapped palindromes in a string. In: Steffen, B., Baier, C., van den Brand, M., Eder, J., Hinchey, M., Margaria, T. (eds.) SOFSEM 2017. LNCS, vol. 10139, pp. 375–386. Springer, Cham (2017). https://doi.org/10.1007/978-3-319-51963-0_29
14. Smith, G.R.: Meeting DNA palindromes head-to-head. Genes Dev. **22**, 2612–2620 (2008)

Maximal Motif Discovery in a Sliding Window

Costas S. Iliopoulos, Manal Mohamed, Solon P. Pissis, and Fatima Vayani[(✉)]

Department of Informatics, King's College London, London, UK
{c.iliopoulos,manal.mohamed,solon.pissis,fatima.vayani}@kcl.ac.uk

Abstract. Motifs are relatively short sequences that are biologically significant, and their discovery in molecular sequences is a well-researched subject. A *don't care* is a special letter that matches every letter in the alphabet. Formally, a *motif* is a sequence of letters of the alphabet and don't care letters. A motif $\tilde{m}_{d,k}$ that occurs at least k times in a sequence is *maximal* if it cannot be extended (to the left or right) nor can it be specialised (that is, its $d' \leq d$ don't cares cannot be replaced with letters from the alphabet) without reducing its number of occurrences. Here we present a new dynamic data structure, and the first on-line algorithm, to discover all maximal motifs in a sliding window of length ℓ on a sequence x of length n in $\mathcal{O}(nd\ell + d\lceil \frac{\ell}{w} \rceil \cdot \sum_{i=\ell}^{n-1} |\text{DIFF}_{i-1}^i|)$ time, where w is the size of the machine word and DIFF_{i-1}^i is the symmetric difference of the sets of occurrences of maximal motifs at $x[i - \ell \mathinner{.\,.} i - 1]$ and at $x[i - \ell + 1 \mathinner{.\,.} i]$.

Keywords: Motif discovery · Sequence motifs
Genome analysis

1 Introduction

As next-generation sequencing technology advances, there is an increase in the production of genomic data that requires *de novo* assembly and analyses. One such analysis is motif discovery [1,9–12,14]. Motifs are relatively short sequences that are biologically significant. Examples of these are protein-binding sites, such as transcription factor recognition sites [6].

We highlight that the maximal motif discovery problem discussed in this paper differs significantly from the well-established *(ℓ, d)-motif search* problem: find all ℓ-length motifs that occur in at least k sequences from a given collection of sequences, where each occurrence of the motif can contain up to d mismatches [16].

The obvious caveat of (ℓ, d)-motif search approaches is that the length of the motif is restricted and in reality, a longer or shorter motif could be more significant. We, therefore, focus on the more general problem of *maximal motif discovery*. A maximal motif $\tilde{m}_{d,k}$ is not determined by a given length, rather, its significance is based on its number of occurrences compared to its substrings. A motif is maximal because it cannot be extended to the left or right without

© Springer Nature Switzerland AG 2018
T. Gagie et al. (Eds.): SPIRE 2018, LNCS 11147, pp. 191–205, 2018.
https://doi.org/10.1007/978-3-030-00479-8_16

reducing its number of occurrences. As importance is given to the number of occurrences, the first parameter k sets a minimum threshold for the number of occurrences of a reported maximal motif. The second parameter d is more restrictive in that mismatches occur in up to d specific positions in the motif, known as *don't care* letters and denoted by $\diamond$. Thus, a motif is also maximal because its don't care letters cannot be specialised without reducing its number of occurrences. For instance, given the sequence ACGTTATGTT and $d = 1$, one should conclude that the significant motif is A$\diamond$GTT rather than, for instance, GTT; both of which have exactly the same number of occurrences. However, if we are restricted to $\ell = 3$, this important observation would be missed. Importantly, we take a purely *de novo* approach, where only one sequence is needed as input.

In [4], Grossi *et al.* proposed, to the best of our knowledge, the most current combinatorial solution for maximal motif discovery: a data structure termed *motif trie*. A motif trie represents all prefixes, suffixes and occurrence positions of each maximal motif $\tilde{m}_{d,k}$ in the set $\mathcal{M}_{d,k}$ of maximal motifs. The authors present an output-sensitive algorithm with a time complexity of $\mathcal{O}(nd + d^3 \cdot \sum_{\tilde{m}_{d,k} \in \mathcal{M}_{d,k}} |\mathrm{OCC}(\tilde{m}_{d,k})|)$, where $\mathrm{OCC}(\tilde{m}_{d,k})$ is the set of occurrences of $\tilde{m}_{d,k}$, assuming the input sequence of length n is built on a constant-sized alphabet.

Our Contribution. Motivated by the aim of discovering interesting regions in large genomic sequences, in this paper, we propose a data structure as sensitive as the motif trie, and crucially, that has the additional advantage of being a dynamic data structure. The motivation behind creating a dynamic structure was to facilitate a sliding window on the input sequence. Specifically, this ensures the additional ability to find interesting ℓ-length regions of the sequence, which is useful in various bioinformatics applications, including the prediction of the origin of chromosomal replication (OriC) [8]. The length of OriC in model bacterial species ranges from 120 to 300bp; for example, it is 240bp in *E. coli* [7]. Furthermore, motifs that occur within OriC, such as DnaA boxes, show that d and k are small constants (for example, $d = 2$ and $k = 4$) in practice [3]. Before presenting the problem formally, let us denote by $\mathcal{M}_{i,d,k}$ the set of the maximal motifs in the ℓ-length window ending at position i in string x, each of which must occur at least k times in the window and contain at most d don't care letters.

MAXIMAL MOTIF DISCOVERY IN A SLIDING WINDOW (MMDSW)
Input: A string x of length n and integers ℓ, $k > 1$ and d.
Output: An array $\mathcal{S}_x$ of scores, where $\mathcal{S}_x[i] = |\mathcal{M}_{i,d,k}|$ and $\ell \leq i < n$.

We present the first on-line algorithm to find the occurrences of all maximal motifs in a sliding window in $\mathcal{O}(nd\ell + d\lceil \frac{\ell}{w} \rceil \cdot \sum_{i=\ell}^{n-1} |\mathrm{DIFF}_{i-1}^i|)$ time, where w is the size of the machine word and DIFF_{i-1}^i is the symmetric difference of the sets of occurrences of maximal motifs at $x[i - \ell .. i - 1]$ and at $x[i - \ell + 1 .. i]$. The space complexity of our algorithm is $\mathcal{O}(\ell^2)$. This result poses an improvement over the time required to solve the same problem using the motif trie [4], which would then be $\mathcal{O}(nd\ell + d^3 \cdot \sum_{i=\ell, \tilde{m}_{d,k} \in \mathcal{M}_{i,d,k}}^{n-1} |\mathrm{OCC}(\tilde{m}_{d,k})|)$. This improvement is significant as a single occurrence of a maximal motif would be reported $\mathcal{O}(\ell)$ times by the latter approach. Therefore, the proposed algorithm results in a speed-up of $\mathcal{O}(d^2w)$ per occurrence of a maximal motif.

2 Definitions and Algorithmic Toolbox

We begin with a few definitions and notation, generally following [2,5]. An *alphabet* Σ is a finite non-empty set of letters of size $|\Sigma|$. A *string* built on Σ is a finite sequence of letters of Σ. In the current context, we assume that the alphabet is fixed, that is, $|\Sigma| = \mathcal{O}(1)$. The *length* of a string x is denoted by $|x|$. We denote the *empty string* by ε. For two positions i and j, we denote by $x[i \mathinner{\ldotp\ldotp} j] = x[i] \mathinner{\ldotp\ldotp} x[j]$ the *factor* (or *substring*) of x that starts at i and ends at j; it is ε if $j < i$. For any string $x = uyv$, where y, u and v are strings, if $u = \varepsilon$ then y is a *prefix* of x. Conversely, if $v = \varepsilon$ then y is a *suffix* of x.

Suffix Tree. Given a string x of length $n > 0$, the *suffix tree* $\mathcal{T}_x$ of x is a compact trie representing all suffixes of x. The nodes of the trie which become nodes of the suffix tree are *explicit* nodes; all other nodes are *implicit*. That is, a node v in the trie with only one outgoing edge is implicit in the suffix tree. The root node r represents the empty string ε. Each edge of the suffix tree can be viewed as a path of implicit nodes from one explicit node to another.

Each implicit node can be represented by a tuple $\langle \gamma, \mu, \lambda \rangle$, where μ is the number of implicit nodes skipped on the edge from explicit node γ, and the edge label begins with $\alpha = x[\lambda]$. The *path-label* $P(v)$ of a node v is the concatenation of the edge labels along the path from r to v. Henceforth, we will use $P(v)$ and v interchangeably to refer to the factor of x that v represents. The *string-depth* $D(v) = |P(v)|$ of a node v is the total number of implicit and explicit nodes in the path from r to v.

Node v is known as a *terminal* node if its path-label is a suffix of x, that is, $P(v) = x[i \mathinner{\ldotp\ldotp} n-1]$, $0 \le i < n$. Note that, each leaf in $\mathcal{T}_x$ is a terminal node. If each terminal node is a leaf node then $\mathcal{T}_x$ is an *explicit suffix tree*, otherwise $\mathcal{T}_x$ is an *implicit suffix tree*. We denote the set of occurrences of a factor v in x by $\mathrm{OCC}(v)$, such that $|\mathrm{OCC}(v)|$ corresponds to the number of terminal nodes in the subtree rooted at v.

The *suffix link* from a *suffix origin*, node v, with path-label $P(v) = \alpha w$, is a pointer to a *suffix target*, node $s(v)$, path-labelled $P(s(v)) = w$, where $\alpha \in \Sigma$ and w is a factor of x.

An *internal* node of $\mathcal{T}_x$ is an explicit, non-root, non-leaf node. The *explicit child* of a node v is the nearest explicit node that has an incoming edge from v. We define an *explicit parent* in a similar way. We define the *ancestors* of a node u as the set of all internal nodes in the path from r to u, if any. Similarly, we define the *descendants* of an internal node v as the set of all internal nodes in the subtree rooted at v, if any.

Maximal Motifs. Each factor of x is uniquely represented by the path-label of a node of $\mathcal{T}_x$. More specifically, each *right-maximal* repeated factor of x is uniquely represented by an internal node of $\mathcal{T}_x$. In other words, at least one occurrence of this factor (of which there are at least two) in x is followed by a letter that is distinct from the rest. Therefore, a right-maximal factor of x cannot be extended to the right without reducing its number of occurrences. A right-maximal factor is also *left-maximal* if the preceding letter of at least one of its occurrences in x is distinct from the rest. If the number of occurrences of a suffix target is not equal to that of its suffix origin, or if it is a target of multiple suffix links, then the suffix target is left-maximal. That is, it cannot be extended to the left without reducing its number of occurrences. If a node is left-maximal, all of its ancestors are also left-maximal. Henceforth, we will refer to repeated factors that are both left- and right-maximal as *seeds*, and their corresponding suffix tree nodes as *seed nodes*. Note that every seed node is an internal node in a suffix tree, but not every internal node corresponds to a seed. The number of seeds are thus $\mathcal{O}(n)$ because the number of nodes in a suffix tree are $\mathcal{O}(n)$.

A *don't care*, denoted as $\diamond$, is a special letter that matches every letter in Σ. We denote a *non-deterministic* string $\tilde{y}$ which contains such letters with a tilde, and say that $\tilde{y}$ is built on $\Sigma^\diamond = \Sigma \cup \{\diamond\}$. An occurrence of $\tilde{y}$ at position i in x is a sequential match of each letter in $\tilde{y}$ with the corresponding letter in $x[i \mathinner{.\,.} i + |\tilde{y}| - 1]$. The set of occurrences of $\tilde{y}$ in x is denoted as $\mathrm{OCC}(\tilde{y})$.

For our purposes and given thresholds d and k, we define a *motif* $\tilde{m}_{d,k}$ that occurs in a given string x, as a sequence of d' don't cares and up to $d' + 1$ seeds, where $0 \leq d' \leq d$ and $|\mathrm{OCC}(\tilde{m}_{d,k})| \geq k$. A motif $\tilde{m}_{d,k}$ is *maximal* as it cannot be extended (to the left or right) nor can it be specialised (that is, its don't cares cannot be replaced with letters from Σ) without reducing its number of occurrences. Each motif must begin and end with a seed, as $\mathrm{OCC}(\tilde{m}_{d,k})$ is not affected by flanking $\tilde{m}_{d,k}$ with don't cares [4]. A singleton seed can be a motif, where $d' = 0$; this will be referred to as a *singleton motif*. We denote the set of all maximal motifs in x as $\mathcal{M}_{d,k}$.

Motif Graph. It is evident that the suffix tree is useful in finding seeds and we now explain how it can be augmented to find maximal motifs. We term this augmented suffix tree a *motif graph*. Each internal node v of $\mathcal{T}_x$ is decorated with (1) an integer variable $|\mathrm{OCC}(v)|$; and (2) a Boolean variable $\mathrm{ISSEED}(v)$, which is TRUE if node v is a seed (and FALSE otherwise). Each node v, where $\mathrm{ISSEED}(v) = $ TRUE, is further augmented with (1) a Boolean variable $\mathrm{ISMOTIF}(v)$, which is TRUE if node v represents a singleton motif (and FALSE otherwise); and (2) a bit-vector $\mathcal{B}(v)$, of total size n bits, indicating the occurrences of v.

A labelled, directed edge $u \xrightarrow{d'} v$, from seed node u to seed node v, indicates that $u \diamond^{d'} v$ occurs at least k times in the string, where $0 < d' \leq d$. Note that, $u = v$ is possible. We will refer to these extra edges as *motif edges*. To facilitate their construction, we store an array E of linear size in which each element keeps a list of pointers to seed nodes which have an occurrence ending at the corresponding position in x.

We define the bit-vector $\mathcal{B}(u \xrightarrow{d'} v)$ of a motif edge as the bit-vector resulting from a SHIFT-AND operation of $\mathcal{B}(u)$ and $\mathcal{B}(v)$, which represents the starting positions of occurrences of $u \diamond^{d'} v$ in x. Note that the shift accounts for $D(u)$ and

d'. If every occurrence of u is succeeded by $\diamond^{d'} v$, and every occurrence of v is preceded by $u \diamond^{d'}$, we say $\mathcal{B}(u) \equiv \mathcal{B}(v) \equiv \mathcal{B}(u \xrightarrow{d'} v)$. We denote as INDEGREE($u$) (resp. OUTDEGREE($u$)) the number of incoming (resp. outgoing) motif edges to (resp. from) the seed node u.

Each maximal motif corresponds to a *maximal path* of motif edges, where the maximality is satisfied by the following two conditions with respect to d and k. Suppose $\tilde{m}_{d,k} = u \diamond^{d'_1} z_1 \diamond^{d'_2} z_2 .. \diamond^{d'_{q-1}} z_{q-1} \diamond^{d'_q} z_q$ corresponds to a path $p = u \xrightarrow{d'_1} z_1 \xrightarrow{d'_2} z_2 .. \xrightarrow{d'_{q-1}} z_{q-1} \xrightarrow{d'_q} z_q$, then $\sum_{i=1}^{q} d'_i \leq d$ and $|\text{OCC}(p)| = |\text{OCC}(\tilde{m}_{d,k})| \geq k$. In other words, p is maximal if its corresponding motif occurs at least k times in the string and contains no more than d don't cares.

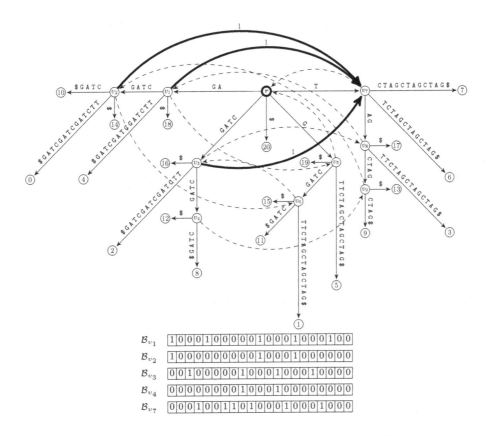

Fig. 1. The motif graph built upon the explicit suffix tree of the string $x =$ AGCTAGTTCTAGCTAGCTAG\$, given $d = 1$ and $k = 2$. Each leaf node has been labelled with the index of the suffix that it represents. Suffix links are shown as dashed directed edges. The set of all internal nodes, $\{v_1, \ldots, v_9\}$, represents the right-maximal repeated factors of x. As $|\text{OCC}(v_5)| = 5 = |\text{OCC}(v_1)|$, v_5 is not a seed; as $|\text{OCC}(v_1)| = 5 \neq |\text{OCC}(v_8)| = 4$, v_1 is a seed; and so on. Thus, the set of all seed nodes is $\{v_1, v_2, v_3, v_4, v_7\}$. Motif edges are shown in bold.

The longest prefix (resp. suffix) of p, denoted by PREFIX(p) (resp. SUFFIX(p)), is the path resulting from the truncation of the last (resp. first) edge in p. If $|\text{OCC}(p)| \neq |\text{OCC}(\text{PREFIX}(p))|$ (resp. $\neq |\text{OCC}(\text{SUFFIX}(p))|$), then PREFIX($p$) (resp. SUFFIX($p$)) is also a maximal path and hence corresponds to a motif. The bit-vector $\mathcal{B}(p)$ of path p can be computed by a series of SHIFT-AND operations of the bit-vectors of the edges in p.

Example 1. Given the string $x =$ AGCTAGTTCTAGCTAGCTAG\$, the set of seeds is $\{v_1 = $ AG$, v_2 = $ AGCTAG$, v_3 = $ CTAG$, v_4 = $ CTAGCTAG$, v_7 = $ T$\}$. For $d = 1$ and $k = 2$, we find the following set $\mathcal{M}_{d,k}$ of motifs from the motif graph shown in Fig. 1.

$\tilde{m}_{d,k}$	AG	AG$\diamond$T	AGCTAG	AGCTAG$\diamond$T	CTAG	CTAG$\diamond$T	CTAGCTAG
$|\text{OCC}(\tilde{m}_{d,k})|$	5	4	3	2	4	3	2

3 Sliding Window

The main computational challenge in reporting motifs in a sliding window is maintaining the left- and rightmost seeds in two respects: checking their maximality (nodes) and updating their relationship with neighbouring seeds (edges). These changes to the motif graph identify and thus efficiently update *only* the subset of motifs occurring at both ends of the window.

Specifically, in what follows, we describe the effect on $\mathcal{M}_{i,d,k}$ and the motif graph when adding a letter to the right of the window, and deleting a letter from the left, thus simulating the sliding window on x.

3.1 Update of Set of Motifs for a Sliding Window

Before proceeding with updates, the set $\mathcal{M}_{i,d,k}$ is copied from the set $\mathcal{M}_{i-1,d,k}$ from the previous window.

Adding a Letter to the Right. When adding a letter $x[i] = \alpha$ to the right of the window, the following cases are checked in order, if $|\text{OCC}(\alpha)| \geq k$ in the window.

1. If α now extends at least k occurrences of some motif $\tilde{m} \in \mathcal{M}_{i,d,k}$, it becomes the suffix of a new motif $\tilde{m}' = \tilde{m} \diamond^{d'} \alpha$, which occurs at least k times in the window, where $0 \leq d' \leq d$. In this case, the new motif $\tilde{m}'$ is added to $\mathcal{M}_{i,d,k}$. If the number of occurrences of $\tilde{m}$ is equal to $\tilde{m}'$, $\tilde{m}$ is deleted from $\mathcal{M}_{i,d,k}$, as it is no longer maximal. Let M be the number of motifs added to $\mathcal{M}_{i,d,k}$.
2. The letter α can be added to $\mathcal{M}_{i,d,k}$ as a singleton motif if it is not already there and if $M = 0$; if $M = 1$ and $|\text{OCC}(\alpha)| > |\text{OCC}(\tilde{m}')|$; or if $M > 1$.

Deleting a Letter from the Left. When deleting the leftmost letter α of the window, every motif $\tilde{m}' = \alpha\tilde{m} \in \mathcal{M}_{i,d,k}$ must be deleted if now $|\text{occ}(\tilde{m}')| < k$ in the window. After this possible deletion, the following cases are considered.

- If $\tilde{m} = \varepsilon$, and thus $\tilde{m}' = \alpha$, then nothing more is done.
- Otherwise, $\tilde{m}$ is added to $\mathcal{M}_{i,d,k}$, if and only if $\tilde{m} \notin \mathcal{M}_{i,d,k}$ and it is not a prefix of a motif $\tilde{m}'' \in \mathcal{M}_{i,d,k}$ where $|\text{occ}(\tilde{m}'')| = |\text{occ}(\tilde{m})|$.

3.2 On-Line Update of Suffix Tree for a Sliding Window

As the motif graph is fundamentally a suffix tree, we will first provide an overview of how a letter can be added to the right and deleted from the left, namely by Ukkonen's [15] and Senft's [13] algorithms, respectively.

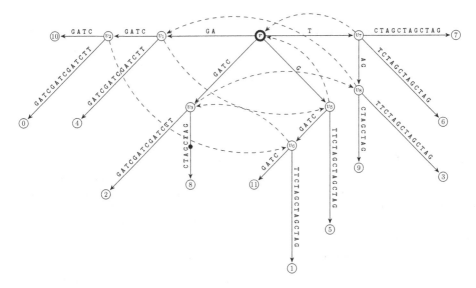

Fig. 2. The implicit suffix tree of the string $x = $ AGCTAGTTCTAGCTAGCTAG. Observe that, the most recent leaf to be added is suffix $j-1 = 11$. The active point, $\mathcal{A} = \langle v_3, 4, 15\rangle$, is represented as a black dot on the path between nodes v_3 and leaf node 8. The longest repeated suffix $x[12..19] = $ CTAGCTAG is the path from r to $\mathcal{A}$.

Adding a Letter to the Right. The following is a summary of the relevant details of Ukkonen's algorithm; for further details, refer to [15]. The algorithm iteratively builds $\mathcal{T}_x$, where the tree $\mathcal{T}_{x_i}$ at each iteration i represents the implicit suffix tree of the prefix $x[0..i]$ of x, where only j suffixes are represented as leaf nodes and leaf $j - 1$ is the most recent leaf added to the suffix tree, where $0 \leq j-1 \leq i < n$. If $j-1 = i$, the suffix tree $\mathcal{T}_x$ is explicit. The algorithm makes use of a special pointer to a node known as the *active point* $\mathcal{A} = \langle \gamma, \mu, \lambda \rangle$ that corresponds to the longest repeated suffix of $x[0..i]$; see Fig. 2.

When adding a letter $x[i] = \alpha$ to the right of the string, and thus extending each existing suffix $\beta \in \{\beta_0, \ldots, \beta_{i-1}\}$, the following three rules are applied.

- If there is no path from r representing $\beta\alpha$, we do either of the following. Let $P(v) = \beta$.
  - If v is a leaf node, we simply append α to the label of the edge ending at v. This is a Rule 1 extension.
  - If v is not a leaf node, observe that $\mathcal{A}$ is pointing to v. We create a new leaf node u, for which the label of its incoming edge from v is α. Thus, u represents the jth suffix of x. If v is an implicit node, it becomes explicit. The active point $\mathcal{A}$ becomes $\langle v, 0, i \rangle$. This is a Rule 2 extension.
- If $\beta\alpha$ already exists within the suffix tree, the structure of the tree is unchanged and μ is incremented. However, if $\mathcal{A}$ reaches an explicit node v', then $\mathcal{A} = \langle v', 0, i \rangle$. This is a Rule 3 extension and we say that $\mathcal{A}$ is *moving along* a branch of $\mathcal{T}_x$, as i moves away from j.

If a Rule 2 extension results in making a node v explicit, then it becomes the suffix origin of a newly created suffix link. Additionally, further leaf nodes may need to be added by moving $\mathcal{A}$ to $s(v)$. In this case, we say that $\mathcal{A}$ is *following a suffix link*, as j moves closer to i.

Example 2. In Fig. 2, leaf nodes 10 and 11 were added when letter $x[16] = $ C was added.

Deleting a Letter from the Left. The following is a summary of the relevant details of Senft's algorithm; for further details, refer to [13]. When deleting a letter α from the left of the window, the longest unique prefix of the window is being deleted, which is in fact the whole window. In doing so, all repeated prefixes of suffixes must be maintained, by giving importance to the longest repeated prefix β, where $\beta[0] = \alpha$. Let $P(u) = \beta\delta$ be the longest unique prefix and $P(v) = \beta$ be the longest repeated prefix; thus v is an ancestor of u.

- If v is an explicit node, we simply delete the leaf u. If v now only has one remaining child u', we delete v and merge the edge that was directed at v with the edge that is directed at u'.
- If v is an implicit node, then β is also the longest repeated suffix. We delete the leaf u and replace it with a leaf u', where $P(u') = \beta$.

The representation of edge labels can be updated efficiently due to the correctness of their offsets relative to the start of the window. Thus, a batch update of all labels can be done after every ℓ window shifts.

Example 3. Considering Fig. 2, the deletion of the leftmost letter (A) would result in the deletion of the leaf node that represents the longest suffix. This would cause the subsequent deletion of node v_2 as it would have one remaining child; the edges from v_1 to v_2 and v_2 to leaf node 10 would be merged.

4 Maximal Motif Discovery Algorithm

The proposed algorithm works in an on-line manner. In order to facilitate this efficiently, we begin by appending to the start of x a string of ℓ letters $\notin \Sigma$. We also append a unique letter $\notin x$ to the end of x to ensure that the motif graph (augmented suffix tree $\mathcal{T}_x$) of the final window is explicit.

First, we must redefine and extend our original definition of the motif graph as follows. For an internal node v, $|\text{OCC}(v)|$ and $\text{ISSEED}(v)$ are now defined relative to the window, not the whole string. The same applies to $\text{ISMOTIF}(v)$ for a seed node v. Similarly, $\mathcal{B}(v)$ is now of size ℓ bits, and in order to maintain it efficiently, we introduce an integer variable $\text{PIVOT}(v)$, which acts as an anchor so that $\mathcal{B}(v)$ is only updated when an occurrence of v is added or deleted, rather than in every step i of the algorithm. Additionally, E is now a dynamic structure, of size $\mathcal{O}(\ell)$, in which each element keeps a list of pointers to seed nodes which have an occurrence ending at the corresponding position in the current window. The aforementioned definition of a motif edge remains; however, the shift operation that produces its bit-vector now also takes the pivot into consideration.

Before proceeding, we define the following subroutines used throughout the algorithm. Given a bit-vector $\mathcal{B}$, the function $\text{POPCOUNT}(\mathcal{B})$ returns the number of set bits in $\mathcal{B}$. Similarly, the Boolean function $\text{KPOPCOUNT}(k, \mathcal{B})$ returns TRUE if the number of set bits in $\mathcal{B}$ is at least k (and FALSE otherwise). The function $\text{CHECKENDPOSITIONS}()$ returns a list E' in which, for each d' and for each pointer to a node v in the list at position $j' = j - d' - 1$ in E, a pair $\langle v, j' \rangle$ is added, where $0 < d' \leq d$ and $j - 1$ is the most recent leaf added to the suffix tree, as described in Sect. 3.2.

Importantly, note that the algorithm assumes that the window is moving with respect to j. Therefore, when a leaf j is added to the motif graph, the leaf $j - \ell$ is deleted and the score is updated accordingly. Therefore, the score of a window represents the number of motifs that occur in the window, such that each motif has at least k starting positions in $x[j - \ell + 1 .. j]$.

4.1 Reading a Letter on the Right

Recall that the active point $\mathcal{A}$ represents the rightmost seed that has an occurrence at position j of x. We, therefore, describe in the following the various cases of how $\mathcal{A}$ is updated when reading letter $x[i]$.

$\mathcal{A}$ **starts moving along a new branch from** r. The active point $\mathcal{A} = \langle r, 1, i \rangle$ is initialised, where $\text{ISSEED}(\mathcal{A}) = \text{TRUE}$ and $|\text{OCC}(\mathcal{A})|$ is computed by incrementing the occurrence of its $\text{EXPLICITCHILD}(\mathcal{A})$ by one. If $|\text{OCC}(\mathcal{A})| \geq k$, $\mathcal{B}(\mathcal{A})$ and $\text{PIVOT}(\mathcal{A})$ are copied from $\text{EXPLICITCHILD}(\mathcal{A})$ and shifted to accommodate the extra occurrence at position j. Incoming motif edges are then added to $\mathcal{A}$ in the following way. First, the list E' is obtained by calling $\text{CHECKENDPOSITIONS}()$. Each pair in E' corresponds to a potential motif edge $v \xrightarrow{d'} \mathcal{A}$. If $\text{KPOPCOUNT}(k, \mathcal{B}(v \xrightarrow{d'} \mathcal{A}))$ is FALSE the edge is discarded. If they exist, the remaining potential motif edges are clustered with respect to $|\text{OCC}(v \diamond^{d'} \mathcal{A})|$. In each cluster, the edges are sorted with respect to $D(v)$, and the motif edge $v \xrightarrow{d'} \mathcal{A}$ is added from the deepest. For $d' > 1$, an edge can only be added if there is no edge from a descendant seed node of v to $\mathcal{A}$ with the same bit-vector as $v \xrightarrow{d'} \mathcal{A}$. Importantly, this is regardless of the label d' of either edge. After the possible addition of motif edges, ISMOTIF($\mathcal{A}$) is set to FALSE if there is any edge $v \xrightarrow{d'} \mathcal{A}$ such that $\mathcal{B}(\mathcal{A}) \equiv \mathcal{B}(v \xrightarrow{d'} \mathcal{A})$, where $0 < d' \leq d$. An update is made to ISMOTIF(v) in a similar way.

$\mathcal{A}$ **advances along a branch and reaches an internal node** u**.** The active point $\mathcal{A} = \langle u, 0, i \rangle$ points to an internal node u, which is updated as follows. First, $|\text{OCC}(u)|$ is incremented and ISSEED(u) is updated. If ISSEED(u) = TRUE and $|\text{OCC}(u)| \geq k$, then u is updated by copying missing information from $\mathcal{A}$ regarding its new occurrence at position j, before the extra structures and incoming edges of $\mathcal{A}$ can be deleted. Specifically, $\mathcal{B}(u)$ and PIVOT(u) are copied from $\mathcal{A}$, and a pointer to u is added to the list of pointers representing position $j + D(u) - 1$ in E. Then, for each incoming motif edge to $\mathcal{A}$, the motif edge is copied to u if it does not already exist. If the motif edge already exists, it is not duplicated, however, it may affect whether u is a singleton motif.

$\mathcal{A}$ **moves further along a branch and passes by a seed node** u**.** The active point $\mathcal{A} = \langle u, 1, i \rangle$ is updated in the same way that is described when $\mathcal{A} = \langle r, 1, i \rangle$. Incoming motif edges do not need to be computed *ab initio*, however, E' must still be computed. For each incoming motif edge to u with label d', where $\langle v, j' \rangle \in E'$ and $0 < d' \leq d$, a motif edge with the same label is copied to $\mathcal{A}$ if the number of set bits in the bit-vector of potential motif edge to $\mathcal{A}$ is at least k. If the bit-vector of the new motif edge to $\mathcal{A}$ is equivalent to that of the corresponding motif edge to u, the duplicate motif edge to u is deleted. Finally, ISMOTIF($\mathcal{A}$) is updated as described earlier.

$\mathcal{A}$ **eventually becomes an explicit node** $v_{\mathcal{A}}$**.** In this case, $\mathcal{A} = \langle v_{\mathcal{A}}, 0, i \rangle$. Therefore, no extra work is being done by initiliasing $\mathcal{A}$ as a seed node prematurely. At this point, all information is copied from $\mathcal{A}$ to $v_{\mathcal{A}}$ and a leaf node representing suffix j is added from $v_{\mathcal{A}}$. In preparation for the next step, E' is initialised as mentioned earlier. Note that, it is at this point that the leaf $j - \ell$ must be deleted; see Sect. 4.2.

$\mathcal{A}$ **moves to another branch following the suffix link from** $v_{\mathcal{A}}$**.** After the leaf node j is added, $\mathcal{A}$ moves to a different branch by following the suffix link from $v_{\mathcal{A}}$ and becomes $\mathcal{A} = \langle s(v_{\mathcal{A}}), 0, i \rangle$. This is in order to prepare to add the leaf node representing the next suffix from $u = s(v_{\mathcal{A}})$; observe that j is incremented. First, $|\text{OCC}(u)|$ is incremented and ISSEED(u) is updated. If ISSEED(u) = TRUE and $|\text{OCC}(u)| \geq k$, then $\mathcal{B}(u)$ and PIVOT(u) are updated to reflect the new occurrence of u at position j. A pointer to u is added to the list of pointers representing position $j + D(u) - 1$ in E. Finally, motif edges are added as described earlier but with one crucial difference: when an edge is added, the cluster to which it belongs is deleted from E'. Lastly, ISMOTIF(u) is updated. Importantly, an update is also done in the aforementioned way for all ancestors of u. There are two possibilities after this step.

- If another suffix link is to be followed due to the addition of the next suffix as a leaf node, then firstly, note that it is at this point that leaf $j - \ell$ must be deleted; see Sect. 4.2. Secondly, E' is updated to reflect the incrementation of j by deleting all pairs where (after the incrementation) $j' = j - 1 - d$ and adding pairs (obtained from E) where $j' = j - 1$. This entire step is repeated until j is no longer incremented.
- There may come a point during the addition of subsequent suffixes as leaf nodes where $j \neq i$ and i once again begins increasing. In other words, $\mathcal{A}$ may follow suffix links around the suffix tree multiple times as j increases, but $\mathcal{A}$ may halt on a branch and begin moving down it. As μ is incremented to 1 after $\mathcal{A} = \langle v, 0, i \rangle$ followed a suffix link to v, all ancestor seed nodes of v are updated, from the shallowest to the deepest, by simulating the movement of $\mathcal{A}$ down the current branch as described at the beginning of this section.

It is evident that as $\mathcal{A}$ moves down a branch in the suffix tree and $D(\mathcal{A})$ elongates, $|\text{OCC}(\mathcal{A})|$ reduces each time it passes an internal node. Thus, each seed node is augmented with a subset of edges of its parent seed node.

4.2 Deleting a Letter from the Left

When the leaf node j is added, a leaf node $j - \ell$ must be deleted and its explicit parent node may also be deleted, as described in Sect. 3.2. Let v' be the deepest remaining ancestor node of the deleted leaf. The following is done for each internal node v in the path from v' to r, inclusive. Note that, every node v is necessarily a seed node. The number of occurrences of v is decremented and ISSEED(v) is updated. Outgoing motif edges are then updated as follows.

We say a motif edge is *relevant* if it originates at v and its destination is a node z which occurs at position $j - \ell + D(v) + d'$, where $0 < d' \leq d$. That is, $v \diamond^{d'} z$ has lost one occurrence. After losing the occurrence, if $|\text{OCC}(v \diamond^{d'} z)| = k - 1$, the edge $v \xrightarrow{d'} z$ must be deleted. Alternatively, we say the edge is *affected*.

If $|\text{OCC}(v)| = k - 1$ or v is no longer a seed, all of its motif edges are outgoing, relevant and must be deleted. If $|\text{OCC}(v)| \geq k$, only a subset of its outgoing edges may be relevant and of those, a subset must be deleted and another subset are affected. Relevant motif edges are dealt with depending on $s(v)$, the suffix target of v, as follows.

- If $s(v) \neq r$, any outgoing motif edge from v that does not exist from $s(v)$, with the same label and destination node, is copied. If $|\text{OCC}(v \diamond^{d'} z)| = k - 1$, then the corresponding motif edge from v is deleted.
- Otherwise, any motif edge such that $|\text{OCC}(v \diamond^{d'} z)| = k - 1$ is deleted, where $0 < d' \leq d$.

Nodes v and $s(v)$ are then updated as follows.

- If $|\text{OCC}(v)| = k - 1$ or v is no longer a seed, there are two possible cases. If the non-empty suffix of v was not a seed, $s(v)$ becomes a seed and all information is moved from v to $s(v)$. If the non-empty suffix of v was already a seed, then pointers to v in E, $\mathcal{B}(v)$, PIVOT(v) and ISMOTIF(v) are all deleted.

– If $|\text{OCC}(v)| \geq k$, then PIVOT(v) and $\mathcal{B}(v)$ are updated.

For every motif edge that is added from $s(v)$ by this update, ISMOTIF of $s(v)$ and the destination nodes must be updated. Finally, ISMOTIF(v) is updated.

4.3   Updating the Score Array

We are now in the position to describe how the algorithm computes the score array $\mathcal{S}_x$. Recall that each motif $m \in \mathcal{M}_{j,d,k}$ contributes to $\mathcal{S}_x[j]$ and m has at least k occurrences in $x[j - \ell + 1 .. j]$. A motif can either be a singleton motif or a maximal path of motif edges. A seed node u can be a singleton motif if it has no incoming or outgoing motif edges, or, it does not have an incoming (resp. outgoing) motif edge from (resp. to) a node v where each occurrence of u is preceded (resp. succeeded) by v.

Before detailing how the score is updated for either side of the window, we describe how a maximal path can be elucidated on the right-hand side of the window (similar logic applies to the left-hand side), given a seed node u and a position j of one of its occurrences. A motif edge $v \xrightarrow{d'} u$, where v occurs at position $j - d' - D(v) + 1$ and KPOPCOUNT($k, \mathcal{B}(v \xrightarrow{d'} u)$) = TRUE, can be extended to the left by following a path of motif edges, where at each extension, two conditions must hold.

- If POPCOUNT($\mathcal{B}(v \xrightarrow{d'} u)$) = k, the bit-vector of the extended path must match exactly with $\mathcal{B}(v \xrightarrow{d'} u)$. Alternatively, if POPCOUNT($\mathcal{B}(v \xrightarrow{d'} u)$) > k, then the bit-vector of the extended path must contain at least k set bits one of which must correspond to position j.
- The cumulative total of the labels of the motif edges in the path must not exceed d.

Reading a Letter on the Right. In Sect. 4.1, we describe how updates are made to the motif graph. Consequently, the score is updated for each relevant seed node u as follows.

- When a new motif edge $v \xrightarrow{d'} u$ is added, the score is incremented by one for each maximal path ending with $v \xrightarrow{d'} u$, if $v \xrightarrow{d'} u$ is not an extension of the prefix of the path. If no such paths exist, then the score is incremented for the motif edge.
- If $v \diamond^{d'} u$ gains an occurrence, the score is decremented for each maximal path ending with $v \xrightarrow{d'} u$, if $v \xrightarrow{d'} u$ is now an extension of the prefix of the path, such that the prefix already contributes to the score.
- If a motif edge is duplicated due to $\mathcal{A}$ passing a seed node, the total score for all paths ending at the given motif edge is doubled. When $\mathcal{A}$ reaches a seed node and both share a motif edge from the same node with the same label, the total score for all paths ending at the given motif edge is halved.
- The score is incremented when a seed becomes a singleton motif; it is decremented when a singleton motif is no longer so. The computation that establishes this has been described in Sect. 4.1 and is done following the addition or deletion of any motif edges.

Deleting a Letter from the Left. In Sect. 4.2, we describe how updates are made to the motif graph. Consequently, the score is updated for each relevant seed node v as follows.

- When a motif edge $v \xrightarrow{d'} z$ from v must be deleted but $s(v) \xrightarrow{d'} z$ already exists, the score is decremented for every maximal path that starts with $v \xrightarrow{d'} z$ if its occurrence positions are distinct from those of the same paths but starting with $s(v) \xrightarrow{d'} z$. Before $v \xrightarrow{d'} z$ is deleted, the score is decremented for each path that begins with $v \xrightarrow{d'} z$, if the occurrence positions of the suffix of the path differ. Then, the score is incremented for the suffix of the path, if it is not a prefix of a longer motif, which would already be contributing to the score.
- For each motif edge copied from v to $s(v)$, ending at some seed node z, the score is incremented for each path starting with $s(v) \xrightarrow{d'} z$ if it has different occurrence positions to $v \xrightarrow{d'} z$. If $v \xrightarrow{d'} z$ has been deleted, the score is incremented without this check. Alternatively, if $s(v)$ was already a seed and a singleton motif, and motif edge $s(v) \xrightarrow{d'} z$ is added to it, if $s(v)$ has the same occurrence positions as $s(v) \diamond^{d'} z$, $s(v)$ is no longer a singleton motif and the score is decremented. A similar check is done for the destination node z whenever such a motif edge is added.
- If $s(v)$ has just become a seed and a singleton motif, the score is incremented. If $|\text{OCC}(v)| = k - 1$ or v is no longer a seed, but v was a singleton motif, the score is decremented. If v is still a seed, $|\text{OCC}(v)| \geq k$ and $\text{ISMOTIF}(v) = \text{FALSE}$ but all of its motif edges have been deleted, v becomes a singleton motif; the score is incremented. If any remaining outgoing motif edge from v has the same occurrence positions as v and v was a singleton motif, it is no longer so; the score is decremented. If no such match is found and v was not a singleton motif, it becomes one; the score is incremented.

5   Algorithm Analysis

The following theorem summarises the complexity of the proposed algorithm.

Theorem 1. *Given a sequence x of length n, a window length ℓ, thresholds k and d, and size w of the machine word, the score array $\mathcal{S}_x$ is computed in $\mathcal{O}(nd\ell + d\lceil \frac{\ell}{w} \rceil \cdot \sum_{i=\ell}^{n-1} |\text{DIFF}_{i-1}^i|)$ time using $\mathcal{O}(\ell^2)$ space.*

Proof. Given a string of length n, the suffix tree can be built for a sliding window in $\mathcal{O}(n)$ time using Ukkonen's [15] and Senft's [13] algorithms. Each time a leaf is added, the number of occurrences on all of its $\mathcal{O}(\ell)$ ancestor nodes must be incremented. This results in $\mathcal{O}(n\ell)$ time complexity for building and maintaining the nodes of the suffix tree. For each node v_i in the suffix tree, where $i < \ell$ per window, at most $\mathcal{O}(d\ell)$ motif edges can be added. Thus, in the worst case, the number of motif edges added are bounded by $\mathcal{O}(nd\ell)$. Each motif corresponds to at least one motif edge, so there cannot be more than $|\mathcal{M}_{i,d,k}|$ motif edges in the motif graph per window. The time required to update the motif graph at each deletion and addition step is proportional to the number of occurrences of motifs deleted and introduced at either end of the window. All bit-operations used in the algorithm can be implemented in $\mathcal{O}(\lceil \frac{\ell}{w} \rceil)$ time. Thus elucidating each maximal path requires $\mathcal{O}(d\lceil \frac{\ell}{w} \rceil)$ time. When a leaf is added, updating E takes $\mathcal{O}(\ell)$ time. Thus the overall time complexity for maintaining E is $\mathcal{O}(n\ell)$. Summing the above gives the overall time complexity.

The size of the motif graph is $\mathcal{O}(\ell \cdot \lceil \frac{\ell}{w} \rceil)$, where the largest extra structure that each node holds is a bit-vector of size $\mathcal{O}(\lceil \frac{\ell}{w} \rceil)$. The lookup table used by POPCOUNT() is of size $\mathcal{O}(2^{\log_2 \ell}) = \mathcal{O}(\ell)$. The dynamic structure E of size $\mathcal{O}(\ell^2)$ gives an upper bound for the space complexity as each of the $\mathcal{O}(\ell)$ positions in E can hold pointers to at most ℓ seed nodes. The array $\mathcal{S}_x$ is not stored in memory as scores are reported in an on-line fashion.   □

6   Concluding Remarks

In this paper, we presented a motif discovery algorithm with the purpose of finding biologically significant regions in genomic sequences.

Our goal is to verify our theoretical findings and claims of improvement compared with the algorithm presented in [4] by implementing our algorithm and testing it using real genomic data.

References

1. Carvalho, A.M., Freitas, A.T., Oliveira, A.L., Sagot, M.: An efficient algorithm for the identification of structured motifs in DNA promoter sequences. IEEE/ACM Trans. Comput. Biol. Bioinform. 3(2), 126–140 (2006)
2. Crochemore, M., Hancart, C., Lecroq, T.: Algorithms on Strings. Cambridge University Press, Cambridge (2007)
3. Fuller, R.S., Funnell, B.E., Kornberg, A.: The dnaA protein complex with the E. coli chromosomal replication origin (oriC) and other DNA sites. Cell 38(3), 889–900 (1984)
4. Grossi, R., Menconi, G., Pisanti, N., Trani, R., Vind, S.: Motif trie: an efficient text index for pattern discovery with don't cares. Theor. Comput. Sci. 710, 74–87 (2018)
5. Gusfield, D.: Algorithms on Strings, Trees and Sequences: Computer Science and Computational Biology. Cambridge University Press, Cambridge (1997)
6. van Helden, J., Andre, B., Collado-Vides, J.: Extracting regulatory sites from the upstream region of yeast genes by computational analysis of oligonucleotide frequencies. J. Mol. Biol. 281(5), 827–842 (1998)
7. Leonard, A.C., Méchali, M.: DNA replication origins. Cold Spring Harb. Perspect. Biol. 5(10), a010116 (2013)
8. Meijer, M., et al.: Nucleotide sequence of the origin of replication of the Escherichia coli K-12 chromosome. Proc. Natl. Acad. Sci. 76(2), 580–584 (1979)
9. Pavesi, G., Mereghetti, P., Mauri, G., Pesole, G.: Weeder web: discovery of transcription factor binding sites in a set of sequences from co-regulated genes. Nucleic Acids Res. 32(Web–Server–Issue), 199–203 (2004)

10. Pisanti, N., Carvalho, A.M., Marsan, L., Sagot, M.-F.: RISOTTO: fast extraction of motifs with mismatches. In: Correa, J.R., Hevia, A., Kiwi, M. (eds.) LATIN 2006. LNCS, vol. 3887, pp. 757–768. Springer, Heidelberg (2006). https://doi.org/10.1007/11682462_69

11. Pissis, S.P.: MoTeX-II: structured MoTif eXtraction from large-scale datasets. BMC Bioinform. **15**, 235 (2014)

12. Pissis, S.P., Stamatakis, A., Pavlidis, P.: MoTeX: a word-based HPC tool for motif extraction. In: Gao, J. (ed.) ACM Conference on Bioinformatics, Computational Biology and Biomedical Informatics, ACM-BCB 2013, Washington, DC, USA, 22–25 September 2013, p. 13. ACM (2013)

13. Senft, M.: Suffix tree for a sliding window: an overview. In: WDS, vol. 5, pp. 41–46 (2005)

14. Sinha, S., Tompa, M.: YMF: a program for discovery of novel transcription factor binding sites by statistical overrepresentation. Nucleic Acids Res. **31**(13), 3586–3588 (2003)

15. Ukkonen, E.: On-line construction of suffix trees. Algorithmica **14**(3), 249–260 (1995)

16. Waterman, M.S.: General methods of sequence comparison. Bull. Math. Biol. **46**(4), 473–500 (1984)

Compressed Range Minimum Queries

Seungbum Jo[1], Shay Mozes[2], and Oren Weimann[1(✉)]

[1] University of Haifa, Haifa, Israel
seungbum.jo@uni-siegen.de,oren@cs.haifa.ac.il
[2] Interdisciplinary Center Herzliya, Herzliya, Israel
smozes@idc.ac.il

Abstract. Given a string S of n integers in $[0, \sigma)$, a range minimum query $\mathsf{RMQ}(i, j)$ asks for the index of the smallest integer in $S[i \ldots j]$. It is well known that the problem can be solved with a succinct data structure of size $2n + o(n)$ and constant query-time. In this paper we show how to preprocess S into a *compressed representation* that allows fast range minimum queries. This allows for *sublinear* size data structures with logarithmic query time. The most natural approach is to use string compression and construct a data structure for answering range minimum queries directly on the compressed string. We investigate this approach using grammar compression. We then consider an alternative approach. Even if S is not compressible, its Cartesian tree necessarily is. Therefore, instead of compressing S using string compression, we compress the Cartesian tree of S using tree compression. We show that this approach can be exponentially better than the former, and is never worse by more than an $O(\sigma)$ factor (i.e. for constant alphabets it is never asymptotically worse).

Keywords: RMQ · Grammar compression · SLP · Tree compression
Cartesian tree

1 Introduction

Given a string S of n integers in $[0, \sigma)$, a range minimum query $\mathsf{RMQ}(i, j)$ returns the index of the smallest integer in $S[i \ldots j]$. A range minimum data structure consists of a preprocessing algorithm and a query algorithm. The preprocessing algorithm takes as input the string S, and constructs the data structure, whereas the query algorithm takes as input the indices i, j and, by accessing the data structure, returns $\mathsf{RMQ}(i, j)$. The range minimum problem is one of the most fundamental problems in stringology, and as such has been extensively studied, both in theory and in practice (see e.g. [11] and references therein).

Range minimum data structures fall into two categories. *Systematic* data structures store the input string S, whereas *non-systematic* data structures do not. A significant amount of attention has been devoted to devising RMQ data

Supported in part by Israel Science Foundation grant 592/17.

T. Gagie et al. (Eds.): SPIRE 2018, LNCS 11147, pp. 206–217, 2018.
https://doi.org/10.1007/978-3-030-00479-8_17

structures that answer queries in constant time and require as little space as possible. There are succinct systematic structures that answer queries in constant time and require fewer than $2n$ bits in addition to the $n \log \sigma$ bits required to represent S [11]. Similarly, there are succinct non-systematic structures that answer queries in constant time, and require $2n + o(n)$ bits [8,11].

The *Cartesian tree* $\mathcal{C}$ of S is a rooted ordered binary tree with n nodes. It is defined recursively. Let i be the index of the smallest element of S (if the smallest element appears multiple times in S, let i be the first such appearance). The Cartesian tree of S is composed of a root node whose left subtree is the Cartesian tree of $S[1, i - 1]$, and whose right subtree is the Cartesian tree of $S[i + 1, n]$. See Fig. 1. By definition, the character $S[i]$ corresponds to the i'th node in an inorder traversal of $\mathcal{C}$ (we will refer to this node as node i). Furthermore, for any nodes i and j in $\mathcal{C}$, their lowest common ancestor $\mathsf{LCA}(i, j)$ in $\mathcal{C}$ corresponds to $\mathsf{RMQ}(i, j)$ in S. It follows that the Cartesian tree of S completely characterizes S in terms of range minimum queries. Indeed, two strings return the same answers for all possible range minimum queries if and only if their Cartesian trees are identical. This well known property has been used by many RMQ data structures including the succinct structures mentioned above. Since there are $2^{2n - O(\log n)}$ distinct rooted binary trees with n nodes, there is an information theoretic lower bound of $2n - O(\log n)$ bits for RMQ data structures. In this sense, the above mentioned $2n + o(n)$ bits data structures [8,11] are nearly optimal.

1.1   Our Results and Techniques

In this work we present RMQ data structures whose size can be *sublinear* in the size of the input string that answer queries in $O(\log n)$ time. This is achieved by using compression techniques, and developing data structures that can answer RMQ/LCA queries directly on the compressed objects. Since we aim for sublinear size data structures, we focus on non-systematic data structures. We consider two different approaches to achieve this goal. The first approach is to use string compression to compress S, and devise an RMQ data structure on the compressed representation. This approach has also been suggested in [1, Sect. 7.1] in the context of compressed suffix arrays. See also [8, Theorem 2], [11, Theorem 4.1], and [3] for steps in this direction. The second approach is to use tree compression to compress the Cartesian tree $\mathcal{C}$, and devise an LCA data structure on the compressed representation. To the best of our knowledge, this is the first time such approach has been suggested. Note that the two approaches are not equivalent. For example, consider a sorted sequence of an arbitrary subset of n different integers from $[1, 2n]$. As a string this sorted sequence is not compressible, but its Cartesian tree is an (unlabeled) path, which is highly compressible. In a nutshell, we show that the tree compression approach can exponentially outperform the string compression approach. Furthermore, it is never worse than the string compression approach by more than an $O(\sigma)$ factor. We next elaborate on these two approaches.

Using String Compression. In Sect. 2.1, we show how to answer range minimum queries on a *grammar compression* of the input string S. A grammar compression is a context-free grammar that generates only S. The grammar is represented as a *straight line program* (SLP) $\mathcal{S}$. I.e., the right-hand side of each rule in $\mathcal{S}$ either consists of the concatenations of two non-terminals or of a single terminal symbol. The size $|\mathcal{S}|$ of the SLP $\mathcal{S}$ is defined as the number of rules in $\mathcal{S}$. Ideally, $|\mathcal{S}| \ll |S|$. Computing the smallest possible SLP is NP-hard [7], but there are many theoretically and practically efficient compression schemes for constructing $\mathcal{S}$ [7,12,13,15] that reasonably approximate the optimal SLP. In particular, Rytter [14] showed an SLP $\mathcal{S}$ of depth $\log n$ (the depth of an SLP is the depth of its parse tree) whose size is larger than the optimal SLP by at most a multiplicative $\log n$ factor.

In [1], it was shown how to support range minimum queries on S with a data structure of size $O(|\mathcal{S}|)$ in time proportional to the depth of the SLP $\mathcal{S}$. Bille et al. [6] designed a data structure of size $O(|\mathcal{S}|)$ that supports random-access to S (i.e. retrieve the i'th symbol in S) in $O(\log n)$ time (i.e. regardless of the depth of the SLP $\mathcal{S}$). We show how to simply augment their data structure within the same $O(|\mathcal{S}|)$ size bound to answer range minimum queries in $O(\log n)$ time (i.e., how to avoid the logarithmic overhead incurred by using the solution of [1] on Rytter's SLP).

Theorem 1. *Given a string S of length n and an SLP-grammar compression $\mathcal{S}$ of S, there is a data structure of size $O(|\mathcal{S}|)$ that answers range minimum queries on S in $O(\log n)$ time.*

Using Tree Compression. In Sect. 2.2, we give a data structure for answering LCA queries on a compressed representation of the Cartesian tree $\mathcal{C}$. By the discussion above, this is equivalent to answering range minimum queries on S. We use DAG compression of the top-tree of the Cartesian tree $\mathcal{C}$ of S. We now explain these concepts.

A *top-tree* [2] of a tree T is a hierarchical decomposition of the edges of T into clusters. Each cluster is a connected subgraph of T with the property that any two crossing clusters (i.e., clusters whose intersection is nonempty and neither cluster contains the other) share at most two vertices; the root of the cluster (called the top boundary node) and a leaf of the cluster (called a bottom boundary node). Such a decomposition can be described by a rooted ordered binary tree $\mathcal{T}$, called a top-tree, whose leaves correspond to clusters with individual edges of T, and whose root corresponds to the entire tree T. The cluster corresponding to a non-leaf node of $\mathcal{T}$ is obtained from the clusters of its two children by either identifying their top boundary nodes (horizontal merge) or by identifying the top boundary node of the left child with the bottom boundary node of the right child (vertical merge). See Fig. 1.

A *DAG compression* [9] of a tree T is a representation of T by a DAG whose nodes correspond to nodes of T. All nodes of T with the same subtree are represented by the same node of the DAG. Thus, the DAG has two sinks, corresponding to the two types of leaf nodes of T (a single edge cluster, either left or right), and a single source, corresponding the root of T. If u is the parent of ℓ and r in T, then the node in the DAG representing the subtree of T rooted at u has edges leading to the two nodes of the DAG representing the subtree of T rooted at ℓ and the subtree of T rooted at r. Thus, repeating rooted subtrees in T are represented only once in the DAG. See Fig. 1.

A *top-tree compression* [5] of a tree T is a DAG compression of T's top-tree $\mathcal{T}$. Bille et al. [5] showed how to construct a data structure whose size is linear in the size of the DAG of $\mathcal{T}$ and supports navigational queries on T in time linear in the depth of $\mathcal{T}$. In particular, given the preorder numbers of two vertices u, v in T, their data structure can return the preorder number of LCA(u, v) in T. We show that their data structure can be easily adjusted to work with inorder numbers instead of preorder, so that, given the inorder numbers i, j of two vertices in T one can return the inorder number of LCA(i, j) in T. This is precisely RMQ(i, j) when T is taken to be the Cartesian tree $\mathcal{C}$ of S.

Theorem 2. *Given a string S of length n and a top-tree compression $\mathcal{T}$ of the Cartesian tree $\mathcal{C}$, there is a data structure of size $O(|\mathcal{T}|)$ that answers range minimum queries on S in $O(\mathbf{depth}(\mathcal{T}))$ time.*

By combining Theorem 2 with the greedy construction of $\mathcal{T}$ given in [5] (in which $\mathbf{depth}(\mathcal{T}) = O(\log n)$), we can obtain an $O(|\mathcal{T}|)$ space data structure that answers RMQ in $O(\log n)$ time.

We already mentioned that, on some RMQ instances, top-tree compression can be much better than any string compression technique. As an example, consider the string $S = 123 \cdots n$. Its Cartesian tree is a single (rightmost, and unlabeled) path, which compresses using top-tree compression into size $|\mathcal{T}| = O(\log n)$. On the other hand, since $\sigma = n$, S is uncompressible with an SLP. By Theorem 2, this shows that the tree compression approach to the RMQ problem can be exponentially better than the string compression approach. In fact, for any string over an alphabet of size $\sigma = \Omega(n)$, any SLP must have $|\mathcal{S}| = \Omega(n)$ while for top-trees $|\mathcal{T}| = O(n/\log n)$ [5]. In Sect. 3 we show that, for small alphabets, $\mathcal{T}$ cannot be much larger nor much deeper than $\mathcal{S}$ for any SLP $\mathcal{S}$.

Theorem 3. *Given a string S of length n over an alphabet of size σ, for any SLP-grammar compression $\mathcal{S}$ of S there is a top-tree compression $\mathcal{T}$ of the Cartesian tree $\mathcal{C}$ with size $O(|\mathcal{S}| \cdot \sigma)$ and depth $O(\mathbf{depth}(\mathcal{S}) \cdot \log \sigma)$.*

Plugging Rytter's [14] SLP into Theorem 3 shows that, at least for small alphabets σ, the top-tree compression approach to RMQ is never far worse than the SLP approach.

Corollary 1. *Given a string S of length n over an alphabet of size σ, let $\mathcal{S}$ denote the smallest possible SLP-grammar compression of S. There is a top-tree compression $\mathcal{T}$ of the Cartesian tree $\mathcal{C}$ of S with size at most $|\mathcal{T}| = \min(O(n/\log n), O(|\mathcal{S}| \cdot \sigma))$, and there is a data structure of size $O(|\mathcal{T}|)$ that answers range minimum queries on S in $O(\log n \cdot \log \sigma)$ time.*

2   RMQ on Compressed Representations

2.1   Compressing the String

Given an SLP compression $\mathcal{S}$ of S, Bille et al. [6] presented a data structure of
size $O(|\mathcal{S}|)$ that can report any $S[i]$ in $O(\log n)$ time. The proof of Theorem 1
is a rather straightforward extension of this data structure to support range
minimum queries.

   The key technique used in [6] is an efficient representation of the *heavy path
decomposition* of the SLP's parse tree. For each node v in the parse tree, we
select the child of v that derives the longer string to be a *heavy* node. The other
child is *light*. Heavy edges are edges going into a heavy node and light edges are
edges going into a light node. The heavy edges decompose the parse tree into
heavy paths. The number of light edges on any path from a node v to a leaf is
$O(\log |v|)$ where $|v|$ denotes the length of the string derived from v. A traversal
of the parse tree from its root to the i'th leaf $S[i]$ enters and exists at most $\log n$
heavy paths. Bille et al. show how to simulate this traversal in $O(\log n)$ time on
a representation of the heavy path decomposition that uses only $O(|\mathcal{S}|)$ space
(note that we cannot afford to store the entire parse tree as its size is n which
can be exponentially larger than $|\mathcal{S}|$). We do not go into the internals of their
representation but it is important to note that for each heavy path P encountered
during the traversal their structure computes the total size (number of leaves)
of all subtrees hanging with light edges from the left (respectively right) of P
between the entry point and exit point in P. This is achieved with a binary
search tree (called an *interval biased search tree*) that ensures that collecting
these values (as well as finding the entry and exit points) on all encountered
heavy paths telescopes to a total of $O(\log n)$ time (rather than $O(\log^2 n)$).

   In order to extend their structure to support range minimum queries we
need only the following two changes: (1) in the interval biased search tree, apart
from storing for each node the number of leaves in its subtree, we also store the
location of the minimum value leaf. This means that apart from accumulating
subtree sizes we can also compare their minimums. (2) for each heavy path in
their representation we add a standard linear-space constant query-time RMQ
data structure [4] over the left (respectively right) hanging subtree minimums.
This RMQ structure will be queried only on the unique heavy path containing
the lowest common ancestor of the i'th and j'th leaves in the parse tree.

2.2   Compressing the Cartesian Tree

We next prove Theorem 2, i.e. how to support range minimum queries on S using
a compressed representation of the *Cartesian tree* [16]. Recall that the Cartesian
tree $\mathcal{C}$ of S is defined as follows: If the smallest character in S is $S[i]$ (in case of a
tie we choose a leftmost position) then the root of $\mathcal{C}$ corresponds to $S[i]$, its left
child is the Cartesian tree of $S[1, i-1]$ and its right child is the Cartesian tree
of $S[i+1, n]$. By definition, the i'th character in S corresponds to the node in
$\mathcal{C}$ with inorder number i (we will refer to this node as node i). Observe that for

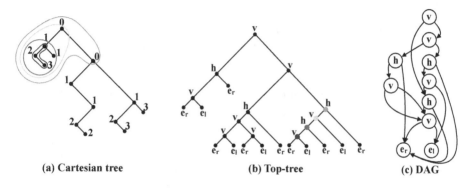

(a) Cartesian tree   **(b) Top-tree**   **(c) DAG**

Fig. 1. The string S = "23110122102313" and its corresponding (a) Cartesian tree, (b) top-tree, and (c) DAG representation of the top-tree. In (a), each node is labeled by its corresponding character in S (these labels are for illustration only, the top-tree construction treats the Cartesian tree as an unlabeled tree). In (b) and (c), each node is labeled by e_l or e_r (atomic edge clusters), v (a vertical merge), or h (a horizontal merge). Four clusters are marked with matching colors in (a) and in (b). (Color figure online)

any nodes i and j in $\mathcal{C}$, the lowest common ancestor $\mathsf{LCA}(i, j)$ of these nodes in $\mathcal{C}$ corresponds to $\mathsf{RMQ}(i, j)$ in S. This implies that without storing S explicitly, one can answer range minimum queries on S by answering LCA queries on $\mathcal{C}$. In this section, we show how to support LCA queries on $\mathcal{C}$ on a *top-tree* compression [5] $\mathcal{T}$ of $\mathcal{C}$. The query time is $O(\mathtt{depth}(\mathcal{T}))$ which can be made $O(\log n)$ using the (greedy) construction of Bille et al. [5] that gives $\mathtt{depth}(\mathcal{T}) = O(\log n)$. We first briefly restate the construction of Bille et al., and then extend it to support LCA queries.

The *top-tree* of a tree T (in our case T will be the Cartesian tree $\mathcal{C}$) is a hierarchical decomposition of T into *clusters*. Let v be a node in T with children $v_1, v_2.$[1] Define $T(v)$ to be the subtree of T rooted at v. Define $F(v)$ to be the forest $T(v)$ without v. A *cluster* with *top boundary node* v can be either (1) $T(v)$, (2) $\{v\} \cup T(v_1)$, or (3) $\{v\} \cup T(v_2)$. For any node $u \neq v$ in a cluster with top boundary node v, deleting from the cluster all descendants of u (not including u itself) results in a *cluster* with *top boundary node* v and *bottom boundary node* u. The top-tree is a binary tree defined as follows (see Fig. 1):

– The root of the top-tree is the cluster T itself.
– The leaves of the top-tree are (atomic) clusters corresponding to the edges of T. An edge $(v, parent(v))$ of T is a cluster where $parent(v)$ is the top boundary node. If v is a leaf then there is no bottom boundary node, otherwise v is a bottom boundary node. If v is the right child of $parent(v)$ then we label the $(v, parent(v))$ cluster as e_r and otherwise as e_ℓ.

---

[1] Bille et al. considered trees with arbitrary degree, but since our tree T is a Cartesian tree we can focus on binary trees.

- Each internal node of the top-tree is a *merged* cluster of its two children. Two edge disjoint clusters A and B whose nodes overlap on a single boundary node can be merged if their union $A \cup B$ is also a cluster (i.e. contains at most two boundary nodes). If A and B share their top boundary node then the merge is called *horizontal*. If the top boundary node of A is the bottom boundary node of B then the merge is called *vertical* and in the top-tree A is the left child and B is the right child.

Bille et al. [5] proposed a greedy algorithm for constructing the top-tree: Start with n identical clusters, one for each edge of T, and at each step merge all possible clusters. More precisely, at each step, first do all possible horizontal merges and then do all possible vertical merges. After constructing the top-tree, the actual compression $\mathcal{T}$ is obtained by representing the top-tree as a directed acyclic graph (DAG) using the algorithm of [9]. Namely, all nodes in the top-tree that have a child with subtree X will point to the same subtree X (see Fig. 1). Bille et al. [5] showed that using the above greedy algorithm, one can construct $\mathcal{T}$ of size $|\mathcal{T}|$ that can be as small as $\log n$ (when the input tree T is highly repetitive) and in the worst-case is at most $O(n/\log_\sigma^{0.19} n)$. Dudek and Gawrychowski [10] have recently improved the worst-case bound to $O(n/\log_\sigma n)$ by merging in the i'th step only clusters whose size is at most α^i for some constant α. Using either one of these merging algorithms to obtain the top-tree and its DAG representation $\mathcal{T}$, a data structure of size $O(|\mathcal{T}|)$ can then be constructed to support various queries on T. In particular, given nodes i and j in T (specified by their position in a *preorder* traversal of T) Bille et al. showed how to find the (preorder number of) node $\mathsf{LCA}(i, j)$ in $O(\log n)$ time. Therefore, the only change required in order to adapt their data structure to our needs is the representation of nodes by their *inorder* rather than preorder numbers.

The *local preorder number* u_C of a node u in T and a cluster C in $\mathcal{T}$ is the preorder number of u in a preorder traversal of the cluster C. To find the preorder number of $\mathsf{LCA}(i, j)$ in $O(\log n)$ time, Bille et al. showed it suffices if for any node u and any cluster C we can compute u_C in constant time from u_A or u_B (the local preorder numbers of u in the clusters A and B whose merge is the cluster C) and vice versa. In Lemma 6 of [5] they show that indeed they can compute this in constant time. The following lemma is a modification of that lemma to work when u_A, u_B and u_C are *local inorder numbers*.

Lemma 1 (Modified Lemma 6 of [5]). *Let C be an internal node in $\mathcal{T}$ corresponding to the cluster obtained by merging clusters A and B. For any node u in C, given u_C we can tell in constant time if u is in A (and obtain u_A) in B (and obtain u_B) or in both. Similarly, if u is in A or in B we can obtain u_C in constant time from u_A or u_B.*

Proof. We show how to obtain u_A or u_B when u_C is given. Obtaining u_C from u_A or u_B is done similarly. For each node C, we store a following information:

- $\ell(A)$ $(r(A))$: the first (last) node visited in an inorder traversal of C that is also a node in A.

- $\ell(B)$ $(r(B))$: the first (last) node visited in an inorder traversal of C that is also a node in B.
- the number of nodes in A and in B.
- u'_C, where u' is the common boundary node of A and B.

Consider the case where C is obtained by merging A and B vertically (when the bottom boundary node of A is the top boundary node of B), and where B includes vertices that are in the left subtree of this boundary node, the other case is handled similarly:

- if $u_C < \ell(B)$ then u is a node in A and $u_A = u_C$.
- if $\ell(B) \le u_C \le r(B)$ then u is a node in B and $u_B = u_C - \ell(B) + 1$. For the special case when $u_C = u'_C$ then u is also the bottom boundary node in A and $u_A = \ell(B)$.
- if $u_c > r(B)$ then u is a node in A visited after visiting all the nodes in B then $u_A = u_C - |B| + 1$.

When C is obtained by merging A and B horizontally (when A and B share their top boundary node and A is to the left of B):

- if $u_C < r(A)$ then u is a node in A and $u_A = u_C$.
- if $u_C \ge r(A)$ then u is a node in B and $u_B = u_C - |A| + 1$. For the special case when $u_C = u'_C$ then u is also the top boundary node in A and $u_A = |A|$.

3   Compressing the String vs. the Cartesian Tree

In this section we compare the sizes of the SLP compression $\mathcal{S}$ and the top-tree compression $\mathcal{T}$. We show that given any SLP $\mathcal{S}$ of height h we can construct a top-tree compression $\mathcal{T}$ based on $\mathcal{S}$ (i.e. non-greedily) such that $|\mathcal{T}| = O(|\mathcal{S}| \cdot \sigma)$ and the height of $\mathcal{T}$ is $O(h \log \sigma)$. Using $\mathcal{T}$, we can then answer range minimum queries on $\mathcal{S}$ in time $O(h \log \sigma)$ as done in Sect. 2.2. Furthermore, we can construct $\mathcal{T}$ using Rytter's SLP [14] as $\mathcal{S}$. Then, the height of $\mathcal{S}$ is $h = \log n$ and the size of $\mathcal{S}$ is larger than the optimal SLP by at most a multiplicative $\log n$ factor. Combined with Rytter's SLP, and since every unlabeled tree has a top-tree compression $\mathcal{T}$ of size $O(n/\log n)$ and height $\log n$ [5], we obtain Theorem 3.

Consider a rule $C \to AB$ in the SLP. We will construct a top-tree (a hierarchy of clusters) of C (i.e. of the Cartesian tree of the string derived by the SLP variable C) assuming we have the top-trees of A and of B. We show that the top-tree of C contains only $O(\sigma)$ new clusters that are not clusters in the top-trees of A and of B, and that the height of the top-tree is only $O(\log \sigma)$ larger than the height of the top tree of A or the top tree of B. To achieve this, for any variable A of the SLP, we will make sure that certain clusters (associated with its rightmost and leftmost paths) must be present in its top-tree. See Fig. 2.

We first describe how the Cartesian tree $CT(C)$ of the string derived by variable C can be described in terms of the Cartesian trees $CT(A)$ and $CT(B)$. We label each node in a Cartesian tree with its corresponding character in the string. These labels are only used for the sake of this description, the actual Cartesian tree is an unlabeled tree. By definition of the Cartesian tree, the labels are monotonically non-decreasing as we traverse any root-to-leaf path.

214   S. Jo et al.

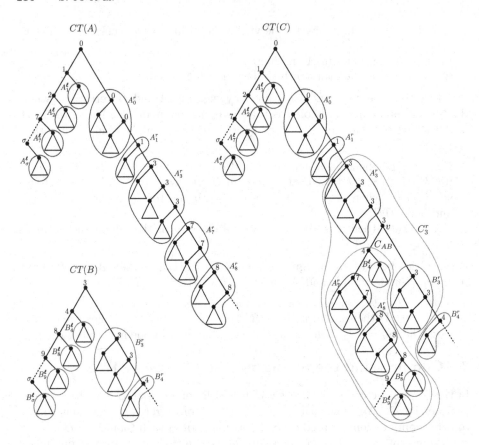

Fig. 2. The Cartesian tree of SLP variables A, B, C where $C \to AB$. The single additional clusters of C_3^r (in green) is formed by merging existing clusters from A (in blue) and from B (in red). First, cluster C_{AB} is formed by alternating subpaths of the leftmost path in $CT(B)$ and the rightmost path in $CT(A)$ (here, $x = 3, y = 7$, and $z = 8$). Then, C_{AB} is merged with B_3^r, v, and A_3^r. In this example, $A_s = \{A_i^r \mid i > 3\}$ and $B_p = \{B_i^\ell \mid i > 3\}$. (Color figure online)

Let $\ell(A)$ (respectively $r(A)$) denote the path in $CT(A)$ starting from the root and following left (respectively right) edges. Since we break ties by taking the leftmost occurrence of the same character we have that the path $\ell(A)$ is strictly increasing (the path $r(A)$ is just non-decreasing).

Let x be the label of the root of $CT(B)$. To simplify the presentation we assume that the label of the root of $CT(A)$ is smaller or equal to x (the other case is handled similarly). Split $CT(A)$ by deleting the edge connecting the last occurrence of x on $r(A)$ with its right child (again, for simplicity of presentation we assume without loss of generality that this node exists). The resulting two subtrees are the Cartesian trees $CT(A_p)$ and $CT(A_s)$ of a prefix A_p and a suffix of A_s of A whose concatenation is A. Split $CT(B)$ by deleting the edge connecting the root to its left child. The resulting two subtrees are the Cartesian trees $CT(B_p)$ and $CT(B_s)$ of a prefix and a suffix of B. The Cartesian tree $CT(C)$ of the concatenation $C = AB$ is obtained as follows. Compute recursively the Cartesian tree $CT(A_s B_p)$ of the concatenation of A_s and B_p, and attach $CT(A_s B_p)$ as the left child of the rightmost leaf in $CT(A_p)$. Then attach $CT(B_s)$ as the right child of the rightmost leaf in $CT(A_p)$. See Fig. 2.

We move on to describing the clusters of the top-tree. For a node with label i appearing in $\ell(A)$ we define A_i^ℓ to be the subtree rooted at the node's right child. We do this for all nodes except for the first node of $\ell(A)$ (i.e. the root of $CT(A)$). Next consider the path $r(A)$. For every label i there can be multiple vertices with label i that are consecutive on $r(A)$. We define A_i^r to be the union of all vertices of $r(A)$ that have label i together with the subtrees rooted at their left children. Again, we treat the first node of $r(A)$ (i.e. the root of $CT(A)$) differently: if its label is i then A_i^r does not include this vertex (the root) nor its left subtree. See Fig. 2 (left).

We define the top-tree recursively by describing how to obtain the clusters for the top-tree of the Cartesian tree $CT(C)$ from the top-trees of $CT(A)$ and $CT(B)$. For each variable (say A) of the SLP $\mathcal{S}$ of S, we require that in the top-tree of S there is a cluster for every A_i^ℓ and every A_i^r. We will show how to construct all the C_i^ℓ and C_i^r clusters of C by merging clusters of A and B while introducing only $O(\sigma)$ new clusters, and with $O(\log \sigma)$ increase in height. First observe that for every i we have that $C_i^\ell = A_i^\ell$ so we already have these clusters. Next consider the clusters C_i^r. Let x denote the label of the root of $CT(B)$. It is easy to see that $C_i^r = A_i^r$ for every $i < x$ and that $C_i^r = B_i^r$ for every $i > x$. Therefore, the only new cluster we need to create is C_x^r.

The cluster C_x^r is composed of the following components: First, it contains the cluster A_x^r. Then, the root of $CT(B)$ (denoted v, and whose label is x) is connected as the right child of the bottom boundary node of A_x^r. The right child of v in C_x^r is the top boundary node of B_x^r and all of B_x^r is contained in C_x^r. The left child of v in C_x^r is the top boundary node of a single new cluster C_{AB} consisting of $O(\sigma)$ existing clusters.

The cluster C_{AB} consist of all clusters B_i^ℓ and the clusters A_i^r for $i > x$. More precisely, let y denote the smallest number larger than x such that A_y^r appears in $r(A)$. Starting from top to bottom, C_{AB} first contains a leftmost path that is a prefix of $\ell(B)$. More precisely, it is the prefix of $\ell(B)$ containing all nodes with labels i for $x < i < y$. For each such node, its right subtree is the cluster B_i^ℓ. After this leftmost path C_{AB} then continues with a rightmost path that is a subpath of $r(A)$ consisting of all nodes in $r(A)$ with labels i for $y \leq i \leq z$. Here z is the smallest number greater or equal to y such that B_z^ℓ appears in $\ell(B)$. In this way, C_{AB} keeps alternating between subpaths of $\ell(B)$ and of $r(A)$ (along with the subtrees hanging from these subpaths). Overall, C_{AB} composes to $O(\sigma)$ clusters consisting of single edges, clusters A_i^r, and clusters B_i^ℓ. We merge these clusters into the single cluster C_{AB} by first doing a horizontal merge for every B_i^ℓ with a single edge cluster and then greedily doing vertical merges for all $O(\sigma)$

clusters of the path. This adds $O(\sigma)$ new clusters and adds $O(\log \sigma)$ to the height of the cluster's hierarchy. Finally, we obtain C_x^r by merging C_{AB}, A_x^r, and B_x^r.

To conclude, once we have all clusters of the SLP's start variable, we merge them into a single cluster (i.e. obtain the top-tree of the entire Cartesian tree of S) by greedily merging all its $O(\sigma)$ clusters (introducing $O(\sigma)$ new clusters and increasing the height by $O(\log \sigma)$) similarly to the above.

4 Conclusions

In this paper we have investigated compressed RMQ. We have shown that compressing the Cartesian tree can be exponentially better than compressing the string itself, and is never worse by more than an $O(\sigma)$ factor. Improving this $O(\sigma)$ factor or finding a counter example that actually exhibits an $\Omega(\sigma)$ factor remains an interesting open question.

References

1. Abeliuk, A., Cánovas, R., Navarro, G.: Practical compressed suffix trees. Algorithms **6**(2), 319–351 (2013)
2. Alstrup, S., Holm, J., de Lichtenberg, K., Thorup, M.: Maintaining information in fully-dynamic trees with top trees. ACM Trans. Algorithms **1**, 243–264 (2003)
3. Barbay, J., Fischer, J., Navarro, G.: LRM-trees: compressed indices, adaptive sorting, and compressed permutations. Theor. Comput. Sci. **459**, 26–41 (2012)
4. Bender, M.A., Farach-Colton, M.: The LCA problem revisited. In: Gonnet, G.H., Viola, A. (eds.) LATIN 2000. LNCS, vol. 1776, pp. 88–94. Springer, Heidelberg (2000). https://doi.org/10.1007/10719839_9
5. Bille, P., Gørtz, I.L., Landau, G.M., Weimann, O.: Tree compression with top trees. Inf. Comput. **243**, 166–177 (2015)
6. Bille, P., Landau, G.M., Raman, R., Sadakane, K., Satti, S.R., Weimann, O.: Random access to grammar-compressed strings and trees. SIAM J. Comput. **44**(3), 513–539 (2015)
7. Charikar, M., et al.: The smallest grammar problem. IEEE Trans. Inf. Theory **51**(7), 2554–2576 (2005)
8. Davoodi, P., Raman, R., Satti, S.R.: Succinct representations of binary trees for range minimum queries. In: Gudmundsson, J., Mestre, J., Viglas, T. (eds.) COCOON 2012. LNCS, vol. 7434, pp. 396–407. Springer, Heidelberg (2012). https://doi.org/10.1007/978-3-642-32241-9_34
9. Downey, P.J., Sethi, R., Tarjan, R.E.: Variations on the common subexpression problem. J. ACM **27**(4), 758–771 (1980). https://doi.org/10.1145/322217.322228
10. Dudek, B., Gawrychowski, P.: Slowing down top trees for better worst-case compression. In: Annual Symposium on Combinatorial Pattern Matching. CPM 2018, 2–4 July 2018, Qingdao, China, pp. 16:1–16:8 (2018). https://doi.org/10.4230/LIPIcs.CPM.2018.16
11. Fischer, J., Heun, V.: Space-efficient preprocessing schemes for range minimum queries on static arrays. SIAM J. Comput. **40**(2), 465–492 (2011)
12. Goto, K., Bannai, H., Inenaga, S., Takeda, M.: Fast q-gram mining on SLP compressed strings. J. Discrete Algorithms **18**, 89–99 (2013)

13. Jez, A., Lohrey, M.: Approximation of smallest linear tree grammar. In: 31st International Symposium on Theoretical Aspects of Computer Science (STACS 2014). STACS 2014, pp. 445–457 (2014)
14. Rytter, W.: Application of Lempel-Ziv factorization to the approximation of grammar-based compression. Theor. Comput. Sci. **302**(1–3), 211–222 (2003)
15. Takabatake, Y., I, T., Sakamoto, H.: A space-optimal grammar compression. In: 25th Annual European Symposium on Algorithms. ESA 2017, pp. 67:1–67:15 (2017)
16. Vuillemin, J.: A unifying look at data structures. Commun. ACM **23**(4), 229–239 (1980)

Fast Wavelet Tree Construction
in Practice

Yusaku Kaneta[✉]

Rakuten Institute of Technology, Rakuten, Inc., Setagaya, Japan
yusaku.kaneta@rakuten.com

Abstract. The wavelet tree is a compact data structure that supports various types of operations on a sequence of n integers in $[0, \sigma)$. Although Munro et al. (SPIRE 2014 and Theoretical Computer Science 2016) and Babenko et al. (SODA 2015) showed that wavelet trees can be constructed in $O(n\lceil \lg \sigma / \sqrt{\lg n} \rceil)$ time, there has been no empirical study on their construction methods possibly due to its heavy use of precomputed tables, seemingly limiting its practicality. In this paper, we propose practical variants of their methods. Instead of using huge precomputed tables, we introduce new techniques based on broadword programming and special CPU instructions available for modern processors. Experiments on real-world texts demonstrated that our proposed methods were up to 2.2 and 4.5 times as fast as the naive ones for the wavelet tree and the wavelet matrix (a variant of wavelet trees), respectively, and up to 1.9 times as fast as a state of the art for the wavelet matrix.

1 Introduction

The *wavelet tree* is a compact data structure that efficiently answers to various types of queries on a sequence of integers, including *rank* and *select* queries known as important primitives for many compact data structures. After invented for compressed text indexing [9], it has found a wide range of applications like space-efficient representations of inverted indexes in information retrieval and grids of points in computational geometry. Figure 1 shows an example of wavelet trees over an alphabet $[0, 16) = \{0, \ldots, 15\}$. For more details on wavelet trees, see, e.g., an excellent survey [15] and textbook [16].

Given an input sequence S of n integers over $[0, \sigma)$, it is easy to construct its wavelet tree in $O(n \lg \sigma)$ time. Almost ten years after its invention, Munro et al. [14] and Babenko et al. [1] independently improved this construction time to $O(n \lg \sigma / \sqrt{\lg n})$ by exploiting the bit-level parallelism of the RAM of word size $w \geq \lg n$ (we assume $\sigma \leq n$). More recently, Shun [20] improved the parallel construction time of wavelet trees based on the idea of [1,14].

To our best knowledge, however, there is no empirical study on these methods. There is thus a gap between the theory and practice of wavelet tree construction. This gap is possibly because the idea of [1,14] requires precomputed tables of $O(2^b b\tau)$ bits of space for some integers $1 \leq b \leq w$ and $1 \leq \tau \leq \lg \sigma$.

© Springer Nature Switzerland AG 2018
T. Gagie et al. (Eds.): SPIRE 2018, LNCS 11147, pp. 218–232, 2018.
https://doi.org/10.1007/978-3-030-00479-8_18

Although $b = \frac{1}{2} \lg n$ and $\tau = \sqrt{\lg n}$ are chosen in theory to minimize the total construction time within $o(n)$ space, they can be chosen independently of the input size n in practice. Assume that, for example, $b = w = 64$ (i.e., bits in a word) and $\tau = 8$ (i.e., bits in a byte) that are appropriate for modern CPUs. This combination of b and τ, however, requires precomputed tables of more than $2^6 4 \cdots 2^3$ words, apparently limiting the practicability.

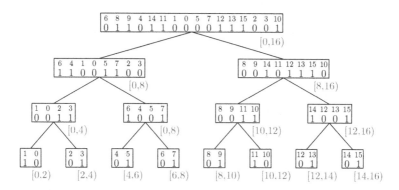

Fig. 1. An example wavelet tree on an input sequence $S = 6\ 8\ 9\ 4\ 14\ 11\ 1\ 1\ 0\ 5\ 7\ 12\ 13$ $15\ 2\ 3\ 10$ or, in binary form, $S = 0110_2\ 1000_2\ 1001_2\ 0100_2\ 1110_2\ 1011_2\ 0001_2\ 0000_2$ $0101_2\ 0111_2\ 1100_2\ 1101_2\ 1111_2\ 0010_2\ 0011_2\ 1010_2$ of 4-bit integers over an alphabet $[0, 16)$. The binary and decimal numbers in the box represent the bit vector and the input integers for each node, respectively. The corresponding interval to each node is attached to the bottom right of the box.

Our Contribution. In this paper, we propose practical variants of fast theoretical wavelet tree construction by Munro et al. [14] and Babenko et al. [1]. The key of our variants is efficient implementations of *packed lists* of integers that exploit special CPU instructions, called *Packed Shuffle Bytes* (pshufb) and *Parallel Bits Extract* (pext), in addition to so-called *broadword programming* techniques. Experiments on real-world texts demonstrated that our proposed methods were up to 2.2 times as fast as a naive one for levelwise wavelet trees (a variant of wavelet trees), and that ours were up to 4.5 and 1.9 as fast as the naive and state of the art [5], respectively, for wavelet matrices (another variant of wavelet trees). Note that unlike the recent literature on the *parallel* construction of wavelet trees [5,6,12,19,20], we study the *sequential* construction. Although our techniques can be applied to the standard wavelet tree, our experiments focus on two variants of wavelet trees: the levelwise wavelet tree [2] and the wavelet matrix [3].

In this paper, we are not concerned with $o(n)$-time construction of rank and select indexes on bit vectors of length n. although Munro et al. [14] and Babenko et al. [1] have improved the construction time of the indexes as well. This is because (1) as Shun [19] pointed out, there are various choices of rank and select indexes in practice, (2) query time and index space are the main concern of rank and select indexes, and (3) practical variants of $o(n)$-time construction of rank and select indexes are already implemented in sdsl [7], a library of succinct data structures, or easily derived from its current code[1].

Related Work. Despite extensive studies on the wavelet tree and its applications, there had been no theoretical work focusing on its efficient sequential construction, except for a few papers [4,21] on how to reduce its construction space. Recently, Munro et al. [14] and Babenko et al. [1] proved that wavelet trees can be constructed in $O(n\lceil \lg\sigma/\sqrt{\lg n}\rceil)$ time on the standard word RAM. In contrast, its efficient parallel construction has attracted much attention both in theory and practice. The first practical parallel wavelet tree construction was presented by Fuentes-Sepúlveda et al. [6], and subsequently improved by Shun [19], Labeit et al. [12], and again Shun [20]. Very recently, Fischer et al. [5] have proposed bottom-up approaches to both sequential and parallel wavelet tree construction. The authors of [5] reported that their sequential methods were faster than the previous state of the art [19] using less space.

2   Preliminaries

We assume the standard RAM of w-bit words with $w \geq \lg n$ as our model of computation: basic bitwise and arithmetic operations on $O(1)$ w-bit integers can be executed in constant time. Throughout this paper, we follow the notations for bitwise operations used by Knuth in [11]: bitwise *and* $x \& y$, bitwise *or* $x \mid y$, bitwise *xor* $x \oplus y$, bitwise *not* $\overline{x}$, and bitwise *shift* $x \ll k$ and $x \gg k$ for any integers x, y, and k in $[0, 2^w)$.

Let $\Sigma = [0, \sigma)$ be a set of integers, called the *alphabet*, and S be a sequence of n integers in Σ. For such S, we denote by $S[i]$ its i-th element and by $|S|$ its length n. Let x be any integer in $[0, 2^w)$. We denote by $|x|_0$ (resp. $|x|_1$) the number of 0's (resp. 1's) in the binary representation of x, and by $(x_{w-1}\cdots x_0)_2$ the binary representation of x with $x = \sum_{i=0}^{w-1} x_i 2^i$. When there is no confusion, we omit the parentheses. Finally, we define $\mathsf{bit}(x, i)$ as the i-th least significant bit in x for $0 \leq i < w$, $\mathsf{rank}_1(x, i)$ as the number of 1's up to position i in x for $0 \leq i < w$, $\mathsf{select}_1(x, i)$ as the position of the i-th 1 in x for $1 \leq i \leq |x|_1$, and $\mathsf{select}_0(x, i)$ as the position of the i-th 0 in x for $1 \leq i \leq |x|_0$.

2.1   Wavelet Trees

We assume that $\sigma \leq n$. Given S of length n over Σ as input, its *wavelet tree* is a perfect binary tree of $\sigma - 1$ nodes, each of which covers an interval in

---

[1] For a practical variant of $o(n)$-time construction of rank indexes, see the class sdsl::rank_support_v5 that supports rank queries in constant time using $0.0625n$ additional bits and note that sdsl builds it word by word. To our best of knowledge, there exists no practical variant of $o(n)$-time construction of select indexes. However, the combined sampling technique [17] of reusing sampled answers to rank in addition to those of select can be implemented in $o(n)$ time using sdsl::rank_support_v5 because sampling answers to select takes $o(w)$ time per word by using an efficient implementation of select in a w-bit word developed in [8,18,22].

$[0, \sigma)$ and stores a bit vector, recursively defined as follows. The root covers the alphabet $[0, \sigma)$ and stores a bit vector that sets its i-th bit to 0 if $S[i]$ belongs to $\Sigma_0 = [0, \sigma/2)$ and to 1 if $S[i]$ belongs to $\Sigma_1 = [\sigma/2, \sigma)$. Let S_0 (resp. S_1) be the subsequence of S that consists of integers in Σ_0 (resp. Σ_1). Then, the left (resp. right) child of the root is the wavelet tree of S_0 (resp. S_1) over Σ_0 (resp. Σ_1). For each node v in the wavelet tree, we denote by B_v its bit vector, by S_v its subsequence, by Σ_v its corresponding interval of the alphabet.

For convenience, we assume that each edge to the left (resp. right) child is labeled by 0 (resp. 1). For node v in the wavelet tree, we define the *label* of v to be the concatenation of the label on the path from the root to v and the *depth* of v to be the length of the label. In general, every bit vector is augmented by auxiliary data structures for supporting rank and select queries on it in constant time. Overall, the wavelet tree uses $n\lceil \lg \sigma \rceil + o(n \lg \sigma) + O(\sigma \lg n)$ bits of space.

The Levelwise Wavelet Tree. The levelwise wavelet tree [2] is a variant of wavelet trees that eliminates the pointers in the standard wavelet trees, saving $O(\sigma \lg n)$ bits of space. A levelwise wavelet tree consists of $\lceil \lg \sigma \rceil$ bit vectors of length n, each of which is the concatenation of the bit vectors of all the nodes of the same depth from left to right. For any integer $0 \le \ell < \lceil \lg \sigma \rceil$, we denote by B_ℓ the bit vector of level ℓ obtained from the nodes of depth ℓ. It is known that levelwise wavelet trees can simulate the traversal of pointers with rank and select queries on the concatenated bit vectors, thus preserving most of the functionality of the standard wavelet trees. At the left side of Fig. 2, we show an example levelwise wavelet tree of the same sequence S as Fig. 1.

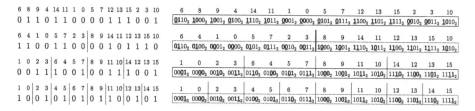

Fig. 2. The levelwise wavelet tree (left) and packed lists (right) of an example sequence over $\sigma = [0, 16)$. The decimal numbers represent the subsequence S_ℓ for each level $\ell \in [0, 4)$. The vertical lines represent the boundaries of the nodes. At the left side, the bit sequences represent B_ℓ for level $\ell \in [0, 4)$. At the right side, each binary number represents its above number in binary form, where the binary numbers surrounded by solid lines are those of big nodes, the binary numbers in bold are actually stored in packed lists, and the bits that compose B_ℓ are underlined in case of $\tau = 2$.

The Wavelet Matrix. The wavelet matrix [3] is another variant of wavelet trees that discards the tree structure of the (levelwise) wavelet tree. A wavelet matrix consists of $\lceil \lg \sigma \rceil$ bit vectors of length n and an array of size $\lceil \lg \sigma \rceil$ for storing how many 0's exist in each bit vector. The difference between the (levelwise) wavelet tree and wavelet matrix of the same input sequence S is how to shuffle S at each level: the levelwise wavelet tree shuffles S according to the *prefix* of each input integer $S[i]$, while the wavelet matrix shuffles S according to the *reversed prefix* of $S[i]$. At the left side of Fig. 3, we show an example wavelet matrix of the same sequence S as Fig. 1.

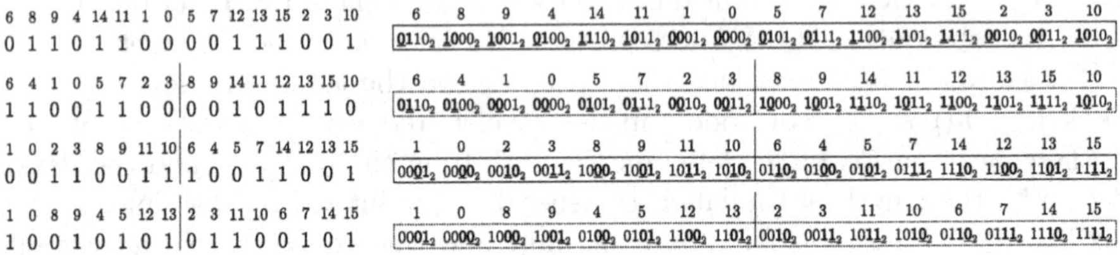

Left (wavelet matrix):

Level 0:
```
6 8 9 4 14 11 1 0 5 7 12 13 15 2 3 10
0 1 1 0 1  1  0 0 0 0 1  1  1  0 0 1
```
Level 1:
```
6 4 1 0 5 7 2 3 | 8 9 14 11 12 13 15 10
1 1 0 0 1 1 0 0 | 0 0 1  0  1  1  1  0
```
Level 2:
```
1 0 2 3 8 9 11 10 | 6 4 5 7 14 12 13 15
0 0 1 1 0 0 1  1  | 1 0 0 1 1  0  0  1
```
Level 3:
```
1 0 8 9 4 5 12 13 | 2 3 11 10 6 7 14 15
1 0 0 1 0 1 0  1  | 0 1 1  0  0 1 0  1
```

Right (packed lists):

Level 0:
```
6     8     9     4     14    11    1     0     5     7     12    13    15    2     3     10
0110₂ 1000₂ 1001₂ 0100₂ 1110₂ 1011₂ 0001₂ 0000₂ 0101₂ 0111₂ 1100₂ 1101₂ 1111₂ 0010₂ 0011₂ 1010₂
```
$0110_2\ 1000_2\ 1001_2\ 0100_2\ 1110_2\ 1011_2\ 0001_2\ 0000_2\ 0101_2\ 0111_2\ 1100_2\ 1101_2\ 1111_2\ 0010_2\ 0011_2\ 1010_2$

Level 1:
$0110_2\ 0100_2\ 0001_2\ 0000_2\ 0101_2\ 0111_2\ 0010_2\ 0011_2\ \mid\ 1000_2\ 1001_2\ 1110_2\ 1011_2\ 1100_2\ 1101_2\ 1111_2\ 1010_2$
(numbers above: 6 4 1 0 5 7 2 3 | 8 9 14 11 12 13 15 10)

Level 2:
$0001_2\ 0000_2\ 0010_2\ 0011_2\ 1000_2\ 1001_2\ 1011_2\ 1010_2\ \mid\ 0110_2\ 0100_2\ 0101_2\ 0111_2\ 1110_2\ 1100_2\ 1101_2\ 1111_2$
(numbers above: 1 0 2 3 8 9 11 10 | 6 4 5 7 14 12 13 15)

Level 3:
$0001_2\ 0000_2\ 1000_2\ 1001_2\ 0100_2\ 0101_2\ 1100_2\ 1101_2\ \mid\ 0010_2\ 0011_2\ 1011_2\ 1010_2\ 0110_2\ 0111_2\ 1110_2\ 1111_2$
(numbers above: 1 0 8 9 4 5 12 13 | 2 3 11 10 6 7 14 15)

Fig. 3. The wavelet matrix (left) and packed lists (right) of an example sequence over $\sigma = [0, 16)$. The decimal numbers represent the subsequence S_ℓ for each level $\ell \in [0, 4)$. The vertical lines represent the boundaries of the intervals. At the left side, the bit sequences represent the B_ℓ for each level $\ell \in [0, 4)$. At the right side, each binary number represents its above number in binary form, where the binary numbers surrounded by solid lines are those of big nodes, the binary numbers in bold are actually stored in packed lists, and the bits that compose B_ℓ are underlined in case of $\tau = 2$.

3 Proposed Wavelet Tree Construction

We show our proposed methods for wavelet tree and matrix construction. Our methods combine the idea of Munro et al. [14] and Babenko et al. [1] with practical implementations of core operations, called *bit packing* and *list splitting*. First, we describe their construction method. Then, we introduce two special CPU instructions used later in this section. Finally, we present our techniques for efficient implementation of bit packing and list splitting.

3.1 Two-Phase Wavelet Tree Construction

We describe the $O(n \lceil \lg \sigma / \sqrt{\lg n} \rceil)$-time construction of wavelet trees proposed by Munro et al. [14] and Babenko et al. [1]. In this section, we refer to their method as the *two-phase construction* of wavelet trees since it conceptually consists of two phases. Although we assume the standard wavelet tree, it can be also applied to the levelwise wavelet tree and the wavelet matrix.

Let τ be an integer in $[0, \lceil \lg \sigma \rceil)$. For some integer α with $0 \le \alpha\tau < \lceil \lg \sigma \rceil$, we call a node v of depth $\alpha\tau$ a *big node*. For simplicity, we assume $\lg \sigma$ and $\lg \sigma / \tau$ to be integers. The two-phase construction is based on two observations:

1. For every big node u of depth $\alpha\tau$, we can build the subsequences of all its big descendants of depth $(\alpha + 1)\tau$ from S_u.
2. For nodes v whose deepest big ancestor is u, we can build their bit vectors B_v from relevant τ bits of each $S_u[i]$.

According to these observations, the two-phase construction of wavelet trees builds the subsequences of all big nodes at its first phase, and it builds the bit vectors of all nodes at its second phase.

Before describing each phase in detail, we introduce the key data structure, called *packed lists*, used for the second phase of the two-phase construction. For each node v of depth $\alpha\tau + t$ $(0 \le t < \tau)$, the two-phase construction stores the concatenation of the τ relevant bits in each $S_v[i]$, starting at the $\alpha\tau$-th most significant bit, into $\lceil |S_v|\tau/w \rceil$ words. For some integer $b \le w$, such a representation enables us to process $\lfloor b/\tau \rfloor$ τ-bit integers at one time. We call this representation the *packed list* of v and denote by X_v. For simplicity, we assume τ divides b and w and thus each b-bit block can hold exactly $N = b/\tau$ τ-bit integers. Then, we define two core operations on packed lists as follows:

Definition 1 (Bit packing operation). Let x be any packed list of N τ-bit integer with $N = b/\tau$, and t be an integer in $[0, \tau)$. The *bit packing* operation $\mathsf{pack}(x, t)$ is defined as follows:

> $\mathsf{pack}(x, t)$:
> return a b-bit integer z such that $\mathsf{bit}(z, i) = \mathsf{bit}(x[i], t)$ for $0 \le i < N$ and $\mathsf{bit}(z, i) = 0$ for $N \le i < b$.

Definition 2 (List splitting operation). Let x be any packed list of N τ-bit integer with $N = b/\tau$, and t be an integer in $[0, \tau)$. The *list splitting* operation $\mathsf{split}(x, t)$ is defined as follows:

> $\mathsf{split}(x, t)$:
> return a pair (z_0, z_1) of b-bit integers both interpreted as packed lists such that $z_c[i] = x[\mathsf{select}_c(r, i+1)]$ for $0 \le i < |r|_c$ and $z_c[i] = 0$ for $|r|_c \le i < N$, where $c \in \{0, 1\}$ and $r = \mathsf{pack}(x, t)$.

In what follows, we explain each phase in more detail.

At the first phase, for every big node v, we build its subsequence S_v recursively as follows. The root is a big node of depth 0 and its subsequence is the input sequence S itself. Suppose that for a big node u of depth $\alpha\tau$, its subsequence S_u is already built. Then, all the subsequences of its big descendants of depth $(\alpha+1)\tau$ can be built in $O(|S_u|)$ time in total by scanning through S_u and appending each $S_u[i]$ to an appropriate subsequence S_v if $S_u[i]$ belongs to Σ_v. This phase takes $O(n \lg \sigma/\tau)$ time in total because the total length of all the subsequences of depth $\alpha\tau$ is always n and α ranges in $[0, \lg \sigma/\tau)$.

At the second phase, for every node v, we build its bit vector B_v recursively as follows. Suppose that for a node v of depth $\alpha\tau + t$ $(0 \le t < \tau)$, its packed list X_v is already built. Then, we build three components by scanning through X_v: the bit vector B_v of v, the packed list X_{v_0} of the left child v_0 of v, and the packed list X_{v_1} of the right child v_1 of v. The bit vector B_v can be built by iteratively reading the next b bits x (i.e., the next $N = b/\tau$ τ-bit integers) from X_v to process and appending $\mathsf{pack}(x, t)$ to B_v. The packed list X_{v_0} and X_{v_1} can be built by iteratively reading the next b bits x from X_v and splitting x into z_0

and z_1 by executing $(z_0, z_1) \leftarrow \mathsf{split}(x, t)$. By precomputing universal tables of $O(2^b b\tau)$ bits, the three components can be built in $O(|S_u|\tau/b)$ time. Finally, we recursively build B_{v_0} (resp. B_{v_1}) from X_{v_0} (resp. X_{v_1}) of v_0 (resp. v_1) of depth $\alpha\tau + t + 1$. We can start this process with its deepest big ancestor u of depth $\alpha\tau$ because its subsequence S_u is already built at the first phase. This phase takes $O(n \lg \sigma\tau/b + \sigma) = O(n \lg \sigma\tau/b)$ time for $\sigma \leq n$ because the total length of the lists is $O(n \lg \sigma)$.

The total time can be minimized by setting $\tau = \sqrt{\lg n}$, and it become $O(n\lceil \lg \sigma/\sqrt{\lg n}\rceil)$. Figures 2 and 3 show the packed lists of the levelwise wavelet tree and the wavelet matrix, respectively, of the same input sequence as Fig. 1 for $\tau = 2$, where each bit in bold is stored in packed lists. For example, the packed list of level 0 is $(01_2, 10_2, 10_2, 01_2, 11_2, 10_2, 00_2, 00_2, 01_2, 01_2, 11_2, 11_2, 11_2, 00_2, 00_2, 10_2)$ in both the levelwise wavelet tree and the wavelet matrix.

The main practical disadvantage of their approach, however, is that they cannot fully exploit the bit-level parallelism of the RAM if w is much greater than $\lg n$ due to the universal tables. Later in this section, we introduce alternative approaches to both the bit packing and list splitting based on broadword computation and advanced CPU instructions. In what follows, we assume that $b = w$ and thus $N = b/\tau = w/\tau$.

3.2   CPU Instructions for Efficient Bit and Byte Manipulation

For fast wavelet tree and matrix construction, we introduce two advanced CPU instructions pshufb and pext, called *Packed Shuffle Bytes* and *Parallel Bits Extract*, respectively. Later in this section, we present practical implementations of bit packing and list splitting based on pshufb and pext. Also in Sect. 4, we empirically demonstrate that both pshufb and pext are effective in practice.

The packed shuffle bytes instruction, pshufb, is an advanced CPU instruction for reordering bytes efficiently. It receives two 64-bit integers x and y as input: x is a packed list of bytes to be shuffled; y is another packed list of bytes to specify how to shuffle x. Formally, pshufb is defined as follows.

Definition 3 (Packed Shuffle Bytes). Given two integers x and y interpreted as packed lists $x = (x[0], \ldots, x[7])$ and $y = (x[0], \ldots, x[7])$ of 8 bytes, packed shuffle bytes $\mathsf{pshufb}(x, y)$ is defined as follows for i in $[0, 8)$:

$$\mathsf{pshufb}(x, y)[i] = \begin{cases} x[y[i]] \bmod 2^3 & \text{if } y[i] < 2^7 \\ 0 & \text{otherwise.} \end{cases}$$

The parallel bits extract, pext, is an advanced CPU instruction for packing bits efficiently. It is included in advanced CPU instruction sets tailored for bit manipulation, called *Bit Manipulation Instruction Sets 2* (BMI2). It receives two 64-bit integers x and y as input: x is a bit vector to be packed; y is another bit vector to specify which bits in x are packed. Formally, pext is defined as follows.

Definition 4 (Parallel Bits Extract). Given two 64-bit integers x and y viewed as bit vectors, *parallel bits extract* $\mathsf{pext}(x, y)$ is defined as follows for i in $[0, 64)$:

$$\mathsf{bit}(\mathsf{pext}(x, y), i) = \begin{cases} \mathsf{bit}(x, \mathsf{select}_1(y, i + 1)) & \text{for } 0 \leq i < |y|_1 \\ 0 & \text{for } |y|_1 \leq i < 64. \end{cases}$$

Compact data structures heavily use bit manipulation, and thus it is often effective in practice to use the so-called *broadword programming* [11] and/or advanced CPU instructions beyond basic bitwise and arithmetic ones, both of which can process multiple chunks of bits in parallel. Vigna [22] initiated a line of research of speeding up compact data structures by broadword programming or SWAR (SIMD Within A Register) techniques for aiming to exploit 64-bit (or longer) registers of modern processors. Gog and Petri [8] studied the effect of SSE instructions in their practical implementation of compact data structures. More recently, Pandey [18] introduced the parallel bits deposit instruction in BMI2 for fast select queries. The most famous example is popcnt (introduced in SSE4.2) that counts 1's in one register, which can speed up rank and select queries on bit vectors [8,23]. In what follows, we show how to use pshufb and pext for the two-phase construction of wavelet trees and matrices.

3.3   Practical Techniques for Bit Packing

For bit packing $\mathsf{pack}(x, t)$, we introduce two techniques: our first technique is based on broadword computation; our second technique is based on the parallel bits extract instruction pext. Let $N = \lceil w/\tau \rceil$ be the number of τ-bit integers per w-bit word, and x be a packed list of N packed τ-bit integers. For simplicity, we assume that τ divides w and thus $N = w/\tau$.

Let $L = (2^0, \ldots, 2^0) = (1, \ldots, 1)$ be a packed list of τ-bit integers with only the least significant bit set. We use an auxiliary function on packed lists: $\mathsf{check}_1(x, t)$, whose i-th τ-bit integer becomes 1 if $\mathsf{bit}(x[i], t) = 1$ and 0 otherwise. This can be implemented in constant time and space by $\mathsf{check}_1(x, t) = (x \gg t) \,\&\, L$.

Broadword Programming. Our first (folklore) technique for $\mathsf{pack}(x, t)$ is based on the so-called *broadword programming* [11,22]. This assumes $\tau \geq N = w/\tau$ and thus $\tau \geq \sqrt{w}$. Then, $\mathsf{pack}(x, t)$ can be implemented as follows:

$$\mathsf{pack}(x, t) = (\mathsf{check}_1(x, t) \times B) \gg (w - N).$$

First, we extract $\mathsf{bit}(x[i], t)$ for i in $[0, N)$ by $\mathsf{check}_1(x, t)$. Then, we multiply $\mathsf{check}_1(x, t)$ with a precomputed bit vector B with $\mathsf{bit}(B, i) = 1$ iff $i \in \{w - N - (\tau - 1)k \mid 0 \leq k < N\}$. This multiplication virtually makes N copies of $\mathsf{check}_1(x, t)$, shifts the k-th copy to the left by $w - N - (\tau - 1)k$ for $k \in [0, N)$, and takes the bitwise or of all the shifted copies simultaneously. For example, $\mathsf{bit}(B, i) = 1$ holds for $i \in \{0, 7, 14, 21, 28, 35, 42, 49, 56\}$ in case of $w = 64$ and $\tau = 8$. Finally, we shift the N most significant bits to be the N least significant ones. This techniques implements $\mathsf{pack}(x, t)$ in constant time and space (in words).

Parallel Bits Extract. Our second technique for $\mathsf{pack}(x,t)$ uses parallel bits extract pext, introduced in Sect. 3.2. With pext and $L = (1, \ldots, 1)$, $\mathsf{pack}(x,t)$ can be implemented as follows:

$$\mathsf{pack}(x,t) = \mathsf{pext}(x, L \ll t).$$

This is much simpler than the folklore technique based on broadword programming without any assumption on τ. This technique implements $\mathsf{pack}(x,t)$ in constant space (in words).

3.4 Practical Techniques for List Splitting

For list splitting $\mathsf{split}(x,t)$, we propose four practical techniques: our first and second techniques are both based on the idea of monotone routing [13], our third technique is based on packed shuffle bytes pshufb, and our fourth technique is based on parallel bits extract pext.

Let $H = (2^{\tau-1}, \ldots, 2^{\tau-1})$ be a packed list of N τ-bit integers with only the most significant bit set. In addition to $\mathsf{check}_1(x,t)$, we use two auxiliary functions on packed lists: $\mathsf{check}_0(x,t)$, whose i-th element becomes 1 if $\mathsf{bit}(x[i],t) = 0$ and 0 otherwise; $\mathsf{fill}(x)$, whose i-th element is filled with 1's if $\mathsf{bit}(x[i],0) = 1$ and filled with 0's otherwise. These can be also implemented in constant time and space by $\mathsf{check}_0(x,t) = ((x \gg t)\,\&\,L) \oplus L$ and $\mathsf{fill}(x) = (H - (x\,\&\,L)) \oplus H$.

Dynamic Monotone Routing. Our first technique for list splitting $\mathsf{split}(x,t)$ dynamically determines how to move τ-bit integers based on the idea of monotone routing [13]. We call this technique *dynamic monotone routing*. We assume that $\tau \geq 1 + \lfloor \lg N \rfloor$ such that any integer in $[0,N)$ can be held in τ bits. Then, $\mathsf{split}(x,t)$ can be implemented as follows. We describe how to build z_1. In a similar way, z_0 can be built. First, we check if $\mathsf{bit}(x[i],t) = 1$ by $r \leftarrow \mathsf{check}_1(x,t)$. Then, we build another packed list d such that each $d[i]$ holds the distance between the position in x and that in z_1, i.e., $d[i] = i - \mathsf{rank}_1(r, i-1)$. To obtain d, we execute $P - ((r \times L) \gg \tau)$, where P is a precomputed packed list with $P[i] = i$. Now that we obtain d, we can move all $x[i]$ with $\mathsf{bit}(x[i],t) = 1$ at $O(\lg N)$ steps, where each $x[i]$ with $d[i] \bmod 2^k = 1$ is shifted by 2^k at step k, based on the idea of monotone routing. Algorithm 1 shows the whole procedure. As a consequence, we obtain the following lemma:

Lemma 5. *For* $1 + \lfloor \lg(w/\tau) \rfloor \leq \tau \leq w$, *list splitting on n packed τ-bit integers can be implemented in* $O((n\tau/w) \lg(w/\tau))$ *time using* $O(1)$ *w-bit masks.*

Static Monotone Routing. Our second technique for list splitting $\mathsf{split}(x,t)$ uses precomputed tables to speed up dynamic monotone routing. We call this technique *static monotone routing*. This technique assumes that each τ-bit integer can hold the distance between its source and destination, i.e., $\tau \geq 1 + \lfloor \lg w/\tau \rfloor$ holds. Notice that in Algorithm 1, bit mask m in the k-th loop can be determined

Algorithm 1. Our implementation of list splitting $\mathsf{split}(x,t)$ based on dynamic monotone routing for x in $[0, 2^w)$ and t in $[0, \tau)$. Here, L, H, and P are precomputed packed lists of τ-bit integers such that $L[i] = (0 \cdots 01)_2$, $H[i] = (10 \cdots 0)_2$, and $P[i] = i$, respectively, for i in $[0, N)$. As auxiliary operations, we use $\mathsf{check}_1(x,t) = (x \gg t) \mathbin{\&} L$, $\mathsf{check}_0(x,t) = ((x \gg t) \mathbin{\&} L) \oplus L$, and $\mathsf{fill}(x) = (H - (x \mathbin{\&} L)) \oplus H$.

1:    $z_0 \leftarrow 0; z_1 \leftarrow 0;$
2:    **for** $i \leftarrow \{0,1\}$ **do**
3:       $r \leftarrow \mathsf{check}_i(x,t);$
4:       $m \leftarrow \mathsf{fill}(r);$
5:       $d \leftarrow P - ((r \times L) \gg \tau);$
6:       $z_i \leftarrow x \mathbin{\&} m;$
7:       **for** $k \leftarrow 0, \ldots, \lfloor \lg w/\tau \rfloor$ **do**
8:          $m \leftarrow \mathsf{fill}((d \gg k) \mathbin{\&} L);$
9:          $z_i \leftarrow (z_i \mathbin{\&} \overline{m}) \mid ((z_i \mathbin{\&} m) \gg (\tau \ll k)));$
10:      $d \leftarrow (d \mathbin{\&} \overline{m}) \mid ((d \mathbin{\&} m) \gg (\tau \ll k)));$
11: **return** $(z_0, z_1);$

---

by k and $\mathsf{bit}(x[i], t)$ stored in r. Because there exist 2^N possible values for r, it is sufficient to precompute a table of 2^N w-bit masks for each k. With $w = 64$, $\tau = 8$, and thus $N = 8$, such precomputed tables require only $3 \cdot 2^8 \cdot 8 \approx 6k$ bytes. As a consequence, we obtain the following lemma:

Lemma 6. *For $\tau \geq 1 + \lfloor \lg w/\tau \rfloor$, list splitting on n packed τ-bit integers can be implemented in $O(\lceil n\tau/w \rceil \lg(w/\tau))$ time using $O(2^{w/\tau} \lg(w/\tau))$ w-bit masks.*

Packed Shuffle Bytes. Our third technique for list splitting $\mathsf{split}(x,t)$ uses packed shuffle bytes pshufb. This technique assumes $w = 64$, $\tau = 8$, and thus $N = w/\tau = 8$ due to the specification of pshufb. The main difficulty is how to compute an appropriate bit mask y for packing x as desired. Assume that we want to compute z_1 as $z_1 = \mathsf{pshufb}(x, y_1)$ with an appropriate bit mask y_1. To obtain such y_1 efficiently, we precompute a universal table using $O(2^N)$ words, associating 2^N possible values of N-bit integers $r \leftarrow \mathsf{pack}(\mathsf{check}_1(x,t), 0)$ with their corresponding packed lists y_r that hold integers in $[0, 8) \cup \{2^7\}$. The corresponding packed list y_r is defined to be $(\mathsf{select}_1(r, 1), \ldots, \mathsf{select}_1(r, |r|_1), 2^7, \ldots, 2^7)$. By reusing the same table with the N least significant bits of the complement $\overline{r}$ of r, we can compute z_0 as well. This technique implements $\mathsf{split}(x,t)$ in constant time using $O(2^N) = O(2^{w/\tau})$ space (in words).

Parallel Bits Extract. Our fourth technique for $\mathsf{split}(x,t)$ uses parallel bits extract pext. This technique just assumes $w = 64$. With pext, $\mathsf{split}(x,t)$ can be implemented as follows. First, we execute $r_0 \leftarrow \mathsf{check}_0(x,t)$ and $r_1 \leftarrow \mathsf{check}_1(x,t)$, such that $r_0[i]$ (resp. $r_1[i]$) becomes 1 if $\mathsf{bit}(x[i], t) = 0$ (resp. $\mathsf{bit}(x[i], t) = 1$) and 0 otherwise for $i \in [0, N)$. Then, we build bit masks y_0 and y_1 used with pext by $y_0 \leftarrow \mathsf{fill}(r_0)$ and $y_1 \leftarrow \mathsf{fill}(r_1)$. Note that each $y_0[i]$

(resp. $y_1[i]$) is filled with τ 1's if $\mathsf{bit}(x[i], t) = 0$ (resp. $\mathsf{bit}(x[i], t) = 1$) and filled with τ 0's otherwise. Finally, we build z_0 and z_1 as output by $z_0 \leftarrow \mathsf{pext}(x, y_0)$ and $z_1 \leftarrow \mathsf{pext}(x, y_1)$. This technique implements $\mathsf{split}(x, t)$ in constant time and space (in words).

4   Experiments

We empirically compare our four methods based on dynamic monotone routing (route-d), static monotone routing (route-s), packed shuffle bytes (pshufb), and parallel bits extract (pext), with three existing ones: a naive method (naive), the bottom-up method based on prefix counting [5] (pc), and the bottom-up method based on prefix sorting [5] (ps).

As our datasets, we used 15 real-world text collections from the Pizza and Chilli Corpus[2] and Lightweight Corpus[3]. The data sizes n and alphabet sizes σ of our datasets are shown in Table 1 (and Table 2). All our experiments were conducted on a machine with Intel Core i7-4790 processors (3.60 GHz and 8 MB cache) and 16 GB main memory running Ubuntu 18.04. All our code was implemented in C++ and integrated into an existing library[4] that included naive, pc, and ps implemented and used by the authors of [5]. Then, all our and their code was compiled by g++8 with -O3 and -march=native flags. All our methods were configured with $w = 64$ and $\tau = 8$, and used the parallel bit extract technique for bit packing because all of them except for route-d[5] showed slightly better performances with the technique on most of our datasets.

Implementation Notes. We explain some details of our implementations. To store the packed lists of the current and next levels, we allocated two buffers of $\lceil n\tau/w \rceil = \lceil n/8 \rceil$ words. To maintain the boundaries of the node or intervals of the current and next levels, we kept two arrays of σ words for the wavelet tree and of just 2 words for the wavelet matrix. To avoid multiple scans over the packed list of each level, we determined the boundaries of the next level while computing the bit vector and packed list of the current level. The packed shuffle bytes and parallel bits extract instructions were used via intrinsics _mm_shuffle_pi8 and _pext_u64, respectively [10].

Time for Wavelet Tree Construction. We show experimental results for wavelet trees in Table 1. First, we compare our methods to the baseline naive. For wavelet tree construction, all our methods outperformed naive on any dataset. As expected, our pext and pshufb outperformed our route-d and route-s by exploiting CPU instructions tailored for complex bit and byte manipulation. In particular, both of our pshufb and pext were 1.9 times as fast as naive on average. Notably, they were much faster than naive on our largest dataset english. Note that even

---

[2] http://pizzachili.dcc.uchile.cl/.
[3] http://people.unipmn.it/manzini/lightweight/corpus/.
[4] https://github.com/kurpicz/pwm.
[5] route-d showed better performances in combination with bit packing based on multiplication for wavelet matrix construction.

Table 1. Elapsed times (in seconds) for constructing wavelet trees without rank and select indexes, as in [5]. For each combination of datasets and methods, the median of five trials is reported. The best construction time on each dataset is underlined.

Text	n	σ	naive	pc [5]	ps [5]	route-d	route-s	pshufb	pext
dblp.xml	$2.96 \cdot 10^8$	97	5.57	2.99	3.03	4.33	3.65	3.09	03.04
dna	$4.04 \cdot 10^8$	16	4.43	2.42	2.72	2.47	2.29	2.07	2.05
english	$2.21 \cdot 10^9$	238	53.0	27.2	28.8	32.1	27.9	23.7	23.5
pitches	$5.58 \cdot 10^7$	132	1.25	0.685	0.812	0.741	0.659	0.576	0.570
proteins	$1.18 \cdot 10^9$	27	16.1	8.29	8.67	12.8	10.9	9.27	9.12
sources	$2.11 \cdot 10^8$	229	4.94	2.54	2.61	3.21	3.09	2.37	2.55
chr22.dna	$3.46 \cdot 10^7$	5	0.233	0.143	0.188	0.190	0.173	0.157	0.156
etext99	$1.05 \cdot 10^8$	145	2.32	1.31	1.62	1.57	1.35	1.16	1.14
gcc-3.0.tar	$8.66 \cdot 10^7$	149	1.91	1.32	1.12	1.467	1.105	0.949	0.935
howto	$3.94 \cdot 10^7$	196	0.832	0.478	0.496	0.592	0.512	0.438	0.432
jdk13c	$6.97 \cdot 10^7$	113	1.30	0.708	0.789	1.03	0.877	0.829	0.755
linux-2.4.5.tar	$1.16 \cdot 10^8$	255	2.76	1.41	1.45	2.24	1.95	1.30	1.51
rctail96	$1.15 \cdot 10^8$	93	2.25	1.18	1.20	1.66	1.40	1.19	1.17
rfc	$1.16 \cdot 10^8$	120	2.28	1.25	1.27	1.62	1.42	1.20	1.19
sprot34.dat	$1.10 \cdot 10^8$	66	2.12	1.14	1.36	1.54	1.70	1.13	1.13
w3c2	$1.04 \cdot 10^8$	255	2.30	1.30	1.28	1.66	1.41	1.30	1.18

our route-d, which requires many bitwise and arithmetic instructions, was 1.4 times as fast as naive on average. Next, we compare our methods with pc since it outperformed ps except for four datasets (jdk13c, rctail96, rfc, and w3c2). Although our pshufb and pext were 1.4 times as fast as pc on gcc-3.0.tar, no clear winner existed on other datasets. In fact, on average our pext and pshufb were just 1.1 times as fast as pc, and ours became slightly slower than pc on some datasets. Overall, our experiments for wavelet tree construction demonstrated that our practical variants of the two-phase construction by [14] and [1] ran well on real-world datasets, although our improvement depended on datasets.

Time for Wavelet Matrix Construction. We show experimental results for wavelet matrices in Table 2. Our improvement for wavelet matrices is more notable than that for wavelet trees. First, as in the case of wavelet trees, all our methods outperformed naive on any dataset. On average, our pshufb and pext improved naive by factors of 3.0–4.6 and 2.5–4.5, respectively. Unlike the case of wavelet trees, our pshufb and pext always outperformed pc by factors of 1.1–1.9. This difference between wavelet trees and matrices can be explained by the fact that our implementation for wavelet trees tends to require more instructions than that for wavelet matrices to treat the boundaries of intervals in bit vectors.

Space for Wavelet Tree and Matrix Construction. On our datasets with $\sigma \ll n$, pc was the most space-efficient method for both wavelet tree and matrix

Table 2. Elapsed times (in seconds) for constructing wavelet matrices without rank and select indexes, as in [5]. For each combination of datasets and methods, the median of five trials is reported. The best construction time on each dataset is underlined.

Text	n	σ	naive	pc [5]	ps [5]	route-d	route-s	pshufb	pext
dblp.xml	$2.96 \cdot 10^8$	97	6.20	3.00	3.01	3.65	2.74	<u>2.02</u>	2.05
dna	$4.04 \cdot 10^8$	16	5.88	2.43	2.70	1.81	1.53	<u>1.29</u>	1.30
english	$2.21 \cdot 10^9$	238	57.0	27.2	28.5	26.7	20.6	<u>15.8</u>	15.9
pitches	$5.58 \cdot 10^7$	132	1.37	0.684	0.709	0.595	0.495	<u>0.429</u>	0.547
proteins	$1.18 \cdot 10^9$	27	22.4	8.29	8.41	11.1	8.44	<u>6.36</u>	6.43
sources	$2.11 \cdot 10^8$	229	5.81	2.54	2.95	2.69	2.28	<u>1.57</u>	1.59
chr22.dna	$3.46 \cdot 10^7$	5	0.385	0.143	0.164	0.132	0.110	0.130	<u>0.092</u>
etext99	$1.05 \cdot 10^8$	145	3.01	1.27	1.34	1.30	1.00	0.803	<u>0.771</u>
gcc-3.0.tar	$8.66 \cdot 10^7$	149	2.18	1.05	1.29	1.13	0.828	<u>0.633</u>	0.639
howto	$3.94 \cdot 10^7$	196	1.011	0.478	0.494	0.495	0.384	<u>0.295</u>	0.298
jdk13c	$6.97 \cdot 10^7$	113	1.57	0.708	0.705	1.17	0.665	<u>0.500</u>	0.506
linux-2.4.5.tar	$1.16 \cdot 10^8$	255	3.14	1.41	1.64	1.46	1.14	<u>0.872</u>	1.11
rctail96	$1.15 \cdot 10^8$	93	2.37	1.22	1.19	1.39	1.27	<u>0.779</u>	0.792
rfc	$1.16 \cdot 10^8$	120	2.65	1.30	1.28	1.34	1.05	<u>0.791</u>	0.811
sprot34.dat	$1.10 \cdot 10^8$	66	2.81	1.14	1.38	1.27	0.982	0.905	<u>0.855</u>
w3c2	$1.04 \cdot 10^8$	255	2.63	1.54	1.27	1.73	1.07	<u>0.80</u>	0.81

construction, and our methods needed about twice the space of pc because ours kept $2\lceil n\tau/w \rceil = 2\lceil n/8 \rceil$ words of packed lists. The bottom-up methods pc and ps aggressively exploit an assumption that $\sigma \leq n$. However, such an assumption does not hold in some applications in numerical and geometrical data analysis [3]. We leave as future work investigating the space on other datasets with $\sigma \geq n$.

5   Conclusion

In this paper, we introduced new techniques for fast wavelet tree and matrix construction, making theoretical work by [14] and [1] feasible in practice. Our experimental results demonstrated that our methods based on special CPU instructions pshufb and pext were attractive choices in practice especially for wavelet matrix construction. Important future work includes conducting more comprehensive experiments and presenting an experimental map to choose the best method for given datasets and resource. It is an interesting challenge to extend our technique by using SSE/AVX instructions on 128-bit or 256-bit registers and/or by combining them with recent improved parallel wavelet tree and matrix construction by Shun [20].

Acknowledgments. I would like to thank the authors of [5] for making their code public, the anonymous reviewers for their helpful comments that greatly improved the correctness and presentation of this paper, and Kunihiko Sadakane for a presentation copy of his book that enhanced my understanding of this field.

References

1. Babenko, M., Gawrychowski, P., Kociumaka, T., Starikovskaya, T.: Wavelet trees meet suffix trees. In: Proceedings of the 26th Annual ACM-SIAM Symposium on Discrete Algorithms (SODA 2015), pp. 572–591 (2015)
2. Claude, F., Navarro, G.: Practical rank/select queries over arbitrary sequences. In: Amir, A., Turpin, A., Moffat, A. (eds.) SPIRE 2008. LNCS, vol. 5280, pp. 176–187. Springer, Heidelberg (2008). https://doi.org/10.1007/978-3-540-89097-3_18
3. Claude, F., Navarro, G., Ordóñez, A.: The wavelet matrix: an efficient wavelet tree for large alphabets. Inf. Syst. **47**, 15–32 (2015)
4. Claude, F., Nicholson, P.K., Seco, D.: Space efficient wavelet tree construction. In: Grossi, R., Sebastiani, F., Silvestri, F. (eds.) SPIRE 2011. LNCS, vol. 7024, pp. 185–196. Springer, Heidelberg (2011). https://doi.org/10.1007/978-3-642-24583-1_19
5. Fischer, J., Kurpicz, F., Löbel, M.: Simple, fast and lightweight parallel wavelet tree construction. In: Proceedings of the 20th Workshop on Algorithm Engineering and Experiments (ALENEX 2018), pp. 9–20 (2018)
6. Fuentes-Sepúlveda, J., Elejalde, E., Ferres, L., Seco, D.: Parallel construction of wavelet trees on multicore architectures. Knowl. Inf. Syst. **51**(3), 1043–1066 (2017)
7. Gog, S., Beller, T., Moffat, A., Petri, M.: From theory to practice: plug and play with succinct data structures. In: Gudmundsson, J., Katajainen, J. (eds.) SEA 2014. LNCS, vol. 8504, pp. 326–337. Springer, Cham (2014). https://doi.org/10.1007/978-3-319-07959-2_28
8. Gog, S., Petri, M.: Optimized succinct data structures for massive data. Softw. Pract. Exp. **44**(11), 1287–1314 (2014)
9. Grossi, R., Gupta, A., Vitter, J.S.: High-order entropy-compressed text indexes. In: Proceedings of the Fourteenth Annual ACM-SIAM Symposium on Discrete Algorithms (SODA 2003), pp. 841–850 (2003)
10. Intel: Intel intrinsics guide. https://software.intel.com/sites/landingpage/Intrinsics Guide/
11. Knuth, D.E.: The Art of Computer Programming, Volume 4, Fascicle 1: Bitwise Tricks & Techniques; Binary Decision Diagrams. Addison-Wesley Professional, Boston (2009)
12. Labeit, J., Shun, J., Blelloch, G.E.: Parallel lightweight wavelet tree, suffix array and fm-index construction. J. Discret. Algorithms **43**, 2–17 (2017)
13. Leighton, F.T.: Introduction to Parallel Algorithms and Architectures: Array, Trees, Hypercubes. Morgan Kaufmann, Burlington (1992)
14. Munro, J.I., Nekrich, Y., Vitter, J.S.: Fast construction of wavelet trees. Theor. Comput. Sci. **638**(C), 91–97 (2016)
15. Navarro, G.: Wavelet trees for all. J. Discret. Algorithms **25**, 2–20 (2014)
16. Navarro, G.: Compact Data Structures - A Practical Approach. Cambridge University Press, Cambridge (2016)
17. Navarro, G., Providel, E.: Fast, small, simple rank/select on bitmaps. In: Klasing, R. (ed.) SEA 2012. LNCS, vol. 7276, pp. 295–306. Springer, Heidelberg (2012). https://doi.org/10.1007/978-3-642-30850-5_26

18. Pandey, P., Bender, M.A., Johnson, R., Patro, R.: A general-purpose counting filter: making every bit count. In: Proceedings of the 2017 ACM International Conference on Management of Data, (SIGMOD 2017), pp. 775–787 (2017)

19. Shun, J.: Parallel wavelet tree construction. In: Proceedings of the 2015 Data Compression Conference (DCC 2015), pp. 92–101 (2015)

20. Shun, J.: Improved parallel construction of wavelet trees and rank/select structures. In: Proceedings of the 2017 Data Compression Conference (DCC 2017), pp. 92–101 (2017)

21. Tischler, G.: On wavelet tree construction. In: Giancarlo, R., Manzini, G. (eds.) CPM 2011. LNCS, vol. 6661, pp. 208–218. Springer, Heidelberg (2011). https://doi.org/10.1007/978-3-642-21458-5_19

22. Vigna, S.: Broadword implementation of rank/select queries. In: McGeoch, C.C. (ed.) WEA 2008. LNCS, vol. 5038, pp. 154–168. Springer, Heidelberg (2008). https://doi.org/10.1007/978-3-540-68552-4_12

23. Zhou, D., Andersen, D.G., Kaminsky, M.: Space-efficient, high-performance rank and select structures on uncompressed bit sequences. In: Bonifaci, V., Demetrescu, C., Marchetti-Spaccamela, A. (eds.) SEA 2013. LNCS, vol. 7933, pp. 151–163. Springer, Heidelberg (2013). https://doi.org/10.1007/978-3-642-38527-8_15

Faster Recovery of Approximate Periods
over Edit Distance

Tomasz Kociumaka(iD), Jakub Radoszewski(iD), Wojciech Rytter(iD),
Juliusz Straszyński(✉)(iD), Tomasz Waleń(iD), and Wiktor Zuba(iD)

Institute of Informatics, University of Warsaw, Warsaw, Poland
{kociumaka,jrad,rytter,jks,walen,w.zuba}@mimuw.edu.pl

Abstract. The approximate period recovery problem asks to compute all *approximate word-periods* of a given word S of length n: all primitive words P ($|P| = p$) which have a periodic extension at edit distance smaller than τ_p from S, where $\tau_p = \lfloor \frac{n}{(3.75+\epsilon)\cdot p} \rfloor$ for some $\epsilon > 0$. Here, the set of periodic extensions of P consists of all finite prefixes of P^∞.

We improve the time complexity of the fastest known algorithm for this problem of Amir et al. [Theor. Comput. Sci., 2018] from $\mathcal{O}(n^{4/3})$ to $\mathcal{O}(n \log n)$. Our tool is a fast algorithm for Approximate Pattern Matching in Periodic Text. We consider only verification for the period recovery problem when the candidate approximate word-period P is explicitly given up to cyclic rotation; the algorithm of Amir et al. reduces the general problem in $\mathcal{O}(n)$ time to a logarithmic number of such more specific instances.

Keywords: Edit distance · Periods · Approximate pattern matching

1 Introduction

The aim of this work is computing periods of words in the approximate pattern matching model (see e.g. [8,10]). This task can be stated as the *approximate period recovery (APR) problem* that was defined by Amir et al. [2]. In this problem, we are given a word; we suspect that it was initially periodic, but then errors might have been introduced in it. Our goal is to attempt to recover the periodicity of the original word. If too many errors have been introduced, it might be impossible to recover the period. Hence, a requirement is imposed that the distance between the original periodic word and the word with errors is upper bounded, with the bound being related to the period length. Here, edit

J. Radoszewski and J. Straszyński—Supported by the "Algorithms for text processing with errors and uncertainties" project carried out within the HOMING programme of the Foundation for Polish Science co-financed by the European Union under the European Regional Development Fund.

W. Rytter—Supported by the Polish National Science Center, grant no. 2014/13/B/ST6/00770.

T. Gagie et al. (Eds.): SPIRE 2018, LNCS 11147, pp. 233–240, 2018.
https://doi.org/10.1007/978-3-030-00479-8_19

distance is used as a metric. The fastest known solution to the APR problem is due to Amir et al. [1].

A different version of the APR problem was considered by Sim et al. [16], who bound the number of errors per occurrence of the period. The general problem of computing approximate periods over weighted edit distance is known to be NP-complete; see [15,16]. Other variants of approximate periods have also been introduced. One direction is the study of approximate repetitions, that is, subwords of the given word that are approximately periodic in some sense (and, possibly, maximal); see [3,12,17,18]. Another is the study of quasiperiods, occurrences of which may overlap in the text; see, e.g., [4–6,11,14].

Let ed-dist(S, W) be the edit distance (or Levenshtein distance) between the words S and W, that is, the minimum number of edit operations (insertions, deletions, or substitutions) necessary to transform S to W. A word P is called *primitive* if it cannot be expressed as $P = Q^k$ for a word Q and an integer $k \geq 2$. The APR problem can now formally be defined as follows.

Approximate Period Recovery (APR) Problem

Input: A word S of length n

Output: All primitive words P (called *approximate word-periods*) for which the infinite word P^∞ has a prefix W such that ed-dist$(S, W) < \tau_p$, where $p = |P|$ and $\tau_p = \lfloor \frac{n}{(3.75+\epsilon)\cdot p} \rfloor$ with $\epsilon > 0$

Remark 1. Amir et al. [1] show that each approximate word-period is a subword of S and thus can be represented in constant space. Moreover, they show that the number of approximate word-periods is $\mathcal{O}(n)$. Hence, the output to the APR problem uses $\mathcal{O}(n)$ space.

The solution of Amir et al. [1] works in $\mathcal{O}(n^{4/3})$ time[1]. Our result is an $\mathcal{O}(n \log n)$-time algorithm for the APR problem.

Let us recall that two words U and V are *cyclic shifts* (denoted as $U \approx V$) if there exist words X and Y such that $U = XY$ and $V = YX$. The algorithm of Amir et al. [1] consists of two steps. First, a small number of candidates are identified, as stated in the following fact.

Fact 2 (Amir et al. [1, Sect. 4.3]). In $\mathcal{O}(n)$ time, one can find $\mathcal{O}(\log n)$ subwords of S (of exponentially increasing lengths) such that every approximate word-period of S is a cyclic shift of one of the candidates.

For a pattern S and an infinite word W, by ED(S, W) let us denote the minimum edit distance between S and a prefix of W. By Fact 2, the APR problem reduces to $\mathcal{O}(\log n)$ instances of the following problem.

---

[1] Also the APR problem under the Hamming distance was considered [2] for which an $\mathcal{O}(n \log n)$-time algorithm was presented [1] for the threshold $\lfloor \frac{n}{(2+\epsilon)\cdot p} \rfloor$ with $\epsilon > 0$.

> Approximate Pattern Matching in Periodic Text (APM Problem)
>
> **Input:** A word S of length n, a word P of length p, and a threshold k
>
> **Output:** For every cyclic shift U of P, compute $\mathsf{ED}(S, U^\infty)$ or report that this value is greater than k

Amir et al. [1] use two solutions to the APM problem that work in $\mathcal{O}(np)$ time and $\mathcal{O}(n + k(k+p))$ time, respectively. The main tool of the first algorithm is *wrap-around dynamic programming* [9] that solves the APM problem without the threshold constraint k in $\mathcal{O}(np)$ time. The other solution is based on the Landau–Vishkin algorithm [13]. For each p and $k < \tau_p$, either algorithm works in $\mathcal{O}(n^{4/3})$ time.

Our Results. We show that:

- The APM problem can be solved in $\mathcal{O}(n + kp)$ time.
- The APR problem can be solved in $\mathcal{O}(n \log n)$ time.

Our solution to the APM problem involves a more efficient combination of wrap-around dynamic programming with the Landau–Vishkin algorithm.

2   Approximate Pattern Matching in Periodic Texts

We assume that the length of a word U is denoted by $|U|$ and the letters of U are numbered 0 through $|U| - 1$, with $U[i]$ representing the ith letter. By $U[i \mathinner{..} j]$ we denote the subword $U[i] \cdots U[j]$; if $i > j$, it denotes the empty word. A prefix of U is a subword $U[0 \mathinner{..} i]$ and a suffix of U is a subword $U[i \mathinner{..} |U| - 1]$, denoted also as $U[i \mathinner{..}]$.

The length of the longest common prefix of words U and V is denoted by $\mathsf{lcp}(U, V)$. The following fact specifies a well-known efficient data structure answering such queries over suffixes of a given text; see, e.g., [7].

Fact 3. *Let S be a word of length n over an integer alphabet of size $\sigma = n^{\mathcal{O}(1)}$. After $\mathcal{O}(n)$-time preprocessing, given indices i and j ($0 \le i, j < n$) one can compute $\mathsf{lcp}(S[i \mathinner{..}], S[j \mathinner{..}])$ in $\mathcal{O}(1)$ time.*

2.1   Wrap-Around Dynamic Programming

Following [9], we introduce a table $T[0 \mathinner{..} n, 0 \mathinner{..} p-1]$ whose cell $T[i, j]$ denotes the minimum edit distance between $S[0 \mathinner{..} i - 1]$ and some subword of the periodic word P^∞ ending on the $(j - 1)$th character of the period. More formally, for $i \in \{0, \dots, n\}$ and $j \in \mathbb{Z}_p$, we define

$$T[i, j] = \min\{\mathsf{ed\text{-}dist}(S[0 \mathinner{..} i - 1], P^\infty[i' \mathinner{..} j']) : i' \in \mathbb{N},\ j' \equiv j - 1 \pmod{p}\};$$

see Fig. 1. The following fact characterizes T in terms of ED.

Fact 4. *We have $\min\{\mathsf{ED}(S, U^\infty) : U \approx P\} = \min\{T[n, j] : j \in \mathbb{Z}_p\}$.*

	A	**A**	**B**	**C**	A	A	B	C	A	A	B	C	A	A
	0	**0**	**0**	**0**	0	0	0	0	0	0	0	0	0	0
C	**1**	**1**	**1**	**0**	1	1	1	0	1	1	1	0	1	1
B	**1**	**2**	**1**	**1**	1	2	1	1	1	2	1	1	1	2
A	**1**	1	**2**	**2**	1	1	2	2	1	1	2	2	1	1
A	**2**	1	2	**3**	2	1	2	3	2	1	2	3	2	1
C	**3**	2	2	**2**	3	2	2	3	2	2	2	3	2	
A	**2**	3	3	**3**	2	3	3	3	2	3	3	3	2	3
A	**3**	2	3	*****	3	2	3	*	3	2	3	*	3	2
B	*****	3	2	**3**	*	3	2	3	*	3	2	3	*	3
C	**3**	*	3	**2**	3	*	3	2	3	*	3	2	3	*
A	**2**	3	*	**3**	2	3	*	3	2	3	*	3	2	3

Fig. 1. The first four columns show the table T for $S = $ CBAACAABCA and $P = $ ABCA. The asterisks represent values that are greater than $k = 3$; these values need not be computed in our algorithm. The next columns contain copies of T; the highlighted diagonals show the computation of the array D (see below). Note that $T[3,1] = 1$ because $T[2,0] = 1$ and $S[2] = $ A $= P[0]$.

Proof. First, let us observe that the definition of T immediately yields

$$\min\{T[n,j] : j \in \mathbb{Z}_p\} = \min\{\text{ed-dist}(S, P^\infty[i' \mathrel{..} j']) : i', j' \in \mathbb{N}\}.$$

In other words, $\min\{T[n,j] : j \in \mathbb{Z}_p\}$ is the minimum edit distance between S and any subword of P^∞. On the other hand, $\min\{\mathsf{ED}(S, U^\infty) : U \approx P\}$ by definition of ED is the minimum edit distance between S and a prefix of U^∞ for a cyclic shift U of P. Finally, it suffices to note that the sets of subwords of P^∞ and of prefixes of U^∞ taken over all $U \approx P$ are the same. □

Below, we use $\oplus$ and $\ominus$ to denote operations in $\mathbb{Z}_p$.

Lemma 5 ([9]). *The table T is the unique table satisfying the following formula:*

$$T[0,j] = 0,$$

$$T[i+1, j \oplus 1] = \min \begin{cases} T[i, j \oplus 1] + & 1 \\ T[i,j] & + [S[i] \neq P[j]] \\ T[i+1, j] + & 1 \end{cases}.$$

Let us mention that the above formula contains cyclic dependencies that emerge due to wrapping (the third value in the minimum). Nevertheless, the table can be computed using a graph-theoretic interpretation. With each $T[i,j]$ we associate a vertex (i,j). The arcs are implied by the formula in Lemma 5: the arcs pointing to $(i+1, j \oplus 1)$ are from $(i, j \oplus 1)$ with weight 1 (deletion), from (i,j) with weight 0 or 1 (match or substitution), and from $(i+1, j)$ with weight 1 (insertion). Then $T[i,j]$ is the length of the shortest path from any vertex $(0, j')$ to the vertex (i,j). With this interpretation, the table T is computed using Breadth-First Search, with the 0-arcs processed before the 1-arcs.

2.2   Wrap-Around DP with Kangaroo Jumps

Our next goal is to compute all the values $T[n,j]$ not exceeding k. In the algorithm, we exploit two properties that our dynamic programming array has.

First of all, let us consider a diagonal modulo length of the period, that is, cells of the form $T[i, j \oplus i]$ for a fixed $j \in \mathbb{Z}_p$. We can notice that the sequence of values on every diagonal is non-decreasing. This stems from the fact that on each diagonal the alignment of the pattern is the same and extending a prefix of S and a subword of P^∞ by one letter does not decrease their edit distance. This results in a conclusion that if we would like to iteratively compute the set of reachable cells within a fixed distance, then we can convey this information with just the indices of the furthermost reachable cells in each of the diagonals. Our task is to check whether we can reach some cell in the last row within the distance k. To achieve this, we can iteratively find the set of cells reachable within subsequent distances $0, 1, \dots$. More formally, for $d \in \{0, \dots, k\}$ and $j \in \mathbb{Z}_p$, we define

$$D[d,j] = \max\{i : T[i, j \oplus i] \le d\};$$

see Fig. 1.

Secondly, we observe that it is cheap to check how many consecutive cost-0 transitions can be made from a given cell. Let us remind ourselves that our only free transition checks whether the next letters of the pattern and the periodic word are equal. To know how far we can stack this transition is, in other words, finding the longest common prefix of appropriate suffixes of S and P^∞. We obtain the following recursive formulae for $D[d,j]$; see Fig. 2.

Fact 6. *The table D can be computed using the following formula:*

$$\mathcal{D}[0,j] = \mathsf{lcp}(S, P^\infty[j\,..]),$$
$$D[d+1,j] = i + \mathsf{lcp}(S[i\,..], P^\infty[i \oplus j\,..]),$$

where $i = \min(n, \max\{D[d,j]+1,\ D[d, j \ominus 1],\ D[d, j \oplus 1]+1\})$.

Proof. We will prove the fact by considering the interpretation of $T[i,j]$ as distances in a weighted graph (see Sect. 2.1). By Lemma 5, from every vertex (i,j) we have the following outgoing arcs:

- $(i,j) \xrightarrow{1} (i+1,j)$,
- $(i,j) \xrightarrow{[S[i] \neq P[j]]} (i+1, j \oplus 1)$,
- $(i,j) \xrightarrow{1} (i, j \oplus 1)$.

Moreover, the value $T[i,j]$ is equal to the minimum distance to (i,j) from some vertex $(0,j')$. The only arc of cost 0 is $(i,j) \xrightarrow{0} (i+1, j \oplus 1)$ when $S[i] = P[j]$. Therefore, when we have reached a vertex (i,j), the only vertices we can reach from it by using only 0-arcs are $(i,j), (i+1, j \oplus 1), \dots, (i+k, j \oplus k)$, where k is the maximum number such that $S[i] = P[j]$, $S[i+1] = P[j \oplus 1]$, $\dots$, $S[i+(k-1)] = P[j \oplus (k-1)]$. Therefore, $k = \mathsf{lcp}(S[i\,..], P^\infty[j\,..])$.

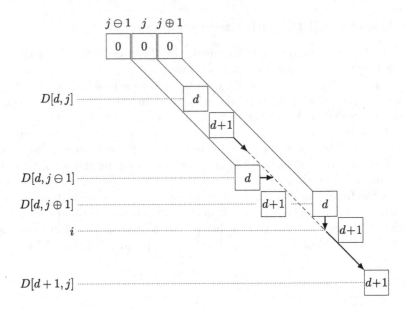

Fig. 2. Illustration of definition and computation of the array D.

Hence, $D[0,j] = \mathsf{lcp}(S, P^\infty[j\mathinner{..}])$ holds for distance 0. Taking advantage of monotonicity of distances on each diagonal, we know that full information about reachable vertices at distance d can be stored as a list of the furthest points on each diagonal. Moreover, to reach a vertex of distance $d + 1$ we need to pick a vertex of distance d, follow a single 1-arc and then zero or more 0-arcs. Combining this with the fact that arcs changing diagonal can be arbitrarily used at any vertex, it suffices to consider only the bottom-most point of each diagonal with the distance d as the starting point of the 1-arc, as we can greedily postpone following an arc that switches diagonals.   □

To conclude, assuming we know the indices of furthest reachable cells in each of the diagonals for an edit distance d, we can easily compute indices for the next distance. In the beginning, we update the indices by applying available 1-arcs and afterwards, we increase indices by the results of appropriate lcp-queries. In the end, we have computed the furthest reachable cells in each of the diagonals within distance $d+1$ and achieved that in linear time with respect to the number of diagonals, i.e., in $\mathcal{O}(p)$ time. This approach is shown as Algorithm 1.

Lemma 7. *Algorithm 1 for each $j \in \mathbb{Z}_p$ computes $T[n,j]$ or reports that $T[n,j] > k$. It can be implemented in $\mathcal{O}(n + pk)$ time.*

Proof. We use Fact 3 to answer each lcp-query in constant time, by creating a data structure for lcp queries for the word $S\#P^r$ where $\#$ is a sentinel character and r is an exponent large enough so that $|P^r| \geq n + p$.   □

Algorithm 1. Compute all values $T[n, j]$ not exceeding k

$T[n, 0 .. p - 1] := (\bot, \ldots, \bot)$
for $d := 0$ **to** k **do**
    foreach $j \in \mathbb{Z}_p$ **do**
        if $d = 0$ **then**
        | $i := 0$
        else
        | $i := \min(n, \max(D[d - 1, j] + 1, D[d - 1, j \ominus 1], D[d - 1, j \oplus 1] + 1))$
        $D[d, j] := i + \mathsf{lcp}(S[i ..], P^\infty[i \oplus j ..]);$
        if $D[d, j] = n$ **and** $T[n, j \oplus n] = \bot$ **then**
        | $T[n, j \oplus n] := d$

2.3 Main Results

The table T specifies the last position of an approximate match within the period of the periodic word. However, in our problem we need to know the starting position, which determines the sought cyclic shift of the period. Thus, let T^R be the counterpart of T defined for the reverse words S^R and P^R. Its last row satisfies the following property:

Fact 8. *For every $j \in \mathbb{Z}_p$, we have*

$$T^R[n, p \ominus j] = \mathsf{ED}(S, U^\infty) \quad \text{where} \quad U = P[j .. p - 1] \cdot P[0 .. j - 1].$$

Here, U a cyclic shift of P with the leading j characters moved to the back.

Proof. By definition of T^R and T, for $0 \le i \le n$ and $j \in \mathbb{Z}_p$, we have

$$\begin{aligned}
T^R[n, j] &= \min\{\text{ed-dist}(S^R, (P^R)^\infty[i' .. j']) : i' \in \mathbb{N}, j' \equiv j - 1 \ (\text{mod } p)\} \\
&= \min\{\text{ed-dist}(S, P^\infty[j' .. i']) : i' \in \mathbb{N}, j' \equiv -j \ (\text{mod } p)\} \\
&= \min\{\text{ed-dist}(S, P^\infty[p \ominus j .. i']) : i' \in \mathbb{N}\} \\
&= \mathsf{ED}(S, P^\infty[p \ominus j ..]).
\end{aligned}$$

Consequently,

$$T^R[n, p \ominus j] = \mathsf{ED}(S, P^\infty[j ..]) = \mathsf{ED}(S, (P[j .. p - 1] \cdot P[0 .. j - 1])^\infty)$$

holds as claimed.   □

Example 9. If $P = \text{ABCA}$ and $S = \text{CBAACAABCA}$ (as in Fig. 1), then $T^R[10, 2] = \mathsf{ED}(\text{CBAACAABCA}, (\text{CAAB})^\infty) = \text{ed-dist}(\text{CBAACAABCA}, \text{CAABCAABCA}) = 2$.

Running Algorithm 1 for the reverse input, we obtain the solution to the APM problem.

Theorem 10. *The Approximate Pattern Matching in Periodic Text problem can be solved in $\mathcal{O}(n + kp)$ time.*

By combining Fact 2 and Theorem 10 with $k < \tau_p$, we arrive at an improved solution to the APR problem.

Theorem 11. *The Approximate Period Recovery problem can be solved in $\mathcal{O}(n \log n)$ time.*

References

1. Amir, A., Amit, M., Landau, G.M., Sokol, D.: Period recovery of strings over the Hamming and edit distances. Theor. Comput. Sci. **710**, 2–18 (2018). https://doi.org/10.1016/j.tcs.2017.10.026
2. Amir, A., Eisenberg, E., Levy, A., Porat, E., Shapira, N.: Cycle detection and correction. ACM Trans. Algorithms **9**(1), 13:1–13:20 (2012). https://doi.org/10.1145/2390176.2390189
3. Amit, M., Crochemore, M., Landau, G.M., Sokol, D.: Locating maximal approximate runs in a string. Theor. Comput. Sci. **700**, 45–62 (2017). https://doi.org/10.1016/j.tcs.2017.07.021
4. Apostolico, A., Ehrenfeucht, A.: Efficient detection of quasiperiodicities in strings. Theor. Comput. Sci. **119**(2), 247–265 (1993). https://doi.org/10.1016/0304-3975(93)90159-Q
5. Apostolico, A., Farach, M., Iliopoulos, C.S.: Optimal superprimitivity testing for strings. Inf. Process. Lett. **39**(1), 17–20 (1991). https://doi.org/10.1016/0020-0190(91)90056-N
6. Breslauer, D.: An on-line string superprimitivity test. Inf. Process. Lett. **44**(6), 345–347 (1992). https://doi.org/10.1016/0020-0190(92)90111-8
7. Crochemore, M., Hancart, C., Lecroq, T.: Algorithms on Strings. Cambridge University Press, Cambridge (2007). https://doi.org/10.1017/cbo9780511546853
8. Crochemore, M., Rytter, W.: Jewels of Stringology. World Scientific, Singapore (2003). https://doi.org/10.1142/4838
9. Fischetti, V.A., Landau, G.M., Sellers, P.H., Schmidt, J.P.: Identifying periodic occurrences of a template with applications to protein structure. Inf. Process. Lett. **45**(1), 11–18 (1993). https://doi.org/10.1016/0020-0190(93)90245-5
10. Gusfield, D.: Algorithms on Strings, Trees, and Sequences: Computer Science and Computational Biology. Cambridge University Press, Cambridge (1997). https://doi.org/10.1017/cbo9780511574931
11. Kociumaka, T., Kubica, M., Radoszewski, J., Rytter, W., Waleń, T.: A linear time algorithm for seeds computation. In: Rabani, Y. (ed.) 23rd Annual ACM-SIAM Symposium on Discrete Algorithms. SODA 2012, pp. 1095–1112. SIAM (2012). https://doi.org/10.1137/1.9781611973099
12. Kolpakov, R.M., Kucherov, G.: Finding approximate repetitions under Hamming distance. Theor. Comput. Sci. **303**(1), 135–156 (2003). https://doi.org/10.1016/s0304-3975(02)00448-6
13. Landau, G.M., Vishkin, U.: Fast parallel and serial approximate string matching. J. Algorithms **10**(2), 157–169 (1989). https://doi.org/10.1016/0196-6774(89)90010-2
14. Li, Y., Smyth, W.F.: Computing the cover array in linear time. Algorithmica **32**(1), 95–106 (2002). https://doi.org/10.1007/s00453-001-0062-2
15. Popov, V.Y.: The approximate period problem for DNA alphabet. Theor. Comput. Sci. **304**(1–3), 443–447 (2003). https://doi.org/10.1016/S0304-3975(03)00211-1
16. Sim, J.S., Iliopoulos, C.S., Park, K., Smyth, W.F.: Approximate periods of strings. Theor. Comput. Sci. **262**(1), 557–568 (2001). https://doi.org/10.1016/S0304-3975(00)00365-0
17. Sokol, D., Benson, G., Tojeira, J.: Tandem repeats over the edit distance. Bioinformatics **23**(2), 30–35 (2007). https://doi.org/10.1093/bioinformatics/btl309
18. Sokol, D., Tojeira, J.: Speeding up the detection of tandem repeats over the edit distance. Theor. Comput. Sci. **525**, 103–110 (2014). https://doi.org/10.1016/j.tcs.2013.04.021

Searching for a Modified Pattern
in a Changing Text

Amihood Amir[✉] and Eitan Kondratovsky[✉]

Department of Computer Science, Bar Ilan University, Ramat Gan, Israel
amir@esc.biu.ac.il, kondrae@cs.biu.ac.il

Abstract. Much attention has been devoted recently to the dynamic model of pattern matching. In this model the input is updated or changed locally. One is interested in obtaining the appropriate search result in time that is shorter than the time necessary to search without any previous knowledge. In particular, searching for a pattern P in an indexed text is done in optimal $O(|P|)$ time. There has been work done in searching for a fixed pattern in a dynamic text, as well as finding all maximum common substrings of two strings in a dynamic setting.

There are real-world applications where the text is unchanged and the pattern is slightly modified at every query. However, in the current state-of-the-art, a new search is required if the pattern is modified. In this paper we present an algorithm that reduces this search time to be sublinear, for a variety of types of pattern modification - in addition to the insertion, deletion, and replacement of symbols, we allow copy-paste and delete substring operations.

We also make a step toward a fully dynamic pattern matching model by also supporting text changes, albeit much more modest than the pattern changes. We support dynamic pattern matching where symbols may also be either added or deleted to either the beginning or the end of the text. We show that we can support such a model in time $O(\log n)$ for every pattern modification or text change. We can then report all occ occurrences of P in the text in $O(occ)$ time.

1 Introduction

Historical pattern matching in which one seeks all occurrences of a pattern in a text is a widely known problem that has been motivated by many fields such as digital libraries, Molecular Biology, Medicine, and more [1,2,9,13,22,25,26,32]. In this problem the text and the pattern are given as an input and the algorithm outputs all the indices in which the pattern is located in the text. Several linear-time solutions were offered, the first being the classic Knuth-Morris-Pratt algorithm [22].

Another important model of the problem is *Indexing* [35]. In this model we preprocess the text T so that one can answer a query of the form 'find

This work was partially supported by ISF grant 571/14 and BSF grant 2014028.
This work is part of the second author's Ph.D. dissertation.

a pattern P in the text T', without the need to scan the text for each query. The suffix tree [6,8,14,15,23,28,33,35], suffix array [21,27] and Burrows-Wheeler transform [3] are all data structures that resulted from the study of the indexing problem. They are constructed in the preprocessing stage and allow answering the query in time $O(m + occ)$, where m is the pattern length and occ is the number of occurrences of the pattern in the text. The indexing problem has an *online* version, where the text is input one symbol at the time and the new letters are appended or prepended to the text. Algorithms such as Ukkonen's [33] were developed to solve the online variation of indexing. In these algorithms symbol insertion or deletion is handled in an amortized time and thus the preprocessing time of the text is linear on the input size.

The next generalization of the problem is when one wants to support a *dynamic* text, a text which can be modified. Various types of modifications were considered - insertion, update or deletion of a single letter in the text, copy-pasting a substring of the text to a new location, or deleting a substring. This model also led to the development of efficient algorithms [16,17,20,30,31]. Recently, Gawrychowski et al. [18] showed an $O(\log^2 n)$ algorithm per text update and $O(m)$ query time, where m is the query pattern's length. In their algorithm a modification changes the text data structure which then requires another search query to report new pattern occurrences.

Amir et al. [7] introduced a dynamic text indexing algorithm where the pattern is fixed. They save query time by not reporting all of the occurrences but only the difference between the new and old occurrences of the pattern when a letter in the text is updated. They achieve a $O(\log \log n + occ_{new} + occ_{old})$ time per text update, where n is the text length, occ_{new} is the number of new occurrences and occ_{old} is the number of old occurrences which no longer exist.

Recently, Bille et al. [10] consider a more comprehensive case in which a source string S is compressed relatively to a reference string R. In this compression S is covered by substrings of R. Their compression is proved to be 2-competitive to the optimal compression under edit distance operations on S, insertion, deletion and update of single characters of S. They support the edit distance operations in $O(\log \log |R| + \frac{\log n}{\log \log n})$ time using $O(|R| + n)$ space when n is the optimal cover size.

Reporting the longest common factor (LCF) of two strings S and T dynamically is a new problem. The first result on dynamic LCF was given by Amir et al. [4]. They achieved $\widetilde{O}(1)$ time reporting the LCF after a single edit operation, i.e. either insertion, deletion or update of a character, in either S or T. This result was soon generalized to support the fully dynamic LCP in sublinear time per character modification [5]. Both algorithms preprocessing time and space is $\widetilde{O}(n)$.

In this paper we tackle two challenges: (1) We would like to spend time sublinear in the pattern length to find all pattern occurrences, when the pattern has been changed. As an example, modern applications often display the search results while the pattern is being typed by the user. If, in the middle of the pattern, a change is made, the current search algorithms require starting the text search from the beginning.

We present an algorithm that supports fast searches of the pattern when the pattern is modified by two new operations: **copy-pasting** a substring of the pattern to a new location or **deleting** a substring from the pattern in addition to edit distance operations, that were considered by Bille et al. [10]. Our algorithm achieves this goal in time $O(\log n)$ for each pattern modification and then reports all occurrences of the pattern in the text.

(2) We take a step toward a fully dynamic pattern matching algorithm. As described above, we allow many types of modifications to the pattern, but we also support text changes, albeit much more modest. We support dynamic pattern matching when symbols are added to the text at its ends - added to either the beginning or the end of the text.

2   Problem Formulation

Definition 1. *A modification of a string S is one of the following operations:*

- *Remove the single symbol at index i of S, where $i \in [1, |S|]$. The resulting string's length is decreased by 1.*
- *Insert a single character σ following index $i-1$ of S, where $\sigma \in \Sigma$ and i is the index of the inserted character within the resulted string, i.e. $i \in [1, |S|+1]$. The resulting string's length is incremented by 1.*
- *Rename $S[i] = a$, where $i \in [1, |S|]$ and $a \in \Sigma$.*
- *Copy-paste a substring of S to start following index $i-1$ of S, where $i \in [1, |S|+1]$. The length of the string is incremented by the length of the copied substring.*
- *Delete a substring of S. The length of S is decremented by the length of the deleted substring.*

Definition 2 (The modified pattern reporting problem).
Input: *Let T be a text and P be a pattern (the pattern might be empty).*
Preprocessing: *We wish to process both the text and the initial pattern in a manner that supports modifications to the pattern.*
Pattern Modification: *For each modification, we efficiently update the data structures in a manner that allows reporting of pattern occurrences.*
Occurrence Reporting: *For a given X, report the first X occurrences of the pattern in the text in time $O(X)$. Also, in time $O(occ)$ report all occ occurrences of the pattern in the text.*

Theorem 1. *Given a string T and an initial pattern P, let n be the text length. The* modified pattern reporting problem *can be solved in the following complexity: Preprocessing is done in $O(n)$ time and space. Subsequently, a single letter modification, text extension and pattern modification, are solved in $O(\log n)$ time per change. A substring modification, copy-pasting a substring of P and deleting a substring of P, in $O(\log n + l)$ time per change, where l is the substring length. The algorithm returns an iterator which can be used to report the occ occurrences using $O(occ)$ time or X first occurrences in $O(X)$ time.*

3 Preliminaries

Let Σ be an alphabet. A *string* T over Σ is a finite sequence of letters from Σ. By $T[i]$, for $1 \leq i \leq |T|$, we denote the ith letter of T. The *empty string* is denoted by ϵ. By $T[i..j]$ we denote the string $T[i] \ldots T[j]$ called a *substring* of T (if $i > j$, then the substring is an empty string). A substring is called a *prefix* if $i = 1$ and a *suffix* if $j = |T|$. By S_i we denote the suffix which starts from index i in T. By $lcp(S, S')$ we denote the *longest common prefix (lcp)* of S and S'. In case S and S' are suffixes S_i and S_j, respectively, we denote $lcp(i, j) = lcp(S_i, S_j)$ for short. By T^R we denote the reversal (the mirror image) of T.

A *suffix tree* of a string T, denoted $ST(T)$, is a compacted trie containing all the suffixes of $T\$$, where $\$$ is a unique character not occurring in Σ. In a compacted trie we define the *depth* of a node to be its number of explicit ancestors, and the *string depth* to be the length of the string it represents. In a suffix tree we define the *suffix link* of a node representing the string as to be a pointer to the node representing s. Every explicit node v stores such a link $sl(v)$.

Definition 3 (suffix array and inverse suffix array). *Let T be an n-length string. Let $\{S_{j_1}, \ldots, S_{j_n}\}$ be the set of T's suffixes sorted in lexicographic order. Then the* suffix array *of T is the array SA, such that $SA[i] = j_i$, $i = 1, \ldots, n$, i.e. the ith suffix in the sorted list is at index i of the suffix array. The inverse* suffix array *is an array in which i^{th} element indicates the rank of S_i in the sorted array of suffixes.*

Definition 4 (lcp array). *Let T be an n-length string. The* lcp array *of T stores the lengths of the longest common prefixes of adjacent suffixes in the suffix array. Formally, $LA[i] = lcp(SA[i], SA[i + 1]), i = 1, \ldots, n - 1$.*

4 The Cover Idea and Previous Work

The basic and simplest case is when both the pattern and the modified pattern (after a single modification) occur in the text. Based on the knowledge about the pattern locations in the text, it is possible to quickly find the modified pattern in the text. For example, via a binary search on the suffix array.

The general case, when there is a sequence of modifications such that only after applying the last modification the pattern starts to occur, turns to be difficult. We, therefore, need a data structure to store the intermediate representations of the pattern. The idea is to represent the pattern by substrings of the text that "cover" it. Ultimately, if the pattern is represented by a single substring of the text then there exists an occurrence of the pattern in the text.

In order to implement this idea we need a cover scheme whose elements have a maximality property which allows us to minimize the number of text elements covering the pattern. We use the cover definition that was introduced in [7]. The idea is to cover the pattern by substrings of T such that a concatenating of every two consecutive substrings is not a substring of T. Formally,

Definition 5 ([7]). *Let S and $S' = s'_1 \ldots s'_n$ be strings over alphabet Σ. A cover of S by S' is a partition of S, $S = \tau_1 \ldots \tau_v$, each τ_i, $i = 1, \ldots, v$, satisfying the following conditions.*

- substring property: *τ_i is a substring of S',*
- maximality property: *$\tau_i \tau_{i+1}$ is not a substring of S', $i = 1, \ldots, v - 1$.*

When the context is clear we call a cover of S by S' simply a cover. We also say that τ_h is an element of the cover. A cover element τ_h is represented by a triple $[i, j, k]$ where $\tau_h = s'_i \ldots s'_j$, and k, the index of the element, is the location in S where the element appears, i.e. $k = \Sigma_{l=1}^{h-1} |\tau_l| + 1$.

A pattern symbol that does not exist in the text is represented by a special substring of T which is an imaginary character (substring of length 1) found after the last text character. This scenario exists in real life applications. For example in C and $C + +$, every string ends with a special null-terminated character.

Minimizing the number of cover elements relies on the idea of *substrings concatenation*. A substring concatenation query has two substrings of T: S' and S'', as its parameters. It returns whether their concatenation is a substring of T or not. If yes, the query returns one of the locations of $S'S''$ in T. This query is performed in $O(\log \log n)$ time and using $O(n)$ space, following a linear time preprocessing for a static text [10]. In Sect. 5.2 we show how to support the online query.

The next step is to store the cover in a data structure that supports splitting and merging of cover elements and a search query that returns the element which covers a given index in the pattern. While under hamming distance modifications a *van Emde Boas tree* [34] can be used to store the cover elements, a *dynamic partial sums* [10] data structure is used to store the cover under edit distance operations.

Definition 6 ([10]). *The* dynamic partial sums problem *is to maintain an array of integers $Z[1..s]$ under the following operations.*

- *$sum(i)$: returns the sum of the first i elements, i.e. $\Sigma_{j=1}^{i} Z[j]$,*
- *$update(i, \Delta)$: update $Z[i] = Z[i] + \Delta$,*
- *$search(t)$: return $1 \leq i \leq |Z|$ such that $sum(i - 1) < t \leq sum(i)$.*
- *$insert(i, \Delta)$, inserts new entry in Z with value Δ before $Z[i]$,*
- *$delete(i)$, deletes the entry $Z[i]$ of value at most Δ,*
- *$merge(i)$, replace entry $Z[i]$ and $Z[i + 1]$ with a new entry with value $Z[i] + Z[i + 1]$,*
- *$divide(i, t)$, where $0 \leq t \leq Z[i]$, replace entry $Z[i]$ by two new consecutive entries with value t and $Z[i] - t$, respectively.*

Assume we are using the RAM model in which accessing memory by indexes and w-bit integers arithmetical operations are supported in constant time. Assume Z is an array of w-bit integers and $\Delta < 2^\delta$, for some constant δ. All the above operations can be answered in $O(\frac{\log |Z|}{\log(w/\delta)})$ time per operation using linear space [10].

The idea is to store an array Z in which at index i we store $|\tau_i|$, the length of the ith element in the cover. This allows us to calculate the beginning location of each element as the sum of the lengths of the previous array elements. Therefore, a search query is used to locate an element which covers a given index in the pattern. Merging and splitting cover elements is done by the merge and split queries respectively.

Theorem 2. *Let T be a text, P be a pattern and a cover of P by T. Then using the dynamic partial sums data structure it is possible to support the following three queries: locate an element which covers a given index, merge two elements to one, and split an element into two elements.*

- *in space $O(m)$ and time $O(\frac{\log m}{\log\log n})$ per operation if substring modifications, copy-pasting or deleting of substrings, are not allowed.*
- *in space $O(m)$ and time $O(\log m)$ per operation if all pattern modifications are allowed.*

Proof. The difference between the cases relies on the choice of Δ, which is the maximal bound on the increasing or decreasing amount allowed to be added to an element in the dynamic partial sums array Z. If we are assuming that no substring modifications occur then Δ is chosen to be 1, because appending or removing single letter result in increasing or decreasing an element in Z by 1. Otherwise if allowing substring modifications, $\Delta = m$ because one might copy-paste or delete substrings of size at most m, which then causes an element in Z to be increased or decreased by $O(m)$. Based on those choices we take $\delta = \log(\Delta + 1)$, such that $\Delta < 2^\delta$ is true.

Other parameters are the same for both cases, $w = O(\log n)$ is the word size in the RAM model and $|Z| \leq m$, the number of elements in the cover.
In the first case, $O(\frac{\log |Z|}{\log(w/\delta)}) = O(\frac{\log m}{\log\log n})$.
While in the second case, $O(\frac{\log |Z|}{\log(w/\delta)}) = O(\frac{\log m}{\log(\log n/\log m)}) = O(\log m)$.
Notice that m can be $O(n)$ and therefore the denominator is a constant.   □

5   Supporting the Online Text

5.1   Idea

We wish to report the pattern occurrences online in a text which is input symbol by symbol, w.l.o.g assume the text is input online by prependings symbols at the beginning. The major problem that needs to be addressed when supporting an online text is the following. Since the method we use is covering the pattern with text substrings that are maximal, in the sense that the concatenation of any two adjacent cover elements is not a substring of T, then prepending letters to the text may invalidate the maximality property. In the worst case scenario, the fear is that after every letter was prepended the algorithm may need to concatenate $O(m)$ cover elements in order to sustain the maximality property.

A second problem that needs addressing is that the pattern might start to occur in the text as a result of new prepended letters. It turns out that by trying to concatenate the last two elements of the cover when a new symbol arrives it is possible to report new occurrences of the pattern if the pattern start to appear in the text. This technique works when changes are not applied to the pattern until the pattern starts to occur in the text.

Theorem 3. *Let T be a text, P be a pattern, C be a cover of P by T. Assume the text is input online by prepending symbols. Assume also that after every prepended text symbol we concatenate the last two cover elements, if possible. Then new occurrences of the pattern are reported correctly when they start to appear at the beginning of the text.*

Proof. Let A and B be the last two cover elements. Due to the maximality property AB is not a substring of T. Let $R(T, P)$ be the longest string which is a prefix of T and a suffix of P, then $R(T, P)$ is a proper suffix of AB because AB is not a substring in T. Let $T' = \sigma T$ be the text after $\sigma \in \Sigma$ was prepended. If we cannot concatenate A and B then the following properties remain correct: AB is not a substring of T' and the new $R(T', P)$ must be a suffix of AB. If A and B can be concatenated then $B' = AB$. Let A' and $B' = AB$ be the last two cover elements. Then $A'B'$ is not a substring of T because B' exists only once as a prefix of T. Furthermore, $R(T', P)$ is a substring of $A'B'$, in particular $R(T', P) = B'$. By induction, any cover C where $|C| \geq 2$ satisfies these two properties. When a concatenation results in a cover with a single element, then the pattern is a prefix of T.   □

We are now ready to tackle the case where symbols are being prepended to the text online as well as the pattern being modified. We will see that this requires a greater number of concatenations of cover elements. Nevertheless, we shows that the number of concatenation of cover elements is *competitive* with the smallest number of operations that one needs to apply so that the pattern will occur in the text, when *operation* means either a letter prepending to the text or a modification of the pattern (in the online algorithms sense, i.e. the number of concatenations does not exceed some constant times the number of operations).

Definition 7. *Let T and P be a text and a pattern. The occurring distance of the pattern P from the text T, denoted by $D_T(P)$, is the smallest number of pattern modifications and text prependings that one needs to apply in order for the resulting pattern to occur in the text.*

Formally, let $G = \{XT \mid X \in \bigcup_{0 \leq i \leq |P|} \Sigma^i\}$ a set of all possible texts after at most $|P|$ prependings.

$$D_T(P) = \min\{|T'| - |T| + \mathrm{Modif}(T', P) \mid T' \in G\} \qquad (1)$$

Where $|P| = m$, $|T| = n$, and $\mathrm{Modif}(S_1, S_2)$ is the smallest number of modifications of S_2 that causes it to appear in S_1.

Lemma 1 ([10]). *Let P and T be a pattern and a text, respectively. Then the size of every cover C that holds the maximality property is 2-competitive to the optimal cover, the cover which has the smallest number of elements. And it holds that $|C| \leq 2|C'| - 1$, where C' is the optimal cover.*

Lemma 2. *Let P and T be a pattern and a text, respectively. Then $|C|$ is 4-competitive to the occurring distance $D_T(P)$, if C holds the maximality property. And it holds that $|C| \leq 4D_T(P) - 1$.*

Proof. Let C be a cover that holds the maximality property. Assume that the occurring distance is achieved by performing q text prepending operations and p pattern modifications. If $q = 0$, only pattern modification are performed. Based on Lemma 1 the cover with maximality property is 2-competitive to the optimal cover. The optimal cover in this case has at most $2p$ elements. In the worst case scenario, all the changes in the pattern are of deletion of letters which are not in the text. And each of the p changes has its own cover element. Thus, $|C| \leq 4p - 1$ Otherwise, $q > 0$. It means that the pattern starts to occur at the prefix of T, since if this not the case, we can take a smaller q in contradiction to the minimality of occurring distance. The first q character of P are covered by at most q elements, while the remaining pattern of size $|P| - q$ occurs at the initial text after performing p modifications. Thus, $|C| \leq q + 4p - 1$. □

Lemma 3. *For all $k > 0$ and $j > 0$ integers it holds that $\lceil \frac{k}{2^j} \rceil = \lceil \frac{k}{2^{j+1}} \rceil + \lfloor \frac{k}{2^{j+1}} \rfloor$.*

Proof. Let $k = c \cdot 2^{j+1} + d$, where c is the quotient of 2^{j+1} and d is the remainder of the division of k by 2^{j+1}, $0 \leq d < 2^{j+1}$. Then, $\lceil \frac{k}{2^j} \rceil = 2c + \lceil \frac{d}{2^j} \rceil$. And, $\lceil \frac{k}{2^{j+1}} \rceil + \lfloor \frac{k}{2^{j+1}} \rfloor = c + \lceil \frac{d}{2^{j+1}} \rceil + c$. Where $d = 0$, the expressions equal to $2c$, otherwise if $d > 0$, they equal to $2c + 1$. □

Corollary 1. *For all $k > 0$,*
$$k = \lceil \tfrac{k}{2} \rceil + \lfloor \tfrac{k}{2} \rfloor = \lceil \tfrac{k}{4} \rceil + \lfloor \tfrac{k}{4} \rfloor + \lfloor \tfrac{k}{2} \rfloor = \lceil \tfrac{k}{2^j} \rceil + \Sigma_{i=1}^{j} \lfloor \tfrac{k}{2^i} \rfloor$$

Theorem 4. *We use the same notations as in the previous theorem. Let k' be the occurring distance of P from T at the first occasion of the cover C in which the pattern does not occur in T. Then the algorithm is α-competitive to k'. We show that $\alpha = 8$. Furthermore, we can maintain a competitive cover by applying 16 concatenations to the cover elements in a cyclic manner.*

Proof. Assume ℓ operations were applied, where after operation ℓ the pattern occurs in the text. Let $\{k_i\}_{i=0}^{\ell}$ be the sequence of the occurring distances, where k_i is the occurring distance after applying the ith operation, $1 \leq i \leq \ell$. $k_\ell = 0$, and $k_0 = k'$ is the value before any operation was applied. An operation is called *good* if all consecutive operations have smaller occurring distances. Formally, the ith operation is *good* if $\forall j > i$, $k_j < k_i$.

Let $k = \max_{1 \leq i \leq \ell} \{k_i\}$ the maximal occurring distance.

We want to prove that the cover size approaches 1 when the pattern appears in the text. By induction we show that after $\Sigma_{i=1}^{j} \lfloor \frac{1}{2^i} k \rfloor$ good operations, $|C| \leq 2 \lceil \frac{1}{2^{j-1}} k \rceil - 1$.

The base case where $j = 0$ and no operation has been done, we know that $|C| \leq 4k' - 1 \leq 4k - 1$ due to the preprocessing stage.

The induction step, assume correctness for j and proof for $j + 1$. Assume $\Sigma_{i=1}^{j} \lfloor \frac{1}{2^i} k \rfloor$ good operations have been done, during the next $\lfloor \frac{1}{2^{j+1}} k \rfloor$ good operations there were at least $16 \lfloor \frac{1}{2^{j+1}} k \rfloor \geq 8 \lceil \frac{1}{2^{j+1}} k \rceil \geq 2 \lceil \frac{1}{2^{j-1}} k \rceil > |C|$ concatenations. Thus by Lemma 2, $|C| \leq 2 \lceil \frac{1}{2^j} k \rceil - 1$, because the cover is 2-competitive to the occurring distance after $\Sigma_{i=1}^{j} \lfloor \frac{1}{2^i} k \rfloor$ which is $\lceil \frac{1}{2^j} k \rceil$.

Let $1 \leq \lceil \frac{1}{2^j} k \rceil \leq 2$, it means that the pattern is very close to the text, in the sense of occurring distance. In this case we know from the induction that $|C| \leq 2 \lceil \frac{1}{2^{j-1}} k \rceil - 1 \leq 4 \lceil \frac{1}{2^j} k \rceil - 1 \leq 8 - 1 = 7$. This means that by trying to concatenate an most 16 elements each time we can detect when the pattern starts to appear in the text. □

5.2 Substring Concatenation

The ideas for a changing text rely heavily on *substring concatenation*. This was the tool in all previous papers for dynamic source string (e.g. the text) and static reference string (e.g. the pattern) [7,10,19]. The problem is that in all previous papers, one string, either the text or pattern, is assumed to be fixed, and thus many results were developed for extremely efficient substring matching. We are exploring the first steps toward a fully dynamic algorithm. Our pattern is heavily modified, and our text may increase at either end (for simplicity we describe prepending symbols to the text, but the algorithm is general enough to handle adding symbols at both ends of the text). As a result of the changing text, we need to revisit the substring concatenation tool.

The concatenation query on the online text is based on two suffix tree constructions and data structures are built on these suffix trees. We build two suffix trees for both T and T^R. Each leaf of the suffix tree corresponds to a suffix. We label each two suffixes that represent the full text, i.e. $t_{i+1} \ldots t_n$ and $t_i \ldots t_1$, with the same value $i + 1$. When a query of the form $S'S''$ is given we search for a node that correspond to $(S')^R$ in the suffix tree of T^R and a node that correspond to S'' in a suffix tree of T. This search can be done in a constant time by locating the suffix leaf whose prefix is the desired string and then performing a weighted ancestor query [19]. By a range query (also called tree cross product query) [12] we find whether $S'S''$ exist in the text. If it does, then we find one of the locations in the text where this string is located.

Implementation: Breslauer and Italiano [11] show how to construct a suffix tree, both with additions at the beginning and additions at the end, in time $O(\log \log n)$ per symbol change. The dynamic weighted ancestor can be supported in $O(\log n)$ worst case time and $O(n)$ space [24]. Finally, a dynamic tree cross product can be supported in time $O(\log n)$ per change [12]. The overall space is $O(n\sqrt{\log n})$.

6   Supporting Copy-Pasting and Deleting Substrings

Bille et al. [10] presented a construction for the *dynamic partial prefix sum* problem. The classical *partial prefix sum* problem is to support three operations on an array of integers Z.

- $sum(i)$: returns the sum of the first i elements, i.e. $\Sigma_{j=1}^{i} Z[j]$,
- $update(i, \Delta)$: update $Z[i] = Z[i] + \Delta$,
- $search(t)$: return $1 \le i \le |Z|$ such that $sum(i-1) < t \le sum(i)$.

In the dynamic variation, Bille et al. [10] consider also the following operations: $insert(i, \Delta)$, inserts new entry in Z with value Δ before $Z[i]$, $delete(i)$, deletes the entry $Z[i]$ of value at most Δ, $merge(i)$, replace entry $Z[i]$ and $Z[i+1]$ with a new entry with value $Z[i] + Z[i+1]$, $divide(i, t)$, where $0 \le t \le Z[i]$, replace entry Z[i] by two new consecutive entries with value t and $Z[i] - t$, respectively.

Assume we are using the RAM model in which accessing memory by indexes and w-bit integers arithmetical operations are supported in constant time. Assume Z is an array of w-bit integers and $\Delta < 2^{\delta}$, for some constant δ. All the above operations can be answered in $O(\frac{\log |Z|}{\log(w/\delta)})$ time [10]. Their data structure is based on B-trees in which each node stores a small data structure which has the same functionality but is of size $O(B) = w^{O(1)}$ and answers the queries in a constant time. This data structure extends an data structure of [29] to support all the above operations. Each small data structure is valid for $O(B)$ insertions and afterwards a new one is needed to be reconstructed in $O(B)$ time. By spending an additional constant time at each insertion, it is possible to reconstruct the data structure.

Deleting a substring $P[i..j]$ is done by finding the cover elements which contain the first and the last indexes i and j. Then a *divide* operation is called to split these intervals so that we can safely remove the substring from P. By removing all the values between these two intervals we achieve a substring deletion in $O(\log n + |j - i + 1|)$ time. The $\log n$ exists because after the deletion we perform a concatenation query on the divided elements with their neighbor elements to ensure the cover remain valid. Similarly, we can copy a string to another location by spending $O(\log n + |j - i + 1|)$.

7   Reporting Pattern Occurrences in $O(occ)$ Time

Based on an online suffix tree and knowledge about one of the indexes in which the pattern occurs, we show how to report all occ occurrences in $O(occ)$ time. We also show how to represent an iterator to report all these occurrences. Let i be one of the pattern locations in the text, we start from a leaf that corresponds to the suffix S_i in the suffix tree, then we go to the ancestor node whose depth is the minimal depth that is at least $|P|$, all the suffixes in the rooted tree are occurrences of P and no other occurrences are in the text. Traversing to a such a node is done by a special weighted ancestor construction [19]. We define the weight of each node to be the length of the string from the root that one needs to treat. The preprocessing time is $O(n)$ and online suffix is supported. And weighted ancestor query is answered in a constant worst case time. Thus, the iterator is represented by the pair $(i, |P|)$, and it allows to iterate all pattern occurrences in the text.

8 Conclusion

We have shown how to report all pattern occurrences in a changing text under pattern modifications: copy-pasting substrings of the pattern to a new locations and deleting substrings of the pattern in addition to insertions, deletions and updates of single letters in the pattern. After each operation, modification of the pattern or extension of the text by one symbol, we detect in sublinear time whether the modified pattern now appears in the text. If it does, then we provide a subroutine that reports all pattern occurrences in $O(\log n)$ time.

Our solution relies on a *dynamic partial prefix sums* data structure, which then implies the lower bound of $\Omega(\frac{\log m}{\log \log m})$. It would be interesting to store the cover elements in a different structure that, perhaps, reduces this bound or, on the other hand, to show that it is impossible, i.e. this bound stands also for the cover storage problem.

Moreover, it would be useful to know a solution for the fully dynamic case in which both the pattern and the text are allowed to be modified when the pattern is reported in a sublinear time after each modification.

References

1. The new oxford english dictionary. http://db.uwaterloo.ca/OED
2. The responsa project. http://www.biu.ac.il/JH/Responsa/
3. Adjeroh, D., Bell, T., Mukherjee, A.: The Burrows-Wheeler Transform: Data Compression, Suffix Arrays, and Pattern Matching. Springer, Boston (2008). https://doi.org/10.1007/978-0-387-78909-5. ISBN 00387789081
4. Amir, A., Charalampopoulos, P., Iliopoulos, C.S., Pissis, S.P., Radoszewski, J.: Longest common factor after one edit operation. In: Fici, G., Sciortino, M., Venturini, R. (eds.) SPIRE 2017. LNCS, vol. 10508, pp. 14–26. Springer, Cham (2017). https://doi.org/10.1007/978-3-319-67428-5_2
5. Amir, A., Charalampopoulos, P., Pissis, S.P., Radoszewski, J.: Longest common factor made fully dynamic. CoRR, abs/1804.08731 (2018)
6. Amir, A., Kopelowitz, T., Lewenstein, M., Lewenstein, N.: Towards real-time suffix tree construction. In: Consens, M., Navarro, G. (eds.) SPIRE 2005. LNCS, vol. 3772, pp. 67–78. Springer, Heidelberg (2005). https://doi.org/10.1007/11575832_9
7. Amir, A., Landau, G.M., Lewenstein, M., Sokol, D.: Dynamic text and static pattern matching. ACM Trans. Algorithms **3**(2), 19 (2007)
8. Amir, A., Nor, I.: Real-time indexing over fixed finite alphabets. In: Proceedings of 19th Annual ACM-SIAM Symposium on Discrete Algorithms (SODA), pp. 1086–1095 (2008)
9. Aoe, J.: Computer Algorithms: String Pattern Matching Strategies (Practitioners). Wiley Blackwell, London (1994). ISBN 0818654627

10. Bille, P., et al.: Dynamic relative compression, dynamic partial sums, and substring concatenation. Algorithmica **16**(4), 464–497 (2017)
11. Breslauer, D., Italiano, G.F.: Near real-time suffix tree construction via the fringe marked ancestor problem. J. Discret. Algorithms **18**, 32–48 (2013)
12. Buchsbaum, A.L., Goodrich, M.T., Westbrook, J.R.: Range searching over tree cross products. In: Paterson, M.S. (ed.) ESA 2000. LNCS, vol. 1879, pp. 120–131. Springer, Heidelberg (2000). https://doi.org/10.1007/3-540-45253-2_12
13. Clifford, R., Efremenko, K., Porat, E., Rothschild, A.: From coding theory to efficient pattern matching. In: Proceedings of 20th Annual ACM-SIAM Symposium on Discrete Algorithms (SODA), pp. 778–784 (2009)
14. Cole, R., Hariharan, R.: Faster suffix tree construction with missing suffix links. SIAM J. Comput. **33**(1), 26–42 (2003)
15. Farach, M.: Optimal suffix tree construction with large alphabets. In: Proceedings of 38th IEEE Symposium on Foundations of Computer Science, pp. 137–143 (1997)
16. Ferragina, P.: Dynamic text indexing under string updates. J. Algorithms **22**(2), 296–328 (1997)
17. Ferragina, P., Grossi, R.: Optimal on-line search and sublinear time update in string matching. SIAM J. Comput. **27**(3), 713–736 (1998)
18. Gawrychowski, P., Karczmarz, A., Kociumaka, T., Lacki, J., Sankowski, P.: Optimal dynamic strings. CoRR, abs/1511.02612 (2015)
19. Gawrychowski, P., Lewenstein, M., Nicholson, P.K.: Weighted ancestors in suffix trees. In: Schulz, A.S., Wagner, D. (eds.) ESA 2014. LNCS, vol. 8737, pp. 455–466. Springer, Heidelberg (2014). https://doi.org/10.1007/978-3-662-44777-2_38
20. Gu, M., Farach, M., Beigel, R.: An efficient algorithm for dynamic text indexing. In: Proceedings of 5th Annual ACM-SIAM Symposium on Discrete Algorithms, pp. 697–704 (1994)
21. Kärkkäinen, J., Sanders, P.: Simple linear work suffix array construction. In: Baeten, J.C.M., Lenstra, J.K., Parrow, J., Woeginger, G.J. (eds.) ICALP 2003. LNCS, vol. 2719, pp. 943–955. Springer, Heidelberg (2003). https://doi.org/10.1007/3-540-45061-0_73
22. Knuth, D.E., Morris, J.H., Pratt, V.R.: Fast pattern matching in strings. SIAM J. Comput. **6**, 323–350 (1977)
23. Kopelowitz, T.: On-line indexing for general alphabets. In: Proceedings of 53rd IEEE Symposium on the Foundation of Computer Science (FOCS) (2012)
24. Kopelowitz, T., Lewenstein, M.: Dynamic weighted ancestors. In: Proceedings of 18th ACM-SIAM Symposium on Discrete Algorithms, SODA, pp. 565–574 (2007)
25. Lemer, M.R., Rooman, M.J., Wodak, S.J.: Protein structure prediction by threading methods: evaluation of current techniques. Proteins **23**, 337–355 (1995)
26. Levenshtein, V.I.: Binary codes capable of correcting, deletions, insertions and reversals. Soviet Phys. Dokl. **10**, 707–710 (1966)
27. Manber, U., Myers, G.: Suffix arrays: a new method for on-line string searches. In: Proceedings of 1st ACM-SIAM Symposium on Discrete Algorithms (SODA), pp. 319–327 (1990)
28. McCreight, E.M.: A space-economical suffix tree construction algorithm. J. ACM **23**, 262–272 (1976)
29. Patrascu, M., Thorup, M.: Dynamic integer sets with optimal rank, select, and predecessor search. In: Proceedings of 55th Annual IEEE Symposium on Foundations of Computer Science (FOCS), pp. 166–175 (2014)
30. Rauhe, T., Alstrup, S., Brodal, G.S.: Pattern matching in dynamic texts. In: Proceedings of 11th ACM-SIAM Symposium on Discrete Algorithms (SODA), pp. 819–828 (2000)

31. Sahinalp, S.C., Vishkin, U.: Efficient approximate and dynamic matching of patterns using a labeling paradigm. In: Proceedings of 37th FOCS, pp. 320–328 (1996)
32. Smith, T., Waterman, M.: Identification of common molecular subsequences. J. Mol. Biol. **147**, 195–197 (1981)
33. Ukkonen, E.: On-line construction of suffix trees. Algorithmica **14**, 249–260 (1995)
34. van Emde Boas, P.: Preserving order in a forest in less than logarithmic time and linear space. Inf. Process. Lett. **6**(3), 80–82 (1977)
35. Weiner, P.: Linear pattern matching algorithm. In: Proceeings of 14 IEEE Symposium on Switching and Automata Theory, pp. 1–11 (1973)

Recovering, Counting and Enumerating Strings from Forward and Backward Suffix Arrays

Yuki Kuhara[(✉)], Yuto Nakashima, Shunsuke Inenaga, Hideo Bannai, and Masayuki Takeda

Department of Informatics, Kyushu University, Fukuoka, Japan
{yuki.kuhara,yuto.nakashima,inenaga,bannai,takeda}@inf.kyushu-u.ac.jp

Abstract. The *suffix array* SA_w of a string w of length n is a permutation of $[1..n]$ such that $SA_w[i] = j$ iff $w[j, n]$ is the lexicographically i-th suffix of w. In this paper, we consider variants of the reverse-engineering problem on suffix arrays with two given permutations P and Q of $[1..n]$, such that P refers to the *forward suffix array* of some string w and Q refers to the *backward suffix array* of the reversed string w^R. Our results are the following: (1) An algorithm which computes a solution string over an alphabet of the smallest size, in $O(n)$ time. (2) The exact number of solution strings over an alphabet of size σ. (3) An efficient algorithm which computes all solution strings in the lexicographical order, in time near optimal up to $\log n$ factor.

1 Introduction

Text indexing is a task to build a data structure for a given text string w so that subsequent pattern matching queries can be answered quickly. The most well-known text indexing structure is the *suffix tree* [26], which is a compacted trie that represents all the suffixes of w. Another classical indexing structure is the *suffix array* [17], which is an array of length $|w|$ such that its i-th entry stores the beginning position of the lexicographically i-th suffix of w.

In some applications such as bidirectional pattern searches, it is helpful to build indexing structures for both w and its reversed string w^R. For an arbitrarily fixed string w, we call w as a forward string and its reverse w^R as a backward string. Also, we call an indexing structure for w as a *forward structure* and that for w^R as a *backward structure*.

There have been a few studies on the structural relations between forward and backward indexing structures. For instance, it is known that the suffix tree of w is isomorphic to the suffix link tree of the *directed acyclic word graph (DAWG)* [3] of w^R. This relation is preserved in the compacted versions of the DAWG and suffix tree, called the compact DAWG *(CDAWG)* [2], in such a manner that the CDAWGs of w and w^R share the same nodes. The *affix tree* [25] is another modification of the suffix tree such that both the affix trees of w and w^R share

T. Gagie et al. (Eds.): SPIRE 2018, LNCS 11147, pp. 254–267, 2018.
https://doi.org/10.1007/978-3-030-00479-8_21

the same nodes. However, no explicit, non-trivial properties are known for the relationship between the forward and backward suffix trees/arrays.

In this paper, we aim to reveal new relationships between the forward and backward suffix arrays in the context of reverse-engineering problems. Namely, we are given two permutations P and Q of $[1..n]$ as inputs, and the task is to recover a string, count and/or enumerate all strings for which P is the forward suffix array and Q is the backward suffix array. We call a string w, a *solution string*, if P is the forward suffix array and Q is the backward suffix array for w. This paper presents:

1. An $O(n)$-time algorithm to find the lexicographically smallest solution string w.
2. The exact number of solution strings.
3. An $O(M \log n)$-time algorithm to enumerate all solution strings in the lexicographical order where M is the number of solution strings.

Technically speaking, our results can be seen as a generalization of the known results for recovering, counting and/or enumerating solution string(s) in the mere case of forward strings.

Duval and Lefebvre [9], and Bannai et al. [1] independently showed how to recover the lexicographically smallest solution string for a given permutation P in $O(n)$ time. While there always exists a solution string for any single permutation P, in our case there do not exist solution strings for some pair of permutations P and Q.

Schürmann and Stoye [23] showed the exact number of solution strings for a given permutation P. Our analysis for the exact number of solution strings for a given pair of permutations P and Q is based on their result. Schürmann and Stoye also pointed out that the problem of computing all solution strings for a given single permutation P is equivalent to computing all non-decreasing sequences of length n. While it is easy to enumerate non-decreasing sequences in their lexicographical order, this does not directly provide us with an algorithm which enumerates the solution strings in the lexicographical order of the strings. We first show that a compact representation of all the solutions for a given single permutation P can be enumerated in lexicographical order. Then, we will remark that it is straightforward to extend this result to our case of two given permutations P and Q.

Related Work. The string recovering/counting/enumerating problems for various string-oriented data structures have been studied, such as suffix arrays [1, 9,23], DAWGs [1], suffix trees [4,13,24], border arrays [8,10,16], and many others (e.g., [5–7,11,12,14,15,18,20–22]). One of the main motivations for studying string recovering/counting/enumerating problems is to gain further insights into the characteristics of the data structures, which may be of future use for developing better algorithms for their construction and use. To our knowledge, however, there have been no studies on recovering/counting/enumerating problems that deal with both forward and backward strings.

2   Preliminaries

2.1   Strings

Let Σ be an integer *alphabet* $[1..\sigma]$ of size σ. An element of Σ^* is called a *string*. The length of a string w is denoted by $|w|$. The empty string ε is a string of length 0. Let Σ^+ be the set of non-empty strings, i.e., $\Sigma^+ = \Sigma^* - \{\varepsilon\}$. For a string $w = xyz$, x, y and z are called a *prefix*, *substring*, and *suffix* of w, respectively. The i-th character of a string w is denoted by $w[i]$, where $1 \leq i \leq |w|$. For a string w and two integers $1 \leq i \leq j \leq |w|$, let $w[i, j]$ denote the substring of w that begins at position i and ends at position j. For convenience, let $w[i, j] = \varepsilon$ when $i > j$.

2.2   Suffix Arrays and Permutations

Let $[1..n]$ be the set of n distinct integers such that each element i satisfies $1 \leq i \leq n$. If a sequence s of length n satisfies $\bigcup_i \{s[i]\} = [1..n]$, we call s a *permutation* of $[1..n]$. A permutation of $[1..n]$ is said to be the *suffix array* [17] of a string w, denoted by SA_w, if the i-th entry $SA_w[i]$ stores the index of lexicographically i-th suffix among all the non-empty suffixes of w in increasing order. We will also consider the suffix array of w where each suffix is identified by the reversed index, and denote it by rSA_w. Namely, $rSA_w[i] = n - j + 1$ iff $SA_w[i] = j$ for any $1 \leq i \leq n$. We will use this suffix array with reversed indices in order that the same indices can be used for the suffix arrays of string w and its reversal w^R. For any permutation P of $[1..n]$, P^{-1} denotes the inverse array of P, namely, $P[i] = j$ iff $P^{-1}[j] = i$ for any $1 \leq i \leq n$. For any integer sequences s and t, $s \equiv t$ denotes the fact that the set of all elements of s and the set of all elements of t is the same. Let $\langle\langle i \rangle\rangle_j$ be the integer sequence of length j such that each element is i.

In this paper, we consider strings w such that $SA_w = P$ and $rSA_{w^R} = Q$ for two given permutations P and Q of $[1..n]$. P is called a *forward suffix array* of a string w if $SA_w = P$ and Q is called a *backward suffix array* if $rSA_{w^R} = Q$ for the reversed string w^R.

Example 1. Let $w = 1, 3, 1, 2, 3$. Then, $SA_w = 3, 1, 4, 5, 2$ (forward suffix array of w) and $rSA_{w^R} = 1, 3, 4, 2, 5$ (backward suffix array of w^R). Moreover, $SA_w^{-1} = 2, 5, 1, 3, 4$ and $SA_w[3, 5] \equiv rSA_{w^R}[3, 5]$.

3   Strings over an Alphabet of Smallest Size

In this section, we solve the following problem. Given two permutations P, Q of $[1..n]$, determine whether there exists a string w such that P is the forward suffix array and Q is the backward suffix array of w. If so, compute such a string over an alphabet of the smallest size.

Duval and Lefebvre [9] solved the problem for a single permutation P. More formally, they proposed a linear time algorithm that computes a string w over an alphabet of the smallest size such that $SA_w = P$ where P is a given permutation of $[1..n]$. It is clear that, for a single permutation, there exists a string w such that $SA_w = P$ for any P, while for the problem, a solution string does not necessarily exist for any P and Q.

In this section, we give the following result.

Theorem 1. *Given two permutations P, Q of $[1..n]$, we can determine whether there exists a string w such that P is the forward suffix array and Q is the backward suffix array of w in $O(n)$ time and space. If it exists, we can compute such a string over an alphabet of the smallest size in $O(n)$ time and space.*

Firstly, in Sect. 3.1, we give an overview of the algorithm in [9] since our algorithm is a natural extension of theirs. In Sect. 3.2, we show our algorithm.

3.1 Computing a String from the Forward Suffix Array

The following lemma ensures the correctness of their algorithm.

Lemma 1 (Theorem 1 of [23]). *Let P be a permutation of $[1, n]$ and w a string of length n. P is the suffix array of w iff the following conditions hold for all $i \in [1, n]$: (1) $w[P[i]] \leq w[P[i+1]]$ and (2) $P^{-1}[P[i]+1] > P^{-1}[P[i+1]+1] \Rightarrow w[P[i]] < w[P[i+1]]$.*

This lemma implies that solution strings can be obtained by the set

$$I_P = \{i \mid P^{-1}[P[i] + 1] > P^{-1}[P[i + 1] + 1]\}.$$

In other words, $w[P[i]]$ has to be smaller than $w[P[i + 1]]$ for any $i \in I_P$.

Let $P = 3, 1, 4, 5, 2$ and $\Sigma = \{1, 2, 3\}$. Then, $I_P = \{2, 3\}$. This means that each string w such that P is the forward suffix array of w must satisfy the condition $w[P[2]] \prec w[P[3]] \prec w[P[4]]$. A string w over the alphabet of the smallest size satisfies $w[P[1]] = w[P[2]] \prec w[P[3]] \prec w[P[4]] = w[P[5]]$. We can obtain $w = 1, 3, 1, 2, 3$ since $w[3] = w[1] = 1 \prec w[4] = 2 \prec w[5] = w[2] = 3$.

It is known that I_P and w can be computed in $O(n)$ time and space [9].

3.2 Computing a String from Forward and Backward Suffix Arrays

We consider the set I_Q that is similar to I_P as follows:

$$I_Q = \{i \mid Q^{-1}[Q[i] - 1] > Q^{-1}[Q[i + 1] - 1]\}.$$

Notice that we can also compute I_Q and a string w such that Q is the backward suffix array of w in $O(n)$ time and space. Let $I_{PQ} = I_P \cup I_Q = \{i_1, \ldots, i_d\}$ where $i_1 < \ldots < i_d$ (for convenience, $i_0 = 0, i_{d+1} = n$). We consider the factorization $P_1, \ldots, P_{d+1}$ of P (resp. $Q_1, \ldots, Q_{d+1}$ of Q) based on I_{PQ} such that $P_j = P[i_{j-1} + 1], \ldots, P[i_j]$ (resp. $Q_j = Q[i_{j-1} + 1], \ldots, Q[i_j]$) for any $1 \leq j \leq d + 1$. Note that $i_d < n$ by the definition.

The key idea of our algorithm is shown in the following lemma, which states a necessary and sufficient condition for the existence of a solution string.

Lemma 2. *There exists a string w such that $SA_w = P$ and $rSA_{w^R} = Q$ iff $P_i \equiv Q_i$ for all $1 \leq i \leq d+1$.*

Proof. ($\Leftarrow$) Let w be a string which can be obtained as follows:

$$\forall j. \; w[P[j]] = i \text{ s.t. } P[j] \in P_i. \tag{1}$$

It is clear from Lemma 1 that $SA_w = P$. Since $P_i \equiv Q_i$ for any $1 \leq i \leq d+1$, then $rSA_{w^R} = Q$. ($\Rightarrow$) From the definition of P_j and Q_j, $|P_j| = |Q_j|$ holds. Assume for a contradiction that there exists $k = \min\{j \mid P_j \not\equiv Q_j\}$. This implies that there exist integers α, β such that $\alpha \in P_k, \alpha \notin Q_k, \beta \in Q_k, \beta \notin P_k$, and $\alpha \neq \beta$. Let k_1 (resp. k_2) be the integer such that $\beta \in P_{k_1}$ (resp. $\alpha \in Q_{k_2}$). It is clear that $k < k_1$ and $k < k_2$. Due to Lemma 1, $w[i] < w[i']$ must hold for any $i \in P_k$ and $i' \in P_{k_1}$. This means that $w[\alpha] < w[\beta]$ holds. Similarly, $w[i] < w[i']$ must hold for any $i \in P_k$ and $i' \in P_{k_2}$. This means that $w[\beta] < w[\alpha]$ holds. Hence, w cannot exist in this case.

Therefore, the lemma holds. □

Based on this lemma, we can compute w (obtained by Eq. (1)) over an alphabet of the smallest size such that P is the forward suffix array of w and Q is the backward suffix array of w. Since we can compute I_P and I_Q in $O(n)$ time, we can also compute I_{PQ} and w explained by Eq. (1) in $O(n)$ time. Therefore, we get Theorem 1.

Let $P = 8, 4, 1, 9, 3, 5, 6, 7, 2$ and $Q = 1, 4, 8, 9, 3, 5, 6, 2, 7$. Then, $I_{PQ} = \{3, 5, 7\}$ since $I_P = \{3, 7\}$ and $I_Q = \{3, 5, 7\}$. The factorization of P is $8, 4, 1 \mid 9, 3 \mid 5, 6 \mid 7, 2$. The factorization of Q is $1, 4, 8 \mid 9, 3 \mid 5, 6 \mid 2, 7$. We notice from the above lemma that there exists a solution string w since $P_j \equiv Q_j$ for any j. Since a solution string w over an alphabet of the smallest size has to satisfy $w[1] = w[4] = w[8] < w[3] = w[9] < w[5] = w[6] < w[2] = w[7]$, then we can obtain $w = 1, 4, 2, 1, 3, 3, 4, 1, 2$.

4   Counting Strings from Forward and Backward Suffix Arrays

In this section, we discuss the number of solution strings, for given permutations P and Q, over an alphabet Σ, and give Theorem 2. For a single permutation, Schürmann and Stoye [23] showed the number of strings w such that P is the forward suffix array of w where P is a given permutation of $[1..n]$.

We first summarize their idea since our proof follows them. Let b_P be the string of length n obtained by the algorithm described in Sect. 3.1, and m a non-decreasing integer sequence of length n of elements in $[0, \sigma - d - 1]$ where σ is the alphabet size and d is the size of I_P. $\mathcal{M}_P$ denotes the set of all m. Consider a string $s_{(P,m)}$ defined as $s_{(P,m)}[P[i]] = b_P[P[i]] + m[i]$ $(1 \leq i \leq n)$. Then, P is the forward suffix array of $s_{(P,m)}$. They also showed that $\bigcup_{m \in \mathcal{M}_P} \{s_{(P,m)}\}$ is the set of all solution strings. This implies that the number of solution strings is equal to the size of $\mathcal{M}_P$.

Now we consider the extension to our problem. Let $I_{PQ} = \{i_1, \ldots, i_d\}$ such that $i_j < i_{j+1}(1 \le j < d)$. For convenience, $i_0 = 0$ and $i_{d+1} = n$. We consider the set of positions I'_{PQ} defined as follows: $I'_{PQ} = \bigcup_{j \in [1..d+1]} \{i' \mid P_j[i_{j-1} + 1, i'] \equiv Q_j[i_{j-1}+1, i'], P_j[i'+1, i_j] \equiv Q_j[i'+1, i_j], i_{j-1}+1 < i' < i_j\}$. It is easy to see that $I_{PQ} \cap I'_{PQ} = \emptyset$ holds. We show an example of this set if $P = 1, 4, 2, 6, 9, 5, 3, 8, 7$ and $Q = 1, 2, 6, 4, 5, 9, 3, 7, 8$. Then, $I_{PQ} = \{4, 6\}$ and $I'_{PQ} = \{1, 7\}$.

By using I_{PQ} and I'_{PQ}, we obtain the following result.

Theorem 2. *Let P, Q be permutations of $[1..n]$ such that $|I_{PQ}| = d$ and $|I'_{PQ}| = d'$, and Σ an alphabet of size σ. The number of strings w such that $SA_w = P$ and $rSA_{w^R} = Q$ is*

$$\binom{d' + \sigma}{\sigma - d - 1}.$$

To prove this result, we first characterize all solution strings for given P and Q. We refer to the string obtained by our algorithm in the previous section as the *basic string*, denoted by b_{PQ}. $\mathcal{I}$ denotes $I_{PQ} \cup I'_{PQ}$. Let $\mathcal{I} = \{i_1, \ldots, i_{d+d'}\}$ such that $i_j < i_{j+1}(1 \le j < d+d')$. For convenience, $i_0 = 0, i_{d+d'+1} = n$. We consider the factorization $P'_1, \ldots, P'_{d+d'+1}$ of P (resp. $Q'_1, \ldots, Q'_{d+d'+1}$ of Q) based on $\mathcal{I}$ such that $P'_j = P[i_{j-1} + 1], \ldots, P[i_j]$ (resp. $Q'_j = Q[i_{j-1} + 1], \ldots, Q[i_j]$) for any $1 \le j \le d + d' + 1$. Let c_{PQ} be the sequence of length $d + d' + 1$ such that $c_{PQ}[i] = b_{PQ}[j]$ where $P[j] \in P'_i$. Notice that $b_{PQ}[P[j_1]] = b_{PQ}[P[j_2]]$ for any j_1, j_2 such that $P[j_1], P[j_2] \in P'_i$. Let m be a non-decreasing integer sequence of length $d + d' + 1$ of elements in $[0, \sigma - d - 1]$, and $\mathcal{M}$ the set of all m. We define $C_{(PQ,m)}$ as $C_{(PQ,m)}[i] = c_{PQ}[i] + m[i]$ for any $1 \le i \le d + d' + 1$. We also define $s_{(PQ,m)}$ as $s_{(PQ,m)}[P[i]] = C_{(PQ,m)}[\ell]$ such that $i_{\ell-1} < i \le i_\ell$.

We give an example of these sequences in Fig. 1. For any $P[i], P[i'] \in P'_j$, $w[P[i]] = w[P[i']]$ has to hold where w is a solution string. $c_{PQ}[j]$ stores the character $b_{PQ}[P[i]]$ such that $P[i] \in P'_j$. For example, in Fig. 1, $b_{PQ}[5] = b_{PQ}[9] = 2$ is stored in $c_{PQ}[3]$ since $P'_3 = 9, 5$. These correspondences are represented by arrowed lines in Fig. 1. If we are given m, $C_{(PQ,m)}$ is determined. $C_{(PQ,m)}[j]$ stores the new character which is applied to $s_{(PQ,m)}[P[i]]$ such that $P[i] \in P'_j$.

We prove $\bigcup_{m \in \mathcal{M}} \{s_{(PQ,m)}\}$ is the set of solution strings. Lemma 3 shows that $s_{(PQ,m)}$ is a solution string for any $m \in \mathcal{M}$. Lemma 4 shows that $s_{(PQ,m')}$ is not a solution string for any integer sequence $m' \notin \mathcal{M}$ of length $d + d' + 1$.

Lemma 3. *For any $m \in \mathcal{M}$, $s_{(PQ,m)} \in \Sigma^*$, $SA_{s_{(PQ,m)}} = P$ and $rSA_{s^R_{(PQ,m)}} = Q$.*

Proof. By the definition of c_{PQ} and m, $c_{PQ}[j] \le c_{PQ}[j + 1]$ and $m[j] \le m[j + 1]$ $(1 \le j < d + d' + 1)$. Then, $C_{(PQ,m)}[j] \le C_{(PQ,m)}[j + 1]$ by the definition of $C_{(PQ,m)}$. Assume that $P[i] \in P'_j$. If $P[i + 1] \in P'_j$, $s_{(PQ,m)}[P[i]] = s_{(PQ,m)}[P[i + 1]] = C_{(PQ,m)}[j]$. If $P[i + 1] \in P'_{j+1}$, then $s_{(PQ,m)}[P[i]] \le s_{(PQ,m)}[P[i + 1]]$ since $s_{(PQ,m)}[P[i]] = C_{(PQ,m)}[j]$ and $s_{(PQ,m)}[P[i + 1]] = C_{(PQ,m)}[j + 1]$. Thus, Condition (1) of Lemma 1 holds for $s_{(PQ,m)}$ w.r.t. P. On the other hand, for any i such that $P^{-1}[P[i] + 1] > P^{-1}[P[i + 1] + 1]$ (i.e., $i \in I_{PQ}$), there exists j such that $P[i] \in P'_j$ and $P[i + 1] \in P'_{j+1}$ holds. This implies that $c_{PQ}[j] <$

	1	2	3	4	5	6	7	8	9
P	1	4	2	6	9	5	3	8	7
Q	1	2	6	4	5	9	3	7	8
b_{PQ}	1	1	3	1	2	1	3	3	2

	1		2		3		4		5
c_{PQ}	1		1		2		3		3
m	0		1		1		1		2
$C_{(PQ,m)}$	1		2		3		4		5

	1	2	3	4	5	6	7	8	9
$s_{(PQ,m)}$	1	2	3	2	3	2	5	5	3

Fig. 1. $s_{(PQ,m)} = 1, 2, 4, 2, 3, 2, 5, 5, 3$, for $m = 0, 1, 1, 1, 2 \in \mathcal{M}$, is a solution string.

$c_{PQ}[j + 1]$ ($\because b_{PQ}[P[i]] < b_{PQ}[P[i + 1]]$). Then, $C_{(PQ,m)}[j] < C_{(PQ,m)}[j + 1]$ and $s_{(PQ,m)}[P[i]] < s_{(PQ,m)}[P[i + 1]]$. Hence, Condition (2) of Lemma 1 holds for $s_{(PQ,m)}$ w.r.t. P. Thus, the forward suffix array of $s_{(PQ,m)}$ is P. We can also prove that the backward suffix array of $s_{(PQ,m)}$ is Q in a similar way. On the other hand, $C_{(PQ,m)}[d + d' + 1] \leq \sigma$ since $c_{PQ}[d + d' + 1] = d + 1$ and $m[d + d' + 1] \leq \sigma - d - 1$. By the definition, $C_{(PQ,m)}[i] \leq C_{(PQ,m)}[d + d' + 1] \leq \sigma$ for any $1 \leq i \leq d + d' + 1$. This implies that $s_{(PQ,m)}$ is a string over Σ. $\qquad \square$

Lemma 4. *Let m' be a non-decreasing integer sequence of length $d + d' + 1$. For any $m' \notin \mathcal{M}$, $s_{(PQ,m')} \notin \Sigma^*$ or $SA_{s_{(PQ,m')}} \neq P$ or $rSA_{s_{(PQ,m')}^R} \neq Q$.*

Proof. Assume that m' is not a non-decreasing sequence. There exists j ($1 \leq j < d + d' + 1$) such that $m'[j] > m'[j + 1]$. Let $i \in \mathcal{I}$ be the position in P such that $P[i] \in P'_j$ and $P[i + 1] \in P'_{j+1}$. If $i \in I'_{PQ}$, then $c_{PQ}[j] = c_{PQ}[j + 1]$ holds. Then, $C_{(PQ,m')}[j] = c_{PQ}[j] + m'[j] > c_{PQ}[j + 1] + m'[j + 1] = C_{(PQ,m')}[j + 1]$. Hence, $s_{(PQ,m')}[P[i]] > s_{(PQ,m')}[P[i + 1]]$. This contradicts Condition (1) of Lemma 1. If $i \in I_{PQ}$, then $c_{PQ}[j] = c_{PQ}[j + 1] - 1$ holds. Then, $C_{(PQ,m')}[j] = c_{PQ}[j] + m'[j] \geq (c_{PQ}[j + 1] - 1) + (m'[j + 1] + 1) = C_{(PQ,m')}[j + 1]$ ($\because m'[j] \geq m'[j + 1] + 1$). Hence, $s_{(PQ,m')}[P[i]] \geq s_{(PQ,m')}[P[i + 1]]$. Moreover, since $i \in I_{PQ}$, $P^{-1}[P[i] + 1] > P^{-1}[P[i + 1] + 1]$ holds. This contradicts Condition (2) of Lemma 1.

Assume that m' is a non-decreasing integer sequence of length $d + d' + 1$ such that $m'[i] > \sigma - d - 1$ for some i. Then, $m'[d + d' + 1] > \sigma - d - 1$. By the definition, $c_{PQ}[d + d' + 1] = d + 1$. Hence, $C_{(PQ,m')}[d + d' + 1] = c_{PQ}[d + d' + 1] + m'[d + d' + 1] > \sigma$, and $s_{(PQ,m')}[P[i]] > \sigma$ for any $P[i] \in P'_{d+d'+1}$. Thus, $s_{(PQ,m')} \notin \Sigma^*$.

Assume that m' is a non-decreasing integer sequence of length $d + d' + 1$ such that $m'[i] < 0$ for some i. Then, $m'[1] < 0$. By the definition, $c_{PQ}[1] = 1$. Hence,

$C_{(PQ,m')}[1] = c_{PQ}[1] + m'[1] \leq 0$, and $s_{(PQ,m')}[P[i]] \leq 0$ for any $P[i] \in P'_1$. Thus, $s_{(PQ,m')} \notin \Sigma^*$.

Therefore, the lemma holds. □

By using these facts and the following lemma, we show Theorem 2. The following lemma describes about the number of non-decreasing sequences.

Lemma 5 (Lemma 9 of [23]). *Let $M(s,t)$ be the number of non-decreasing sequence of length s of elements in $[0, t-1]$. For any positive integers s and t,*

$$M(s,t) = \binom{s+t-1}{t-1}.$$

Proof (of Theorem 2). It is clear from the definition of $s_{(PQ,m)}$ that $s_{(PQ,m_1)} \neq s_{(PQ,m_2)}$ for any distinct sequences $m_1, m_2 \in \mathcal{M}$. From Lemmas 3, 4, $\mathcal{M}$ produces all strings w such that P is the forward suffix array and Q is the backward suffix array of w. Hence, the number of all solution strings is equal to the size of $\mathcal{M}$. From Lemma 5, the number of elements in $\mathcal{M}$ is $\binom{d'+\sigma}{\sigma-d-1}$ (by setting $s = d+d'+1$ and $t = \sigma - d$). □

5 Enumerating Strings from Suffix Arrays

In this section, we consider enumeration problems. Due to the previous section, each m produces a solution string w, and the w can be computed by using m and given permutations. In this paper, we consider enumerating all m instead of all solution strings. Our algorithm computes all m in lexicographically increasing order w.r.t. solution strings. We propose two enumeration algorithms, one is for a single permutation and another is for two permutations. We explain only the first algorithm (for a single permutation) in this paper (in Sect. 5.1) since the second algorithm can be obtained by a natural extension based on the previous section.

5.1 Enumerating Strings from the Forward Suffix Array

Let S_P be the set of strings which have P as the forward suffix array, namely, $S_P = \bigcup_{m \in \mathcal{M}_P} s_{(P,m)}$. $m_k \in \mathcal{M}_P$ denotes the non-decreasing sequence of length n of elements in $[0, \sigma-d-1]$ such that $s_{(P,m_k)}$ is the lexicographically k-th smallest string in S_P. If $m = \langle\langle 0 \rangle\rangle_n$, it is clear that $s_{(P,m)}$ is the lexicographically smallest string in S_P (i.e., $m_1 = \langle\langle 0 \rangle\rangle_n$). Similarly, if $m = \langle\langle \sigma - d - 1 \rangle\rangle_n$, $s_{(P,m)}$ is the lexicographically largest string in S_P (i.e., $m_{|\mathcal{M}_P|} = \langle\langle \sigma - d - 1 \rangle\rangle_n$).

We show a way to compute m_{k+1} when we know m_k in the following lemma. Due to a technical reasons, we assume that $m_k[n+1] = \sigma - d - 1$ for all k.

Lemma 6. *Let $i_k = \arg\max_{\ell} P[\ell]$ where $\ell \in \{i \mid m_k[i] < m_k[i+1], 1 \leq i \leq n\}$ for any $1 \leq k < |\mathcal{M}_P|$. Then,*

$$m_{k+1}[i] = \begin{cases} m_k[i] + 1 & (\text{if } P[i] = P[i_k]), \\ m_k[i] & (\text{if } P[i] < P[i_k]), \\ m_{k+1}[i-1] & (\text{if } P[i] > P[i_k]). \end{cases} \tag{2}$$

Proof. From the definition of $s_{(P,m)}$, we show the correctness of the following in order to prove the correctness of Eq. (2):

$$\begin{cases} s_{(P,m_{k+1})}[P[i]] = s_{(P,m_k)}[P[i]] + 1 & (\text{if } P[i] = P[i_k]), \\ s_{(P,m_{k+1})}[P[i]] = s_{(P,m_k)}[P[i]] & (\text{if } P[i] < P[i_k]), \\ s_{(P,m_{k+1})}[P[i]] \leq s_{(P,m_k)}[P[i]] & (\text{if } P[i] > P[i_k]). \end{cases}$$

It is clear that $s_{(P,m_k)} \prec s_{(P,m_{k+1})}$ holds since $s_{(P,m_k)}[1, P[i_k] - 1] = s_{(P,m_{k+1})}[1, P[i_k] - 1]$ and $s_{(P,m_k)}[P[i_k]] < s_{(P,m_{k+1})}[P[i_k]]$. We prove that there does not exist k' such that $s_{(P,m_k)} \prec s_{(P,m_{k'})} \prec s_{(P,m_{k+1})}$. Assume for a contradiction that there exists k' such that $s_{(P,m_k)} \prec s_{(P,m_{k'})} \prec s_{(P,m_{k+1})}$. By the assumption, $s_{(P,m_k)}[1, P[i_k] - 1] = s_{(P,m_{k'})}[1, P[i_k] - 1] = s_{(P,m_{k+1})}[1, P[i_k] - 1]$. This implies that either $s_{(P,m_{k'})}[P[i_k]] = s_{(P,m_k)}[P[i_k]]$ or $s_{(P,m_{k'})}[P[i_k]] = s_{(P,m_{k+1})}[P[i_k]]$ holds.

Suppose that $s_{(P,m_{k'})}[P[i_k]] = s_{(P,m_k)}[P[i_k]]$ (see also Fig. 2). Let $j = \min\{i \mid s_{(P,m_k)}[i] \prec s_{(P,m_{k'})}[i]\}$ and i' be the integer such that $P[i'] = j$. Then, $m_k[i'] < m_{k'}[i']$ ($\because s_{(P,m_k)}[j] = b_P[j] + m_k[i']$ and $s_{(P,m_{k'})}[j] = b_P[j] + m_{k'}[i']$). Let $i'' = \min\{i \mid m_{k'}[i'] \leq m_k[i], i' < i\}$. Then, $m_k[i] < m_{k'}[i']$ for any $i \in [i' + 1..i'' - 1]$. Since $m_{k'}$ is a non-decreasing sequence, $m_{k'}[i'] \leq m_{k'}[i]$ for any $i \in [i' + 1..i'' - 1]$. Therefore, for any $i \in [i' + 1..i'' - 1]$, we have $m_k[i] < m_{k'}[i]$ and thus $s_{(P,m_k)}[P[i]] < s_{(P,m_{k'})}[P[i]]$. Since $s_{(P,m_k)}[1, j - 1] = s_{(P,m_{k'})}[1, j - 1]$, $P[i] > j$ for any $i \in [i' + 1..i'' - 1]$. Thus, $P[i'' - 1] > j \ (= P[i']) > P[i_k]$ holds. By the definition of i'', $m_k[i'' - 1] < m_k[i'']$. Hence, $m_k[i'' - 1] < m_k[i'']$ and $P[i_k] < P[i'' - 1]$, which contradicts the definition of i_k.

Suppose that $s_{(P,m_{k'})}[P[i_k]] = s_{(P,m_{k+1})}[P[i_k]]$. Let $j = \min\{i \mid s_{(P,m_{k'})}[i] \prec s_{(P,m_{k+1})}[i]\}$ and i' be the integer such that $P[i'] = j$. Then, $m_{k'}[i'] < m_{k+1}[i']$. Let $i'' = \max\{i \mid m_{k+1}[i] \leq m_{k'}[i'], i < i'\}$. Then $m_{k'}[i'] < m_{k+1}[i]$ for any $i \in [i'' + 1..i' - 1]$. Since $m_{k'}$ is a non-decreasing sequence, $m_{k'}[i] \leq m_{k'}[i']$ for any $i \in [i'' + 1..i' - 1]$). Therefore, for any $i \in [i'' + 1..i' - 1]$, we have $m_{k'}[i] < m_{k+1}[i]$ and thus $s_{(P,m_{k'})}[P[i]] < s_{(P,m_{k+1})}[P[i]]$. Since $s_{(P,m_{k'})}[1, j - 1] = s_{(P,m_{k+1})}[1, j - 1]$, $P[i] > j$ for any $i \in [i' + 1..i'' - 1]$. Thus, $P[i'' + 1] > j \ (= P[i']) > P[i_k]$ holds. Although, this implies that $m_{k+1}[i''] = m_{k+1}[i'' + 1]$ has to hold by the third case of Eq. (2), $m_{k+1}[i''] < m_{k+1}[i'' + 1]$ holds by the definition of i''. This is a contradiction.

Hence, such k' cannot exist, showing that Eq. (2) correctly updates m_k to m_{k+1}. Finally, we show that this update procedure eventually produces $\langle\langle \sigma - d - 1 \rangle\rangle_n$. Suppose that $m_k \neq \langle\langle \sigma - d - 1 \rangle\rangle_n$. This implies that there exists $i \geq 1$ such that $m_k[i] < \sigma - d - 1$. Thus, there always exists i_k such that $1 \leq i_k \leq n$, and we can update m_k to m_{k+1}. □

Now we show an efficient algorithm that traverses all $m \in \mathcal{M}_P$. We can overwrite m_{k+1} on m_k from left to right, due to Eq. (2). Let $m_{(k,i)}$ be the non-decreasing sequence of integers which is updated from the first to the i-th elements, namely, $m_{(k,i)} = m_{k+1}[1, i]m_k[i + 1, n]$. Notice that $m_{(k,n)} = m_{k+1}$ (an example is given in Fig. 3).

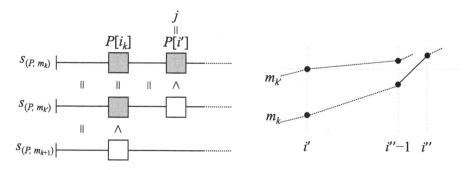

Fig. 2. This figure shows the conditions of strings (left) and m (right), when $s_{(P,m_{k'})}[P[i_k]] = s_{(P,m_k)}[P[i_k]]$ holds.

	1	2	3	4	5	6	7	8	9	(10)
P	1	4	2	6	9	5	3	8	7	-
m_k	0	0 ↗ 1 ↗ 2			2	2 ↗ 3 ↗ 5			5	5
$m_{(k,4)}$	0	0 ↗ 1		$\underline{1}$ ↗ 2		2 ↗ 3 ↗ 5			5	5
$m_{(k,5)}$	0	0 ↗ 1		1	$\underline{1}$ ↗ 2 ↗ 3 ↗ 5				5	5
$m_{(k,6)}$	0	0 ↗ 1		1	1 ↗ $\underline{3}$		3 ↗ 5		5	5
$m_{(k,8)}$	0	0 ↗ 1		1	1 ↗ 3		3	$\underline{3}$ ↗ 5		5
$m_{(k,9)} = m_{k+1}$	0	0 ↗ 1		1	1 ↗ 3		3	3	$\underline{3}$	5

Fig. 3. This is an example of computing m_{k+1} from P and m_k which are shown in the figure. An arrowed line which is drawn between two adjacent values indicates that the left value is strictly smaller than the right. An underlined value is different from the value which is the same position in the previous array. We have omitted $m_{(k,i)}$ from the figure if equal to $m_{(k,i-1)}$ (e.g., $m_{(k,7)} = m_{(k,6)}$).

In our algorithm, we maintain sets $U_{(k,i)}$ and $D_{(k,i)}$ defined as follows:

$$U_{(k,i)} = \{P[j] \mid m_{(k,i)}[j] < m_{(k,i)}[j+1], 1 \leq j \leq n\},$$
$$D_{(k,i)} = \{(j, P[j]) \mid m_{(k,i)}[j-1] < m_{(k,i)}[j], 1 \leq j \leq n\}.$$

Remark that $m_k[0] = 0, m_k[n+1] = \sigma - d - 1$ for any $1 \leq k \leq |\mathcal{M}_P|$. We can see that the maximum element of $U_{(k-1,n)}$ is $P[i_k]$, which is required for updating m_k to m_{k+1} (Eq. (2)). Values in $D_{(k,n)}$ are searched to find i where $P[i] > P[i_k]$ and $m_k[i] \neq m_{k+1}[i]$ to update the remaining positions (third case of Eq. (2)).

By the following operations, we can update $U_{(k,i-1)}$ to $U_{(k,i)}$ (respectively, $D_{(k,i-1)}$ to $D_{(k,i)}$).

When $m_k[i]$ is rewritten as $m_k[i] + 1$ (the first case of Eq. (2)), we

- insert $P[i-1]$ to $U_{(k,i-1)}$ (if not a member),
- insert $P[i]$ to $D_{(k,i-1)}$ (if not a member),
- if $m_{k+1}[i] = m_k[i+1]$,

- delete $P[i]$ from $U_{(k,i-1)}$,
- delete $P[i+1]$ from $D_{(k,i-1)}$.

When $m_k[i]$ is rewritten as $m_{k+1}[i-1]$ (the third case of Eq. (2)), we

- insert $P[i]$ to $U_{(k,i-1)}$ (if not a member),
- insert $P[i+1]$ to $D_{(k,i-1)}$ (if not a member),
- delete $P[i-1]$ from $U_{(k,i-1)}$,
- delete $P[i-1]$ from $D_{(k,i-1)}$.

We can correctly update $U_{(k,i)}$ and $D_{(k,i)}$ by the above operations, due to simple observations on m_k and Lemma 6. Roughly speaking, $U_{(k,i)}$ stores each position which is the left position of an arrowed line (in Fig. 3) in $m_{(k,i)}$, and $D_{(k,i)}$ stores each positions which is the right position of an arrowed line in $m_{(k,i)}$.

The number of operations is constant for each changed value in m_k. The total number of operations to compute $U_{(|\mathcal{M}_P|-1,n)}$ and $D_{(|\mathcal{M}_P|-1,n)}$ can be bounded by $O(|\mathcal{M}_P|)$, which can be seen from the following arguments: For each k, there is exactly one update on m_k, corresponding to the first case of Eq. (2), which increments a value for m_k. Thus, the total number of such updates is $|\mathcal{M}_P|$. For each update that corresponds to the third case of Eq. (2) and $m_k[i] \neq m_{k+1}[i]$, a value of m_k is decreased. Since only one value is incremented when updating m_k to m_{k+1}, the total number of values which can be decreased is also bounded by $|\mathcal{M}_P|$.

By maintaining $U_{(k,i)}$ by using a balanced search tree, we can insert or delete an element in $O(\log n)$ time since the size of the above set is $O(n)$. We can also find the maximum element in the set in $O(\log n)$ time. This implies that we can find $P[i_k]$ (and i_k) in $O(\log n)$ time. On the other hand, we maintain $D_{(k,i)}$ by using a priority search tree [19].

Lemma 7 ([19]). *Let S be a dynamic set of ordered pairs (x,y) over the set $[1,j]$, and consider the following operations applied to S:*

1. *Insert (delete) a pair (x,y) into (from) S.*
2. *Given query integers x_0, x_1, and y_0, among all pairs (x,y) in S such that $x_0 \leq x \leq x_1$ and $y \leq y_0$, find a pair with the smallest x.*

These operations can be done in $O(\log n)$ time with an $O(n)$ space data structure where n is the cardinality of S.

Note that we can easily change the condition of $y \leq y_0$ to $y \geq y_0$ by considering the reversed y-axis. Let i' be some position in m such that $m_{k+1}[i'] \neq m_k[i']$, and i'' the largest position in m such that $m_{k+1}[i''] \neq m_k[i'']$ and $i'' < i'$ if it exists, or $i'' = 0$ otherwise. Assume that we have computed $m_{(k,i'')}$. By setting query integers as $x_0 = i'' + 1, x_1 = n$ and $y_0 = P[i_k] + 1$ we can find i' in $O(\log n)$ time. Hence, we can traverse all $m \in \mathcal{M}_P$ (with no outputs) in $O(|\mathcal{M}_P| \log n)$ time in total.

Theorem 3. *We can traverse all $m \in \mathcal{M}_P$ in lexicographically increasing order w.r.t. solution strings in $O(|\mathcal{M}_P| \log n)$ time and $O(n)$ space.*

It is easy to see that we can output all $m \in \mathcal{M}_P$ (instead of strings) explicitly.

Corollary 1. *We can compute all $m \in \mathcal{M}_P$ in lexicographically increasing order w.r.t. solution strings in $O(|\mathcal{M}_P|n)$ time and $O(n)$ working space.*

We propose a compact representation of all $m \in \mathcal{M}_P$. Let μ_k be the set of pairs (i, δ_i), for any i which satisfies $m_k[i] \neq m_{k+1}[i]$, where $\delta_i = m_{k+1}[i] - m_k[i]$. Our data structure is defined as follows:

- the ordered set of μ_k for all $1 \leq k < |\mathcal{M}_P|$, and
- m_i for all $i = j\tau$ $(1 \leq j \leq \lceil \frac{|\mathcal{M}_P|}{\tau} \rceil)$ where τ is a parameter.

It is clear from the above algorithm that this data structure is $O(\frac{|\mathcal{M}_P|}{\tau}n + |\mathcal{M}_P|)$ space $(O(\frac{|\mathcal{M}_P|}{\tau}n)$ space for all m_i and $O(|\mathcal{M}_P|)$ space for all $\mu_k)$, and it can be computed in $O(\frac{|\mathcal{M}_P|}{\tau}n + |\mathcal{M}_P| \log n)$ time. By using this data structure, we can return the lexicographically j-th solution string, for any given $1 \leq j \leq |\mathcal{M}_P|$, in $O(\tau n)$ time (we first find the most nearest explicit m, and we decode all m from the nearest one to the j-th by using μ). If we set $\tau = n$, we can compute the j-th solution string in $O(n^2)$ time with a linear space data structure.

Theorem 4. *We can compute in $O(\frac{|\mathcal{M}_P|}{\tau}n + |\mathcal{M}_P| \log n)$ time, an $O(\frac{|\mathcal{M}_P|}{\tau}n + |\mathcal{M}_P|)$-space data structure that can answer the lexicographically j-th solution string in $O(\tau n)$ time for any given j.*

Finally, we state our result for the problem of two permutations. We can obtain the following results by natural extensions of the above arguments.

Theorem 5. *We can traverse all $m \in \mathcal{M}$ in lexicographically increasing order w.r.t. solution strings in $O(|\mathcal{M}| \log n)$ time and $O(n)$ space.*

Theorem 6. *We can compute $O(\frac{|\mathcal{M}|}{\tau}n + |\mathcal{M}|)$-space data structure which returns the lexicographically j-th solution strings in $O(\tau n)$ for any given j in $O(\frac{|\mathcal{M}|}{\tau}n + |\mathcal{M}| \log n)$ time.*

Acknowledgments. This work was supported by JSPS KAKENHI Grant Numbers JP18K18002 (YN), JP17H01697 (SI), JP16H02783 (HB), and JP18H04098 (MT).

References

1. Bannai, H., Inenaga, S., Shinohara, A., Takeda, M.: Inferring strings from graphs and arrays. In: Rovan, B., Vojtáš, P. (eds.) MFCS 2003. LNCS, vol. 2747, pp. 208–217. Springer, Heidelberg (2003). https://doi.org/10.1007/978-3-540-45138-9_15
2. Blumer, A., Blumer, J., Haussler, D., Mcconnell, R., Ehrenfeucht, A.: Complete inverted files for efficient text retrieval and analysis. J. ACM **34**(3), 578–595 (1987)
3. Blumer, A., Blumer, J., Haussler, D., Ehrenfeucht, A., Chen, M.T., Seiferas, J.: The smallest automaton recognizing the subwords of a text. Theor. Comput. Sci. **40**, 31–55 (1985)

4. Cazaux, B., Rivals, E.: Reverse engineering of compact suffix trees and links: a novel algorithm. J. Discret. Algorithms **28**, 9–22 (2014)
5. Clément, J., Crochemore, M., Rindone, G.: Reverse engineering prefix tables. In: Proceedings of 26th International Symposium on Theoretical Aspects of Computer Science (STACS 2009), pp. 289–300 (2009)
6. Crochemore, M., Iliopoulos, C.S., Pissis, S.P., Tischler, G.: Cover array string reconstruction. In: Amir, A., Parida, L. (eds.) CPM 2010. LNCS, vol. 6129, pp. 251–259. Springer, Heidelberg (2010). https://doi.org/10.1007/978-3-642-13509-5_23
7. Daykin, J.W., Franek, F., Holub, J., Islam, A.S., Smyth, W.: Reconstructing a string from its Lyndon arrays. Theor. Comput. Sci. **710**, 44–51 (2018)
8. Duval, J., Lecroq, T., Lefebvre, A.: Efficient validation and construction of border arrays and validation of string matching automata. ITA **43**(2), 281–297 (2009)
9. Duval, J., Lefebvre, A.: Words over an ordered alphabet and suffix permutations. ITA **36**(3), 249–259 (2002)
10. Gawrychowski, P., Jeż, A., Jeż, L.: Validating the Knuth-Morris-Pratt failure function, fast and online. Theor. Comput. Syst. **54**(2), 337–372 (2014)
11. He, J., Liang, H., Yang, G.: Reversing longest previous factor tables is hard. In: Dehne, F., Iacono, J., Sack, J.-R. (eds.) WADS 2011. LNCS, vol. 6844, pp. 488–499. Springer, Heidelberg (2011). https://doi.org/10.1007/978-3-642-22300-6_41
12. I, T., Inenaga, S., Bannai, H., Takeda, M.: Counting and verifying maximal palindromes. In: Chavez, E., Lonardi, S. (eds.) SPIRE 2010. LNCS, vol. 6393, pp. 135–146. Springer, Heidelberg (2010). https://doi.org/10.1007/978-3-642-16321-0_13
13. I, T., Inenaga, S., Bannai, H., Takeda, M.: Inferring strings from suffix trees and links on a binary alphabet. In: Proceedings of the Prague Stringology Conference 2011, pp. 121–130 (2011)
14. I, T., Inenaga, S., Bannai, H., Takeda, M.: Verifying and enumerating parameterized border arrays. Theor. Comput. Sci. **412**(50), 6959–6981 (2011)
15. Kärkkäinen, J., Piatkowski, M., Puglisi, S.J.: String inference from longest-common-prefix array. In: Proceedings of 44th International Colloquium on Automata, Languages, and Programming (ICALP 2017), pp. 62:1–62:14 (2017)
16. Lu, W., Ryan, P.J., Smyth, W.F., Sun, Y., Yang, L.: Verifying a border array in linear time. J. Comb. Math. Comb. Comput **42**, 223–236 (2002)
17. Manber, U., Myers, E.W.: Suffix arrays: a new method for on-line string searches. SIAM J. Comput. **22**(5), 935–948 (1993)
18. Matsubara, W., Ishino, A., Shinohara, A.: Inferring strings from runs. In: Proceedings of the Prague Stringology Conference vol. 2010, pp. 150–160 (2010)
19. McCreight, E.M.: Priority search trees. SIAM J. Comput. **14**(2), 257–276 (1985)
20. Nakashima, Y., Okabe, T., I, T., Inenaga, S., Bannai, H., Takeda, M.: Inferring strings from Lyndon factorization. Theor. Comput. Sci. **689**, 147–156 (2017)
21. Nakashima, Y., Takagi, T., Inenaga, S., Bannai, H., Takeda, M.: On reverse engineering the Lyndon tree. In: Proceedings of the Prague Stringology Conference vol. 2017, pp. 108–117 (2017)
22. Nishida, M., I, T., Inenaga, S., Bannai, H., Takeda, M.: Inferring strings from full abelian periods. In: Elbassioni, K., Makino, K. (eds.) ISAAC 2015. LNCS, vol. 9472, pp. 768–779. Springer, Heidelberg (2015). https://doi.org/10.1007/978-3-662-48971-0_64
23. Schürmann, K., Stoye, J.: Counting suffix arrays and strings. Theor. Comput. Sci. **395**(2–3), 220–234 (2008)

24. Starikovskaya, T.A., Vildhøj, H.W.: A suffix tree or not a suffix tree? J. Discrete Algorithms **32**, 14–23 (2015)
25. Stoye, J.: Affix trees. Technical report 2000-04, Universität Bielefeld, Technische Fakultät (2000)
26. Weiner, P.: Linear pattern-matching algorithms. In: Proceedings of 14th IEEE Annual Symposium on Switching and Automata Theory, pp. 1–11 (1973)

Optimal In-Place Suffix Sorting

Zhize Li[1(✉)], Jian Li[1(✉)], and Hongwei Huo[2]

[1] Institute for Interdisciplinary Information Sciences, Tsinghua University, Beijing, China
zz-li14@mails.tsinghua.edu.cn, lijian83@mail.tsinghua.edu.cn
[2] Department of Computer Science, Xidian University, Xi'an, China
hwhuo@mail.xidian.edu.cn

Abstract. The suffix array is a fundamental data structure for many applications that involve string searching and data compression. Designing time/space-efficient suffix array construction algorithms has attracted significant attentions and considerable advances have been made for the past 20 years. We obtain the *first* in-place linear time suffix array construction algorithms that are optimal both in time and space for (read-only) integer alphabets. Our algorithm settles the open problem posed by Franceschini and Muthukrishnan in ICALP 2007. The open problem asked to design in-place algorithms in $o(n \log n)$ time and ultimately, in $O(n)$ time for (read-only) integer alphabets with $|\Sigma| \le n$. Our result is in fact slightly stronger since we allow $|\Sigma| = O(n)$. Besides, we provide an optimal in-place $O(n \log n)$ time suffix sorting algorithm for read-only general alphabets (i.e., only comparisons are allowed), recovering the result obtained by Franceschini and Muthukrishnan which was an open problem posed by Manzini and Ferragina in ESA 2002.

Keywords: Suffix sorting · Suffix array · In-place

1 Introduction

In SODA 1990, suffix arrays were introduced by Manber and Myers [25] as a space-saving alternative to suffix trees [9,29]. Since then, it has been used as a fundamental data structure for many applications in string processing, data compression, text indexing, information retrieval and computational biology [1,10,12,14,15]. Particularly, the suffix arrays are often used to compute the Burrows-Wheeler transform [5] and Lempel-Ziv factorization [39]. Comparing with suffix trees, suffix arrays use much less space in practice. Abouelhoda et al. [2] showed that any problem which can be computed using suffix trees can also be solved using suffix arrays with the same asymptotic time complexity, which makes suffix arrays very attractive both in theory and in practice. Hence, suffix arrays have been studied extensively over the last 20 years (see e.g., [11,18,19,22,31,33,34]). We refer the readers to the surveys [8,35] for many suffix sorting algorithms.

© Springer Nature Switzerland AG 2018
T. Gagie et al. (Eds.): SPIRE 2018, LNCS 11147, pp. 268–284, 2018.
https://doi.org/10.1007/978-3-030-00479-8_22

In 1990, Manber and Myers [25] obtained the first $O(n \log n)$ time suffix sorting algorithm over general alphabets. In 2003, Ko and Aluru [22], Kärkkäinen and Sanders [18] and Kim et al. [21] independently obtained the first linear time algorithm for suffix sorting over integer alphabets. Clearly, these algorithms are optimal in terms of asymptotic time complexity. However, in many applications, the computational bottleneck is the *space* as we need the space-saving suffix arrays instead of suffix trees, and significant efforts have been made in developing *lightweight* (in terms of space usage) suffix sorting algorithms for the last decade (see e.g., [4,11,13,22,26,28,31–34]). In particular, the ultimate goal in this line of work is to obtain *in-place algorithms* (i.e., $O(1)$ additional space), which are also asymptotically optimal in time.

1.1 Problem Setting

Problem: Given a string $T = T[0 \ldots n - 1]$ with n characters, we need to construct the *suffix array* (SA) which contains the *indices* of all sorted suffixes of T (see Definition 1 for the formal definition of SA).

Here, we consider the following two popular settings. We measure the space usage of an algorithm in the unit of *words* same as [11,31]. A word contains $\lceil \log n \rceil$ bits. One standard arithmetic or bitwise boolean operation on word-sized operands costs $O(1)$ time.

1. Read-only integer alphabets: The input string T is *read-only*. Each $T[i] \in [1, |\Sigma|]$, where $|\Sigma| = O(n)$. Note that the constant alphabets (e.g., ASCII code) is a special case of integer alphabets, and the read-only integer alphabets is commonly used in practice.
2. Read-only general alphabets: The input string T is read-only and the only operations allowed on the characters of T are comparisons. Each comparison takes $O(1)$ time. We *cannot* write the input space, make bit operations, even copy an input character $T[i]$ to the work space. Clearly, $\Omega(n \log n)$ time is a lower bound for suffix sorting in this case, as it generalizes comparison-based sorting.

The *workspace* used by an algorithm is the total space needed by the algorithm, excluding the space required by the input string T and the output suffix array SA. An algorithm which uses $O(1)$ words workspace to construct SA is called an *in-place* algorithm. See Tables 1[1] and 2 for existing and new results.

1.2 Related Work and Our Contributions

Read-Only Integer Alphabets. In ICALP 2007, Franceschini and Muthukrishnan [11] posed an open problem for designing an in-place algorithm that takes $o(n \log n)$ time or ultimately $O(n)$ time for (read-only) integer alphabets with

---

[1] Some previous algorithms state the space usages in terms of bits. We convert them into words.

Table 1. Time and workspace of suffix sorting algorithms for read-only integer alphabets Σ

Time	Workspace (words)	Algorithms
$O(n^2 \log n)$	$cn + O(1)$ $c < 1$	[26–28]
$O(n^2 \log n)$	$|\Sigma| + O(1)$	[16]
$O(n^2)$	$O(n)$	[38]
$O(n \log^2 n)$	$O(n)$	[36]
$O(n \log n)$	$O(n)$	[23,25]
$O(vn)$	$O(n/\sqrt{v})$ $v \in [1, \sqrt{n}]$	[19]
$O(n\sqrt{|\Sigma|}\log(n/|\Sigma|))$	$O(n)$	[3]
$O(n \log \log n)$	$O(n)$	[20]
$O(n \log \log |\Sigma|)$	$O(n \log |\Sigma| / \log n)$	[13]
$O(n \log |\Sigma|)$	$|\Sigma| + O(1)$	[32]
$O(n)$	$O(n)$	[18,19,21,22]
$O(n)$	$n + n/\log n + O(1)$	[33,34]
$O(n)$	$|\Sigma| + O(1)$	[31]
$O(n)$	$O(1)$	This paper

$|\Sigma| \leq n$ (in fact, they did not specify whether the input string T is read-only or not). The current best result along this line is provided by Nong [31], which used $|\Sigma|$ words workspace (Nong's algorithm is in-place if $|\Sigma| = O(1)$, i.e., constant alphabets). Note that in the worst case $|\Sigma|$ can be as large as $O(n)$. We list several previous results and our new result in Table 1.

In this paper, we settle down this open problem by providing the first optimal linear time in-place algorithm, as in the following theorem. Note that our result is in fact slightly stronger since we allow $|\Sigma| = O(n)$ instead of $|\Sigma| \leq n$ mentioned in the open problem [11].

Theorem 1 (Main Theorem). *There is an in-place linear time algorithm for suffix sorting over integer alphabets, even if the input string T is read-only and the size of the alphabet $|\Sigma|$ is $O(n)$.*

Read-Only General Alphabets. Now, we consider the case where the only operations allowed on the characters of string T (read-only) are comparisons. See Table 2 for an overview of the results. In 2002, Manzini and Ferragina [28] posed an open problem, which asked whether there exists an $O(n \log n)$ time algorithm using $o(n)$ workspace. In 2007, Franceschini and Muthukrishnan [11] obtained the first in-place algorithm that runs in optimal $O(n \log n)$ time. Their conference paper is somewhat complicated and densely-argued.

We also give an optimal in-place algorithm which achieves the same result, as in the following theorem. In addition, our algorithm does not make any bit

Table 2. Time and workspace of suffix sorting algorithms for read-only general alphabets

Time	Workspace (words)	Algorithms
$O(n \log n)$	$O(n)$	[23, 25]
$O(vn + n \log n)$	$O(v + n/\sqrt{v})$ $v \in [2, n]$	[4]
$O(vn + n \log n)$	$O(n/\sqrt{v})$ $v \in [1, \sqrt{n}]$	[19]
$O(n \log n)$	$O(1)$	[11]
$O(n \log n)$	$O(1)$	This paper

operations while theirs uses bit operations heavily. Our algorithm is also arguably simpler.

Theorem 2. *There is an in-place $O(n \log n)$ time algorithm for suffix sorting over general alphabets, even if the input string T is read-only and only comparisons between characters are allowed.*

1.3   Difficulties and Our Approach

Difficulties: Typically, the suffix sorting algorithms are recursive algorithms. The size of the recursive (reduced) sub-problem is usually less than half of the current problem. See e.g., [11, 19, 22, 31, 33–35]. However, all previous algorithms require extra arrays, e.g., *bucket array* (which needs $|\Sigma|$ words at the top recursive level and $n/2$ words at the deep recursive levels), *type array* (which needs $n/\log n$ words) and/or other auxiliary arrays (which need up to $O(n)$ words), to construct the reduced problems and use the results of the reduced problems to sort the original suffixes.[2]

In particular, Nong et al. [33] made a breakthrough by providing the SA-IS algorithm which only required one bucket array (which needs $\max\{|\Sigma|, n/2\}$ words) and one type array ($n/\log n$ words). Note that the bucket array and type array are reused for each recursive level.

Currently, the best result was provided by Nong [31]. However, Nong's algorithm still requires the bucket array for the top recursive level, but not for the deeper levels. Hence, it needs $|\Sigma|$ words instead of $\max\{|\Sigma|, n/2\}$ words. Note that $|\Sigma|$ can be $O(n)$ in the worst case for integer alphabets. For the type array, Nong used this bucket array to indicate the type information at the top recursive level. For the deeper levels, Nong removed the type array.

Thus, *the main technical difficulty is to remove the workspace for the bucket array at the top recursive level since there is no extra space to use.* Note that it is non-trivial since T is read-only and SA needs to store the final order of all suffixes. Besides, the previous sorting steps or tricks may not work if one removes the bucket array. For example, Nong [31] used the bucket array to indicate the

---

[2] The definitions of bucket array and type array can be found in Sect. 2.

type information. If the bucket array was removed, one would need the type array.

Our Approach: We briefly describe our optimal in-place linear time suffix sorting algorithms that overcome these difficulties. We provide an *interior counter trick* which can implicitly represent the dynamic *LF/RF-entry* information (see Sect. 2 for the definition) in SA. Besides, we provide a *pointer data structure* which can represent the bucket heads/tails in SA. Combining these two techniques, we can remove the workspace needed by the bucket array entirely. Note that it is non-trivial for the top recursive level which is the most difficult part, since the pointer data structure needs *nonconstant* workspace and we only have $O(1)$ extra workspace. As a result, we divide the sorting step into two stages to address this issue. In order to remove the type array, we provide some useful properties and observations which allows us to retrieve the type information efficiently. For the general alphabets case, we provide simple sorting steps and extend the interior counter trick to obtain an optimal in-place $O(n \log n)$ time suffix sorting algorithm.

Organization: The remaining of the paper is organized as follows. Section 2 covers the preliminary knowledge. In Sect. 3, we describe the framework and the details of our optimal in-place suffix sorting algorithm for the read-only integer alphabets. Finally, we conclude in Sect. 4. For the read-only general alphabets, we defer the details of our optimal in-place algorithm to the full version of this paper [24].

2   Preliminaries

Given a string $T = T[0 \ldots n-1]$ with n characters, the suffixes of T are $T[i \ldots n-1]$ for all $i \in [0, n-1]$, where $T[i \ldots j]$ denotes the substring $T[i]T[i+1] \ldots T[j]$ in T. To simplify the argument, we assume that the final character $T[n-1]$ is a sentinel which is lexicographically smaller than any other characters in Σ. Without loss of generality, we assume that $T[n-1] = 0$.[3] Any two suffixes in T must be different since their lengths are different, and their lexicographical order can be determined by comparing their characters one by one until we see a difference due to the existence of the sentinel.

Definition 1. *The suffix array* SA *contains the indices of all suffixes of T which are sorted in lexicographical order, i.e.,* $\mathsf{suf}(\mathsf{SA}[i]) < \mathsf{suf}(\mathsf{SA}[j])$ *for all* $i < j$, *where* $\mathsf{suf}(i)$ *denotes the suffix* $T[i \ldots n-1]$.

For example, if $T = $ "1220", then all suffixes are $\{1220, 220, 20, 0\}$ and SA $= [3, 0, 2, 1]$. Note that SA always uses n words no matter what the alphabets Σ are, since it contains the permutation of $\{0, \ldots, n-1\}$, where n is the length of T.

A suffix $\mathsf{suf}(i)$ is said to be *S-suffix* (S-type suffix) if $\mathsf{suf}(i) < \mathsf{suf}(i+1)$. Otherwise, it is *L-suffix* (L-type suffix) [22]. The last suffix $\mathsf{suf}(n-1)$ containing

---

[3] Some previous papers use $ to denote the sentinel.

only the single character 0 (the sentinel) is defined to be an S-suffix. Equivalently, the $\mathsf{suf}(i)$ is S-suffix if and only if (1) $i = n - 1$; or (2) $T[i] < T[i + 1]$; or (3) $T[i] = T[i + 1]$ and $\mathsf{suf}(i + 1)$ is S-suffix. Obviously, the types can be computed by a linear scan of T (from $T[n - 1]$ to $T[0]$). We further define the type of a character $T[i]$ to *S-type* (or *L-type* resp.) if $\mathsf{suf}(i)$ is S-suffix (or L-suffix resp.). For the same example, the types are *"SLLS"*.

A suffix $\mathsf{suf}(i)$ is called an *LMS-suffix* (Leftmost S-type) if $T[i]$ is S-type and $T[i - 1]$ is L-type, for $i \geq 1$ [33]. Similarly, a character $T[i]$ is called *LMS-character* if $\mathsf{suf}(i)$ is LMS-suffix. A substring $T[i \ldots j]$ is called an *LMS-substring* if both $T[i]$ and $T[j]$ are LMS-characters, and there is no other LMS-characters between them, or $i = j = n - 1$ (the single sentinel). We also define the *LML-suffix* (Leftmost L-type), *LML-character* and *LML-substring* similarly.

Obviously, the indices of all suffixes, which begin with the same character, must appear consecutively in SA. We denote a subarray in SA for these suffixes with the same beginning character as a *bucket*, where the *head* and the *tail* of a bucket refer to the first and the last index of the bucket in SA respectively. Moreover, we define the first common character as its *bucket character*. For the same example SA $= [3, 0, 2, 1]$, the buckets are $\{\mathsf{SA}[0], \mathsf{SA}[1], \mathsf{SA}[2, 3]\}$ and the bucket characters are $0, 1, 2$, respectively. If the bucket character is $T[i]$, we refer to the bucket as bucket $T[i]$. The bucket head and tail of bucket 2 is 2 and 3, respectively. Note that S-suffixes always appear after the L-suffixes in any bucket, i.e., if an S-suffix and an L-suffix begin with the same character, the L-suffix is always smaller than the S-suffix.

Induced Sorting: The *induced sorting* technique, developed by Ko and Aluru [22], is responsible for many recent advances of suffix sorting algorithms [11,31, 33–35], and is also crucial to us. It can be used to induce the lexicographical order of L-suffixes from the sorted S-suffixes. Now, we briefly introduce the standard induced sorting technique which needs the *bucket array* and *type array* explicitly. The bucket array contains $|\Sigma|$ integers and each denotes the position of a bucket head/tail (depending on induced sorting the L-suffixes or S-suffixes) in SA. The type array contains n bits and each entry denotes an L/S-type information for T (i.e., 0 for L-type and 1 for S-type).

Inducing the Order of L-suffixes from the Sorted S-suffixes: Assume that all indices of the sorted S-suffixes are already in their correct positions in SA (i.e., in the tail of their corresponding buckets in SA). Now, we define some new notations (e.g., *LF/RF-entry*) to simplify the representation. We scan SA from left to right (i.e., from SA[0] to SA[$n - 1$]). We maintain an *LF-pointer* (leftmost free pointer) for each bucket which points to the leftmost free entry (called the *LF-entry*) of the bucket. The LF-pointers initially point to the head of their corresponding buckets. When we scan SA[i], let $j = \mathsf{SA}[i] - 1$. If $\mathsf{suf}(j)$ is an L-suffix (indicated by the type array), we place the index of $\mathsf{suf}(j)$ (i.e., j) into the LF-entry of bucket $T[j]$, and then let the LF-pointer of this bucket $T[j]$ point to the next free entry. The LF-pointers are maintained in the bucket array. If $\mathsf{suf}(j)$ is an S-suffix, we do nothing (since all suffixes are already sorted in the correct positions). We give a running example in our full version [24].

Sorting all S-suffixes from the sorted L-suffixes is completely symmetrical: we scan SA from right to left, maintaining an *RF-pointer* (rightmost free pointer) for each bucket which points to the *RF-entry* (rightmost free entry) of the bucket.

The idea of induced sorting is that the lexicographical order between $\mathsf{suf}(i)$ and $\mathsf{suf}(j)$ is decided by the order of $\mathsf{suf}(i+1)$ and $\mathsf{suf}(j+1)$ if $\mathsf{suf}(i)$ and $\mathsf{suf}(j)$ are in the same bucket (i.e., $T[i] = T[j]$). We only need to specify the correct order of these L-suffixes in the same buckets since we always place the L-suffixes in their corresponding buckets. Consider two L-suffixes $\mathsf{suf}(i)$ and $\mathsf{suf}(j)$ in the same bucket. We have $\mathsf{suf}(i+1) < \mathsf{suf}(i)$ and $\mathsf{suf}(j+1) < \mathsf{suf}(j)$ by the definition of L-suffix. Since we scan SA from left to right, $\mathsf{suf}(i+1)$ and $\mathsf{suf}(j+1)$ must appear earlier than $\mathsf{suf}(i)$ and $\mathsf{suf}(j)$. Hence the correctness of induced sorting is not hard to prove by induction.

Actually, Nong et al. [33] observed that one can sort all L-suffixes from the sorted LMS-suffixes (instead of S-suffixes). Roughly speaking, the idea is that in the induced sorting, only LMS-suffixes are useful for sorting L-suffixes. We also provide a running example in the full version [24]. They also showed that one can use the same induced sorting step to sort all LMS-substrings from the sorted LMS-characters of T.

Note that in this preliminary section, the induced sorting steps are not *in-place* since they require explicit storage for the bucket and type arrays.

3   Suffix Sorting for Read-Only Integer Alphabets

In this section, we provide an *interior counter trick* which can implicitly represent the dynamic LF/RF-entry information in SA. Besides, we provide a *pointer data structure* which can represent the bucket heads/tails in SA. Combining these two techniques, we can remove the workspace needed by the bucket array entirely. To address the issue of the hardest part (i.e. the top recursive level), we divide the sorting step into two stages. For removing the type array, we give some useful properties and observations between string T and SA to obtain the L/S-type information.

3.1   Framework

First, we define some notations. Let n_L and n_S denote the number of L-suffixes and S-suffixes, respectively. Let n_1 denote the length of the reduced problem T_1, i.e., n_1 equals to the number of LMS-suffixes (Case 1) or LML-suffixes (Case 2). Note that the number of LMS-characters, LMS-suffixes, and LMS-substrings are the same. Now, we describe the framework of our algorithm as follows:

1. If $n_L \leq n_S$ (i.e., the number of L-suffixes is no larger than that of S-suffixes), then:
   (1) (Sect. 3.2) Sort all LMS-characters of T.
       We use counting sort to sort all LMS-characters of T in $\mathsf{SA}[n-n_1 \ldots n-1]$. In the counting sort step, we use $\mathsf{SA}[0 \ldots n/2]$ as the temporary space (counting array). After this step, all indices of the sorted LMS-characters are stored in $\mathsf{SA}[n - n_1 \ldots n - 1]$.

(2) (Sect. 3.4) Induced sort all LMS-substrings from the sorted LMS-characters.

This induced-sorting step is the same as Step (4) below where we induced-sort all suffixes from the sorted LMS-suffixes. Thus, we only describe the details of this step in Sect. 3.4. After this step, all indices of the sorted LMS-substrings are stored in $SA[n - n_1 \ldots n - 1]$.

(3) (Sect. 3.3) Construct and solve the reduced problem T_1 from the sorted LMS-substrings.

We construct the reduced problem T_1 using the ranks of all sorted LMS-substrings which are stored in $SA[n - n_1 \ldots n - 1]$, where the ranks of LMS-substrings correspond to the lexicographical order of the sorted LMS-substrings. Then we get the reduced problem T_1 in $SA[0 \ldots n_1 - 1]$ and solve T_1 recursively to obtain the sorted LMS-suffixes. In the recursive step, we use $SA_1 = SA[n - n_1 \ldots n - 1]$ as the output space for T_1. After this step, all indices of the sorted LMS-suffixes are stored in $SA[n - n_1 \ldots n - 1]$.

(4) (Sect. 3.4) Induced sort all suffixes of T from the sorted LMS-suffixes (T_1).

We induced-sort all suffixes of T from the sorted LMS-suffixes which are stored in $SA[n - n_1 \ldots n - 1]$. Note that the in-place implementation of this induced sorting step is the main technical part of our optimal in-place algorithm. As we discussed before, we develop the interior counter trick and the pointer data structure, and then divide this sorting step into two stages to remove the workspace. After this step, all indices of the suffixes of T are sorted and stored in $SA[0 \ldots n - 1]$.

2. Otherwise, execute the above steps switching the role of LMS with LML.

Without loss of generality, we assume that $n_L \leq n_S$. Note that we compare the number of L-suffixes and S-suffix at the beginning since we need half of the space of SA to construct our pointer data structure for induced-sorting the L-suffixes (from the sorted LMS-suffixes) and S-suffixes (from the sorted L-suffixes) in Step (4). Note that the empty space is enough since the number of LMS-suffixes (i.e., n_1) and L-suffixes (i.e., n_L) both are less than or equal to $n/2$, where $n_1 \leq n/2$ since any two LMS-characters are not adjacent by the definition of LMS-characters, and $n_L \leq n/2$ since $n_L \leq n_S$. Note that for previous algorithms (e.g., [31,33]), they do not need the comparison at the beginning since they use the bucket array (which needs $|\Sigma|$ words workspace) in the induced sorting step (i.e. Step (4)). Here, we construct the pointer data structure and combine our interior counter trick to remove the bucket array.

Now, we describe the details of our in-place algorithm in the following sections.

3.2   Sort All LMS-Characters of T

In this section, we sort all LMS-characters of T and place their indices in $SA[n - n_1 \ldots n - 1]$. Recall that n_1 denotes the number of LMS-characters.

Now, we describe the details. Since $|\Sigma| = O(n)$, we can assume that $|\Sigma| \leq dn$ for some constant d. We divide the LMS-characters of T into $2d$ partitions and sort each partition one by one. The partition i contains the LMS-characters which belong to $\left[\frac{i|\Sigma|}{2d} + 1, \frac{(i+1)|\Sigma|}{2d}\right]$, for $0 \leq i < 2d$. We use m_i to denote the number of LMS-characters in partition i. Then for each partition i, we use the standard *counting sort* (see e.g., [7, Chap. 8]) to sort these m_i LMS-characters (the LMS-characters can be identified by scanning T once from right to left). Concretely, we use $\mathsf{SA}[0 \ldots n/2]$ as the temporary counting array, and use $\mathsf{SA}[n/2 + \sum_{j=0}^{i-1} m_j + 1 \ldots n/2 + \sum_{j=0}^{i} m_j]$ as the output array. After this counting sort step, the indices of these m_i sorted LMS-characters have been placed in $\mathsf{SA}[n/2 + \sum_{j=0}^{i-1} m_j + 1 \ldots n/2 + \sum_{j=0}^{i} m_j]$.

Note that we can use the counting sort step for each partition. Because the gap of each partition is $\frac{|\Sigma|}{2d} \leq \frac{dn}{2d} = \frac{n}{2}$, the space of $\mathsf{SA}[0 \ldots n/2]$ is enough for the temporary counting array (its size equals to the gap) of counting sort step. It is not hard to see that the sorting step takes $O(n)$ time and uses $O(1)$ workspace since we only make $2d$ times of counting sort steps (each step takes linear time).

After sorting all $2d$ partitions, all indices of the sorted LMS-characters are placed in $\mathsf{SA}[n/2 + 1, n/2 + \sum_{j=0}^{2d-1} m_j]$ (i.e., $\mathsf{SA}[n/2 + 1, n/2 + n_1]$). Then we move them to $\mathsf{SA}[n - n_1 \ldots n - 1]$, which can be easily done in linear time and $O(1)$ workspace.

3.3   Sort All LMS-Suffixes of T by Solving the Reduced Problem T_1

Construct the Reduced Problem T_1: We construct the reduced problem T_1 using the ranks of all sorted LMS-substrings which are stored in $\mathsf{SA}[n - n_1 \ldots n - 1]$ from the Step (2) (see the framework in Sect. 3.1), where the ranks of LMS-substrings are corresponding to the lexicographical order of the sorted LMS-substrings. Note that this construction step is not difficult and similar to the previous algorithms (e.g., [31,33]).

Now, we spell out the details for this step. Initially, all LMS-substrings are sorted in $\mathsf{SA}[n - n_1 \ldots n - 1]$. First, we let the rank of the smallest LMS-substring (i.e., the LMS-substring which begins from index $\mathsf{SA}[n - n_1]$) be 0 (it must be the sentinel). Then, we scan $\mathsf{SA}[n - n_1 + 1 \ldots n - 1]$ from left to right to compute the rank for each LMS-substring. When scanning $\mathsf{SA}[i]$, we compare the LMS-substring corresponding to $\mathsf{SA}[i]$ and that corresponding to $\mathsf{SA}[i - 1]$. If they are the same, $\mathsf{SA}[i]$ gets the same rank as $\mathsf{SA}[i - 1]$. Otherwise, the rank of $\mathsf{SA}[i]$ is the rank of $\mathsf{SA}[i - 1]$ plus 1. Since we have no extra space, we need to store the ranks in SA as well. In particular, the rank of $\mathsf{SA}[i]$ is stored in $\mathsf{SA}[\lfloor \frac{\mathsf{SA}[i]}{2} \rfloor]$. There is no conflict since any two LMS-characters are not adjacent. Finally, we shift nonempty entries in $\mathsf{SA}[0 \ldots n - n_1 - 1]$ to the head of SA, so that the ranks occupy a consecutive segment of the space. Now, we have obtained the reduced problem T_1 which is stored in $\mathsf{SA}[0 \ldots n_1 - 1]$. In other words, $\mathsf{SA}[i]$ ($i \in [0, n_1 - 1]$) stores the new name of the i-th LMS-substring with respect to its appearance in the input string T. An example of this step can be found in our full version [24].

Now, we have the following lemma.

Lemma 1. T_1 *can be constructed and stored in* $\mathsf{SA}[0\ldots n_1 - 1]$ *using* $O(n)$ *time and* $O(1)$ *workspace.*

The proof easily follows from the following observation, i.e., the whole comparison process takes $O(n)$ time because the total length of all LMS-substrings (each of them is identified by this observation) is less than $2n$.

Observation 1. *For any index* i *of* T, *let* $j \in [i+1, n-1]$ *be the smallest index such that* $T[j] < T[j+1]$ *(So* $T[j]$ *is S-type). Furthermore let* $k \in [i+1, j]$ *be the smallest index such that* $T[l] = T[j]$ *for any* $k \le l \le j$. *Then* $T[k]$ *is the first S-type character after index* i. *Moreover, all characters between* $T[i]$ *and* $T[k]$ *are L-type, and characters between* $T[k]$ *and* $T[j]$ *are S-type.*

Solve T_1 Recursively: Now, we sort all LMS-suffixes by solving T_1 recursively and place their indices in the tail of SA (i.e. $\mathsf{SA}[n - n_1 \ldots n - 1]$). This step is carried out as follows:

1. We first solve T_1 recursively. Recall that T_1 is stored in $\mathsf{SA}[0 \ldots n_1 - 1]$. We define SA_1 to be $\mathsf{SA}[n - n_1 \ldots n - 1]$ and use SA_1 to store the output of the subproblem T_1.
2. Now, we put all indices of LMS-suffixes in SA. First we move SA_1 to $\mathsf{SA}[0 \ldots n_1 - 1]$ (i.e., move $\mathsf{SA}[n - n_1 \ldots n - 1]$ to $\mathsf{SA}[0 \ldots n_1 - 1]$). Then we scan T from right to left. For every LMS-character $T[i]$, place i (i.e., index of $\mathsf{suf}(i)$) in the tail of SA.
3. For notational convenience, we define $\mathsf{LMS}[0 \ldots n_1] \triangleq \mathsf{SA}[n - n_1 \ldots n - 1]$. Now, we obtain the sorted order of all LMS-suffixes of the original string T by letting $\mathsf{SA}[i] = \mathsf{LMS}[\mathsf{SA}[i]]$ for all $i \in [0, n_1 - 1]$.
4. Finally, we finish this step by moving $\mathsf{SA}[0 \ldots n_1 - 1]$ to $\mathsf{SA}[n - n_1 \ldots n - 1]$. Now, all indices of the sorted LMS-suffixes are stored in $\mathsf{SA}[n - n_1 \ldots n - 1]$.

Lemma 2. *All LMS-suffixes can be sorted by solving the reduced problem* T_1 *recursively and placed in the tail of* SA *using* $O(n)$ *time and* $O(1)$ *workspace.*

Proof. The time and space used in this step are easy to verify.[4] We only show the correctness of this step. Each character of T_1 corresponds to an LMS-substring of T and this character is the rank of the corresponding sorted LMS-substring. Hence, the lexicographical order of LMS-suffixes of T is the same as the order of suffixes in T_1.

3.4   Induced-Sort All Suffixes of T from the Sorted LMS-Suffixes

In this section, we show how to *in-place* induced-sort all suffixes from the sorted LMS-suffixes which have been placed in $\mathsf{SA}[n - n_1 \ldots n - 1]$ from the previous step (see Lemma 2). Let $\mathsf{SA}_L = \mathsf{SA}[0 \ldots n_L - 1]$ and $\mathsf{SA}_S = \mathsf{SA}[n_L \ldots n - 1]$. Recall

---

[4] If one worries the $O(\log n)$ workspace in the recursion, one can use the highest bits in SA (i.e., n bits) to store them since the size of the reduced sub-problem is no larger than $n/2$.

that n_S and n_L denote the number of S-suffixes and L-suffixes, respectively. Also note that $n_L + n_S = n$. First, we sort all n_L L-suffixes from the sorted LMS-suffixes which are stored in $\mathsf{SA}[n - n_1 \ldots n - 1]$ and store the sorted L-suffixes in SA_L. Then, we sort all n_S S-suffixes from the sorted L-suffixes and store the sorted S-suffixes in SA_S. Note that sorting the L-suffixes from the sorted LMS-suffixes is totally symmetrical as sorting the S-suffixes from the sorted L-suffixes, as stated in Sect. 2. Thus, we only need to show the details of how to sort all n_S S-suffixes from the sorted L-suffixes which has already been stored in SA_L, and then store the sorted S-suffixes in SA_S.

We briefly recall the original (not in-place) induced sorting step here. We scan SA from right to left (i.e., from $\mathsf{SA}[n - 1]$ to $\mathsf{SA}[0]$). When we scan $\mathsf{SA}[i]$, let $j = \mathsf{SA}[i] - 1$. If $\mathsf{suf}(j)$ is an S-suffix (indicated by the type array), we place the index of $\mathsf{suf}(j)$ (i.e. j) into the RF-entry of bucket $T[j]$, and then let the RF-pointer of this bucket $T[j]$ point to the next free entry. If $T[j]$ is L-type, we do nothing (since all L-suffixes are already sorted). The RF-pointers are maintained by the bucket array.

Inducing the Order of S-suffixes from the Sorted L-suffixes: In order to obtain the in-place algorithm, we develop the interior counter trick and the pointer data structure to remove the workspace needed by the bucket array and type array in the induced sorting step. Briefly speaking, the purpose of the pointer data structure is to indicate the bucket tails of S-suffixes, and the purpose of the interior counter trick is to maintain the RF-pointers of the buckets dynamically. Thus, for a query of RF-entry for $\mathsf{suf}(j)$ in bucket $T[j]$, we know the tail of the bucket $T[j]$ from the pointer data structure in constant time (Lemma 6), then we use the interior counter trick to indicate the RF-entry in this bucket (Lemma 3). For removing the type array, we use the Lemma 4 to identify the L/S-suffixes in the induced sorting step.

Now, we describe the details step by step. First, we introduce our interior counter trick assuming that the tail of the bucket of any S-suffix is known (which is indicated by the Lemma 6).

Interior Counter Trick: Note that the buckets of the S-suffixes we discussed in this section are in $\mathsf{SA}_S = \mathsf{SA}[n_L \ldots n - 1]$, since we already have placed the sorted L-suffixes in $\mathsf{SA}_L = \mathsf{SA}[0 \ldots n_L - 1]$. Thus, we only need to sort all S-suffixes to their corresponding buckets in SA_S and the buckets only contains S-suffixes now.

Here we only describe the details of interior counter trick for one bucket since other buckets are the same. Recall that we assume that the tail of the bucket of any S-suffix is known (Lemma 6). Thus, to simplify the representation, we assume the bucket from index 0 to index $m - 1$ of SA_S, where m is the size of this bucket (i.e. the number of S-suffixes in this bucket is m). We only describe the case where $m > 3$ since other cases with $m \leq 3$ are similar and simpler. We define five special symbols B_H (head of the bucket), B_T (tail of the bucket), E (Empty), R_1 (one remaining S-suffix) and R_2 (two remaining S-suffixes)[5].

First, we use three special symbols to initialize this bucket, i.e., let $SA_S[0] = B_H$, $SA_S[m-2] = E$ and $SA_S[m-1] = B_T$. Let S_i denote the index of the i-th S-suffix which needs to be placed into the RF-entry of this bucket. Now, we describe how to place the indices of these m S-suffixes into the RF-entry of this bucket one by one. We distinguish the following four cases (To demonstrate these four cases more clearly, we also provide a demonstration in our full version [24].):

(1) If $SA_S[m-1] = B_T$, and $SA_S[m-2] = E$ or $SA_S[m - SA_S[m-2] - 3] \neq B_H$: In this case, we place the index of the current S-suffix (i.e., S_i) into the RF-entry of this bucket, where $1 \leq i \leq m-3$. Concretely, we know the position of the tail of this bucket in SA_S, i.e., $m-1$ according to the assumption. Then, we use $SA_S[m-2]$ as the counter to denote the number of the indices of S-suffixes has been placed so far. Note that the RF-entry of this bucket is pointed by this counter (i.e. RF-pointer). Thus, we can place the index of the current S-suffix (S_i) into the RF-entry of this bucket in constant time, and then update the counter $SA_S[m-2]$.

(2) If $SA_S[m-1] = B_T$ and $SA_S[m - SA_S[m-2] - 3] = B_H$: In this case, we place the index of the third to last S-suffix (i.e. S_{m-2}) into the RF-entry of this bucket. Concretely, we shift the previous $m-3$ S-suffixes which stored in $SA_S[1, \ldots, m-3]$ to $SA_S[2, \ldots, m-2]$. Then, we place S_{m-2} into $SA_S[1]$ and let $SA_S[m-1] = R_2$. This step takes $O(m)$ time since we shift $m-3$ S-suffixes.

(3) If $SA_S[m-1] = R_2$: In this case, we place the index of the second to last S-suffix (i.e. S_{m-1}) into the RF-entry of this bucket. We shift the previous $m-2$ S-suffixes which stored in $SA_S[1, \ldots, m-2]$ to $SA_S[2, \ldots, m-1]$. Then, we place S_{m-1} into $SA_S[1]$ and let $SA_S[0] = R_1$. This step takes $O(m)$ time since we shift $m-2$ S-suffixes.

(4) Otherwise: In this case, we place the index of the last S-suffix (i.e. S_m) into the RF-entry of this bucket. First, we know the tail of the bucket indicated by our pointer data structure in constant time. Then, we search the entries before the tail one by one until that we find the special symbol R_1. We let this entry to be S_m. This step takes $O(m)$ time since we search $m-1$ S-suffixes.

Note that this step uses $O(1)$ workspace since there is no bucket array and type array, and the space needed by our interior counter trick and pointer data structure is in SA_S. The purpose of the interior counter trick is to dynamic maintain the RF-pointers of the buckets. E.g., for a query of RF-entry for $\mathsf{suf}(j)$ in bucket $T[j]$, first we know the tail of the bucket $T[j]$ by the assumption, then

---

[5] We use at most five special symbols in this paper. The special symbol is only used to simplify the argument and we do not have to impose any additional assumption to accommodate these symbols (including the read-only general alphabets case). These special symbols can be handled using an extra $O(1)$ workspace. The details can be found in our full version [24].

we use the interior counter trick to indicate the RF-entry in this bucket. We have the following lemma.

Lemma 3. *If the tail of the bucket of any S-suffix is known, one can sort the S-suffixes from the sorted L-suffixes using the induced sorting step with the interior counter trick in linear time and $O(1)$ workspace.*

Note that in the induced sorting step, one uses the type array to identify whether the suf(j) is S-suffix or not. For removing the type array, we use the following Lemma 4 to identify the type of the L- or S-suffix in the induced-sorting step. Note that it is not hard to decide whether all S-suffixes in the current scanning bucket $T[\mathsf{SA}[i]]$ are already sorted or not by using an extra variable (reused for all buckets).

Lemma 4. *If $T[j] \neq T[\mathsf{SA}[i]]$, the type of suf($j$) can be obtained immediately, where $j = \mathsf{SA}[i] - 1$. Otherwise $T[j] = T[\mathsf{SA}[i]]$ (this case suf(j) belongs to the current scanning bucket $T[\mathsf{SA}[i]]$), if all S-suffixes of T that belong to bucket $T[\mathsf{SA}[i]]$ are not already sorted, then the suf(j) is S-suffix.*

Get the Tails of the Buckets: Now, there is only one thing left: how to know the tails of the bucket of S-suffixes in the induced sorting step (this is the only assumption we used above). The purpose of the pointer data structure is to indicate the tails of the bucket of S-suffixes. However, the pointer data structure requires c_p words, where the value of c_p will be specified later. Thus, we need to divide this induced-sorting step into two stages. The first stage is to sort the first $n_S - c_p$ S-suffixes (i.e. the largest $n_S - c_p$ S-suffixes), where our pointer data structure exists. The second stage is to sort the last c_p S-suffixes, where there is no space for the pointer data structure.

The First Stage: Now, we construct our pointer data structure which supports to find the tails of the buckets in constant time. We store the pointer data structure in the tail of SA_S, recall that $\mathsf{SA}_S = \mathsf{SA}[n_L, \ldots, n-1]$. Now, we describe the details. We divide the S-suffixes of T into $4d$ parts according to their first characters, and construct the pointer data structure for each part respectively. The $4d$ parts are divided by $T[j] \in \left[\frac{i|\Sigma|}{4d} + 1, \frac{(i+1)|\Sigma|}{4d} \right]$, for $0 \leq i < 4d$. Let D_i denote the pointer data structure of the i-th part. We only show the details how we construct the pointer data structure D_0 as follows, since constructing D_i is similar for $0 < i < 4d$ (i.e., shift $T[j]$ with $\frac{i|\Sigma|}{4d}$).

(1) First, we let $\mathsf{SA}_S[i] = 1$ for all $i \in [1, \frac{|\Sigma|}{4d}]$. Then we scan T from right to left. For every S-type $T[i] \in [1, \frac{|\Sigma|}{4d}]$, we increase $\mathsf{SA}_S[T[i]]$ by one.

(2) Then we scan $\mathsf{SA}_S[1 \ldots \frac{|\Sigma|}{4d}]$ from left to right. We use a variable *sum* to count the sum, first initialize *sum* $= -1$. For each $\mathsf{SA}_S[i]$ which is being scanned, first let *sum* $=$ *sum* $+ \mathsf{SA}_S[i]$, then let $\mathsf{SA}_S[i] =$ *sum*. Now, for any S-suffix suf(i) satisfying $T[i] \in [1, \frac{|\Sigma|}{4d}]$, $\mathsf{SA}_S[T[i]] - T[i]$ must indicate the tail of bucket $T[i]$ in SA_S. Since we want every entry in $\mathsf{SA}_S[1 \ldots \frac{|\Sigma|}{4d}]$ to be

distinct, we initialize $\mathsf{SA}_S[i] = 1$ for all $i \in [1, \frac{|\Sigma|}{4d}]$ in Step (1). Hence the tail of bucket $T[i]$ is $\mathsf{SA}_S[T[i]] - T[i]$.

(3) Finally, we construct D_0 for $\mathsf{SA}_S[1 \dots \frac{|\Sigma|}{4d}]$ according to Lemma 5. D_0 uses at most $c(n + \frac{|\Sigma|}{4d})/\log n$ words space. We store D_0 in the tail of SA_S (i.e., $\mathsf{SA}_S[n_S - c(n + \frac{|\Sigma|}{4d})/\log n \dots n_S - 1]$). D_0 supports to find the tail of the bucket of any S-suffix $\mathsf{suf}(i)$ satisfying $T[i] \in [1, \frac{|\Sigma|}{4d}]$ in constant time.

Lemma 5. *For any m distinct integers $0 \leq a_0 < a_1 \dots < a_{m-1} \leq n$, where $m \leq n$ and $n > 1024$, one can construct a data structure using linear time (i.e., $O(n)$ time) and at most $cn/\log n$ words, where $1 < c < 2$, such that each query to the i-th smallest integer a_i (select(i)) can be answered in constant time.*

The Lemma 5 is proved by using the classical select query in a bitmap (see e.g., [6,17,30]). The proof can be found in our full version [24]. After this step, the pointer data structure (i.e. D_i for all $0 \leq i < 4d$) is stored in $\mathsf{SA}_S[n_S - c_p \dots n_S - 1]$, where $c_p = \lceil 4d \cdot (c(n + \frac{|\Sigma|}{4d})/\log n) \rceil \leq \lceil 5dcn/\log n \rceil$. Now, we have the following lemma.

Lemma 6. *We can construct the pointer data structure in linear time, and this pointer data structure uses at most c_p words and can support to find the bucket tail of any S-suffix in constant time.*

Now according to Lemmas 3, 4 and 6, we can sort the first largest $n_S - c_p$ S-suffixes from the sorted L-suffixes which stored in SA_L using the induced sorting step.

The Second Stage: Now, we describe the details to sort the last c_p S-suffixes which is occupied by our pointer data structure. First, we move the sorted largest $n_S - c_p$ S-suffixes to the tail of SA_S, i.e., $\mathsf{SA}_S[c_p, n_S - 1]$. Then we scan the T from right to left to place the smallest c_p S-suffixes into $\mathsf{SA}_S[0, c_p - 1]$. Now, we use merge sort with the in-place linear time merging algorithm [37] to sort these c_p S-suffixes, the sorting key for each S-suffix is its beginning character. After this sorting step, these c_p S-suffixes have been placed in their corresponding buckets in $\mathsf{SA}_S[0, c_p - 1]$. Note that we can use the same sorting step (which we used for sorting the first $n_S - c_p$ S-suffixes) to sort the last c_p S-suffixes without the pointer data structure.

The key point is that we can use the binary search (instead of the pointer data structure) to find the tails of the bucket for these c_p S-suffixes, since $c_p \leq \lceil 5dcn/\log n \rceil$ is small enough (i.e. $c_p \log n = O(n)$) to maintain that the time complexity of our algorithm is $O(n)$. Using the binary search to extend interior counter trick is not very difficult, one can find the details in our full version [24] where we induced sort all L-suffixes from the sorted S-suffixes for the read-only general alphabets.

After the second stage, all n_S S-suffixes are sorted in SA_S. Now we have all sorted L-suffixes in SA_L (i.e., $\mathsf{SA}[0 \dots n_L - 1]$) and all sorted S-suffixes in SA_S (i.e., $\mathsf{SA}[n_L \dots n - 1]$). Then, we use the stable, in-place, linear time merging algorithm [37] to merge the ordered SA_L and SA_S (the merging key for $\mathsf{SA}[i]$ is

$T[\mathsf{SA}[i]]$, i.e., the first character of $\mathsf{suf}(\mathsf{SA}[i])$). After this merging step, all suffixes of T have be sorted in $\mathsf{SA}[0 \ldots n-1]$.

Theorem 3 (Main Theorem). *Our Algorithm takes $O(n)$ time and $O(1)$ workspace to compute the suffix array of string T over integer alphabets Σ, where T is read-only and $|\Sigma| = O(n)$.*

4 Conclusion

In this paper, we present the optimal in-place algorithms for suffix sorting over (read-only) integer alphabets and read-only general alphabets. All of them are optimal both in time and space. Concretely, we provide the first optimal linear time in-place suffix sorting algorithm for (read-only) integer alphabets. Our algorithms solve the open problem posed by Franceschini and Muthukrishnan in ICALP 2007 [11]. For the read-only general alphabets (the details of this part can be found in our full version [24]), we provide simple sorting steps to obtain an optimal in-place $O(n \log n)$ time suffix sorting algorithm, which recovers the result obtained by Franceschini and Muthukrishnan [11] which was an open problem posed by Manzini and Ferragina [28].

Acknowledgments. This research is supported in part by the National Basic Research Program of China Grant 2015CB358700, the National Natural Science Foundation of China Grant 61772297, 61632016, 61761146003, and a grant from Microsoft Research Asia. The authors would like to thank Ge Nong for his help in our experiments, and Gonzalo Navarro for helpful suggestions.

References

1. Abouelhoda, M.I., Kurtz, S., Ohlebusch, E.: The enhanced suffix array and its applications to genome analysis. In: Guigó, R., Gusfield, D. (eds.) WABI 2002. LNCS, vol. 2452, pp. 449–463. Springer, Heidelberg (2002). https://doi.org/10.1007/3-540-45784-4_35
2. Abouelhoda, M.I., Kurtz, S., Ohlebusch, E.: Replacing suffix trees with enhanced suffix arrays. J. Discret. Algorithms **2**(1), 53–86 (2004)
3. Baron, D., Bresler, Y.: Antisequential suffix sorting for bwt-based data compression. IEEE Trans. Comput. **54**(4), 385–397 (2005)
4. Burkhardt, S., Kärkkäinen, J.: Fast lightweight suffix array construction and checking. In: Baeza-Yates, R., Chávez, E., Crochemore, M. (eds.) CPM 2003. LNCS, vol. 2676, pp. 55–69. Springer, Heidelberg (2003). https://doi.org/10.1007/3-540-44888-8_5
5. Burrows, M., Wheeler, D.J.: A block-sorting lossless data compression algorithm. Technical report 124 (1994)
6. Clark, D.: Compact pat trees. Ph.D. thesis, University of Waterloo (1996)
7. Cormen, T.H., Leiserson, C.E., Rivest, R.L., Stein, C.: Introduction to Algorithms. MIT Press, Cambridge (2001)
8. Dhaliwal, J., Puglisi, S.J., Turpin, A.: Trends in suffix sorting: a survey of low memory algorithms. In: Proceedings of the Thirty-fifth Australasian Computer Science Conference, vol. 122, pp. 91–98. Australian Computer Society, Inc. (2012)

9. Farach, M.: Optimal suffix tree construction with large alphabets. In: Proceedings of the 38th Annual Symposium on Foundations of Computer Science (FOCS), pp. 137–143. IEEE (1997)
10. Ferragina, P., Manzini, G.: Opportunistic data structures with applications. In: Proceedings of the 41st Annual Symposium on Foundations of Computer Science (FOCS), pp. 390–398. IEEE (2000)
11. Franceschini, G., Muthukrishnan, S.: In-place suffix sorting. In: Arge, L., Cachin, C., Jurdziński, T., Tarlecki, A. (eds.) ICALP 2007. LNCS, vol. 4596, pp. 533–545. Springer, Heidelberg (2007). https://doi.org/10.1007/978-3-540-73420-8_47
12. Grossi, R., Vitter, J.S.: Compressed suffix arrays and suffix trees with applications to text indexing and string matching. SIAM J. Comput. 35(2), 378–407 (2005)
13. Hon, W.K., Sadakane, K., Sung, W.K.: Breaking a time-and-space barrier in constructing full-text indices. In: Proceedings of the 44th Annual Symposium on Foundations of Computer Science (FOCS), pp. 251–260. IEEE (2003)
14. Huo, H., Chen, L., Vitter, J.S., Nekrich, Y.: A practical implementation of compressed suffix arrays with applications to self-indexing. In: Data Compression Conference (DCC), pp. 292–301. IEEE (2014)
15. Huo, H., et al.: CS2A: a compressed suffix array-based method for short read alignment. In: Data Compression Conference (DCC), pp. 271–278. IEEE (2016)
16. Itoh, H., Tanaka, H.: An efficient method for in memory construction of suffix arrays. In: String Processing and Information Retrieval Symposium, 1999 and International Workshop on Groupware, pp. 81–88. IEEE (1999)
17. Jacobson, G.: Space-efficient static trees and graphs. In: Proceedings of the 30th Annual Symposium on Foundations of Computer Science (FOCS), pp. 549–554. IEEE (1989)
18. Kärkkäinen, J., Sanders, P.: Simple linear work suffix array construction. In: Baeten, J.C.M., Lenstra, J.K., Parrow, J., Woeginger, G.J. (eds.) ICALP 2003. LNCS, vol. 2719, pp. 943–955. Springer, Heidelberg (2003). https://doi.org/10.1007/3-540-45061-0_73
19. Kärkkäinen, J., Sanders, P., Burkhardt, S.: Linear work suffix array construction. J. ACM (JACM) 53(6), 918–936 (2006)
20. Kim, D.K., Jo, J., Park, H.: A fast algorithm for constructing suffix arrays for fixed-size alphabets. In: Ribeiro, C.C., Martins, S.L. (eds.) WEA 2004. LNCS, vol. 3059, pp. 301–314. Springer, Heidelberg (2004). https://doi.org/10.1007/978-3-540-24838-5_23
21. Kim, D.K., Sim, J.S., Park, H., Park, K.: Linear-time construction of suffix arrays. In: Baeza-Yates, R., Chávez, E., Crochemore, M. (eds.) CPM 2003. LNCS, vol. 2676, pp. 186–199. Springer, Heidelberg (2003). https://doi.org/10.1007/3-540-44888-8_14
22. Ko, P., Aluru, S.: Space efficient linear time construction of suffix arrays. In: Baeza-Yates, R., Chávez, E., Crochemore, M. (eds.) CPM 2003. LNCS, vol. 2676, pp. 200–210. Springer, Heidelberg (2003). https://doi.org/10.1007/3-540-44888-8_15
23. Larsson, N.J., Sadakane, K.: Faster suffix sorting. Theor. Comput. Sci. 387(3), 258–272 (2007)
24. Li, Z., Li, J., Huo, H.: Optimal in-place suffix sorting. arXiv preprint arXiv:1610.08305 (2016)
25. Manber, U., Myers, G.: Suffix arrays: a new method for on-line string searches. In: Proceedings of the First Annual ACM-SIAM Symposium on Discrete Algorithms (SODA), pp. 319–327. Society for Industrial and Applied Mathematics (1990)

26. Maniscalco, M.A., Puglisi, S.J.: Faster lightweight suffix array construction. In: Proceedings of International Workshop On Combinatorial Algorithms (IWOCA), pp. 16–29. Citeseer (2006)
27. Maniscalco, M.A., Puglisi, S.J.: An efficient, versatile approach to suffix sorting. J. Exp. Algorithmics (JEA) **12**, 1–2 (2008)
28. Manzini, G., Ferragina, P.: Engineering a lightweight suffix array construction algorithm. In: Möhring, R., Raman, R. (eds.) ESA 2002. LNCS, vol. 2461, pp. 698–710. Springer, Heidelberg (2002). https://doi.org/10.1007/3-540-45749-6_61
29. McCreight, E.M.: A space-economical suffix tree construction algorithm. J. ACM (JACM) **23**(2), 262–272 (1976)
30. Navarro, G., Providel, E.: Fast, small, simple rank/select on bitmaps. In: Klasing, R. (ed.) SEA 2012. LNCS, vol. 7276, pp. 295–306. Springer, Heidelberg (2012). https://doi.org/10.1007/978-3-642-30850-5_26
31. Nong, G.: Practical linear-time O (1)-workspace suffix sorting for constant alphabets. ACM Trans. Inf. Syst. (TOIS) **31**(3), 15 (2013)
32. Nong, G., Zhang, S.: Optimal lightweight construction of suffix arrays for constant alphabets. In: Dehne, F., Sack, J.-R., Zeh, N. (eds.) WADS 2007. LNCS, vol. 4619, pp. 613–624. Springer, Heidelberg (2007). https://doi.org/10.1007/978-3-540-73951-7_53
33. Nong, G., Zhang, S., Chan, W.H.: Linear suffix array construction by almost pure induced-sorting. In: Data Compression Conference (DCC), pp. 193–202. IEEE (2009)
34. Nong, G., Zhang, S., Chan, W.H.: Two efficient algorithms for linear time suffix array construction. IEEE Trans. Comput. **60**(10), 1471–1484 (2011)
35. Puglisi, S.J., Smyth, W.F., Turpin, A.H.: A taxonomy of suffix array construction algorithms. ACM Comput. Surv. (CSUR) **39**(2), 4 (2007)
36. Sadakane, K.: A fast algorithm for making suffix arrays and for burrows-wheeler transformation. In: Data Compression Conference (DCC), pp. 129–138. IEEE (1998)
37. Salowe, J., Steiger, W.: Simplified stable merging tasks. J. Algorithms **8**(4), 557–571 (1987)
38. Schürmann, K.B., Stoye, J.: An incomplex algorithm for fast suffix array construction. Softw.: Pract. Exp. **37**(3), 309–329 (2007)
39. Ziv, J., Lempel, A.: Compression of individual sequences via variable-rate coding. IEEE Trans. Inf. Theory **24**(5), 530–536 (1978)

Computing Burrows-Wheeler Similarity Distributions for String Collections

Felipe A. Louza[1]($\boxtimes$)(iD), Guilherme P. Telles[2], Simon Gog[3], and Liang Zhao[1]

[1] Department of Computing and Mathematics, University of São Paulo,
Ribeirão Preto, Brazil
{louza,zhao}@usp.br
[2] Instituto de Computação, Universidade Estadual de Campinas, Campinas, Brazil
gpt@ic.unicamp.br
[3] ebay Inc., San Jose, USA
sgog@ebay.com

Abstract. In this article we present practical and theoretical improvements to the computation of the Burrows-Wheeler similarity distribution for all pairs of strings in a collection. Our algorithms take advantage of the Burrows-Wheeler transform (BWT) computed for the concatenation of all strings, instead of the pairwise construction of BWTs performed by the straightforward approach, and use compressed data structures that allow reductions of running time while still keeping a small memory footprint, as shown by a set of experiments with real datasets.

Keywords: Burrows-wheeler transform · String similarity
String collections

1 Introduction

Computing similarities among strings is an important task in computational biology and information retrieval [1,16]. Many measures of similarity exist for strings. In particular, measures based on the Burrows-Wheeler transform (BWT) [2,11] are interesting because they may be computed faster than measures based on alignments or block-edit distances while still capturing the notion of similarity between strings.

Mantaci *et al.* [9] introduced an extension of the BWT for string collections, called eBWT, and defined a class of similarity measures [10], which takes into account how much the symbols of two strings S_1 and S_2 are shuffled in their eBWT. The key idea is that the more the symbols are intermixed by the transformation, the greater the number of shared substrings, and as consequence, the more similar S_1 and S_2 are.

Yang *et al.* [21] recrafted the method by Mantaci *et al.* and introduced the Burrows-Wheeler similarity distribution (BWSD) of two strings S_1 and S_2 based on the BWT of their concatenation. The authors evaluated similarity measures

© Springer Nature Switzerland AG 2018
T. Gagie et al. (Eds.): SPIRE 2018, LNCS 11147, pp. 285–296, 2018.
https://doi.org/10.1007/978-3-030-00479-8_23

based on the expectation and entropy of the BWSD to efficiently construct phylogenetic trees for DNA and protein sequences.

In this article we present two new algorithms to compute the BWSD-based distances among all pairs of strings in a collection. Our algorithms compute the BWT for the concatenation of all strings only once, instead of the straightforward pairwise construction of BWTs performed by Yang [21], and use compressed data structures that allow reductions of running time while still keeping a small memory footprint, as shown by a set of experiments with real datasets.

The algorithms introduced here contribute to the solution of phylogenetic tree reconstruction, where a matrix with all pairs of distances is computed and given as input for algorithms like UPGMA and Neighbor-Joining, extensively used in the literature [16]. Improved practical algorithms to evaluate pairwise distances among strings are useful because biological datasets are getting larger over time, both in the number and in the length of sequences. Growing datasets are also a reality for non-biological textual documents, like web-pages, books and other manuscripts, that may also be related by phylogenies to enable visual exploration by content similarity [19].

2   Background

2.1   Notation

Let $S[1, n]$ be a string of length $|S| = n$ over an ordered alphabet Σ of size σ. The i-th symbol of S is denoted by $S[i]$, with $1 \leq i \leq n$. The substring $S[i] \ldots S[j]$ is denoted by $S[i, j]$, for $1 \leq i \leq j \leq n$. $S[i, n]$ is the suffix of S that starts at position i. We assume that $S[n] = \$$ is a terminator symbol which is not present elsewhere in S and precedes every other symbol in Σ. Juxtaposition is the concatenation operator of strings or symbols.

The *suffix array* (SA) [5,8] of a string $S[1, n]$ is an array of integers in the range $[1, n]$ that gives the lexicographic order of all suffixes of S, such that $S[SA[1], n] < S[SA[2], n] < \ldots < S[SA[n], n]$. The suffix array may be constructed in $O(n)$ time [15,20].

The *Burrows-Wheeler transform* (BWT) [2] of a string S is a reversible transformation that tends to group identical symbols in runs. The BWT may be defined in terms of the suffix array, such that

$$\text{BWT}[i] = S[SA[i] - 1] \text{ if } SA[i] \neq 1 \text{ or } \text{BWT}[i] = \$ \text{ otherwise.} \quad (1)$$

We define the context i of the BWT as the prefix of the i-th sorted suffix up to and including the terminal symbol $\$$. The BWT can be obtained from the text and its SA or can be computed directly, without computing SA, in linear time [18]. Figure 1(a) and (b) show the BWTs and the contexts for $S_1 = $ banana$\$$ and $S_2 = $ anaba$\$$.

Let $\mathcal{S} = S_1, S_2, \ldots, S_d$ be a collection of d strings over Σ of lengths $n_1, n_2, \ldots, n_d$, such that $N = \sum_{i=1}^{d} n_i$. The suffix array for collection $\mathcal{S}$ can be obtained by computing the SA of the concatenated string $S = S_1 S_2 \ldots S_d$,

(a)

i	BWT	context
1	a	$
2	n	a$
3	n	ana$
4	b	anana$
5	$	banana$
6	a	na$
7	a	nana$

(b)

i	BWT	context
1	a	$
2	b	a$
3	n	aba$
4	$	anaba$
5	a	ba$
6	a	naba$

(c)

i	DA	BWT	context
1	1	a	$_1
2	2	a	$_2
3	1	n	a$_1
4	2	b	a$_2
5	2	n	aba$_2
6	1	n	ana$_1
7	2	$_1	anaba$_2
8	1	b	anana$_1
9	2	a	ba$_2
10	1	$_2	banana$_1
11	1	a	na$_1
12	2	a	naba$_2
13	1	a	nana$_1

Fig. 1. BWTs for $S_1 = $ banana$, $S_2 = $ anaba$ and $S = S_1 S_2 = $ banana$_1$anaba$_2$.

such that each terminal symbol is replaced by a symbol $\$_i$, with $\$_i < \$_j$ iff $i < j$. The BWT for collection S can be also obtained by the SA of the concatenated string as in Eq. 1.

The suffix array of $S[1, N]$ is commonly accompanied by the *document array* (DA), where DA$[i]$ stores the index of the string which context SA$[i]$ came from. Figure 1(c) shows the BWT, the document array and the contexts for $S = S_1 S_2 = $ banana$_1$anaba$_2$.

The suffix array for S may be constructed in $O(N)$ time on the concatenated string without replacing the terminators by distinct symbols while still preserving the order among equal contexts [7], thus avoiding increasing the alphabet size. DA can also be computed in $O(N)$ time together with the suffix array of $S[1, N]$ [7].

A *rank query* on a bitvector $B[1, n]$, denoted by rank$_1(B, i)$, returns the number of occurrences of bit 1 in $B[1, i]$. A *select query* on a bitvector $B[1, n]$, denoted by select$_1(B, i)$, returns the position of the i-th occurrence of bit 1 in $B[1, n]$. B can be preprocessed in $O(n)$ time so that rank/select queries are supported in $O(1)$ time using $o(n)$ bits of additional space [12].

A *wavelet tree* [6] for an array $A[1, n]$ with σ distinct symbols supports rank/select queries in $O(\lg \sigma)$ time. The wavelet tree uses $n \lg \sigma + o(n \lg \sigma)$ bits of space and can be built in $O(n \lceil \frac{\lg \sigma}{\sqrt{\lg n}} \rceil)$ time [13].

A *range minimum query* (rmq) on an array $A[1, n]$ returns the smallest value in a given interval of A, that is, rmq$(i, j) = \min_{i < k \leq j}\{A[k]\}$, for $1 \leq i < j \leq n$, whereas a *range maximum query* (RMQ) returns the largest value in a given interval. The rmq and RMQ operations may be solved in constant time with a linear time preprocessing [3].

2.2   Burrows-Wheeler Similarity Distribution

The *Burrows-Wheeler similarity distribution* (BWSD) of a pair of sequences is constructed as follows. Given the BWT of $S = S_1S_2$, we create a bitvector $\alpha_{1,2}$ of size $n_1 + n_2$ such that $\alpha_{1,2}[i] = 0$ if BWT$[i] = \$_2$ or BWT$[i]$ is a symbol from string S_1 and BWT$[i] \neq \$_1$, and $\alpha_{1,2}[i] = 1$ otherwise. In other words, $\alpha_{x,y}[i] = 0$ if DA$[i] = x$, that is, the i-th context came from string S_x, and $\alpha_{x,y}[i] = 1$ if DA$[i] = y$.

The bitvector $\alpha_{1,2}$ may be represented as a sequence of runs in the form $r = 0^{k_1}1^{k_2}0^{k_3}1^{k_4}\ldots0^{k_m}1^{k_{m+1}}$, where i^{k_j} indicates that i repeats k_j times and such that only k_1 and k_{m+1} may be zero. Note that $|r| = m + 1$ is at most $2 \times (\min(n_1, n_2) + 1)$. Let t_{k_j} be the number of occurrences of 0^{k_j} and 1^{k_j} in r. The largest possible value for k_j is $k_{\max} = \max(n_1, n_2)$. Let $s = t_1 + t_2 + \ldots + t_{k_j} + \ldots + t_{k_{\max}}$.

Definition 1. BWSD(S_1, S_2) is the probability mass function $P\{k_j = k\} = t_k/s$ for $k = 1, 2, \ldots, k_{\max}$.

For example, given strings $S_1 = $ banana$\$_1$ and $S_2 = $ anaba$\$_2$ we have

$$\text{BWT}(S_1S_2) = \text{aanbnn}\$_1\text{ba}\$_2\text{aaa}$$

$$\alpha_{1,2} = \{0, 1, 0, 1, 1, 0, 1, 0, 1, 0, 0, 1, 0\}$$

$$r = 0^11^10^11^20^11^10^11^10^21^10^11^0$$

Therefore, $t_1 = 9$, $t_2 = 2$ and $s = 11$. The BWSD(S_1, S_2) is

$$P\{k_j = 1\} = 9/11, P\{k_j = 2\} = 2/11.$$

Yang *et al.* [21] defined the following distances between S_1 and S_2.

Definition 2. $D_M(S_1, S_2) = E(k_j) - 1$, *where* $E(k_j)$ *is the expectation of* BWSD(S_1, S_2).

Definition 3. $D_E(S_1, S_2) = -\sum_{k \geq 1, t_k \neq 0}(t_k/s)\log_2(t_k/s)$ *is the Shannon entropy of* BWSD(S_1, S_2).

Note that if $S_1 = S_2$, then the BWSD is $P\{k_j = 1\} = \frac{n_1 + n_2}{n_1 + n_2} = 1$ and $D_M(S_1, S_2) = D_E(S_1, S_2) = 0$. Also, since $\alpha_{1,2}$ is equal to the complement of $\alpha_{2,1}$, then both have the same distribution and $D_E(S_1, S_2) = D_E(S_2, S_1)$ and $D_M(S_1, S_2) = D_M(S_2, S_1)$ for any two strings.

BWSD(S_1, S_2) can be computed straightforward by first building the BWT of S_1S_2 and $\alpha_{1,2}$ and then obtaining $t_1, t_2, \ldots, t_{k_{\max}}$ and s. The BWT and $\alpha_{1,2}$ may be constructed in linear time [7] and computing t_{k_j} also takes linear time. Then computing BWSD(S_1, S_2) takes $O(n_1 + n_2)$ time. D_M and D_E can be computed in $O(\max(n_1, n_2))$ time.

Therefore, given a collection of d strings of total length $N = n_1 + n_2 + \cdots + n_d$, computing all pairs of distances will take $\sum_{i=1}^{d}\sum_{j>i}^{d}O(n_i + n_j) = O(dN)$ time.

3 Algorithm 1

Given a collection of strings $S = \{S_1, S_2 \ldots, S_d\}$ as input, Algorithm 1 outputs a strictly upper triangular matrix M, where each entry $M(i, j)$ is either $D_M(S_i, S_j)$ or $D_E(S_i, S_j)$.

Algorithm 1 concatenates all strings into $S = S_1 S_2 \ldots S_d$. Then it computes the BWT and the document array of S. In the sequel, the algorithm builds d bitvectors B_i, $|B_i| = N$, where $B_i[j] = 1$ if $DA[j] = i$ or $B_i[j] = 0$ otherwise, and builds an $O(1)$ rank/select structure over each B_i. The algorithm then proceeds line by line on the matrix. To evaluate the distances among S_i and $S_{j>i}$, the algorithm selects the intervals over DA that contain consecutive occurrences of i. For each interval the algorithm counts the k_j occurrences of j, which corresponds to the existence of the run 1^{k_j} in the sequence of runs for S_i and S_j. The runs 0^{ℓ_j+1} are computed when ℓ_j consecutive intervals do not contain any occurrence of j.

The pseudocode for the algorithm is shown in Fig. 1. At each step $i = 1, \ldots, d$, it computes the distances in line i of M as follows. Initially, q_s is set to 1. For $p = 1, \ldots, n_i$, the algorithm sets q_e such that $DA[q_e]$ corresponds to the p-th value equal to i in $DA[1, N]$. Then, for each $j \in [i+1, d]$, it counts the number of j's in the interval $DA[q_s, q_e]$ by computing $\text{rank}_1(B_j, q_e) - \text{rank}_1(B_j, q_s)$ and stores it in k_j. If $k_j > 0$ it means that the run $0^{\ell_j} 1^{k_j}$ occurs in $r_{i,j}$, thus $t^j_{k_j}$ and $t^j_{\ell_j}$ are increased by 1 and ℓ_j gets 1 for the next iteration. Otherwise, if $k_j = 0$, it means that the block $0^{\ell_j} 1^0 0^1$ in $r_{i,j}$ can be collapsed into 0^{ℓ_j+1}. To this end, ℓ_j must be increased by one. In a next iteration, when $k_j > 0$, counter $t^j_{\ell_j}$ is increased by one. At the end of the iteration, q_s receives q_e.

The document array will enable selecting up to the last symbol of S_i but there can be symbols from S_j, $j > i$, to the right of such position. Then, lines 22-29 will deal with the last blocks of 0s and 1s accordingly and invoke the computation of the distance measure from t^j.

We remark that the second rank operation (lines 10 and 23) can be avoided by storing the result of the first rank of the previous iteration. Also, another practical improvement can be achieved by storing, in an auxiliary array, for each position $DA[i] = j$ the position of next value equal to j in DA, such that, in the for loop of line 9, if the next position j in DA is greater than q_e, we can avoid two rank operations and go to line 17 (in this case $k_j = 0$).

3.1 Theoretical Costs

The BWT and DA construction for the concatenated string S can be done in $O(N)$ time [7]. The construction of all bitvectors B_i with rank/select support takes $O(dN)$ time. For each string S_i the algorithm performs n_i select operations (line 8), each one in $O(1)$ time, and performs $(n_i + 1)d$ rank operations (lines 10 and 23), each one in $O(1)$ time. The cost to compute each distance (line 28) is $O(n_i + n_j)$. Therefore, the total running time is $O(dN)$ time. The space used by the algorithm is $N \lg \sigma$ bits for S, $N \lg \sigma$ bits for the BWT, $N \lg d$ bits for DA and $dN + o(dN)$ bits for the bitvectors.

Algorithm 1. Compute Distances

Data: $S = \{S_1, S_2, \ldots, S_d\}$, $|S_i| = n_i$
Result: result matrix M
1 Build BWT and DA for $S = S_1 S_2 \ldots S_d$
2 Compute B_i, for $i = 1, 2, \ldots, d$;
3 **for** $i \leftarrow 1$ **to** d **do**
4 $\quad q_s \leftarrow 1$;
5 $\quad \ell_j \leftarrow 0$ for all j;
6 $\quad t_{k_j}^j \leftarrow 0$ for all k_j;
7 $\quad$ **for** $p \leftarrow 1$ **to** n_i **do**
8 $\quad\quad q_e \leftarrow \mathsf{select}_1(B_i, p)$;
9 $\quad\quad$ **for** $j \leftarrow i + 1$ **to** d **do**
10 $\quad\quad\quad k_j \leftarrow \mathsf{rank}_1(B_j, q_e) - \mathsf{rank}_1(B_j, q_s)$;
11 $\quad\quad\quad$ **if** $k_j > 0$ **then**
12 $\quad\quad\quad\quad t_{\ell_j}^j$ ++ ;   // 0^{ℓ_j}
13 $\quad\quad\quad\quad t_{k_j}^j$ ++ ;   // 1^{k_j}
14 $\quad\quad\quad\quad \ell_j \leftarrow 1$;
15 $\quad\quad\quad$ **end**
16 $\quad\quad\quad$ **else**
17 $\quad\quad\quad\quad \ell_j$++;
18 $\quad\quad\quad$ **end**
19 $\quad\quad$ **end**
20 $\quad\quad q_s \leftarrow q_e$;
21 $\quad$ **end**
22 $\quad$ **for** $j \leftarrow i + 1$ **to** d **do**
23 $\quad\quad k_j \leftarrow \mathsf{rank}_1(B_j, N) - \mathsf{rank}_1(B_j, q_s)$;
24 $\quad\quad t_{\ell_j}^j$ ++ ;   // 0^{ℓ_j}
25 $\quad\quad$ **if** $k_j > 0$ **then**
26 $\quad\quad\quad t_{k_j}^j$ ++ ;   // 1^{k_j}
27 $\quad\quad$ **end**
28 $\quad\quad \mathsf{M}[i][j] \leftarrow compute\_distance(t^j, n_i, n_j)$;
29 $\quad$ **end**
30 **end**

3.2 Implementation Alternatives

Sparse Bitvectors: Each bitvector $B_i[1, N]$ is very sparse, containing exactly n_i bits equal to 1. We can use Elias-Fano compressed bitvectors with rank/select support [17], and then each B_i will take $n_i \lg \frac{N}{n_i} + 1.92n_i + o(n_i)$ bits of space. The total space will be reduced to $\sum_{i=1}^{d} (n_i \lg \frac{N}{n_i} + 1.92n_i + o(n_i)) = \sum_{i=1}^{d} (n_i \lg \frac{N}{n_i}) + 1.92N + o(N) = N \sum_{i=1}^{d} (\frac{n_i}{N} \lg \frac{N}{n_i}) + 1.92N + o(N) = N H_0(\mathsf{DA}) + 1.92N + o(N)$ bits, where $H_0(\mathsf{DA})$ is the entropy compressed size of DA. The running time will increase to $O(dN \times \log \frac{N}{avg(n_i)})$, because each rank operation will take $O(\log(\frac{N}{n_i}))$ time, where $avg(n_i)$ is the average length of the strings.

Wavelet Trees: Another alternative is replacing all bitvectors by a single wavelet tree built over $\mathsf{DA}[1, N]$. The alphabet size of such wavelet tree is $\sigma = d$. The space used by the d bitvectors will be reduced to $N \lg d + o(N \log d)$ bits for the wavelet tree. The running time will increase to $O(dN \lg d)$, because each rank and select operations will take $O(\lg d)$ time.

4   Algorithm 2

For collections of unsimilar strings the number of runs in all B_i, say z, is much smaller than the maximal possible $O(dN)$. In the extreme case each B_i consists of only two runs and the sum of all runs is therefore as small as $z = d^2 - d$, but Algorithm 1 would still require $O(dN)$ steps to compute all $\alpha_{i,j}$. We will now show how to improve the running time to $O(N + z)$.

We precompute again the document array DA of the concatenation $S = S_1 S_2 \ldots S_d$. Next, we compute an array L_i for each string S_i, with $L_i[j]$ equal to the index of the j-th occurrence of i in DA and $L_i[0] = -1$. Then, we compute arrays prev and next, such that $\mathsf{prev}[i] = \max\{j | j < i \text{ and } \mathsf{DA}[j] = \mathsf{DA}[i]\}$ or -1 if no such j exists and $\mathsf{next}[i] = \min\{j | j > i \text{ and } \mathsf{DA}[j] = \mathsf{DA}[i]\}$ or n if no such j exists. We add a range minimum query structure on prev ($\mathsf{rmq}_{\mathsf{prev}}$) and a range maximum query structure on next ($\mathsf{RMQ}_{\mathsf{next}}$) in order to extract the leftmost and the rightmost occurrence of all r distinct documents in any arbitrary range in DA in $O(r)$ time; see [14] for details. Adding an array R, where $R[i] = rank_{\mathsf{DA}[i]}(\mathsf{DA}, i)$, allows to get the frequency of each distinct document in $O(1)$ time.

Now for each string i, we can compute the number and length of all runs which break the runs of string i as follows. We traverse all intervals $\mathsf{DA}[1, L_i[1] - 1]$, $\mathsf{DA}[L_i[n_i] - 1, N - 1]$ and $\mathsf{DA}[L_i[j - 1] + 1, L_i[j] - 1]$ for $j = 2, \ldots, n_i$. For each interval we use $\mathsf{rmq}_{\mathsf{prev}}$ and $\mathsf{RMQ}_{\mathsf{next}}$ to determine all r distinct documents and their frequencies in r time. Note that it is not necessary in this step to maintain the number and length of runs of string i as this is calculated symmetrically when the other strings $\neq i$ are traversed.

4.1   Theoretical Costs

The precomputation of DA, prev, next, $\mathsf{rmq}_{\mathsf{prev}}$, $\mathsf{RMQ}_{\mathsf{next}}$ and R requires $O(N)$ time and space. Generating all intervals requires $\sum_{i=1}^{d} (n_i + 1) = O(N)$ time and each run of every $\alpha_{i,j}$ is handled in constant time. So overall we achieve a time complexity which is upper bounded by $O(N + z)$, where z is the sum of all runs in all $\alpha_{i,j}$ ($1 \leq i < j \leq d$), improving the computation of all $\alpha_{i,j}$ by Algorithm 1, which is $O(dN)$. The cost to compute all pairs of distances is still $O(dN)$. Therefore, the total running time is $O(dN)$.

5   Experiments

We have analyzed the performance of the algorithms for computing the upper triangular entries of the distance matrix $\mathsf{M}_{d \times d}$. We computed the expectation based distances D_M (Definition 2). We compared the straightforward approach (SF) [21] to compute the distances with three versions of Algorithm 1, using plain bitvectors (BIT), using Elias-Fano compressed bitvectors (BIT_sd) and using a wavelet tree (WT).

Although Algorithm 2 has a better theoretical running time, the higher constants in the RMQ queries degrades its practical performance. The worst case for Algorithm 1 would be exhibited when the bitvector has the form $\{0^{n_i}1^{n_j}\}^*$, an unlikely situation in practice where two strings are completely "different", for instance when they come from interleaved and disjoint alphabets. In a situation like this, Algorithm 2 could pay off. Thus, results for Algorithm 2 were not included below.

The algorithms were implemented in C++ using the SDSL library [4] version 2.0[1]. We computed the BWTs and document arrays using gSACA-K[2] [7]. The source code of all algorithms are freely available at https://github.com/felipelouza/bwsd.

The experiments were conducted on a machine with Debian GNU/Linux 8 (kernel 3.16.0-4) 64 bits operating system with an Intel Xeon Processor E5-2630 v3 20M Cache 2.40-GHz, with 384 GB of RAM and a 13 TB SATA storage. The sources were compiled by g++ v 4.7.2, with flags std=c++14, -O3, -m64 and -fomit-frame-pointer.

We used four different real data collections with up to $d = 15{,}000$ strings, described in Table 1.

Table 1. Datasets used in our experiments and their attributes.

Dataset	σ	Total length	No. of strings	Max length	Avg length
READS	4	1,422,718	15,000	101	94.85
UNIPROT	25	3,454,210	15,000	2,147	230.28
ESTS	4	11,313,165	15,000	1,560	754.21
WIKIPEDIA	208	25,430,657	15,000	150,768	1,695.38

READS: is a collection of reads from Human Chromosome 14 (library 1)[3].
UNIPROT: is a collection of protein sequences from Uniprot/TrEMBL protein database release 2015_09[4].
ESTS: is a collection of DNA sequences of ESTs from *C. elegans*[5].
WIKIPEDIA: is a collection of pages from a snapshot of the English-language edition of Wikipedia[6].

---

[1] https://github.com/simongog/sdsl-lite.
[2] https://github.com/felipelouza/gsa-is/.
[3] http://gage.cbcb.umd.edu/data/index.html.
[4] http://www.ebi.ac.uk/uniprot/download-center/.
[5] http://www.uni-ulm.de/in/theo/research/seqana.html.
[6] http://algo2.iti.kit.edu/gog/projects/ALENEX15/collections/ENWIKIBIG/.

5.1   Running Time

Figure 2(a) shows the running time (in seconds) of each algorithm. The running time includes the time spent in building all auxiliary data structures, which is a small fraction of the total time, less than 1%. The elapsed time was recorded using the clock() function of ANSI/C.

BIT and BIT_sd were the fastest algorithms in all experiments. Comparing with the straightforward approach, BIT was 2.4 times faster than SF and BIT_sd was 2.0 times faster than SF, on the average. For WIKIPEDIA, BIT was 2.9 times faster than SF, whereas BIT_sd was approximately 2.4 times faster. WT was 1.4 times faster than SF, on the average.

This result shows that Algorithm 1 represents a practical improvement, even with the additional time taken by the rank/select operations when plain bitvectors (BIT) are replaced by compressed bitvectors (BIT_sd) or wavelet trees (WT), been always better than the straightforward approach.

5.2   Peak Memory

Figure 2(b) shows the $\log_2$ peak memory usage (in GB) of each algorithm. The input collection uses N bytes, whereas the output matrix takes $(d^2 - d)/2$ entries (upper triangular matrix), each one of 8 bytes (double variable). The total size of the output matrix was approximately 868 MB for collections with 15,000 strings. We measured memory usage with the malloc_count library[7].

The space used by SF was the smallest. As expected it was very close to what is needed for the input and output, as only $O(\max(n_i))$ bytes are added for the BWT and auxiliary variables. BIT_sd and WT were also lightweight. BIT_sd used approximately 1.02 GB and WT used approximately 1.23 GB when $d = 15,000$. The space used by BIT was, however, much larger. For WIKIPEDIA, BIT used approximately 64 times more space than SF. We remark that the data structures used by the algorithms were the same, except for bitvectors and wavelet tree.

This result shows that the space used by the d plain bitvectors (BIT) can be a bottleneck for Algorithm 1. On the other hand, the compressed data structures used by BIT_sd and WT provide good space-efficient alternatives comparable to SF.

We may conclude that time and memory requirements of BIT_sd show that this version of Algorithm 1 provides a good time/space trade-off, being the best alternative in our experiments.

---

[7] http://panthema.net/2013/malloc_count.

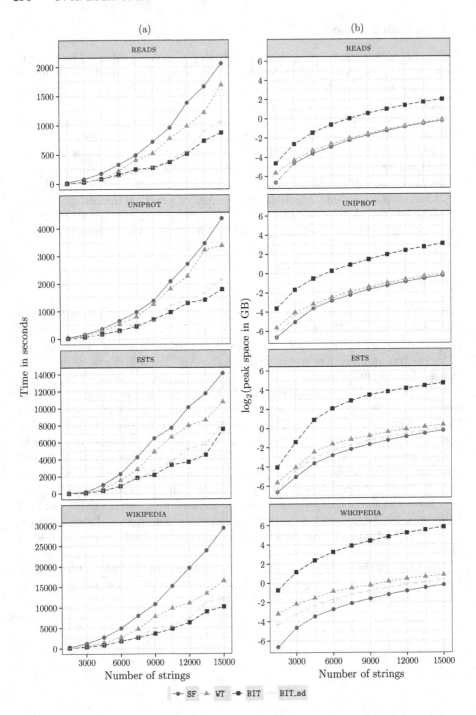

Fig. 2. Running time in seconds and peak memory in GB (in logarithmic scale) for the aternatives of Algorithm 1 and for the straightforward approach on all datasets.

6   Conclusions

In this paper we presented two new algorithms to compute the Burrows-Wheeler similarity distribution (BWSD) for collections of strings. We evaluated our algorithms with a set of real collections. Our experimental results showed that the three different versions of Algorithm 1 outperformed the straightforward approach by a factor of up to 2.9, and that two versions have a small memory footprint.

Our algorithms contribute for solving the problem of comparing strings in practice and are specially interesting for the case of biological sequences and other large datasets. The approach may be extended to different distance measures, broadening its application. Parallel versions for our algorithms may improve practical applications as well.

Acknowledgments. The authors thank Prof. Nalvo Almeida for granting access to the machine used for the experiments.

Funding. FAL was supported by the grant #2017/09105-0 from the São Paulo Research Foundation (FAPESP). GPT acknowledges the support of CNPq grants 425340/2016-3 and 310685/2015-0.

References

1. Baeza-Yates, R.A., Ribeiro-Neto, B.A.: Modern Information Retrieval: The Concepts and Technology Behind Search, 2nd edn. Pearson Education Ltd., Harlow (2011)
2. Burrows, M., Wheeler, D.J.: A block-sorting lossless data compression algorithm. Technical report, Digital SRC Research Report (1994)
3. Fischer, J., Heun, V.: Theoretical and practical improvements on the RMQ-problem, with applications to LCA and LCE. In: Lewenstein, M., Valiente, G. (eds.) CPM 2006. LNCS, vol. 4009, pp. 36–48. Springer, Heidelberg (2006). https://doi.org/10.1007/11780441_5
4. Gog, S., Beller, T., Moffat, A., Petri, M.: From theory to practice: plug and play with succinct data structures. In: Gudmundsson, J., Katajainen, J. (eds.) SEA 2014. LNCS, vol. 8504, pp. 326–337. Springer, Cham (2014). https://doi.org/10.1007/978-3-319-07959-2_28
5. Gonnet, G.H., Baeza-Yates, R.A., Snider, T.: New indices for text: pat trees and pat arrays. In: Information Retrieval, pp. 66–82. Prentice-Hall Inc., Upper Saddle River (1992)
6. Grossi, R., Gupta, A., Vitter, J.S.: High-order entropy-compressed text indexes. In: Proceedings of ACM-SIAM Symposium on Discrete Algorithms (SODA), pp. 841–850. ACM/SIAM (2003)
7. Louza, F.A., Gog, S., Telles, G.P.: Inducing enhanced suffix arrays for string collections. Theor. Comput. Sci. **678**, 22–39 (2017)
8. Manber, U., Myers, E.W.: Suffix arrays: a new method for on-line string searches. SIAM J. Comput. **22**(5), 935–948 (1993)
9. Mantaci, S., Restivo, A., Rosone, G., Sciortino, M.: An extension of the burrows wheeler transform and applications to sequence comparison and data compression. In: Apostolico, A., Crochemore, M., Park, K. (eds.) CPM 2005. LNCS, vol. 3537, pp. 178–189. Springer, Heidelberg (2005). https://doi.org/10.1007/11496656_16

10. Mantaci, S., Restivo, A., Rosone, G., Sciortino, M.: A new combinatorial approach to sequence comparison. Theory Comput. Syst. **42**(3), 411–429 (2008)
11. Mantaci, S., Restivo, A., Sciortino, M.: Distance measures for biological sequences: some recent approaches. Int. J. Approx. Reason. **47**(1), 109–124 (2008)
12. Munro, J.I.: Tables. In: Chandru, V., Vinay, V. (eds.) FSTTCS 1996. LNCS, vol. 1180, pp. 37–42. Springer, Heidelberg (1996). https://doi.org/10.1007/3-540-62034-6_35
13. Munro, J.I., Nekrich, Y., Vitter, J.S.: Fast construction of wavelet trees. Theor. Comput. Sci. **638**, 91–97 (2016)
14. Muthukrishnan, S.: Efficient algorithms for document retrieval problems. In: Proceedings ACM-SIAM Symposium on Discrete Algorithms (SODA), pp. 657–666. ACM/SIAM (2002)
15. Nong, G.: Practical linear-time O(1)-workspace suffix sorting for constant alphabets. ACM Trans. Inform. Syst. **31**(3), 1–15 (2013)
16. Ohlebusch, E.: Bioinformatics Algorithms: Sequence Analysis, Genome Rearrangements, and Phylogenetic Reconstruction. Oldenbusch Verlag (2013)
17. Okanohara, D., Sadakane, K.: Practical entropy-compressed rank/select dictionary. In: Proceedings of Workshop on Algorithm Engineering and Experimentation (ALENEX). SIAM (2007)
18. Okanohara, D., Sadakane, K.: A linear-time burrows-wheeler transform using induced sorting. In: Karlgren, J., Tarhio, J., Hyyrö, H. (eds.) SPIRE 2009. LNCS, vol. 5721, pp. 90–101. Springer, Heidelberg (2009). https://doi.org/10.1007/978-3-642-03784-9_9
19. Paiva, J.G., Florian, L., Pedrini, H., Telles, G., Minghim, R.: Improved similarity trees and their application to visual data classification. IEEE Trans. Vis. Comput. Graph. **17**(12), 2459–2468 (2011)
20. Puglisi, S.J., Smyth, W.F., Turpin, A.H.: A taxonomy of suffix array construction algorithms. ACM Comp. Surv. **39**(2), 1–31 (2007)
21. Yang, L., Zhang, X., Wang, T.: The Burrows-Wheeler similarity distribution between biological sequences based on Burrows-Wheeler transform. J. Theor. Biol. **262**(4), 742–749 (2010)

Better Heuristic Algorithms for the Repetition Free LCS and Other Variants

Radu Stefan Mincu[1] and Alexandru Popa[1,2(✉)]

[1] Department of Computer Science, University of Bucharest,
Bucharest, Romania
{mincu.radu,alexandru.popa}@fmi.unibuc.ro
[2] National Institute for Research and Development in Informatics,
Bucharest, Romania

Abstract. In Discrete Applied Mathematics 2010, Adi et al. introduce and study a variant of the well known Longest Common Subsequence problem, named *Repetition Free Longest Common Subsequence (RFLCS)*. In RFLCS the input consists of two strings A and B over an alphabet Σ and the goal is to find the longest common subsequence containing only distinct characters from Σ. Adi et al. prove that the problem is $\mathcal{APX}$-hard and show three approximation algorithms. Castelli et al. (Operations Research Letters 2013) propose a heuristic genetic algorithm and Blum and Blesa introduce metaheuristic algorithms (International Conference on Artificial Evolution 2013 and Evolutionary Computation in Combinatorial Optimization 2016).

In this paper we design and test several new heuristic algorithms for RFLCS. The first algorithm, uses dynamic programming and in our testing setup outperforms the algorithms of Adi et al. The second heuristic algorithm improves upon the first and becomes comparable to the state-of-the-art algorithms of Blum and Blesa. The third algorithm transforms the RFLCS instance into an instance of the Maximum Independent Set (MIS) problem with the same value of the optimum solution. Then, we apply known algorithms for the MIS problem. We also augment one of the approximation algorithms of Adi et al. and we prove that we achieve an approximation of factor $2\sqrt{\min\{|A|, |B|\}}$.

Finally, we introduce a new variant of the LCS problem, named *Multiset Restricted Common Subsequence (MRCS)*, that is a generalization of RFLCS. We present an exact polynomial time algorithm for MRCS for constant size alphabet. Additionally, we show that MRCS admits a $2\sqrt{\min\{|A|, |B|\}}$ approximation.

This work was supported by the research programme PN 1819 "Advanced IT resources to support digital transformation processes in the economy and society - RESINFO-TD" (2018), project PN 1819-01-01 "New research in complex systems modelling and optimization with applications in industry, business and cloud computing", funded by the Ministry of Research and Innovation.

T. Gagie et al. (Eds.): SPIRE 2018, LNCS 11147, pp. 297–310, 2018.
https://doi.org/10.1007/978-3-030-00479-8_24

1   Introduction

MOTIVATION AND PREVIOUS WORK. The Longest Common Subsequence problem (LCS) is long studied [3,4,15] and its importance is further emphasized by its wide array of applications in diverse fields such as data compression, computational biology, text editing and comparison (notable examples include the Unix diff utility and plagiarism detection systems), pattern recognition.

In the field of computational biology, advances in genome sequencing techniques are bringing about the need for algorithms to be used in the analysis and reconstruction of genomic data. An important and often occurring task in this field is, given two genomes, to compute the similarity between them. A straightforward solution is to compute the LCS between them as a similarity metric. However, depending on the desired focus of the similarity metric, LCS may not be the best choice. As a consequence, many LCS variants have been developed to interpret the DNA sequence fragments resulting from various DNA sequencing procedures.

There are situations where, for instance, we want to focus on the occurrence of some specific sequence that is known to appear in both inputs. If there exist many copies of other sequences in the inputs they might outweigh the target sequence in the computation of the LCS similarity measure. This is the case for the *Constrained LCS problem (CLCS)* first presented by Tsai [17] and later proven to be equivalent to a particular case of *Constrained Sequence Alignment (CSA)* [12].

Another approach to measure genome similarity is to consider only one representative of each gene appearing in the inputs and disregard duplicates for the purpose of contributing to the value of similarity. This has lead to the exemplar model based LCS variants, namely the *Exemplar LCS (ELCS)* variants [8] and the *Repetition Free LCS (RFLCS)* problem [1]. A generalization of the CLCS and RFLCS problems exists in the *Doubly Constrained LCS problem (DCLCS)* [9].

To have a better overview of the considered common subsequence problem family we present the formal definitions and go over some results regarding these problems:

- LCS: Given a set of strings $\mathcal{S}$, find the longest string that is a subsequence to all the strings in $\mathcal{S}$. A *subsequence* of a string is obtained by deleting some symbols (possibly none). It is well known that the above problem is $\mathcal{NP}$-hard for a set of strings of arbitrary size [16] while 2-LCS is solvable in polynomial time by dynamic programming [15,18].
- CLCS: Given two strings A, B and a set of constraint strings $\mathcal{C}$, find a longest common subsequence R of A and B such that each string in $\mathcal{C}$ is a subsequence of R. For an arbitrary number of constraints the problem is $\mathcal{NP}$-hard [14], while CLCS with a single constraint string is polynomial time solvable [12,17].
- RFLCS: Let there be two strings A and B over an alphabet Σ. Find the longest common subsequence R of A and B such that R contains at most one occurence of each $\sigma \in \Sigma$. The problem is known to be $\mathcal{APX}$-hard even when each symbol can occur at most twice in each input string [1].

- DCLCS is a generalization of CLCS and RFLCS: Given two strings A, B over alphabet Σ, a set of constraint strings $\mathcal{C}$ and a function $occurence : \Sigma \to \mathbb{N}$, find a longest common subsequence R of A and B such that each string in $\mathcal{C}$ is a subsequence of R and R contains no more than $occurence(\sigma)$ of each symbol σ. Because it is a generalization, DCLCS inherits the hardness properties of CLCS and RFLCS and is therefore $\mathcal{APX}$-hard [9].

- ELCS has four versions and is based on splitting the alphabet Σ into two disjoint sets, namely the set of mandatory symbols Σ_m and the set of optional symbols Σ_o. The problems consist of finding R the LCS of two strings A and B over alphabet $\Sigma = \Sigma_m \cup \Sigma_o$ such that:
  - ELCS(1): R has exactly 1 of each $\sigma \in \Sigma_m$ and arbitrary many $\sigma \in \Sigma_o$.
  - ELCS($\geq$1): R has at least 1 of each $\sigma \in \Sigma_m$ and arbitrary many $\sigma \in \Sigma_o$.
  - ELCS(1,$\leq$1): R has exactly 1 of each $\sigma \in \Sigma_m$ and at most one of each $\sigma \in \Sigma_o$.
  - ELCS($\geq$1,$\leq$1): R has at least 1 of each $\sigma \in \Sigma_m$ and at most one of each $\sigma \in \Sigma_o$.

  Note that RFLCS is a special case of the last two problems when $\Sigma_m = \emptyset$. For two input strings, it is known that 2-ELCS(1,$\leq$1) and 2-ELCS($\geq$1,$\leq$1) are $\mathcal{APX}$-hard even when each symbol may appear at most twice in each input sequence [9]. Moreover, the existence of a feasible solution for 2-ELCS can be determined in polynomial time if there are at most *3 occurrences in total* of each symbol in the input strings, but determining a feasible solution becomes $\mathcal{NP}$-hard if at most 3 occurrences of each symbol are allowed *in each of the input strings*.

In this paper we select the RFLCS problem and design practical heuristic algorithms for obtaining approximate solutions and give a new theoretical result regarding a previous approximation algorithm. Motivated by genome similarity metrics, we further introduce a new LCS variant, MRCS.

In the comparison of our designed algorithms, we often refer to the first heuristic algorithm for RFLCS, namely Algorithm 1 from [1], henceforth called $\mathcal{A}1$. For the definition of $\mathcal{A}1$ see Sect. 6.

It is noteworthy that in [10] Castelli et al. present a hybrid genetic algorithm for approximating RFLCS which is noticeably better than $\mathcal{A}1$ on shorter inputs but not as good on longer input strings. In parallel with Castelli et al., Blum et al. present an alternative metaheuristic-based approach, Beam-ACO [7]. Afterwards, Blum and Blesa apply a new metaheuristic named CMSA [5]. For a comprehensive review of the state-of-the-art algorithms for RFLCS, refer to [6].

OUR RESULTS. We focus our efforts on the RFLCS problem for which we obtain these new results:

1. A dynamic programming heuristic algorithm for RFLCS is presented in Sect. 2 which obtains good solutions in practice. Our algorithm produces better average solution lengths than $\mathcal{A}1$ in all tested cases (see Table 1).

2. An improvement to the previous dynamic programming heuristic, named Top-k is described in Sect. 3. The designed algorithm performance becomes comparable to that of the state-of-the-art algorithms [5–7,11] while maintaining low computation time.

3. In Sect. 4 we design a way to transform any RFLCS instance into a *Maximum Independent Set (MIS)* problem instance. The solution for the MIS problem can be transformed back into a solution for our RFLCS instance. As a consequence, any heuristic for MIS can provide a solution for RFLCS.

4. We present experimental results regarding the heuristics in Sect. 5.

5. Section 6 describes a $2\sqrt{\min(n,m)}$-approximation for RFLCS based on $\mathcal{A}1$. We modify $\mathcal{A}1$ to achieve an approximation that is not dependent on the number of occurrences of the most frequent common symbol, but on the length of the input sequences.

In this paper we also define and study a RFLCS generalization, named *Multiset Restricted Common Subsequence (MRCS)*. The formal definition follows.

Problem 1 (MRCS). The input consists of two strings A and B of length n and m, respectively, over an alphabet Σ and a *multiset* $\mathcal{M}$ of characters from Σ. The goal is to find *a common subsequence* R between A and B, that contains the maximum number of characters from $\mathcal{M}$.

More precisely, the objective of MRCS as an optimization problem is to minimize $|\mathcal{M} \setminus R|$ as a multiset difference or, equivalently, to maximize $|\mathcal{M} \cap R|$ as a multiset intersection.

$$A = \texttt{abccbaa} \qquad \text{MRCS}(A,B,\texttt{bba}) \in \{\ \texttt{abb, bba, abba, abbaa}\}$$
Example 1. $B = \texttt{cabbaac} \qquad \text{MRCS}(A,B,\texttt{abc}) \in \{\ \texttt{abc, cba, cbaa}\}$
$$\text{MRCS}(A,B,\texttt{cc}) = \texttt{cc}$$

The solutions for the RFLCS problem are included in the special case of MRCS where $\mathcal{M} = \Sigma$. The MRCS solution set includes all RFLCS solutions of the optimum length as well as all common subsequences of A and B which contain these optimum solutions as a subsequence. To obtain RFLCS solutions, one can find $\text{MRCS}(A, B, \Sigma)$ and remove all repeated occurrences of each $\sigma \in \Sigma$. As such, if $\text{MRCS}(A, B, \Sigma)$ is solvable in polynomial time, then $\text{RFLCS}(A, B)$ can be solved in polynomial time as well. However, since RFLCS is $\mathcal{APX}$-hard, MRCS is $\mathcal{APX}$-hard as well.

Regarding the newly introduced MRCS problem we are able to present the following results:

1. An approximation algorithm for MRCS is given in Sect. 7. LCS is a natural approximation for MRCS, almost in the same way $\mathcal{A}1$ approximates RFLCS. The difference is that it is not required to eliminate the symbols that appear more than the required number of times, since such solutions are equally as good as the optimum, according to the definition.

2. For a constant size alphabet we show that MRCS is solvable in polynomial time in Sect. 8. Thus, the difficult cases of MRCS are like those of RFLCS when the alphabet size grows linearly as a function of the input size.

2   Dynamic Programming (DP) Heuristic for RFLCS

Given $A = a_1 a_2 \ldots a_n$, a string of length n, we denote the non-empty substring between positions i and j as $A[i..j] = a_i a_{i+1} \ldots a_{j-1} a_j$, with $1 \leq i \leq j \leq n$. The length of such a substring is $j - i + 1$. We denote the empty substring of A as any $A[i..j]$ where $i > j$ or that has $j = 0$.

Let $S(i,j)$ be the subset of alphabet Σ that is used in the solution of our DP heuristic algorithm for substrings $A[1..i]$ and $B[1..j]$. Let $S_{A,B}$ denote $S(n,m)$ on inputs A and B of length n and m, respectively. We define $S(i,j)$ as:

$$S(i,j) = \begin{cases} S(i-1,j-1) \cup \{a_i\}, & \text{if } a_i = b_j = \sigma_t \text{ and } \sigma_t \notin S(i-1,j-1) \\ S(i-1,j), & \text{if } |S(i-1,j)| \geq |S(i,j-1)| \\ S(i,j-1), & \text{otherwise} \end{cases}$$

$$(1)$$

Boundary conditions: $S(i,0) = \emptyset$ and $S(0,j) = \emptyset$, for all $0 \leq i \leq n$, $0 \leq j \leq m$.

By backtracking through the dynamic programming table that is constructed from position (n,m) to $(0,0)$ we can easily recover the solution (common subsequence). Otherwise, assume that $S(i,j)$ is an ordered set (i.e. repetition free subsequence) and the solution is always $S(n,m)$ after algorithm termination.

The following example shows that this algorithm cannot have an approximation factor better than $\sqrt{OPT}$.

Example 2. Let $rev : \Sigma^* \rightarrow \Sigma^*$ be the function that reverses a string. With the previous notation together with the colon operator : denoting string concatenation we define recursively the following strings:

$$P_{i+1} = rev(R_{i+1}) : \quad P_i \quad : R_{i+1}$$
$$Q_{i+1} = \quad Q_i \quad : rev(R_{i+1}) : R_{i+1}$$

Additionally, let $P_1 = Q_1 = \sigma$ (some start symbol) and let R_{i+1} share no symbols with P_i, have no repeated symbols and be of length $i + 1$. For instance:

P_i	Q_i	$|S_{P_i,Q_i}|$	$|OPT|$
a	a	1	1
cb:a:bc	a:cb:bc	2	3
fed:cbabc:def	acbbc:fed:def	3	6
jihg:fedcbabcdef:ghij	acbbcfeddef:jihg:ghij	4	10

In other words, we are able to describe a case where the optimum of the solution increases by i at each step, while the solution size given by our algorithm increases by 1. In the general case we get a solution of size n when the optimum is $n(n+1)/2$. This is possible because of the way $S(i,j)$ always selects $S(i-1,j)$ instead of $S(i,j-1)$ when they are of equal size.

The above example also brings us to the conclusion that:

Lemma 1. *The DP algorithm is not symmetrical on the input strings i.e. $S_{A,B}$ is not necessarily equal to $S_{B,A}$.*

In fact, on Example 2 S_{Q_i,P_i} is always the optimum.

3 Top-k Heuristic for RFLCS

Analyzing the traces of our previously described DP algorithm on random instances, we notice that we can perform some improvements. In the following, we present our Top-k heuristic algorithm which builds upon DP.

First, let us consider the example in Fig. 1. The inputs are A=bdacbd and B=abdcbd and the optimum solution is acbd. We observe that our DP algorithm (pictured top left in Fig. 1) fails to reach the optimum because of the limitation to select $S(i,j)$ to be the $S(i-1,j)$ set, in case that $|S(i-1,j)| = |S(i,j-1)|$. More specifically, the highlighted cell in the top left table does not contain a, which is a component of the optimum. However, even if such choices are flipped (the table of the modified algorithm is pictured top right in Fig. 1), we still fail to retain a, because it is of smaller size than the bd set.

Top left table:

	a	b	d	c	b	d
b		b	b	b	b	b
d		b	bd	bd	bd	bd
a	a	b	bd	bd	bd	bd
c	a	b	bd	bdc	bdc	bdc
b	a	ab	bd	bdc	bdc	bdc
d	a	ab	abd	bdc	bdc	bdc

Top right table:

	a	b	d	c	b	d
b		b	b	b	b	b
d		b	bd	bd	bd	bd
a	a	a	bd	bd	bd	bd
c	a	a	bd	bdc	bdc	bdc
b	a	ab	ab	bdc	bdc	bdc
d	a	ab	abd	abd	abd	abd

Bottom table:

	a	b	d	c	b	d
b		b	b	b	b	b
d		b	b,bd	b,bd	b,bd	b,bd
a	a	a,b	a,bd	a,bd	a,bd	a,bd
c	a	a,b	a,bd	ac,bdc	ac,bdc	ac,bdc
b	a	a,ab	ab,bd	ac,bdc	acb,bdc	acb,bdc
d	a	a,ab	ab,abd	abd,bdc	acb,abd	acb,acbd

Fig. 1. Three dynamic programming tables illustrating our Top-k heuristic. The inputs **bdacbd** and **abdcbd** are displayed as the first column and line, respectively, for each table. The top left table corresponds to our base DP algorithm where, upon encountering equally sized set candidates for (i,j), the set in the above cell $(i-1,j)$ is preferred. Similarly, in the top right, is the same DP algorithm with the modification that now $(i,j-1)$ is preferred when the set candidates are equal size. The bottom table corresponds to a Top-2 heuristic and obtains the optimum solution, **acbd**. The traces of the obtained solutions are in bold and the critical decision points are highlighted.

Our idea is to retain several sets for each cell in the DP table, such that we may reach a better solution. Keeping all of the sets leads to an exponential time algorithm, so we keep at most k in each cell. A natural question that follows is: how do we select which sets to keep? Retaining the largest sets alone hampers the quality of the solution, as seen in Fig. 1. Given the example, what would be a good heuristic to retain a in order to reach the optimum?

One answer is to also keep the sets that overlap the least with the remainder of the two inputs. To be exact, retain the sets that have the smallest intersection with the intersection of the alphabets of the remainder of the inputs. For an example, consider the moment we decide the contents of the highlighted a,bd cell. We have chosen bd because of its size and then we have chosen a over b because $|a \cap cbd| < |b \cap cbd|$.

For our implementation of this algorithm, each cell in the DP table will be a set of sets. We consider for the contents of cell (i, j) the union of the sets at $(i-1, j-1)$, $(i-1, j)$, $(i, j-1)$. If $a_i = b_j$ we are careful to add a_i to each of the sets inside set $(i-1, j-1)$. Note that, since they are sets, nothing is changed if a_i is already present. We sort the entire collection in (i, j) by set size. In the case of equally sized sets, the ones that overlap the remaining alphabet of the inputs less, take precedence over the others. We then discard all but the top k results. The solution is the largest of the sets in cell (n, m) for $A[1..n]$, $B[1..m]$.

4   A Polynomial Time Reduction from RFLCS to MIS

Given a graph $G = (V, E)$, the objective of the Maximum Independent Set (MIS) problem problem is to find the largest subset $S \subseteq V$ such that no two vertices from S are adjacent. The MIS problem is long studied and there are heuristic approaches to approximating it that work well in practice, e.g. [2], as well as exact algorithms, e.g. [19].

Theorem 1. *Instances of RFLCS can be reduced in polynomial time to MIS instances with the same optimum.*

Proof. We describe how to transform a RFLCS instance into a MIS instance that has the same value of the optimal solution. The resulting graph has a vertex set $V = \{(i, j) | a_i = b_j\}$ corresponding to all matching symbols between the two input strings A, B. The solution for the MIS problem is a subset $S \subseteq V$ and each vertex (i, j) in S corresponds to a symbol a_i contained in the solution for the RFLCS problem. More precisely, each (i, j) corresponds to a matching in the two input strings of symbol a_i that we want in our solution. By building a suitable edge set we can model the two constraints of our string problem:

1. Common subsequence: two matchings (i, j) and (k, ℓ) can exist in a common subsequence only if (k, ℓ) are both either smaller or larger than (i, j). Otherwise the matchings are mutually exclusive. For the MIS problem this becomes an edge i.e. for all distinct (i, j) and (k, ℓ) we add an edge between them if $(i < k)$ and $(j > \ell)$.
2. Repetition-free: Two matchings (i, j) and (k, ℓ) are mutually exclusive if $a_i = a_k$ because we require no more than one a_i in the final solution. Therefore we need to add edges between all such vertices, forming a clique for every distinct symbol.

Moreover, since we require the *maximum* independent set, that immediately leads to a *longest* repetition free common subsequence.   □

5   Experimental Results Regarding Our Heuristics

In this section we showcase the results of testing our designed algorithms (DP and Top-k). To analyze our RFLCS-to-MIS reduction method, we have chosen to employ a basic greedy vetex cover algorithm as a proof of concept. The complement of such a cover gives a solution for the MIS problem from which we recover a solution to the initial RFLCS instance.

We compare in Table 1 the average solution length of the algorithms and we use as a reference our own implementation of $\mathcal{A}1$, which we consider representative amongst the three algorithms in [1].

Our test instances are pairs of strings of length n composed of uniformly random strings (i.e. for each position in such a string, each symbol from the alphabet Σ has equal chance to be selected). We prefer using a larger number of instances (400) than the experiments of [1,5–7]. While this allows for much more accurate values for the mean of the solution length, it is impossible to obtain the optimum for each solution (in reasonable time) without a highly specialized algorithm. As such, we follow the guidelines from [13] and provide the expected value for the optimum solution for each batch of tests.

Remarks regarding the tests in Table 1:

1. Our testing shows that the mean of the solution length for our DP and Top-20 algorithms is superior to that of $\mathcal{A}1$ on the same set of instances.
2. The solutions of Top-20 are consistently the best across all test instances.
3. However basic, our greedy vertex cover heuristic shows that there is much potential for MIS heuristics in solving RFLCS. Best performance is observed in the $n/8$ and $2n/8$ cases, where its solutions are superior to that of $\mathcal{A}1$ even on length 512 inputs.
4. There is a missing value for the column MIS on length 512 and alphabet size $n/8$. That is because the edge set of the constructed instances din not fit into the test machine memory (8GB).
5. Due to lack of space, the running times of the algorithms were omitted. We report that the highest average running time per instance was achieved by Top-20 on length 512 and alphabet size $n/8$ at 6.94 s. For the same case, the highest average time for the greedy vertex cover algorithm (including graph construction in memory) reaches 3.55 s.
6. Although we cannot directly compare our results with those in [5,6] due to the different number of test instances, we observe that our average solutions for Top-20 are within 4% of the average solutions in [5,6].

6   A $2\sqrt{\min(n,m)}$-approximation for RFLCS

In [1] Adi et al. construct three algorithms that are p-approximations for the RFLCS problem, where $p = \max_{\sigma \in \Sigma} m_\sigma(A, B)$ and the amount $m_\sigma(A, B)$ represents the minimum between the number of occurrences of σ in A and the occurrences of σ in B.

We give here the definition of $\mathcal{A}1$:

Table 1. Comparison between the average solution lengths of our algorithms and our implementation of $\mathcal{A}1$ from [1]. The first column is the size of the alphabet Σ and the second column is the length n of the two strings A, B we approximate RFLCS on. The third coumn is the value reported by $\mathcal{A}1$. The next column represents the value of the complement of a greedy vertex cover on reduced MIS instances. After that is the average solution length of our DP algorithm. Then follows the average length reported by the Top-20 heuristic. The column $\mathbb{E}_{OPT}$ is the expected value of the optimum solution calculated according to [13]. Finally, in the last column are plots describing the fraction $\frac{\text{average solution}}{\mathbb{E}_{OPT}}$ over n and separately for each $|\Sigma|$. The data is computed by averaging the results of 400 instances per case.

$|\Sigma|$	n	$\mathcal{A}1$	MIS	DP	Top-20	$\mathbb{E}_{OPT}$	x-axis=n and y-axis = avg. / $\mathbb{E}_{OPT}$
$\frac{n}{8}$	32	3.98	4.00	4.00	4.00	3.99	
	64	7.84	7.99	7.99	7.99	7.97	
	128	15.25	15.87	15.98	15.99	15.7	
	256	28.91	31.07	31.78	31.96	30.1	
	512	52.47	-	60.66	62.66	55.33	
$\frac{2n}{8}$	32	6.77	7.27	7.47	7.60	7.52	
	64	12.26	13.36	13.88	14.56	13.83	
	128	21.40	23.25	24.54	25.86	24.22	
	256	36.04	38.49	40.71	42.72	40.45	
	512	58.63	60.93	65.19	67.55	64.88	
$\frac{3n}{8}$	32	7.85	8.30	8.62	8.93	9.42	
	64	13.16	14.09	14.63	15.30	15.92	
	128	21.99	22.91	24.21	25.14	25.77	
	256	35.00	35.53	37.79	39.15	40.29	
	512	54.77	54.17	58.37	59.77	61.34	
$\frac{4n}{8}$	32	7.80	8.23	8.53	8.80	10.11	
	64	12.94	13.43	14.05	14.49	16.22	
	128	20.96	21.37	22.51	23.14	25.18	
	256	32.70	32.37	34.69	35.47	38.11	
	512	50.15	48.67	52.29	53.22	56.62	
$\frac{5n}{8}$	32	7.72	8.00	8.27	8.50	10.22	
	64	12.51	12.77	13.27	13.56	15.88	
	128	19.91	19.71	20.90	21.31	24.06	
	256	30.40	29.70	31.60	32.21	35.76	
	512	46.00	44.30	47.54	48.20	52.41	
$\frac{6n}{8}$	32	7.49	7.58	7.88	8.01	10.07	
	64	11.91	12.02	12.48	12.70	15.33	
	128	18.55	18.21	19.29	19.55	22.87	
	256	28.47	27.72	29.39	29.83	33.61	
	512	42.71	40.64	43.75	44.20	48.85	
$\frac{7n}{8}$	32	6.94	7.02	7.30	7.38	9.82	
	64	11.33	11.26	11.79	11.94	14.73	
	128	17.53	17.19	18.18	18.38	21.75	
	256	26.76	25.88	27.39	27.70	31.72	
	512	40.17	38.18	40.86	41.21	45.85	

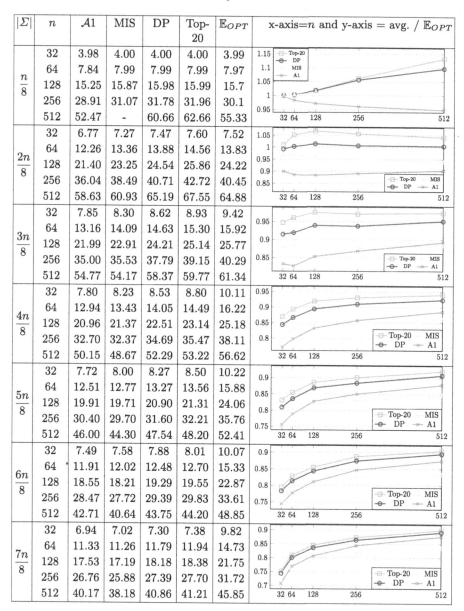

Algorithm 1. A p-approximation for RFLCS

1. Compute the LCS of the input strings.
2. Remove all duplicates of each $\sigma \in \Sigma$ (i.e. keep a random occurrence, if any).

We can use the results for $\mathcal{A}1$ to obtain a $2\sqrt{\min(n,m)}$-approximation for RFLCS, where $n = |A|$, $m = |B|$. The modified algorithm is as follows:

Algorithm 2. A $2\sqrt{\min(n,m)}$-approximation for RFLCS

1. Remove all the symbols σ from both A and B that have $m_\sigma(A,B) > \sqrt{\min(n,m)}$.
2. Apply $\mathcal{A}1$ on the resulting subsequences A' and B' over Σ'.

Theorem 2. *Algorithm 2 is a $2\sqrt{\min(n,m)}$-approximation for RFLCS.*

Proof. The number of symbols $\sigma \in \Sigma$ removed at Step 1 of the algorithm is at most $\sqrt{\min(n,m)}$. If this was not the case, by removing more than $\sqrt{\min(n,m)}$ symbols, each symbol occurring at least $\sqrt{\min(n,m)}$ times in each string, the length of the removed subsequences exceeds the length of the shorter string, contradiction. Thus, the value of the optimum solution OPT for the original strings A, B is $OPT \leq (\sqrt{\min(n,m)} + OPT_2)$ where OPT_2 is the optimum for the two subsequences A', B' from Step 2 of the algorithm.

At Step 2 we apply the analysis from [1]. $\mathcal{A}1$ gives us a solution S of size greater or equal to $\dfrac{OPT_2}{\max_{\sigma \in \Sigma} m_\sigma(A',B')}$.

Since for each $\sigma \in \Sigma$ it is true that $m_\sigma(A',B') \leq \sqrt{\min(n,m)}$ then $\max_{\sigma \in \Sigma} m_\sigma(A',B') \leq \sqrt{\min(n,m)}$.

Therefore $\dfrac{OPT_2}{\max_{\sigma \in \Sigma} m_\sigma(A',B')} \geq \dfrac{OPT_2}{\sqrt{\min(n,m)}}$ so that $\mathcal{A}1$ gives us a $\sqrt{\min(n,m)}$-approximation for RFLCS(A',B') in this case. Assume that there exists at least 1 common symbol between A' and B'. Then the following holds and completes our proof:

$$S \geq \max\left(1, \frac{OPT_2}{\sqrt{\min(n,m)}}\right) \geq \frac{\sqrt{\min(n,m)} + OPT_2}{2\sqrt{\min(n,m)}} \geq \frac{OPT}{2\sqrt{\min(n,m)}} \qquad \square$$

7   Approximation Algorithm for MRCS

A straightforward approximation for MRCS is the LCS of the input strings A, B. By definition, an optimal solution for MRCS$(A,B,\mathcal{M})$ is a common subsequence R that maximizes $|\mathcal{M} \cap R|$. We observe that:

$$|\mathcal{M} \cap \text{MRCS}(A,B,\mathcal{M})| \geq |\mathcal{M} \cap \text{LCS}(A,B)| \geq |\mathcal{M} \cap \mathcal{A}1(A,B)|$$

Consider the special case when $\mathcal{M} = \Sigma$. All common subsequences of A, B that have RFLCS(A, B) as a subsequence are an optimal solution of this special case of MRCS. The LCS of A, B has the same objective function value as $\mathcal{A}1$ and gives us the same approximation ratios. In other words:

$$|\Sigma \cap \mathrm{MRCS}(A, B, \Sigma)| \geq |\Sigma \cap \mathrm{LCS}(A, B)| = |\Sigma \cap \mathcal{A}1(A, B)|$$

Therefore, in the general case, the LCS of the input strings also approximates MRCS. In fact, this is a $2\sqrt{\min(n, m)}$-approximation.

8 A Polynomial Time Algorithm for MRCS with Constant Size Alphabet

We show that solving the MRCS problem for a constant size alphabet $|\Sigma| = \ell$ can be done in polynomial time.

Let $A = a_1 a_2 \ldots a_n$ and $B = b_1 b_2 \ldots b_m$ be the two input strings over alphabet $\Sigma = \{\sigma_1, \sigma_2, \ldots, \sigma_\ell\}$. If $\mathcal{M} = \{\sigma_1{}^{c_1}, \sigma_2{}^{c_2}, \ldots, \sigma_\ell{}^{c_\ell}\}$ is the multiset of symbols whose occurrences we want to maximize in the resulting subsequence, then let $\mathcal{C} = \{c_1, c_2, \ldots, c_\ell\}$ be count set of each σ_i in $\mathcal{M}$. With this formulation, we are searching for a solution with a count set $\mathcal{X} = \{x_1, x_2, \ldots, x_\ell\}$ that minimizes the objective function $\sum_{i=1}^{\ell} \max(c_i - x_i, 0)$.

We use a boolean function $F(i, j, x_1, x_2, \ldots, x_\ell)$ to denote the existence of a solution with *exactly* x_t occurrences of each symbol σ_t for substrings $A[1..i]$ and $B[1..j]$.

Lemma 2. *For $1 \leq i \leq n$, $1 \leq j \leq m$ and $x_t \neq 0$:*

$$F(i, j, x_1, x_2, \ldots, x_\ell) = \begin{cases} 1, \text{if } a_i = b_j = \sigma_t \text{ and} \\ \quad F(i-1, j-1, x_1, x_2, \ldots, x_t - 1, \ldots, x_\ell) = 1 \\ F(i-1, j, x_1, x_2, \ldots, x_\ell) \vee \\ \vee F(i, j-1, x_1, x_2, \ldots, x_\ell), \text{ otherwise} \end{cases} \quad (2)$$

The boundary conditions are:

1. $F(i, j, 0, 0, \ldots, 0) = 1$ i.e. if no symbol is required then any common subsequence of A and B is a solution (in particular, the empty subsequence is certainly a solution).
2. $F(i, 0, x_1, x_2, \ldots, x_t, \ldots, x_\ell) = 0$ where $x_t \neq 0$: if there exists a nonzero x_t, since we cannot match any more σ_t from A then there is no solution.
3. $F(0, j, x_1, x_2, \ldots, x_t, \ldots, x_\ell) = 0$ where $x_t \neq 0$: if there exists a nonzero x_t, since we cannot match any more σ_t from B then there is no solution.

Proof. We prove by induction that F is correctly defined. For the first step we consider two strings A and B and a multiset $\mathcal{M} = \{\sigma_t\}$ containing a single required symbol. Thus we are in the case where we are concerned with the value of $F(i, j, 0, 0, \ldots, x_t = 1, \ldots, 0)$. To solve the problem we evaluate if $a_i = b_j =$

σ_t. Should this be true, the problem is reduced to $F(i-1, j-1, 0, 0, \ldots, 0)$ which is known to be true (first boundary condition). Otherwise if $a_i \neq b_j$, the problem is reduced to whether $F(i-1, j, 0, 0, \ldots, x_t = 1, \ldots, 0)$ is true or $F(i, j-1, 0, 0, \ldots, x_t = 1, \ldots, 0)$ is true. Because the strings are finite, we will locate a pair such that $a_p = b_q = \sigma_t$ for some p, q with $1 \leq p \leq i$, $1 \leq q \leq j$ if such a solution exists. Otherwise we end up finishing searching the strings and obtain the value of boundary conditions 2 and 3 which is false. Thus, there is no solution because $A[1..i]$ and $B[1..j]$ do not each contain at least one σ_t.

In the general step, we focus on satisfying the x_t-th occurrence of some σ_t, knowing the truth value of all F for up to x_i occurrences of all σ_i and for up to $x_t - 1$ occurrences of σ_t. If $a_i = b_j$ and $F(i-1, j-1, x_1, x_2, \ldots, x_t - 1, \ldots, x_\ell) = 1$ from the induction hypothesis then $F(i, j, x_1, x_2, \ldots, x_t, \ldots, x_\ell)$ is immediately true by using the first case of the recurrence. Otherwise if $a_i \neq b_j$ we go back searching for one $F(p, q, x_1, x_2, \ldots, x_t, \ldots, x_\ell)$ with $1 \leq p \leq i$, $1 \leq q \leq j$ that verifies $a_p = b_q$. If such a $F(p, q, x_1, x_2, \ldots, x_t, \ldots, x_\ell)$ with $a_p = b_q$ exists, then we have to apply the first case of the definition to find its truth value and we can immediately determine it because we know the truth values for all $F(p, q, x_1, x_2, \ldots, x_t - 1, \ldots, x_\ell)$ from the induction hypothesis. Otherwise, we run into a boundary condition and a solution that satisfies x_t occurrences of σ_t does not exist, resulting in $F(i, j, x_1, x_2, \ldots, x_t, \ldots, x_\ell) = 0$.

Theorem 3. *The MRCS of two input strings* $A = a_1 a_2 \ldots a_n$ *and* $B = b_1 b_2 \ldots b_m$ *over alphabet* $\Sigma = \{\sigma_1, \sigma_2, \ldots, \sigma_\ell\}$, *given multiset* $\mathcal{M} = \{\sigma_1^{c_1}, \sigma_2^{c_2}, \ldots, \sigma_\ell^{c_\ell}\}$ *can be computed in time* $O(nmt^\ell)$, *where* $t = \max\limits_{\sigma_i^{c_i} \in \mathcal{M}} c_i$.

Proof. Using the dynamic programming approach we may construct a multidimensional array to hold all values of F as we compute them starting with the boundaries. The space required to store the array is $O(nmt^\ell)$. Each element is visited once for storing its value. To compute the value for a specific index in the array we are either in the first case where memory lookups are performed in constant time or we are in the second case where we compute the logical or $\vee$ of two elements in the array also in constant time. During the construction of the array, we may record the index $(i, j, x_1, x_2, \ldots, x_\ell)$ that has the best solution size $x_1 + x_2 + \cdots + x_\ell$. The total time required to find the solution is the size of the array multiplied by the time needed to fill up each cell. Consequently, this algorithm takes $O(nmt^\ell)$ time.

9   Conclusions and Future Work

We present polynomial time dynamic programming-based algorithms for RFLCS whose average solutions are comparable to the state-of-the-art algorithms, while maintaining a low computation time. It would be interesting to see how far the average solution length can be pushed by further improving on these heuristics. In particular, our Top-k heuristic can be used to quickly solve small instances or provide useful initial solutions for exact methods (e.g. ILP model solving).

We introduce a new problem, MRCS, which is $\mathcal{APX}$-hard in the general case and admits a $2\sqrt{\min(n, m)}$-approximation. For constant size alphabet, we show that MRCS is polynomial time solvable.

We describe a way to use MIS heuristics to obtain a solution for RFLCS from the transformed problem. Our comparative study regarding the solution length given using this approach and the previous algorithms yields encouraging results. It is worthwhile to employ and modify MIS heuristics in order to obtain better algorithms for approximating RFLCS. The reduction is also suitable for exact methods. Because we also have extra information about the cliques in the graph we create, it is possible to obtain a speedup for the heuristic methods used. In this way we may see good, fast solutions even if the heuristic considered does not normally perform that well on general graphs.

For RFLCS we modify $\mathcal{A}1$ to achieve an approximation factor that is dependent on input length and not on the frequence of the most common symbol. As stated by Adi et al. [1], it is interesting to see if there exists a constant factor approximation algorithm for RFLCS.

Acknowledgments. We thank the anonymous reviewers for their useful comments and for pointing out some ideas which led to the development of the Top-k heuristic in Sect. 3.

References

1. Adi, S.S., et al.: Repetition-free longest common subsequence. Discret. Appl. Math. **158**(12), 1315–1324 (2010). https://doi.org/10.1016/j.dam.2009.04.023, traces from LAGOS07 IV Latin American Algorithms, Graphs, and Optimization Symposium Puerto Varas - 2007
2. Andrade, D.V., Resende, M.G.C., Werneck, R.F.: Fast local search for the maximum independent set problem. J. Heuristics **18**(4), 525–547 (2012). https://doi.org/10.1007/s10732-012-9196-4
3. Apostolico, A.: String editing and longest common subsequences. In: Rozenberg, G., Salomaa, A. (eds.) Handbook of Formal Languages, pp. 361–398. Springer, Heidelberg (1997). https://doi.org/10.1007/978-3-662-07675-0_8
4. Bergroth, L., Hakonen, H., Raita, T.: A survey of longest common subsequence algorithms. In: Proceedings Seventh International Symposium on String Processing and Information Retrieval, SPIRE 2000, pp. 39–48 (2000). https://doi.org/10.1109/SPIRE.2000.878178
5. Blum, C., Blesa, M.J.: Construct, merge, solve and adapt: application to the repetition-free longest common subsequence problem. In: Chicano, F., Hu, B., García-Sánchez, P. (eds.) EvoCOP 2016. LNCS, vol. 9595, pp. 46–57. Springer, Cham (2016). https://doi.org/10.1007/978-3-319-30698-8_4
6. Blum, C., Blesa, M.J.: A comprehensive comparison of metaheuristics for the repetition-free longest common subsequence problem. J. Heuristics **24**(3), 551–579 (2018). https://doi.org/10.1007/s10732-017-9329-x
7. Blum, C., Blesa, M.J., Calvo, B.: Beam-ACO for the repetition-free longest common subsequence problem. In: Legrand, P., Corsini, M.-M., Hao, J.-K., Monmarché, N., Lutton, E., Schoenauer, M. (eds.) EA 2013. LNCS, vol. 8752, pp. 79–90. Springer, Cham (2014). https://doi.org/10.1007/978-3-319-11683-9_7

8. Bonizzoni, P., Della Vedova, G., Dondi, R., Fertin, G., Rizzi, R., Vialette, S.: Exemplar longest common subsequence. IEEE/ACM Trans. Comput. Biol. Bioinform. **4**(4), 535–543 (2007). https://doi.org/10.1109/TCBB.2007.1066

9. Bonizzoni, P., Vedova, G.D., Dondi, R., Pirola, Y.: Variants of constrained longest common subsequence. Inf. Process. Lett. **110**(20), 877–881 (2010). https://doi.org/10.1016/j.ipl.2010.07.015

10. Castelli, M., Beretta, S., Vanneschi, L.: A hybrid genetic algorithm for the repetition free longest common subsequence problem. Oper. Res. Lett. **41**(6), 644–649 (2013). https://doi.org/10.1016/j.orl.2013.09.002

11. Castelli, M., Dondi, R., Mauri, G., Zoppis, I.: The longest filled common subsequence problem. In: Kärkkäinen, J., Radoszewski, J., Rytter, W. (eds.) 28th Annual Symposium on Combinatorial Pattern Matching (CPM 2017). Leibniz International Proceedings in Informatics (LIPIcs), vol. 78, pp. 14:1–14:13. Schloss Dagstuhl-Leibniz-Zentrum fuer Informatik, Dagstuhl, Germany (2017). https://doi.org/10.4230/LIPIcs.CPM.2017.14

12. Chin, F.Y., Santis, A.D., Ferrara, A.L., Ho, N., Kim, S.: A simple algorithm for the constrained sequence problems. Inf. Process. Lett. **90**(4), 175–179 (2004). https://doi.org/10.1016/j.ipl.2004.02.008

13. Fernandes, C.G., Kiwi, M.: Repetition-free longest common subsequence of random sequences. Discret. Appl. Math. **210**, 75–87 (2016). https://doi.org/10.1016/j.dam.2015.07.005. lAGOS13: Seventh Latin-American Algorithms, Graphs, and Optimization Symposium, Playa del Carmen, Mxico (2013)

14. Gotthilf, Z., Hermelin, D., Lewenstein, M.: Constrained LCS: hardness and approximation. In: Ferragina, P., Landau, G.M. (eds.) CPM 2008. LNCS, vol. 5029, pp. 255–262. Springer, Heidelberg (2008). https://doi.org/10.1007/978-3-540-69068-9_24

15. Hirschberg, D.S.: Algorithms for the longest common subsequence problem. J. ACM (JACM) **24**(4), 664–675 (1977). https://doi.org/10.1145/322033.322044

16. Maier, D.: The complexity of some problems on subsequences and supersequences. J. ACM **25**(2), 322–336 (1978). https://doi.org/10.1145/322063.322075

17. Tsai, Y.T.: The constrained longest common subsequence problem. Inf. Process. Lett. **88**(4), 173–176 (2003). https://doi.org/10.1016/j.ipl.2003.07.001

18. Wagner, R.A., Fischer, M.J.: The string-to-string correction problem. J. ACM **21**(1), 168–173 (1974). https://doi.org/10.1145/321796.321811

19. Xiao, M., Nagamochi, H.: Exact algorithms for maximum independent set. Inf. Comput. **255**, 126–146 (2017). https://doi.org/10.1016/j.ic.2017.06.001

Linear-Time Online Algorithm Inferring the Shortest Path from a Walk

Shintaro Narisada, Diptarama Hendrian, Ryo Yoshinaka$^{(\boxtimes)}$, and Ayumi Shinohara

Graduate School of Information Sciences, Tohoku University, Sendai, Japan
shintaro_narisada@shino.ecei.tohoku.ac.jp,
{diptarama,ryoshinaka,ayumis}@tohoku.ac.jp

Abstract. We consider the problem of inferring an edge-labeled graph from the sequence of edge labels seen in a walk of that graph. It has been known that this problem is solvable in $O(n \log n)$ time when the targets are path or cycle graphs. This paper presents an online algorithm for the problem of this restricted case that runs in $O(n)$ time, based on Manacher's algorithm for computing all the maximal palindromes in a string.

Keywords: Graph inference · Walk · Palindrome

1 Introduction

Aslam and Rivest [2] proposed the problem of *minimum graph inference from a walk*. Let us consider an edge-labeled undirected (multi)graph G. A *walk* of G is a sequence of edges $e_1, \ldots, e_n$ such that each e_i connects v_{i-1} and v_i for some (not necessarily pairwise distinct) vertices $v_0, v_1, \ldots, v_n$. The *output* of the walk is the sequence of the labels of those edges. For a string w, *minimum graph inference from a walk* is the problem to compute a graph G with the smallest number of *vertices* such that w is the output of a walk of G. We give an example in Fig. 1. With no assumption on graphs to infer, trivially the graph with a single vertex with self-loops labeled with all output symbols is always minimum. The problem has been studied for different graph classes in the literature.

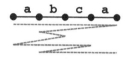

Fig. 1. Minimum path graph that has `abcaacbbbaabccbbca` as a walk output

S. Narisada—Currently affiliated with KDDI Corporation, Tokyo, Japan.

T. Gagie et al. (Eds.): SPIRE 2018, LNCS 11147, pp. 311–324, 2018.
https://doi.org/10.1007/978-3-030-00479-8_25

Aslam and Rivest [2] proposed polynomial time algorithms for the minimum graph inference problem for path graphs and cycle graphs, which include the variant of minimum path graph inference where a walk must start from an end of a path graph and end in the other end (Table 1), which we call an *end-to-end* walk. Raghavan [6] studied the problem further and showed that both minimum path and cycle graph inference from walk can be reduced to path graph inference from an end-to-end walk in $O(n)$ time. Moreover, he presented an $O(n \log n)$ time algorithm for inferring minimum path/cycle graph from a walk, while showing inferring minimum graph with bounded degree k is NP-hard for any $k \geq 3$. Maruyama and Miyano [4] strengthened Raghavan's result so that inferring minimum tree with bounded degree k is still NP-hard for any $k \geq 3$. On the other hand, Maruyama and Miyano [5] showed that it is solvable in linear time when trees have no degree bound. They also studied a variant of the problem where the input consists of multiple path labels rather than a single walk label, which was shown to be NP-hard. Akutsu and Fukagawa [1] considered another variant, where the input is the numbers of occurrences of vertex-labeled paths. They showed a polynomial time algorithm with respect to the size of output graph, when the graphs are trees of unbounded degree and the lengths of given paths are fixed. They also proved that the problem is strongly NP-hard even when the graphs are planar of unbounded degree.

Table 1. Time complexity of minimum graph inference bounded degree 2 from a walk

Algorithms	Connected graph bounded degree 2		
	Path		Cycle
	End-to-end walk	General walk	
Aslam and Rivest [2]	$O(n^3)$	$O(n^3)$	$O(n^5)$
Raghavan [6]	$O(n \log n)$	$O(n \log n)$	$O(n \log n)$
Proposed	$O(n)$	$O(n)$	$O(n)$

This paper focuses on the problem on graphs of bounded degree 2, i.e., path and cycle graphs. We propose a linear-time online algorithm that infers a minimum path graph from an end-to-end walk. Thanks to Raghavan's result [6], this entails that one can infer a minimum path/cycle graph in linear time from a walk, which is not necessarily end-to-end. Aslam and Rivest [2] showed that the minimum path graphs that have end-to-end walks xyy^Ryz and xyz coincide, where x, y, z are label strings and y^R is the reverse of y. Let us call a nonempty string of the form yy^Ry a *Z-shape*. Their result implies that to obtain the minimum path graph of a label string, one can repeatedly contract an arbitrary occurrence of a Z-shape yy^Ry to y until the sequence contains no such substring. Then the finally obtained string is just the sequence of labels of the edges of the minimum path graph. Raghavan [6] achieved an $O(n \log n)$ time algorithm by introducing a sophisticated order of rewriting, which always contract the smallest Z-shapes in the sequence. We follow their approach of repetitive contraction of Z-shapes but with a different order. The order we take might appear more naive; We read letters of the input string one by one and always contract the firstly found Z-shape. This approach makes our algorithm online. Apparently finding Z-shapes is closely related to finding palindromes. Manacher [3] presented a linear-time "online" algorithm that finds all the maximal palindromes in a string. To realize linear-time Z-shape elimination, we modify Manacher's algorithm for Z-shape detection and elimination. Our experimental results show that our algorithm is faster than Raghavan's in practice, too.

2   Preliminaries

For a tuple $e = (e_1, \ldots, e_m)$ of elements, we represent $(e_0, e_1, \ldots, e_m)$ by $e_0; e$ or $(e_0; e)$. For two integers i, j, we define $[i : j] = \{ k \mid i \le k \le j \}$.

Let Σ be an alphabet. A sequence of elements of Σ is called a *string* and the set of strings is denoted by Σ^*. The empty string is denoted by ε and the set of nonempty strings is $\Sigma^+ = \Sigma^* \setminus \{\varepsilon\}$. For a string $w = xyz$, x, y, and z are called a *prefix*, a *substring*, and a *suffix* of w, respectively. The length of w is denoted by $|w|$. The i-th letter of w is denoted by $w[i]$ for $1 \le i \le |w|$. For $1 \le i \le j \le |w|$, $w[i : j]$ represents $w[i] \ldots w[j]$. The reversed string of w is denoted by $w^R = w[|w|] \cdots w[1]$. The string repeating w k times is w^k.

A string y is called an *even palindrome* if $y = xx^R$ for a string $x \in \Sigma^*$. The *radius* of y is $r = |x|$. We will call an even palindrome simply a palindrome, because we consider only even palindromes in this paper. When y occurs as a substring $w[i : j]$ of a string w, the position $c = i + r - 1$ is called the *center* (of the occurrence) of y. Especially, y is said to be the *maximal palindrome* centered at c iff either $i = 1$, $j = |w|$, or $w[i-1] \ne w[j+1]$. By $\rho_w(c)$ we denote the radius of the maximal palindrome centered at c in w. The sets $\{c - \rho_w(c) + 1, \ldots, c\}$ and $\{c + 1, \ldots, c + \rho_w(c)\}$ of positions are called the *left* and *right arms* of the maximal palindrome centered at c, respectively.

A string z is called a *Z-shape* if $z = xx^Rx$ for a non-empty string $x \in \Sigma^+$. The *tail* of z is the suffix x^Rx. When z occurs as a substring $z = w[i : j]$ of a string w, the positions $p_1 = i + s - 1$ and $p_2 = i + 2s - 1$ are called the *left* and *right pivots* (of the occurrence) of z. The occurrence of the Z-shape is represented by a pair $\langle p_1, p_2 \rangle$. Note that the left and right pivots are the centers of the constituent palindromes xx^R and x^Rx, respectively.

Example 1. For a string $w = \text{ab}\underline{\text{abccbaabc}}\text{a}$, $\langle 5, 8 \rangle$ is an occurrence of Z-shape $w[3 : 11] = \text{abccbaabc}$.

Minimum graph inference from a walk

Let us define a binary relation $\rightarrow$ over nonempty strings by $xyy^Ryz \rightarrow xyz$ for $x, z \in \Sigma^*$ and $y \in \Sigma^+$. We call a string w *irreducible* if there is no string w' such that $w \rightarrow w'$. Aslam and Rivest [2] proved that every string w admits a unique irreducible string w' such that $w \to^* w'$, where $\to^*$ is the reflexive and transitive closure of $\to$. Let us call the string w' the Z-*normal form* of w and denote it by $\hat{w}$. Their result can be written as follows.

Theorem 1. ([2]) *The sequence of the labels of the edges of the minimum path graph with output T of an end-to-end walk is its Z-normal form $\hat{T}$.*

Therefore, to infer the minimum path graph from an end-to-end walk is to calculate its Z-normal form.

Example 2. The Z-normal form of $T = $ cbaaaabccbaabba is $\hat{T} = $ cba, which is obtained by cba<u>aaa</u>bccbaabba $\to$ <u>cbaabccbaabba</u> $\to$ cb<u>aabba</u> $\to$ cba. Here, underlines show Z-shapes to contract. Another way to obtain $\hat{T}$ is cbaaaabcc<u>baabba</u> $\to$ cba<u>aaa</u>bccba $\to$ <u>cbaabccba</u> $\to$ cba.

3   Irreducible and Suffix-Reducible Strings

We call a string w *suffix-reducible* if every proper prefix of w is irreducible but w is reducible. Clearly a Z-shape occurs in a suffix-reducible string as a suffix. By deleting its tail, we obtain an irreducible string. A string w is said to be *pseudo-irreducible* if every proper prefix of w is irreducible.

Starting with $w = u_0 = \varepsilon$, our algorithm repeats the following procedure. We extend $w = u_{i-1}$ by reading letters from the input string T one by one until it becomes a suffix-reducible string $w = v_i$. Then we reduce v_i to $u_i = \hat{v}_i$ by deleting the tail of the Z-shape and resume reading letters of T. By repeatedly applying the procedure, we finally obtain the normal form $w = \hat{T}$.

Therefore, strings our algorithm handles are all pseudo-irreducible. We first study mathematical properties of such strings.

Lemma 1. *Every suffix-reducible string has a unique nonempty suffix palindrome and thus has a unique Z-shape.*

There can be several suffix palindromes in an irreducible string. Lemma 1 implies that only one among those can become[1] the tail of the unique Z-shape in a suffix-reducible string (Lemma 1), in which moment the other ones that used to be suffix palindromes are not suffix palindromes any more. This lemma suggests us to keep watching just one (arbitrary) suffix palindrome when reading letters from the input in order to detect a Z-shape. When the palindrome we are watching has become a non-suffix palindrome, we look for another suffix palindrome to track. Suppose we are tracking a suffix palindrome centered at c of radius $r = \rho_w(c) = |w| - c$ in w. When appending a new letter t from the input to w, it

---

[1] To avoid lengthy expressions, we casually say that a palindrome centered at c in x *becomes* or *grows* to a bigger palindrome in xy when $\rho_x(c) < \rho_{xy}(c)$, without explicitly mentioning several involved mathematical objects that should be understood from the context or that are not important. Other similar phrases should be understood in an appropriate way.

is still a suffix palindrome in wt if and only if $wt[c - r] = wt[c + r + 1] = t$. In that case, it is the tail of a Z-shape if and only if $\rho_w(c - r - 1) \geq r + 1$. Apparently we need to know the maximal radii at all positions to detect a Z-shape but appending a new letter or deleting the tail of a Z-shape disturbs those values even on positions that are not deleted. It takes more than linear time if we keep recalculating the maximal radius at every position. Therefore, we have to partly give up to maintain the exact values of maximal radii. However, there is a moment when maximal radii are stable.

Definition 1. Let w be an irreducible string and c a position in w. We say that c is *stable* in w, if for any string y, either

- there is a prefix x of y for which $|\widehat{wx}| < c$, or
- for any prefix x of y, $\rho_{\widehat{wx}}(c) = \rho_w(c)$.

Moreover, c is *strongly stable* if the former never happens.

That is, if c is stable, the maximum radius at c need not be recalculated when appending letters or deleting a Z-shape's tail at the end of the string, unless the position itself is deleted. In the remainder of this section, we present conditions for a position to be stable.

Let us write $c \sqsubset_w d$ if $c \leq d - \rho_w(d) < d \leq c + \rho_w(c) \leq d + \rho_w(d)$, which roughly means that the right arm of the palindrome centered at c includes the left arm of the one at d. Clearly $c \sqsubset_w d$ implies $\rho_w(c) \geq \rho_w(d)$. Moreover if $c \sqsubset_w d$ and $c = d - \rho_w(d)$ then $\langle c, d \rangle$ is a Z-shape in w. Note that the condition $c \leq d - \rho_w(d)$ in the above definition is redundant for a pseudo-irreducible string; one can see that if $c < d \leq c + \rho_w(c) \leq d + \rho_w(d)$ and $d - \rho_w(d) < c$, then $\langle c, d \rangle$ is a non-suffix Z-shape.

A *palindrome chain from c_0* in w is a sequence $\mathbf{c} = (c_0, \ldots, c_k)$ of positions in w such that $c_{i-1} \sqsubset c_i$ for each $i = 1, \ldots, k$. The *frontier of the palindrome chain $\mathbf{c}$* in w is the position $F_w(\mathbf{c}) = c_k + \rho_w(c_k)$, and the *maximum frontier from a position c* is

$$\mathscr{F}_w(c) = \max\{ F_w(\mathbf{c}) \mid \mathbf{c} \text{ is a palindrome chain from } c \}.$$

The *originator* $\mathscr{A}(d)$ of a position d in w is the smallest position $\mathscr{A}(d) = c$ such that $c \leq d \leq \mathscr{F}_w(c)$. Figure 2 illustrates a palindrome chain in a string $w = \texttt{xabbcddeeddcbbaabbcddcddcy}$.

The stability property can be rephrased in various ways.

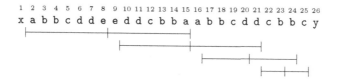

Fig. 2. In a string $w = \texttt{xabbcddeeddcbbaabbcddcbbcy}$, $(8, 15, 20, 23)$ is a palindrome chain, whose frontier is 25. The originator of any position between 8 and 25 is 8

Algorithm 1. Z-detector

```
 1  Let Pals be an empty array and w = ε;
 2  Function ZDetect(T)
 3      T := $T#;                                    // $ and # are sentinel symbols
 4      w.append(T);                                 // append a new letter from T to w
 5      while  there remains to read in T do
 6          w.append(T);
 7          ZDetectInChain(|w| − 1);

 8      output "No Z-shape" and halt;

 9  Function ZDetectInChain(c)
10      b = |w|;
11      Extend(c);
12      for d := b to c + Pals[c] do                 // in increasing order
13          if d + Pals[2c − d] < c + Pals[c] then Pals[d] := Pals[2c − d] ;
14          else ZDetectInChain(d) and break;

15  Function Extend(c)
16      r := |w| − c − 1;
17      while w[c + r + 1] = w[c − r] do
18          r := r + 1;
19          if Pals[c − r] ≥ r then output ⟨c − r, c⟩ and halt;
20          w.append(T);
21      Pals[c] := r;
```

Proposition 1. *The following four are equivalent:*

(1) c is stable in w,

(2) $\mathscr{F}_w(c) < |w|$,

(3) for any string y, either
  – there is a prefix x of y for which $|\widehat{wx}| < c$, or
  – for any prefix x of y, $|\widehat{wx}| > \mathscr{F}_w(c)$,

(4) $c \sqsubset_w d$ implies that d is stable in w for all d.

Here is another rephrasing.

Corollary 1. *Suppose that positions $c + 1, \ldots, |w| − 1$ are all stable in an irreducible string w. Then a position c is stable if and only if $c + \rho_w(c) < |w|$.*

It is not hard to see that a position c is strongly stable if and only if all the positions $d \leq c$ are stable. If a position c is strongly stable in w, then $|\widehat{wx}| > c$ for any x.

4 Algorithm

Our algorithm is based on Manacher's [3] for calculating the radius of the maximal palindrome at every position in an input. Algorithm 1 detects the first occurrence of a Z-shape in the input string T. Commenting out Line 19 gives his original algorithm with slightly different appearance. The algorithm reads letters from the input one by one, while focusing on the left-most suffix palindrome among possibly many others. The algorithm computes the maximum radius at each position from left to right and stores those values in the array $Pals$. The function $\mathsf{Extend}(c)$ calculates $Pals[c]$ naively comparing letters on the left and right in the same distance from c, knowing that the radius is at least $|w| - c - 1$. Due to the symmetry, the maximum radii at positions in the right arm of a big palindrome coincide those at the corresponding positions in the left arm, unless those palindromes in the right arm may go beyond the right end of the big palindrome. The function $\mathsf{ZDetectInChain}(c)$ copies the value of $Pals[c - r]$ to $Pals[c + r]$ ($d = c + r$ in the algorithm) for $r \leq Pals[c]$ as long as $c + r + Pals[c - r] < c + Pals[c]$. If $c + r + Pals[c - r] \geq c + Pals[c]$, which means $c \sqsubset c + r$, $\mathsf{ZDetectInChain}(c)$ recursively calls $\mathsf{ZDetectInChain}(c + r)$. If there is no such r, it means that we have reached the frontier of the originator of c. By the correctness of his algorithm and Lemma 1, we see that Algorithm 1 outputs the Z-shape occurrence of the shortest suffix-reducible prefix of the input. If the input has no Z-shape, it halts with the array $Pals$ such that $Pals[c] = \rho_w(c)$ for all the positions c. One may think of using this algorithm to compute the normal form by deleting the tail of the found Z-shape. However, deleting a Z-shape tail alters the maximal radii, which have been calculated before, and maintaining those values is not a trivial issue. As we have discussed earlier, to keep recalculating the exact values of the maximal radii takes more than linear time.

4.1   Outline of Our Algorithm

Our online algorithm for calculating the Z-normal form of an input string T is shown as Algorithm 2. Throughout the algorithm, the string w in the working space is kept pseudo-irreducible. That is, $w^\lhd = w[1 : |w| - 1]$ is irreducible and we would like to know if w itself is still irreducible. Algorithm 2 consists of functions $\mathsf{Stabilize}$, $\mathsf{SlowExtend}$ and $\mathsf{FastExtend}$ in addition to the main function $\mathsf{ZReduce}$. Among those, $\mathsf{Stabilize}$ plays the central role. The data structures we use are very simple: a working string w, an array $Pals$ for the maximal radius at each position of w, and a stack of positions. Those are all global variables in Algorithm 2. At the beginning, we add extra fresh symbols \$ and # to the left and right ends of the input, respectively. Those work as sentinel symbols so that we never try to access the working string beyond the ends when extending a suffix palindrome.

The working string is initialized to be the empty string and is expanded by appending letters from T one by one by append. Suppose that we have read u from the input and $w = \hat{u}$ is in the working space. When the function $\mathsf{Stabilize}(c)$ is called, we know that $c + \rho_{w^\lhd}(c) = |w^\lhd|$ but not yet sure if $c + \rho_w(c) = |w|$ holds. Then $\mathsf{Stabilize}(c)$ processes the shortest prefix v of the unprocessed suffix of T such that c is stable in the resultant string $w' = \widehat{wv}$, i.e., $\mathscr{F}_{w'}(c) = |w'| - 1$. In an extreme case, we have $w' = w$ and just confirm $\mathscr{F}_w(c) = |w| - 1$. After the execution of $\mathsf{Stabilize}(c)$, unless it returns true, it is guaranteed that all positions $d \in [c : \mathscr{F}_{w'}(c)]$ are stable in w' and satisfy $Pals[d] = \rho_{w'}(d)$. This is why we

---

Algorithm 2. Z-reducer

```
 1  Let Stack be an empty stack, Pals an empty array and w = ε;
 2  Function ZReduce(T)
 3      T := $T#;                                    // $ and # are sentinel symbols
 4      w.append(T);
 5      while there remains to read in T do
 6          w.append(T); Stack.clear();
 7          Stabilize(|w| − 1);
 8      return w[2 : |w| − 1];                        // strip the sentinel symbols

 9  Function Stabilize(c)
10      b = |w|; unstable := true;
11      while unstable do
12          unstable := false;
13          if SlowExtend(c) then return true;
14          for d := c + Pals[c] downto b do         // in decreasing order
15              if d + Pals[d] ≥ c + Pals[c] then
16                  if FastExtend(d) then
17                      if Stabilize(d) then
18                          if c = |w| then return true;
19                          if d = |w| then Pals[d] := Pals[2c − d];
20                          w.append(T); unstable := true;
21                          break;
22                  Stack.push(d);

23      return false;

24  Function SlowExtend(c)
25      r := |w| − c − 1;
26      while w[c + r + 1] = w[c − r] do
27          r := r + 1;
28          if Pals[c − r] ≥ r then                   // detect a suffix Z-shape ⟨c − r, c⟩
29              w := w[1 : c − r];                     // contract the suffix Z-shape
30              Pals := Pals[1 : c − r];               //      same as above
31              return true;
32          Pals[c + r] := Pals[c − r];                // transfer the value
33          w.append(T);
34      Pals[c] := r;                                  // Pals[c] = ρ_w(c)
35      return false;

36  Function FastExtend(d)
37      while Stack is not empty do
38          r := Stack.top() − d;
39          if Pals[d − r] ≥ Pals[d + r] then Stack.pop();
40          else Pals[d] := r + Pals[d − r]; return false;   // Pals[d] = ρ_w(d)
41      return true;
```

name the function Stabilize. Moreover if the call of Stabilize(c) was from the main function ZReduce(T), $c = \mathscr{A}_{w'}(c)$ and those positions d are all strongly stable.

To stabilize all the positions up to the (future) frontier of c, Stabilize(c) recursively calls Stabilize(d) for positions d such that $c \sqsubset d$. This accords with the definition of the frontier. To determine positions d on which we should recursively call Stabilize(d), we need to know the value of $\rho_w(c)$ first of all. The function Stabilize(c) first calls SlowExtend(c). When the function SlowExtend(c) is called, we are sure $c + \rho_{w^{\triangleleft}}(c) \geq |w^{\triangleleft}|$. By reading more letters from the input, it does three tasks. One is to calculate the maximal radius at c exactly, taking the unread part of the input into account. One is to detect and contract a Z-shape whose right pivot is c. The last one is to transfer the values of $Pals$ on the left arm to the right arm. We extend the palindrome at c by comparing values of $w[c - r]$ and $w[c+r+1]$. When it happens that $Pals[c-r] \geq r$, this means that we find a Z-shape occurrence $\langle c-r, c\rangle$. In this case, the suffix palindrome shall be deleted, and the function returns true. When the palindrome has become non-suffix, it returns false. During the extension of the palindrome at c, it copies the value of $Pals[c - r]$ to $Pals[c+r]$. This transfer might appear nonsense, since it might be the case that $\rho_w(c-r) \neq \rho_w(c+r)$. However, this "sloppy calculation" of radii is advantageous over the exactly correctly calculated values. Those copied values are "adaptive" in extensions and deletions of succeeding part of the working string (and thus the maximal radius at c), in the sense that they can always be used to certainly detect a Z-shape occurrence where the concerned position is the left-pivot. The exactly correct values are too rigid to have this property. Those values will be fixed in the recursive calls of Stabilize.

On Line 14 of Algorithm 2, we recursively call Stabilize(d) in decreasing order for positions on the right arm of the palindrome at c. This "reversed" order might appear unnatural, but this is also related to the adaptability of values in $Pals$. To stabilize positions, anyway we have to calculate the maximal radius at some positions, though they are not yet stable. If we calculate $\rho_w(d)$ in increasing order, they are not adaptive any more. In this case, once some suffix of the working string is deleted and then extended, those exact values would become useless. Contrarily, we calculate $\rho_w(d)$ in the opposite order. Then the previously copied values of $Pals$ on the left are adaptive and remain useful, unless they are deleted.

Palindromes overlap a lot even in an irreducible string and we must avoid scanning the same position multiple times. The function FastExtend(d) tells us whether the palindrome at d is a suffix of $w^{\triangleleft}$ without looking at letters in the working space. The computation is quickly done by using a stack which stores positions $c_0, \ldots, c_k$ forming a palindrome chain with d such that $F_{w^{\triangleleft}}(d, c_0, \ldots, c_k) = |w^{\triangleleft}|$. Moreover, it is guaranteed that those positions c_i are stable and $Pals[c_i] = \rho_w(c_i)$. If the right arm of the palindrome centered at d can reach $|w^{\triangleleft}|$, the left arm of it must have the structure that can be seen as the "reversed" palindrome chain symmetric to the one in $Stack$. By examining whether $Pals[2d - c_i] = Pals[c_i]$ for each i, one can tell whether the right arm of the maximal palindrome at d can reach the position $|w| - 1$. If it is the case, FastExtend(d) returns true and lets SlowExtend extend the palindrome by investigating further. Otherwise, FastExtend(d) lets $Pals[d] = \rho_w(d)$ and returns false.

Example 3. We show a running example of Algorithm 2. Consider an input string $T = $ abbaa1221aabbaa11aabbb. Assume that ZReduce(T) has read $w = $ \$abbaa12 and computed $Pals[1 : 7]$, where the red part has been stabilized. Then, Stabilize(8) extends the palindrome at 8 by SlowExtend(8) up to $w = $ \$abbaa1221aabbaa. Next, Stabilize(15), called by Stabilize(8), finds a maximal palindrome aa in $w = $ \$abbaa1221aabbaa1. Then 15 is pushed to the stack. After that, FastExtend(13), called via Stabilize(13) by Stabilize(8), reveals that $\rho_w(13) \geq 3$ in $w = $ \$abbaa1221aabbaa1 using $Stack = (15)$. Then SlowExtend(13) extends the radius of the palindrome at 13 by one as $w = $ \$abbaa1221aabbaa11. Then Stabilize(13) calls Stabilize(17). By reading further letters from T, the working string becomes $w = $ \$abbaa1221aabbaa11aab, where a Z-shape occurrence $\langle 13, 17 \rangle = $ 1aabbaa11aab is found. By deleting the tail of it, we have $w = $ \$abbaa1221aab, on which Stabilize(8) resumes calculation. Now the palindrome is extended as $w = $ \$abbaa1221aabbb. Then Stabilize(18) calls Stabilize(14), which detects and contracts $\langle 13, 14 \rangle = $ bbb. We now have $w = $ \$abbaa1221aa. After that, Stabilize(8) continues extending the palindrome and obtains $w = $ \$abbaa1221aab#. Finally, ZReduce halts with $\hat{T} = w[2 : |w| - 1] = $ abbaa1221aab.

4.2   Correctness and Complexity of the Algorithm

To prove the correctness of our algorithm, we first introduce some technical definitions, which characterize "adaptive" values.

Definition 2. Let us write $i \sim_k j$ if $\min\{i, k\} = \min\{j, k\}$. We say that $Pals$ on w is *accurate enough between c and d* if for any $e \in [c : d]$, it holds that $Pals[e] \sim_{d-e} \rho_w(e)$. We denote this property by $\text{Æ}_w(c, d)$ with implicit understanding of $Pals$.

Let $\nu_w(c)$ denote the largest e such that $e \sqsubset c$. If there is no such e, let $\nu_w(c) = 1$. We say that c is *left-good* in w if $\text{Æ}_w(\nu_w(c), c)$ holds. We say that c is *right-good* in w if $\text{Æ}_w(c, c + \rho_w(c))$ holds.

Clearly $\text{Æ}_w(c_1, d_1)$ implies $\text{Æ}_w(c_2, d_2)$ if $[c_2 : d_2] \subseteq [c_1 : d_1]$.

Lemma 2. *Suppose that c is left-good and $\rho_w(c) = |w| - c$ for a pseudo-irreducible string w. Then w has a Z-shape occurrence $\langle c - \rho_w(c), c \rangle$ if and only if $Pals[c - \rho_w(c)] \geq \rho_w(c)$. Suppose in addition $Pals[c - r] = Pals[c + r]$ for all $r = 1, \ldots, \rho_w(c)$. Then, c is right-good.*

If $\text{Æ}_w(d, c)$ holds, then one can correctly determine whether w has a Z-shape with right pivot c. Namely, $\langle d, c \rangle$ is a Z-shape if and only if $Pals[d] \geq c - d$. We detect a suffix Z-shape whose right pivot is c extending a suffix palindrome at c in SlowExtend(c). Lemma 2 means that this indeed works well when c is left-good and values on the left arm are copied to the corresponding positions on the right arm. Note that the left-goodness depends on $w[1:c]$ only. This means that this property is robust against deletion and extension of the right arm.

We will show that the function Stabilize satisfies the following precondition and postcondition, where w and w' are the working strings before and after a call, respectively.

Condition 1 (Precondition of Stabilize(c)).

- *Stack* is empty,
- $c + \rho_w(c) \geq |w| - 1$,
- c is left-good,
- For all positions $d \in [1 : \mathscr{A}(c) - 1] \cup [c + 1 : |w| - 1]$, d is stable in w and $Pals[d] = \rho_w(d)$.

Condition 2 (Postcondition of Stabilize(c)).

- If it returns true, then
  - $w' = \widehat{w}u$ for the shortest string u appended from the input such that $|w'| \leq c$,
  - *Stack* is empty.
- If it returns false, then $w' = \widehat{w}u$ for the shortest string u appended from the input such that
  - $(c; Stack)$ is a palindrome chain such that $\mathscr{F}_{w'}(c) = F_{w'}(c; Stack) = |w'| - 1$,
  - d is stable in w' and $Pals[d] = \rho_w(d)$ for all $d \in [c : |w'| - 1]$.

Lemma 3 (Stabilize). *Suppose that c satisfies Condition 1. Then after executing Stabilize(c), Condition 2 is satisfied.*

Assuming that Lemma 3 is true, we establish the following proposition.

Proposition 2. *Algorithm 2 calculates the normal form of the input.*

When Stablize(c) tries to fix the value $Pals[c]$ to be $\rho_w(c)$, the right arm of the palindrome at c may be cut in the middle after finding the end of the right arm in a string, unless it has been stabilized. Then we need to extend it again. The **while** loop is repeated until c becomes stable.

Condition 3 (Precondition of the while loop). In addition to Condition 1,

- for all positions $d \in [b : |w| - 1]$, $Pals[d] = Pals[2c - d]$.

In what follows we give some lemmas that explain the behavior of our algorithm in a more formal way.

Lemma 4 (SlowExtend). *Suppose that at the beginning of an iteration of the **while** loop of Stabilize(c), Condition 3 holds. Let w and w' be the working strings before and after execution of SlowExtend(c), respectively. Then either*

- SlowExtend(c) *returns* true,
- $w' = \widehat{wu}$ *for u appended from the input such that wu is suffix-reducible and the right pivot of the Z-shape is c,*

or

- SlowExtend(c) *returns* false,
- $w' = wu$ *for u appended from the input such that $c + \rho_{w'}(c) = |w'| - 1$ and w' is pseudo-irreducible,*
- $Pals[c] = \rho_{w'}(c)$,
- *for all $r \in [1 : Pals[c]]$, $Pals[c + r] = Pals[c - r]$.*

Lemma 5 (FastExtend). *Suppose that FastExtend(d) is called from Stabilize(c) satisfying that*

- *(c; Stack) is a palindrome chain from some $e > d$ such that $F_w(c; Stack) = \max\{\, \mathscr{F}_w(e) \mid d < e \le c + Pals[c]\,\} = |w| - 1$,*
- *c is left-good and right-good,*
- *for all $e \in [d + 1 : |w| - 1]$, e is stable and $Pals[e] = \rho_w(e)$,*

Then after the execution,

- *if it returns* true, *then $d + \rho_w(d) \ge |w| - 1$ and Stack is empty,*
- *if it returns* false, *then*
  - *(d; Stack) is a palindrome chain such that $F_w(d; Stack) = \max\{\, \mathscr{F}_w(e) \mid d \le e \le c + Pals[c]\,\} = |w| - 1$,*
  - *for all $e \in [d : |w| - 1]$, e is stable and $Pals[e] = \rho_w(e)$.*

Lemma 6. *Suppose that c is right-good and $c \sqsubset_w d$ in a pseudo-irreducible string w. Then d is left-good in w.*

Hence, when FastExtend(d) returns true, Condition 1 for d is satisfied.

Now we have prepared enough for analyzing the function Stabilize(c). Our goals is to show that Condition 2 holds for Stabilize(c) provided that Condition 1 holds. The function Stabilize(c) calls Stabilize(d) recursively. For now we assume that Condition 1 implies Condition 2 for those d. Then this inductive argument completes a proof of Lemma 3.

Suppose that Condition 1 holds for Stabilize(c). If SlowExtend(c) returns true, clearly Condition 2 holds by Lemma 4. Hereafter we suppose that SlowExtend(c) returns false.

Lemma 7 (for loop). *Suppose that Condition 3 is satisfied at the beginning of every iteration of the **while** loop. Then, at the beginning of each iteration of the **for** loop of Stabilize(c), the following holds.*

- *(c; Stack) is a palindrome chain such that*

$$F_w(c; Stack) = \max(\{\, \mathscr{F}_w(e) \mid d < e \le c + Pals[c]\,\} \cup \{c + Pals[c]\}) = |w| - 1,$$

- *c is left-good,*

– for all $e \in [c+1:d]$, $Pals[d] = Pals[2c - d]$,
– for all $e \in [d+1:|w|-1]$, e is stable and $Pals[e] = \rho_w(e)$.

Moreover if we **break** the loop, still Condition 3 holds. If we return true on Line 18, Condition 2 holds for c.

Lemma 8 (while loop). At the beginning of an iteration of the **while** loop in Stabilize(c), Condition 3 holds. Moreover if it returns true, Condition 2 holds.

Theorem 2. Algorithm 2 calculates the normal form of the input in linear time.

Proof. The function Stabilize is called from ZReduce or Stabilize itself. In both cases, Stabilize(c) is called right after a new letter is appended at position $c+1$. More precisely, in the latter case, Stabilize(d) is called just after SlowExtend(c) or Stabilize(c) appended a new letter at position $d+1$. Note that when **while** loop repeats, the letters on the positions $d+1$ for which Stabilize(d) was called are deleted. Therefore, the number of calls of Stabilize is bounded by $|T|$.

This explanation about the number of calls of Stabilize also shows that the total number of the execution of the **while** loop is bounded by $|T|$ and this implies the number of calls of SlowExtend is also bounded by $|T|$. The total running time of SlowExtend is bounded by the number of its calls and the times of appending letters from T, which is bounded by $O(|T|)$ in total. The same argument on the number of calls of Stabilize applies to that of executions of the **for** loop. This implies that the total number of positions that is pushed onto the stack is bounded by $|T|$, which implies that total running time of FastExtend is bounded by $O(|T|)$.

All in all, Algorithm 2 runs in linear time. □

By using Algorithm 2 and Raghavan's algorithm [6], the smallest path and cycle can be inferred from walks in linear time.

Corollary 2. Given a string w of length n, the smallest path and cycle on which w is the output of a walk can be inferred in $O(n)$ time.

5   Experiments

This section presents experimental performance of our algorithm comparing with Raghavan's $O(n \log n)$ time algorithm [6].

We implemented these algorithms in C++ and compiled with Visual C++ 12.0 (2013) compiler. The experiments were conducted on Windows 7 PC with Xeon W3565 and 12GB RAM. In the whole experiments, we got the average running time for 10 times of attempts.

First, for randomly generated strings of length between 10^5 and 10^6 over Σ of size $|\Sigma| = 2, 6, 10$, we compared the running time of the algorithms (Fig. 3 (a)). For any alphabet size, our proposed algorithm ran faster.

Furthermore, we conducted experiments for strings of length between 10^6 and 10^7 with the same alphabets, and got a similar result (Fig. 3 (b)). Here,

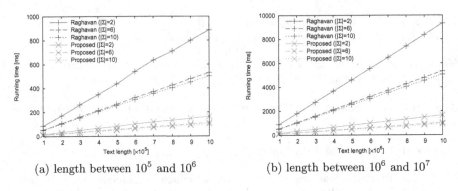

(a) length between 10^5 and 10^6 (b) length between 10^6 and 10^7

Fig. 3. Running time for the random strings with $|\Sigma| = 2, 6, 10$

the slope of Raghavan's algorithm's performance increases slightly as the string length increases. On the other hand, our proposed algorithm keeps the same slope. This shows the proposed algorithm runs in linear time in practice.

Acknowledgments. The research is supported by JSPS KAKENHI Grant Numbers JP15H05706, JP26330013 and JP18K11150, and ImPACT Program of Council for Science, Technology and Innovation (Cabinet Office, Government of Japan).

References

1. Akutsu, T., Fukagawa, D.: Inferring a graph from path frequency. In: Apostolico, A., Crochemore, M., Park, K. (eds.) CPM 2005. LNCS, vol. 3537, pp. 371–382. Springer, Heidelberg (2005). https://doi.org/10.1007/11496656_32
2. Aslam, J.A., Rivest, R.L.: Inferring graphs from walks. In: Computational Learning Theory, pp. 359–370 (1990)
3. Manacher, G.K.: A new linear-time on-line algorithm for finding the smallest initial palindrome of a string. J. ACM **22**(3), 346–351 (1975)
4. Maruyama, O., Miyano, S.: Graph inference from a walk for trees of bounded degree 3 is NP-complete. In: Wiedermann, J., Hájek, P. (eds.) MFCS 1995. LNCS, vol. 969, pp. 257–266. Springer, Heidelberg (1995). https://doi.org/10.1007/3-540-60246-1_132
5. Maruyama, O., Miyano, S.: Inferring a tree from walks. Theor. Comput. Sci. **161**(1), 289–300 (1996)
6. Raghavan, V.: Bounded degree graph inference from walks. J. Comput. Syst. Sci. **49**(1), 108–132 (1994)

Trickier XBWT Tricks

Enno Ohlebusch$^{(\boxtimes)}$, Stefan Stauß, and Uwe Baier

Institute of Theoretical Computer Science, Ulm University, 89069 Ulm, Germany
{Enno.Ohlebusch,Stefan.Stauss,Uwe.Baier}@uni-ulm.de

Abstract. A trie [11] is one of the best data structures for implementing and searching a dictionary. However, to build the trie structure for larger collections of strings takes up a lot of memory. Since the eXtended Burrows-Wheeler Transform (XBWT) [8,9] is able to compactly represent a labeled tree, it can naturally be used to succinctly represent a trie. The XBWT also supports navigational operations on the trie, but it does not support failure links. For example, the Aho-Corasick algorithm [1] for simultaneously searching for several patterns in a text achieves its good worst-case time complexity only with the aid of failure links. Manzini [18] showed that a balanced parentheses sequence P can be used to support failure links in constant time with only $2n + o(n)$ bits of space, where n is the number of internal nodes in the trie. Besides practical algorithms that construct the XBWT, he also provided two different algorithms that construct P. In this paper, we suggest an alternative way for constructing P that outperforms the previous algorithms.

1 Introduction

The eXtended Burrows-Wheeler Transform (XBWT) [8,9] can be used to compactly represent a trie by a character array L and a bit array Last; see Fig. 1 for an example. A recent empirical comparison [19] of string dictionary implementations shows that the XBWT achieves the best compression of all techniques under consideration. Moreover, in contrast to most other methods, the XBWT supports substring searches. The compact representation of the XBWT can be computed as follows. Each internal node v of the trie T is associated with a string that is obtained by concatenating the characters at the edges in the *upward* path from v to the root of T (the root itself is associated with the empty string ε). If T has n internal nodes, then there are n associated strings and the (virtual) array $\Pi[1..n]$ stores them in lexicographical order. We (conceptually) number the internal nodes of T according to Π: If node v is associated with the string $\Pi[i]$, it gets the number i. Let L_i be the set of characters at outgoing edges of node i (in no particular order) and let the character array L contain the concatenation of $L_1, L_2, \ldots, L_n$. Furthermore, the bit array Last stores the borders of L_i: we initialize Last with zeros and for all $i \in \{1, \ldots, n\}$ we set $\mathsf{Last}[j_i] = 1$, where $j_i = \sum_{\ell=1}^{i} |L_\ell|$. As already mentioned, the XBWT representation of the trie consists of the arrays L and Last. These arrays can be calculated with the help of an array MR, which we will define next.

© Springer Nature Switzerland AG 2018
T. Gagie et al. (Eds.): SPIRE 2018, LNCS 11147, pp. 325–333, 2018.
https://doi.org/10.1007/978-3-030-00479-8_26

Suppose the trie T is constructed from the pairwise distinct strings $x_1,\ldots,x_k$. Let $y_i = x_i^R$, where x_i^R denotes the string that is obtained by reversing x_i. Furthermore, let $S = y_1\$y_2\$\ldots y_k\$$ be the concatenation of the y_i, separated by a special character $\$$, which is assumed to be smaller than any other character. In the following, let m be the length of S (note that $m = k + \sum_{i=1}^{k}|x_i|$). The suffix array SA and the Burrows-Wheeler Transform BWT of S are obtained by sorting the suffixes of S lexicographically (this can be done in linear time): If $S[j..m]$ is the i-th lexicographically smallest suffix of S, then $\mathsf{SA}[i] = j$ and $\mathsf{BWT}[i] = S[j-1]$ is the character preceding that suffix (if $j = 1$, then $\mathsf{BWT}[i] = \$$); see Fig. 1 for an example. Fast implementations of (semi-) external suffix sorting algorithms exist [6,16], but multi-string BWT construction algorithms may be competitive in the context of this paper; see [3,17]. The array MR is defined with the help of suffix array intervals. If ω is a substring of S, then the ω-interval is the largest interval $[i..j]$ such that ω is a prefix of all the suffixes in the interval $[i..j]$. Now $\mathsf{MR}[lb] = 1$ if and only if lb is the left boundary of a z-interval, where z is a suffix of some y_i (i.e., z^R is a prefix of some x_i). Note that $\mathsf{MR}[1] = 1$ because ε is a suffix of all y_i and $[1..m]$ is the ε-interval. To avoid case distinctions, we set $\mathsf{MR}[m+1] = 1$. Let $j_1 = 1 < j_2 < \cdots < j_n < j_{n+1} = m+1$ be the indices with $\mathsf{MR}[j_\ell] = 1$. For each i with $1 \leq i \leq n$, the interval $[j_i..j_{i+1} - 1]$ is the $\Pi[i]$-interval. Thus L_i is the set of the characters in $\mathsf{BWT}[j_i..j_{i+1} - 1]$ and $\mathsf{Last}[p_i] = 1$, where $p_i = \sum_{\ell=1}^{i}|L_\ell|$. It is readily verified that the arrays L and Last can be computed in $O(m)$ time by simultaneously scanning the arrays MR and BWT from left to right.

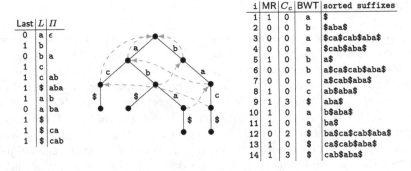

Last	L	Π
0	a	ϵ
1	b	
0	b	a
1	c	
1	c	ab
1	$	aba
1	a	b
0	a	ba
1	$	
1	$	ca
1	$	cab

i	MR	C_c	BWT	sorted suffixes
1	1	0	a	$
2	0	0	b	aba
3	0	0	a	cacababa
4	0	0	a	cababa$
5	1	0	b	a$
6	0	0	b	acacababa
7	0	0	c	acababa$
8	1	0	c	ababa
9	1	3	$	aba$
10	1	0	a	baba
11	1	0	a	ba$
12	0	2	$	bacacababa
13	1	0	$	cacababa$
14	1	3	$	cababa

Fig. 1. Example for the input strings $\mathsf{ab},\mathsf{ac},\mathsf{bac},\mathsf{aba}$. Left: XBWT consisting of the arrays Last and L (the array Π is not stored). Center: Trie of the strings, where failure links of internal nodes are indicated by dashed arrows. Right: MR, C_c, and BWT for the concatenation of the reversed strings (i.e., $S = \mathsf{ba\$ca\$cab\$aba\$}$).

Recall that node i in the trie T is associated with the string $\Pi[i]$. In this context, the *failure link* of i points to the node j so that $\Pi[j]$ is the longest proper prefix of $\Pi[i]$. Failure links are not supported by the XBWT representation of T, but Manzini [18] showed that a balanced parentheses sequence P can be used to support them in constant time with only $2n+o(n)$ bits of space. P can be defined by means of Π: For $i = 1,\ldots,n$ a pair of parentheses is written by repeating the following: (1) For each $\ell < i$, for which its closing parenthesis has not been written yet and $\Pi[\ell]$ is *not* a prefix of $\Pi[i]$, write a closing parenthesis. (2) Write the opening parenthesis for i. After termination of this for-loop, write a closing parenthesis for each ℓ, for which its closing parenthesis has not been written yet. In the example of Fig. 1, we have $P = ((((()))(())(())))$. P can be preprocessed in linear time, using only $o(n)$ bits, so that the operations *rank*, *select*, and *enclose* can be supported in constant time [7,15,20]. Using these operations on P, failure links can be supported in constant time; see [18, Lemma 4] for details. Manzini [18] devised two different algorithms that construct P. In the next section, we suggest an alternative way for constructing P that outperforms his algorithms.

2   The New Algorithm

Our new construction algorithm uses an idea of Belazzougui [4], who devised a rather simple method to build the balanced parenthesis representation of a suffix tree topology. He writes: "Our key observation is that we can easily build a balanced parenthesis representation by enumerating the suffix array intervals. More precisely for every position in $[1..n]$, we associate two counters, one for open and the other for close parentheses implemented through two arrays of counters $C_o[1..n]$ and $C_c[1..n]$. Then given a suffix array interval $[i,j]$ we will simply increment the counters $C_o[i]$ and $C_c[j]$. Then we scan the counters C_c and C_o in parallel and for each i from 1 to n, write $C_o[i]$ opening parentheses followed by $C_c[i]$ closing parentheses. It is easy to see that the constructed sequence is that of the balanced parentheses of the suffix tree." Since we do not want to represent a suffix tree topology, we cannot enumerate *all* suffix array intervals. Instead, we must enumerate all z-intervals for which z is a suffix of some y_i (for then z^R is a prefix of some x_i). Recall that $MR[lb] = 1$ if and only if lb is the left boundary of such a z-interval. Consequently, the array $MR[1..m]$ coincides with the array $C_o[1..m]$. Moreover, observe that if z is a suffix of some y_i, then the left boundary b_z of the z-interval in the suffix array of S coincides with the left boundary $b_{z\$}$ of the $z\$$-interval because $z\$$ is a substring of S and $\$$ is the smallest character.

For the explanation of the pseudo-code of our new construction algorithm (Algorithm 1), we need a few preliminaries. For each character c, $C[c]$ is the overall number of occurrences of characters in $BWT[1..m]$ that are strictly smaller than c. Given the ω-interval $[lb..rb]$ and a character c, the $c\omega$-interval $[i..j]$ can be computed by $i = C[c] + rank_c(BWT, lb-1) + 1$ and $j = C[c] + rank_c(BWT, rb)$, where $rank_c(BWT, lb-1)$ returns the number of occurrences of character c in the prefix $BWT[1..lb-1]$ (we have $i \leq j$ if $c\omega$ is a substring of S; otherwise $i > j$); see [10] for details. The (balanced) *wavelet tree* [14] of the BWT supports such a backward search step in $O(\log \sigma)$ time, where σ is the size of the alphabet. Backward search can be generalized on the wavelet tree as follows: Given an ω-interval $[lb..rb]$, a slight modification of the procedure *getIntervals*$([lb..rb])$

Algorithm 1. Computation of the arrays MR and C_c

1: **function** VISIT($b_{z\$}, e_{z\$}, e_z$)   ▷ the $z\$$-interval is $[b_{z\$}..e_{z\$}]$ and the z-interval is
   $[b_{z\$}..e_z]$, where z is a suffix of some string y_i
2:    MR$[b_{z\$}] \leftarrow 1$
3:    $C_c[e_z] \leftarrow C_c[e_z] + 1$
4:    $list \leftarrow getIntervals([b_{z\$}..e_{z\$}])$
5:    **for** each $(c, [b_{cz\$}..e_{cz\$}])$ with $c \neq \$$ in $list$ **do**
6:       **if** $e_z = e_{z\$}$ **then**
7:          $e_{cz} \leftarrow e_{cz\$}$
8:       **else**
9:          $e_{cz} \leftarrow C[c] + rank_c(\text{BWT}, e_z)$
10:      VISIT($b_{cz\$}, e_{cz\$}, e_{cz}$)

---

described in [5] returns the list $[(c, [i..j]) \mid c\omega$ is a substring of S and $[i..j]$ is the $c\omega$-interval], where the first component of an element $(c, [i..j])$ is a character. The worst-case time complexity of the procedure $getIntervals$ is $O(occ + occ \cdot \log(\sigma/occ))$, where occ is the number of elements in the output list; see [12, Lemma 3].

If $z = \varepsilon$ is the empty string, then the z-interval is $[b_z..e_z] = [1..m]$ and the $z\$$-interval is $[b_{z\$}..e_{z\$}] = [1..k]$. The function call VISIT $(1, k, m)$ computes the arrays MR $= C_o$ and C_c; the pseudo-code of this function can be found in Algorithm 1. The function first counts an opening parenthesis at position $b_z = b_{z\$}$ and a closing parenthesis at position e_z. With the help of the procedure $getIntervals$ it then computes all non-empty $cz\$$-intervals, where $c \in \Sigma$ and $c \neq \$$. The fact that a $cz\$$-interval $[b_{cz\$}..e_{cz\$}]$ is not empty means that cz is a suffix of some y_i. It follows as a consequence that the cz-interval $[b_{cz}..e_{cz}]$ is also not empty. Again, $b_{cz} = b_{cz\$}$ holds true, but the right boundary e_{cz} of the cz-interval is not known yet. Now there are two cases. If the right boundaries of the z-interval and the $z\$$-interval coincided, then so do the right boundaries e_{cz} and $e_{cz\$}$ of the cz-interval and the $cz\$$-interval. If they were not the same, e_{cz} must be computed by evaluating $C[c] + rank_c(\text{BWT}, e_z)$ as in backward search. Finally, the function recursively calls itself with the new parameters $b_{cz\$}, e_{cz\$}, e_{cz}$.

The overall time complexity of the construction of P is $O(m \log \sigma)$ because the BWT can be build in $O(m)$ time, the wavelet tree of the BWT can be constructed in $O(m \log \sigma)$ time, initialization and computation of the arrays MR and C_c takes $O(m + n \log \sigma)$ time (n is the number of internal nodes of the trie and satisfies $n \leq m$), and the computation of P based on MR and C_c requires $O(m)$ time.

Let us consider the working space of Algorithm 1. By the definition of P, there are at most $\max_i |x_i|$ consecutive closing parentheses, thus the array C_c requires $m \log(\max_i |x_i|)$ bits. The array MR occupies only m bits and the wavelet tree of the BWT essentially uses $m\lceil \log \sigma \rceil + o(m \log \sigma)$ bits of space; see e.g. [21]. The stack for the recursion contains (at any point in time) at most $\max_i |x_i|$ elements. Each stack element stores a list returned by the procedure $getIntervals$; this

Algorithm 2. Computation of P with less space

1: **input:** BWT
2: compute the bit array MR of size m
3: preprocess MR so that rank-queries can be answered in constant time
4: initialize an array C'_c of size $n = rank_1(\text{MR}, m)$ with zeros
5: VISIT2$(1, k, m)$
6: initialize an array P of size $2n$ with zeros   ▷ $2n$ opening parentheses
7: $k \leftarrow 1$
8: **for** $i \leftarrow 1$ **to** n **do**
9:     $k \leftarrow k + 1$ ▷ opening parenthesis because $P[k] = 0$
10:    **for** $j \leftarrow 1$ **to** $C'_c[i]$ **do**
11:        $P[k] \leftarrow 1$ ▷ write closing parentheses
12:        $k \leftarrow k + 1$
13: **return:** P

---

list contains at most σ elements of the form $(c, [lb..rb])$. Since every list element requires $O(1)$ space, the whole stack uses $O(\sigma \cdot \max_i |x_i|)$ space.

3   Saving Space

As already observed by Manzini [18], the number n of ones in the bit array MR gives the number of internal nodes of the trie. If one computes MR in a first phase (for instance, by the algorithm in [18, Fig. 4]), then n is known and more space-efficient algorithms for computing P can be deduced. Manzini suggests to use two arrays RCP' and LEN' of length n that use $O(n \log(\max_i |x_i|))$ bits of memory and store only values for which the corresponding entry in the array MR equals 1. His algorithm [18, Fig. 5] calculates P based on these arrays. We would like to follow this approach, but the example from Fig. 1 shows that there are non-zero entries $C_c[i]$ for which $\text{MR}[i] = 0$ ($i = 12$ in Fig. 1). We next derive a version of Algorithm 1 that increments only counters at indices i for which $\text{MR}[i] = 1$. To distinguish the new version from Algorithm 1, we use $\hat{C}_c$ to denote the array of counters (which is still of size m). Recall that Algorithm 1 increments $C_c[e_z]$ by one, where e_z is the right boundary of a z-interval. The new version increments $\hat{C}_c[j]$ instead, where $j = \max\{i \mid i \leq e_z$ and $\text{MR}[i] = 1\}$. In other words, if $\text{MR}[e_z] = 1$, it increments $\hat{C}_c[e_z]$ and if $\text{MR}[e_z] = 0$, it increments the counter at which the previous one in MR can be found. In the example from Fig. 1 it would increment the counter at index 11 instead of that at $i = 12$. To see that this preserves correctness, consider two indices i and j so that $\text{MR}[i] = 1$, $\text{MR}[j] = 1$, and $\text{MR}[k] = 0$ for all k with $i < k < j$ (the case in which i is the last index with $\text{MR}[i] = 1$ follows similarly). On the one hand, if we use the array C_c, an opening parenthesis will be written for $\text{MR}[i] = 1$, followed by $\sum_{k=i}^{j} C_c[k]$ closing parentheses, and then an opening parenthesis will be written for $\text{MR}[j] = 1$. On the other hand, if we use the array $\hat{C}_c$, an opening parenthesis will be written for $\text{MR}[i] = 1$, followed by $\hat{C}_c[i]$ closing parentheses and an opening parenthesis for $\text{MR}[j] = 1$. Since $\hat{C}_c[i] = \sum_{k=i}^{j-1} C_c[k]$, it follows that both algorithms compute the same sequence of parentheses. Algorithm 2 implements the new version of Algorithm 1, however, it uses an array C'_c of length n and size $n \log(\max_i |x_i|)$ bits instead of the array $\hat{C}_c$ of length m. First, it computes the bit array MR and then preprocesses it so that $rank$-queries can be answered in constant time. Then it calls the function VISIT2 with parameters $1, k, m$. Function VISIT2 can be obtained from function VISIT by deleting line 2 in Algorithm 1 and replacing the assignment in line 3 by $C'_c[rank_1(\mathsf{MR}, e_z)] \leftarrow C'_c[rank_1(\mathsf{MR}, e_z)] + 1$. That is, for a z-interval $[b_z..e_z]$, function VISIT2 increments $C'_c[rank_1(\mathsf{MR}, e_z)]$ by one. This simulates the new version of Algorithm 1, in which $\hat{C}_c[j]$ is incremented, where $j = \max\{i \mid i \leq e_z \text{ and } \mathsf{MR}[i] = 1\}$.

In contrast to Algorithm 1, Algorithm 2 uses two passes to compute MR and C'_c separately. That is, it saves space by using C'_c instead of C_c, but the run-time doubles in practice (its time complexity is also $O(m \log \sigma)$).

4   Experimental Results

We experimentally compared our new XBWT construction algorithms with the ones presented in [18]. More precisely, we implemented the following algorithms, as we could not find an implementation of Manzini's algorithms:
- MAN : algorithm by Manzini   [18, Sect. 4]
- MAN-LW : lightweight algorithm by Manzini   [18, Sect. 4]
- OSB : our new algorithm   (Sect. 2)
- OSB-LW : lightweight version of the new algorithm (Sect. 3)

Our test data—the files dblp.xml, dna, proteins, english, and sources—originate from the Pizza & Chili corpus.[1] In our experiments, we constructed tries for each of the files using the above-mentioned algorithms, where the distinct lines of a file were used as input strings for trie construction.

Table 1. Trie construction results. The left column lists test data along with its size and the length of its longest string. The other columns show, for each test case, the construction time in seconds and the memory peak during construction, excluding suffix array and BWT construction.

File		MAN		MAN-LW		OSB		OSB-LW	
		time	peak	time	peak	time	peak	time	peak
dblp.xml $\quad$ 165 MB $\quad$ $\max |x_i| = 685$		66 s	784 MB	122 s	392 MB	39 s	430 MB	68 s	310 MB
dna $\quad$ 384 MB $\quad$ $\max |x_i| = 28{,}515{,}262$		242 s	1,873 MB	885 s	2,741 MB	252 s	1,530 MB	510 s	1,542 MB
proteins $\quad$ 864 MB $\quad$ $\max |x_i| = 36{,}805$		1,247 s	4,322 MB	1,942 s	3,896 MB	572 s	2,594 MB	1,102 s	2,394 MB
english $\quad$ 1,485 MB $\quad$ $\max |x_i| = 2{,}792$		961 s	7,613 MB	5,256 s	5,858 MB	1,600 s	4,592 MB	3,155 s	4,135 MB
sources $\quad$ 143 MB $\quad$ $\max |x_i| = 1{,}491$		65 s	680 MB	189 s	448 MB	53 s	396 MB	99 s	326 MB

---

[1] http://pizzachili.dcc.uchile.cl.

Algorithm 3. Computation of P by a depth-first traversal of a generalized ST

1: **function** DFT(v)
2:     **if** v is leaf and its incoming edge has a label $\neq \$$ **then**
3:         write an opening parenthesis and a closing parenthesis
4:     **if** v is an internal node **then**
5:         **if** v has an outgoing edge with label $\$$ **then** write an opening parenthesis
6:         for each child node w of v (in lexicographical order of the labels of the outgoing edges from v) call DFT(w)
7:             **if** v has an outgoing edge with label $\$$ **then** write a closing parenthesis

---

The experiments were conducted on a 64 bit Ubuntu 16.04.4 LTS system equipped with two 16-core Intel Xeon E5-2698v3 processors and 256 GB of RAM. All programs were compiled with the O3 option using g++ (version 5.4.1). Our programs and the benchmark are publically available.[2] Table 1 shows the results of the experiments. Among all tested algorithms, OSB-LW has the lowest memory peak. Surprisingly, if the trie is built from long strings (dna), Algorithm MAN-LW requires a lot of memory, probably because of a stack that stores items consisting of several components. Algorithms MAN and OSB are the fastest construction methods, but despite of a lower memory peak, OSB often outperforms MAN (we think this is caused by cache-misses in MAN, which occur during accesses to the suffix array and the test data).

Summing up, our new algorithms OSB and OSB-LW outperform the algorithms MAN and MAN-LW in terms of memory consumption, and perform similarly fast or even faster. As OSB requires only a little more memory than OSB-LW, but performs similarly fast as MAN, algorithm OSB has a good space-time tradeoff and therefore is our method of choice for XBWT construction.

Our implementation is based on the sdsl-lite library [13] and we further tried to reduce the memory peak of our algorithms by using compressed wavelet trees supported by the sdsl-lite library. With Huffman-shaped wavelet trees that use rrr-bitvectors [13], it is possible to obtain a 25% reduction of the memory peak on average, but the construction time increases by a factor of 2.5 on average. It might be worth trying other compressed wavelet trees such as the one described in [2], but unfortunately its implementation contained in the sdsl-lite library lacks support for the procedure *getIntervals*.

5   Concluding Remark

Some readers may prefer to construct the balanced parentheses sequence P by means of a suffix tree, and of course this is possible. To this end, build the generalized suffix tree ST of the reversed input strings $y_1, y_2 \ldots, y_k$. In such a generalized suffix tree, all strings are either terminated by $\$$ or they are terminated by pairwise different symbols $\$_1, \$_2 \ldots, \$_k$. Here, we will use $\$$. Then traverse ST in a depth-first fashion, i.e., call function DFT of Algorithm 3 with

---

[2] https://www.uni-ulm.de/in/theo/research/seqana/.

the root of ST as parameter. If an internal node v is visited during the traversal, the algorithm writes parentheses for that node only if v has an outgoing edge with label \$ because in this case the path from the root to v corresponds to a suffix of some y_i. Moreover, leaves whose incoming edge has label \$ are ignored.

References

1. Aho, A.V., Corasick, M.: Efficient string matching: an aid to bibliographic search. Commun. ACM **18**(6), 333–340 (1975)
2. Barbay, J., Claude, F., Gagie, T., Navarro, G., Nekrich, Y.: Efficient fully-compressed sequence representations. Algorithmica **69**(1), 232–268 (2014)
3. Bauer, M.J., Cox, A.J., Rosone, G.: Lightweight algorithms for constructing and inverting the BWT of string collections. Theor. Comput. Sci. **483**, 134–148 (2013)
4. Belazzougui, D.: Linear time construction of compressed text indices in compact space. In: Proceedings of 46th Annual ACM Symposium on Theory of Computing, pp. 148–193 (2014)
5. Beller, T., Gog, S., Ohlebusch, E., Schnattinger, T.: Computing the longest common prefix array based on the Burrows-Wheeler transform. J. Discret. Algorithms **18**, 22–31 (2013)
6. Beller, T., Zwerger, M., Gog, S., Ohlebusch, E.: Space-efficient construction of the Burrows-Wheeler transform. In: Kurland, O., Lewenstein, M., Porat, E. (eds.) SPIRE 2013. LNCS, vol. 8214, pp. 5–16. Springer, Cham (2013). https://doi.org/10.1007/978-3-319-02432-5_5
7. Clark, D.: Compact pat trees. Ph.D. thesis, University of Waterloo, Canada (1996)
8. Ferragina, P., Luccio, F., Manzini, G., Muthukrishnan, S.: Structuring labeled trees for optimal succinctness, and beyond. In: Proceedings of 46th Annual IEEE Symposium on Foundations of Computer Science, pp. 184–193 (2005)
9. Ferragina, P., Luccio, F., Manzini, G., Muthukrishnan, S.: Compressing and indexing labeled trees, with applications. J. ACM **57**(1), Article no. 4 (2009)
10. Ferragina, P., Manzini, G.: Opportunistic data structures with applications. In: Proceedings of 41st Annual IEEE Symposium on Foundations of Computer Science, pp. 390–398 (2000)
11. Fredkin, E.: Trie memory. Commun. ACM **3**(9), 490–499 (1960)
12. Gagie, T., Navarro, G., Puglisi, S.J.: New algorithms on wavelet trees and applications to information retrieval. Theor. Comput. Sci. **426–427**, 25–41 (2012)
13. Gog, S., Beller, T., Moffat, A., Petri, M.: From Theory to practice: plug and play with succinct data structures. In: Gudmundsson, J., Katajainen, J. (eds.) SEA 2014. LNCS, vol. 8504, pp. 326–337. Springer, Cham (2014). https://doi.org/10.1007/978-3-319-07959-2_28
14. Grossi, R., Gupta, A., Vitter, J.S.: High-order entropy-compressed text indexes. In: Proceedings of 14th Annual ACM-SIAM Symposium on Discrete Algorithms, pp. 841–850 (2003)
15. Jacobson, G.: Space-efficient static trees and graphs. In: Proceedings of 30th Annual IEEE Symposium on Foundations of Computer Science, pp. 549–554 (1989)
16. Kärkkäinen, J., Kempa, D., Puglisi, S.J.: Parallel external memory suffix sorting. In: Cicalese, F., Porat, E., Vaccaro, U. (eds.) CPM 2015. LNCS, vol. 9133, pp. 329–342. Springer, Cham (2015). https://doi.org/10.1007/978-3-319-19929-0_28
17. Li, H.: Fast construction of FM-index for long sequence reads. Bioinformatics **30**(22), 3274–3275 (2014)

18. Manzini, G.: XBWT tricks. In: Inenaga, S., Sadakane, K., Sakai, T. (eds.) SPIRE 2016. LNCS, vol. 9954, pp. 80–92. Springer, Cham (2016). https://doi.org/10.1007/978-3-319-46049-9_8

19. Martínez-Prietoa, M.A., Brisaboa, N., Cánovas, R., Claude, F., Navarro, G.: Practical compressed string dictionaries. Inf. Syst. **56**, 73–108 (2016)

20. Munro, J.I.: Tables. In: Chandru, V., Vinay, V. (eds.) FSTTCS 1996. LNCS, vol. 1180, pp. 37–42. Springer, Heidelberg (1996). https://doi.org/10.1007/3-540-62034-6_35

21. Ohlebusch, E.: Bioinformatics Algorithms: Sequence Analysis, Genome Rearrangements, and Phylogenetic Reconstruction. Oldenbusch Verlag, Bremen (2013)

Fast and Effective Neural Networks for Translating Natural Language into Denotations

Tiago Pimentel[1,2(✉)], Juliano Viana[2], Adriano Veloso[1], and Nivio Ziviani[1,2]

[1] CS Department, Universidade Federal de Minas Gerais, Belo Horizonte, Brazil
{adrianov,nivio}@dcc.ufmg.br
[2] Kunumi, Belo Horizonte, Brazil
{tiago.pimentel,juliano}@kunumi.com

Abstract. In this paper we study the semantic parsing problem of mapping natural language utterances into machine interpretable meaning representations. We consider a text-to-denotation application scenario in which a user interacts with a non-human assistant by entering a question, which is then translated into a logical structured query and the result of running this query is finally returned as response to the user. We propose encoder-decoder models that are trained end-to-end using the input questions and the corresponding logical structured queries. In order to ensure fast response times, our models do not condition the target string generation on previously generated tokens. We evaluate our models on real data obtained from a conversational banking chat service, and we show that conditionally-independent translation models offer similar accuracy numbers when compared with sophisticate translation models and present one order of magnitude faster response times.

1 Introduction

Around 38% of American consumers have used virtual-assistant services on their smartphones recently.[1] Conversational banking, for instance, enables users to interact with a non-human about their finances, allowing them to check accounts' balances, request deposits and wire transfers, and find out how much was spent on groceries. A key technology for developing such conversational interfaces is semantic parsing (Liang 2014), which allows mapping natural language utterances into denotations (answers) via intermediate logical forms, such as a structured query (Berant et al. 2013) on which a machine can act.

Typical approaches for semantic parsing are based on domain-specific handcrafted features, lexicons, and grammars (Berant et al. 2013). An alternate and prominent approach to semantic parsing is based on training end-to-end deep architectures (Dong and Lapata 2016; Jia and Liang 2016), thus making very few domain-specific assumptions with minimal feature engineering. In this case, the mapping between questions or commands entered by the user and their logical

---

[1] http://econ.st/1MAEREf.

© Springer Nature Switzerland AG 2018
T. Gagie et al. (Eds.): SPIRE 2018, LNCS 11147, pp. 334–347, 2018.
https://doi.org/10.1007/978-3-030-00479-8_27

forms is learned by presenting a set of translation examples, so that the network parameters are found by minimizing some loss function (Andreas et al. 2013; Dong and Lapata 2016).

Network architectures for semantic parsing have been largely inspired by works in neural machine translation (Gehring et al. 2016; Kalchbrenner et al. 2014, 2016; Vaswani et al. 2017). These works resulted in great improvements, but they also resulted in increasingly complex systems, with networks containing millions (Bahdanau et al. 2015) or billions (Shazeer et al. 2017) of parameters and which demand a lot of computation. While this complexity might be necessary for achieving state-of-the-art performance in natural language translation, we claim that semantic parsing models in which the target representation is machine-readable rather than human-readable, can be greatly simplified, enabling much faster response times without hurting accuracy.

In this paper, we propose models based on deep architectures for semantic parsing. We explicitly assume that target token generation depends only on the meaning of a sentence, and thus we propose end-to-end network architectures that are conditionally independent, that is, the target sentence is translated at once with each token having no dependency on previous outputs. While this assumption is unrealistic and is not correct in general, it usually holds in semantic parsing applications which do not show long-range dependencies. By making independence assumptions we can drastically reduce the complexity of our models, while still achieving close to perfect accuracy.

We built a dataset from the logs of a conversational banking chat system in order to evaluate our models. These logs contain questions and commands entered by different users, along with the corresponding logical outcomes. We also evaluate diverse network architectures and components, including recurrent networks with gated recurrent units (GRU), attention mechanisms (Bahdanau et al. 2015), and ByteNets (Kalchbrenner et al. 2016). The main contributions of this work are:

- We propose three encoder-decoder convolutional architectures that assume conditional independence between the target generation and previously generated tokens. For six different generated models using our proposed architectures, we obtained near 100% accuracy results in conversational banking data.
- Our proposed networks present faster training and response times than competitors. In particular, we show that our best model is more than 9 times faster to respond than ByteNets and recurrent networks, while our fastest model is more than 16 times faster.

2   Related Work

Next, we discuss recent related work focusing on neural semantic parsing models.

Semantic Parsing as Machine Translation. In Andreas et al. (2013), the authors show that standard machine translation components can be adapted into a semantic parser. As a general advantage, semantic parsing approaches based on machine translation are trained considerably faster than conventional alternatives. In Dong and Lapata (2016), the authors also propose to solve semantic parsing using machine translation approaches. Specifically, the authors propose a neural machine translation approach based on recurrent networks, named Seq2Tree, in which the tree structure of logical form is explicitly incorporated into the model. There are many other neural machine translation approaches, which are typically based on the general encoder-decoder translation process, where predictions are made sequentially using inexact inference, such as greedy or beam search Jia and Liang (2016). While these approaches were originally designed for machine translation, they can also be applied to more restricted application scenarios, such as semantic parsing. In Bahdanau et al. (2015), the authors propose a translation model based on an LSTM network with an attention component in the decoder, thus freeing the model from having to encode a whole source sentence into a fixed-length vector. In Gehring et al. (2016), the authors propose an encoder based on a succession of convolutional layers. This network architecture is faster to train than typical bi-directional LSTMs. In Kalchbrenner et al. (2016), the authors propose the ByteNet translation model, which uses a 1-D convolutional network to encode the source sentence and decode the target sentence.

Recent Advances in Neural Machine Translation. In order to achieve superior accuracy numbers, neural machine translation approaches are becoming increasingly complex and hard to train. In Ranzato et al. (2016), the authors propose translation models that employ reinforcement learning to fine-tune translations, improving BLEU scores. In Yang et al. (2017), the authors propose a translation model based on generative adversarial learning, which tries to minimize the distinction between human translation and the translation given by their model. Translation models such as the one proposed in Gehring et al. (2017) takes 37 days to be trained, using 8 GPUs. And the model in Vaswani et al. (2017), significantly faster, still takes +3 days to train using 8 GPUs.

Reliable Conversation Models. In applications such as conversational banking, models must be reliable in the sense that wrong mappings are extremely expensive. In Khani et al. (2016), the authors present the unanimity principle, guaranteeing 100% precision, by proposing a system which can abstain from doubtful mappings. The authors employ a set of models and a response is only provided if all models that are consistent with the training data predict the same output. In Popescu et al. (2003), the authors propose a system which is able to detect questions that cannot be handled correctly and which requests a paraphrase for these questions.

Our Work. The aforementioned works are mainly focused on achieving high translation scores. We advocate that there are other important dimensions that must be taken into account. In particular, we consider application scenarios where lengthy time delays between consecutive responses may hurt user engagement in the conversation. We are also interested in scenarios where users are unwilling to trade reliable and predictable interfaces for intelligent but unreliable ones. In this paper, we are particularly interested in learning semantic parsing models in which the user should wait minimally for receiving the correct answer.

3   Conditionally-Independent Models

Our aim is to learn a model that maps natural language input $x = x_1, x_2, \ldots, x_{|x|}$ to a logical form representation of its meaning $y = y_1, y_2, \ldots, y_{|y|}$. With this objective, we have as input a *training set*, which consists of a set of pairs of source and target statements (that is, the training set is essentially a parallel corpus). The training set is used to construct a probabilistic model which transforms an arbitrary natural language utterance x into its correct formal expression y. The *test set* contains only natural language utterances, and the model learned from the training set produces translations for these utterances. Under this learning scenario, we are particularly interested in semantic parsing models that deal with two potentially conflicting objectives:

- Near perfect accuracy: the model must respond to users' requests accurately, otherwise it gives unhelpful information and wrong answers, exposing users to risk.
- Interactive response time: the model must meet real-time constraints or a level of acceptable asynchronous behavior, otherwise users may get distracted.

The models we propose consist of an encoder, which encodes natural language input x into a vector representation, and a decoder, which learns to generate y conditioned on the encoding vector. These models may vary greatly in terms of their network capacity. Highly accurate models can be learned using sophisticate deep architectures, such as recurrent neural networks coupled with attention mechanisms. Choices of architecture, however, may greatly increase response times. To meet high accuracy numbers and fast interactive response time simultaneously, we propose three encoder-decoder convolutional[2] network architectures that make independence assumptions. The three architectures are described in the following sections.

3.1   Fast Semantic Parsing

The architecture shown in Fig. 1 does not condition the target string generation on previously generated tokens, thus assuming conditional independence:

$$p(y_i|y_{1:i-1}, x) = p(y_i|x)$$

where x is the input sentence and y_i is the token at position i.

---

[2] Feed-forward neural networks have the potential to be much faster than recurrent networks.

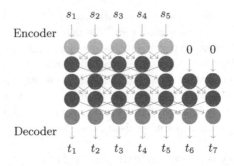

Fig. 1. Fast Semantic Parsing architecture.

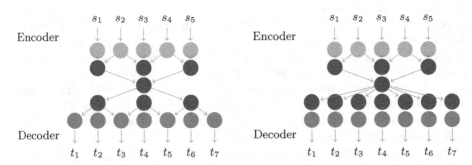

Fig. 2. Reduced Fast Semantic Parsing architecture.

Fig. 3. Reduced MultiLinear Network architecture.

The proposed Fast Semantic Parsing architecture uses full convolutions with dilation (Yu and Koltun 2015) in both the encoder and decoder. The encoder generates distributed representations with the same length as the source sentence, which is then padded with zeros before being sent to the decoder. The decoder then convolves all inputs at once, simultaneously generating all tokens in the target sentence. Convolutional networks with dilated representations have a dependency size which is exponential in the number of layers.

Given a pre-specified kernel-size and maximum input/output sentence lengths, we calculate the number of layers in the encoder and decoder such that each token in the output sentence will have as dependency size the whole input sentence. Models based on this architecture not only generate all target tokens at once during training, but they also do this at test time, since outputs do not depend on the previous ones. As a consequence, models based on this architecture are extremely fast to be trained and to translate text-to-denotation.

3.2 Reduced Fast Semantic Parsing

Next we propose the Reduced Fast Semantic Parsing architecture, as shown in Fig. 2. It also employs an encoder-decoder mechanism, but in this case the encoder generates a single representation of the source sentence, which is then deconvoluted[3] (Shelhamer et al. 2017) to generate the target sentence. Its encoder uses 1-D convolutions with stride to reduce the source sentence to a 1-D representation. Its decoder, then, uses deconvolutions to produce the target sentence from this representation. Again, the target sentence is generated at once with no dependency on previous outputs, which makes translation extremely fast. Since it reduces the size of the representations, it becomes even faster, specially in CPUs.

3.3   Reduced MultiLinear Network

Finally, we propose the Reduced MultiLinear Network architecture, as shown in Fig. 3. It uses a linear layer followed by a softmax to generate an output probability distribution, such as:

$$p(y_i|x) = \text{Softmax}\left(W \cdot d_i\right)$$

where W is a linear transformation and d_i is a representation of the input x for target position i.

Since we are not conditioning our sentences in the previous outputs, we wondered if explicitly conditioning the tokens we generate on their position in the target sentence could improve translations. For this, we create a new type of module, called here MultiLinear Layer, which is composed by a set of independent linear transformations, as follows:

$$W = \left\{W^{(1)}, W^{(2)}, \ldots, W^{(m)}\right\}$$

where m is the maximum target sentence length in the training set. Each $W^{(i)}$ is used coupled with the position of the token to be generated, thus conditioning the output probability distribution on its position in the target sentence, such that:

$$p(y_i|x, pos = i) = \text{Softmax}\left(W^{(i)} \cdot d_i\right)$$

The Reduced MultiLinear Network architecture uses the same encoder as the Reduced Fast Semantic Parsing architecture to create a representation for the source sentence. It then uses MultiLinear transformations to output tokens as follows:

$$d_{:,0} = \text{Encoder}(x)$$
$$d_{i,j} = W^{(i,j)} \cdot \sigma\left(d_{i,j-1}\right), \quad W^{(i,j)} \in W^{\{j\}}$$

where $d_{:,0}$ is the source sentence representation, $d_{i,j}$ is the positional dependent representation in layer j and position i, σ is a non-linearity, and $W^{\{j\}}$ is a MultiLinear transformation. The output probability distribution is given as:

$$p(y_i|x, pos = i) = \text{Softmax}\left(d_{i,l}\right)$$

---

[3] It is technically upconvoluted, but this is typically referenced as deconvolution in the literature.

where l is the number of layers in the decoder. Note that, in this architecture, there are no convolutions in the decoder.

4   Experiments

In this section, we present the dataset and baselines used to evaluate our proposed semantic parsing models. Then, we discuss our evaluation procedure and report the results. In particular, our experiments aim to answer the following research questions:

RQ1 How accurate are the different models based on the architectures described in Sect. 3?
RQ2 What is the speedup of simpler models over sophisticate ones?
RQ3 Are conditionally-independent models effective?
RQ4 Can we select a set of best models for this task?
RQ5 What is the accuracy vs. training size trade-off for the models?

4.1   Dataset

In order to evaluate different models we gathered data from real conversations between customers of a bank institution and trained attendants. Specifically, customers entered natural language sentences into a web chat session, and the attendants interpreted these sentences and then executed queries in order to return the correct answers to the customers. In summary, the corpus contains 4,959 examples of sentences in natural language paired with the corresponding queries in the formal query language, and was obtained from a large bank institution in Brazil. Questions entered by the customers are of diverse types, including:

- 'how much': typically asking how much money was spent on something (e.g., "how much did the client spend on groceries in April?")
- 'did I pay': typically asking if a specific bill was paid (e.g., "did the client pay the electricity last month?")
- 'where did I spend': typically asking where something happened (e.g., "where did the client spent most money in the month?")

Since this data comes from a real bank scenario, questions have a limited scope (banking activities), so several questions have similar contexts or phrasing, which results in the high accuracies seen. This corpus also contains many sentences with construction errors, which the model must learn to translate correctly. The output vocabulary size is 69 and an example of query is "SELECT History FILTER Timestamp EQ MONTH_DAY 5 June KEEP Balance".

4.2   Models

We considered the following models based on the network architectures presented in Sect. 3:

- **FaSP**: it uses the Fast Semantic Parsing architecture followed by a simple linear transformation and a softmax.
- **FaSP (ML)**: it uses the Fast Semantic Parsing architecture followed by a MultiLinear transformation and a softmax.
- **RedFaSP**: it uses the Reduced Fast Semantic Parsing architecture followed by a simple linear transformation and a softmax.
- **RedFaSP (ML)**: it uses the Reduced Fast Semantic Parsing architecture followed by a MultiLinear transformation and a softmax.
- **RedMulNet (1)**: it uses the Reduced MultiLinear Network architecture with a single decoder layer.
- **RedMulNet (2)**: it uses the Reduced MultiLinear Network architecture with two decoder layers.

4.3   Baselines

We considered the following models in order to provide baseline comparison:

- **RNN**: Recurrent Neural Network (Sutskever et al. 2017) using Gated Recurrent Units (GRU) as recurrent modules.
- **Attn-RNN**: Recurrent Neural Network using Gated Recurrent Units (GRU) with an attention mechanism (Bahdanau et al. 2015).
- **Bytenet**: Architecture with a fully convolutional encoder-decoder which has a training time that is linear in the target sentence sizes (Kalchbrenner et al. 2016). This architecture uses masked convolutions in the decoder to condition translations on the previously translated words.
- **Bytenet (ML)**: ByteNet architecture followed by a MultiLinear transformation and a softmax layer.

4.4   Setup

The measure used to evaluate the effectiveness of our models is the standard accuracy of full sentence translations, which means the whole output sentence needs to match the ground truth to be considered correct. We conducted ten-fold cross validation, where the dataset is arranged into ten folds with approximately the same number of examples. At each run, eight folds are used as training set, one fold is used as validation set, and the remaining fold is used as test set. The training set is used to learn the models, the validation set is used to tune hyper-parameters and the test set is used to estimate the accuracy of the models. Unless otherwise stated, the results reported are the average of the ten runs, and are used to assess the overall effectiveness of each model.

Training and Model Selection. We used stochastic gradient descent (Hinton 2012) with learning rate set to 0.01, maximizing the log-likelihood of the training set. We used Exponential Linear Units (ELU, Clevert et al. 2016) as non linear activations and a dropout probability of 0.2. The mini-batch size is fixed to 16 and training was stopped after 50 epochs with no improvement. We trained each of the convolutional architectures with kernel sizes of $\{3, 5, 7\}$ and hidden sizes $\{256, 512\}$. While the recurrent architectures were trained for number of layers in $\{1, 3, 5\}$ and hidden sizes in $\{256, 512\}$. We perform a grid search for these hyper-parameters, tuning on the validation set, with early stopping. The best model for each architecture was chosen as the smallest loss on the validation set.

4.5   Results and Discussion

Next we report results obtained from the execution of the experiments, and discuss these results in the light of our research questions.

Accuracy of the Models. The first experiment is concerned with RQ1. We present a comparison between all considered models in terms of their accuracy numbers. Table 1 shows the average accuracy numbers in the validation and test sets. It is clear that all considered models present very high accuracy on conversational banking data. Specifically, accuracy varies from 98.19% using RedMul-Net(1), to 99.46% using RNN.

Speedup. The next set of experiments is devoted to answer RQ2. Both training and translation times can be seen in Table 2. We can see that the training time per epoch for all convolutional based methods is considerably smaller than for recurrent networks. We can also see that training times per epoch for the architectures with MultiLinear transformations at the top layers are not very different from the ones with common Linear transformations. These MultiLinear architectures have a training time bigger than their counterparts, which is expected since they have more parameters to learn. Nevertheless, the increase in training time in FaSP and ByteNet is not very large when compared with the increase for models based on recurrent architectures.

While the training times from our conditionally-independent models are similar to the one from ByteNet and ByteNet (ML), translation times are considerably different, both for CPU and GPU.[4] Analyzing Table 2 we can see that both ByteNet and ByteNet (ML) take almost 3 min to translate the dataset, while the slowest conditionally-independent model takes only 27 s. FaSP (ML) takes only 18 s. On CPU, ByteNet architectures are even slower than RNN, taking more than 10–12 min, while RNN takes approximately 3.5 min and FaSP only 1 min.

---

[4] Translation times correspond to the time taken to translate the entire dataset, consisting of 4,959 questions. Both training and testing (GPU) were done using a single K40 GPU, on a 12 core dedicated server with 32GB of RAM, while CPU times were collected in a dedicated 16 core server with 36GB of RAM.

Table 1. Results for best configurations.

Model	Accuracy	
	Val	Test
FaSP	98.99%	98.97%
ByteNet	99.01%	98.93%
RedFaSP	98.55%	98.49%
RNN	99.48%	99.46%
Attn-RNN	99.11%	99.17%
FaSP (ML)	98.89%	98.91%
ByteNet (ML)	98.99%	98.97%
RedFaSP (ML)	98.47%	98.57%
RedMulNet (1)	98.23%	98.19%
RedMulNet (2)	98.57%	98.53%

Table 2. GPU training times. GPU and CPU response times. (Best models)

Model	Training (GPU)		Translation	
	Epoch	Total	GPU	CPU
FaSP	0m08s	56m	0m20s	2m28s
ByteNet	0m04s	57m	2m48s	10m09s
RedFaSP	0m04s	38m	0m10s	0m32s
RNN	0m29s	178m	3m16s	3m28s
Attn-RNN	2m11s	539m	4m34s	12m23s
FaSP (ML)	0m06s	67m	0m18s	1m01s
ByteNet (ML)	0m06s	88m	2m59s	12m36s
RedFaSP (ML)	0m06s	95m	0m17s	1m23s
RedMulNet (1)	0m03s	92m	0m21s	0m34s
RedMulNet (2)	0m05s	153m	0m27s	0m53s

Effectiveness of Conditionally-Independent Models. The next set of experiments is devoted to answer RQ3. Table 3 shows if there is a statistical differences between each pair of models evaluated. The statistical difference was evaluated by comparing the ten runs for each pair of models and running a Welch's t-test (unequal variances t-test), with $p = 0.01$. It can be seem that there is no statistical difference between the RNN, Attn-RNN, FaSP (ML) and ByteNet (ML) models, for which the accuracy on the test set vary from 98.91% to 99.46%.

From Table 3, we can also see that the only models that are statistically better than others are RNN, which beats several of the simpler models, and Attn-RNN, which only beats RedMulNet(1), our simplest model. This means that FaSP (ML), a conditionally independent model which uses only convolutions for semantic parsing in conversational banking data, presents statistically similar results to the three best conditional models, ByteNet (ML), Attn-RNN and RNN. Therefore, conditionally independent models, specially FaSP (ML), are effective for conversational banking data. When we apply Bonferroni correction (Bonferroni 1950) to the statistical tests, no differences present statistical significance.

Table 4 shows detailed results for the best models in terms of accuracy in the test set. From this table we can see that RNN indeed is a robust model. What might be surprising is that FaSP(ML) was more robust than both ByteNet(ML) and Attn-RNN. Another important result is that the model with the highest accuracy in the test set was FaSP(ML), with a kernel size of 7 and a hidden size of 512, beating RNN, Attn-RNN and Bytenet(ML) models.

Table 3. (Color online) Statistical difference of results.

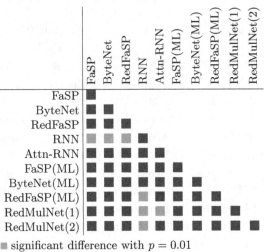

■ significant difference with $p = 0.01$

■ no significant difference with $p = 0.01$

Table 4. Detailed results for best models.

	Test accuracy					
(number of layers, hidden size)	(1, 256)	(3, 256)	(5, 256)	(1, 512)	(3, 512)	(5, 512)
RNN	99.40%	99.19%	99.40%	99.40%	99.40%	**99.46%**
Attn-RNN	92.94%	99.19%	30.85%	55.85%	97.78%	**99.17%**
(kernel size, hidden size)	(3, 256)	(5, 256)	(7, 256)	(3, 512)	(5, 512)	(7, 512)
FaSP (ML)	**98.91%**	99.19%	99.19%	98.79%	98.99%	99.60%
ByteNet (ML)	97.38%	98.79%	**98.97%**	99.19%	99.40%	99.19%

Pareto Optimality. Having the translation times and accuracy numbers of our models, we can find a set of Pareto optimal models in order to answer RQ4. The graphs in Fig. 4(left) and (right) show accuracy numbers and translation times on GPU and CPU, respectively. By analyzing these graphs, we can find this set of Pareto optimal points for either running this system on CPU or GPU. On CPU, this set is composed of RedMulNet(1), RedFaSP, RedMulNet(2), FaSP, FaSP (ML) and RNN, which either have a better accuracy or translation time on CPU than all other models. When running on GPU, this set is composed only of RedFaSP, RedFaSP (ML), FaSP, FaSP (ML), ByteNet (ML) and RNN. Notice that Attn-RNN and ByteNet are in neither of these sets, while ByteNet (ML) is only in the GPU one, but is hardly a good choice, since it has statistically the same result as FaSP (ML), with a much larger translation time.

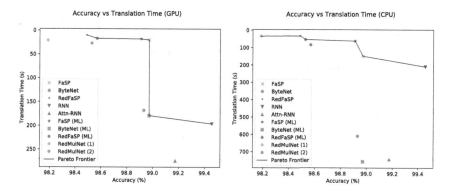

Fig. 4. (Color online) Accuracy and translation times on GPU (left) and on CPU (right). Y-axis is flipped for better visualization of the Pareto frontiers. (Best models)

Training Size vs. Accuracy. The last set of experiments concerns RQ5. Figure 5 shows the accuracy of the models as the size of the dataset increases. To build this graph, we trained each model on smaller parts of the training set $\{6.25\%, 12.5\%, 25\%, 50\%, 100\%\}$, again saving models every epoch and selecting the best one according to the smallest loss on the full validation set. After that we evaluated each model on the full test set.

Analyzing this graph we can see that the models based on recurrent architectures are more robust to training size, almost dominating conditionally-independent models in terms of accuracy. This is expected, since RNN models the entire source sentence in a vector with a constant size, independent of sentence length, while convolutional units have a dependency which is exponential

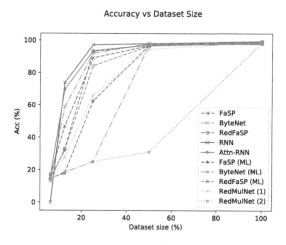

Fig. 5. (Color online) Accuracy numbers for reduced training sets.

with its number of layers, so the minimum number of parameters used by these architectures is usually bigger.

Further, for smaller training sizes, models with Linear transformations at the output layers outperform models with MultiLinear transformations. This is also coherent with theory, since Linear architectures have less parameters and must learn to generalize better, even with fewer samples. With 50% of the training set, most models already generalize well achieving accuracy numbers around 97%. RNN and ByteNet architectures having equal accuracies of 97.97%, FaSP (ML) and Attn-RNN achieving 97.17%, ByteNet (ML) with 97.57% and only RedMulNet(2) still not being able to learn, with only 31.11%.

5   Conclusions

In this paper, we proposed neural models for conversational banking. Our models are based on three new network architectures that assume conditional independence of the target tokens. Although this is a fairly dangerous assumption to make in traditional machine translation and semantic parsing applications, we showed that our models are able to provide results that are statistically equivalent to either recurrent models or more complex convolutional models, like ByteNet, with much faster training time than the recurrent models and an order of magnitude faster translation time in GPU than traditional models. We also proposed the MultiLinear module, which can be plugged in any network architecture used to solve sequence to sequence problems where targets are positionally dependent. As shown in our experiments, the MultiLinear module can improve results, at the cost of needing larger training sets. Our fastest conditionally-independent models, which still achieve 98, 49% accuracy, can translate 4,959 questions in only 10 s using a K40 GPU and in only 32 s on a 16 core CPU. This is relevant because financial institutions have large number of clients and in conversational banking, to maintain user engagement, real-time answers must be given to a large set of these concurrent users simultaneously.

Acknowledgements. We thank the partial support given by the Project: Models, Algorithms and Systems for the Web (grant FAPEMIG/PRONEX/MASWeb APQ-01400-14), and authors' individual grants and scholarships from CNPq and Kunumi.

References

Andreas, J., Vlachos, A., Clark, S.: Semantic parsing as machine translation. In: Proceedings of the 51st Annual Meeting of the Association for Computational Linguistics, pp. 47–52 (2013)

Bahdanau, D., Cho, K., Bengio, Y.: Neural machine translation by jointly learning to align and translate. In: International Conference on Learning Representations (2015)

Berant, J., Chou, A., Frostig, R., Liang, P.: Semantic parsing on freebase from question-answer pairs. In: Proceedings of the 2013 Conference on Empirical Methods in Natural Language Processing, pp. 1533–1544 (2013)

Bonferroni, C.: Sulle medie multiple di potenze. Boll. dell'Unione Mat. Ital. **5**(3–4), 267–270 (1950)

Clevert, D.-A., Unterthiner, T., Hochreiter, S.: Fast and accurate deep network learning by exponential linear units (ELUs). In: International Conference on Learning Representations (2016)

Dong, L., Lapata, M.: Language to logical form with neural attention. In: Proceedings of the 54th Annual Meeting of the Association for Computational Linguistics (2016)

Gehring, J., Auli, M., Grangier, D., Dauphin, Y.N.: A convolutional encoder model for neural machine translation. CoRR, abs/1611.02344 (2016). http://arxiv.org/abs/1611.02344

Gehring, J., Auli, M., Grangier, D., Yarats, D., Dauphin, Y.N.: Convolutional sequence to sequence learning. CoRR, abs/1705.03122 (2017). http://arxiv.org/abs/1705.03122

Hinton, G.E.: A practical guide to training restricted boltzmann machines. In: Montavon, G., Orr, G.B., Müller, K.-R. (eds.) Neural Networks: Tricks of the Trade. LNCS, vol. 7700, pp. 599–619. Springer, Heidelberg (2012). https://doi.org/10.1007/978-3-642-35289-8_32

Jia, R., Liang, P.: Data recombination for neural semantic parsing. In: Proceedings of the 54th Annual Meeting of the Association for Computational Linguistics (2016)

Kalchbrenner, N., Grefenstette, E., Blunsom, P.: A convolutional neural network for modelling sentences. In: Proceedings of the 52nd Annual Meeting of the Association for Computational Linguistics, pp. 655–665 (2014)

Kalchbrenner, N., Espeholt, L., Simonyan, K., van den Oord, A., Graves, A., Kavukcuoglu, K.: Neural machine translation in linear time. CoRR, abs/1610.10099 (2016). http://arxiv.org/abs/1610.10099

Khani, F., Rinard, M.C., Liang, P.: Unanimous prediction for 100% precision with application to learning semantic mappings. In: Proceedings of the 54th Annual Meeting of the Association for Computational Linguistics (2016)

Liang, P.: Talking to computers in natural language. ACM Crossroads **21**(1), 18–21 (2014)

Popescu, A.-M., Etzioni, O., Kautz, H.A.: Towards a theory of natural language interfaces to databases. In: Proceedings of the 8th International Conference on Intelligent User Interfaces, pp. 149–157 (2003)

Ranzato, M.A., Chopra, S., Auli, M., Zaremba, W.: Sequence level training with recurrent neural networks. In: International Conference on Learning Representations (2016)

Shazeer, N., et al.: Outrageously large neural networks: the sparsely-gated mixture-of-experts layer. In: International Conference on Learning Representations (2017)

Shelhamer, E., Long, J., Darrell, T.: Fully convolutional networks for semantic segmentation. IEEE Trans. Pattern Anal. Mach. Intell. **39**(4), 640–651 (2017)

Sutskever, I., Vinyals, O., Le, Q.V.: Sequence to sequence learning with neural networks. In: Advances in Neural Information Processing Systems 27: Annual Conference on Neural Information Processing Systems 2014, pp. 3104–3112 (2014)

Vaswani, A., et al.: Attention is all you need. CoRR, abs/1706.03762 (2017). http://arxiv.org/abs/1706.03762

Yang, Z., Chen, W., Wang, F., Xu, B.: Improving neural machine translation with conditional sequence generative adversarial nets. CoRR, abs/1703.04887 (2017). http://arxiv.org/abs/1703.04887

Yu, F., Koltun, V.: Multi-scale context aggregation by dilated convolutions. CoRR, abs/1511.07122 (2015). http://arxiv.org/abs/1511.07122

Faster and Smaller Two-Level Index
for Network-Based Trajectories

Rodrigo Rivera[1], M. Andrea Rodríguez[1,2], and Diego Seco[1,2(✉)]

[1] Departamento de Ingeniería Informática y Ciencias de la Computación,
Universidad de Concepción, Concepción, Chile
{rodrivera,andrea,dseco}@udec.cl
[2] IMFD, Santiago, Chile

Abstract. Two-level indexes have been widely used to handle trajectories of moving objects that are constrained to a network. The top-level of these indexes handles the spatial dimension, whereas the bottom level handles the temporal dimension. The latter turns out to be an instance of the *interval-intersection* problem, but it has been tackled by non-specialized spatial indexes. In this work, we propose the use of a compact data structure on the bottom level of these indexes. Our experimental evaluation shows that our approach is both faster and smaller than existing solutions.

Keywords: Space-efficient data structures · Moving-objects · Indexing

1 Introduction

Spatio-temporal information has gained popularity in decision making systems, such as optimization of transportation systems, urban planning, and so on. The proliferation of different types of sensors to capture or generate this kind of data has made these applications possible but, at the same time, it has also made challenging the storage and processing of spatio-temporal data. The work in this paper focuses on a subcategory of spatio-temporal data, that is, trajectory of moving objects, which can be reconstructed by the GPS devices of smart-phones or, at a different granularity, by smart transportation cards.

Trajectories can be classified as free-trajectories, in which movement is not constrained, and network-based trajectories, in which movement is constrained to a network and cannot exist outside such network. Hurricanes and animal migrations are examples of the former, whereas public transportation is an example of the latter. Useful queries that can be answered by handling trajectories are: count the number of vessels inside a region during a time period (e.g. fishing

Funded in part by European Union's Horizon 2020 research and innovation programme under the Marie Skłodowska-Curie grant agreement 690941, CONICYT-PFCHA/MagísterNacional/2016 - 22161080 (R.R.), Millennium Institute for Foundational Research on Data and CONICYT FONDECYT 1170497.

© Springer Nature Switzerland AG 2018
T. Gagie et al. (Eds.): SPIRE 2018, LNCS 11147, pp. 348–362, 2018.
https://doi.org/10.1007/978-3-030-00479-8_28

closed season) or find the shortest path between two stops of a transportation system during a time period.

Several spatio-temporal indexes have been proposed to handle both free and network-based trajectories. However, classical solutions to deal with moving-object data are inefficient when facing the data volume collected through new sensor technology and the increasing interest for data analysis. On the other hand, space-efficient data structures have been proved to be successful for handling large volumes of data in many different domains, such as the Web, biological sequences, documents and code repositories, to name some examples.

In this work, we focus on two-level indexes for network-based trajectories and propose a new solution that uses compact data structures on the bottom level. This approach turns out to be smaller and faster than existing solutions.

2   Background and Related Work

A data structure for trajectories must provide access methods that allow the processing of spatio-temporal queries. These queries can be classified into coordinate- and trajectory-based queries [26]. Coordinate-based queries include *time-slice* queries that determine the position of objects at a given time instant, *time-interval* queries that extend time-slice queries to a time range, and queries about *nearby neighbors*. As for trajectory-based queries, they include topological queries, which involve information regarding the movement of an object, and queries related to navigation, which involve information derived from the movement, such as speed or direction. There also exist combinations such as "Where was object X at a given time instant".

Various data structures have been proposed to efficiently support queries on trajectories. These structures can be broadly classified into two categories: (i) Data structures to support free movements on a space, such as 3D R-tree (a three-dimensional extension of the R-tree [17]), TB-tree [26] (which preserves the trajectories while allowing typical range queries on an R-tree) and MV3R-tree [32] (which uses a multi-version R-tree, called MVR-tree, along with an auxiliary 3D R-tree). (ii) Data structures to support movements on networks, such as FNR-tree [14] (which uses a combination of a 2D R-tree with a forest of 1D R-trees), MON-tree [1] (using 2 levels of 2D R-trees) and PARINET [28] (based on graph partitioning and the use of B$^+$-tree). Among the previous structures, FNR-tree and MON-tree have in common the separation of spatial and temporal dimensions, using a spatial structure (two-dimensional) and a forest of temporal structures (one-dimensional) to tackle each of these sub-problems separately.

Like FNR-tree and MON-tree, we focus on these two-level indexes. To solve the spatial problem, that is, the representation of the network in space (two-dimensional plane), aforementioned structures use a 2D R-tree, storing the segments of the network as lines. With the spatial problem solved, time has to be associated with segments in the network. More precisely, it is necessary to look for all the time intervals (times in which some objects pass through a segment) that intersect with a given query interval. This problem is known in the literature as *interval intersection*, an extension of the *interval stabbing problem* [30]. Classical structures to solve this problem are Interval trees and Priority trees [5].

As for the subproblem in the temporal dimension, FNR-tree makes use of a one-dimensional R-tree for each segment. These 1D R-trees index the objects whose trajectories pass through the segments of the network, storing the instant they enter and leave the segment in the form of a time interval (t_{entry}, t_{exit}). Since only these intervals are stored, the structure assumes that objects do not stop or change speed or direction in the middle of a segment, they can only do so at nodes. MON-tree eliminates this restriction by replacing the one-dimensional R-trees with two-dimensional R-trees, where they store the relative movement within the segments as rectangles in the 2D R-tree of the form (p_1, p_2, t_1, t_2), with (p_1, p_2) a range of relative positions and (t_1, t_2) a temporal interval.

While some of aforementioned structures support queries efficiently on large datasets, they are incapable of handling the increasing data volume of current applications. This has forced the use of compression techniques for data storage and transmission. Some techniques are to reduce the number of points in a curve [23] or to use features at each point, such as speed and orientation [27]. Both techniques work in free spaces and, when the movement is restricted to networks, it is even possible to get a better compression, like the ones shown in [18–20, 29].

Previous compression techniques improve storage requirements and transmission time of large datasets. However, the compression can be directly exploited by data structures that can maintain a compact representation of the data while allowing for indexed search capabilities. These structures have been called self-indexes and have been successfully implemented in other domains, such as information retrieval [24].

Recently, compact data structures have been also used for the representation of trajectories. GraCT [9], for free paths, uses a k^2-tree [10] to store the absolute position of the objects in regular time intervals (snapshots) plus compressed logs for the representation of the movements between snapshots. ContaCT [8] improves GraCT with more efficient logs. Both structures answer spatio-temporal queries where space and time are the main filters, such as, "finding trajectories that went through a specific region at a given time instant". On the other hand, CTR [7] supports trajectories restricted to networks by combining compressed suffixes arrays (CSA), to represent the nodes on the network an object passes through, and a balanced Wavelet matrix for the temporal component of the movement. In CTR, trajectories (or trips) are defined as sequences of labels, which represent the nodes of the network. Hence, it solves other types of queries in which the space is represented with such labels, such as "find the number of trajectories that started at X and ended at Y". This is a fundamental difference with our proposal, in which the spatial dimension are coordinates in a two-dimensional space, and not labels. This is also the main difference with CiNCT [20], which boosts CTR in terms of memory storage and query time.

Another difference with previous solutions is that our approach uncouples the network from the trajectories. This model known as Network-Matched has been successfully used [12,22], but without using compact data structures in its implementation. Our approach has the advantage that mapping trajectories to a network facilitates the finding of similar trajectories and, in consequence, it allows a better use of space.

3   Data Structures for Network-Based Trajectories

Similarly to the FNR-tree and MON-tree, we propose an index with two levels: spatial (top level) and temporal (bottom level). In a preliminary experimental evaluation, we observed that the spatial level requires negligible space compared with the temporal level. For example, for the Oldenburg network (see Sect. 4), in the baseline structure, the temporal level uses about 89% of the total memory with 1,000 objects circulating and about 94% with 2,000 objects. The more data are stored, the more negligible the spatial level becomes (due to the almost-static nature of the transportation network in comparison with the moving objects). Hence, we focus on optimizing the temporal level and process the spatial level with a 2D R-tree, as the FNR-tree and MON-tree do. Recall that the R-tree is a balanced tree in which each leaf stores an entry of the form (id, MBB), where id is a reference to the data (in this case to a temporal index) and MBB is the Minimum Bounding Box that covers the spatial object (a line segment, in this domain). The R-tree does not provide worst-case guarantees as it may be forced to examine the entire tree in $O(n)$ time, even when the output is empty. However, it performs well in practice and is ubiquitous in spatial databases.

Each leaf of the R-tree contains a reference to a temporal index. These indexes solve the *Interval Intersection* problem. Before presenting alternatives to solve this problem, we give an overview of a query algorithm for spatio-temporal range queries, which are the most general coordinate-bases queries. First, a spatial query, a 2D window, is solved on the 2D R-tree, which returns a set of leaves whose segment may intersect the window. As in most spatial indexes, a refinement step is then executed to eliminate false positives, i.e. network segments whose MBBs intersect the window, but they do not actually intersect the window. After this refinement, the interval intersection query is executed in each temporal index referenced by the remaining leaves of the R-tree. Results from all these temporal indexes are then combined using an implementation of a set. Hence, all the structures below store object identifiers to allow this merge.

3.1   Temporal Level: Data Structures for the Interval Intersection Problem

Unlike the FNR-tree and MON-tree, which use variants of an R-tree, we explore the use of specialized data structures for the interval-intersection problem.

Interval-Tree [5]. This is a binary tree that is constructed recursively in the following way: (i) The median x_{med} of all the interval endpoints is computed. (ii) Intervals are classified in three sets, I_{med}, I_{left} and I_{right}, which contain intervals stabbed by x_{med}, intervals to the left of x_{med} and intervals to the right of x_{med}, respectively. (iii) I_{med} is stored in a structure composed of two arrays sorted by left and right endpoints, and associated with the root, whereas I_{left} and I_{right} are recursively processed and assigned as left and right child, respectively.

A search for the intervals that intersect with the query interval (l_q, r_q) is solved recursively starting from the root. The intervals within the visiting node that intersect the query interval are returned and the search is continued in the left child if l_q is less than x_{med} and/or in the right child if r_q is greater than x_{med}. This data structure requires linear space and $O(\log n + k)$ query time, where k is the number of reported results.

Schmidt. The structure presented in [30] to solve the Interval Stabbing problem can be extended to solve also the Interval Intersection problem [11]. It defines the *father* of an interval as the rightmost interval among those that cover it completely. This relation forms a tree where siblings are ordered from left to right, and the root of the tree is a special node that acts as the father of all the intervals that are not covered by any other. In addition, for each possible endpoint of an interval, the structure stores an array called `start`, with a pointer to the node representing the rightmost-starting interval that intersects such point, and an array `start2`, storing a pointer to the node representing the rightmost interval starting up to such point (which may not be stabbed by it).

To solve an interval intersection query q, the algorithm first reports the rightmost interval that intersects q, which is $\max(start[l_q], start_2[r_q])$, if it exists. Then, the algorithm recursively reports the siblings to the left of the node while its right endpoint is greater than or equal to l_q, also searching among the right children of the reported nodes. This structure requires linear space and optimal $O(1+k)$ query time. Note, however, that this solution works only for small integer ranges. In order to work with intervals whose endpoints are floats, these endpoints are stored in sorted arrays and two binary searches are used to translate the query to rank space [11], which results in a total complexity of $O(\log n + k)$.

Compact Data Structure Based on Independent Interval Sets (IIS). A set of intervals $I = \{i_1, i_2, ..., i_n\}$ is called an *Independent Interval Set* if no interval $i_j \in I$ is contained in any other interval $i_k \in I$.

Report the k intervals of an *IIS* that intersect a query interval $Q = [l_q, r_q]$ can be easily computed if we have the intervals in order. Note that, by definition of *IIS*, the order of the left endpoints of the intervals is the same as that of the right endpoints. If the first and the last interval intersected by the query are located, it is enough to iterate between them to return all the intersected intervals (see Fig. 1).

In order to locate these two intervals, we could store the left and right coordinates of the intervals in two sorted arrays and use binary search to locate them,

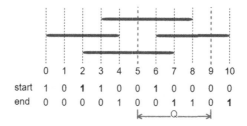

Fig. 1. An Independent Interval Set (IIS) and its representation with two bitvectors. In red, the last interval stabbed in **start** and the first one in **end**. (Color figure online)

which is similar to what we did in previous solution. However, for this domain, we propose a simple solution that facilitates the use of compact data structures. Recall that the endpoints of our intervals are timestamps represented as float numbers. We multiply these timestamps by a scale factor to convert them to integers. For example, if we work with timestamps with up to 6 decimals it is enough to multiply each one of them by 10^6 to discretize the space. With this procedure, we obtain integer endpoints in an universe U and, the larger the scale factor, the larger the universe.

After this discretization, we use two bitvectors, one for the left endpoints, **start**, and another for the right endpoints, **end**, of each interval in the set (see Fig. 1). A 1-bit in these bitvectors indicate that an interval starts (or ends, respectively), at such position. Then, for a query $Q = [l_q, r_q]$ also discretized to this universe, two rank operations on these bitmaps are used to locate the first and last intervals intersected by the query: $rank_1(end, l_q)$ and $rank_1(start, r_q)$, respectively. As we mentioned above, the larger the scale factor, the larger the size of the universe u, which is the number of bits in these bitmaps. However, the number of set bits in them is n, which is the number of intervals (independently of the scale factor). Hence, we use the Elias-Fano representation [25] for this bitmaps, which takes $2n + n \log \frac{u}{n}$ bits of space. Note that, for a constant c and $u = O(n^c)$, it uses $O(n)$ words of space as previous structures. The query time of rank operations on these bitmaps is $O(\log \frac{u}{n})$, thus, this structure can report the k intervals intersecting the query in $O(\log \frac{u}{n} + k)$ time.

Although this solution only works for IIS, a general set of intervals can be decomposed into m independent sets in $O(n \log m)$ time, for example, with Fredman's algorithm [13] to find the optimal number of shuffled upsequences in a permutation (by considering the rightmost endpoints of the intervals as the permuted values). This leads to a solution that requires $O(m \log \frac{u}{n} + k)$ time to report the k solutions. This does not provide worst case guarantees as m can be as large as n, however, this adaptive analysis shows that this is an efficient solution for domains in which m is small. The empirical evaluation in next section shows that this is precisely the case in our domain.

4   Experimental Results

All the implementations evaluated in this paper were coded in C++11. For the baselines, we use some available implementations: R-tree [2], Interval-tree[1] [15] and Schmidt [31]. We also make use of some succinct data structures from the SDSL library [16]. The experiments were run in a computer with an Intel Xeon E3-1220 v5 of 3.00 GHz CPU, 64 GB of RAM, and implementations were compiled with g++ 5.4.0 over Ubuntu 16.04 (64 bits).

We first evaluate the performance of all the implementations for interval intersection on synthetic datasets, and then, the best candidates are evaluated in the complete solution for network-based trajectories.

4.1   Evaluation of Interval Intersection Data Structures

We evaluated the performance in three scenarios with different types of intervals: (i) fixed size (Fig. 2), (ii) random size (Fig. 3), and (iii) intervals of trajectories extracted from a trajectories dataset generated with Brinkhoff's generator [6] over San Francisco's network (Fig. 4). For each of these scenarios, we created a dataset with 800,000 intervals and a queryset with 500 random queries. We report average time per query.

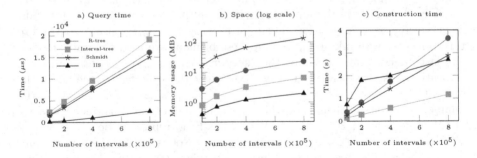

Fig. 2. Fixed size intervals

Figure 2 shows the performance of the structures using fixed size intervals. The compact data structure shows the best performance among the four structures, with a considerable advantage in both query time and memory usage. In this scenario, intervals do not fully cover each other (except for precision issues), which produces a low number of independent sets in the IIS structure (only 6 for 800,000 intervals). This explains the outstanding performance of IIS.

Figure 3 shows the performance of the structures for random size intervals. The compact data structure keeps the best results in query time and memory

---

[1] This implementation uses sequential search in each node, which is not optimal in theory, but performs well in practice.

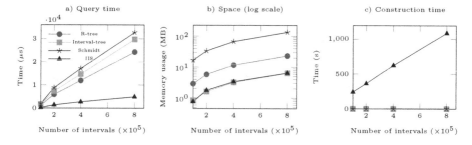

Fig. 3. Random size intervals.

usage (although in a tie with the Interval-tree) while the building time is drastically increased (up to 900 times the building time of the Interval-tree). This is explained by the high number of independent sets (3,273 for 800,000 intervals), which is caused by the frequency with which intervals fully cover each other.

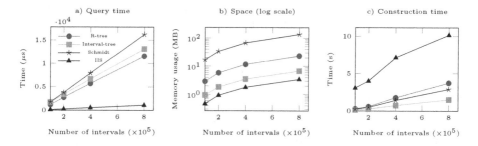

Fig. 4. Intervals from trajectories.

Figure 4 shows the performance of the structures using time intervals extracted from synthetic trajectories obtained with Brinkhoff's generator. The compact data structure shows a performance in between the two previous cases, but more similar to the first one. Note, however, that results in these three scenarios are not directly comparable due to differences in the number of intervals reported in the queries. This shows the sensibility of the structure to the number of independent sets. In this dataset, intervals of trajectories have often similar length, producing a relatively low number of independent sets (29 for 800,000 intervals). Each temporal index is associated with a segment of the network, and moving objects usually traverse a same segment at a similar speed.

We also evaluated the sensibility of the structures to the scale used to transform original float-number times to integers. In this procedure, each time is multiplied by a scale factor and then truncated. In our datasets, original times use up to 8 digits to the right of the decimal point. Hence, a scale factor of 10^8 guarantees a lossless transformation, whereas lower scale factors may produce a lossy transformation. Results are shown in Fig. 5.

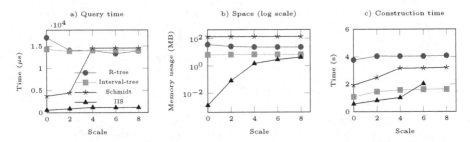

Fig. 5. Performance according the scale of the intervals. The last point of IIS in the last graph was omitted, because it is about 40 times larger than the others.

Query time shows an almost constant behavior, except for the increase suffered by Schmidt, which is caused by the high number of duplicates when only 2 or less digits are used for the fractional part. In terms of space and construction time, the compact data structure is more sensible than the other structures, which is caused by the scale process. As we explain in previous section, the larger the scale factor, the larger the size of the bitmaps in this structure. Even so, this structure obtains the best results in both query time and memory usage, also giving the possibility to improve the performance in applications where the user can afford losing some precision.

4.2 Overall Evaluation

From the experiments in previous section, we conclude that Schmidt's structure is always outperformed by the others, and thus it is not considered in the implementation of data structures for trajectories. In the following experiments we compare our proposal, based on compact data structures, with two baselines: the original FNR-tree and an ad-hoc baseline in which 1D R-trees are replaced by interval trees. Note that in these experiments we are comparing three two-level indexes, all of them using a 2D R-tree on the top level.

The datasets of trajectories were created using Brinkhoff's generator [6] over the real road networks of Oldenburg and San Francisco. The former consists of 6,105 nodes and 7,305 edges, whereas the latter consists of 175,343 nodes and 223,343 edges. We created trajectories for 1,000, 2,000, 3,000, 4,000 and 5,000 objects during 100 units of time for both networks.

Memory Usage. Figure 6 shows the space required by each of the structures. The proposed space-efficient solution (labeled as IIS in the graphs) obtained the best results in all the experiments. In addition, the larger the number of objects moving over the network, the larger the advantage of this structure over the baselines. For small number of moving objects, the total space used by the data structures is dominated by the spatial level, however, as this number increases, the temporal level dominates, and our proposal takes more advantage.

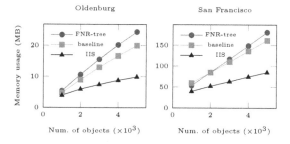

Fig. 6. Total memory usage.

Table 1. Memory usage per object (KB / object) [5,000 objects and 100 time units].

Structure	Old.	S.F.
FNR-tree	5	32
baseline	4	26
IIS	1.5	11

The approximated memory usage per object is shown in Table 1, which shows that our approach requires about 70% less memory than the FNR-tree, and about 60% less memory than the baseline, when there are 5,000 objects moving over the networks. The difference between the two datasets is explained by the size of the network, the San Francisco network being much larger. First, part of the space charged to each object is due to the spatial index. However, the size of the network has also an impact on the distribution of objects per edge of the network. As this distribution is very skewed, the larger the network, the larger the number of nodes with few objects, which means an overhead.

Query Time. The time performance of the structures was evaluated for three types of queries, which are the same used in the original evaluation of the FNR-tree [14]: (i) *Range Queries with Equal Spatial and Temporal Extent*, such as "find all objects within a given area during a given time interval"; (ii) *Range Queries with Larger Temporal Extent*, which query for very large time intervals, including intervals expanding the whole temporal dimension, such as "find all the objects having ever passed through a given area"; and (iii) *Time Slice Queries*, that only consider a time instant, such as "find all the objects that were in a given area at a given time instant". For each of these scenarios, we created three query-sets with 500 random queries for each network.

Figure 7 shows the results for the first type of queries. The first row shows results for Oldenburg and the second row for San Francisco. For both datasets, we show the results of random queries of different sizes, 1%, 10% and 20% in each dimension. Similar frameworks will be used to evaluate the other two types of queries. This is the same experimental setting used in [14].

In all the experiments our proposal outperforms both baselines. Just for small queries, 1% of the dimensions, the FNR-tree shows competitive results with our proposal. This is more evident in the largest network. The justification is the relative importance of the spatial part of the query with respect to the temporal part, which depends on the size of the network. Also important, our proposal shows better scalability on the number of objects moving through the network.

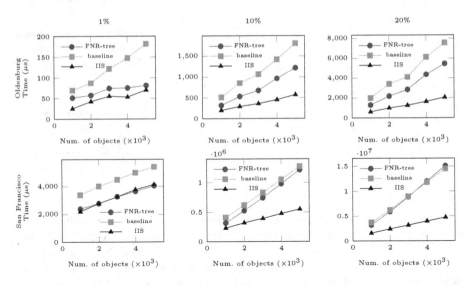

Fig. 7. Range queries. First row for Oldenburg and second row for San Francisco. Each column contains queries of different size from 1% to 20%.

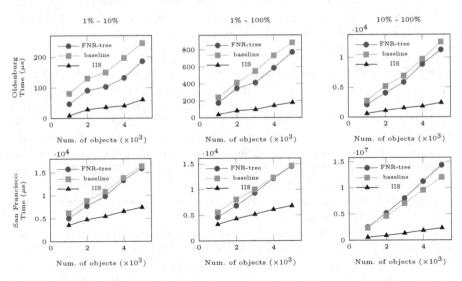

Fig. 8. Range queries with larger temporal extent. First row for Oldenburg and second row for San Francisco. Each column indicates $x\% - y\%$, being x the size of each spatial dimension (1% or 10%) and y the size of the time intervals (10% or 100%).

Figure 8 shows the results for range queries with larger temporal extent. In these experiments the temporal extent is always larger than the spatial extent, expanding the whole temporal dimension in the second and third column.

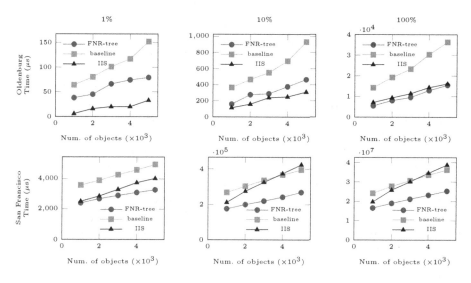

Fig. 9. Time slice queries. First row for Oldenburg and second row for San Francisco. Each columns contains queries of different spatial extent (1% to 100%).

Results in this scenario are similar to the previous one, but the advantage of our proposal is even more obvious. Recall that our structure performs two rank operations in each independent set and then it just iterates over the results, which is very efficient. Finally, Fig. 9 shows the results for time slice queries.

The analysis of these experiments is quite different from the previous ones, as the FNR-tree usually outperforms all the other approaches. There are two main reasons for this. First, large spatial queries lead querying many temporal indexes (all of them for the experiments in the last column). Second, most of these queries to temporal indexes produce empty results or very few results, which is expensive in our proposal. Each of these queries needs to perform the two rank operations in each independent set just to detect that there are no results to iterate through. Hence, this scenario represents the worst case for our proposal.

5   Conclusions

We have proposed a new data structure for trajectories of moving objects, which movement is constrained to a network. Our proposal is inspired by two-level indexes, such as the FNR-tree and MON-tree and, indeed, we use the same two-dimensional R-tree for the spatial dimension. Hence, the difference from previous solutions is in the temporal dimension. This is justified by our experimental evaluation showing that the spatial dimension requires negligible space compared with the temporal dimension. For this dimension, we propose a structure based on a decomposition on independent sets of intervals and the use of succinct data structures. Our experimental evaluation shows that the resulting structure is smaller than previous solutions, and also faster for a broad set of queries.

The interval intersection problem can be reduced to 2-sided range reporting [11], a problem for which efficient data structures have been successfully applied in LZ-indexes [3,4,21]. As these structures are not adaptive to the number of independent interval sets, a combination of both approaches would be interesting as future work. Second, to handle larger datasets, it is necessary to improve construction time. Note, however, that we used larger datasets than those used in the evaluation of the FNR-tree. Third, some parts of the structure could be further optimized. We have observed that the distribution of the moving objects through the network is very skewed, which produces few temporal indexes storing many intervals and many indexes storing very few intervals. Hence, in order to use this index in practice, it is necessary to determine a threshold under which the intervals are just stored in an array and sequentially searched. Finally, bitmaps supporting append operations should be used to support dynamism.

References

1. de Almeida, V.T., Güting, R.H.: Indexing the trajectories of moving objects in networks*. GeoInformatica **9**(1), 33–60 (2005)
2. Barkan, Y.: RTree, GitHub repository (2011). https://github.com/nushoin/RTree
3. Belazzougui, D., Cunial, F., Gagie, T., Prezza, N., Raffinot, M.: Composite repetition-aware data structures. In: Cicalese, F., Porat, E., Vaccaro, U. (eds.) CPM 2015. LNCS, vol. 9133, pp. 26–39. Springer, Cham (2015). https://doi.org/10.1007/978-3-319-19929-0_3
4. Belazzougui, D., Cunial, F., Gagie, T., Prezza, N., Raffinot, M.: Flexible indexing of repetitive collections. In: Kari, J., Manea, F., Petre, I. (eds.) CiE 2017. LNCS, vol. 10307, pp. 162–174. Springer, Cham (2017). https://doi.org/10.1007/978-3-319-58741-7_17
5. de Berg, M., Cheong, O., van Kreveld, M., Overmars, M.: Computational Geometry: Algorithms and Applications, 3rd edn. Springer-Verlag TELOS, Heidelberg (2008). https://doi.org/10.1007/978-3-662-03427-9
6. Brinkhoff, T.: A framework for generating network-based moving objects. GeoInformatica **6**(2), 153–180 (2002)
7. Brisaboa, N.R., Fariña, A., Galaktionov, D., Rodríguez, M.A.: Compact trip representation over networks. In: Inenaga, S., Sadakane, K., Sakai, T. (eds.) SPIRE 2016. LNCS, vol. 9954, pp. 240–253. Springer, Cham (2016). https://doi.org/10.1007/978-3-319-46049-9_23
8. Brisaboa, N.R., Gagie, T., Gómez-Brandón, A., Navarro, G., Paramá, J.R.: Efficient compression and indexing of trajectories. In: Fici, G., Sciortino, M., Venturini, R. (eds.) SPIRE 2017. LNCS, vol. 10508, pp. 103–115. Springer, Cham (2017). https://doi.org/10.1007/978-3-319-67428-5_10
9. Brisaboa, N.R., Gómez-Brandón, A., Navarro, G., Paramá, J.R.: GraCT: a grammar based compressed representation of trajectories. In: Inenaga, S., Sadakane, K., Sakai, T. (eds.) SPIRE 2016. LNCS, vol. 9954, pp. 218–230. Springer, Cham (2016). https://doi.org/10.1007/978-3-319-46049-9_21

10. Brisaboa, N.R., Ladra, S., Navarro, G.: k^2-trees for compact web graph representation. In: Karlgren, J., Tarhio, J., Hyyrö, H. (eds.) SPIRE 2009. LNCS, vol. 5721, pp. 18–30. Springer, Heidelberg (2009). https://doi.org/10.1007/978-3-642-03784-9_3

11. Brisaboa, N.R., Luaces, M.R., Navarro, G., Seco, D.: Space-efficient representations of rectangle datasets supporting orthogonal range querying. Inf. Syst. **38**(5), 635–655 (2013)

12. Ding, Z., Yang, B., Güting, R.H., Li, Y.: Network-matched trajectory-based moving-object database: models and applications. IEEE Trans. Intell. Transp. Syst. **16**(4), 1918–1928 (2015)

13. Fredman, M.L.: On computing the length of longest increasing subsequences. Discret. Math. **11**(1), 29–35 (1975)

14. Frentzos, E.: Indexing objects moving on fixed networks. In: Hadzilacos, T., Manolopoulos, Y., Roddick, J., Theodoridis, Y. (eds.) SSTD 2003. LNCS, vol. 2750, pp. 289–305. Springer, Heidelberg (2003). https://doi.org/10.1007/978-3-540-45072-6_17

15. Garrison, E.: Intervaltree, GitHub repository (2011). https://github.com/ekg/intervaltree

16. Gog, S., Beller, T., Moffat, A., Petri, M.: From theory to practice: plug and play with succinct data structures. In: Gudmundsson, J., Katajainen, J. (eds.) SEA 2014. LNCS, vol. 8504, pp. 326–337. Springer, Cham (2014). https://doi.org/10.1007/978-3-319-07959-2_28

17. Guttman, A.: R-Trees: a dynamic index structure for spatial searching. SIGMOD Rec. **14**(2), 47–57 (1984)

18. Han, Y., Sun, W., Zheng, B.: Compress: a comprehensive framework of trajectory compression in road networks. ACM Trans. Database Syst. **42**(2), 11:1–11:49 (2017)

19. Kellaris, G., Pelekis, N., Theodoridis, Y.: Map-matched trajectory compression. J. Syst. Softw. **86**(6), 1566–1579 (2013)

20. Koide, S., Tadokoro, Y., Xiao, C., Ishikawa, Y.: CiNCT: compression and retrieval for massive vehicular trajectories via relative movement labeling. In: ICDE, pp. 1097–1108 (2018)

21. Kreft, S., Navarro, G.: On compressing and indexing repetitive sequences. Theor. Comput. Sci. **483**, 115–133 (2013)

22. Krogh, B., Pelekis, N., Theodoridis, Y., Torp, K.: Path-based queries on trajectory data. In: SIGSPATIAL, pp. 341–350 (2014)

23. Meratnia, N., de By, R.A.: Spatiotemporal Compression Techniques for Moving Point Objects. In: Bertino, E., Christodoulakis, S., Plexousakis, D., Christophides, V., Koubarakis, M., Böhm, K., Ferrari, E. (eds.) EDBT 2004. LNCS, vol. 2992, pp. 765–782. Springer, Heidelberg (2004). https://doi.org/10.1007/978-3-540-24741-8_44

24. Navarro, G., Mäkinen, V.: Compressed full-text indexes. ACM Comput. Surv. **39**(1), Article No. 2 (2007). https://dl.acm.org/citation.cfm?id=1216372

25. Okanohara, D., Sadakane, K.: Practical entropy-compressed rank/select dictionary. In: ALENEX, pp. 60–70 (2007). http://dl.acm.org/citation.cfm?id=2791188.2791194

26. Pfoser, D., Jensen, C.S., Theodoridis, Y.: Novel approaches in query processing for moving object trajectories. In: VLDB, pp. 395–406 (2000)

27. Potamias, M., Patroumpas, K., Sellis, T.: Sampling trajectory streams with spatiotemporal criteria. In: SSDBM, pp. 275–284 (2006)

28. Sandu Popa, I., Zeitouni, K., Oria, V., Barth, D., Vial, S.: Indexing in-network trajectory flows. VLDB J. **20**(5), 643 (2011)
29. Schmid, F., Richter, K.-F., Laube, P.: Semantic trajectory compression. In: Mamoulis, N., Seidl, T., Pedersen, T.B., Torp, K., Assent, I. (eds.) SSTD 2009. LNCS, vol. 5644, pp. 411–416. Springer, Heidelberg (2009). https://doi.org/10.1007/978-3-642-02982-0_30
30. Schmidt, J.M.: Interval stabbing problems in small integer ranges. In: Dong, Y., Du, D.-Z., Ibarra, O. (eds.) ISAAC 2009. LNCS, vol. 5878, pp. 163–172. Springer, Heidelberg (2009). https://doi.org/10.1007/978-3-642-10631-6_18
31. Schmidt, J.M.: Publications by J.M. Schmidt. http://www4.tu-ilmenau.de/combinatorial-optimization/ShowPub.html (2018). Accessed 1 May 2018
32. Tao, Y., Papadias, D.: MV3R-Tree: a spatio-temporal access method for timestamp and interval queries. In: VLDB, pp. 431–440 (2001)

Author Index

Printed in the United States
By Bookmasters